WILLIAM
ALBERT
ALLARD

WILLIAM ALBERT ALLARD

FIVE DECADES
A RETROSPECTIVE

NATIONAL GEOGRAPHIC · FOCAL POINT

Washington, D.C.

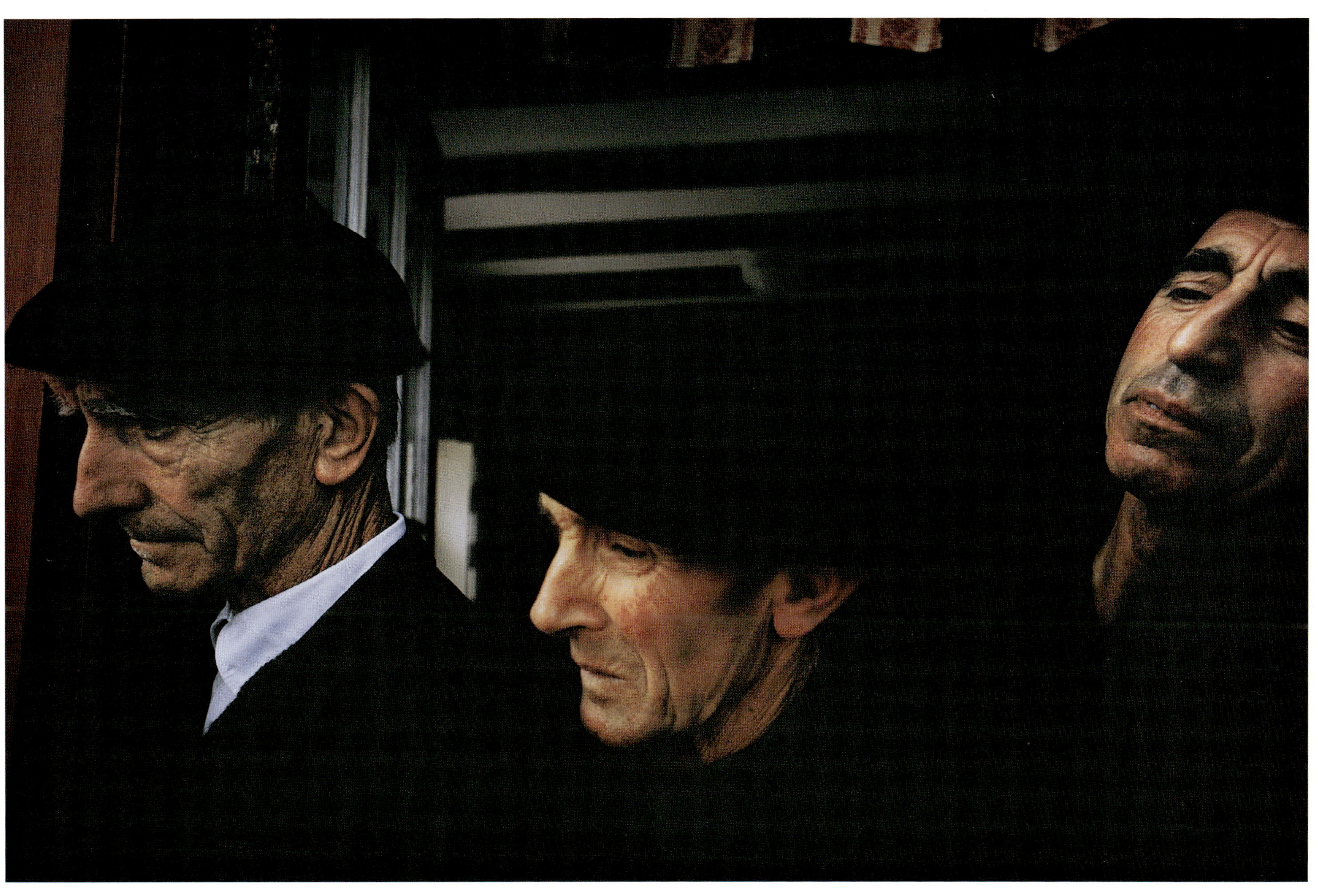

Basque men listening to a poet, Sare, France, 1967

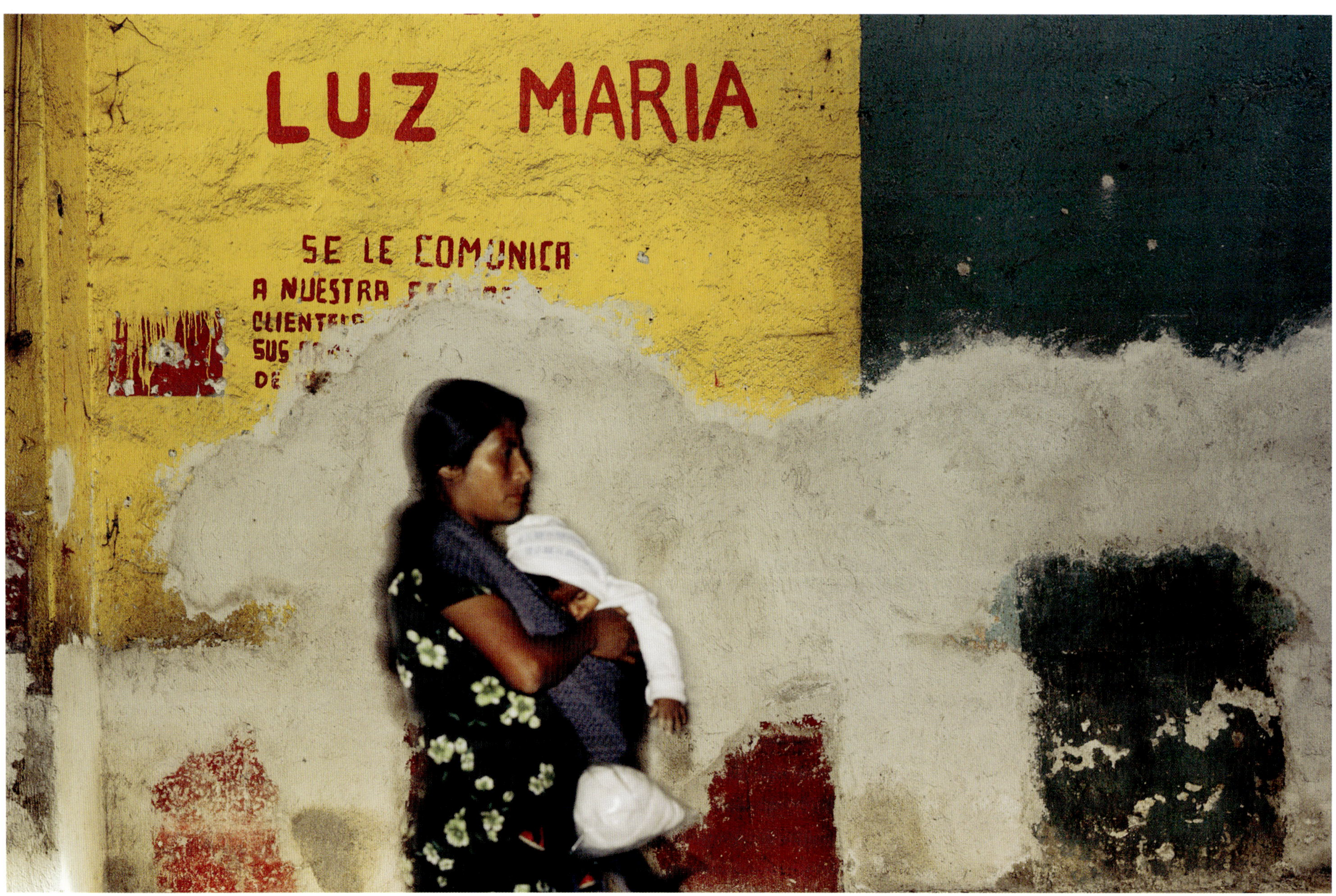

Woman in the market, Oaxaca, Mexico, 1980

To Ani. And to my children: Chris, Terry, David, Anthony, and our beloved Scott.

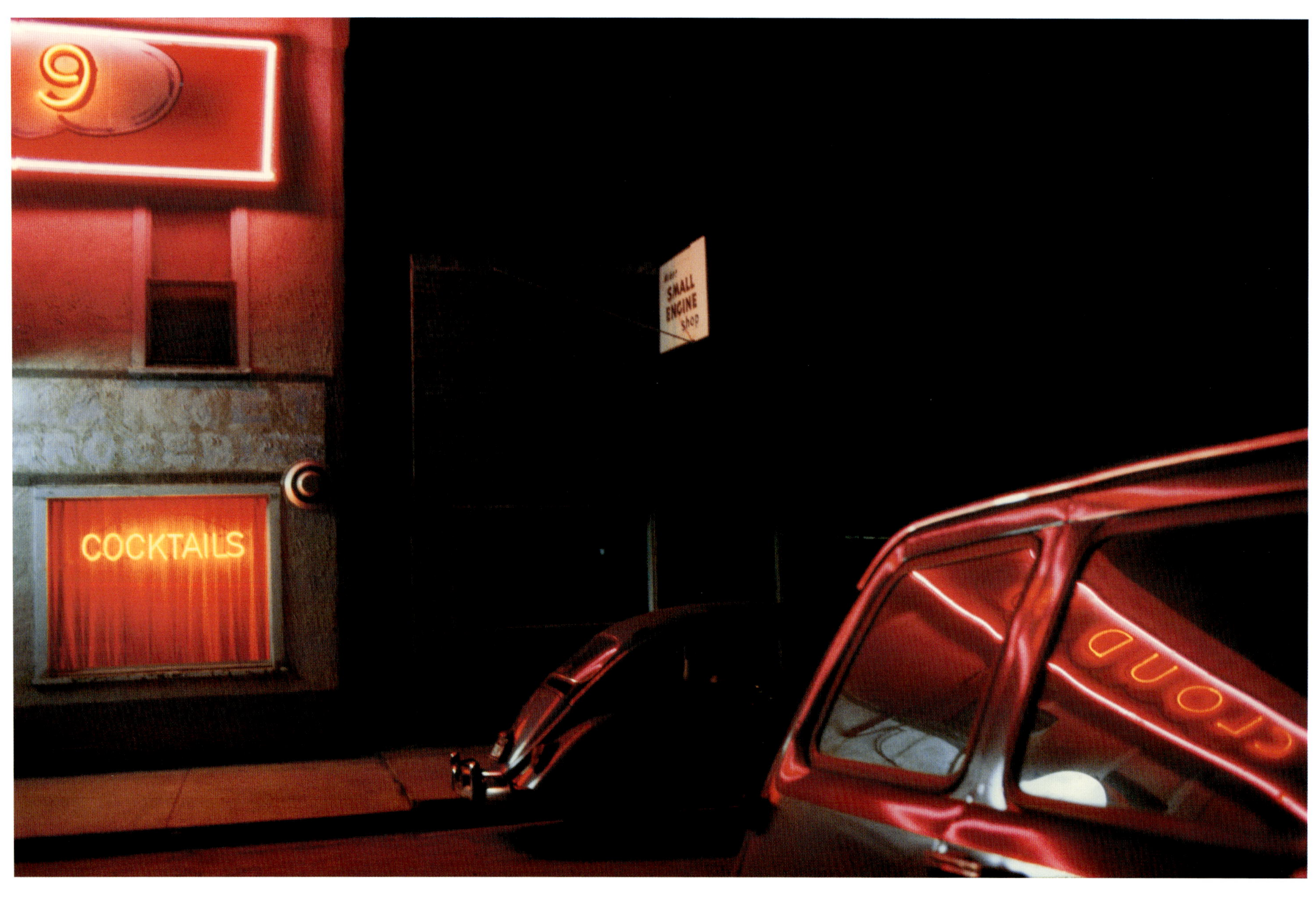

Cloud 9 Bar, Elko, Nevada, 1979

Foreword | William Kittredge

"We live permanently in the recurrence of our own stories, whatever story we tell."
—*Divisadero*, Michael Ondaatje

Friends pass away, on over, wherever they might go—my brother and women I once loved and lifetime pals who knew all the stories. Not much fresh blood came along until Bill Allard bought a house on a hilltop overlooking Missoula, the town where I've lived for decades, and started summering there. We'd been acquaintances before, and soon tracked each other down.

In 1980, editors at *Rocky Mountain Magazine* got a look at the striking photographs Allard took while traveling with chuck wagon buckaroo crews out in the sagebrush reaches of northern Nevada. I'd grown up on one of those cowhand outfits, so those editors hired me to provide the text for an essay to accompany the photographs. It was called "Owyhee Buckaroo," and it worked well for both of us. I keep returning to Bill Allard's photograph *Buckaroo T. J. Symonds, IL cow camp, Nevada, 1979*. There it is, a version of my boyhood, a young man in a chuck wagon camp out in the Great Basin desert country just to the west of the Owyhee River, got up in a fresh white shirt, enjoying camp-made bread with peanut butter and pancake syrup and the possibilities of a new day.

Bill Allard got it dead on. I liked him and admired his work, but ours was a professional relationship. At that time, as he acknowledges with profound candor in his essays, Bill was enduring plenty of personal difficulty—a divorce and the self-inflicted several-year loss of the job with National Geographic that defines his professional life.

But I knew nothing of this. He soldiered on, as he does, and we went off toward other lives.

Allard carries his years of worldwide experience lightly. An amiable and evocative storyteller, intuitive and incisive, he's candidly on to himself while self-assured. Trust your art and leave your worrisome ego behind. *Come fly with me.*

Allard is attentive to elegance and obviously determined to get the look of things just right, a self-described "serious hat man." "I own and wear a lot of them: stylish hats," Allard says, "hand-shaped crowns and brims, fine-quality felt." In Chicago, while covering a story about blues music, Allard attended the funeral of musician Junior Wells, and there he was, Junior in his casket, laid out faceup and dressed high in his best black fedora, stylish to the end. Bill speculates about being laid down and put away like Junior Wells in his own finest hat, "a silver belly 10X with a Montana crease and full pencil rolled brim, custom-built for me in Billings, Montana, by Rand's Custom Hats."

Add old friends and that fine blues music and an occasional riff by Frank Sinatra, and it sounds like a good way to go. But Allard says no, it's going to be ashes, scattered in central Montana and in Minnesota, where *he* grew up.

BILL ALLARD DESCRIBES HIMSELF as a "street shooter." It's a technique based on staying utterly alert to possibility and chance, wherever he goes, along whichever mean streets, camera at hand, "working the edges," trusting his instincts. Great images pass so quickly.

While he may occasionally stage a posed portrait, much more often he's watching patiently for striking men and women, intimate postures and gestures that come along, waiting for moments and glances that reveal personalities and resonate with respect and courage and evasions and love and even disdain. Extemporizing in such passing moments and then vanishing into the next wash of encounter, Allard finds ways to compose profoundly stirring photographs—instantly, on the spot. Experience counts for a lot.

In the 1920s, British novelist E. M. Forster wrote, "The medium we work in is the reader's [audience's] imagination." Artists incite us to imagine and reimagine our own enormous variety of stories and anecdotes, hoping we'll discover order and coherencies that cast light on our own lives.

Raymond Carver, the great American short story writer, would say, "We've seen some things." Ray was talking about all of us, of course, but particularly artists like himself and Allard, who have indeed witnessed vivid moments as they help us toward experiencing a version of what they've seen, and, more usefully, incite us to reexplore our own stories, our idiosyncratic private legends and personal myths. The works of art we most revere tend to move us toward rethinking our own trajectories.

Legends constantly have to be reinvented. Life evolves. Much art goes out of date and doesn't play so well after a while, but Bill Allard's photographs seem to be as valid and emotionally useful as ever. Most likely that's true because, wherever in the world he might be, Allard focuses on the ways isolation and loneliness can cross with friendships and community and self-respect and lead to an adding up and what we end up calling character. His photographs help me recall men and women I have known and admired and modeled my life on—hay hands and field cooks and teachers in the one-room school I attended as a kid, and photographers and poets encountered all up and down the road, each quite utterly idiosyncratic and yet understandable.

Photographers and writers or painters or musicians, from the artists who painted the great bulls in the cave at Lascaux to Andy Warhol and the Rolling Stones, always tend to imply that the range of our emotions can run off any map unto endlessness. The human cortex is the most complicated physical "thing" in the known universe—an electric "grid" capable of trillions of synaptic connections. There are no simple minds. *Electricity is the way nature behaves.* Complexity glows even in Allard's earliest photographs, like the one facing the title page in this book, *Basque men listening to a poet, Sare, France, 1967*—men and their responses to the poet and poetry and emotions they find in recollection, private and implied states of mind that we recognize as innately human and yet very distinct from ours. And of course, since it's Allard, they're wearing their hats, keeping the lid on.

Photographers learn to position their cameras so as to have a chance at staying in contact with the evolving world. Their natural intelligence feeds on their fascination with learning the complexities of a trade. Allard is continually willing to teach, humble about it but also spilling workshop secrets along the way (one of the fine, useful things about this book).

Taking note, noticing, then leading *us* to take note, to see, and to speculate and partway make sense, to fathom—that's the artist's job. Artists like Allard spend decades learning their trade. Such is our good fortune, and, of course, theirs. Over those decades, Allard developed and cultivated confidence like that of ballplayers who rely on judgments and instincts, and have the wit to play to their recognized strengths and away from weaknesses—Brooks Robinson, the Hall of Fame third baseman for Baltimore, it's said, shaded toward his left side, his slightly slower move, and thus cut off many ground balls that might have got past. Bill Allard has obviously learned to play to his own strengths—primary among them his instinctive empathy—and thus earned and enjoyed some extraordinary innings.

IT'S ALSO OUR GOOD FORTUNE that Allard is an evocative essayist. Like the photographs, which stand on their own, his essays lead us to thrashing through thickets in our most meaningful stories.

In 2002, he was on a double assignment, traveling between Paris and India. In the "360-acre pocket called Le Marais," especially in the "immaculately manicured Place des Vosges," he enjoyed French girls bicycling through the "beautiful historical architecture . . . antique shops, and restaurants." He was paid for wandering around amid "sophistication and wealth" with a camera. After those pleasures, however, Allard would catch a long flight to "the vastness and intensity of India" and the "160 million souls born into the dark bottom of India's massive social structure, the Hindu caste system"—the utterly disenfranchised Untouchables. They occupy the bottom rung of a system that's "still brutally intact after 1,500 years" in a country of one billion people. Responsible for cleaning up any human waste; disposing of dead and decaying roadside animals and tanning animal hides; searching through sewage for any usable thing, food or otherwise; descending into and cleaning sewers and village latrines, they dispose of anything foul. It's the life they were born to; they give their lives to honoring that idea. Allard says flying between Paris and the Untouchables was like working on "separate planets." Perhaps this disjunction between worlds inspires some of the insight behind his photographs from each situation.

Trying to make sense of Allard's breadth of experience, his sense of earned worldliness, let's listen to his essays and take a look at a pair of photographs, one of a young woman in a bistro on Rue de Rivoli in Paris, perhaps the most casually sophisticated street in the world; the other of a filthy member of the Untouchable "scavenger caste," the lowest in India, plastered with excrement. Allard's essay on the Untouchables tells of watching Amrutbhai Sarasiya "descend into the sewer on a rope, immersing himself in excrement, to use a simple metal bucket to remove the waste, bucketful after bucketful." Allard says, "This man's pride seemed undiminished by his position in the world." His photograph of "this man" coming up from a sewer "undiminished" though pasted with human waste, both the humanist and political point of it, is examined in Allard's accompanying essay.

Amid an excremental and political stink Allard doubtless found it very difficult to shake on the flight back to Paris, there he goes in his determined and reasonable way, off on his own to yet another set of streets, back to work, seeing to the people James Agee wrote about, survivors who've suffered "the enormous assaults of the universe" and yet remained "as hardly killed, as easily wounded." Allard went back to Rue de Rivoli and walked down another revealing street with his cameras, and crossed bridges amid another swirl of multitudes.

Progressing through this collection of his photographs and essays, I was struck by his continual all-over-the-world drive to celebrate "multitudes" in his art, echoes of thronging medieval carnivals and Walt Whitman at his most inclusive, in "Crossing Brooklyn Ferry": "The glories strung like beads on my smallest sights and hearings, on the walk in the street and the passage over the river."

DURING THE FALL OF 2009, Bill Allard displayed a collection of his favorite photographs of women in a Missoula gallery. The writer Leonard Michaels, long deceased, once began a short story with this line: "Kittredge loves beautiful women but he is blind." I was thankful Bill Allard had seen beauties so vividly and variously. He covered for my blindness with that show of fearless women he'd photographed in the stark Andean highlands of Peru; and in the showbiz glitter of Bollywood in India; and in the redneck clutches of a Mississippi fraternity party; and backstage at Parisian fashion shows; and in what looks to be a bordello in Elko, Nevada; and in his beloved Hutterite colonies in central Montana. There was only one nude, as I recall, posed in a Mexican brothel.

The particular beauty that struck me most vividly in that show was Allard's photograph titled *Girl smoking, Au Gamin de Paris restaurant, Paris, 2002*. It was not simply the physical beauty of the woman that attracted me. I can't stay away from cigarettes. My true companion, Annick Smith, laughed and said it was the smoking, a feather of smoke hanging between the subject and the camera, that attracted me. I said, "No way" (and yet, at least to some degree, maybe it was). Rather, I said, it was the young woman's cool and appraising glance as she eyed an unknown photographer snapping her picture from down the bar. Allard catches her just as she spots him and she commences figuring him out. "Usually in candid photography you hope to not have anyone looking at the camera," Allard writes. "But in this case the momentary contact her eyes had with mine is the essence of the image."

It's a self-portrait, Allard himself unseen but implied, the artist reflected in the mirroring glance of his subject. In "The Maids of Honor," a world masterpiece by Diego Velázquez hanging in the Prado museum, we see the Infanta Margarita charming a palace room where Velázquez is painting a portrait of her parents, the royal family of Spain—the privileged innocent child and ladies and dwarfs and dog steal a moment from power. Reflected in a mirror, we see Velázquez at work on the very painting before us; by implication he's attempting to show the entire complex transaction between a subject and artist. Same thing goes for the Allard portrait of that young woman with her cigarette in Paris—although in this case the artist remains invisible.

"...THE SUBJECT GAVE HERSELF TO ME.... I believe many of the best pictures are given, not taken." In Native American hunting stories, the game is sometimes said to "give" its being to the hunter. "Looking for pictures," Allard goes on, "is a little bit like hunting, watching and waiting."

Back in 1980, when I first saw Allard's photographs taken on the Great Basin sage deserts of northern Nevada, I wondered how a midwestern and cosmopolitan man from National Geographic could get so obviously close to the independent and solitary souls who buckaroo for those chuck wagon crews. I imagined that Allard's success with those men must have been the result of his professionalism, making short-term friends so as to get the job done. Now I know different.

He grew up in midwestern hunting culture. At the age of 12 Bill was given a new .22 rifle by his blue-collar father, who would take him on the hour-long drive from Minneapolis to his uncle Hank's 160-acre farm for squirrel hunting. Back home, it was Bill's job to skin and gut the squirrels and put them to soak in a tub of salt water. His mother would cook and serve them with a Scandinavian white sauce. "I'm a carnivore," Allard says, "and if I didn't eat what I kill I wouldn't hunt."

But why continue hunting in a culture that ordinarily comes by its foodstuffs in commercial ways? Perhaps to escape relentless commodification? That, and small pleasures like being out in the wild with his dog, Buster, engaged in an ageless ritual of pursuit that's "as much a part of the natural world as anything might be." Part of it involves Allard's strong emotional response to the implied paradise of animals once inhabited by Native Americans—the charismatic grizzlies and elk and vast flights of migrating mallards and pintails and snow geese and Canada honkers and prairie birds by the millions in Montana—Allard tells of "almost trembling at the thought of how wonderful it must have been."

With that in the background, it's easy enough to understand how Allard fell into a long-term "love affair with the American West" in the mid-1970s, a powerful attraction that resonates in the prizewinning book that recorded his time with the Nevada buckaroos, *Vanishing Breed*, published in 1982. It's an affair driven by reverence for the "long look" of the prairies and "big sky" over Montana plains and northern Nevada, and for creatures both domestic and wild—farm hogs and tame geese and mule deer in the draws and sage grouse and antelope. But his response to the West seems equally driven by respect for straightforward, resolute citizens who continue to live far from the money-oriented American mix, especially his good friends the Hutterites.

"Along with other pacifists," Allard tells us, "the Amish and Mennonites, Hutterites emerged from the Anabaptist movement of 16th-century Europe." After starting his professional career with successful photographic work among the Amish in Pennsylvania, over decades Allard has gone on through a series of *National Geographic* assignments to form very close friendships in the Hutterite colonies of central and eastern Montana. Allard's daughter once said that one colony in Montana was his "other family." With good reason; the colony was his home away from his home. He lived there with them for months at a time, enjoying his friendships and taking his photographs. And they saw him through an extremely difficult time. It's a personal story involving primal heartbreak, and the ways friends can help us stand against such heartbreak. Bill tells it with restraint and considerable art.

Bill Allard's work and stories lead me to reflect on the usefulness of seeking and finding solace in places where there's order and stability, a kind of tribal order and stability, which is especially releasing since it isn't quite your tribe, and marriage and blood family are not involved—it's a communal dream in which artists have no duties but to record responsibly. Allard has perhaps found such a place with the Hutterites. Anyway, he returns again and again.

Come to the mirror. *Mine enemy grows older.* Through decades, searching out human beauties around the world, working in isolation and finding new friends and loved ones, Bill Allard seems to have hung his days on finding cause for celebration. In this book we all reap the rewards. Bless the man and his work. Gives me heart. ■

Wild colt, Sable Island, Nova Scotia, 1965

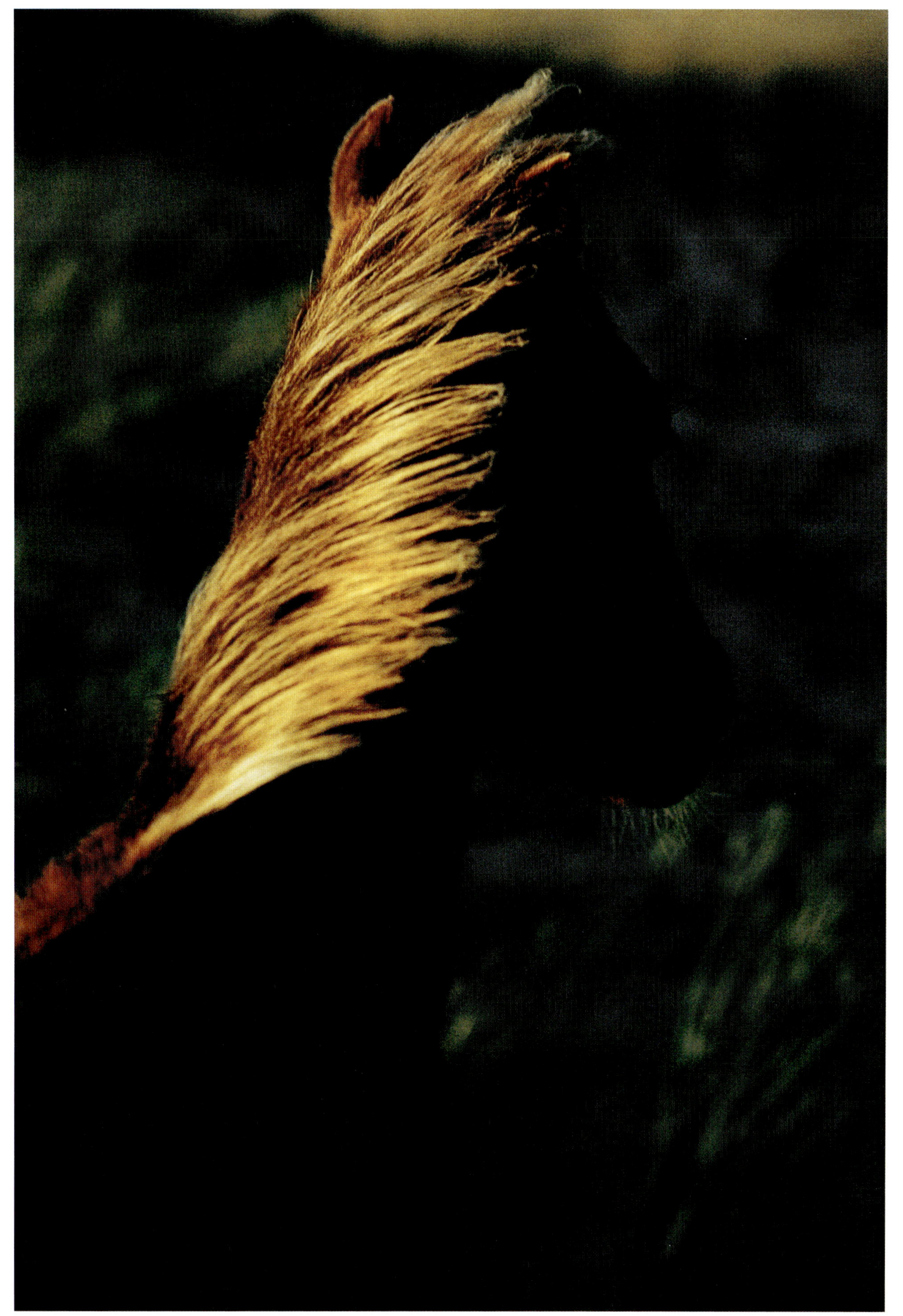

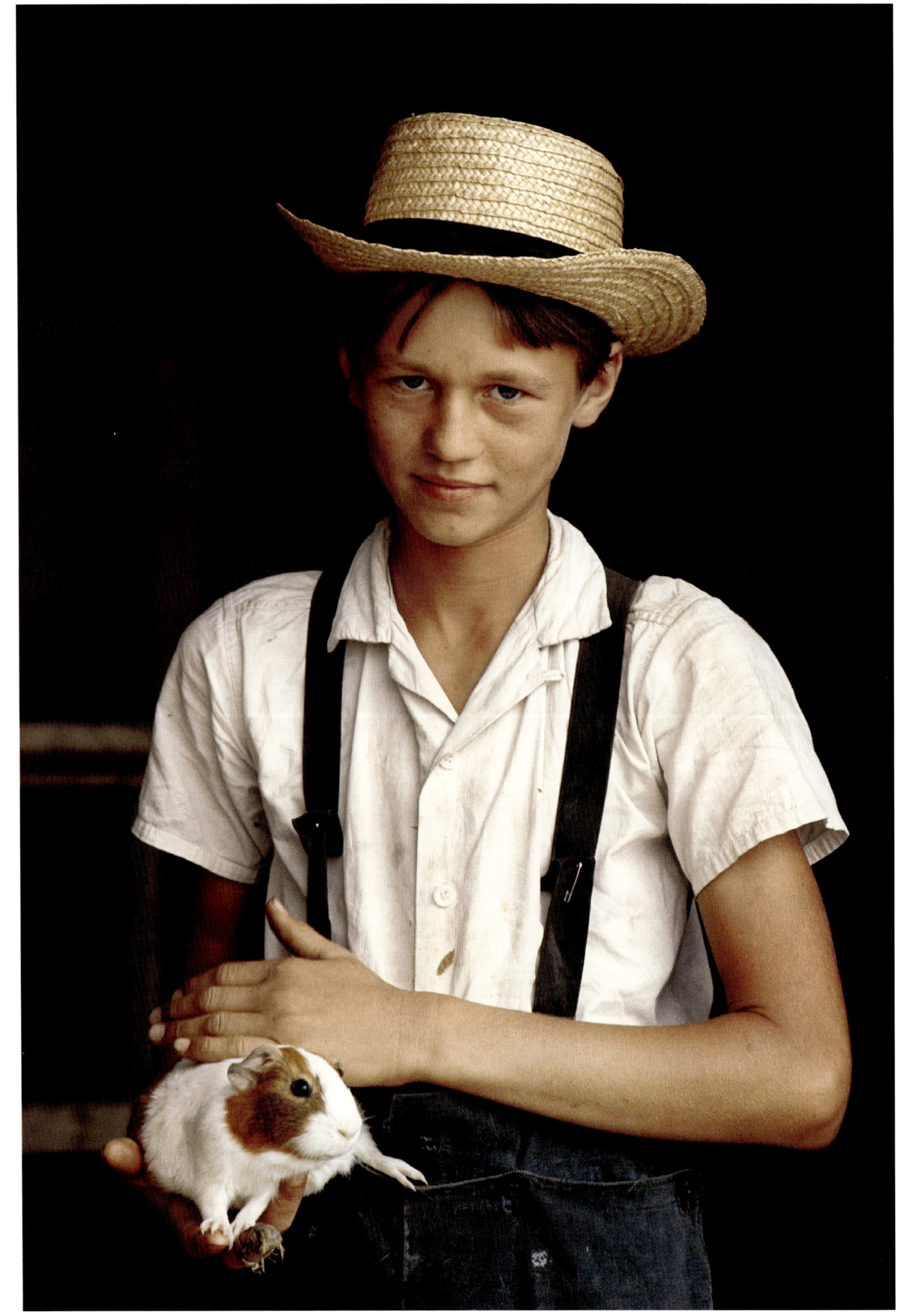

Introduction | William Albert Allard

As a small boy I loved to draw and I loved to listen to the radio.

Many of my afternoons after school were spent with a pad of paper and colored pencils or crayons, sprawled on the living room rug in front of the console radio that stood by the front closet in our home in north Minneapolis, drawing pictures and listening to radio programs like *The Shadow, The Lone Ranger*, or *The Green Hornet.* On some special Friday nights, *Gillette Cavalcade of Sports* would broadcast a world championship fight from Madison Square Garden in New York City. The fight broadcasts might just as well have been coming from the moon as far as my childish geographic knowledge was concerned, but I was transfixed by the drama of the rapid, sharp-voiced, blow-by-blow description by ringside announcer Don Dunphy, coming from within that tall, brown, cathedral-shaped radio with the cloth-covered speaker:

Two sharp jabs followed by an overhand right . . . a left hook . . . a right uppercut that lands solidly. The fighters clinch, and referee Ruby Goldstein breaks them up. Those vicious body punches of the early rounds are showing their effect . . . the challenger is lowering his hands and taking more blows to the head. A cut has appeared over his right eye and is bleeding profusely . . . there's an awful lot of blood flowing into that eye. The other eye is swollen almost shut. They'll definitely have to have the ringside doctor look at him between rounds, if he survives this one. Oh! He's hurt! He's staggered! He's DOWN!

Amish boy with guinea pig, Lancaster County, Pennsylvania, 1964

The announcer would frequently identify fighters by the color of their trunks: which fighter was in the black trunks, which in white with a purple stripe, as though we could see them as they moved about the ring. In my mind I sometimes could.

I was ten years old in 1947 when I listened with my father the night world heavyweight champion Joe Louis defended his title against Jersey Joe Walcott for the first time. We hunkered over the dining room table, listening silently and unbelievingly as Walcott—supposedly a pushover, just another bum-of-the-month—knocked the champion to the canvas twice, and anybody listening, even a kid like me, could tell at the end of the fight that Walcott had defeated the Brown Bomber by a wide margin. But the judges gave the decision to Louis. How could that be? I thought. I felt bad for Jersey Joe. A year later I lay heartbroken in front of that radio listening to my boxing idol, world featherweight champion Willie Pep, getting knocked out and losing his title to Sandy Saddler. It brought me to tears.

In my childhood, words written in books and spoken on the radio nurtured my imagination; they created pictures in my mind. Radio was powerful, a kind of magic that could keep me focused on the voice of someone I couldn't see but willingly surrendered my attention to. In story or song, radio could bring great comedy or drama into my home. We didn't have a television until after it had become quite popular with our friends and neighbors. When we finally got one, a small set that fit snugly beneath the dining room buffet cabinets, my dad and I would sometimes watch the Friday night fights together. By that time I was in my early teens.

That ability to visualize those earlier radio fight broadcasts was a trait that presented itself in my love of art, especially drawing, and eventually led me as a young married man, four years out of high school but with a less than stellar high school grade point average, to study at the Minneapolis School of Fine Arts. There, before the end of the first year, instead of wanting to draw or paint, a desire to write flowered and became my primary creative ambition. Then, after transferring to the school of journalism at the University of Minnesota, I discovered photojournalism, the bringing together of words and pictures to create something potentially more powerful than either of the two by itself. It was a personal revelation that would shortly and fortunately lead to a long career contributing to *National Geographic* and other magazines both as a photographer and a writer. Today, almost 50 years later, my love for words and pictures still flourishes, and my greatest satisfaction is to see them brought together in books. I enjoy the heft and tactile solidity and permanence of books; the worlds, real and imaginary, they can reveal. I love even the smell of them.

I would be extraordinarily happy to earn my living solely from producing books, but that's an aspiration almost impossible to fulfill. It would be wonderful to make lots of money from books, but I believe one's primary motive behind creating a book should be the love for the subject involved. One should feel rewarded and truly grateful if the book in question turns out to be close to what one had hoped it would be. The cruel reality of publishing is that a book is a onetime thing. Should it go south, if for whatever reason or reasons it fails to meet your expectations and desires, that's too bad, because it's over. For better or worse, it's finished. A book can make you immensely happy and proud. It can also break your heart. I've done books on the American cowboy, the Basque Country of Spain and France, the lake country of my home state of Minnesota, a retrospective of my work from 1964 to the early 1980s, and my most recent book—a retrospective of my work on American subjects up until 1998. None of them is perfect, but I'm proud of all of them. Four of the five are out of print but can be found if one searches.

Many of the images I've made on American subjects over the years that have appeared in my previous books will not appear again in this one. Those pictures from American subjects that do appear here are either previously unpublished work, recent work, or older pictures that seem to be iconic—ones that beg to be included in a retrospective that touches on what I feel is the best of my work, domestic and foreign.

Early in my career of doing stories for the National Geographic Society, I gravitated for subject matter to people who represented parts of American society just outside of the common. In my first five years as a photojournalist I photographed both the Amish and the Hutterites, two Anabaptist groups that, with their Old World clothing and rigid religious dictates, are certainly examples of lifestyles apart from the more typical American way.

The American cowboy—the kind who has the skills to work with a horse and a rope in any kind of weather and knows how cows think—has been around since before the Civil War but remains somewhat outside the increasingly automated and computerized American workforce.

On an afternoon in Nevada in the early 1970s I was with Brian Morris, cow boss of the Circle A ranch out of Paradise Valley, Nevada. We were several drinks into the afternoon at a bar called Paradise Hill. Sunlight was slanting in through the windows, skimming across the green felt of the pool table. Brian was wearing his short-brimmed silver belly Stetson; his high-topped, handmade Blucher boots; and a scruffy, wild rag around his neck, and his face was burnished by the sun and wind of the high desert country he knew so well. We were to move out on a cattle drive the next morning and were talking about the state of cowboying and how much was being taken over by modern technology of one sort or another, brought in to do the job of a man with a rope and a horse. I asked him, "Brian, do you ever think you'll be replaced by a machine?"

He looked at me, and in his marvelous, soft drawl he said, "Bill, they just ain't come up with nothin' yet that'll take as much abuse as a cowboy."

The subject of the cowboy and the American West captured my attention and my heart for better than a decade, from the late 1960s through the '70s, and even though I worked in other countries on other stories during those years, I returned whenever possible to the West.

Moving away from the West as subject matter, in the 1980s I visually explored the subject of William Faulkner's Mississippi for *National Geographic* magazine, working in a part of the South steeped in its particular culture, mythology, and racial history, a place my northern born and raised mind didn't attempt to decipher in order to produce pictures that might illustrate the work of a genius. I simply responded to what I saw, hoping to make a connection. In the end, it was really pictures of *my* Mississippi, the one I saw while thinking about Faulkner, that found their way into the magazine.

In 1990 I spent a summer photographing young hopefuls in the world of minor-league baseball, where only 1 out of 14 aspirants ever makes it to the "show," the big leagues. But all of them can tell their children and grandchildren that they once played the game as a professional. I greatly enjoyed doing that story about a game I grew up with, but I never felt driven to stay with it for the purpose of a book.

The following year I tried to portray the traditions and the voices of northern Minnesota's lake country, a landscape I treasured in childhood and one that will forever remain a part of me. One of those lakes, Gladstone—so small it's not even a tiny blue splotch on some Minnesota state maps—is where my family vacationed for a week or so each summer for 60 years. It is also where my older brother Bob's ashes were gently dispersed into the water after the 1982 Memorial Day afternoon in Minneapolis when he took his own life in the garage where my father stored the bamboo fishing poles on the open rafters above the car. The Minnesota lake country essay was deeply personal, not just about a region, but about intimate experience and emotional history, the kind of story I had to do because who else could possibly know it better, who else could really tell it? I photographed and wrote it, and after publication, readers responded to it in greater numbers than to anything else I'd ever done for the magazine. I felt impelled to find a publisher and return again to the lake country a few years later on my own, to try to get it even better, fuller, and to give it the permanency offered by a book.

Some of the most recent work in this five-decade retrospective is the result of my decision in 2005 to return to the Hutterites of Montana for a new story about the people I first knew and portrayed in 1969. By 2005 some of them were like a second family to me. That year, in Minnesota, my son Scott—the firstborn of my five children, in the prime of life at age 45, a father of two—succumbed to the sudden savagery of melanoma while I was with the Hutterites in Montana. Their support of me at that moment, and my writing about Scott while writing about them, eased my grief and may have saved my mind.

In this book are pictures from places I first visited and then felt a need to return to, such as Paris and Peru. In a lifetime of travels, Paris remains my favorite city in the world. Peru changed my life and my world. Other places, such as Sicily, I have been to only once but would like to return to, as I would to almost anywhere in Italy. I waited until the twilight of my career before first visiting India, and I would go back tomorrow if an assignment beckoned, and could probably live at least another lifetime or two and not exhaust the visual stimuli of that country.

In this book are pictures I feel warrant their place on a page even though they may be the only picture selected from a particular essay; some may best represent a step or a moment in my development as a photographer. There is a simple picture, made in 1964, of a wild colt on a windy, often hostile-weathered place off the coast of Nova Scotia called Sable Island, a place famous for its history as a ship graveyard. The picture of the horse is the only one I made that I care about or show from a couple of weeks of trying to do a story on that barren Canadian weather station island, where a handful of civil servants worked and shared the habitat with a herd of wild horses whose ancestors survived some long-ago shipwreck. This picture—with the colt's face in dark profile and its windblown mane a splash of gold against a green background—helped me discover the power of color film.

The light and color in a picture of a bar in Panama City, Panama, made in 1969, is subdued, open enough to show the figures of five men

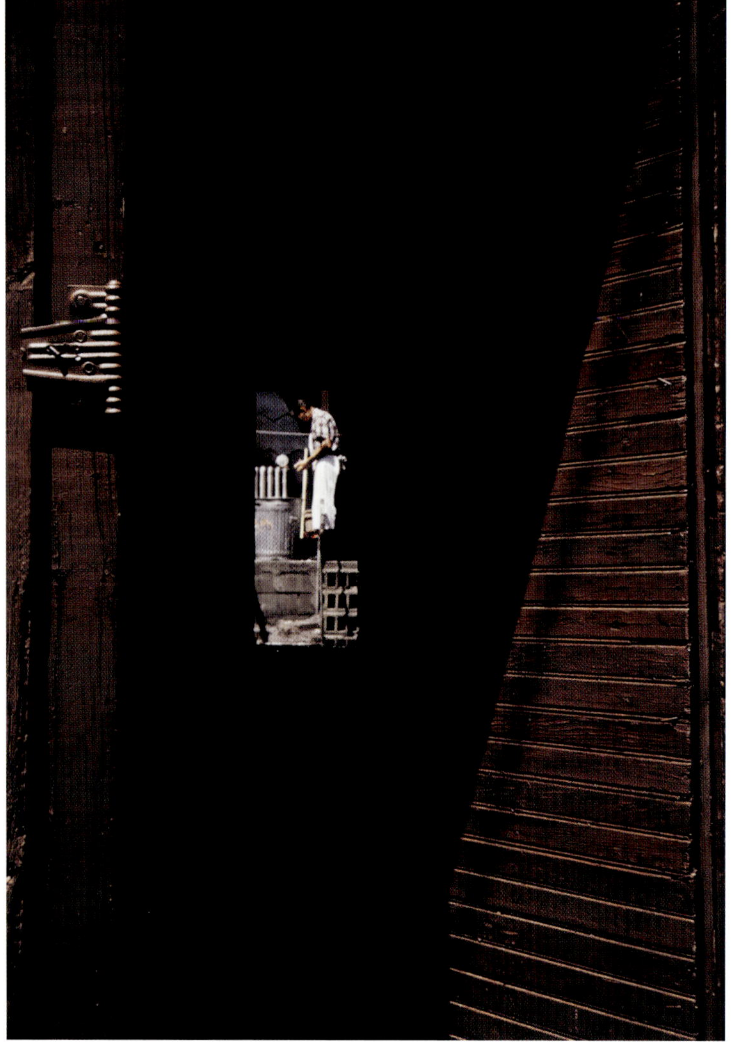

and the painting of a partially nude woman on the wall, and there is just a hint—you have to look close—that one of those men has just exhaled some cigarette smoke that angles upward like a faint funnel in the air. Little moments within pictures are the details that give them life and form.

Photography is all about light. Color photography is about light, the color of the light, and more, but I've never developed the proper vocabulary to be articulate about it. I just feel it. When I started as a professional photographer, at *National Geographic*, color was not mentioned on my brief photography résumé. That day in the spring of 1964, a couple of months away from graduating from the University of Minnesota, I was in the Washington, D.C., office of Bob Gilka, the magazine's director of photography, who was considering me for a possible internship. He asked, "How do you feel about color?" "Doesn't bother me," I answered. I still don't consider my answer anything less than totally honest. How could it bother me? I'd never loaded a roll of color film into my camera.

But as soon as I got home to Minneapolis, I did. I still have that first roll of color film. I didn't like color film too much at first. As an intern at the *Geographic*, the country's only all-color major magazine, it wasn't a matter of choice: I had to work in color. At first it was like sending all my film to the drugstore. It went off to a professional lab for processing and came back as cardboard-mounted transparencies stacked inside yellow boxes. I missed the hands-on darkroom work, the magic

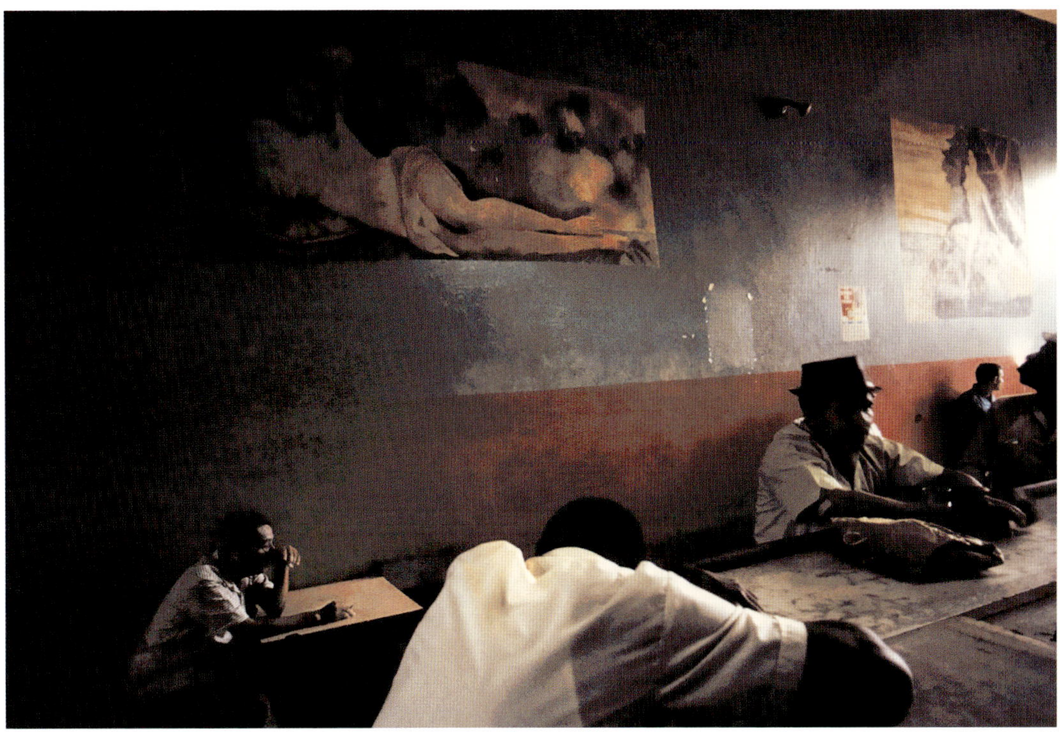

LEFT: *From my first roll of color film, Minneapolis, 1964* ABOVE: *Bar, Panama City, Panama, 1969*

of unspooling film by feel and loading it into a tank; the acrid smell of darkroom chemicals; and the birth of a black-and-white print that lay in a tray, slowly revealing itself while submerged beneath my fingertips. But I came to love color film fairly soon, and since then, although I enjoy looking at beautiful black-and-white prints, I've wanted to work only in color; I am probably one of the few photographers of my generation whose entire body of work is in color.

Many of the pictures in this book were found along a road, in a bar, down a street, maybe while I was wandering through a country. Often I wasn't looking for anything in particular, but was simply allowing myself to be open to what serendipity might offer. Just looking. And many of these pictures were not really taken, they were given. The subjects trusted me. They projected something of themselves to me, and it became my privilege and pleasure to receive that something, look at it, arrange the space in which it resided, find what seemed to be order within chaos, and make the photograph.

AS A SMALL BOY I loved to sing.

I spent parts of my summers on an uncle's farm. My aunt assured my mother: "I always know where Billy is because I can hear him singing." As a teenager I was part of a vocal quartet, and then a trio. After high school, we did singing gigs here and there in clubs in Minneapolis for a while and then split up when I decided to concentrate on my studies at the University of Minnesota. But music has always been a major and necessary force in my life. If I were not a photographer and a writer, if I were lucky enough, I'd make music my work. As with the desire to make photographs or craft words for a living, it isn't really about money. It's about finding some way to go through life truly loving and needing what you do for that living.

When asked, as I sometimes am, to speak to a class of high school or college students, I usually get around to wishing for them something I consider special. I emphasize that it's probably not going to happen to all of them, but I wish it for them nonetheless. I tell them that when they go out to earn a living, as almost everyone must, although everyone would like to have a car they can depend upon, live in a house or dwelling they can feel good about, and be financially comfortable, I wish for them the joy of finding something that they truly *love* to do. People are not running around in great numbers who can say that. I can. I know what it is like to have loved what I've done for a livelihood. And I've known what it's like not to be able to, and how badly I missed it.

There are lyrics from Pink Floyd's "Comfortably Numb" that I think about sometimes. I favor Van Morrison's version, so intense and almost desperate, with a sense of loss. It's the closing lyrics that really tell the story:

When I was a child I caught a fleeting glimpse
Out of the corner of my eye
I turned to look, but it was gone
I cannot put my finger on it now
The child has grown, the dream is gone
And I have become
Comfortably numb

Life does that to some of us. As the years pass, the child within tends to grow up and often goes away, taking along the dreams of childhood. Unlike that teenage son or daughter who goes off to college or to see the world, this inner child does not come back. The absence of that child can sometimes dampen the creative fires; the passions of earlier dreams may change to concerns about benefits accrued in the workplace: 401s, 403s, IRAs, and how soon one can get out of that workplace to have fun or perhaps to just rest. I've been quite lucky—blessed, I suppose. My inner child has never truly grown up. Each time I have the experience of seeing a visually exciting moment and trying to capture that moment in a camera, each time I'm writing about something I really care about, my childhood dreams are very much alive. And I've never wanted out of my workplace, which, for the most part, has been *National Geographic* magazine. During my career I have worked for and been published in many different publications worldwide. But since I made my first photograph for them in 1964, National Geographic has been a kind of primary sponsor that has allowed me to create most of the images in this book. I owe them my sincere gratitude. I've always tried to be worth their faith in me. I guess it's because of their willingness over almost all of my career to support the kind of work I truly love to do that my fire and passion for it still burns. And I've somehow managed to avoid becoming comfortably numb. I'm going to do my best to stay that way. ■

—Missoula, Montana, 2009

Hank Irby, Marks, Mississippi, 1968

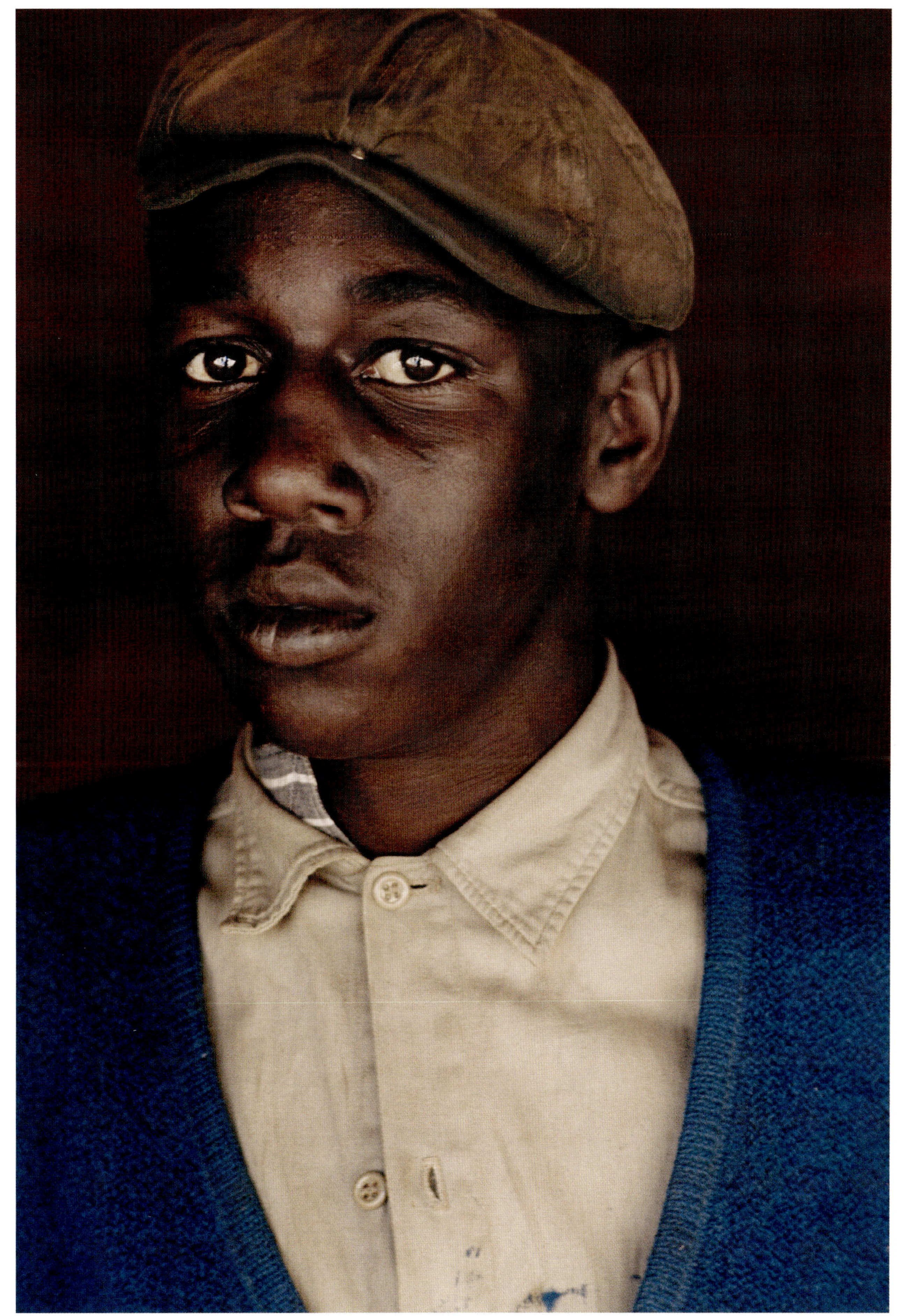

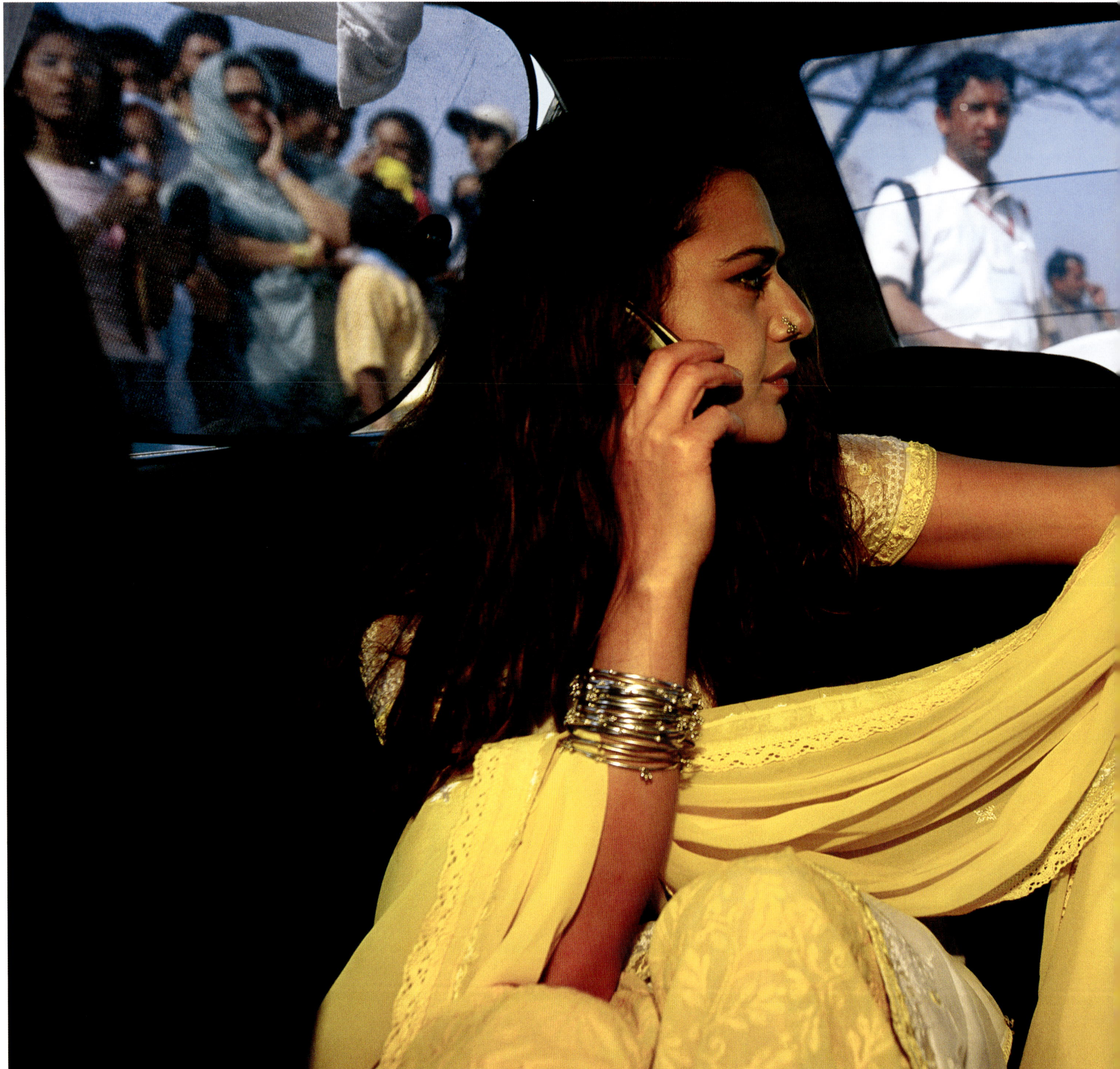

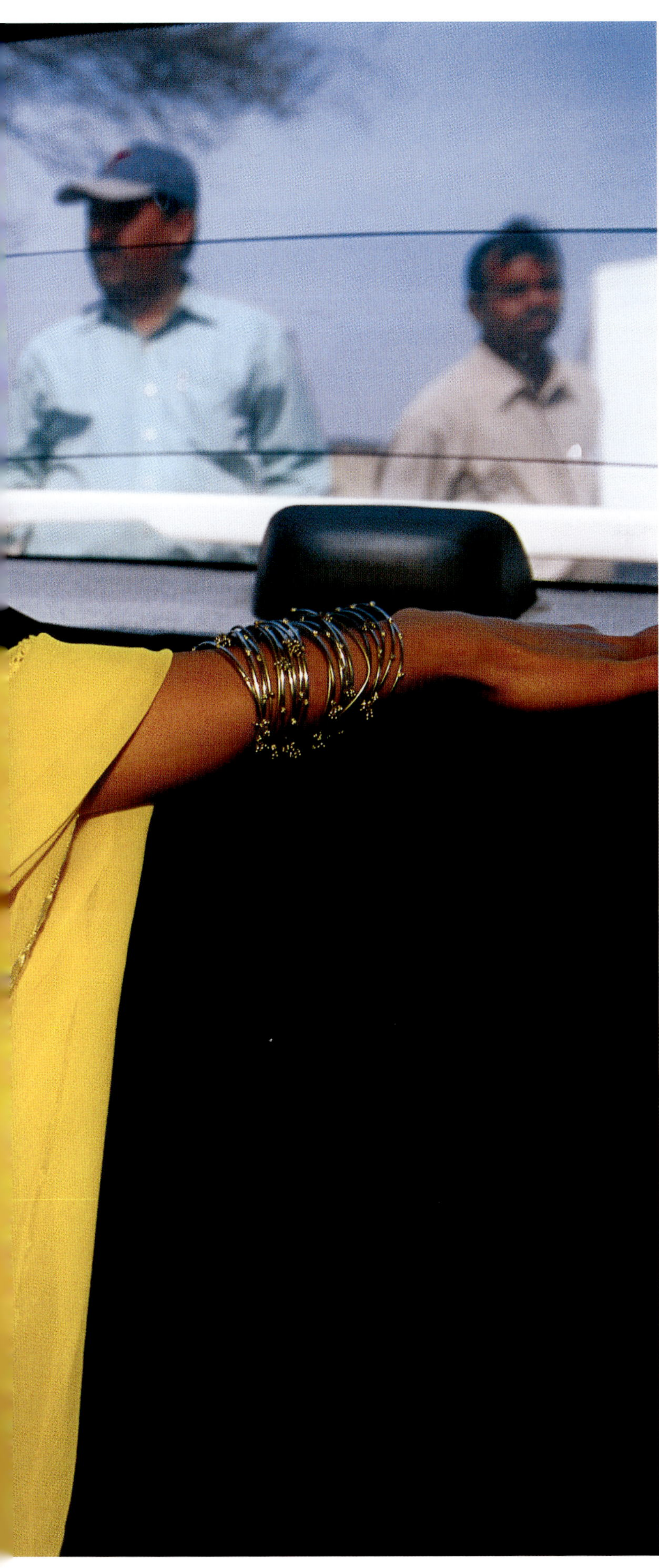

"I think I can feel color... I can't explain it, but I can feel it. In my photography, color and composition are inseparable. I see in color."

Preity Zinta, Bollywood actress, India, 2004

"The picture of Eduardo...is one of the rare times I feel I've been able to give back to one of my subjects in a significant way."

Eduardo Ramos with his dead sheep, Puno, Peru, 1981

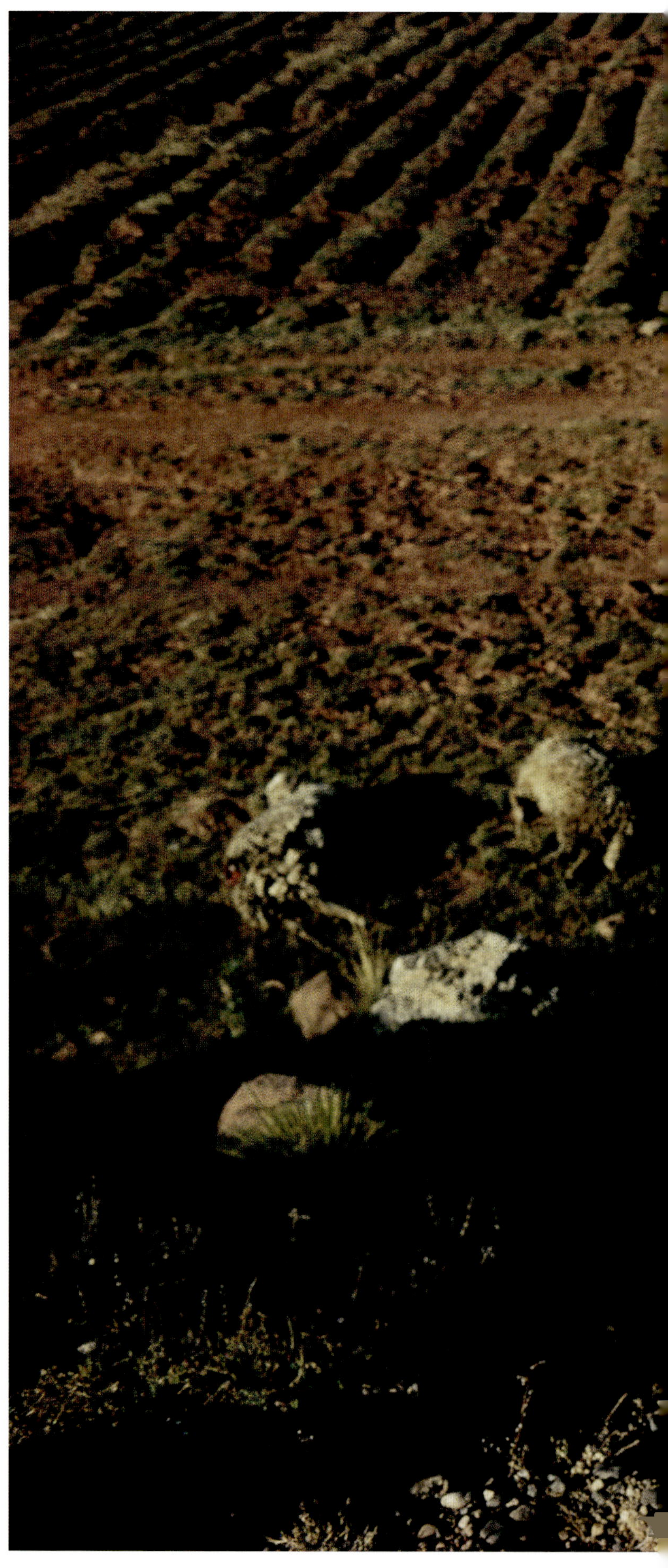

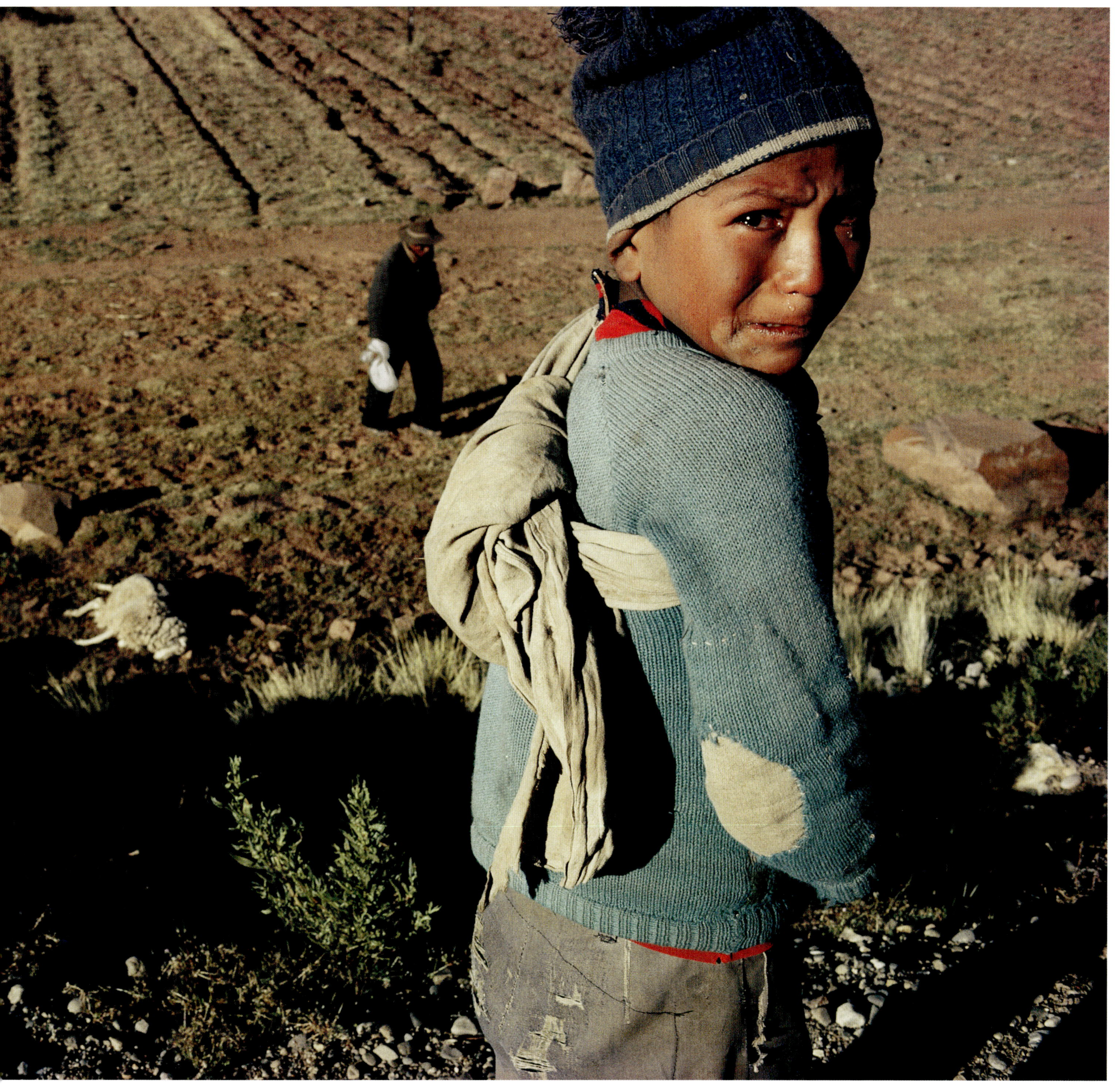

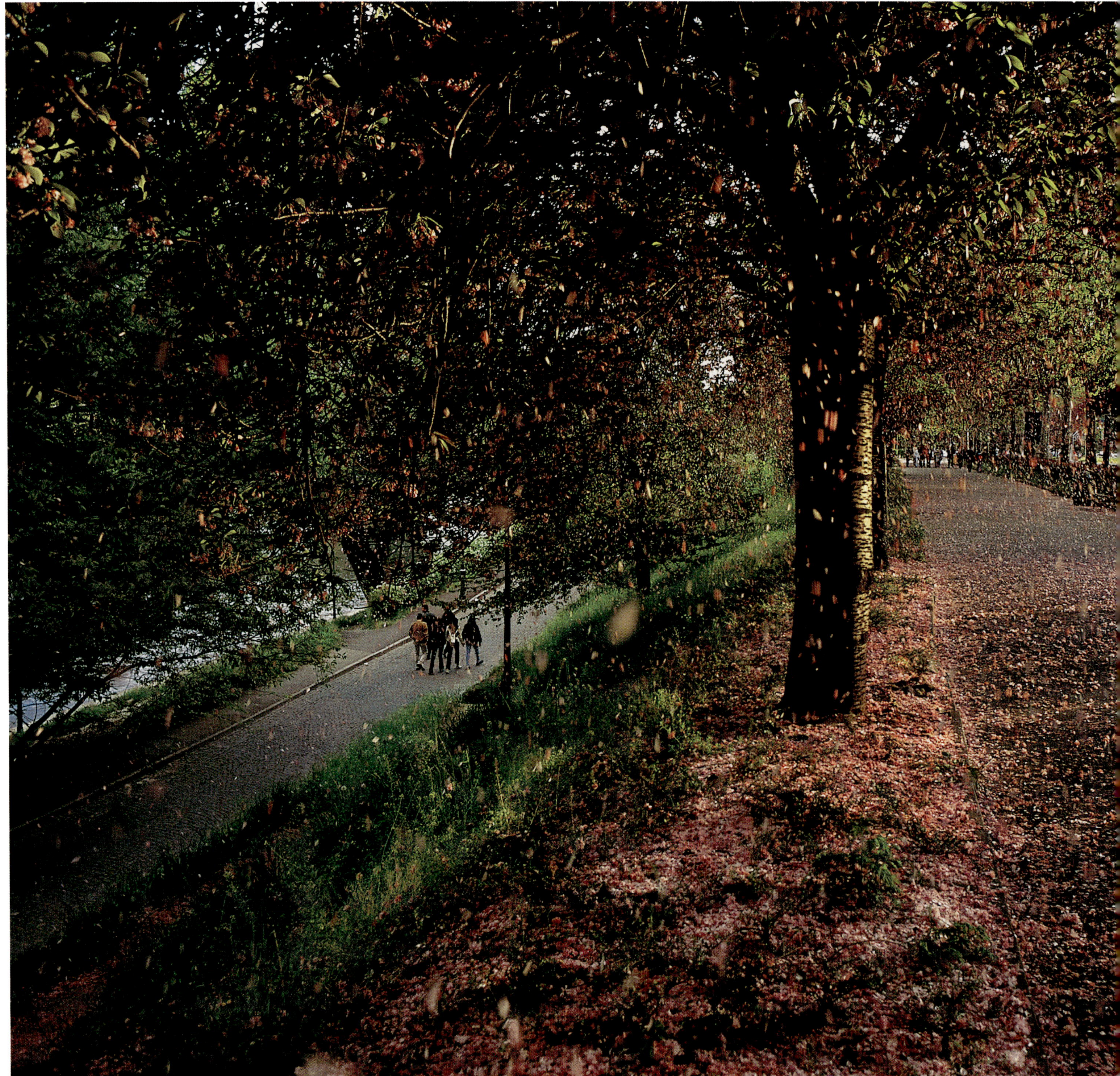

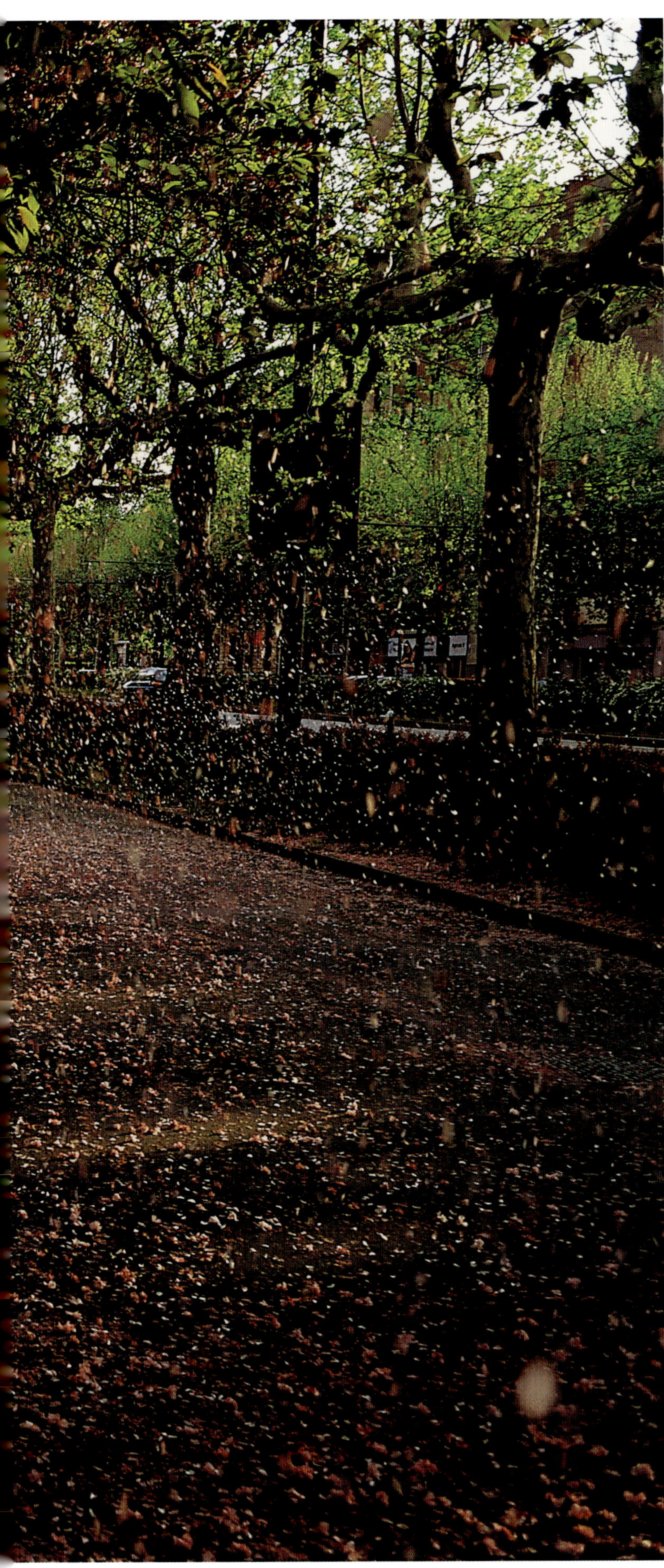

"The best pictures last because they sing, and some people will remember them as they remember songs. Maybe that's a stretch. But I believe it; it works for me to think that way."

Blossoming apricot trees, Valentino Park, Turin, Italy, 2001

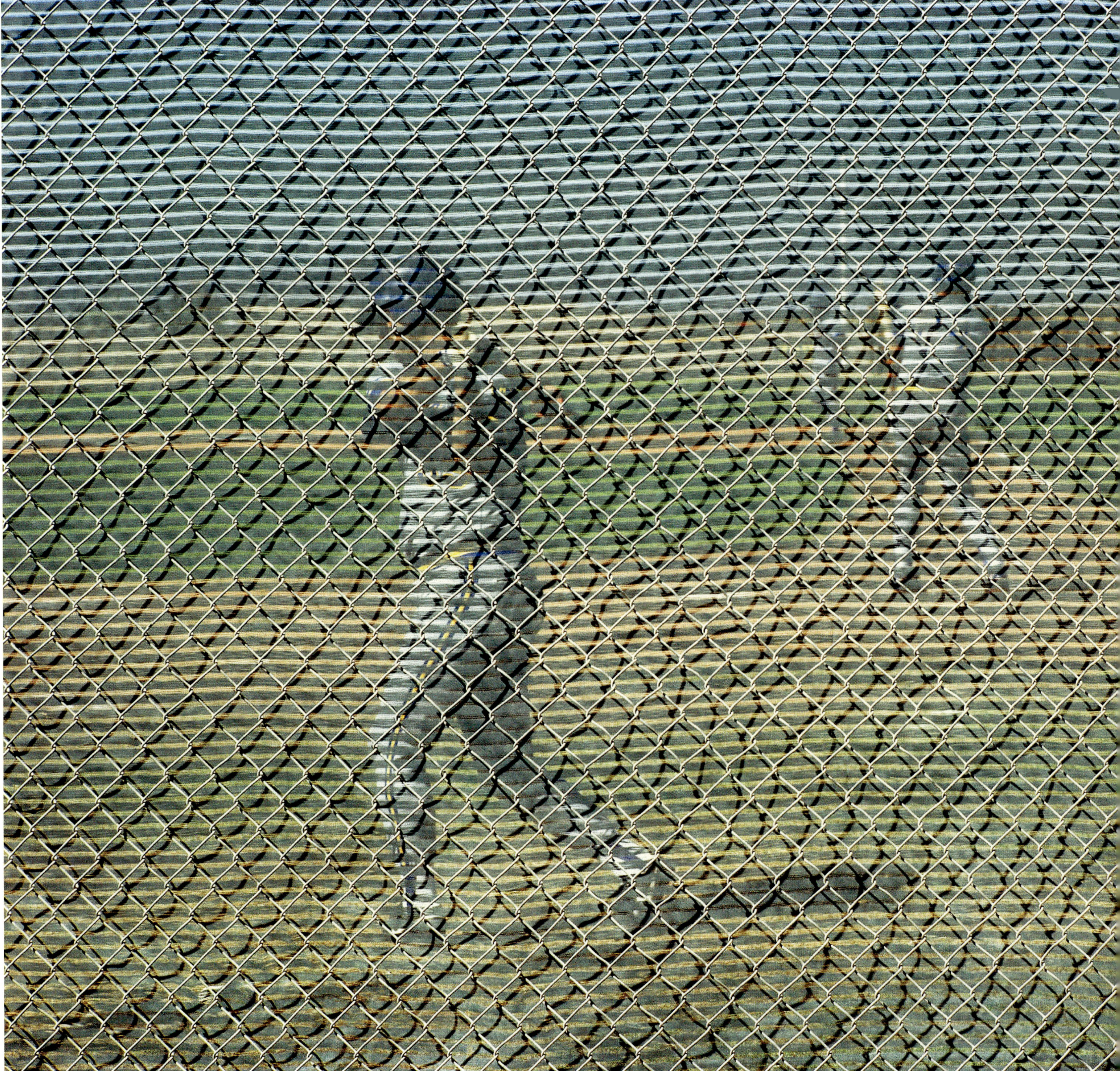

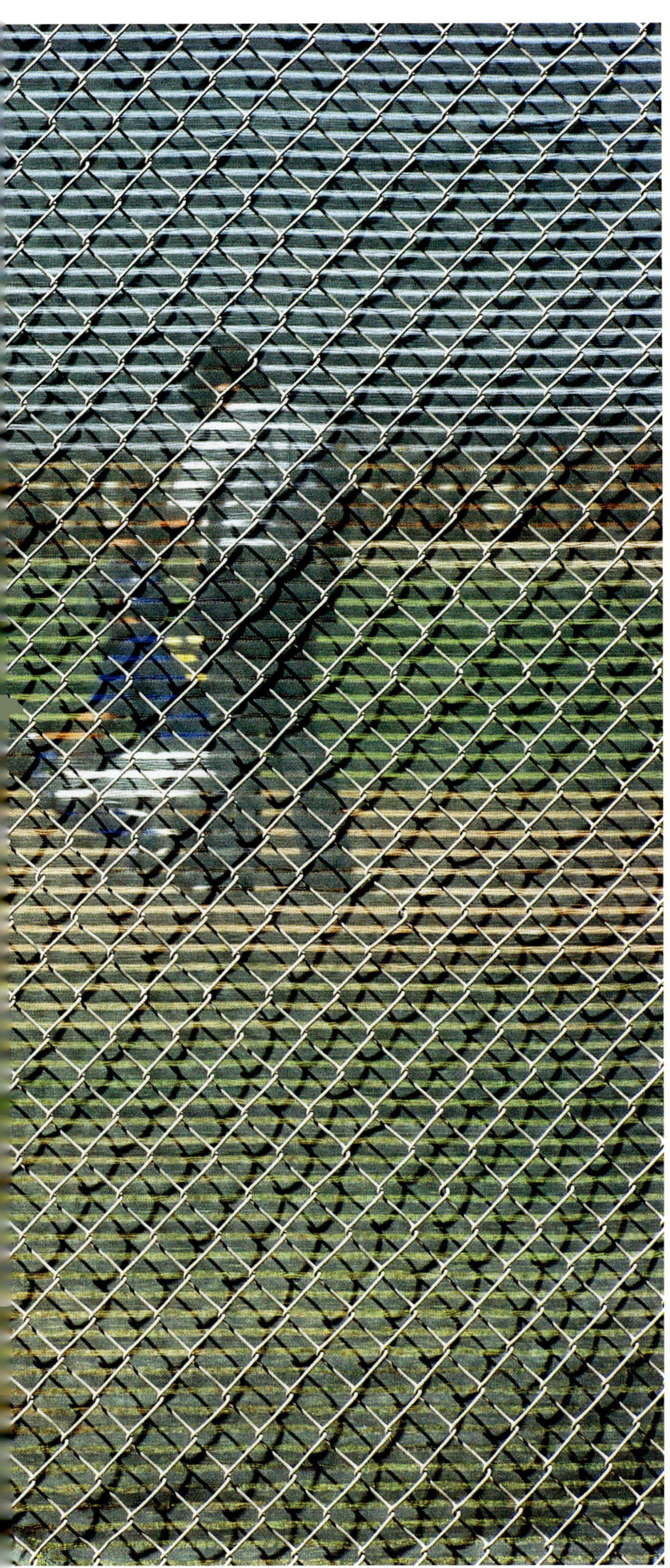

"I hope and look for that one image, totally balanced, complete within itself, perfection framed in a single moment. Well, perhaps not perfection, but the best it can be until I try again to do it even better."

Minor league spring training, Phoenix, Arizona, 1990

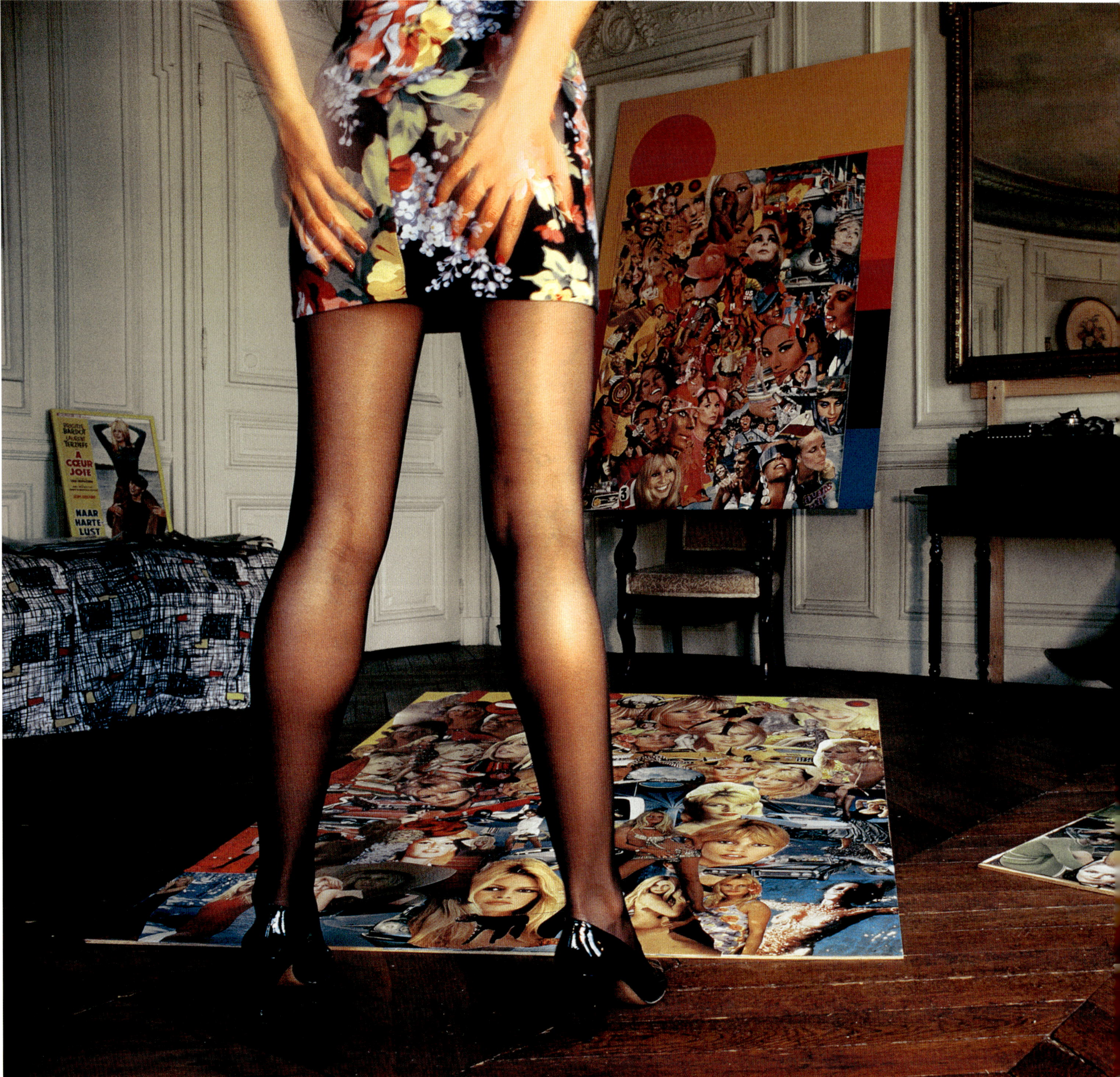

BARDOT
TERZIEFF
A
CŒUR
JOIE
NAAR
HARTE-
LUST

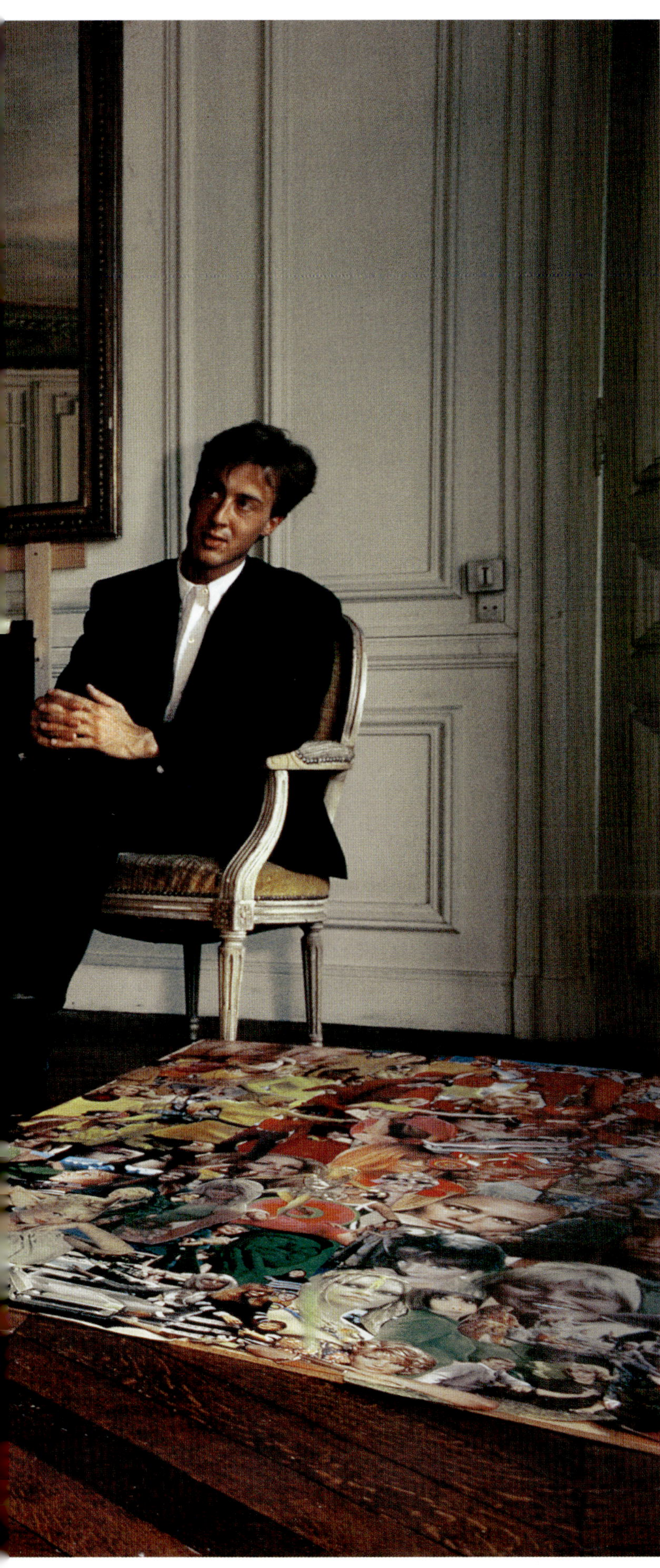

"I want an image to have the harmony and economy of a well-crafted paragraph, the grace and sense of balance found within the geometry of a fine painting. I want my pictures to have intimacy..."

Tanya and Edouard, Paris, 1988

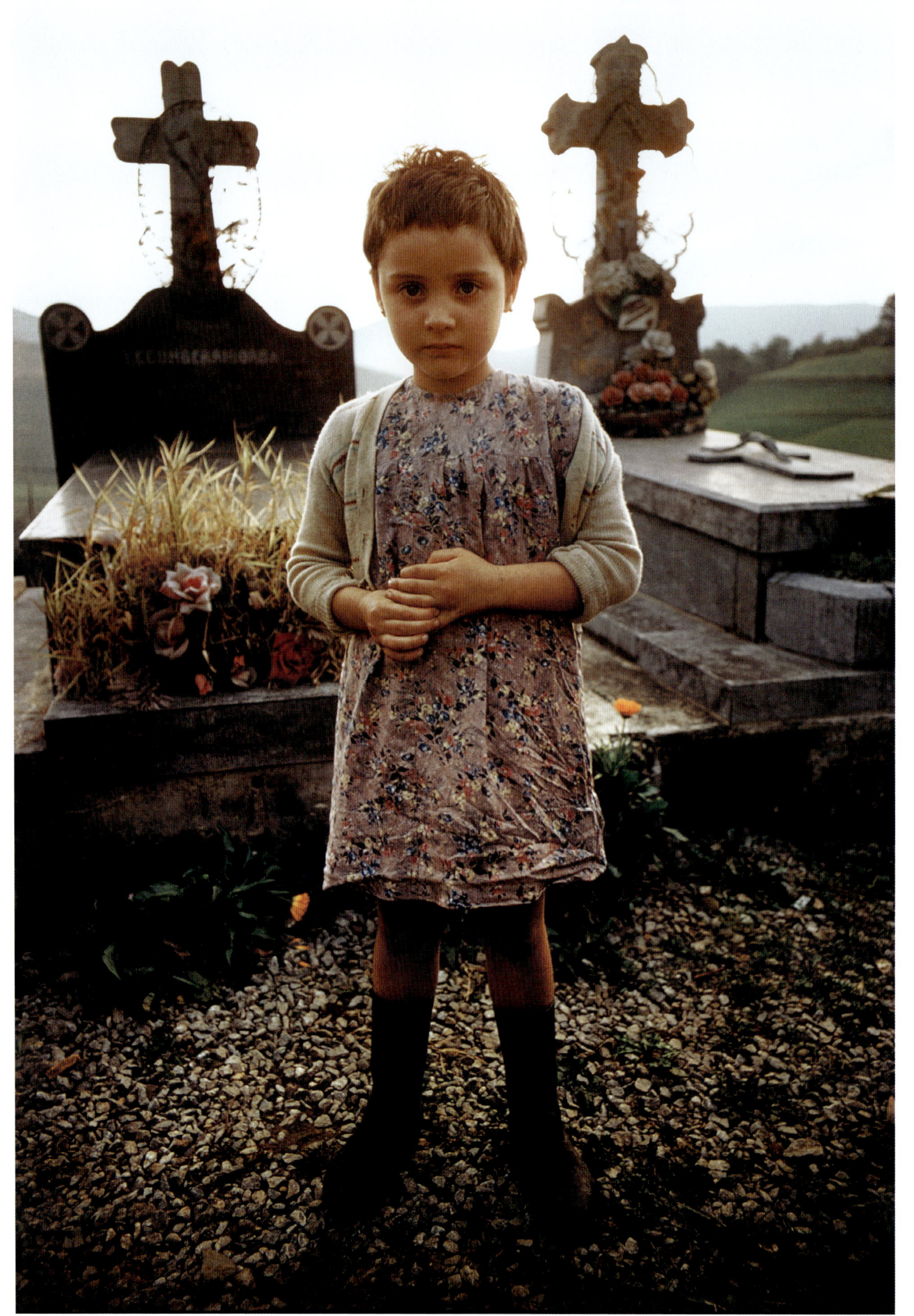

The Basques

In the fall of 1967 I spent several months in the Basque Country of Spain and France to illustrate a *National Geographic* article written by the late Robert Laxalt. Laxalt's father had been an immigrant Basque sheepherder in Nevada in the early 1900s. At one time Bob and his family lived in the French Basque region. Unlike Bob, though, I never lived in the Basque Country; I was merely a visitor.

There was a lot I didn't see during my short stay in the Basque Country—aspects of traditional Basque life I couldn't photograph because I didn't witness them. The few images in this book are drawn from a short visit to a place that probably requires a lifetime to really know and maybe longer to truly understand.

This was my inaugural visit to France and Spain, and I was still very much in a kind of finger painting stage of color photography. I had photographed in color for the first time barely three years earlier, in 1964, when given my first *Geographic* assignment, the Amish of Lancaster County, Pennsylvania. I was still learning to transfer what I would see with my eyes onto the color films I was using, most of which were quite slow in light sensitivity. As a photojournalism and art photography student at the University of Minnesota, I had to work to support my family as well as attend school, and I had to do a lot of my photography projects at night and inside places with not much light. I learned to use slow, handheld exposures to obtain black-and-white pictures in subdued, often

Girl in the cemetery, Béhorléguy, France, 1967

very dim light. Now working in color, using much slower films, I had somehow never thought that I couldn't work the same way as I had in black and white; it often became a matter of trying to hold my camera steady, making a lot of mistakes, losing pictures to subject motion or hand shake, but ultimately getting those images I saw with the feeling and palette that color film offered. I think it was while working in the Basque Country that I truly fell in love with color photography. Even though typically I would not be able to see my efforts from an assignment until long after the pictures had been made, when I returned to Washington to look at them with my picture editor, I was learning intuitively about color. I think I can feel color. I don't have a designer's vocabulary to talk about it, I can't explain it, but I can feel it. In my photography, color and composition are inseparable. I see in color.

In the Basque Country I continued to follow a working mode I'd established at the very beginning of my career when working in the Amish country: going out looking for perhaps something in particular but always leaving myself open to serendipity, to something I might be offered by chance that far surpassed what I thought I'd been looking for. I would haunt the mountain roads, winding through villages, past vineyards and high pastures, hunting for pictures, sometimes alone, sometimes with a translator.

It was always promising if I happened to come upon a village on market day, because market day brought together the women and men of the community for a lot of social interaction, gossiping as well as marketing. Men would show their cattle, sheep, or horses—asking for a price, arguing for it, back and forth, back and forth in a language totally beyond any comprehension on my part. Understanding the Basque language seemed impossible, far beyond something I might pick up easily, even though I have a decent ear for the sounds of a language; Basque is far beyond my linguistic sensitivities.

Women would cluster like the chickens they had brought to sell under the awning of the town's main café, the social center for most days but especially on market day. Gray-furred rabbits were strung by their feet from a scale; others nestled in reed-woven baskets. Some baskets held ducks or perhaps dozens of fresh eggs. As dusk prevailed and the market emptied, the café would slowly fill with diners. The menu would offer *palombre,* doves trapped during their fall migration through the mountain passes, cooked in red wine—perhaps the same local red wine, a bit harsh but full bodied, that filled my glass.

It was always nice to get back to whatever village I was staying in before dark. Some of the mountain roads proved challenging after sunset. Once, while returning to St.-Jean-Pied-de-Port from St.-Jean-de-Luz, where I'd gone to satisfy my new addiction to escargot (we never saw snails on a menu in north Minneapolis, where I grew up, and now at dinner I often had a dozen at one meal, followed by a pepper steak and a full bottle of red wine), I managed to slide my rental car off the edge of the road to where I was staying. There I was, high centered, hung up in a ditch well short of town. A couple of young Basque men passing by stopped, backed up, and offered to help. By themselves—I remember there being only two, but there must have been three; it was a long time ago—they righted my car and sent me on my way. Muscular men, the Basques celebrate feats of strength in some of their festival contests, seeing who can lift the heaviest stone. Perhaps car lifting might be added, but cars wouldn't have the same traditional appeal as the large, smooth, rounded stones used in the age-old contests.

WHEN I LOOK NOW at the *National Geographic* article published in 1968, I think it looks OK; it has some high points in terms of individual pictures, but I also think, Why didn't I push to have some of the other pictures published that were so much better? That was a question that would develop into a cause and at times a calamity as my career continued.

Sometimes a picture is excluded from a layout because it echoes another or repeats a kind of vision or gesture or mood. There were, in my early years, times when a picture might have been said to be too "arty," whatever that was supposed to mean. I had a picture editor tell me once, "You have an awful lot of people looking at the camera." So? I thought. If they aren't doing something vastly more interesting, then why not simply look at them, show their faces, introduce them to the viewer with a portrait strong enough that you might somehow feel you know something about that person, what they actually might be like, what kind of life they live, the music they love? I have always believed that a picture, made well enough, can form that kind of connection and transcend being simply a snapshot on the street or a portrait cranked out with the perfection and predictability of standard studio lighting and backdrop but lacking any insight or feeling. The kind of revealing portrait I seek requires an almost indefinable connection between photographer and subject, but I think it is possible even when there might be the barrier of an unshared language. We communicate with our bodies and our eyes and our attitude so much; that's a language unto itself.

Sometimes I would find myself in agreement with the picture selection for a final layout; other times I would not. At *National Geographic* I have always been included in the picture selection and layout design, although I never truly have a decision-making role. It took me a long time to realize that you can't charge into the layout room and just vent your frustrations with the picture choices being made by people who have that duty assigned them and by the editor in chief, who has the ultimate power of choice. It took me years to finally say to myself, Hell, it's their magazine—let them do what they're going to do and let it go. Just do the work. It's all academic and without value if the work isn't done and done well. There are other ways to put that work to use.

There are always pictures from a completed essay that become favorites, although when asked "What is your favorite picture?" I find that singular selection impossible. But there are images one holds in greater esteem from within any particular body of work. From my Basque work there are a number of pictures I feel as strongly about today as when I first saw them projected in the picture editor's office as what we call selects.

Three men stand in a doorway in the French village of Sare, listening to a *bertsolari*, a poet, during a fête. They are dressed in black. One man displays part of a blue shirt collar, but aside from that wedge of coolness and a bit of interior structure of the room behind them, the light seems to find only those faces rising up out of a mass of black, and they are burnished faces, carved and creviced with an ancient heritage.

A girl stands in a cemetery. Her hair is cut boyishly short. Maybe her mother trimmed it just today. She holds her hands at waist level, her small fingers interlaced, arms held close to her sides. She wears a wrinkled cotton dress with a flowery print, uneven at the hem, and a thin blue sweater slipping off one shoulder, the sleeves tugged up above her wrists. She wears rubber boots and stands firmly on gray pieces of gravel, fully confronting me with a stare that seems protected by the crucifixes rising, ghostly, from the two tombstones behind her. There are flowers, real and artificial, and although I can't see them, I know there are photographs of the dead displayed somewhere on the cold granite of those graves that are as hard and foreboding as she is soft and warm and a well-tended-for child. She may be wondering how long I will take her picture. And so am I, probably. After making a picture I later often think I should have done more, I should have done it better. But I'm not at all sure I would change anything here. She is a child in a cemetery. Nothing more, perhaps, and maybe a lot more, depending upon how and what you read into the picture.

Much more whimsical is the picture of three small boys playing by the wall of a house in the village of St.-Jean-le-Vieux. They were probably playing a child's version of the traditional Basque game of *pelota*, throwing the ball against the wall, but their actions at this moment seem totally separate, each child involved in his own world of movement, the smallest one seeming to perch on the back of the boy in the foreground. The architecture of the picture seems right, the various parts connected and interlocked as in a picture puzzle with few pieces that still must fit, and here, I think, they do.

A simple but elegant picture that remains as important and meaningful for me today as it was in the autumn of 1967 is the one of two children running home. I remember how soft the light was in the waning hours of that afternoon. The sun had settled below the surrounding mountains, but its dying light was reflecting off the clouds and fell in a wonderful caress upon the narrow, curving road leading to the small village of Béhorléguy. I was standing alongside the road, just below a cemetery where the children sometimes played. I was looking off over a vineyard when I heard a woman's voice calling from one of the houses at the edge of the village. Moments later I heard the patter of feet upon the road behind me, and as I turned to the sound, two small girls were running and skipping past me in answer to what must have been their mother calling them home. I raised my Leica, framed them, and made two exposures. I remember thinking, feeling, "That could be something special." If I got it right, that could be something special.

A month or so later, when I was back in Washington, D.C., at National Geographic, looking at my film, I came upon those two frames. One was blurry, useless, an utter, uninteresting failure. The other was simply wonderful. The colors were pastel. The soft, diffused light on the children and the road drew you in to the center of the image. And the two girls were not running, they weren't skipping; they were weightless, floating in the air, as if forever suspended in grace and innocence. I believe that picture will always stand the test of time.

On another late afternoon, with dusk approaching, I was driving down out of the mountains with my friend, and sometimes guide and translator, Jean Garicoitz, to his home in St.-Jean-Pied-de-Port. The fading light became a hazy gray veil cast over the rugged landscape and all it contained. Shadows took the shape of objects, and objects became shadows. "We have a saying for this time of day," Jean said. *"Le temps entre chiens et loups,"* he said. "The time between dogs and wolves." I have often thought of that phrase in the years since my brief stay among the Basques, and how different that time was from the soon-to-come years of bloodshed and tears that cursed both sides of the Basque Country because of the brutal and deathly conflict of *Euskadi Ta Askatasuna* (ETA) separatism, beginning in 1968, which lasted for decades.

On the night of the last day of September 1967, I celebrated my 30th birthday alone in a small café in St.-Jean-Pied-de-Port. I was reading a book and drinking a Basque liquor called Izarra. The word means "star," and the throat-warming drink is said to be made from flowers of the Pyrenees. The café had a jukebox, and I played James Brown's "Kansas City" and the Beatles' "Penny Lane." I think I was reading Hemingway's *For Whom the Bell Tolls*; I know I had it with me then. I recall that evening, not so much for the significance attached to having left the decade of my 20s but for the memorable, quiet solitude of the night; the clean, clear air of the mountains; and the feeling of being in the midst of a country and its people unlike any other place in the world. Although alone and unable to speak the language, I somehow felt in tune with the place. I loved it but couldn't quite say why. In retrospect, I suppose it was simply the right moment to be there. I was a young man in an ancient land at a time between dogs and wolves. ■

Workman, Bacáicoa, Spain, 1967

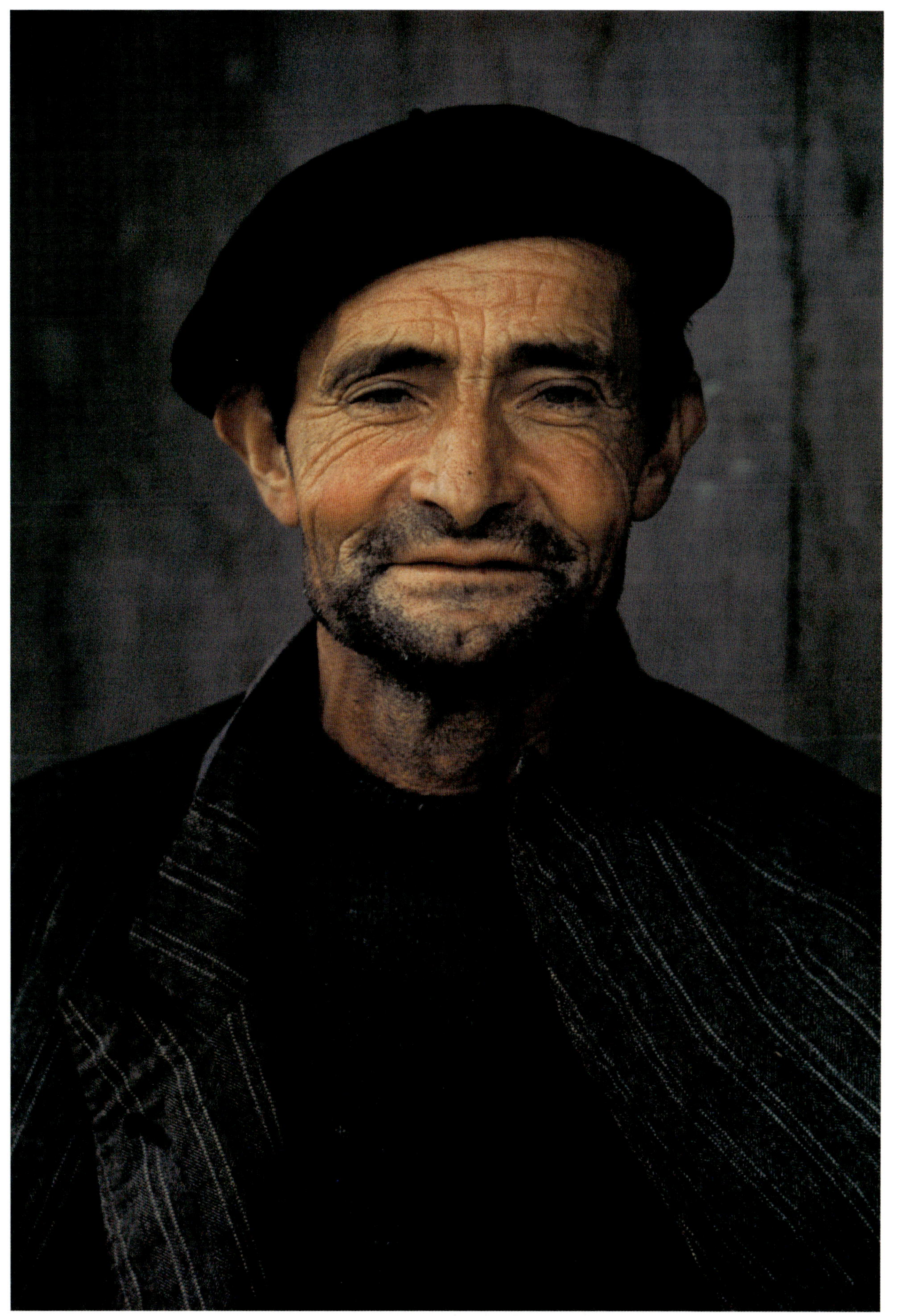

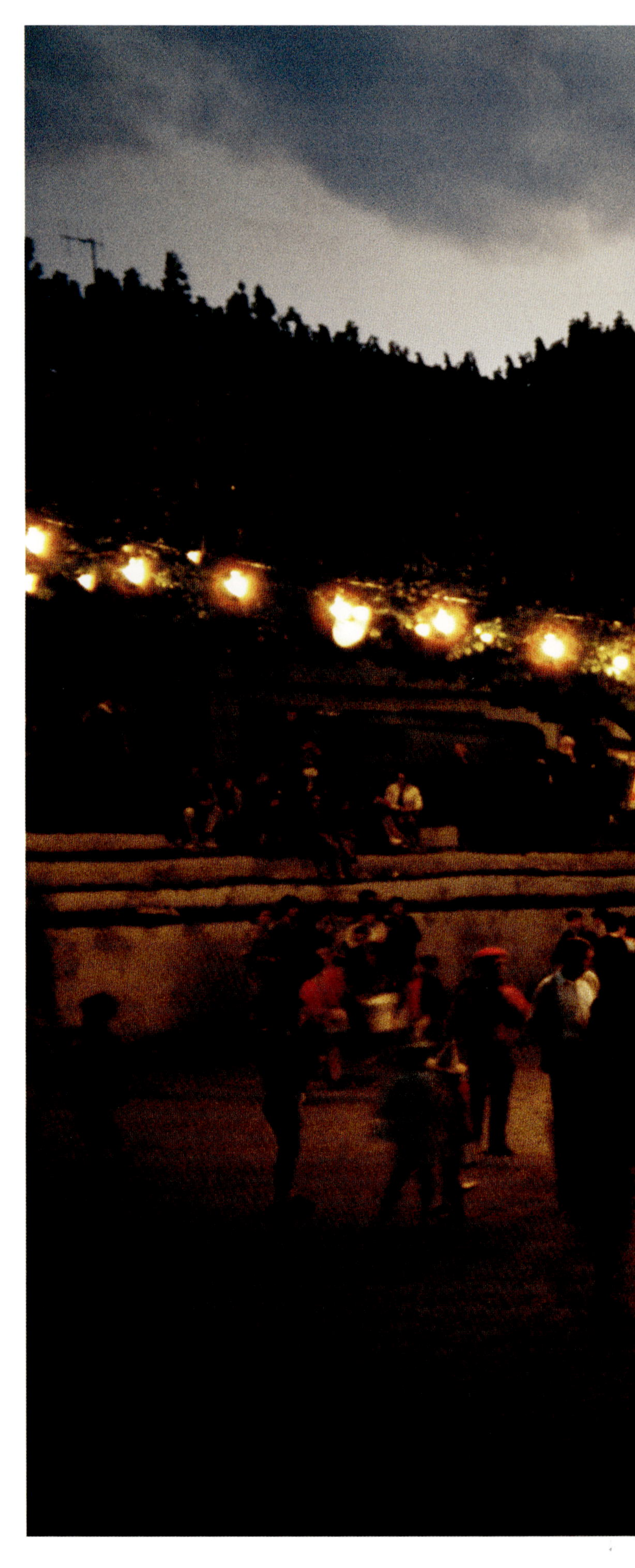

Festival evening, Sare, France, 1967

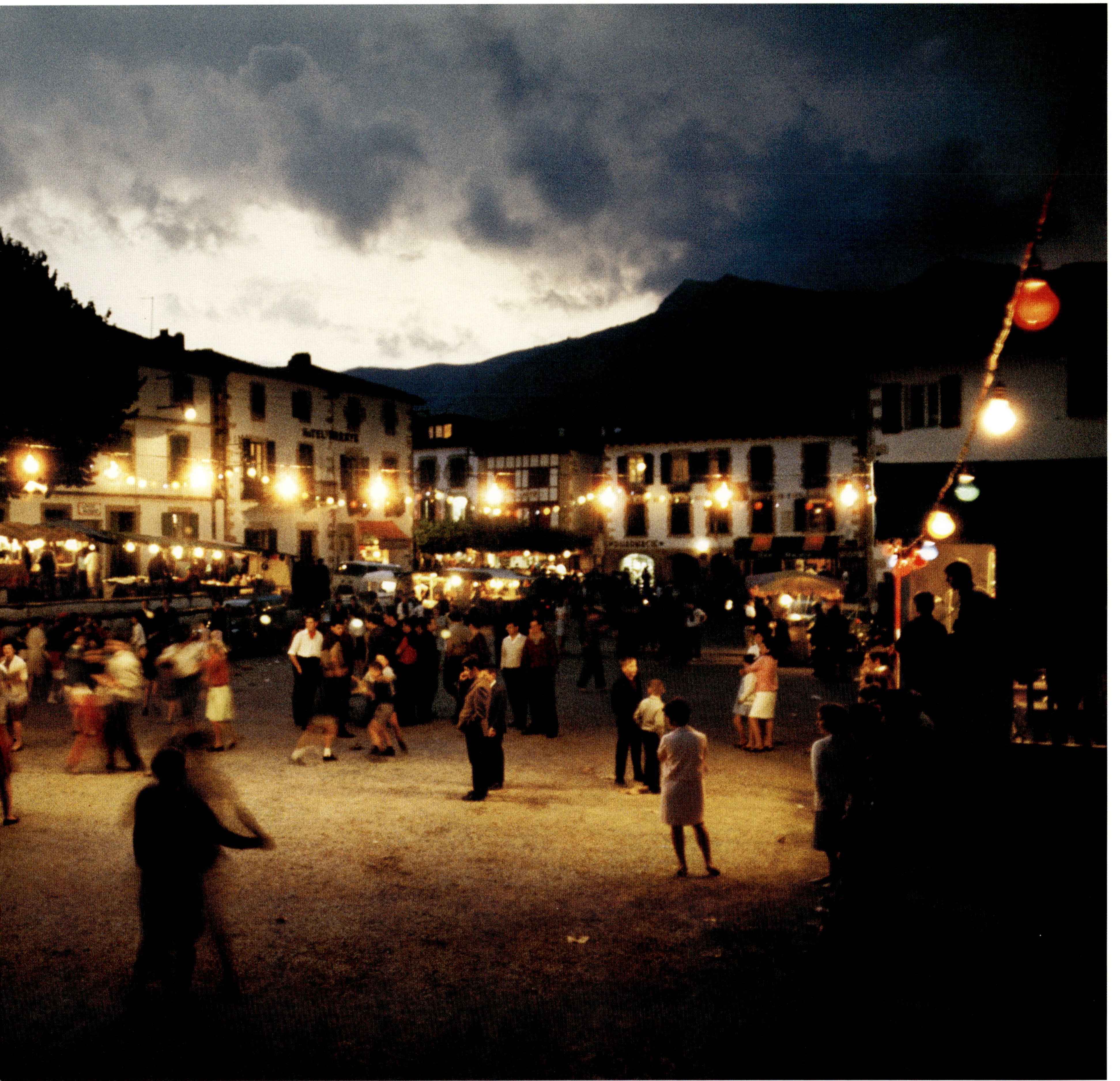

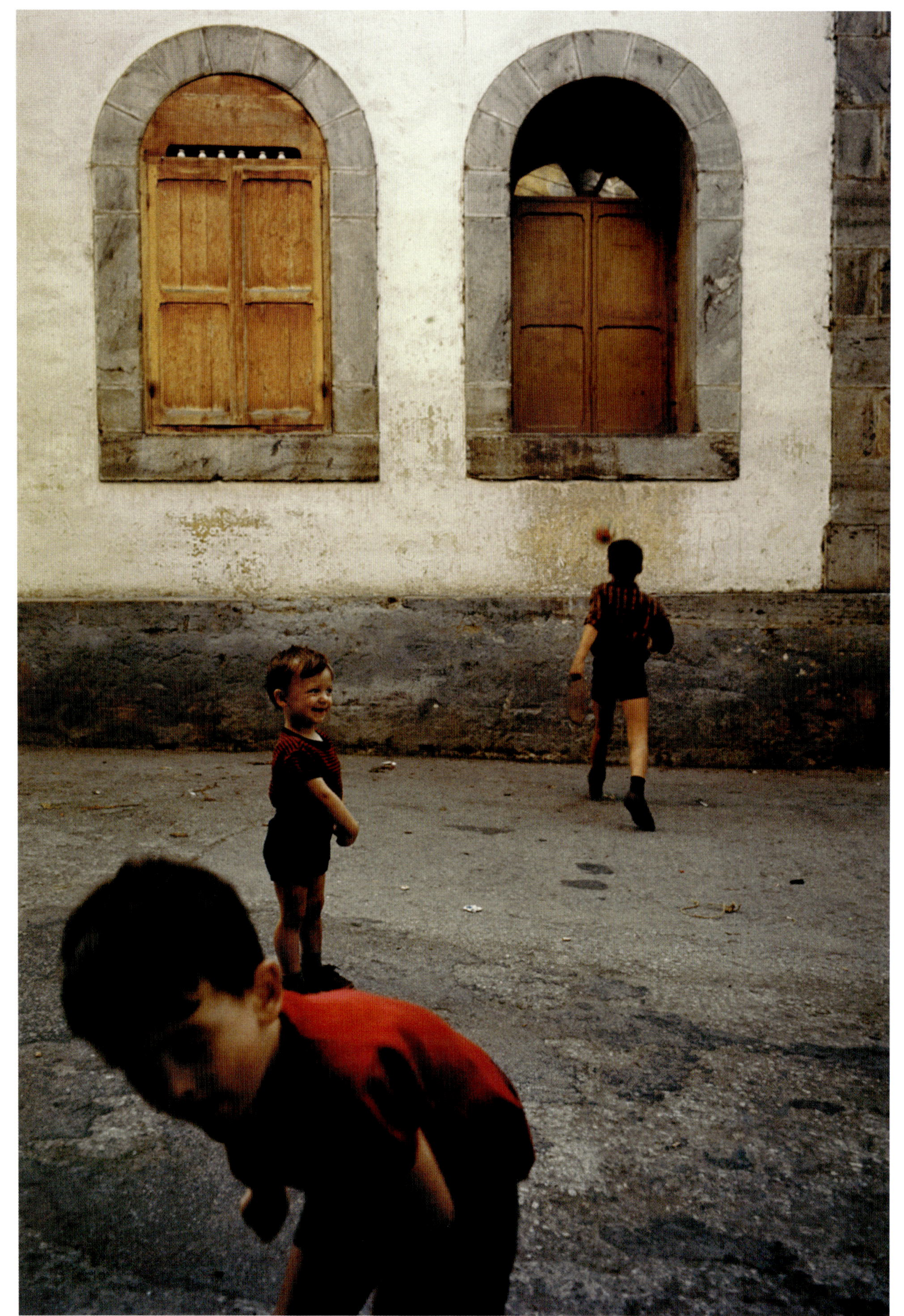

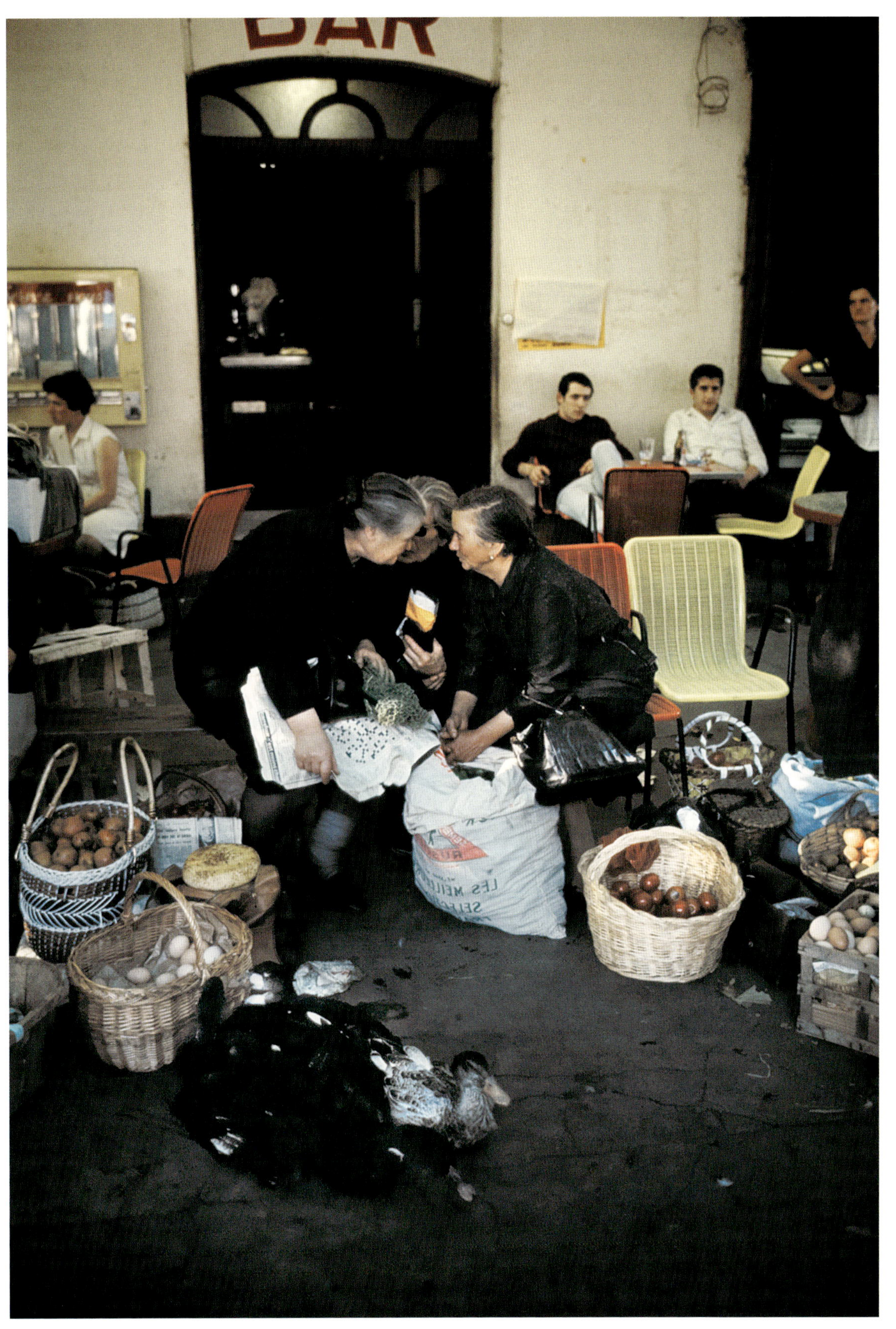

LEFT: *St.-Jean-le-Vieux, France, 1967* ABOVE: *St.-Jean-Pied-de-Port, France, 1967*

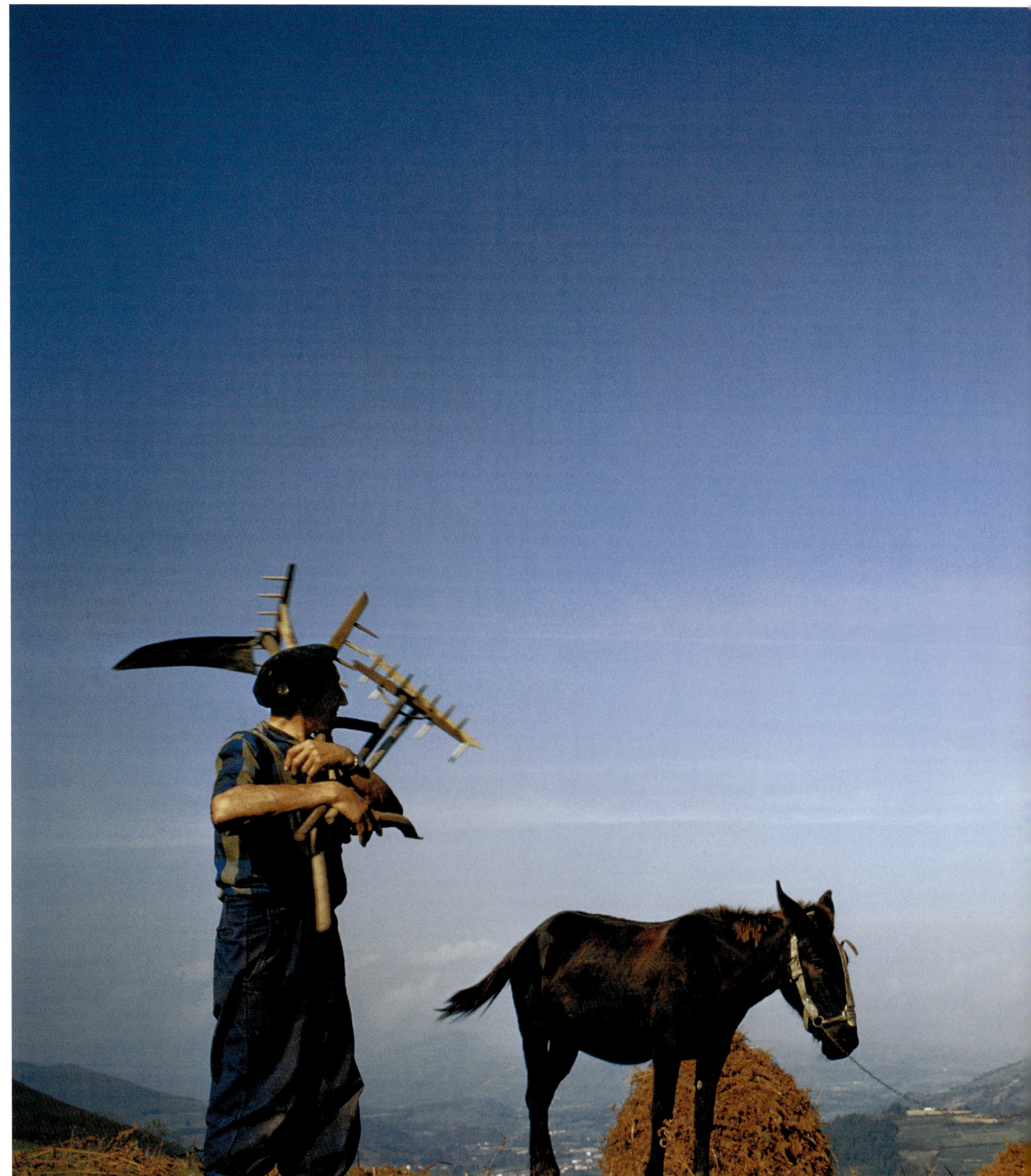

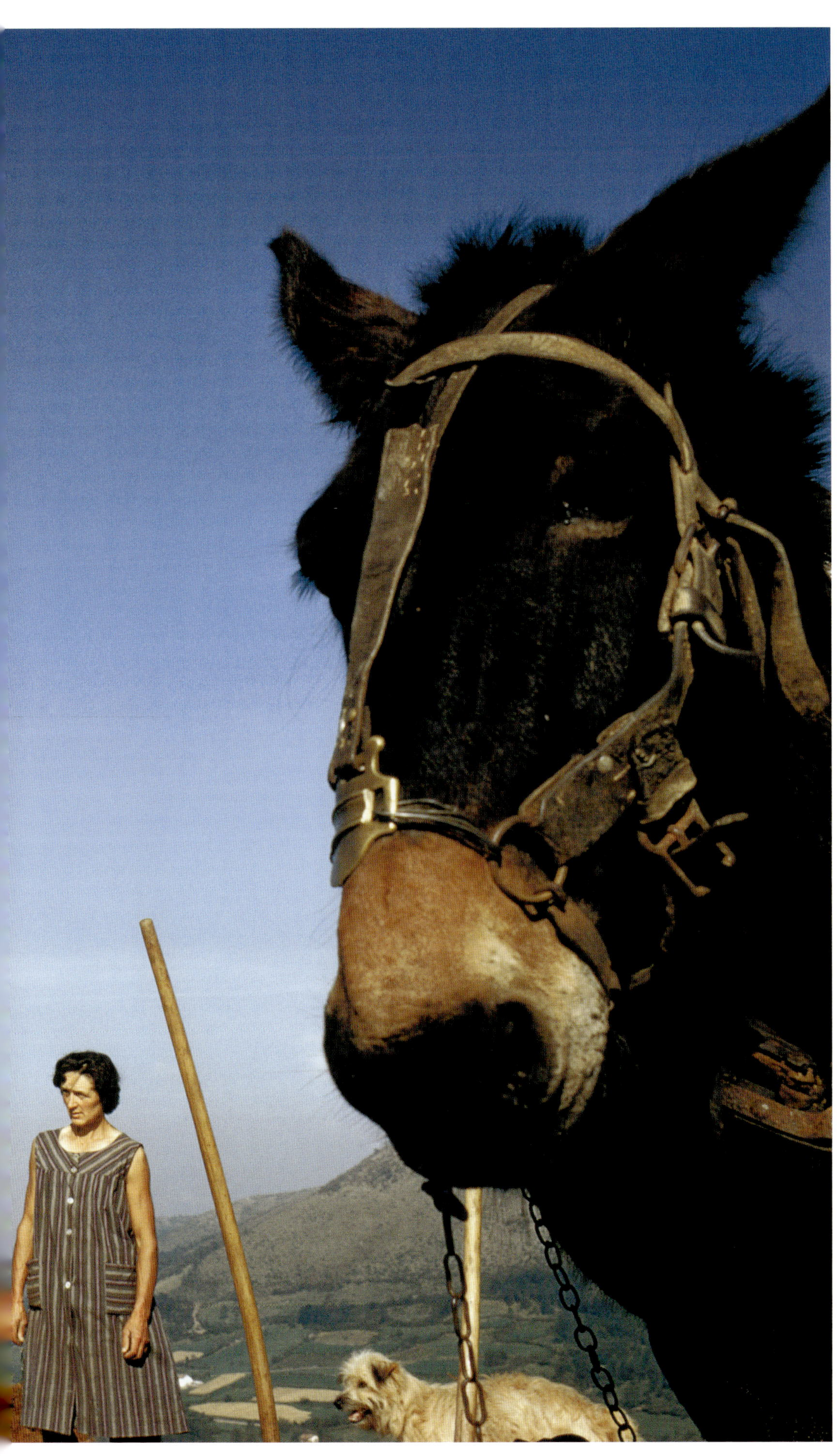

Farmer and his wife, Béhorléguy, France, 1967

"...the two girls were not running, they weren't skipping; they were weightless, floating in the air, as if forever suspended in grace and innocence."

Girls running home, Béhorléguy, France, 1967

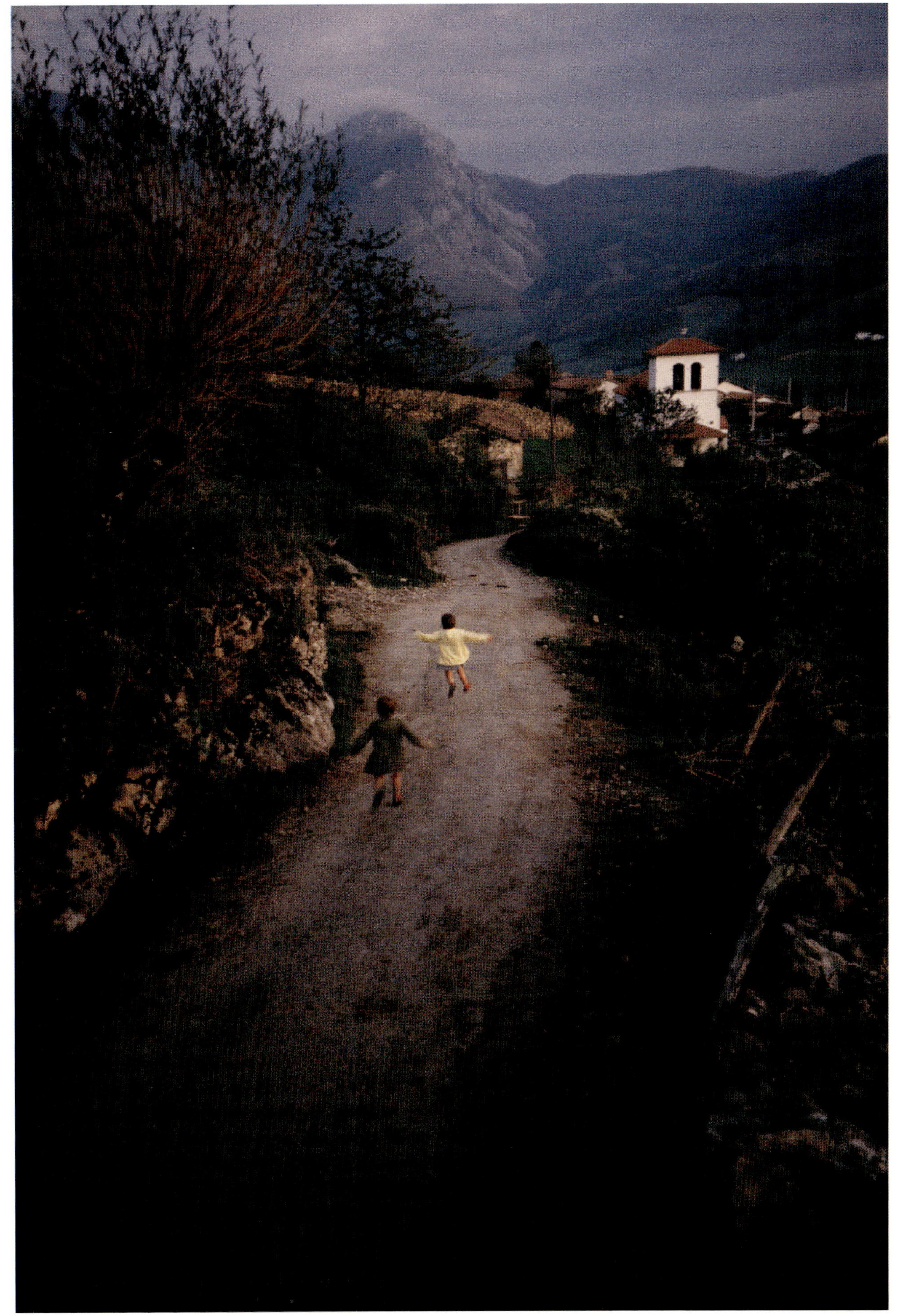

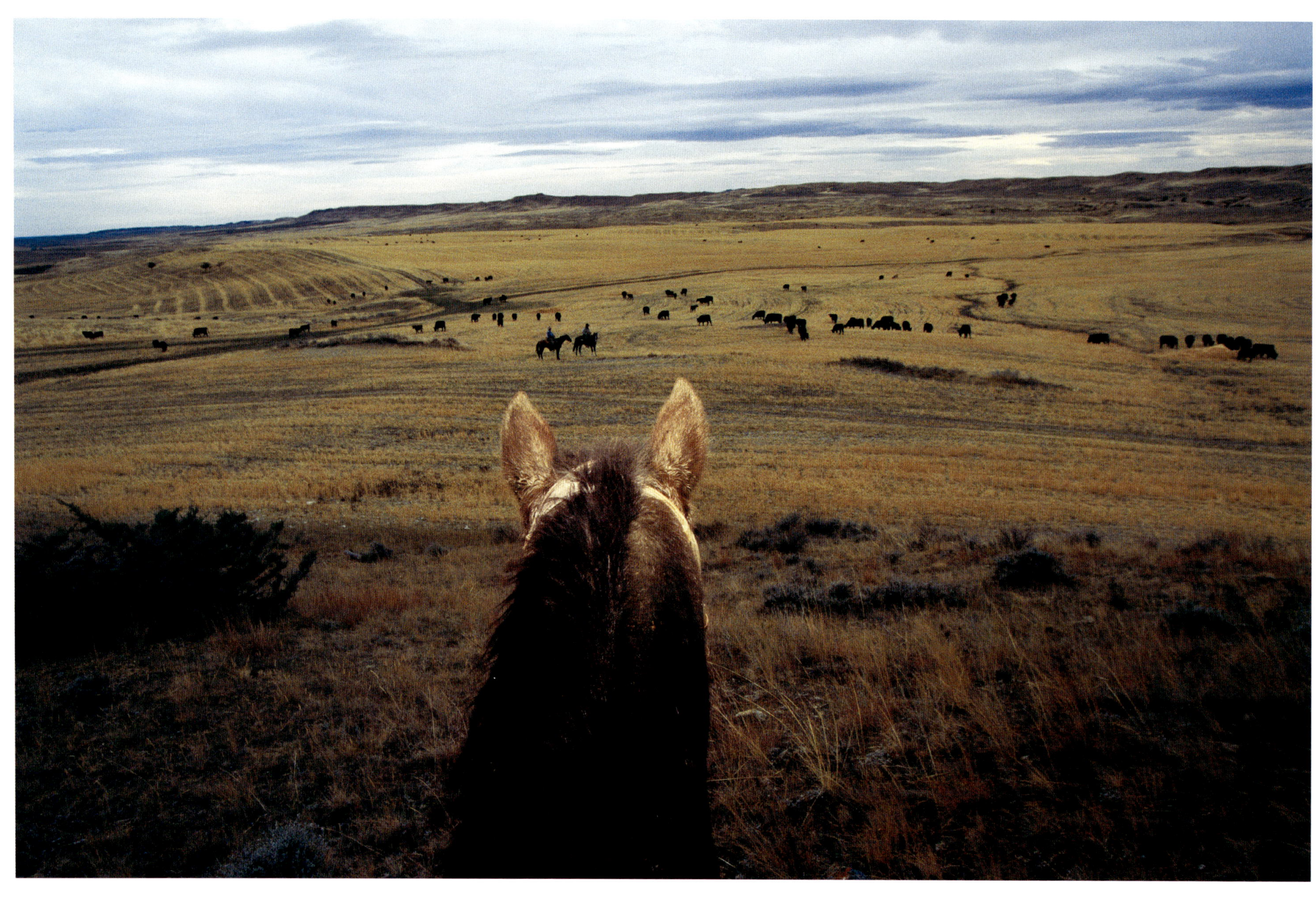

Knox ranch, Missouri Breaks, 1996

Montana Stories

I've loved photographing throughout the American West, and the pictures in this chapter document my experiences from Texas to Montana. But Montana in particular has become a second home. From the first time I visited the state in 1966, I've always felt at home in Montana. As a young man, it was love at first sight for reasons I can't really explain and don't try to. I've done good work in Montana; I've made lifelong friends there, too. And I've heard some good stories while hanging out in cow camps, in the colonies of my Hutterite friends; just about anywhere I've been in Montana, I've seen or heard something worth remembering. It took me an awful long time, but in 2007 I finally made a move and I'm now living in Montana, no longer young but still happily in love with the place. My wife, Ani, and I divide each year between Charlottesville, Virginia, where I've lived more than half my life, and Missoula.

A friend of mine, Swede Anderson, now in his late 50s, was born and raised in Stanford, Montana, in the central part of the state. Swede grew up one of nine kids on a combination farm-ranch where his father ran some cows and raised good saddle horses. When he was not quite 17 Swede fell off a hayrack and lost all hearing in one ear and about 75 percent in the other. As an adult he tried raising some sheep and hogs but eventually moved to Missoula, where he runs his own handyman service. When I'm in Missoula in the summer and fall, Swede stops at our place some afternoons. He and I drink a beer or two and he tells me stories about growing up in central

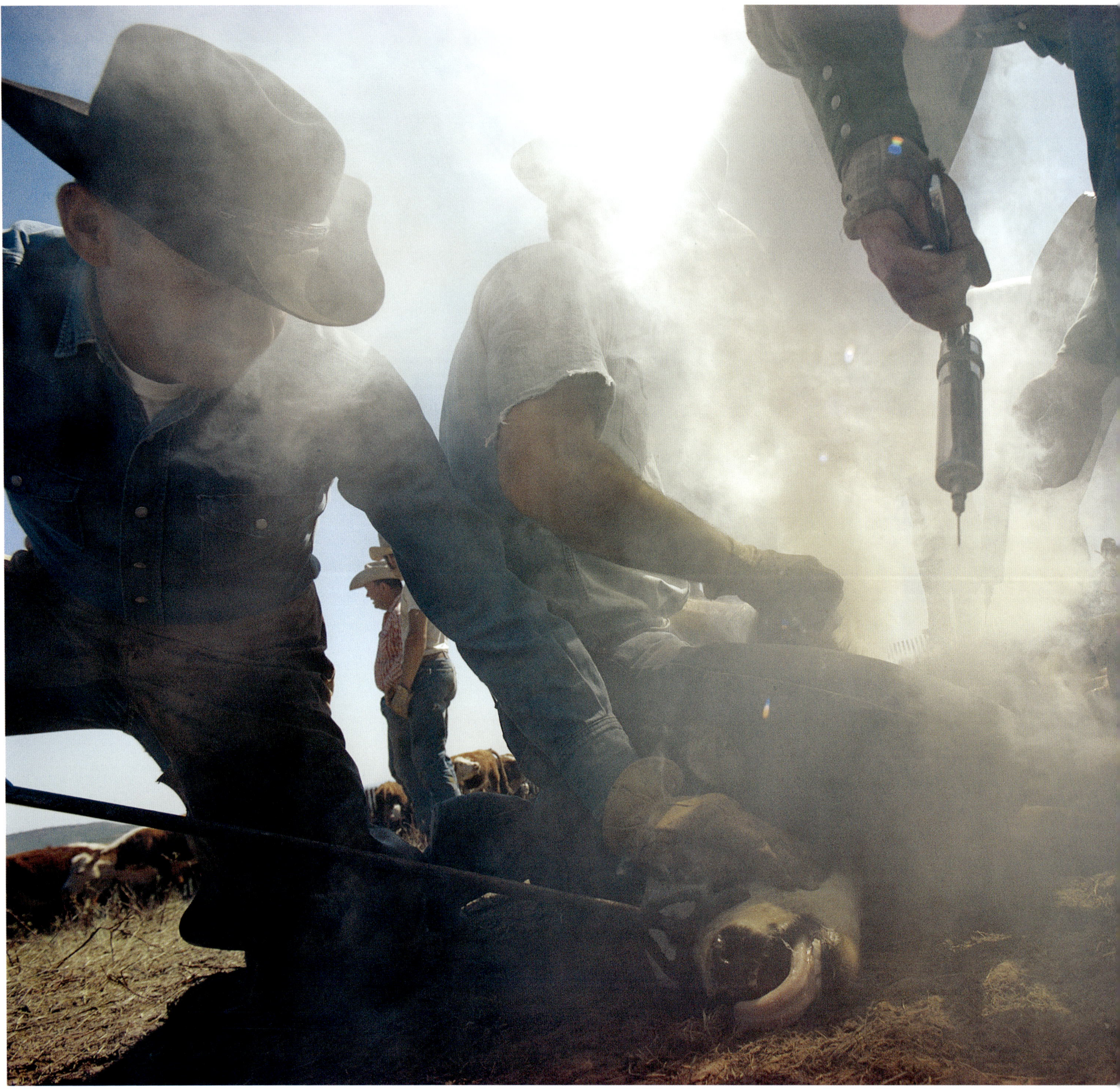

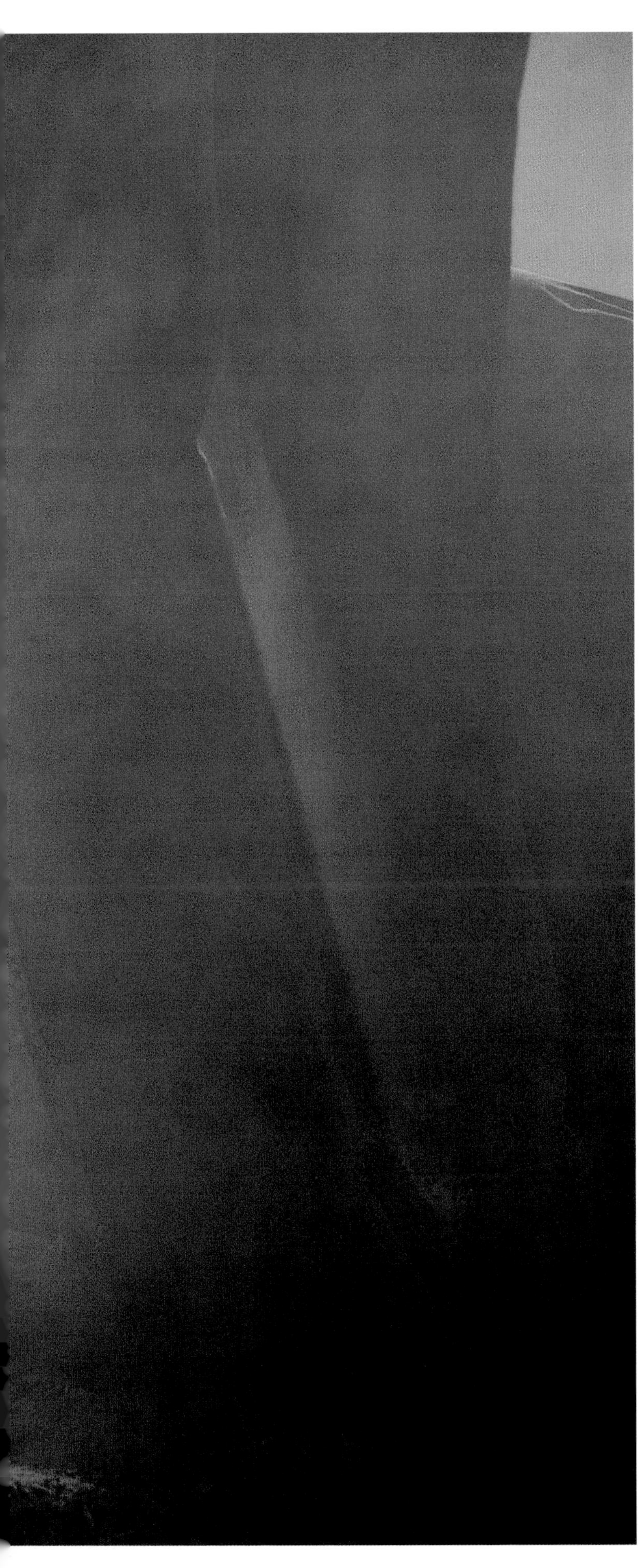

Calf branding, Padlock ranch, Montana, 1972

Montana. "Some of these stories," he says with a smile and mischievous eyes, "are even true!"

Like the day years ago on Halloween when he and some other young men from neighboring ranches were driving about 350 head of cattle out of the Big Snowy Mountains so they could load them on trucks and get them to winter range near Stanford. It was blowing snow and it was cold—twelve below zero.

"God," Swede said, "it was cold. We had to warm the horses' bits in a fire before we could put 'em in their mouths. We were able to stay in our saddles, but God, it was cold. It was just awful. Lenny Ernst was up front, riding lead, trying to keep the cows bunched up and not going too fast. A guy came along that mountain road in a propane truck, and as he got closer, he looked at Lenny and those cows and calves and rolled down the window of his truck a crack and said, 'Jesus! I don't believe this.' And Lenny said, 'I don't believe it either.' "

Swede said his aunt Belle had been a schoolteacher in Stanford, and his uncle Clifford, a cowboy. "But cowboys couldn't make much of a living," said Swede, "so he and Belle moved to Great Falls, where Cliff took up glassblowing and became well known throughout Montana for his ability as a glassblower. They called him the dean of Montana glassblowers." Swede's uncle Cliff created some of the neon signs that can still be seen glowing in the windows of Montana drinking establishments.

"Uncle Cliff loved horses and became a member of the Great Falls Saddle Club that was full of doctors and lawyers and high society. One fall he and another guy promised the members of the club an elk for their annual fall feed. They meant well, but you know, sometimes things don't work out. Uncle Cliff thought for sure they'd get an elk, but they didn't get one in time for the banquet. Well, another friend had a two-year-old stud colt that they decided to kill and butcher and donate in place of the elk. They cooked it up with all the trimmings. The ladies and the men in the club all raved about how good it was. Didn't know it was horse. 'Why that's the best damn elk meat I've tasted,' they said. Cliff was high society for a couple of weeks. But then I guess the word somehow got around and they found out. They booted Uncle Cliff out of the club—for life."

Swede told me how his grandfather had grown up one of 13 kids in the Red River country of North Dakota in difficult times in a family that didn't have much. "His parents would take away the kids' shoes in summer to save them for winter or for wearing to town. In summer months they would do all their chores around the place and in the fields barefoot," he said. Years later, as an adult in Montana, his grandfather homesteaded a place near Stanford. "He had the reputation of being the hardest-working guy on Sage Creek," said Swede. "Other guys would be quitting for the day, and Grandpa would just come in to change horses and go right back out." Swede said his grandfather could often be heard out in the fields on moonlit nights, singing as he walked barefoot in the dirt furrows behind his four-horse plow.

Swede told me, "My mother asked him once, 'Why in the world do you work out there in your bare feet?'" "Because it takes me back to my childhood," his grandfather had said. "It takes me home."

IT WAS SUMMER 1969 and I was photographing and writing my first story about some Hutterite colonies in central Montana. I was horseback riding along with a young Hutterite, the son of the colony's preacher.

There had been no rain for weeks, and although we walked our horses, the sun brought sweat to their withers. The 17-year-old Hutterite boy from Surprise Creek Colony near Stanford told me that you can tell it's really dry when a single rider can kick up a dust trail.

We stopped at a stream. The water we drank had come down from the mountains, and it was cool and tasted of the earth. In the thick heat of midday we drank carelessly, splashing our faces until our shirtfronts hung wet and the falling droplets made pockmarks in the dust.

"Do you ever feel like going away?" I asked.

"What do you mean?" he asked.

"You know—do you ever feel like leaving the colony?"

"No," he said. "I've never felt a temptation to leave here. It must be a pretty rough life on the outside, all alone, trying to make a living. Don't you think?"

We let the horses drink and then rode on.

"Yes," I told him. "It can be all of that."

IN THE SUMMER OF 1972 I brought my sons, Scott, 12, and David, 8, out to Montana to spend a week with me at a branding camp where I was working on a story for *National Geographic* about the Padlock, a family-owned ranch that stretched across parts of northern Wyoming and southwestern Montana. The Padlock was then one of the few outfits in that part of the country that still ran a horse-drawn branding wagon. The branding crew moved from one camp to another with chuck wagon and bed wagon and a procession of about 40 saddle horses loping along, flanking both sides of the trail the wagons followed. It was a pretty sight to see. When my sons arrived we were camped at a place called Bear Creek on the Crow Agency, not far from the Little Big Horn, where Custer and his 7th Cavalry troopers had met their demise on a hot summer afternoon just a little less than a hundred years earlier. My sons saddled up with us most days to ride on morning gatherings, then watched from perches on the top rails of the catch pens when calves were roped and wrestled and branded. After lunch in the afternoon we all napped in the coolness of canvas tents.

One night after supper my boys and I, wagon boss Floyd Workman, and the rest of the crew were sitting around the fire—we always had a campfire blazing after supper—and some of the older hands were telling stories. The talk got around to the gear a cowboy uses. All the best cowboys I encountered in my travels took great pride in what they wore and used, from their saddles to their boots and hats and chaps.

We got to talking about chaps. Chaps protect a cowboy's legs from getting roughed up against brush or mesquite, if he's in that kind of country, and maybe even trees, if he's trying to chouse a cow on the fight out of closely spaced timber along a twisting creek bed. Chaps also provide cover from wind and rain. And they come in different styles. "Batwing" chaps flare out like the kind rodeo rough stock riders wear that flap wildly as their legs churn rhythmically, spurring a bareback or saddle bronc. "Chinks," a kind of abbreviated chaps, are narrower than batwings, come down to just below the knees, and are often fringed along the edges. "Shotguns" are full-length leather leggings closed snuggly with clips or zippers. In country where cold is a factor—and that certainly includes Montana—one might see "woollies," chaps covered with thick sheep wool. They are usually white or black but sometimes dyed to a color the owner finds pleasing.

Veteran hand Harold "Smitty" Smith liked to reminisce about other outfits he'd worked on and cowhands he'd known. Smitty usually had a couple of toothpicks tucked into his hatband, and as he talked he'd work a toothpick around in his mouth, the tip of it spearing out sporadically from beneath his mustache.

"A cowboy I worked with on one outfit had a pair of bright orange wool chaps," Smitty recalled. "Orange woollies, they were. Another fella on the outfit took a likin' to those chaps. Decided he had to have 'em. Finally traded the man for 'em. Gave him his wife and $25. He sure liked them orange chaps."

My oldest son laughed at that story and probably thought Smitty had made it up. Of course, my son had never seen a pair of orange woollies. I saw a pair of green ones once, and they were beautiful.

PADLOCK WAGON BOSS Floyd Workman always had a pouch of Bull Durham tucked into his shirt pocket. He could roll a cigarette while riding at a trot and not spill a flake. Floyd was kind of a quiet man; he didn't tell too many stories. But I learned a lot about cowboying, listening to him talk about his crew and other outfits he'd worked on in Montana.

"I guess these boys don't know what it's like to work for a tough outfit," Floyd once told me. "The horses here are pretty good, mostly broke before we get 'em. I've worked for outfits with trashy horses where the foreman tried to get you bucked off every morning. I guess it used to be fun watching the young hands gettin' bucked off them rank horses. Maybe that's why cowboys on rough outfits used to eat a light breakfast. I got so I couldn't eat breakfast. It was a low feeling in the morning, worrying if you could cut it because if you didn't, they'd put you to doin' somethin' else.

"I tell these young kids on this crew that if they really want to punch cows in these hills, all they need is a good bed and a good saddle. You can take a pretty rough day if you've got a good bed. I don't mean one of them expensive sleepin' bags. Just a couple of blankets, maybe a piece of foam rubber, and a good canvas. Hell, a man can climb in according to the weather, put what he don't need on top underneath for a cushion. Sleepin' bag's either too hot or too cold, never seems just right. And then, with a good saddle to ride, a man's ready to cowboy."

THE STUBBY REMAINS of a Bull Durham smoke dangling from his lips, Floyd shook out a broad loop in his rope and slowly stalked across the dusty corral, looking for a white-footed sorrel with a burr-tangled mane. The horses eyed his approach, and with ears flattened back they suddenly whirled away. The white-footed sorrel was buried deep among them as they crowded wedgelike into a corner of the corral. There they stood with bodies tensed, their heavily muscled hindquarters turned toward the man. He closed a step or two. For a moment they held fast. Then, in an explosion of pounding hooves and flashing legs, they came apart, some dashing to the other end of the corral. For a second or two the sorrel was exposed. He knew it and made his move. Floyd made his. The horse feinted left, then rolled back on his hocks and broke to his right. Swiftly, smoothly, Floyd cast the rope, his wrist turning downward at the moment of release, like a pitcher throwing an overhand curve. The open loop seemed to skim over the other horses by only inches and fell softly on target. With a quick jerk, Floyd threw his weight behind the rope and it made a zipping sound as the loop tightened around the sorrel's neck. His role in the drama completed, the horse dropped his head slightly in resignation, waiting to be led away.

AT THE PADLOCK BRANDING corral the morning turned hot, and the young hands were like athletes struggling through the first day of training. Muscles quickly grew tired. One calf wrestler had been bloodied from a kick in the jaw. Another had been kicked in the groin and sat crumpled up against the fence like a pile of dirty clothes, his head cradled in his arms.

We were headed back to the wagon by noon. Sweat lathered the necks of our horses and they threw their heads nervously, bothered by the nose flies. Floyd looked over at a young cowboy riding a flea-bit gray.

"You know something?" he said. "If we'd branded 270 calves today instead of just 170, it probably would've taken all the fun out of it."

Hungry, hot, and aching for a rest, the young man silently looked at the wagon boss with eyes that were dust rimmed and weary. A big grin broke over Floyd's face as he tapped spurs to his bay and we loped for camp, leaving tawny plumes of dust behind us.

IT STARTED TO SNOW the night before we were to trail a thousand Padlock steers 12 miles to the shipping pens. The first flakes melted quickly, becoming dirty streaks on the windowpanes. Outside the bunkhouse door, Butch's cow dog Bill whimpered to be let in. Jim Martin walked out to see if the sky might clear. When he returned I asked how he thought the weather would be by morning.

"Deep and still," he said slowly in his high-pitched Texas accent.

"What's *that* mean?" I asked.

"Deep as your ass and still snowing," he replied.

IN 1976 I WROTE and photographed a *National Geographic* article about the sad story of Chief Joseph and the Nez Perce Indian war of 1877. Joseph and his band of perhaps 800 tribal members—half of them warriors, the rest women, children, and elderly men—evaded the pursuit of 5,000 U.S. Army troops in a 1,700-mile chase that ended in surrender at a place called Snake Creek, near the Bear Paw Mountains of northern Montana. They were just two days short of Joseph's goal of finding respite with Sitting Bull and the Sioux residing in southern Canada.

I ENDED MY MONTHS of tracing the flight of Chief Joseph at the site of the Bear Paw battlefield, where Gen. Nelson A. Miles and his troops, with their devastating artillery, caught what was left of the Nez Perce exiles 16 miles south of present-day Chinook, Montana. The end began in the cold of dawn on September 30, 1877, 60 years before the day I was born in not-so-faraway Minneapolis, Minnesota. Five days later, Joseph, both his brothers killed during the flight, gave up his rifle and the chase, making his famous statement: "From where the sun now stands, I will fight no more forever."

On a quiet October morning I walked the battlefield in solitude, with just my thoughts and the knowledge of how impossible it was to truly appreciate the depths of sorrow that must have been in the hearts of those people so close to what they hoped was freedom; how tragic an episode in American history.

In the willows by the creek I saw a rabbit and it saw me and stopped, its velvet body frozen in anticipation, unsure of my intent. "Have you ever tried to tame a wild rabbit?" an Indian friend of mine had asked me miles ago. "It may seem yours for a while, and then one day it flees if it can, or if it can't, then it dies because it willed itself to die. They must be free. That is the way of wild things."

The rabbit, its eyes like liquid sensors, watched intensely as I moved slowly along a path that would cross the creek and take me away from that place.

I looked back a moment later and it was gone.

ON A GRAY FALL AFTERNOON a few years back, I was driving along a narrow strip of Highway 81 between Coffee Creek and the route to Lewistown, which is just about in the dead center of the state. I saw in the distance a couple of metal grain bins flanking a wooden shed out on the edge of what had been a wheat field. The light was dull, kind of somber, but the structures standing in solitude seemed both desolate and yet decorative. The local high school seniors had targeted the ensemble for some multicolored graffiti, marking the shed with a big '06 and one of the metal grain bins with a salutation they evidently felt appropriate:

"Welcome to the Middle of Nowhere"

I couldn't help wondering if they'll feel the same way after being out for a few years in the middle of whatever else life has in store for them. The middle of Montana has always looked pretty good to me. ■

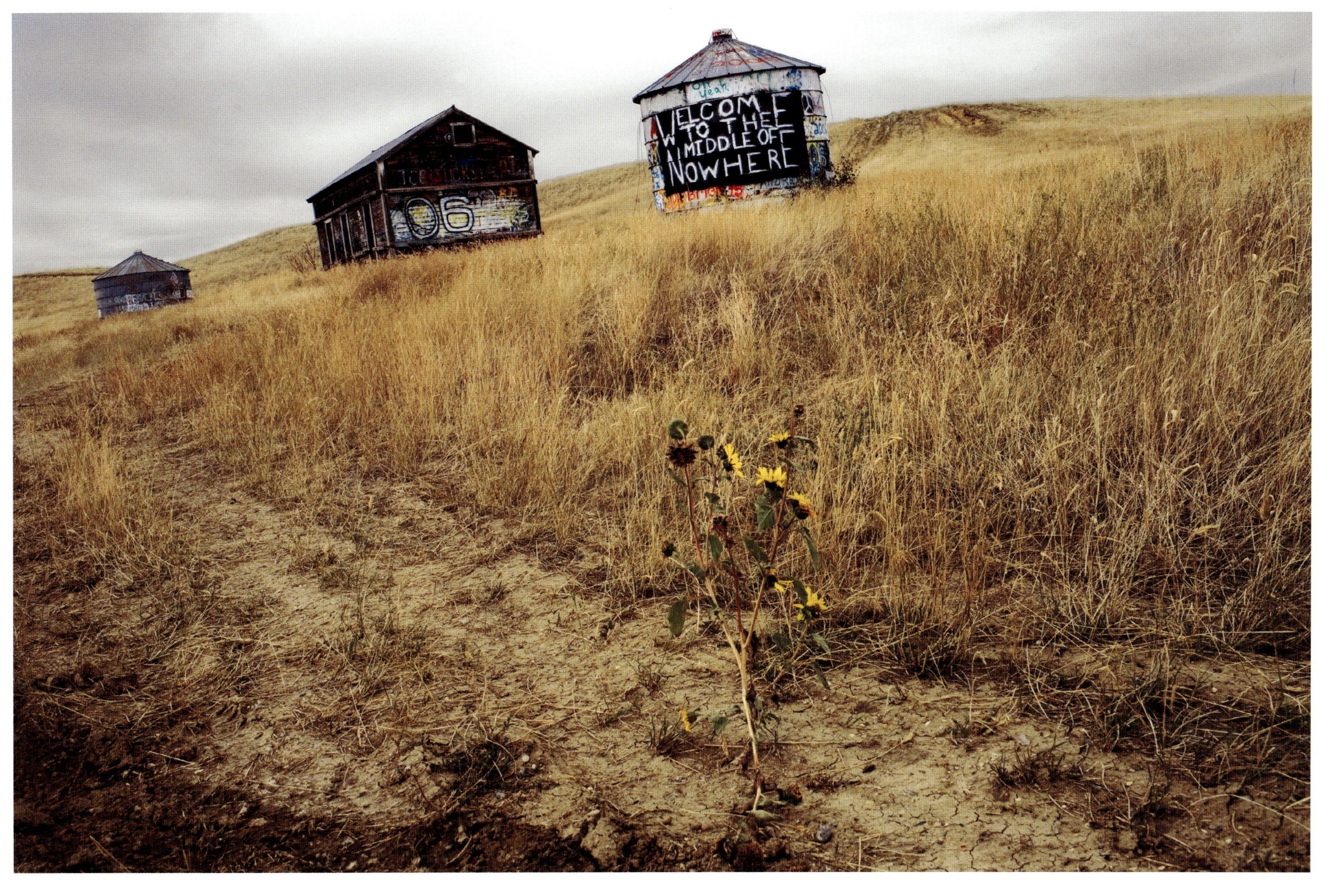

Coffee Creek, Montana, 2006

Lone rider, Texas, 1974

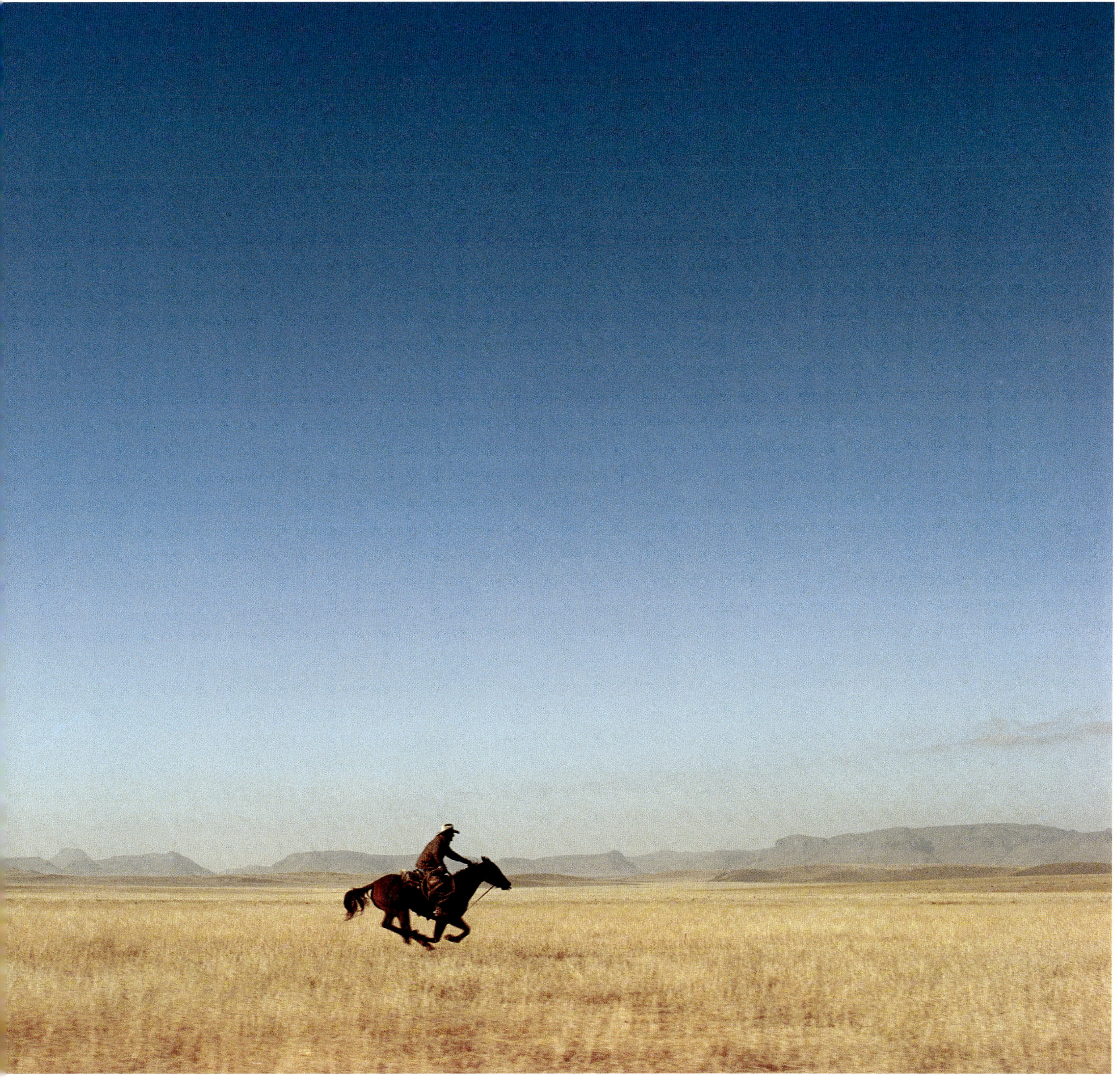

"...why not... show their faces, introduce them to the viewer with a portrait strong enough that you might somehow feel you know something about that person ..."

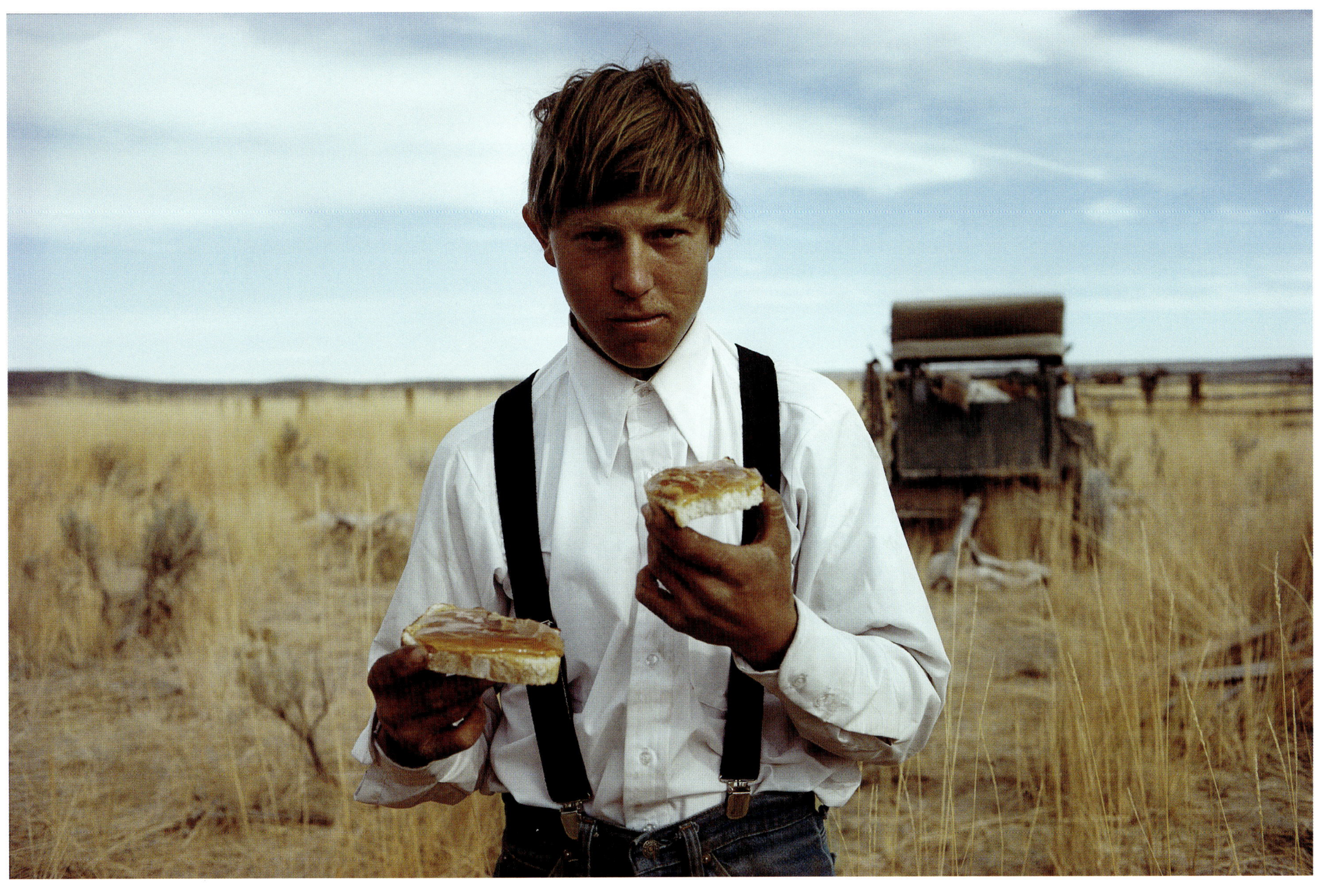

Buckaroo T. J. Symonds, IL cow camp, Nevada, 1979

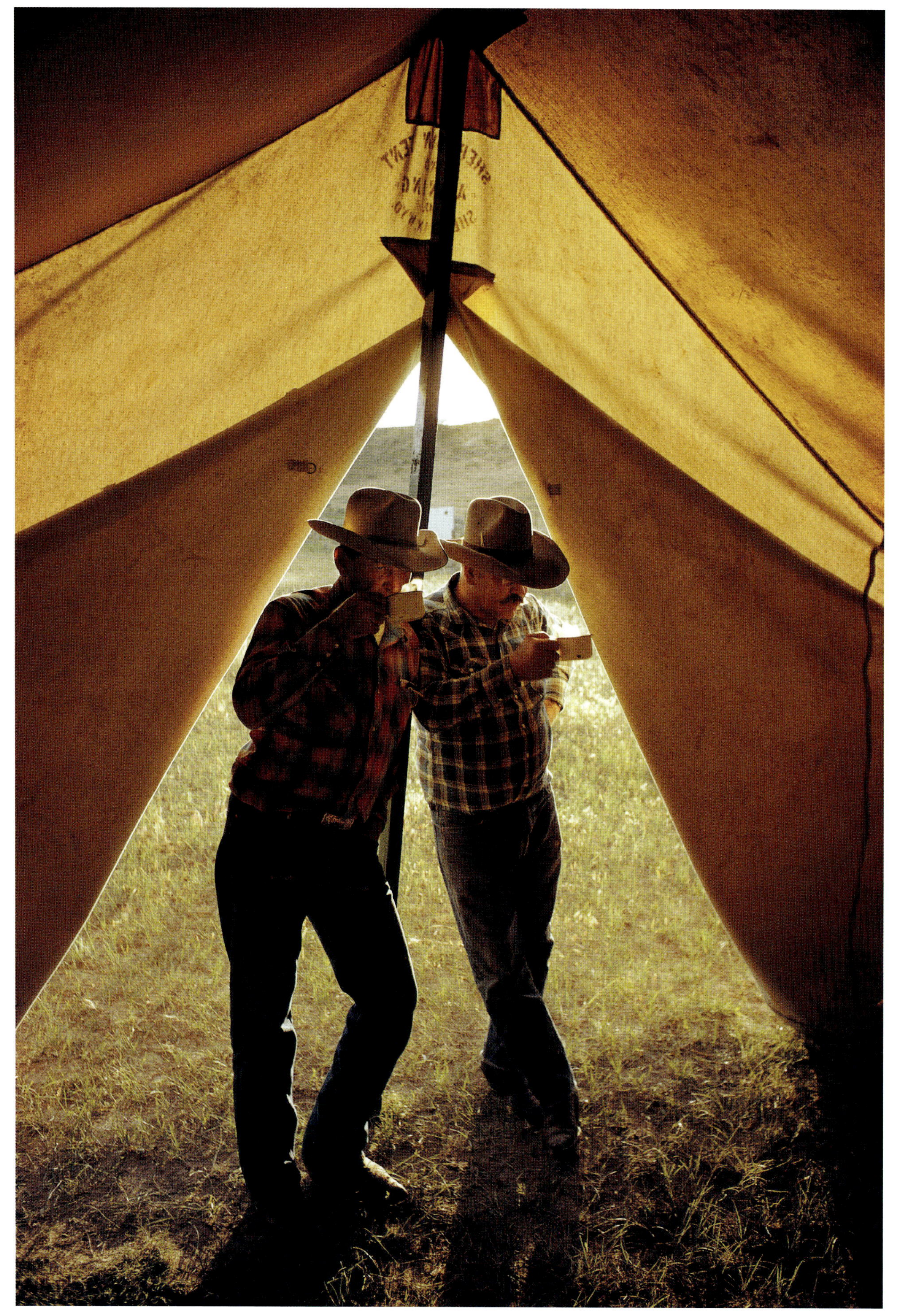

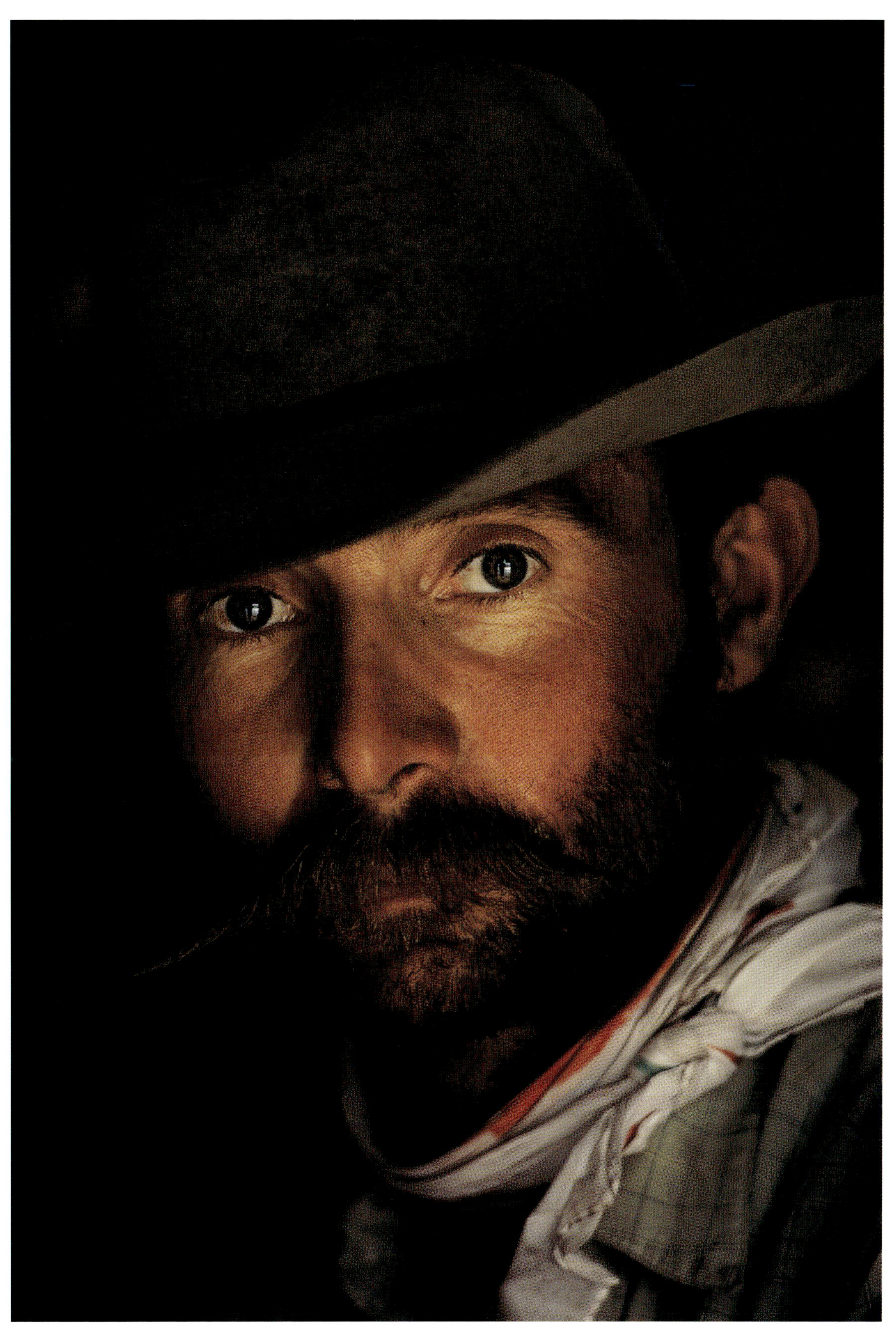

LEFT: *Floyd and Smitty, Padlock, Montana, 1972* ABOVE: *Brian Morris, Circle A boss, Paradise Valley, Nevada, 1970*

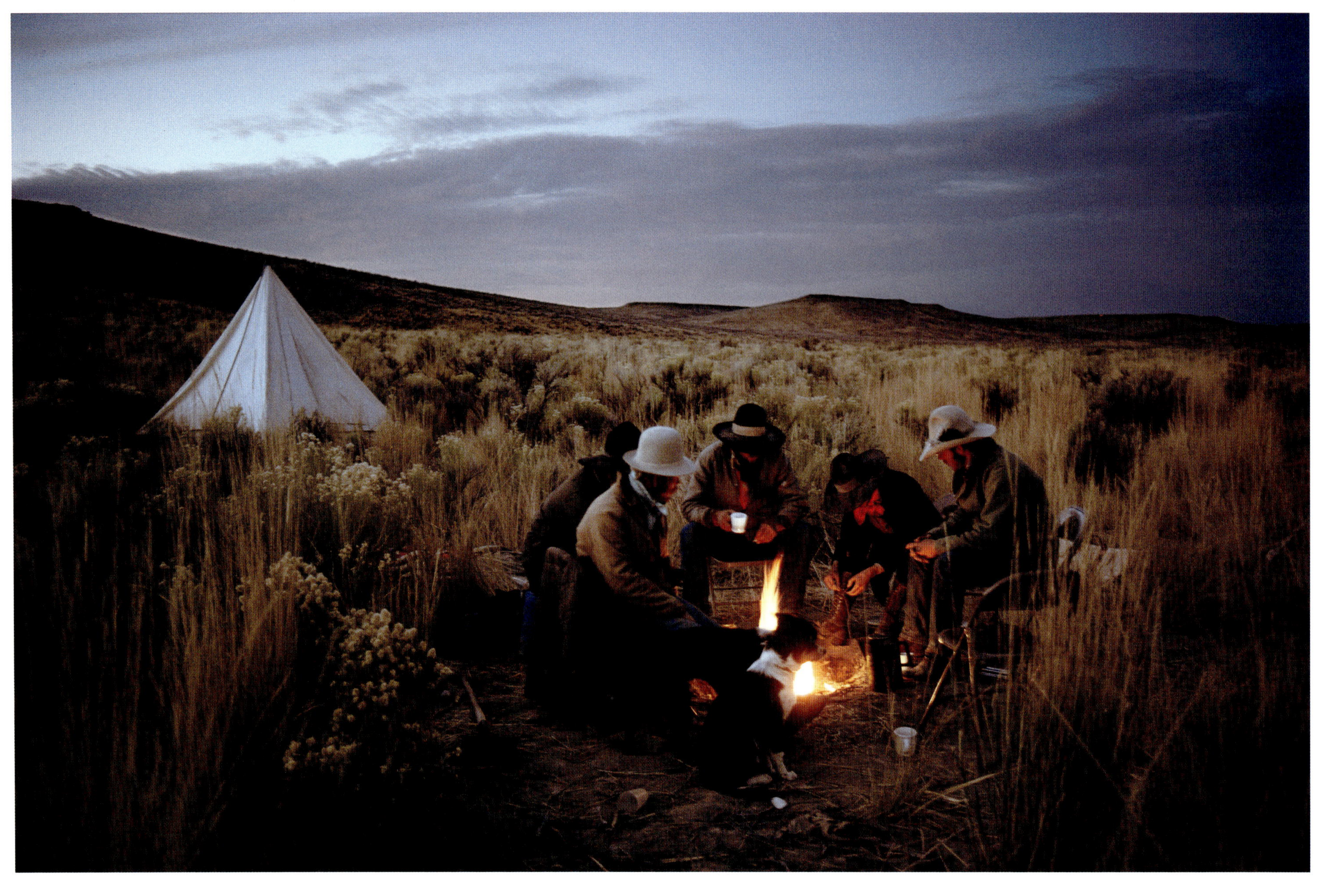

IL cow camp at dawn, Nevada, 1979

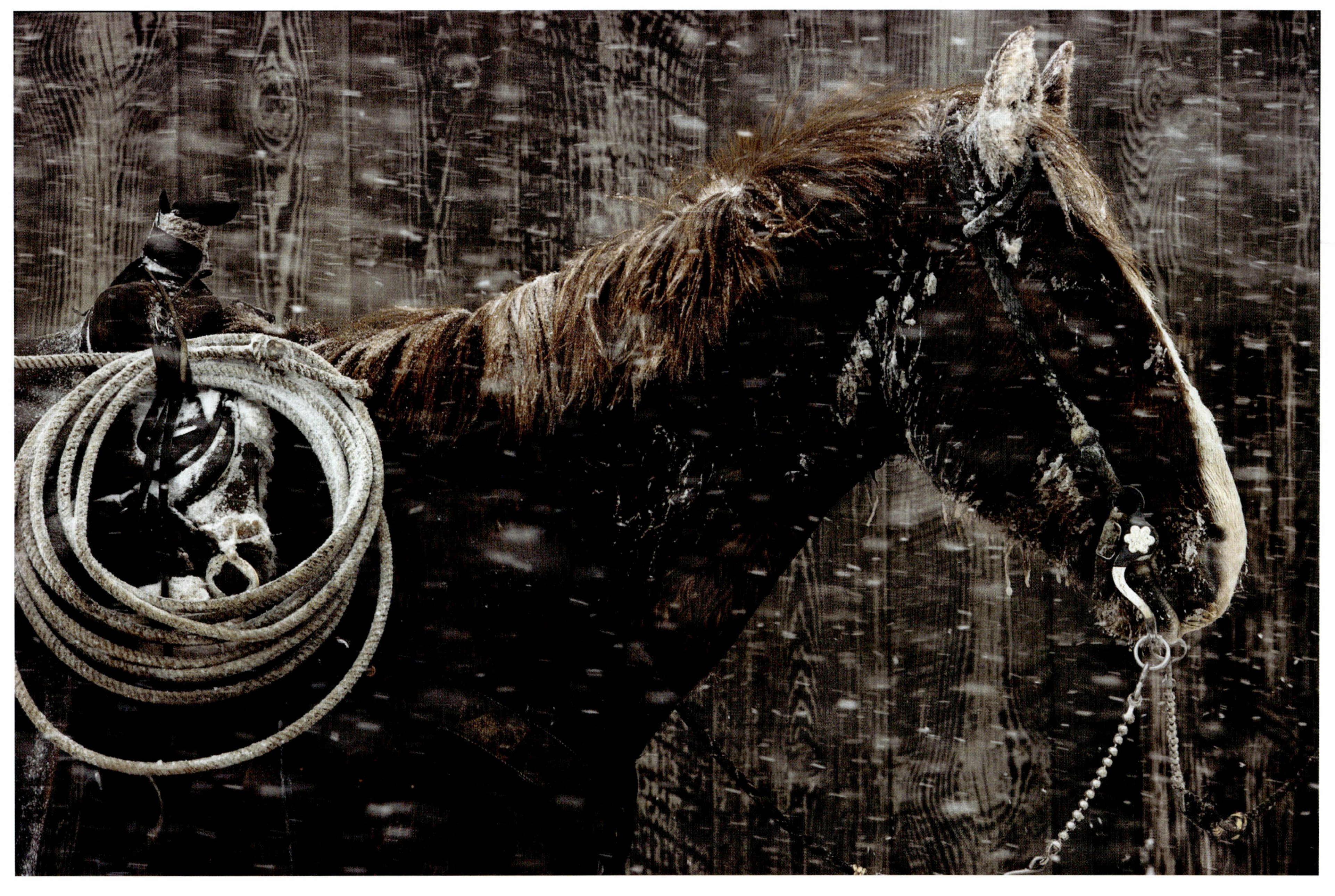

Calving time, Padlock ranch, Montana, 1975

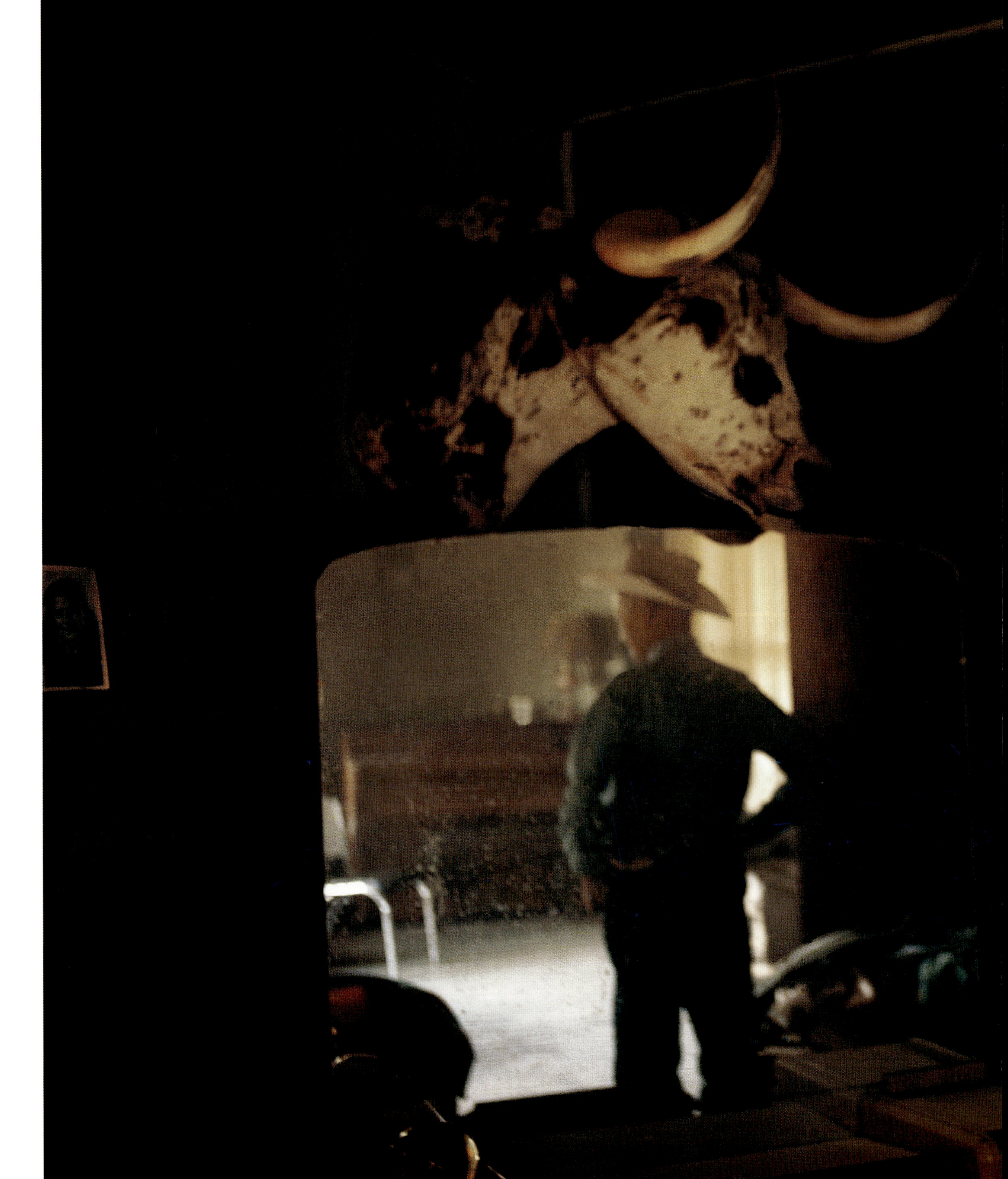

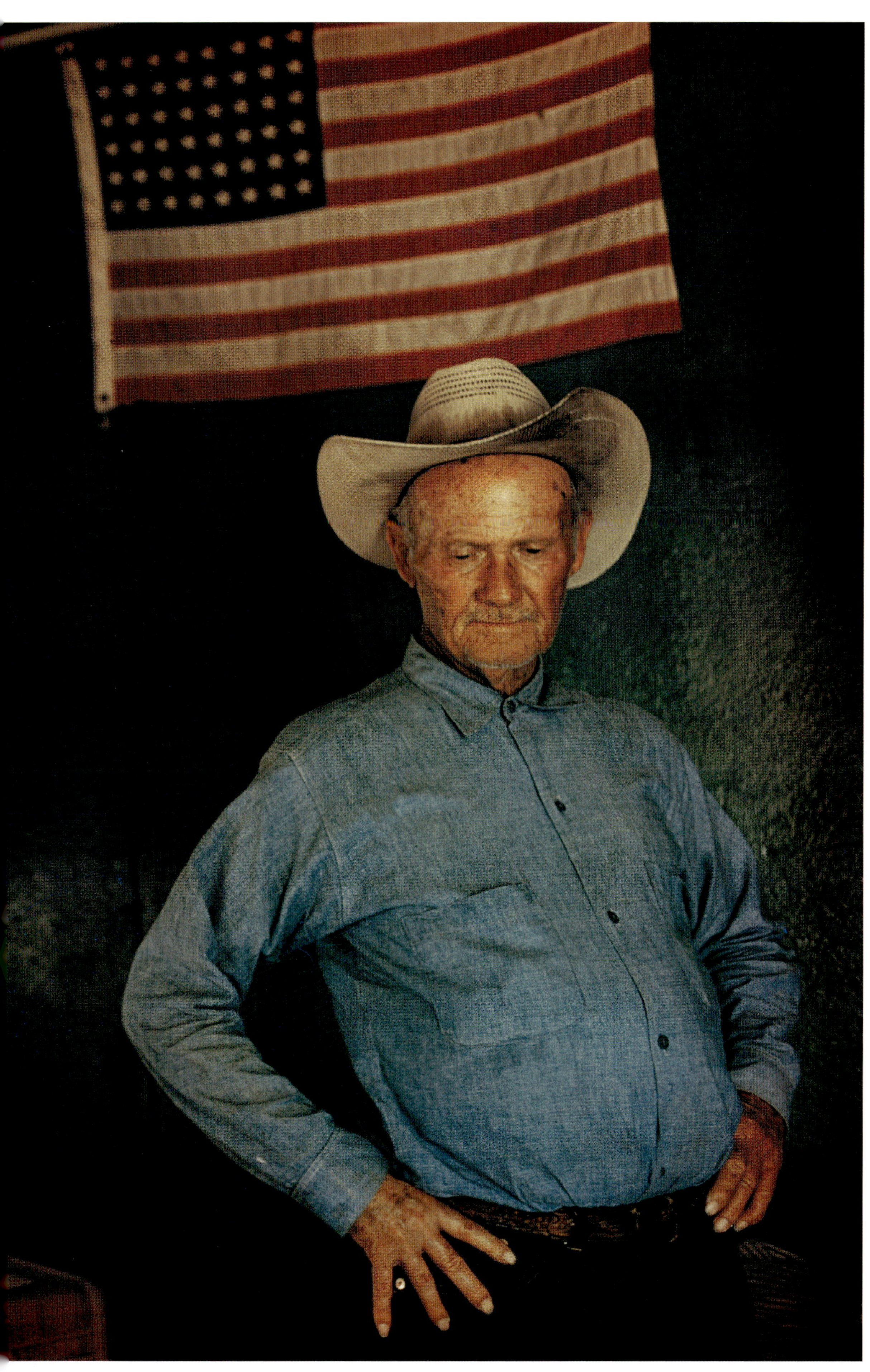

Henry Gray, rancher, Arizona, 1970

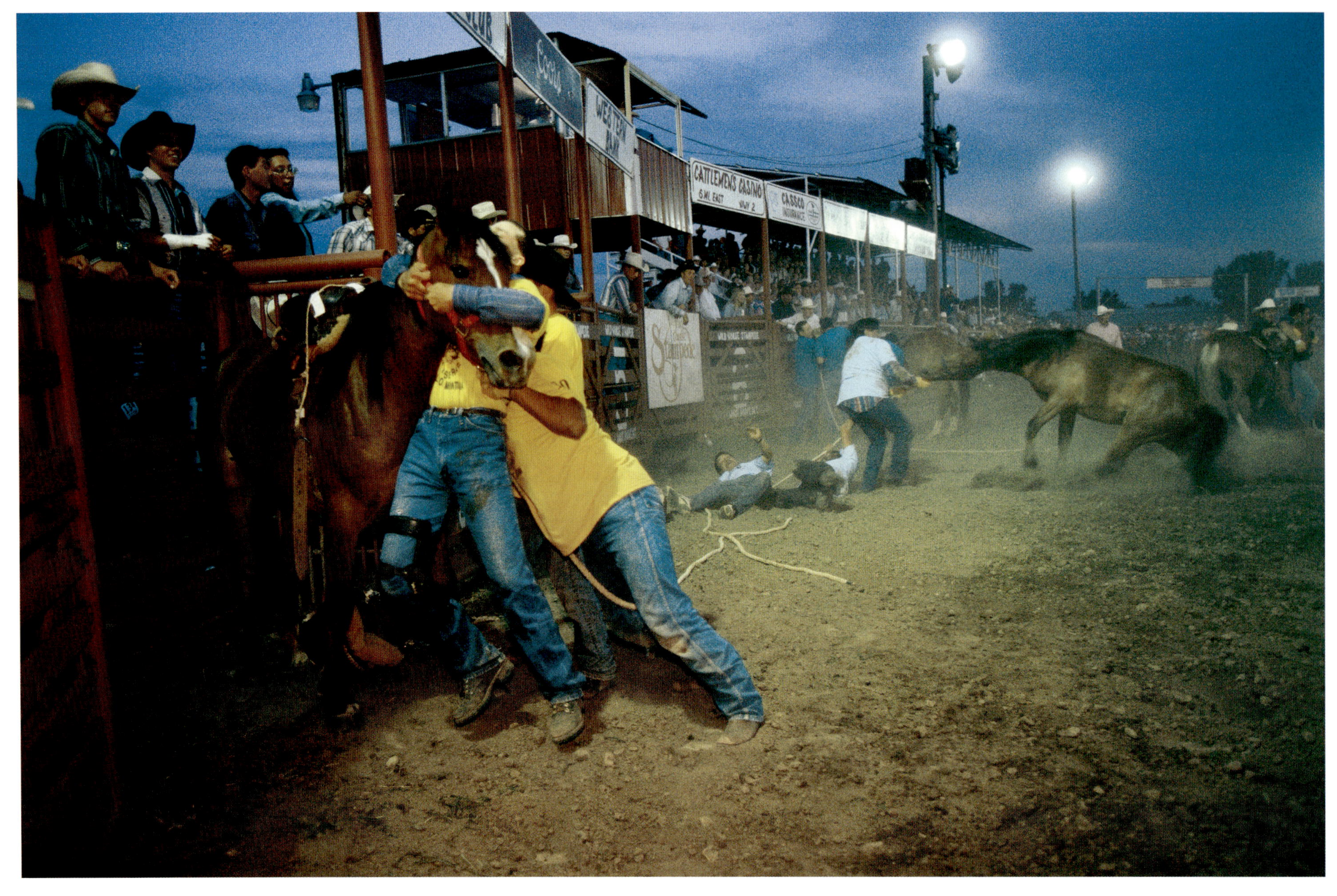

Wild-horse race, Wolf Point, Montana, 1998

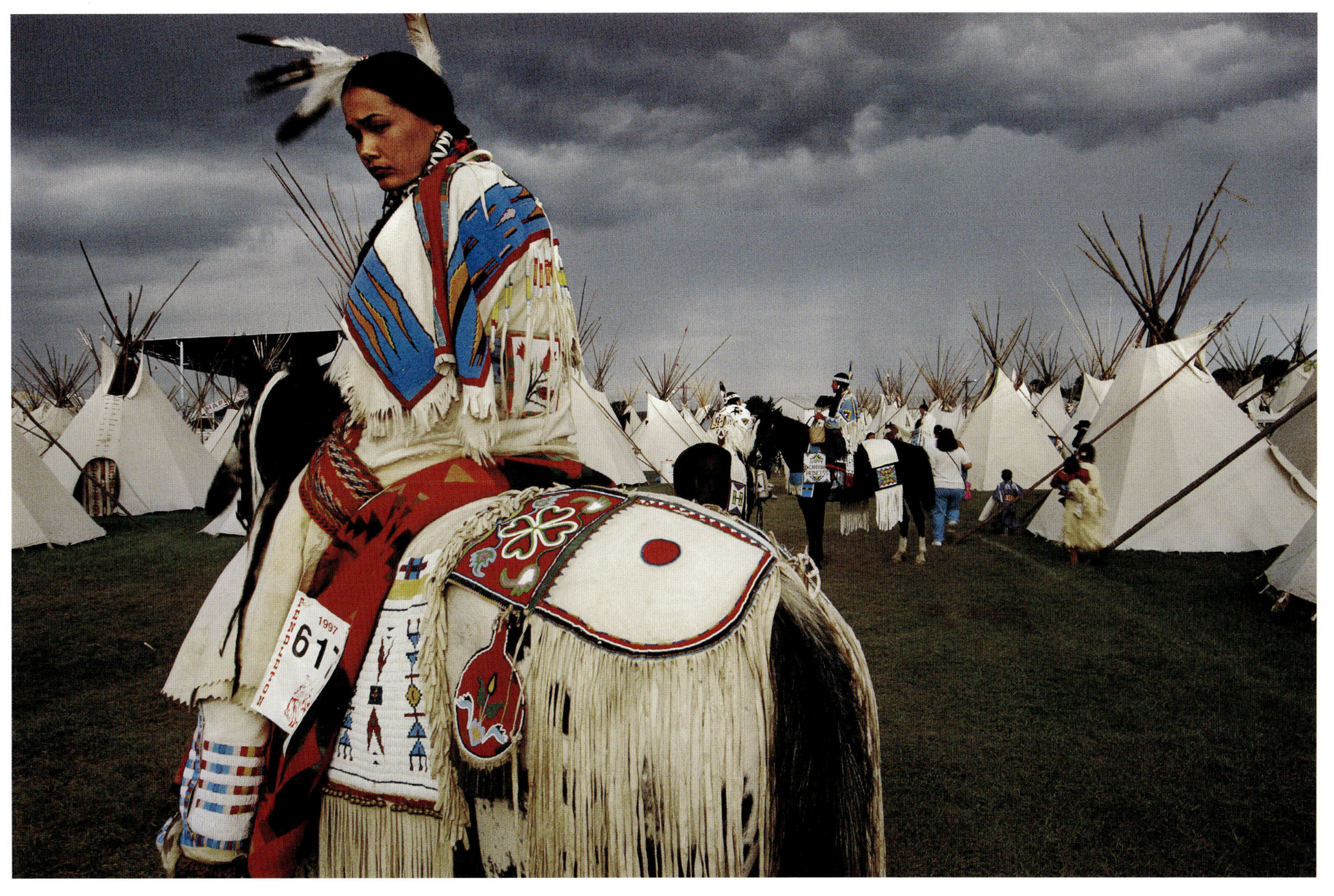

Acosia Red Elk, Indian princess, at rodeo, Pendleton, Oregon, 1998

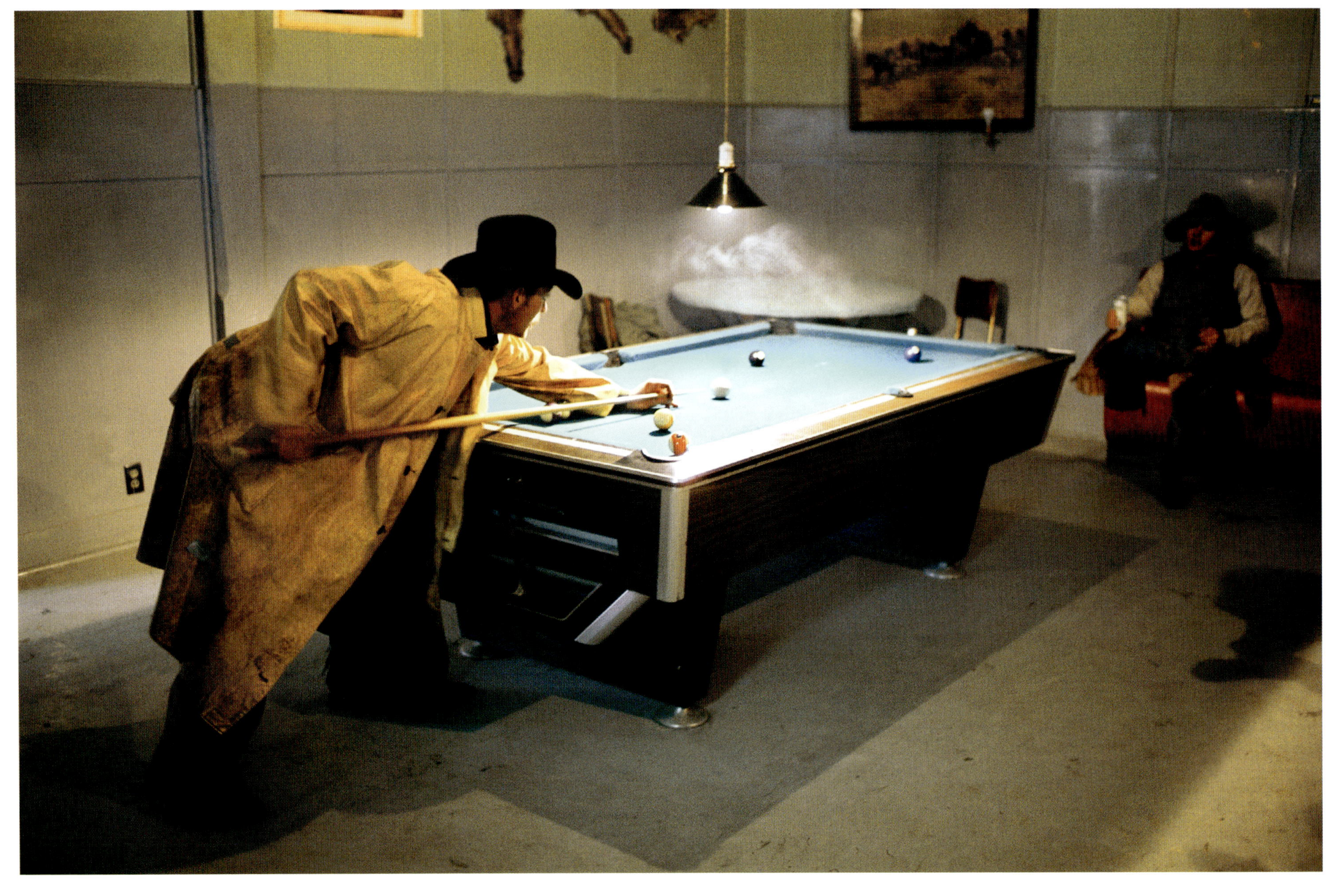

Circle A buckaroos, Paradise Valley, Nevada, 1970

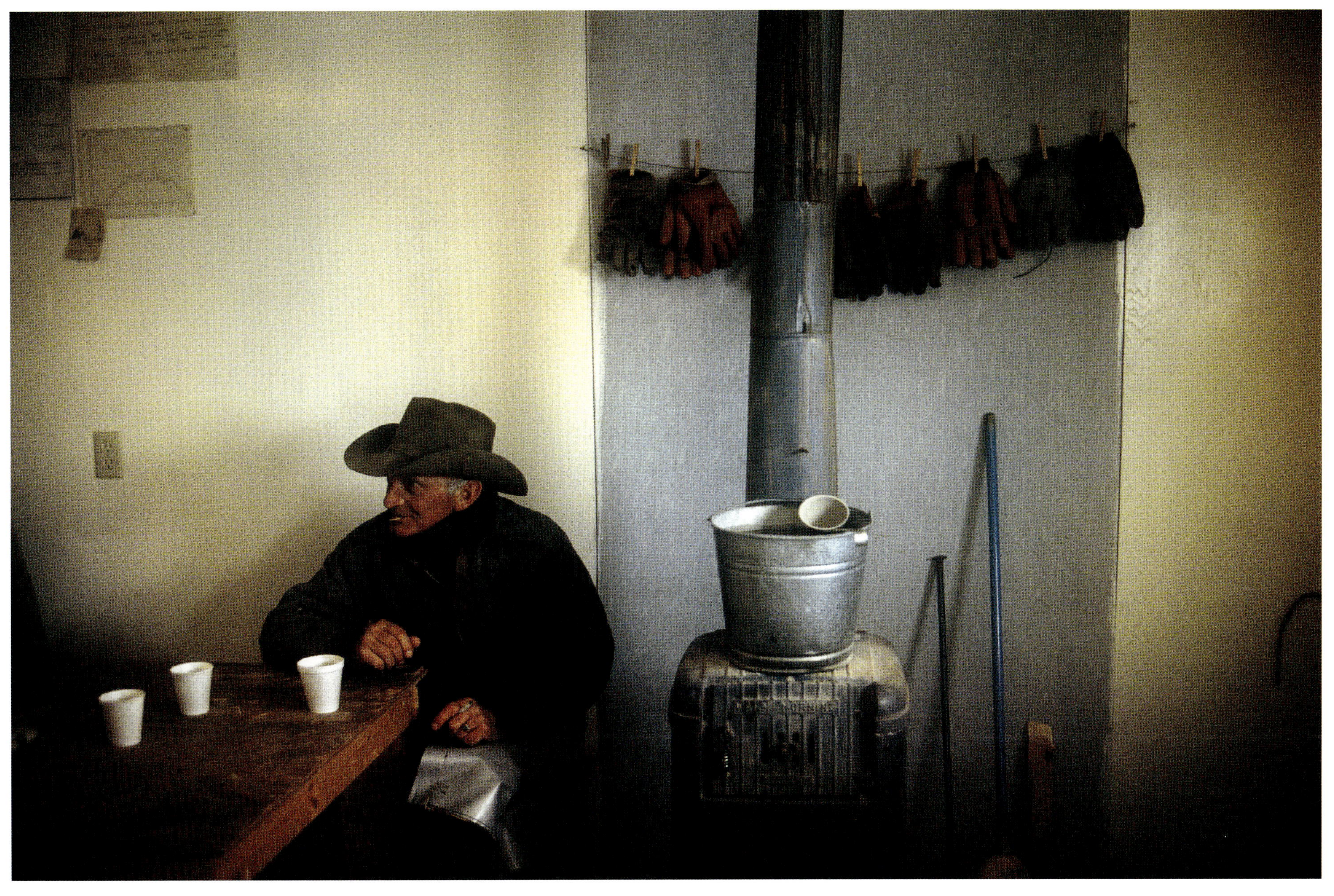

Ruben Weigand, Padlock calving shack, Montana, 1978

"We were several drinks into the afternoon at a bar...Sunlight was slanting in through the windows, skimming across the green felt of the pool table...I asked him, 'Do you ever think you'll be replaced by a machine?' He looked at me, and in his marvelous, soft drawl he said, 'Bill, they just ain't come up with nothin' yet that'll take as much abuse as a cowboy.'"

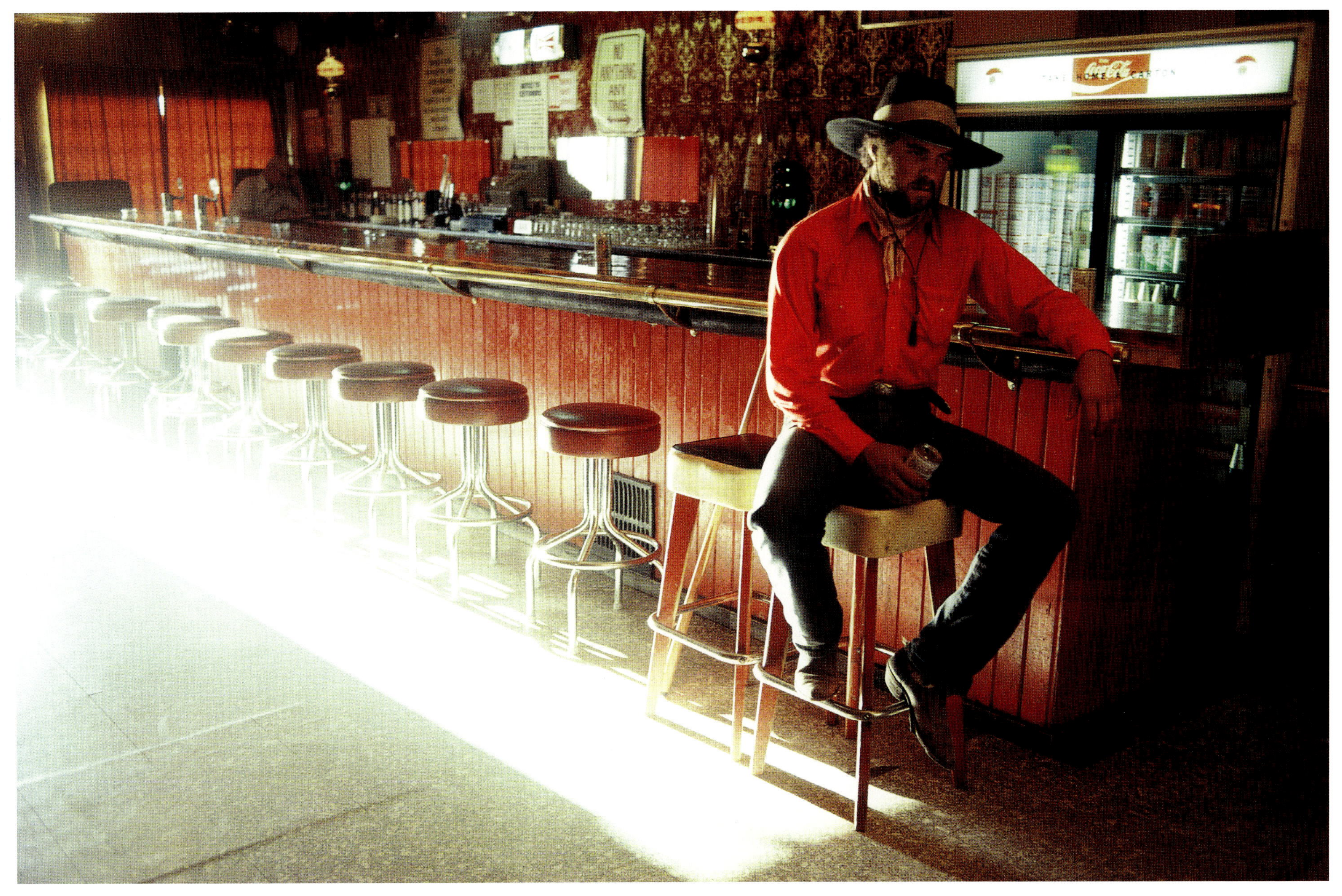

IL buckaroo Stan Kendall at the bar, Mountain City, Nevada 1979

Remnants of a homestead, Winifred, Montana, 1996

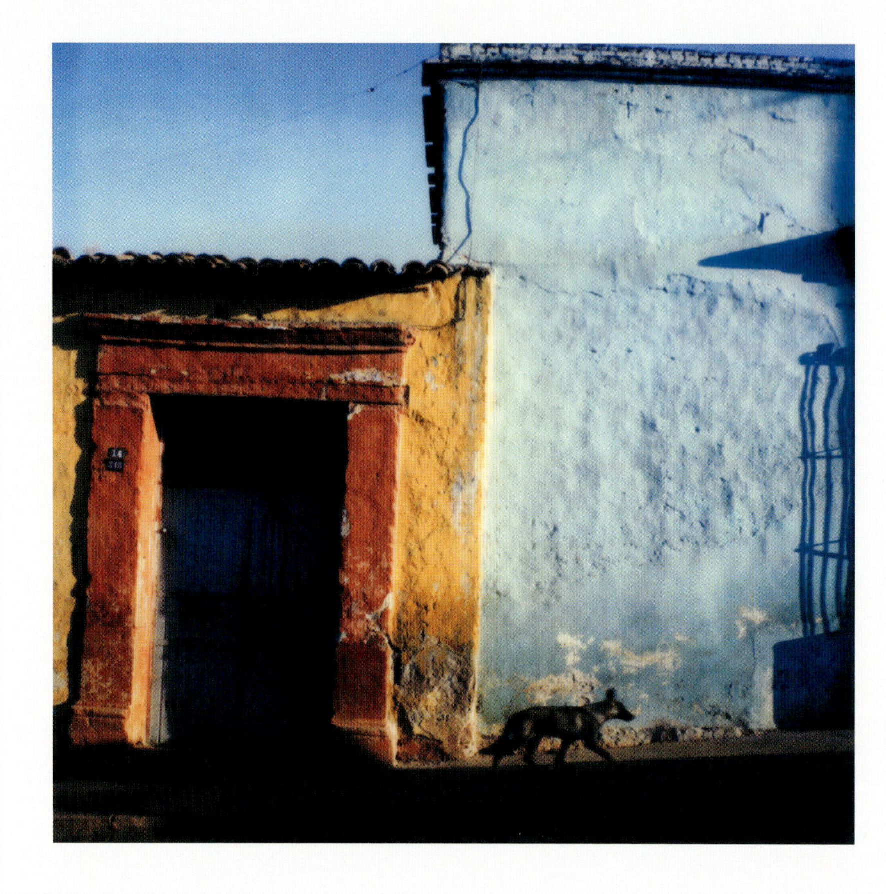

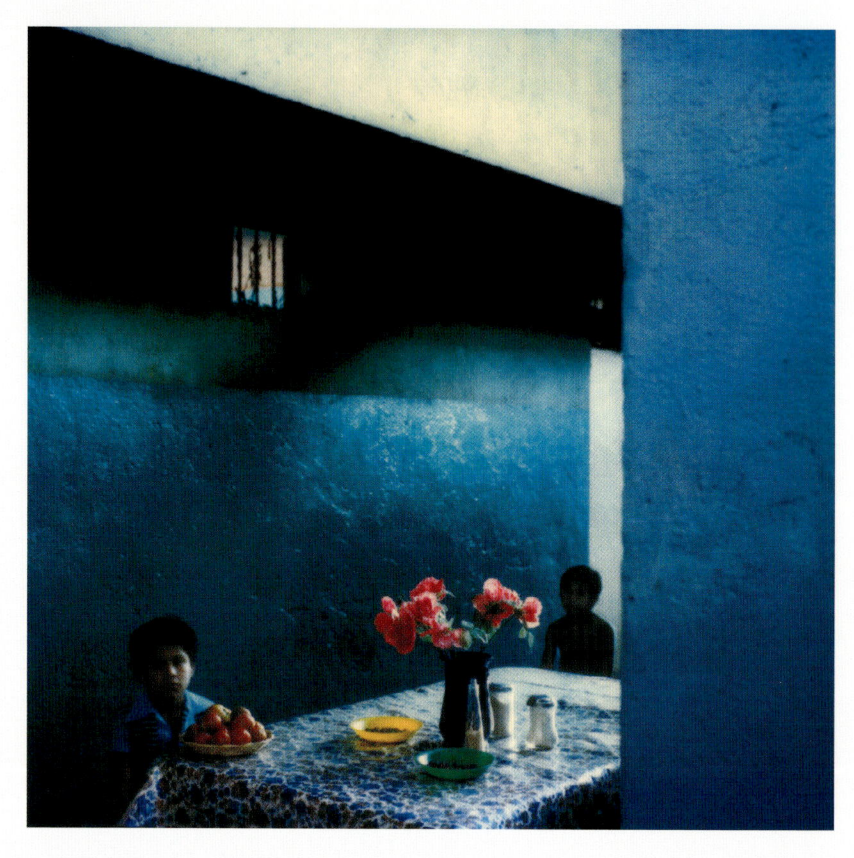

LEFT: *Dog by the wall, Oaxaca, 1980* RIGHT: *Boys at a market café table, Oaxaca, 1980, SX-70 Polaroids*

A Coincidence of Color

I entered the world of magazine photojournalism two days after getting my degree from the University of Minnesota in June 1964. I was hugely fortunate to start at the top, coming in off the street and working as a photographic intern for *National Geographic.* I was also fortunate at the University of Minnesota, where I studied photojournalism under R. Smith Schuneman, who demanded excellence from his students in their camera and darkroom efforts, and at the university's fine arts school, where I'd studied with Jerome Liebling, a former student of Paul Strand's. Liebling was a fine photographer and a provocative teacher. For me it was never simply about getting good grades in my photography courses; I did. But more important, inspired by my teachers and by writers and photographers and painters, I had a passion for making good pictures. One book, *Let Us Now Praise Famous Men,* by writer James Agee and photographer Walker Evans, was a profound influence on me as a student. Other writers also had great influence.

Inside my photo lab locker I had taped a quote I think was attributed to Ernest Hemingway that was something like:

"Who is the best bullfighter of them all?"

"I am," he said.

"And who is next best?"

"All the others."

It sounds like Hemingway, although I'm not sure where in his work it might have appeared. I kept the quote where I could see it daily. It took me a while to grow out of that. On the other hand, it fueled my passion for photography in those beginning years.

Within weeks after arriving at *National Geographic* to start my summer internship, I got an opportunity that would jump-start my career. Bob Gilka, director of photography at the magazine, sent me to photograph a Pennsylvania Dutch festival in Lancaster County, Pennsylvania, and told me, "See if you can get some pictures of the Amish while you're there."

They gave me one of the oldest cars in the Geographic garage. I stopped at a surplus store in Baltimore and bought a used pair of navy blue coveralls I thought would be good for working in farm country. I was soon in southwestern Pennsylvania, cruising two-lane rural roads wrapped like gray ribbons around the emerald and gold fields that encompassed Old Order Amish farms, with their white-painted houses and formidable barns. If I stopped by one of the antique covered bridges and cut my car's engine and waited, I would eventually hear the hollow staccato sound of horse hooves pacing across the wooden board flooring of the bridge as a black, high-wheeled Amish buggy passed through. Gilka's expectations regarding my getting pictures of the Amish could not have been too high. After all—and it was probably a good thing that he hadn't told me—they'd sent out a staff photographer months earlier, and he'd come back with no pictures. He'd gone to the local Amish bishop to request permission and been refused. Well, I didn't go to the bishop; I don't think I even knew there was one. But I knew being photographed is contrary to the Amish religion, so it stands to reason that Amish bishops pretty much have to say no; that's what they do.

Upon arrival in Lancaster, I went to the bar in my motel and made friends with some local young people. The father of one of them owned a stone quarry. He gave me a few names, and I started making the rounds, stopping at each Amish farm. I explained who I was, who I represented, and why I thought it was important to tell the story of the Amish way of life. After being turned down by many of the bearded patriarchs, I finally found one who would let me visit his family and photograph them. Melvin Stoltzfus and his wife, Barbara, were, I think, just a few years older than I and were warm and hospitable people. I'd stop at their farm often on my daily drives around the county. I'd been sent to Pennsylvania to stay for about a week. I immediately began shipping film with my Amish pictures back to the *Geographic*, so Bob Gilka told me to stay. I spent a good part of that summer in Amish country.

When my internship ended, Gilka put me on contract, and I went back to do more on the Amish in the fall. Six months later, I was asked to join the staff. My portrait of the Amish boy holding his pet guinea pig, which opened the essay, was one of the first pictures I made as a professional, as well as one of the first I made in color. Published in July 1965, that story is credited by some as the beginning of a more intimate way for *National Geographic* to look at people.

As I matured a little I shook off that supposed Hemingway quote about being the best there is and began to focus on just being a better photographer than I had been a year earlier, or two years earlier. To be better than I had been before, if even to a small degree, was most important to me; I didn't worry about all the others.

By the late summer of 1967 I felt a need to leave my staff position at *National Geographic* to freelance and work for other magazines, but I also wanted to continue to work for the *Geographic*. I guess I'd thought then that the New York–based magazines might have an edge to their use of photography that *National Geographic* didn't have, and I felt the need to be independent. So I borrowed some money, bought some cameras, and left the *Geographic* in late August of that year. Immediately, though, I took a freelance assignment from them to do a story about the Basque Country of Spain and France. I would continue to freelance for the next 29 years, working for *Life* and the *Saturday Evening Post*, *Look*, *Fortune*, and *GEO*. Much more often, though, I worked for *National Geographic*, which, as the years passed and the editorship passed from Melville Bell Grosvenor to his son, Gil Grosvenor, to Bill Garrett, to Bill Graves, to Bill Allen, was evolving into a much stronger, more visually dynamic magazine. And as it did, many of those New York–based magazines foundered.

As a freelance photographer, I would occasionally get some commercial work from ad agencies. They paid well, although the work wasn't always interesting. But every once in a long while in my career I got paid very well to just wander around taking pictures that I liked without concern for editors or anybody else back somewhere, because there *wasn't* anybody else back somewhere. To be paid handsomely to make pictures with absolutely no strings attached is a rarity in this profession. It's like a grant with no obligations. It's been a long time since I've had that kind of opportunity. The first time was more than 30 years ago.

In Rockport, Maine, in 1979, I was teaching a weeklong workshop at the Maine Photographic Workshops; I was showing my work during an evening presentation open to the public. I mentioned that I was hoping eventually to do a book of my work on the American West and the cowboy, with pictures drawn from *National Geographic* assignments from over the years throughout the West. But I told the audience I needed to do more work. I've never been a believer in what I think of as the "quick" book, one that is created out of a single magazine assignment. In general, I believe one needs to put more into a book, to go back on one's own nickel, or however one can, to do more on the subject until that work is truly worthy of a book.

Then as now, I think of a book of one's work as almost sacred. A finely produced book of photographs should not be just an extended magazine essay, but something special, a tactile creation to hold in one's hands that with each turn of a page reveals strong vision, its images printed well and displayed intelligently, with a union that flows from beginning to end; it should have a depth and personality one can return to again and again with a pleasure similar to that of enjoying the company of a good and trusted friend.

In the audience that evening in Rockport was Sam Yanes, then, as I recall, in charge of publicity and marketing for the Polaroid Corporation. He was vacationing in Rockport and taking in the workshop's evening presentations at the theater. Sam approached me after my presentation, introduced himself, complimented me on my pictures, and offered to help me continue my work on the American cowboy. He told me Polaroid was coming out with a new film for its SX-70 camera. The film was to be called Time-Zero. Sam said he wanted to hire me to be the first professional to test it in the field. All I had to do was pick a place, go there, and make lots of SX-70 pictures with the new film. Polaroid hoped to announce the new film by mounting an exhibition of my SX-70 pictures in a one-man show at the Clarence Kennedy Gallery near the Polaroid Corporation in Cambridge, Massachusetts. They would supply the cameras and the film and pay all my expenses. And for making the pictures, they would pay me $600 a day for 30 days. I was quite happy that evening when Sam Yanes and I said goodnight. A few months later I was headed back out West, taking with me a half dozen Polaroid SX-70 cameras and a lot of the regular SX-70 film. But the new Time-Zero film had not yet been released. Sam said Polaroid would ship it to me once I was out West. I was excited to start this lucrative freelance commercial assignment that would take me right back into a subject I loved: the American West.

In 1979 many commercial photographers were making day rates greater than $600, sometimes twice that much or more, photographing advertising campaigns. I'd done just a little myself, contributing to a couple of Marlboro campaigns in the early 1970s that I think paid around $1,500 a day. But those days were full of frustration because what I was asked to do with the subject of the cowboy in those cigarette advertisements had nothing to do with what I knew about the reality of cowboys, how they looked, and their way of working.

I could deal with the campaign's stylized and sanitized clothing: the sheepskin coats I'd never seen on a working cowhand; the absence of "wild rags," those neck scarves, often wrinkled and ratty but warming in winter, sun shielding in summer; and the pristine cowboy hats lacking a single sweat stain or any signs of having been scuffed up by the manure-smeared dirt of a horse corral, with no evidence at all of really ever having been worked in. The Marlboro cowboys I photographed were certainly genuine; they came out of ranch country in the West and were thoroughly versed in cowboy skills. But they knew how their bread was buttered: They were paid well to dress a certain way to portray a romantic image of the West fashioned in the minds of a creative team at an advertising agency based in Chicago, which was hired to help sell a product made in the Southeast. It was all about image, and I acknowledged that. Sort of. I found it exasperating not being truly free to make what I thought were good pictures, and watching opportunities for excellent pictures fade away with the day's best light while trying to make something special out of what were sometimes an art director's not-so-good ideas. Part of my problem at the time was probably my inexperience with how some of the creative people in advertising thought; their concept of reality versus mine; and my early success in the photojournalism profession as a documentary photographer, where I worked with reality and welcomed it.

Also clouding my reasoning and perspective was the fact that my father never made more than $95 a week in his life. In the years before his retirement at 65 he had been shoveling flaxseed at a mill in northeast Minneapolis for a living, a job for which I can't believe he had much love, and certainly no passion. Working as a freelance photographer and writer for *National Geographic* I had been doing what I absolutely loved to do, while establishing a reputation in the profession, and getting paid reasonably well. When an advertising agency offered me more money for a day's work than my father could ever have dreamed of making in a month, I actually thought it was because they wanted me to make the kinds of pictures I was becoming known for. I found out it often wasn't quite like that in advertising. A smart person, of course, would simply do the work as the art director thought best, say "Thank you very much; it's been wonderful," and take the check with all those numbers on it to the bank.

To begin the Polaroid work, I made the cross-country drive to northeastern Nevada in my '76 Dodge van, which I'd outfitted with excellent speakers so I had good music. I planned to hang out with the buckaroos on the IL, a big, corporation-owned ranch based near Elko. I hadn't ever been on the IL before, but I'd called and made a connection with the ranch manager. Once I got out there, I stayed in the cow camps with the IL buckaroo boss, Hank Brackenberry, and his crew; rode horseback with them on their daily gatherings; went into town with them; visited the brothels of Elko; and generally blended in pretty well, although they were all younger than I.

In Nevada I had the Polaroid SX-70 cameras and lots of the regular SX-70 film. I still had no Time-Zero film, though, because Edwin Land, founder of Polaroid and still running the show, refused to release it to the public as a result of its tendency to turn blue in certain light conditions. So I practiced with the SX-70s and the regular film. I also used my Leica film cameras to do work that might be good enough for my book.

When I first started working with the Polaroid SX-70 cameras, I thought I'd be frustrated by the square format, which differed from the rectangular format of my 35mm cameras. But I soon adapted and become fond of it, seeing how one could work within the corners in a kind of compact way. I was so used to taking candid pictures in relatively low light by framing them quickly with my Leicas, though, that the slower lens and less light-sensitive Polaroid film often forced me to really jam the SX-70 camera's viewfinder against my face to hold it steady enough to make the picture. By the end of the day I'd have a groove pressed into the side of my nose.

As time passed I was getting concerned about not having the new Time-Zero film. The weather was starting to cool, and Polaroid film, which was sensitive to temperature extremes, didn't respond well if the weather was cold. I finally called Sam Yanes back East and told him I thought we'd have to stop our efforts and rethink where to go when the film finally became available. As I recall, about two weeks had passed since I had arrived out in the high desert to join Hank and his buckaroos. I was getting paid, but I said, "Sam, this isn't going to work. I think I'd better start the long drive home, and we'll have to try someplace else when Doctor Land lets loose of that film." "OK," said Sam. "OK."

I packed up the van and drove east. With me were a number of rolls of 35mm Kodachrome film I had shot on my Leicas. These would yield quite a few pictures that would eventually find their way into my first book, *Vanishing Breed* (published by Little Brown/New York Graphic Society Books two years later). That book of my pictures and writing about the cowboy would be nominated for the 1982 American Book Award. It received the Leica Medal of Excellence and the Western Heritage Wrangler Award for Best Western Art Book of 1982. It was the first time that award had been given to a photographer rather than a painter.

WHEN I GOT BACK HOME to Virginia from Nevada, after thinking a lot during the long drive about where to go to complete my Polaroid commission (I've always liked to call it a commission; it has such a nice, noncommercial sound), I called Sam Yanes and told him I thought I ought to go to Oaxaca, Mexico. Why I thought of Oaxaca, a place I'd never been to, I can't say. It just kind of came out. I must have read about it somewhere, but can't now, for the life of me, remember where or when. It may have been in a travel magazine, in which I could see it was a place of great physical color. I expected that it was probably warm, and thus favorable to the Polaroid film, and that there would be lots of good light. Sam said, "Fine. Great idea." He told me he had once been a member of writer Ken Kesey's Merry Pranksters, who bused their way across America in the psychedelic sixties. Sam said he'd spent some time down in Oaxaca before he was a corporation man. Maybe he had, and maybe he was just kidding. But he told me to go, and I went. And I now had the new SX-70 Time-Zero film.

Oaxaca offered, as I'd suspected, a wonderful color palette to play with as I visually explored the town and nearby villages. There were markets with people and their produce and animals for sale, and all within a rainbow of color I had never experienced photographically before, certainly not while hanging out in cow camps in Nevada or Montana. Vibrant color seemed to be everywhere, not just in the often multicolored buildings, but also in the clothing of the people, the woven cloth offered in the markets, and the furniture in the cafés. And there always seemed to be flowers.

Because I wasn't fluent in Spanish I had to hire a local woman as an interpreter. Otherwise, I worked alone—just me and the streets of Oaxaca. I worked with both the Polaroid cameras and my Leica film cameras. I was no longer, of course, making pictures for my book on the American West and the cowboy. But I was making pictures with my Leicas that would eventually fit into a book called *The Photographic Essay*, a retrospective published by Little Brown/Bulfinch Press in 1989.

I spent most nights in Oaxaca looking over my day's production of SX-70 prints and soon became aware of something I came to think of as the *coincidence of color* that was part of the physicality of Oaxaca. It was something I would come to love. In the market I saw a girl sitting on a yellow chair by a yellow wall. In her dress was a small pattern that echoed the color of another wall nearby. A second girl was leaning against a wall of vivid red, wearing a dress with a pattern that repeated the color. A woman walking down the street, passing a building painted in burnt ocher, was wearing something that repeated that color, and hanging on her arm was a straw basket that matched. Time and again I would see examples of how the colors of this place and the appearance of its people were virtually interwoven. I couldn't always make pictures that showed this, but it was there, constantly.

Following my work in Oaxaca, Polaroid hung a one-man show of my SX-70 photographs at the Clarence Kennedy Gallery in Cambridge, Massachusetts. The experience of taking on that assignment to work with the new Polaroid film was a total pleasure. It was fun to make pictures I enjoyed finding by wandering, open to everything. I was also able to make pictures with my Leicas. And Polaroid paid me well.

I returned to Oaxaca in 1985 when Polaroid hired me again, this time to make pictures with their new Spectra camera and film.

Over the years, although I've done relatively little commercial work, I always hope for a commercial project that will allow me to use my vision in the same way I would if I were on a journalism assignment in Paris or India, working serendipitously, making pictures that are real and have an aesthetic strength that makes you want to hang them on a wall. It's rare to have the kind of commercial assignments I had with Polaroid, which offered such total aesthetic freedom.

Would I be happy doing only commercial work, where the money is very good but my personal involvement might not be? No, I know I wouldn't. ■

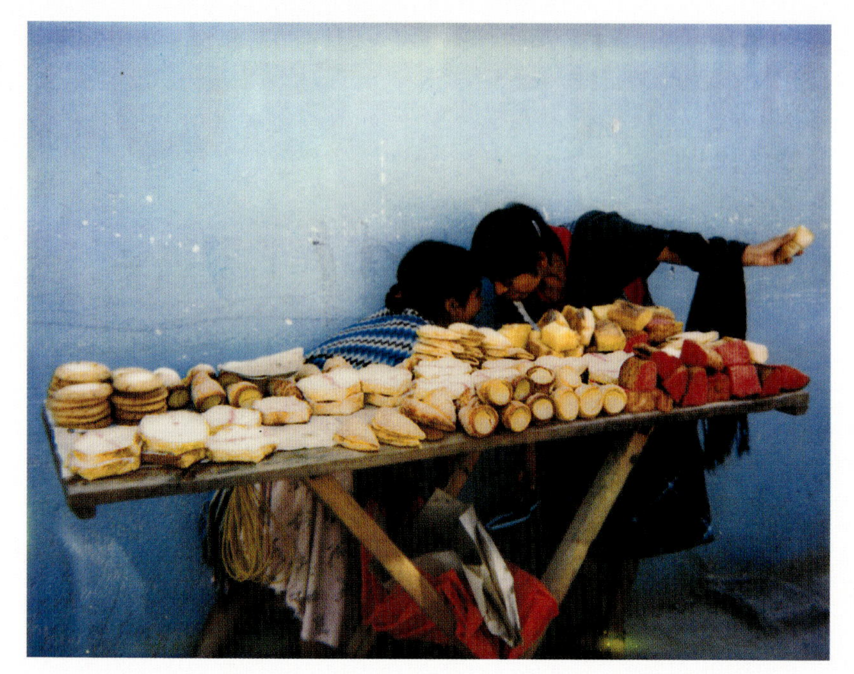

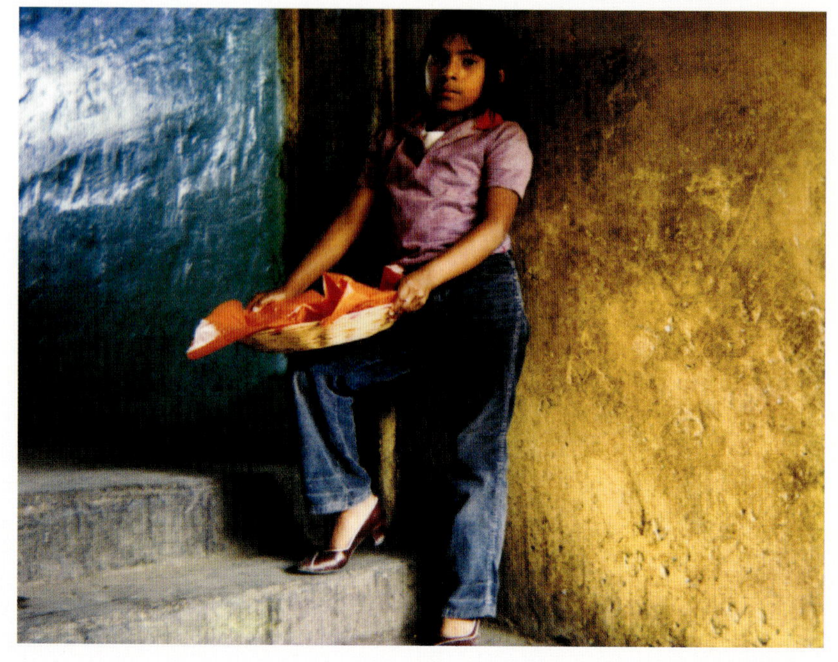

LEFT: *Two girls talking, Oaxaca, 1980* RIGHT: *Girl in her mother's shoes, Oaxaca, 1980, SX-70 Polaroids*

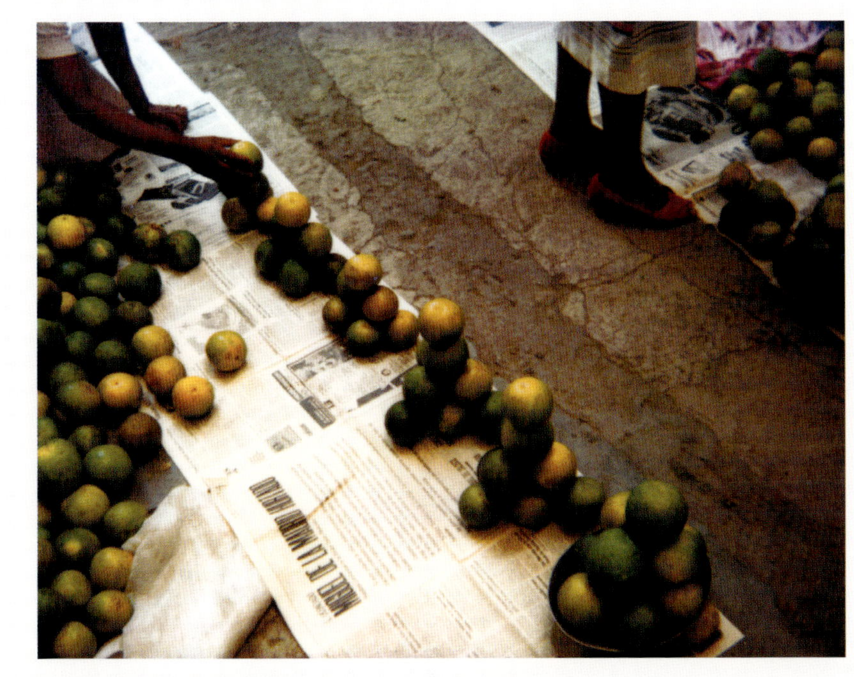

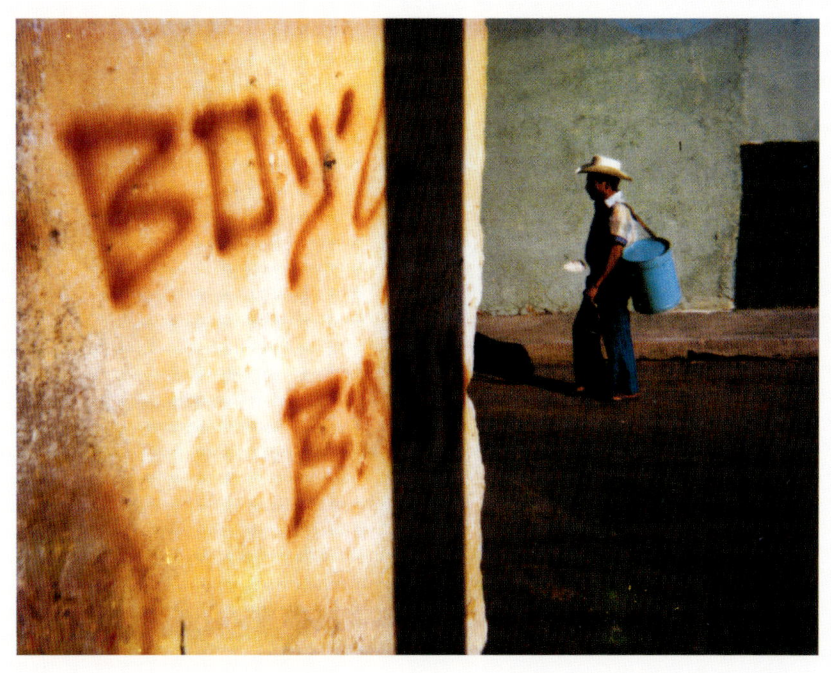

LEFT: *Limes in the market, Oaxaca, 1980* RIGHT: *Walls and the street, Oaxaca, 1980, SX-70 Polaroids*

"In the market I saw a girl sitting on a yellow chair by a yellow wall. In her dress was a small pattern that echoed the color of another wall nearby."

Woman with red rose, Oaxaca, 1985, Spectra Polaroid

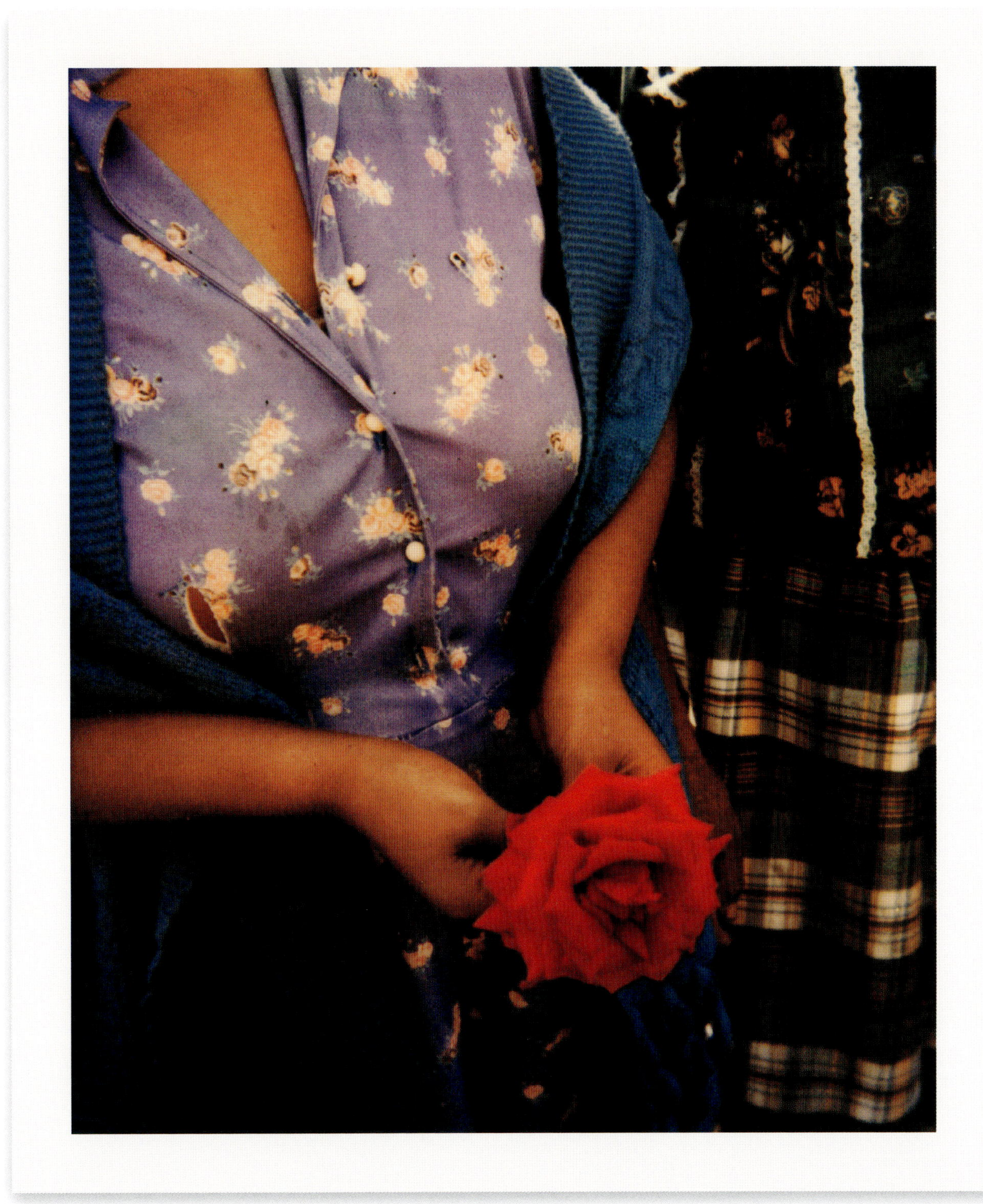

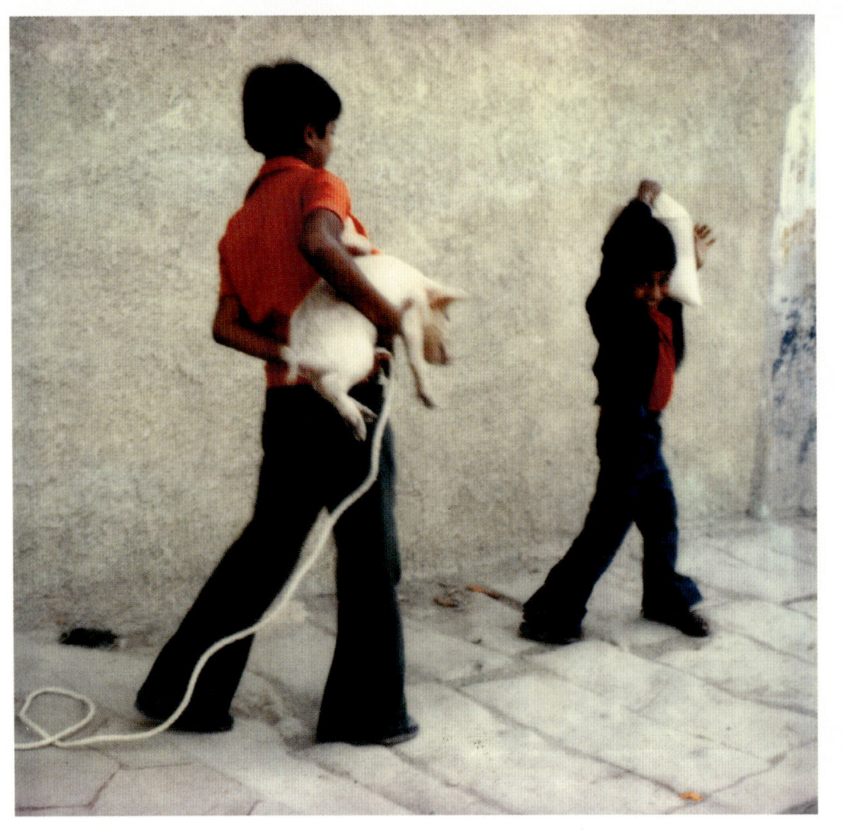

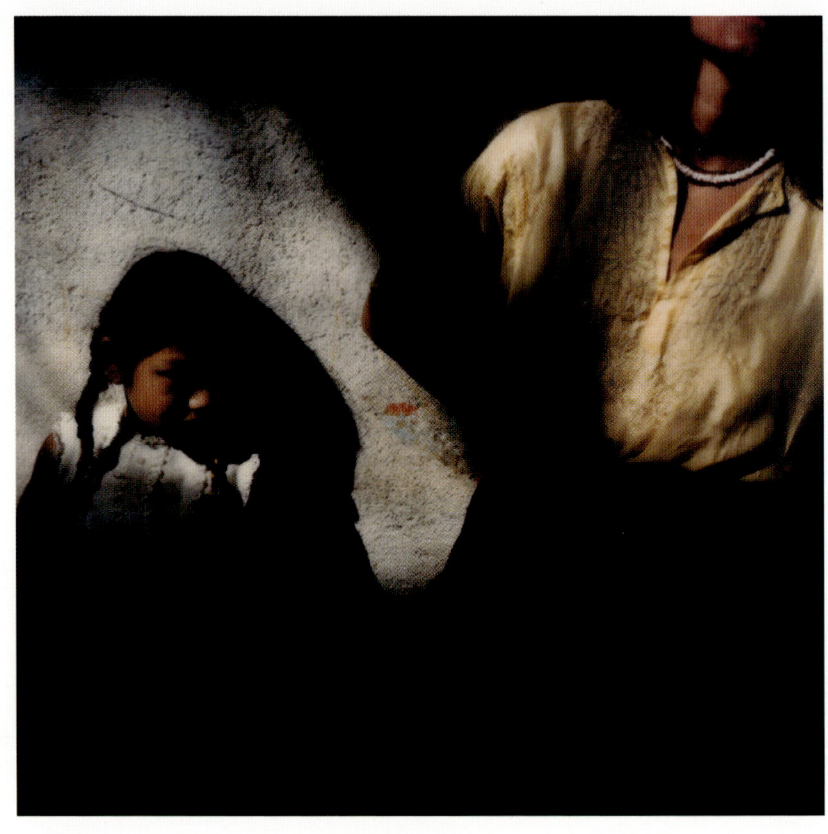

LEFT: *Boy with a pig, Oaxaca, 1980* RIGHT: *Woman and girl in the shadows, Oaxaca, 1980, SX-70 Polaroids*

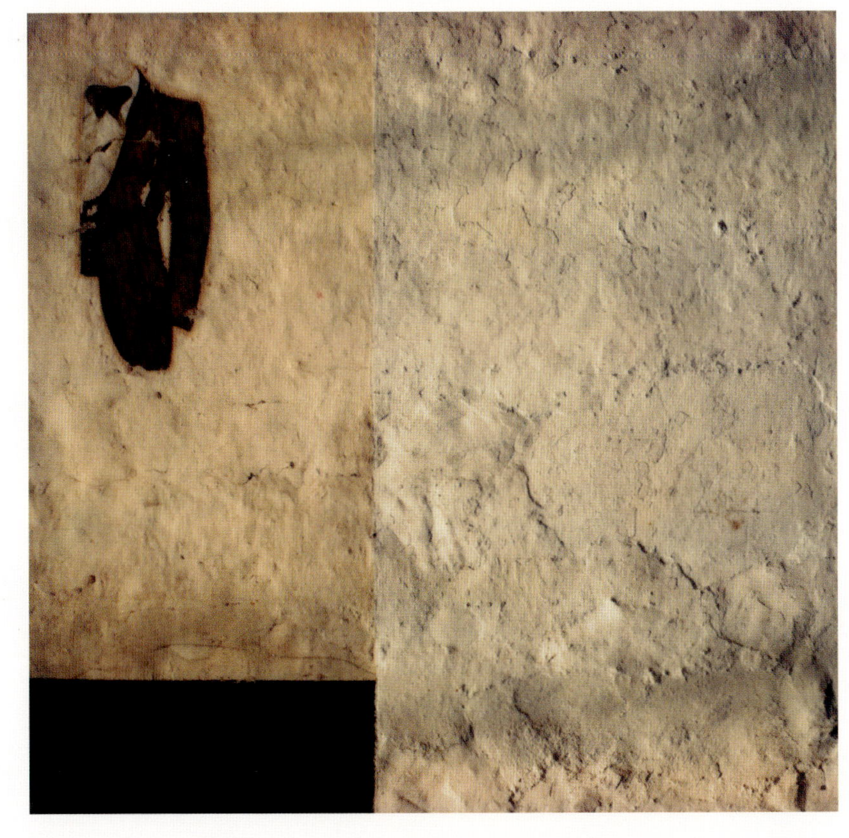

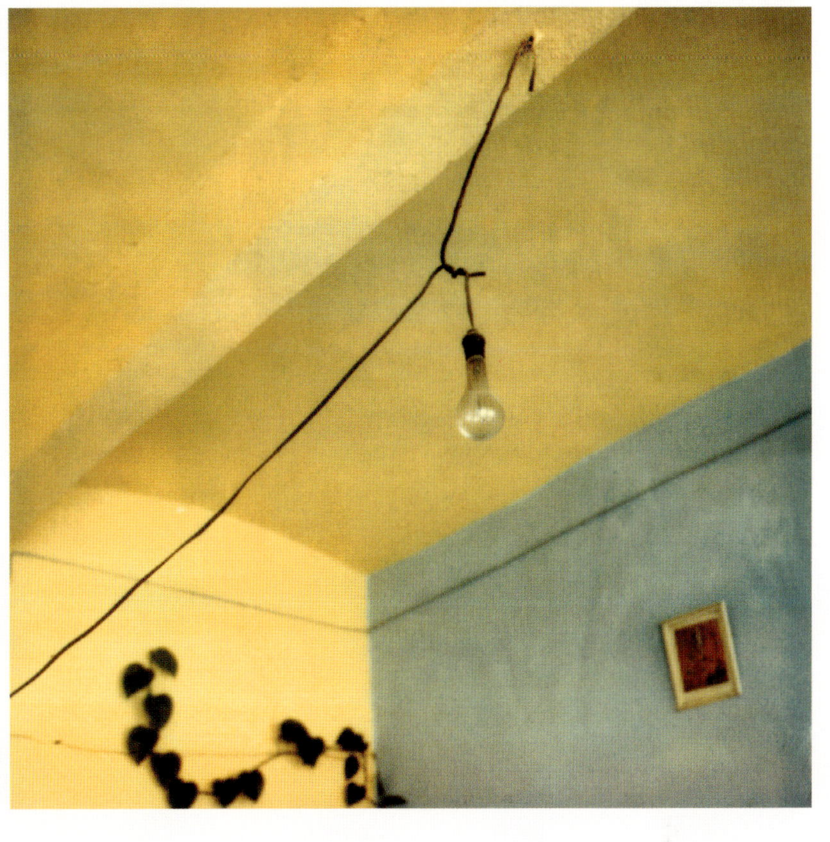

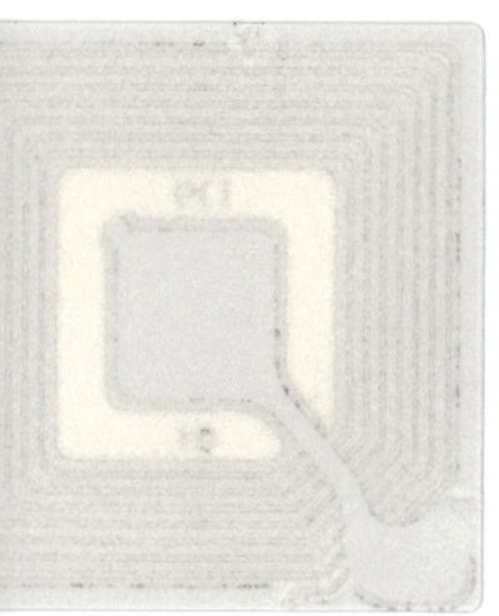

LEFT: *Wall of a tailor's shop, Oaxaca, 1980* RIGHT: *Ceiling light and picture, Oaxaca, 1980, SX-70 Polaroids*

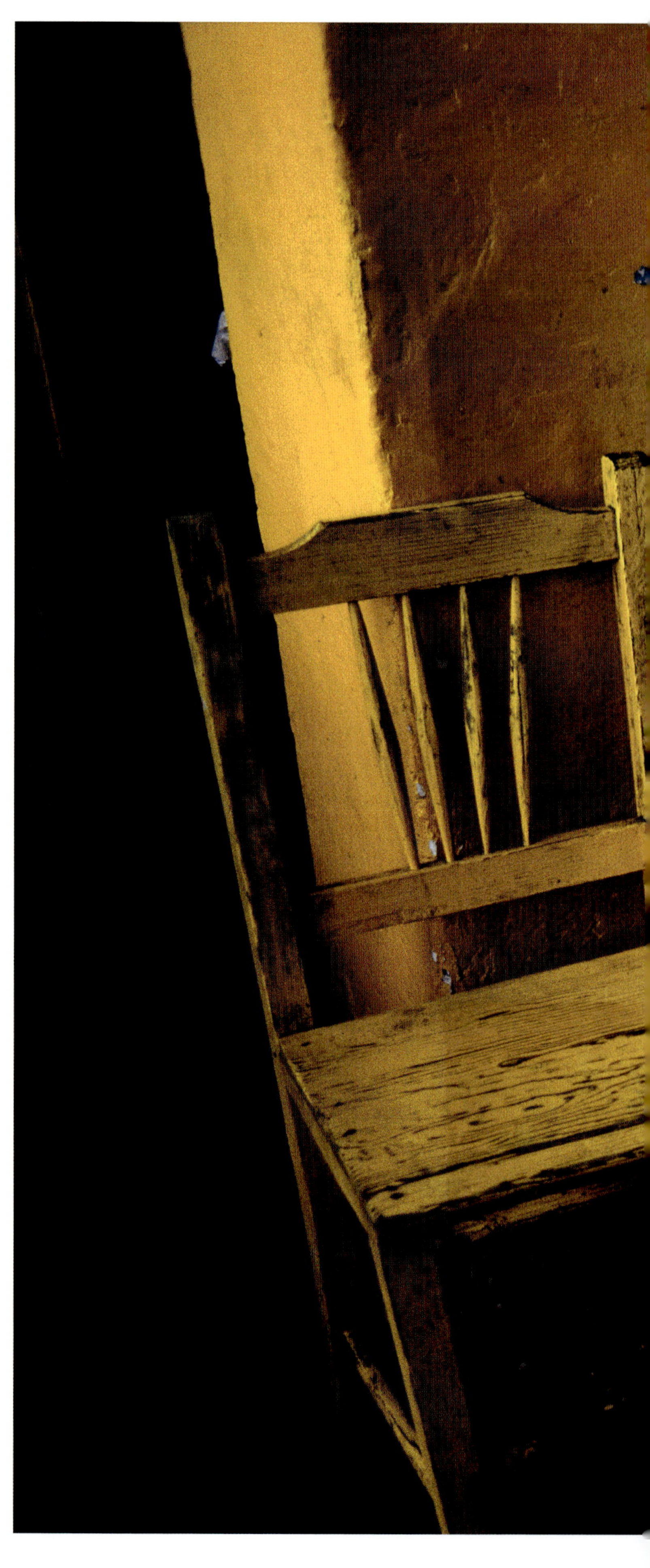

Girl by a yellow wall and yellow chair, Oaxaca, 1980, 35mm Kodachrome film

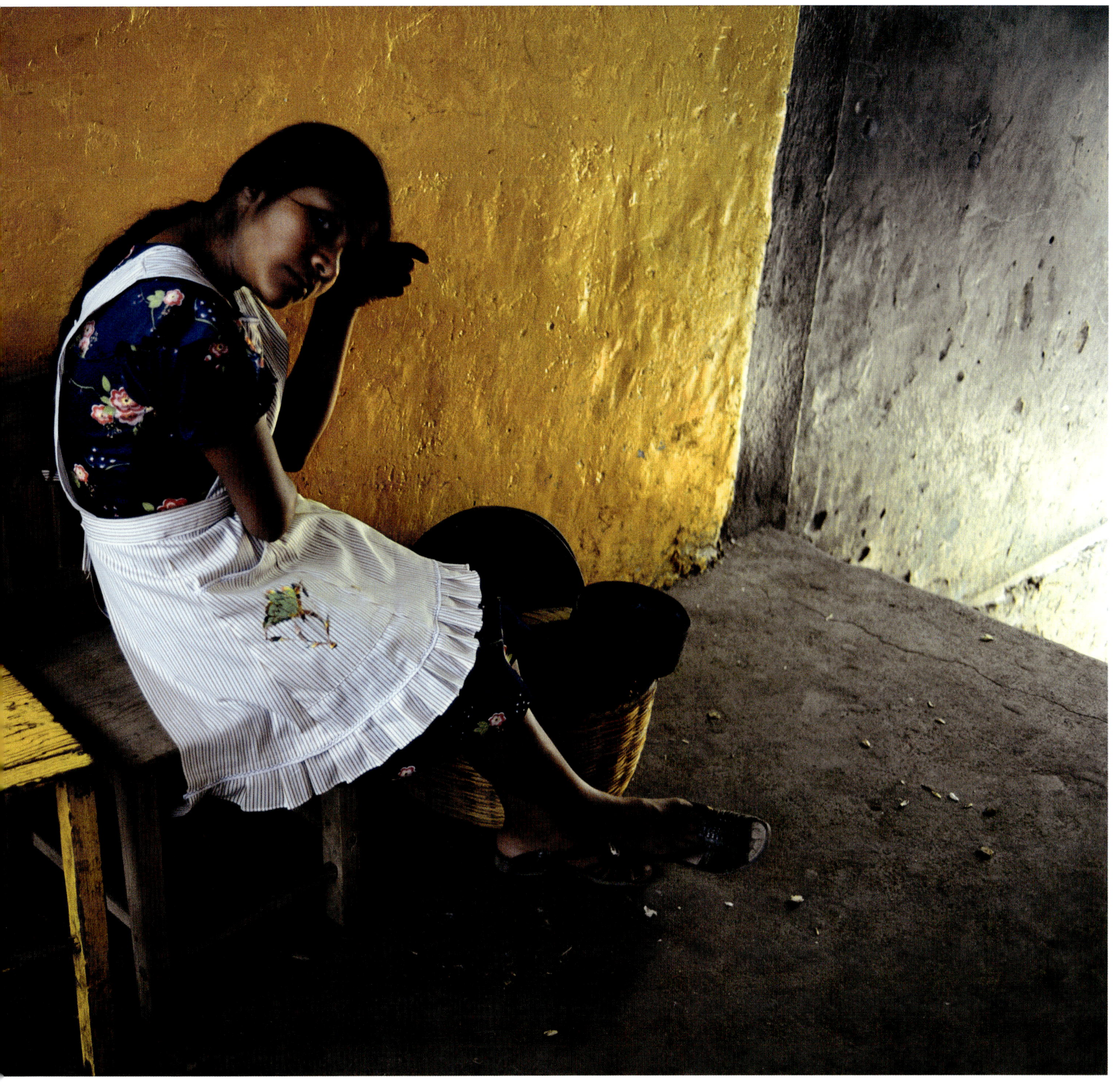

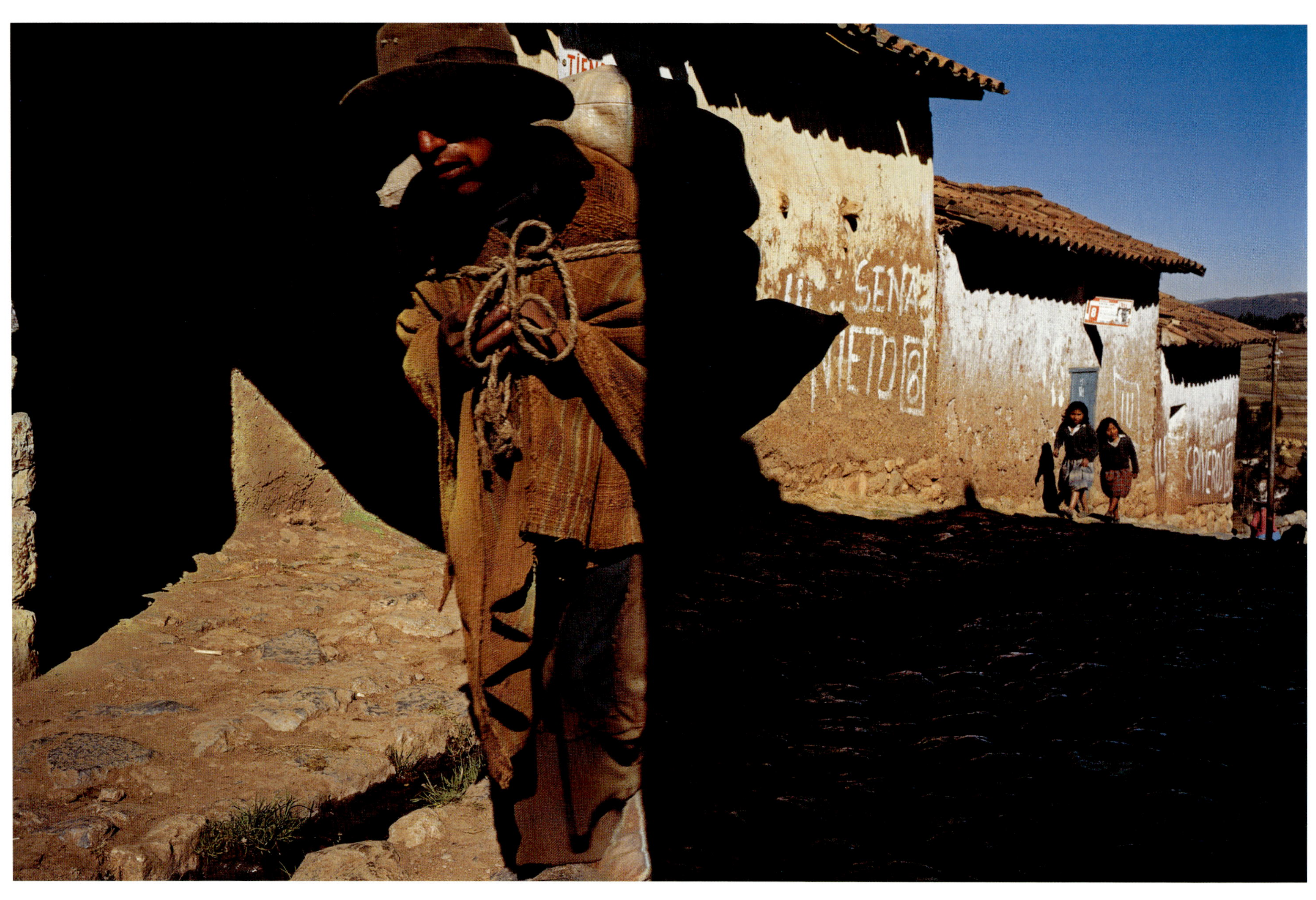

Man emerging from shadows, Chincheros, 1985

Peru

I've been criticized over the years, probably justifiably so, for using too many four-letter words in my everyday speech. Well, *Peru* is a four-letter word. So, also, is *life.* And when I think of the word "Peru," I can't help but think of how much the country has influenced my life since I first saw it while on assignment for *National Geographic* in 1981. Ultimately, that first Peru visit would prove to be life changing. Initially, I had—literally—an earthshaking introduction to the country.

Shortly after my arrival in Lima that spring (our spring, their fall) to begin a country story on Peru, I traveled with my assistant to Ayacucho. The Andean town is celebrated for its Easter week processions and traditions and was the birthplace, only a year earlier, of the Sendero Luminoso (Shining Path), whose guerrillas terrorized Peru for more than a decade with such butchery that Amnesty International called it "the most brutal terrorist movement in the world."

All went well my first few days in Ayacucho, although I didn't think my assistant's command of the English language was as good as I needed it to be, and I would eventually have to find someone else.

On the evening of Good Friday, I was preparing to photograph an evening candlelight procession due to make its way through the streets of the little town. While inside one of its many churches, waiting for the procession

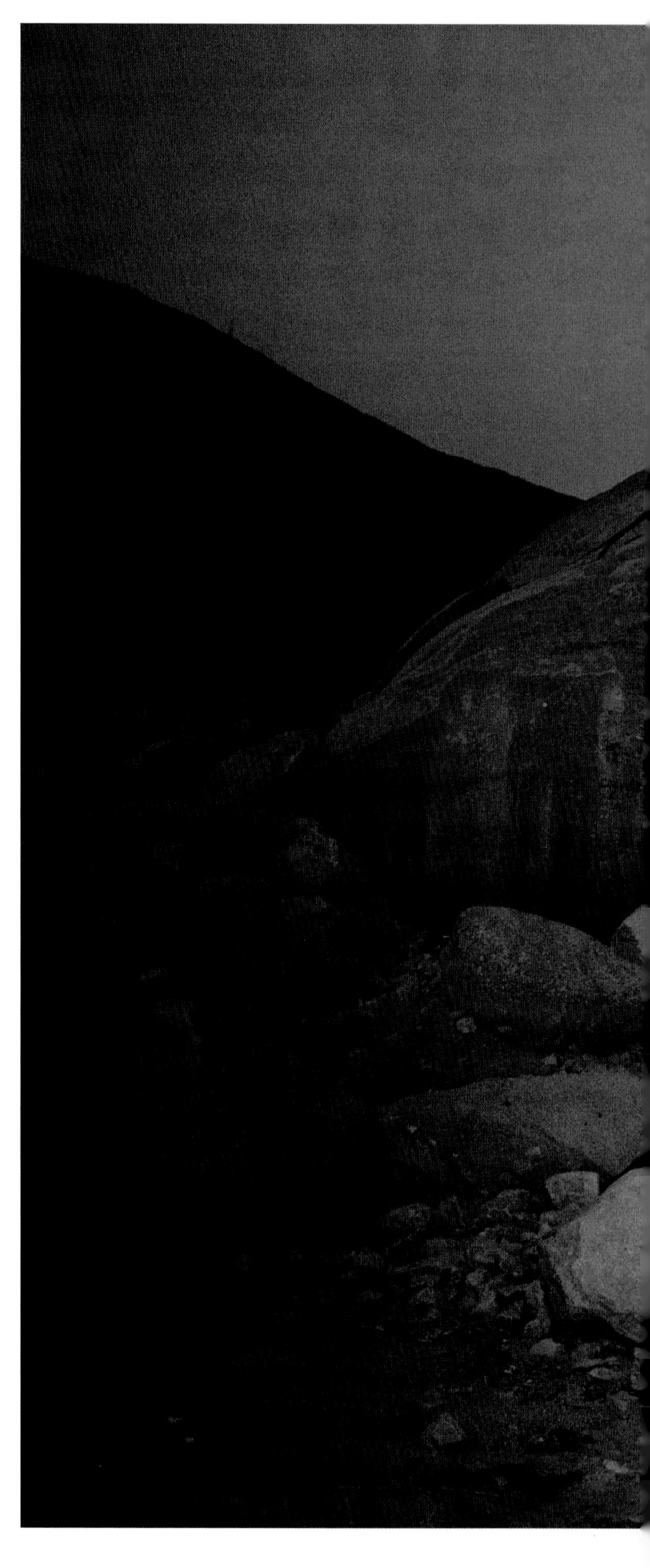

Girl walking through earthquake rubble, Pedregal, 1984

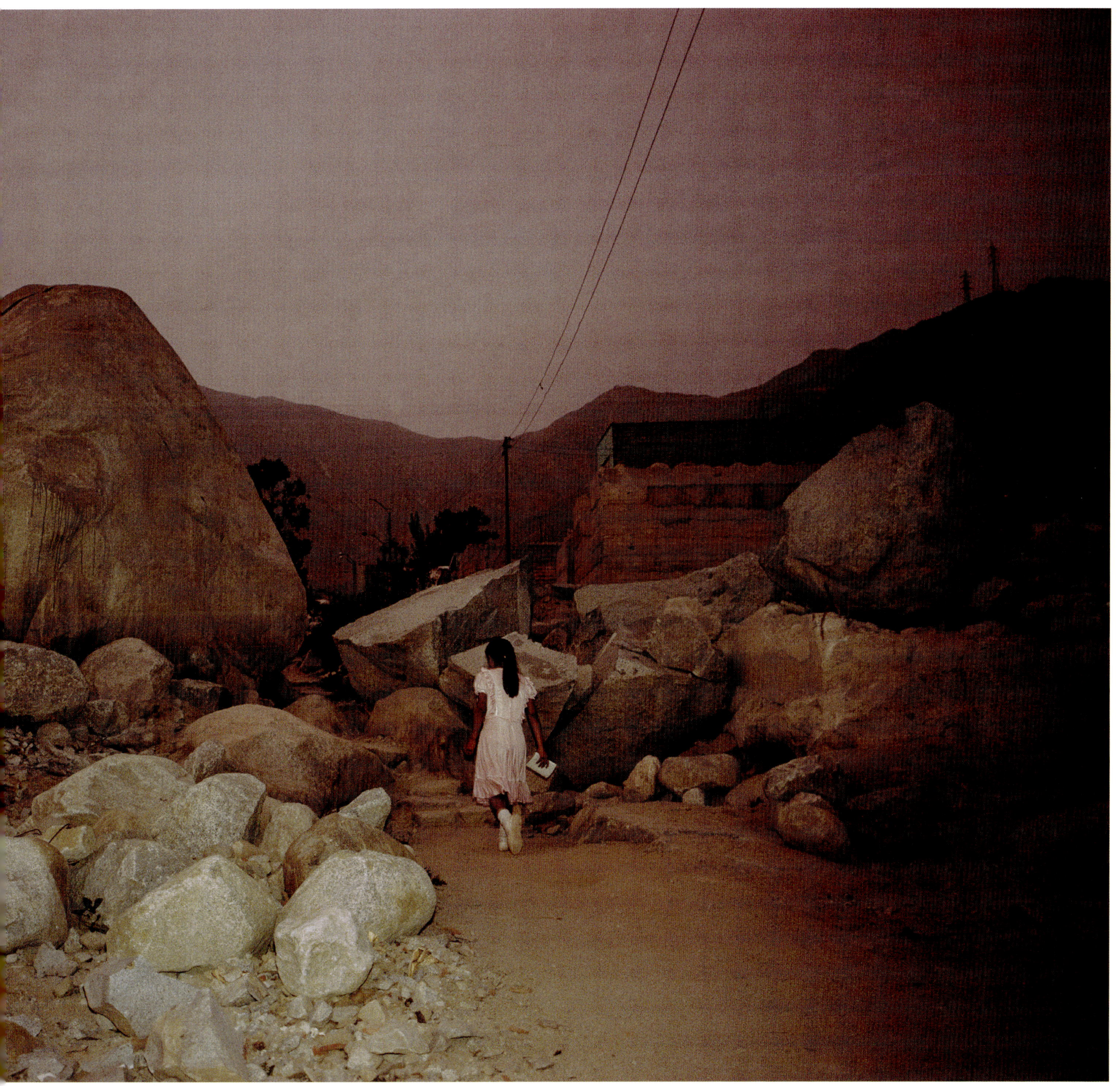

to begin, I felt a sudden, startling movement of the earth beneath my feet, like nothing I'd ever felt before. Then I heard screams:

"Terremoto! Terremoto!"

I was near the church entrance and struggled to leave, trying not to panic. Once outside, I was encompassed by a crushing wave of bodies, elbow to elbow with hundreds of other people, fear masking their faces. My heart was pounding. If there are more tremors, I thought, many of us will be trampled to death, victims of a futile attempt to escape something perhaps inescapable.

I'd never been in an earthquake before. I knew before arriving in Lima that a U.S. physicist had predicted a series of cataclysmic earthquakes for Peru, to take place in the summer of 1981. That proved false, but Peru does have an alarming history of devastating earthquakes, dating back to 1746, when a quake destroyed much of Lima. A horrendous earthquake in 1970 killed 70,000 people to the north of Lima, literally burying the Andean village of Yungay and turning it into a cemetery, the center of which is now marked by three palm trees covered up to about half their height with rubble, earth, and wildflowers.

The Good Friday tremor in 1981, later reported as 5.1 on the Richter scale, was not to repeat itself that evening. *National Geographic* staff writer Harvey Arden told me later that night, "It sounded like two subway trains had collided beneath our feet." I, however, couldn't recall hearing *anything*. I remembered only the horrible feeling of the earth tearing apart beneath me. Perhaps the shock of that moment temporarily muted my sense of hearing; I really don't know. The rest of the evening passed uneventfully. But all was not to stay that way.

Two days later, in midmorning, my assistant appeared outside my motel room, pounding loudly on the door. When I opened it, her eyes were wide, and she kept repeating what sounded like *"Irwauk! Irwauk! Irwauk!"* I finally realized she was trying to tell me there had been an earthquake elsewhere in the region and that people had died. Evidently the same quake we'd experienced Good Friday evening had devastated several villages a good distance away, deep in a roadless Andean valley. A half dozen campesinos had walked to Ayacucho to tell of the deaths of eight in the tiny village of Paccha and to plead for help. I heard that the military was going to fly emergency supplies and a medical team to the village. I managed to hitch a ride with them.

Once we landed, a medical tent was set up and the team began to examine the people of the tiny village. The villagers, in turn, closely watched the doctors and nurses at work, peering at them through a mosquito-netted tent window, as though they were witnessing some kind of exotic species on display at a county fair.

The doctors, with their stethoscopes and flashlights, were probing the chests and the backs of the village men, shining their flashlights into mouths gaped open and eyes rolled back. It was a mesmerizing sight for three young girls looking in, sunlight and shadow carving their faces into relief behind the mosquito netting of the window. They seemed in complete awe. Most likely, no one in this village had ever seen a real doctor before. And most likely, none of them ever would again.

The archbishop of Ayacucho had flown in on another helicopter to hold a Catholic Mass for the earthquake victims. A woman with a worn, weather-creased face wept, her hands, with toil-blackened fingers, clasped in prayer.

Later, on my helicopter flight back to Lima, I watched a village woman next to me, who was being taken to Ayacucho to be treated for a crushed ankle, as she huddled on the floor of the chopper, her eyes wide in terror. I think if I had reached out to try to comfort her, she might have recoiled even deeper into fear. I couldn't help thinking, my God! What must this be like for someone who may never even have been to a town where there are cars and trucks, now being taken up by strangers into the vast sky in this huge, shuddering, and ear-shattering machine?

In 1981 Peru was, and it still is now, a country with many people existing on the borderline of subsistence. Much later during that assignment, on a crystal-clear day in the Altiplano near Puno, I was ending an afternoon of wandering, driving back to town, when I saw a small boy crying by the side of the road. His blue knit sweater was patched at the elbows, and the seat of his pants was tattered and crosshatched with stitches.

His name was Eduardo Ramos. He was nine and had been taking his family's small band of about a dozen sheep home from where they'd been grazing. Eduardo's daily responsibility was to take the sheep out in the morning and bring them home in the late afternoon. In Andean villages livestock often represent a family's well-being. They may have a few sheep, perhaps a cow, some chickens, a pig. Whatever they own is often critical to their existence.

A taxi driver, carelessly speeding back to town, had slammed into Eduardo's sheep as they crossed the road, killing half of them, throwing their broken bodies out into a field, where they lay like discarded stuffed animals. I don't think the driver had even stopped to check his cab for damage. Eduardo's family's economy had suddenly been devastated by something completely beyond his responsibility and control. It was emotionally wrenching to the boy. He was shattered, tears running down his sun- and wind-burned face. So many of his sheep—dead. What could he tell his family?

I made a few pictures—very few—and left. It's always difficult to decide in times like that: What do you do to try to make things better? Do you pay someone for a picture? You can't go around handing out dollars for pictures; that isn't good even if you really want to. You can quickly develop a following if you leave a trail of dollars, obviously; in a poor neighborhood you can count on it. It would be better to have a supply of food, maybe fruit, to give, especially to the children. I don't remember myself or anyone I was with giving Eduardo anything. We had no food with us. I'm sure we tried to comfort him with words, but to what end? I didn't see the pictures of him for more than a month, not until I returned to the States and went to the *Geographic* to look at my film.

When I finally saw Eduardo's picture, with the dead sheep behind his half-turned, crying face, I told my editors I thought we needed to run the picture, because it talked simply but clearly about how difficult life can be in Peru for the many who live a marginal existence. The picture ran large in the published story.

What I didn't expect, although perhaps I should have, was how the *National Geographic* readers responded. Classes of schoolchildren sent in small donations of a couple of dollars; many people sent in more, all responding to the plight of Eduardo. Eventually, almost $7,000 was sent to *National Geographic* to help the boy. The Society contacted CARE, the international humanitarian organization, which in turn located Eduardo's village. The family's sheep were replaced, a water pump for the village was installed, and the remaining amount was designated to go into a fund for Peruvian schoolchildren.

To that little nine-year-old and his family, the readers' response to the picture I took must have seemed unbelievable, like something from out of the sky. In their world, things die around them all the time, sometimes violently, like livestock destroyed by a careless taxi; or a drunken mine worker killed in a fall off an overloaded truck; or passengers crushed when their bus slews off a mudslide-ruined mountain road and tumbles down, over and over, for 500 feet. Sometimes death comes quietly and stealthily, perhaps as a common respiratory fever in a baby; the mother either has no knowledge of the need for an antibiotic or, if she does, she has no access to it, and her baby dies because the traditional herbal treatment doesn't work. In a world where death can come easily, and often early in life, rarely does anyone ever come along to make bad things better.

The readers' response to Eduardo was also a gift to me, because it lifted away that heavy stone of guilt for once again having taken but not really given in return.

I haven't often photographed human grief. The earthquake in Peru was the last time. I never served as a photographer at a newspaper, where one is often assigned to cover death by accident or intent. My emotional stress bulwarks have not frequently been put to the test on a professional basis. I wonder, sometimes, how those who often photograph wars or famine or natural disasters manage to keep emotionally stable. I would think that to become personally, emotionally involved in every situation that shows human grief would probably take almost anyone into too dark a place to remain unaffected. They must somehow remain apart from the horrors they see. But I'm convinced that the best photographers, at least the best ones I know personally who frequently document human tragedy, are doing it because they sincerely believe someone must bear witness to the assaults of man against humanity, and to other disasters, because maybe, just maybe, their pictures will somehow make a difference.

I think of James Nachtwey, a photographer who makes images of the horrors of war and the sorrows of famine and disease. He has put his life at great risk again and again to show the worst of man; and he continues to do so because he believes we must bear witness.

My friend Eugene Richards has often visited the bottom of America's society, people ravaged by drugs, poverty, mental illness. He says he becomes very angry politically and works out his anger through his photographs. Photographer Vince Musi, when introducing Richards at the 2009 LOOK3 Festival of the Photograph, in Charlottesville, Virginia, referred to his work as "the photograph as evidence; the photograph as testimony." The same certainly could be said of the work of James Nachtwey.

One must wonder, however, just how Nachtwey and Richards can maintain themselves emotionally, having seen as much evidence and making as much testimony as both of them have. In the case of Richards, his subjects are often part of his life far after he's ceased to document them. He maintains contact with some of them as he would with family.

In my career, although I have established relationships with some of my subjects, such as the Hutterites, that have endured far beyond a given assignment, many of my best pictures have been made of people in passing, people I will never see again, of serendipitous moments, wistful, perhaps of joy, of reflection. But seldom have I made a photograph that caused me to look into a heart that was broken or dead.

I remember many years ago, I think it was 1968, being on assignment for *Life* to photograph a mine disaster in West Virginia. I was one of the first press photographers to reach the community, where families of the miners feared dead were gathered in the small company store, waiting for news from mine officials. Hopelessness and dread seemed to hang in the air as I made a few photographs of a woman sitting in a stuffed chair, holding a paper coffee cup with the symbol of the Red Cross on it. Her eyes were red rimmed and fatigued, her face haggard and pale. Her young daughter stood by her side, her eyes staring out the storefront window to where the mine entrance was, not far away. I quietly tried to make a few nonintrusive pictures of them.

Then I stopped, and said to the woman, "I'm sorry I have to do this."

"That's all right," she said. "I understand."

I remember thinking at the time that perhaps she understood, but I wasn't at all sure that I did.

Susan Sontag implied in her book *On Photography* that photographers are of a predatory nature, and I believe she was right in many ways. I think photographers are certainly not all the same and should be judged by their individual discretion and professional behavior when in pursuit of a picture. On the other hand, listen to the vocabulary we commonly share: We "take," we "capture," we "shoot," we "get," and on and on. That does tend to speak for itself.

Over the years, I've taken so many pictures of so many people without giving much of anything in return other than a thank-you, maybe a few prints, often not even that. Still, in the end I know I've made, and have had published, many pictures that have introduced a subject or a person to viewers far removed, pictures that may have educated them, told them something about the world someone else inhabits. I know I've entertained viewers, given them visual pleasure, maybe even some kind of comfort. The picture of Eduardo, however, is one of the rare times I feel I've been able to give back to one of my *subjects* in a significant way.

Although I think its aesthetics merit hanging the picture on a gallery wall, I don't imagine the image will ever warrant a mention in the history of photojournalism. It didn't help stop a war or contribute to the eradication of a disease; it didn't raise a million dollars for a just cause. I suppose it's just another picture of a poor kid in a backward place. But it did, in fact, actually make a positive difference in someone's life. In my experience, that simply doesn't happen very often.

WHILE WORKING IN PERU in 1981 I wanted to show the country in ways that would illustrate subjects peculiar to Peruvians living in certain regions. I knew, for instance, that meat was, at that time, rationed in the Andes; it was available only on certain days of the week. So one day I went to where cattle, sheep, and pigs were brought to slaughter, thinking I would possibly show meat being made available to the people of the area. However, what I was to see on my first visit to that slaughterhouse, and in other slaughterhouses in Peru, seemed to mirror some basic elements of life in Peru that can be harsh, cruel, primitive, and well beyond the simple rationing of meat.

What I saw was nothing like one might expect in the meat industry in the United States today, perhaps not even early in the last century, when Upton Sinclair revealed the cruelty and crudeness on the killing floors of Chicago's slaughterhouses in his book *The Jungle*.

Here, in a slaughterhouse, *el camal*, there were no men in hard hats and rubber boots and smocks; here, to a place of violence and sudden death, a mother might bring her children to play barefoot on the blood-slick floor while she helped her husband hold down a screaming pig so he could make the fatal knife thrust; here an elderly woman might dash in to collect a cup of cascading blood to drink hot from the dying animal. Here, amid the squealing and the carnage, I saw a girl selling chewing gum from a cardboard box, dead pigs sprawled at her feet. Another girl stood nearby, her skirt and her sweater sleeves soaked, her forearms and even her face splotched in scarlet from helping collect in plastic buckets the blood spilling from the jugulars of glass-eyed steers toppled by a dagger stab to the spinal column at a point where the neck meets the head. I saw a man in a nice sweater and neatly pressed trousers attending the butchering of his pig. A cow lay on its back, its feet hacked off, its head resembling something from Picasso's "Guernica."

In 1995, I photographed another story about Peru for *National Geographic*, and in the finished and approved layout was a picture I had made in an Ayacucho slaughterhouse when the workers were butchering hogs. A woman, seen from the chest down, stands in a blue skirt flared out above blood-splattered sneakers; in her gore-coated hands she holds red-smeared plastic buckets, and she is flanked by two small girls, each holding their hands over their ears. Behind them stand three other observers.

I was at home one morning when Editor in Chief Bill Allen called to tell me he was going to take that picture out of the story. Too tough, I guess he figured at the time. I asked to explain why I thought it should remain.

"The reason the children are holding their hands over their ears is because the pigs are screaming as they are being wrestled to the ground and bled to death," I said.

"Ayacucho," I reminded him, "was the birthplace of the Shining Path guerrilla movement. They slaughtered many people in their homes," I said to Bill. "Sometimes entire families. There must have been a lot of screaming."

He left the picture in.

It's the only time in 46 years that I've had an editor in chief call me at home to tell me he was going to change a layout, that he wanted to take out a picture he knew I felt strongly about. It's also the only time I can remember successfully explaining a picture of mine back into a layout.

Incredible as it may sound, I found a kind of beauty in the reality of what I witnessed in those Peruvian slaughterhouses.

One would naturally want to question what I consider "beauty," but I believe beauty can sometimes be found in dire conditions. Look at the work of Goya. Look at the elegance within the black-and-white photographs of Sebastiao Salgado or James Nachtwey. In 1968, while I was looking for freelance work, Dick Pollard, the director of photography at *Life* magazine, commented after I'd shown him a portfolio of my color prints that "you can't photograph war in color." Although I wasn't looking to do so, I left his office thinking, Why can't war be photographed in color? Death from war or famine or murder happens every day under beautiful blue skies. I think a kind of beauty can be found in conditions not considered beautiful in a traditional way, and perhaps not at all, in the eyes of those who dwell within the imagery. William Stott, in his book *Documentary Expression and Thirties America*, comments on the "beauty" to be found in the formal images by Walker Evans of the dirt-poor Alabama tenant farmers in Evans and James Agee's *Let Us Now Praise Famous Men*, a book that greatly influenced me while at the University of Minnesota. In the Peruvian slaughterhouses I saw images that could easily shock—which was not my intent—and yet at the same time have a strikingly strong aesthetic that draws you in, makes you want to look.

IN 1985, WHILE IN PERU, in the small Urubamba Valley village of Chincheros, not far from Cusco, I made a complicated picture of a man passing by on his way to the weekly market, a bundle of something on his back. As he passed under an archway, a mosaic of light and shadow encompassed him. It is a favorite picture of mine, one I worked and reworked in an attempt to best use the light and shadow of that place. I'd been there four years earlier and had made some interesting pictures under that archway, but I always felt I could do better. So, on this market day, I went back and forth between photographing the general market scene and crouching under the archway, watching with passing time how the shadows changed, looking through different focal length lenses, moving slightly this way or that, wedging myself against a low retaining wall, making small adjustments in angle—virtually making myself into a tripod.

I was putting a picture puzzle together in my mind and eye, waiting for something or someone to come along to create the moment and complete the picture.

What was it that the poet James Dickey said about the freshness of a poem? How it seemed to come out of nowhere, so natural, but in reality: "It takes me a hundred drafts to get a poem right," he said. "And fifty more to make it sound spontaneous."

It is sometimes like that to photograph in the streets, to find that chunk of space between a storefront and an alley entrance, or some light/shadow combination where one might wait, almost in ambush, to take what passes through that space, to fit it into the puzzle and make the whole work. It might take many different attempts to make it work, maybe only a few; maybe it never does. But the hope is always to find the best way to make it happen, which is simply to wait and watch. Henri Cartier-Bresson's earliest work was like that, the man leaping a puddle, the individual form crossing through a maze of spatial relationships in what appears to be the perfect placement. How many ambushes took place in Cartier-Bresson's eye before that perfection was obtained? How many attempts to capture spontaneity?

I hope and look for that one image, totally balanced, complete within itself, perfection framed in a single moment. Well, perhaps not perfection, but the best it can be until I try again to do it even better. ■

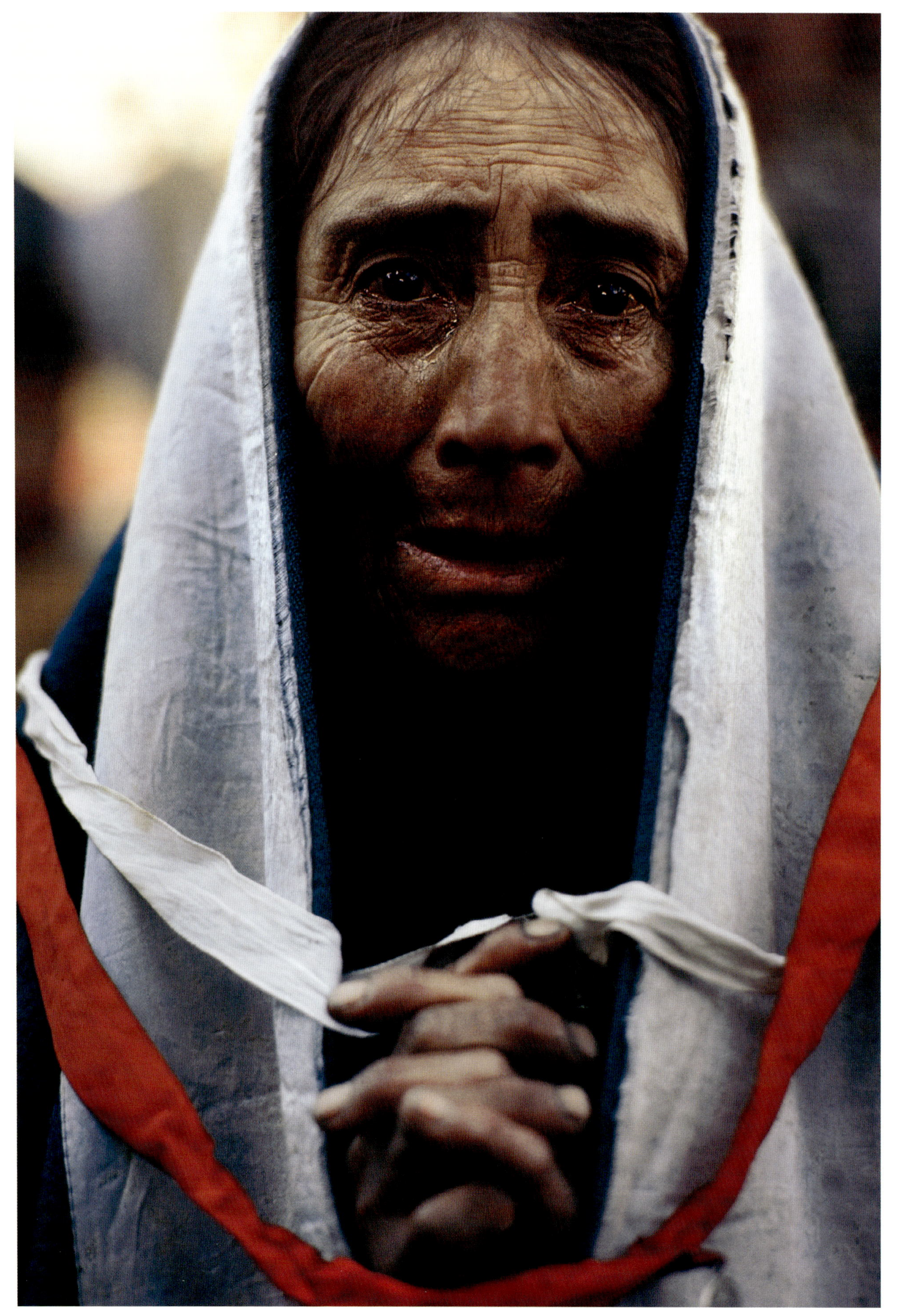

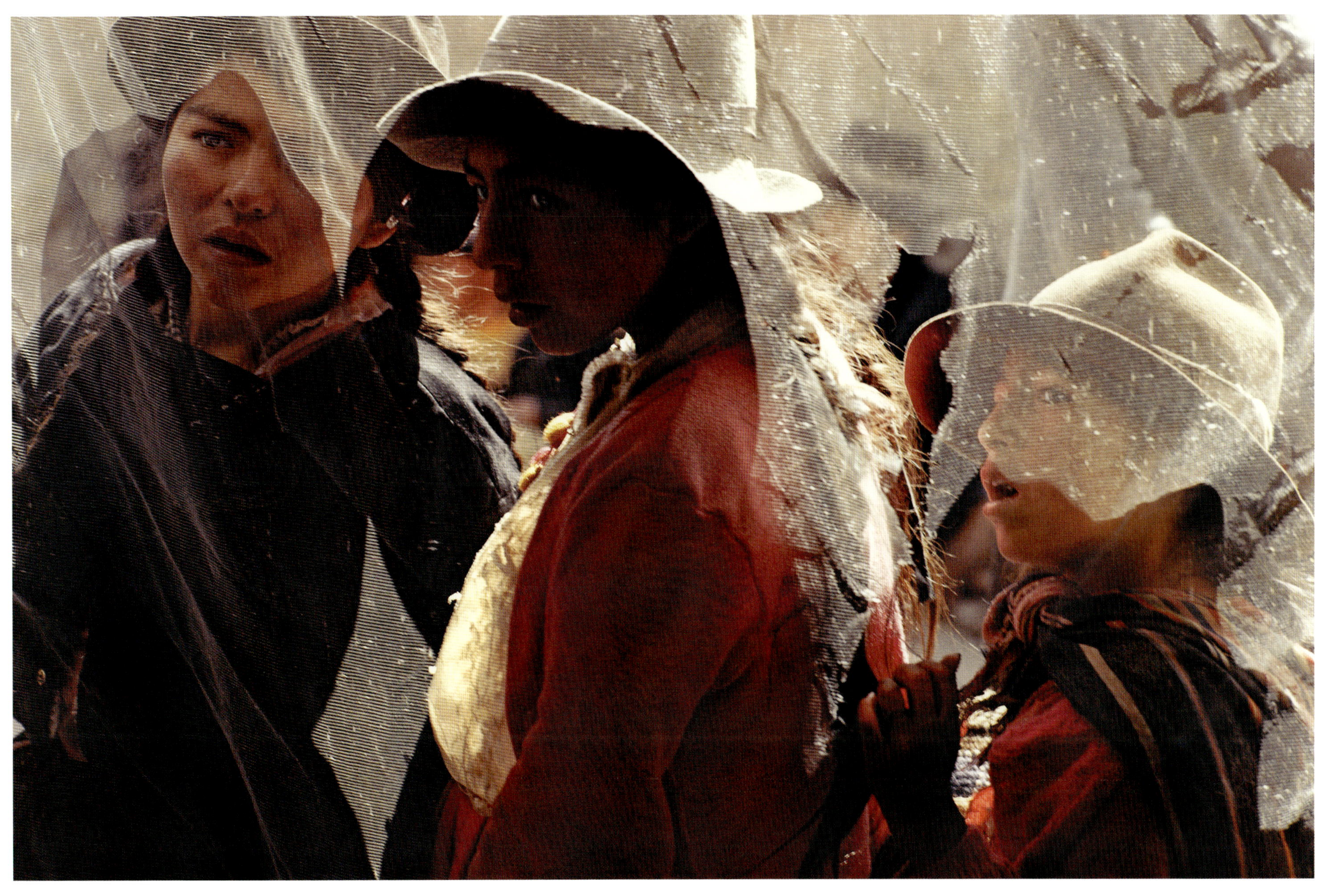

LEFT: *Woman praying for earthquake victims, Paccha, 1981* ABOVE: *Girls looking into medical tent, Paccha, 1981*

"Here, again, is a picture basically quite simple, few moving parts, but it poses a question. Just what the hell is going on here?"

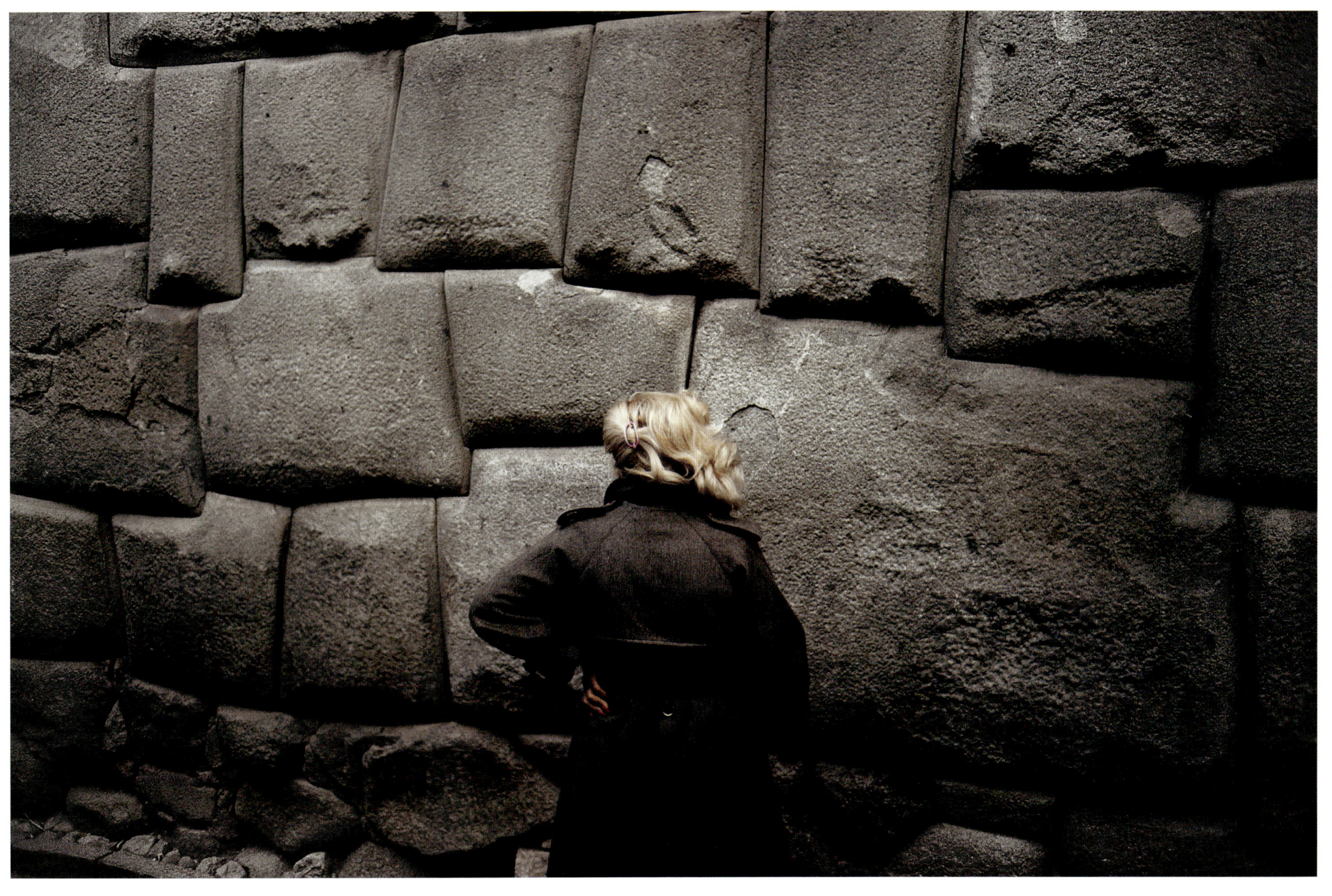

Inca wall of 12 angles, Cusco, 1981

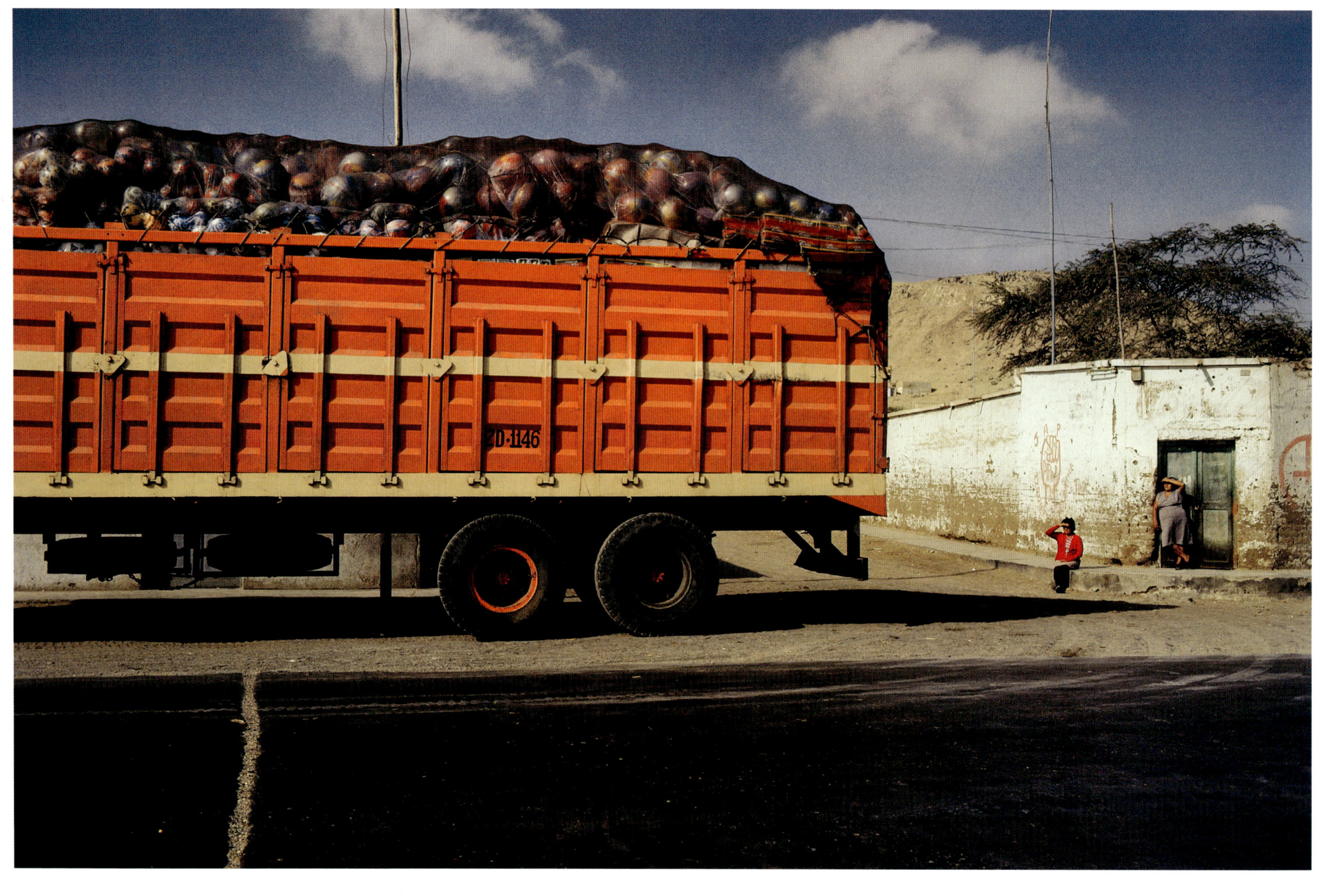

Truckload of beach balls near Trujillo, 1981

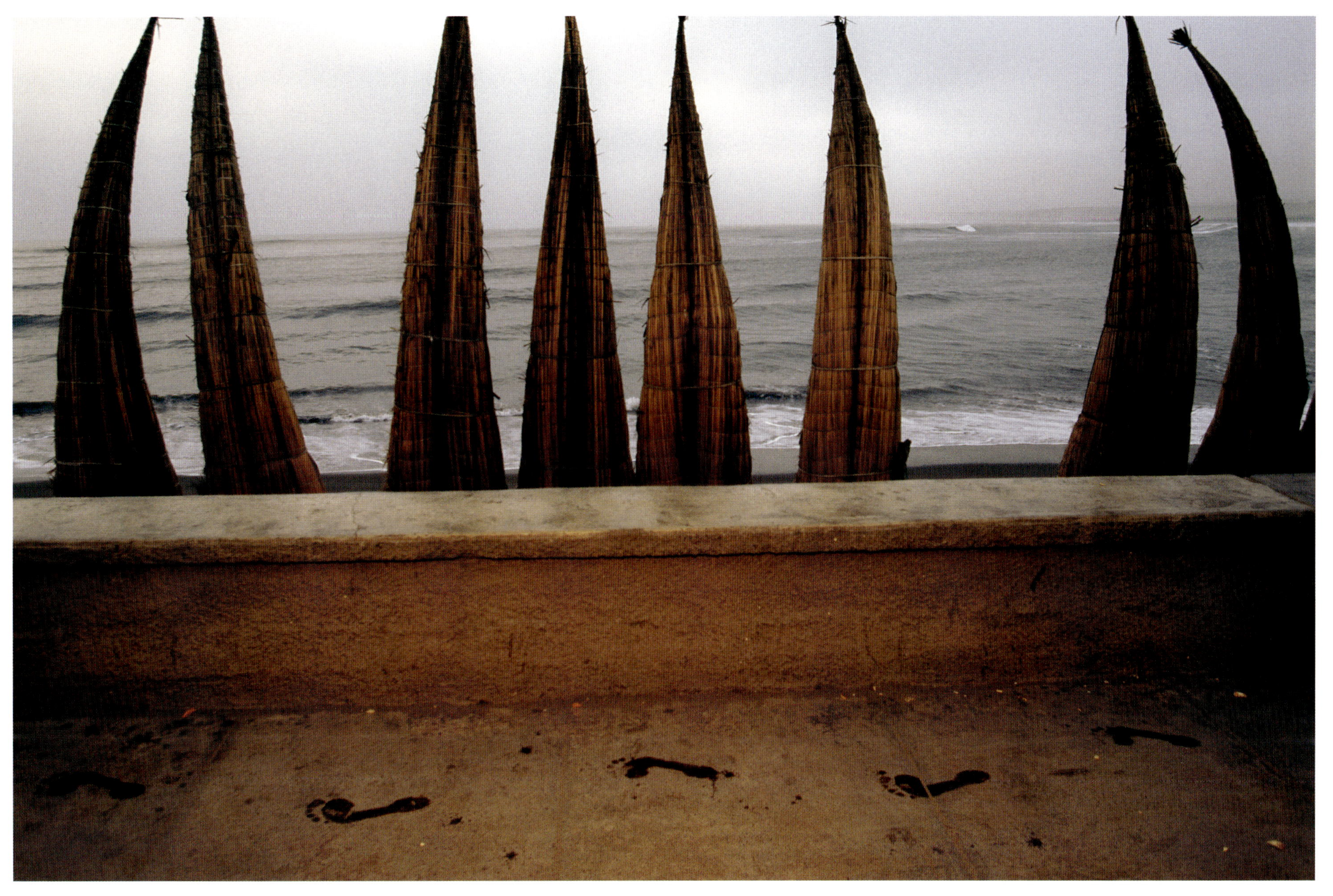

Reed boats and footprints, Trujillo, 1995

"Looking for pictures is always a little bit like hunting: watching and waiting."

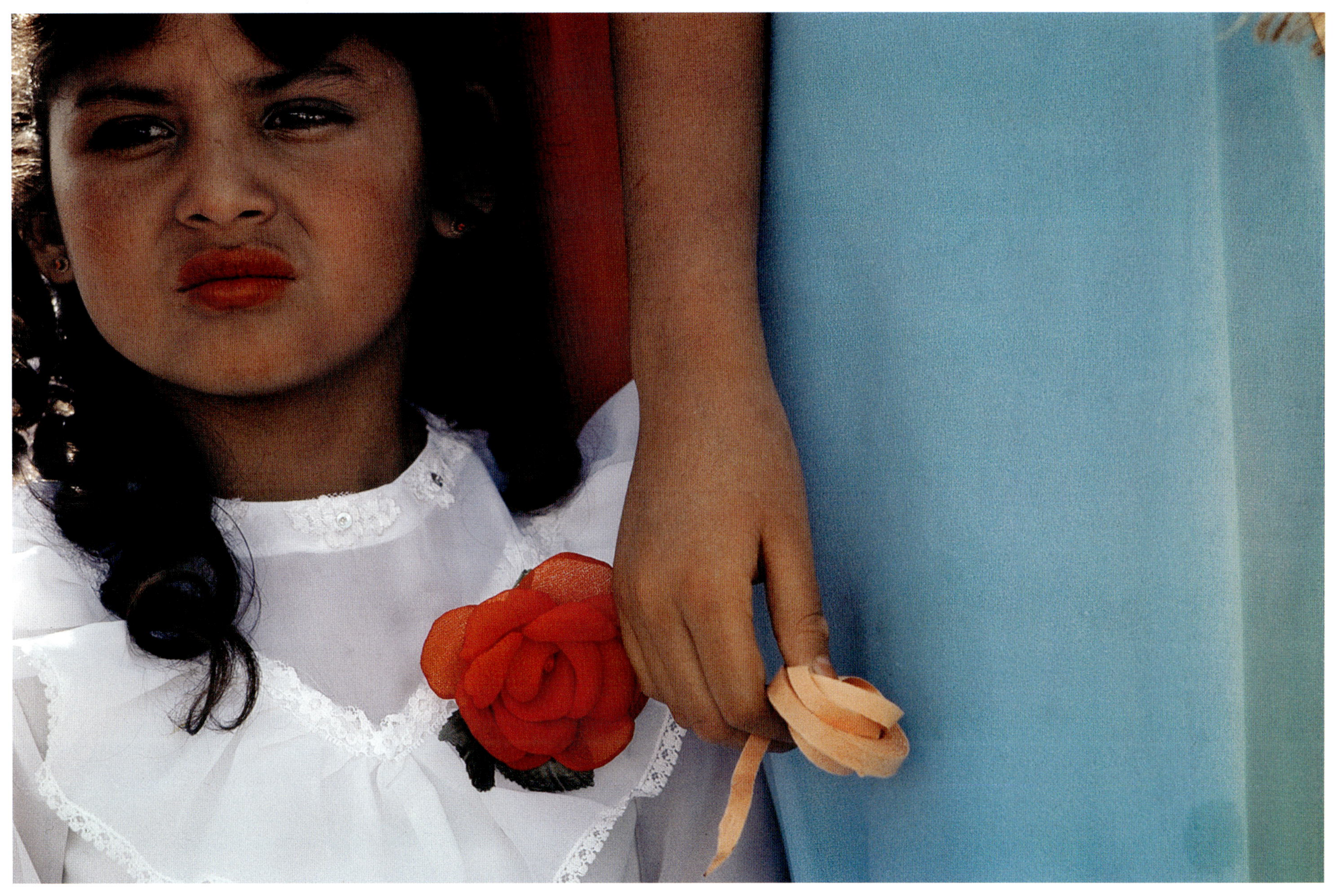

Girl with red lips and red rose, Trujillo, 1981

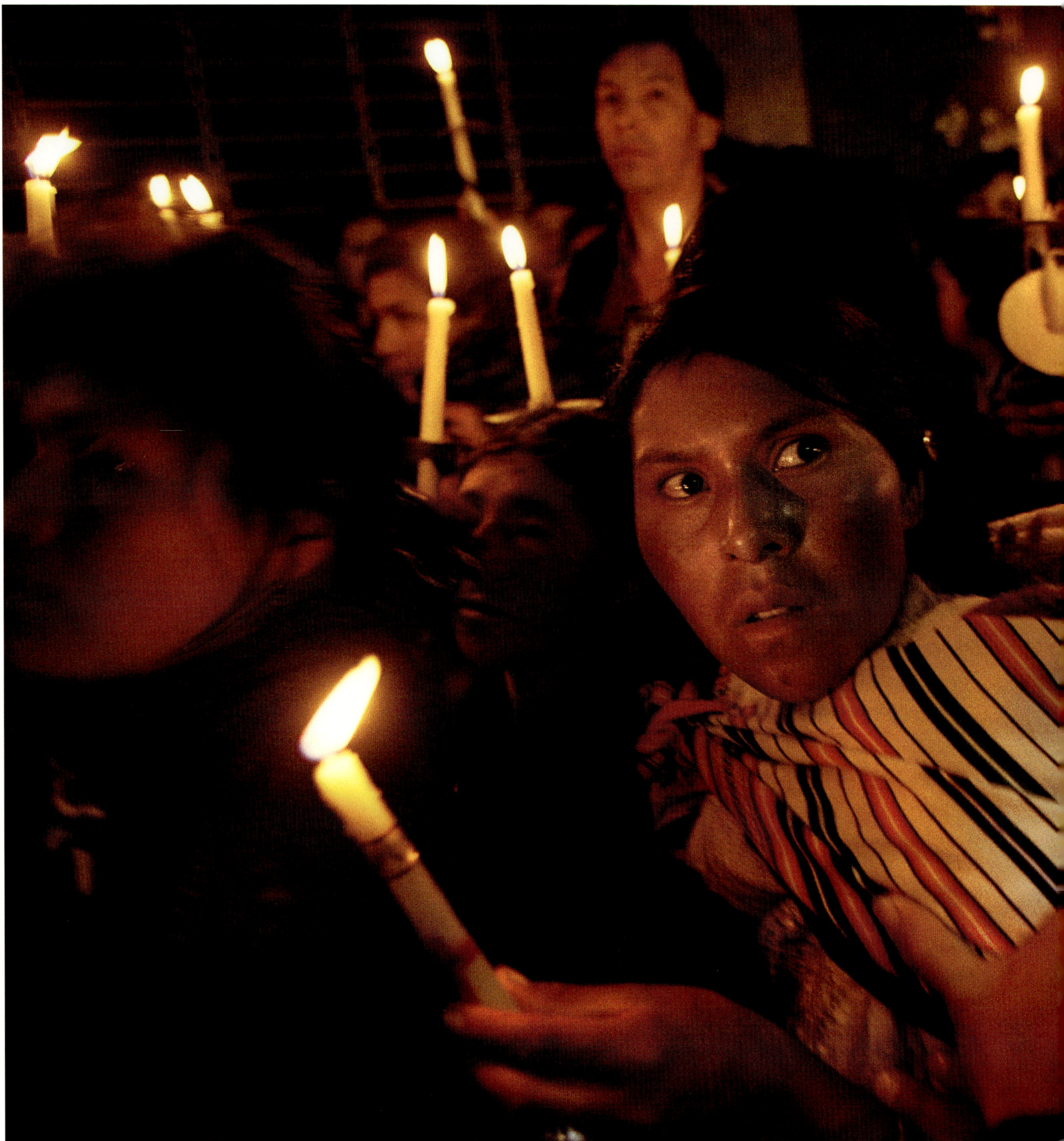

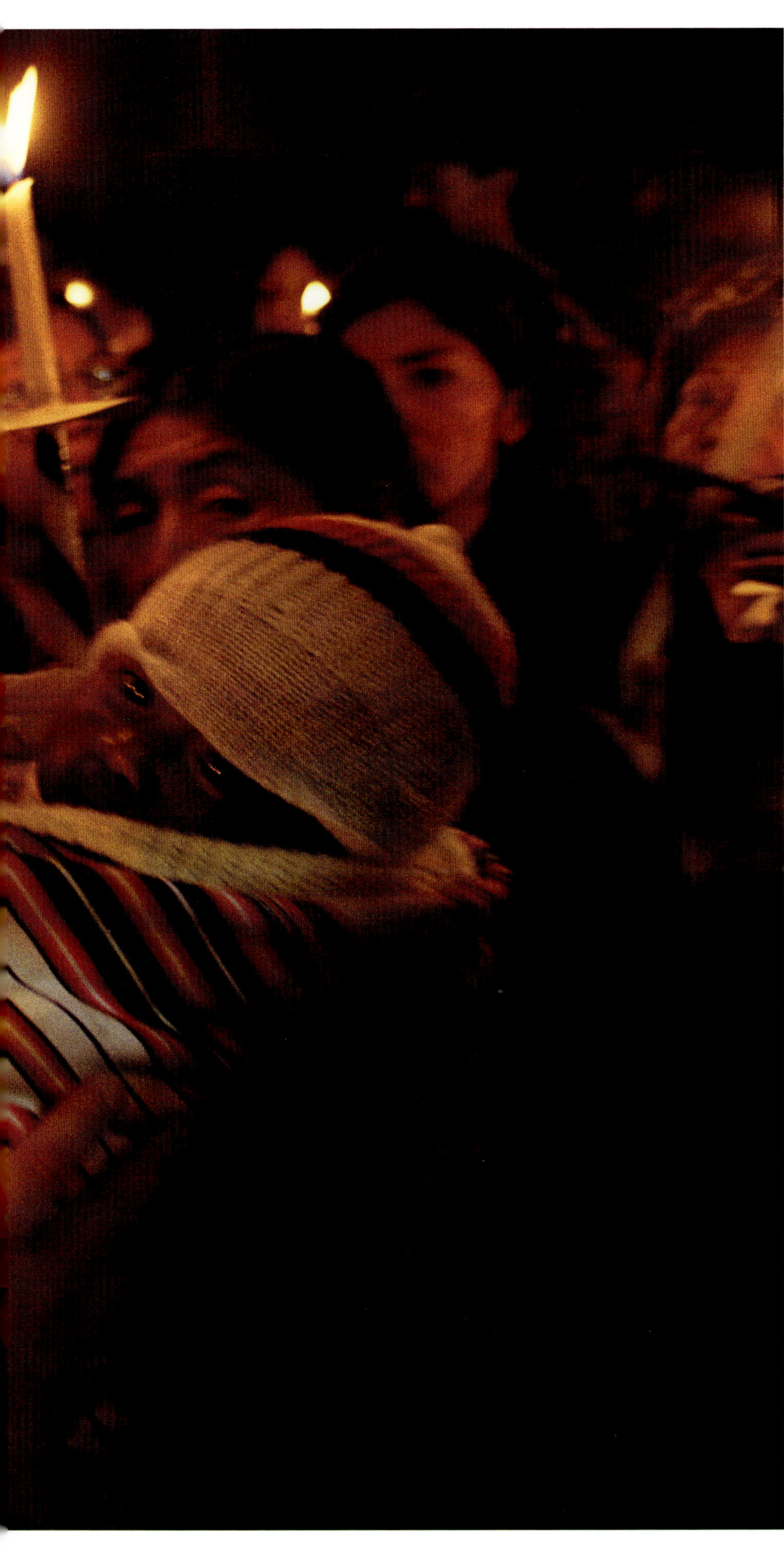

Woman and baby in Easter procession, Ayacucho, 1995

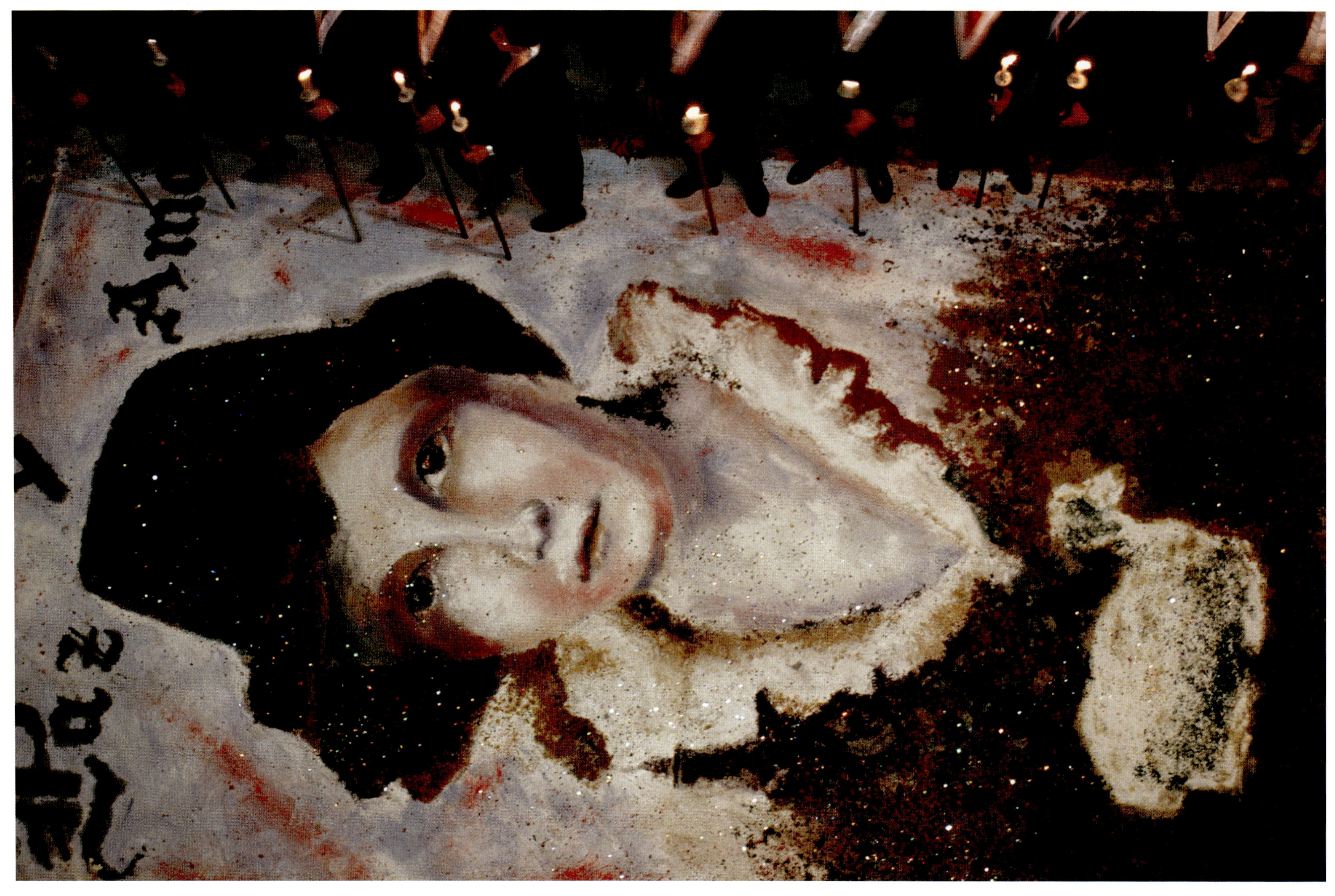

Easter procession, Ayacucho, 1995

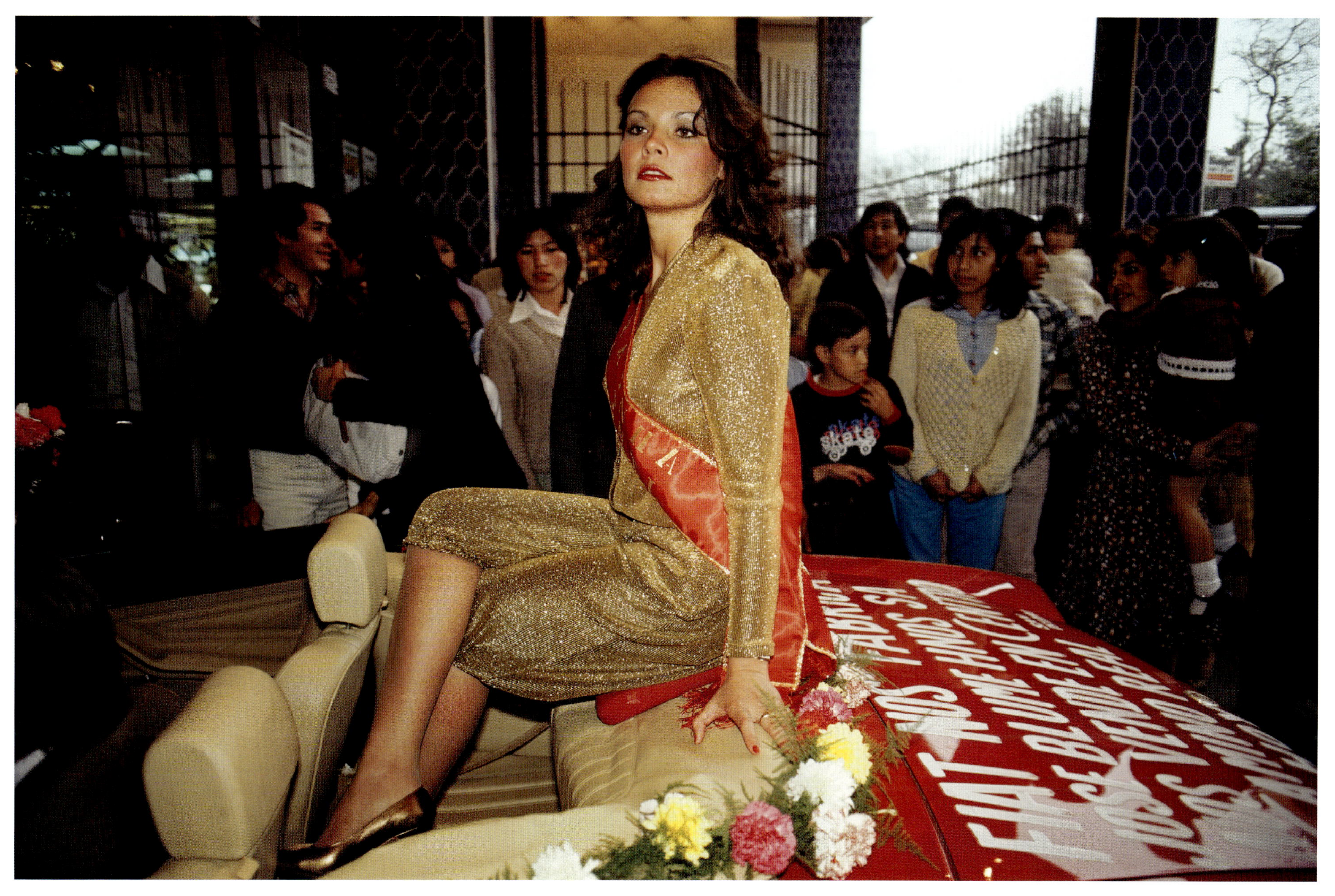

Beauty queen, Lima, 1981

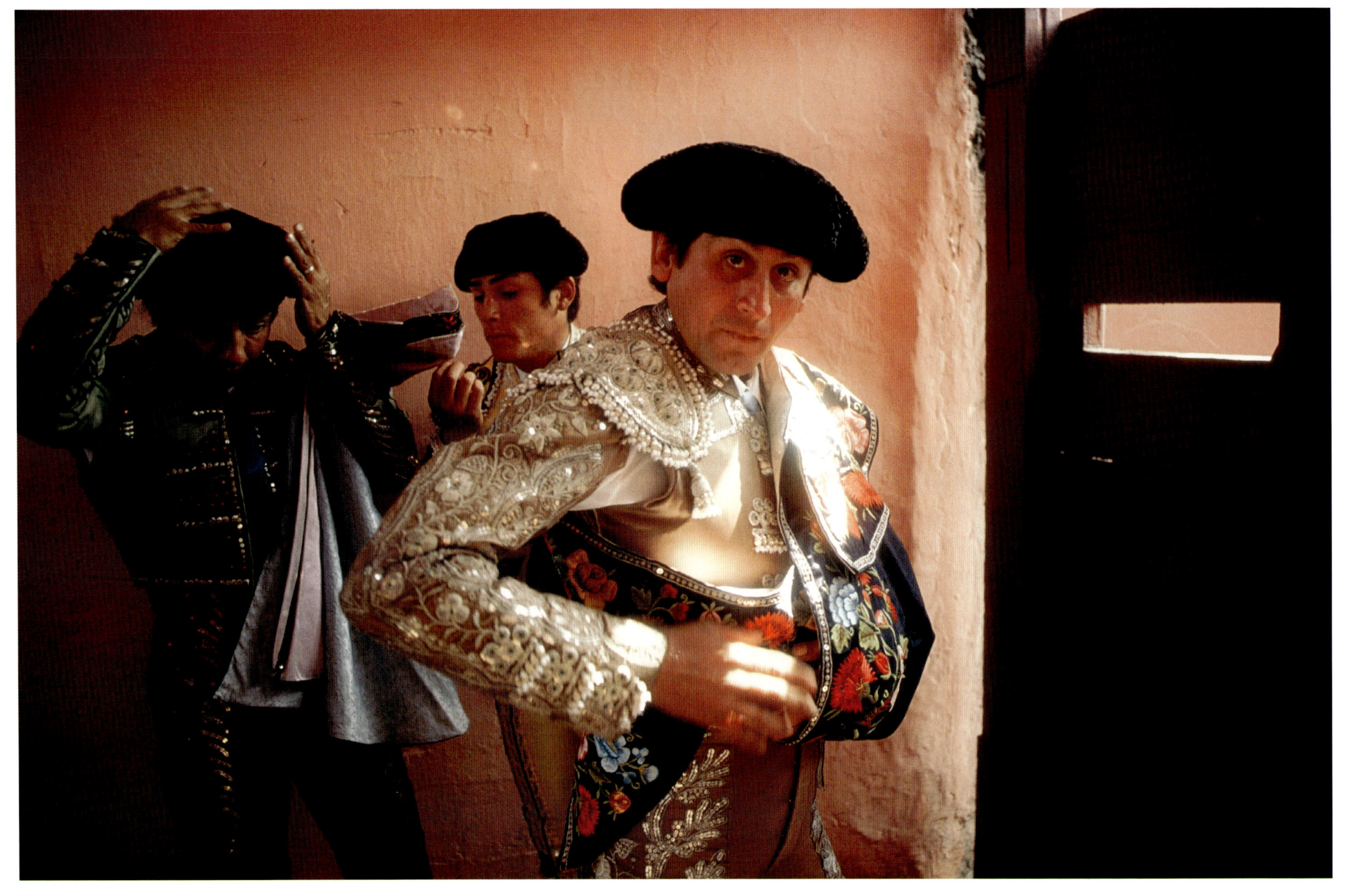

Three bullfighters, Lima, 1981

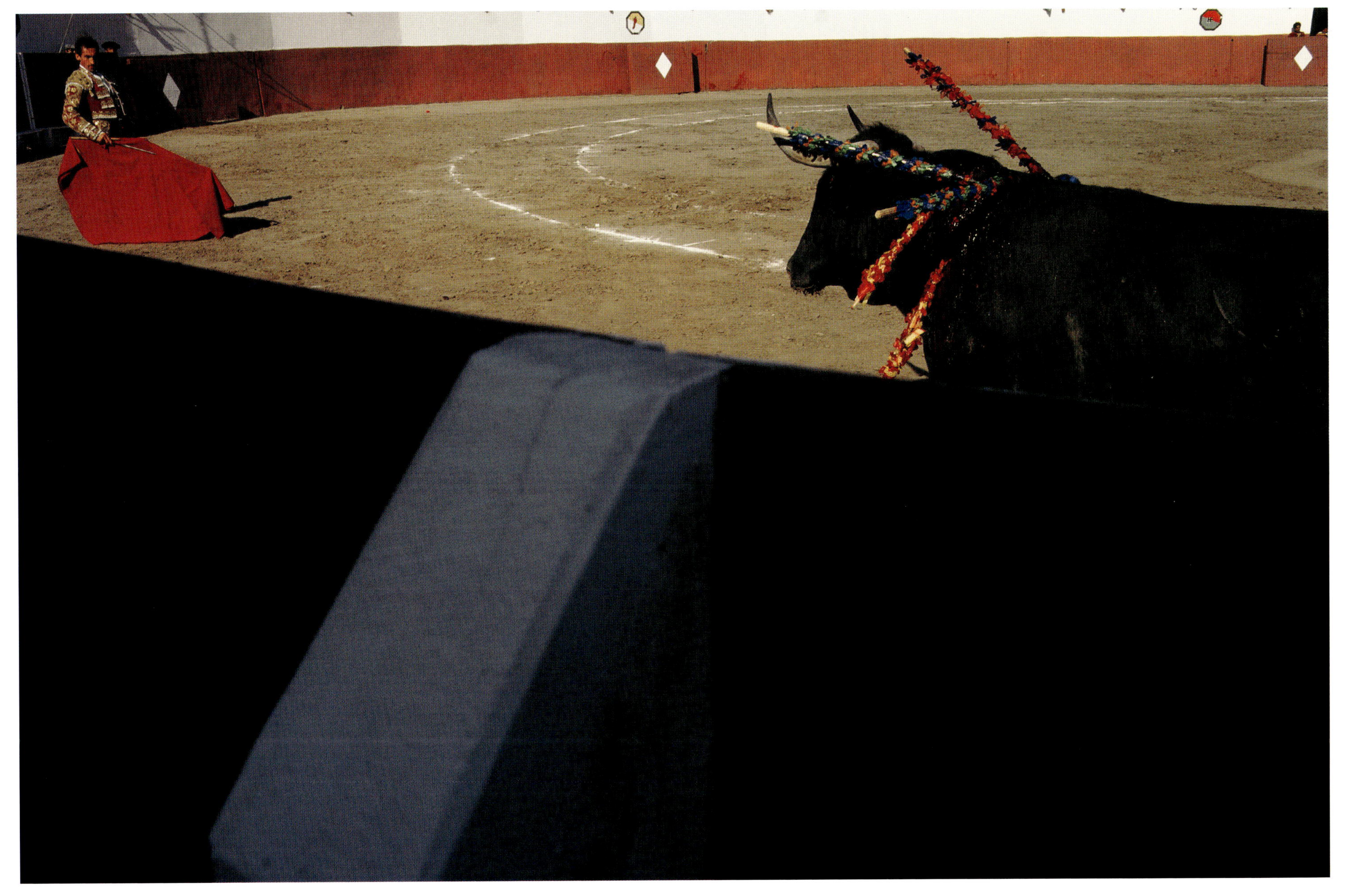

Bullfight, Trujillo, 1995

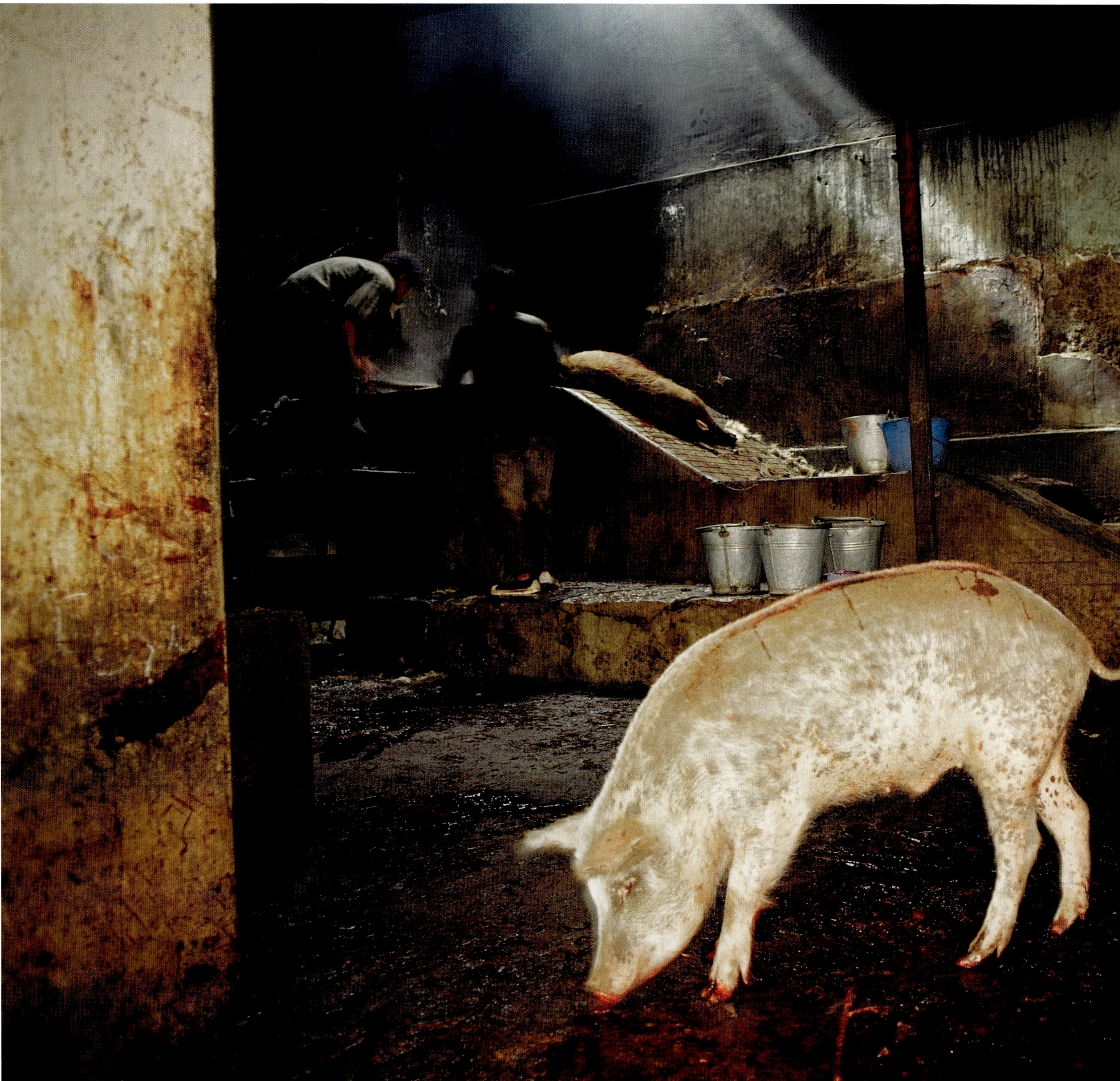

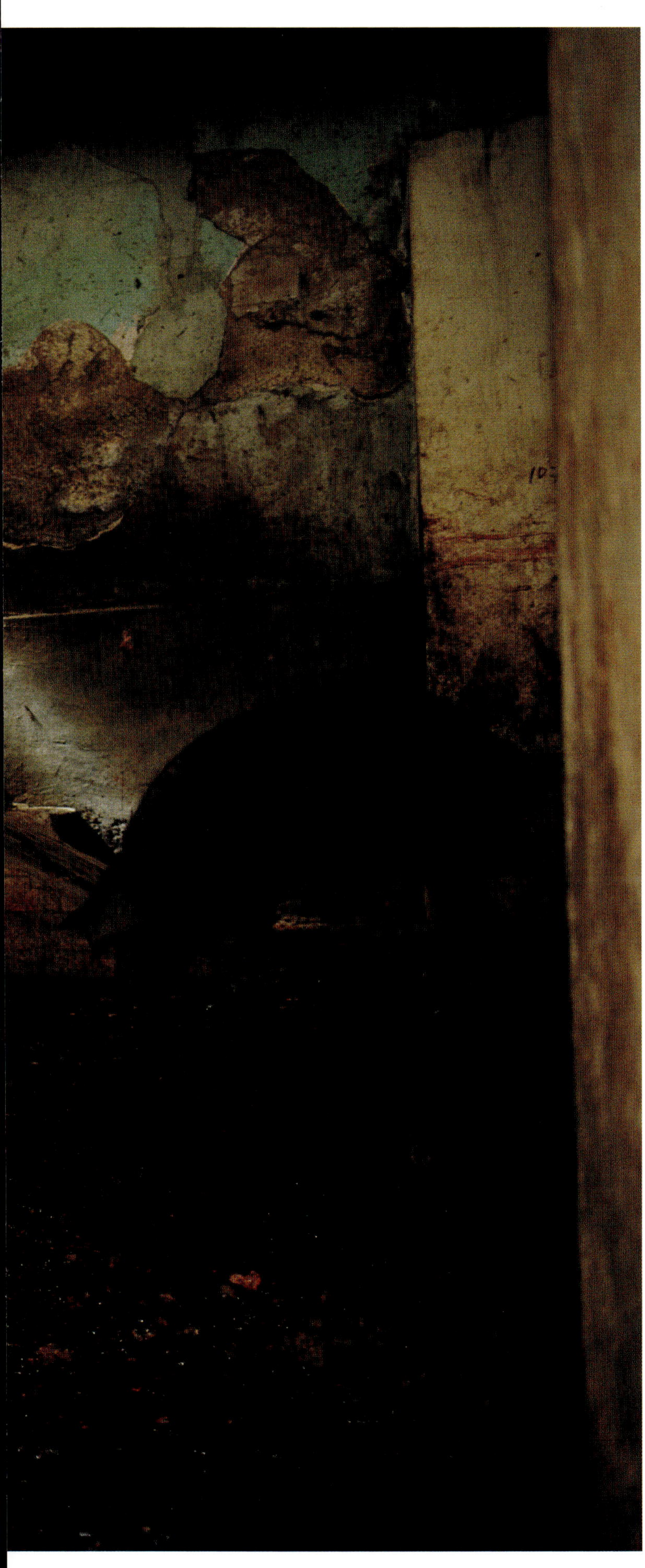

White pig, slaughterhouse, Huancayo, 1981

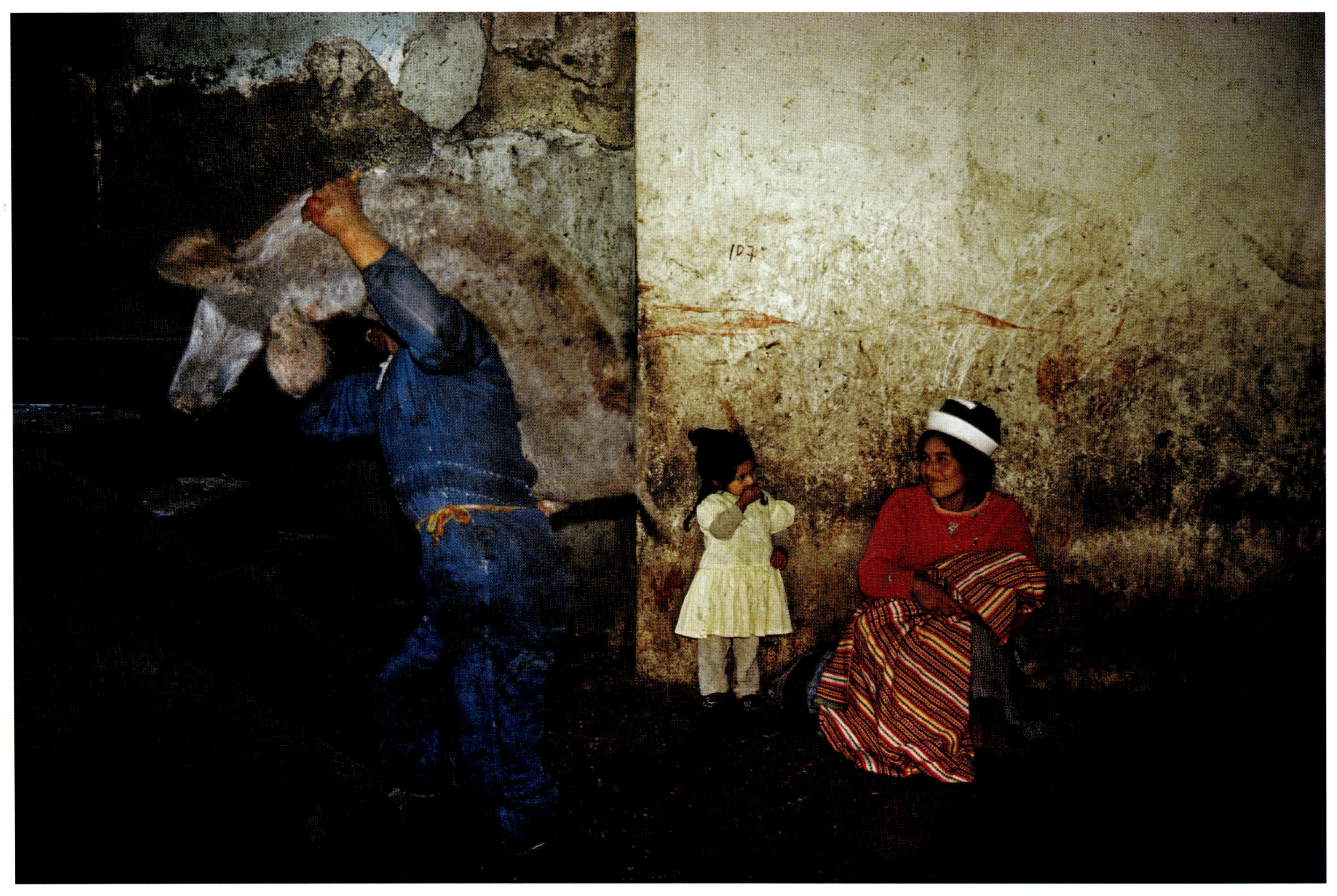

Ghost pig, slaughterhouse, Huancayo, 1981

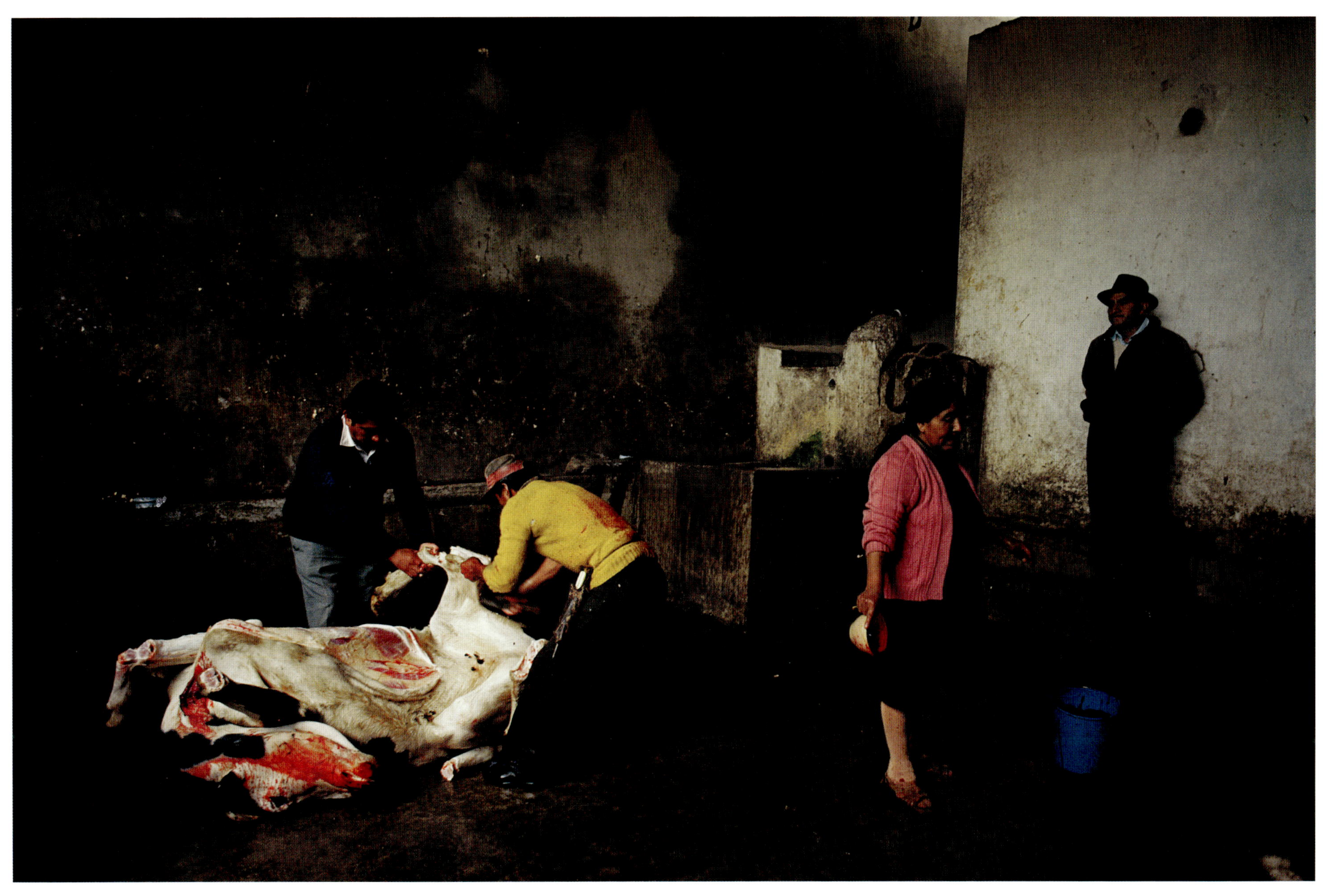

Woman in pink sweater, slaughterhouse, Huancayo, 1981

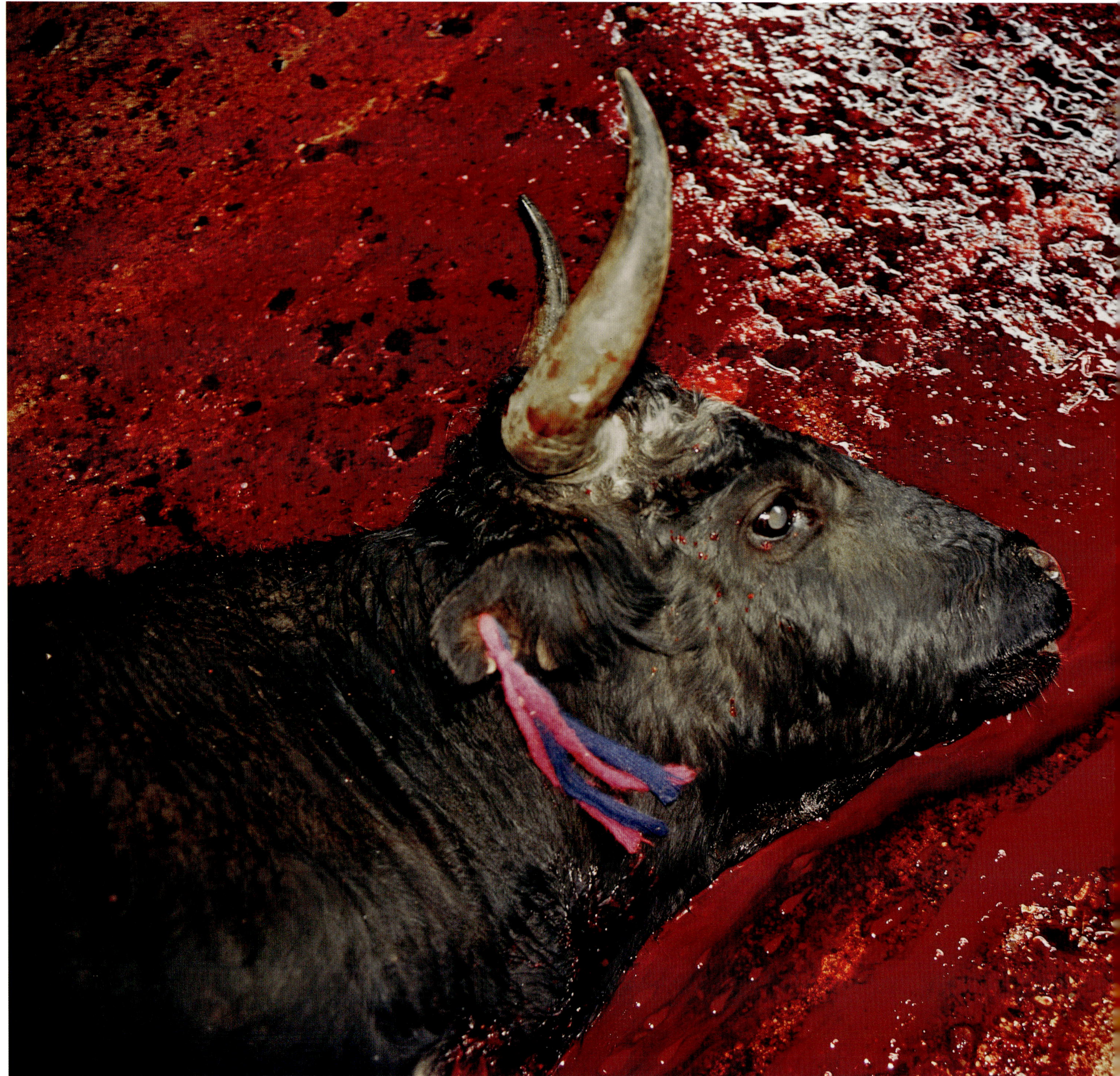

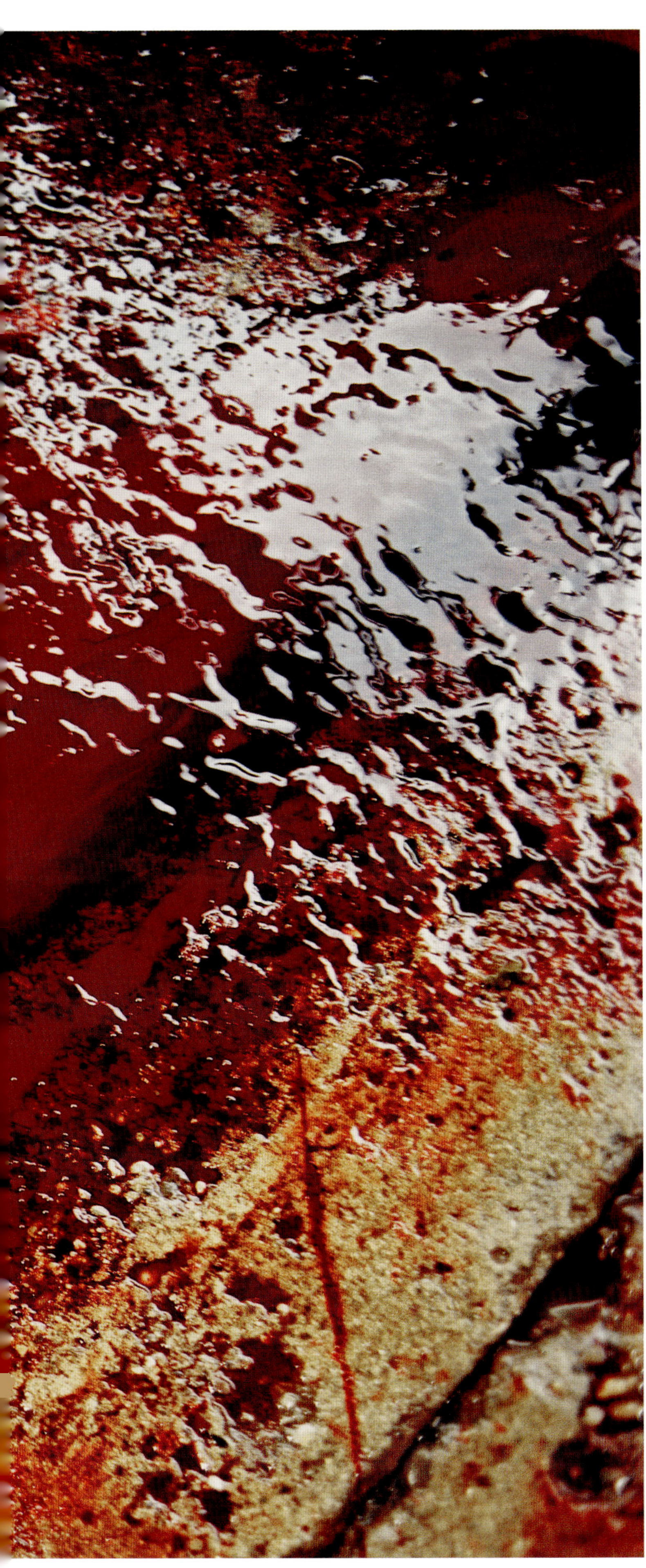

Steer's head on slaughterhouse floor, Huancayo, 1981

"They slaughtered many people in their homes," I said… "Sometimes entire families. There must have been a lot of screaming."

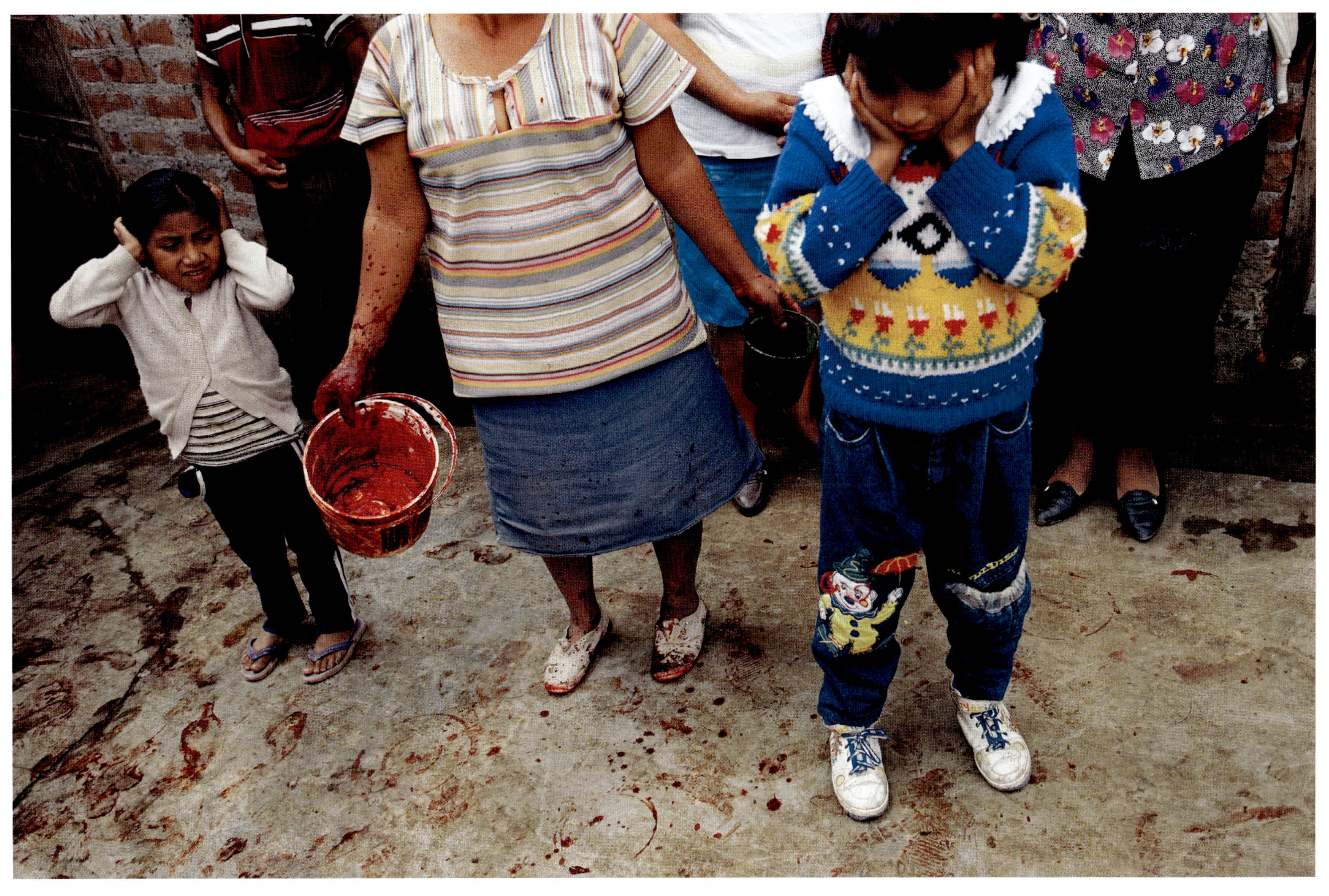

The pigs are screaming, Ayacucho, 1995

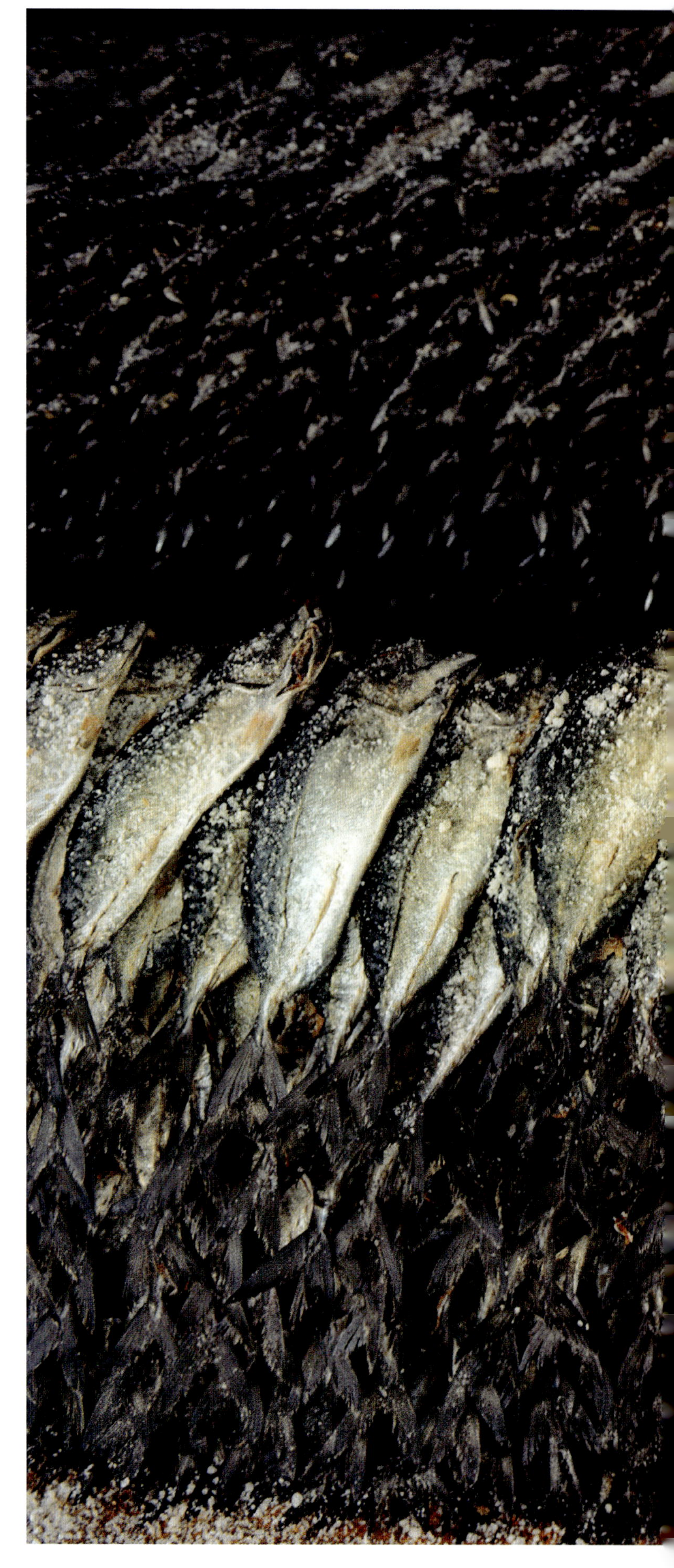

Woman with salted fish, Huaraz, 1981

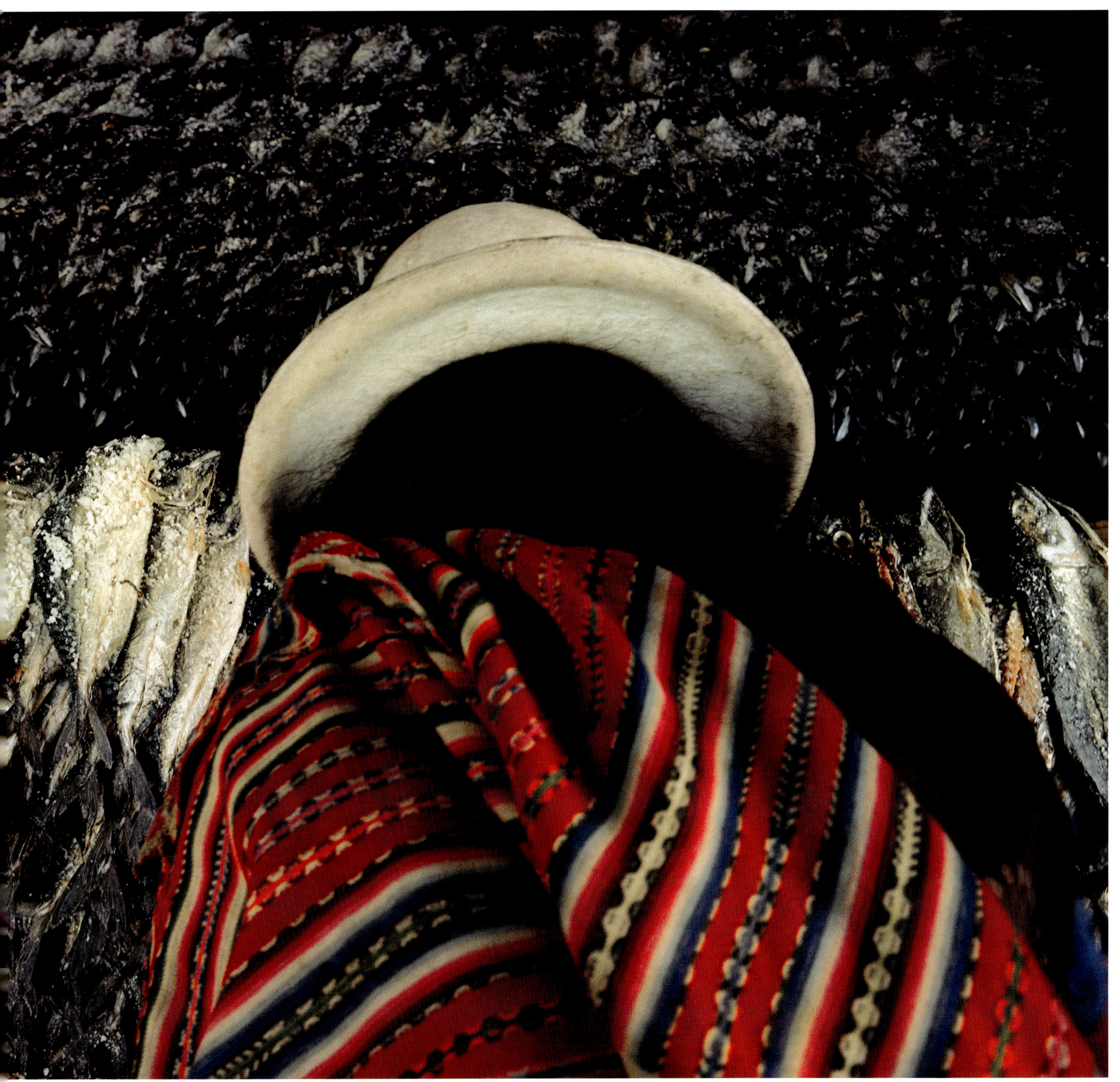

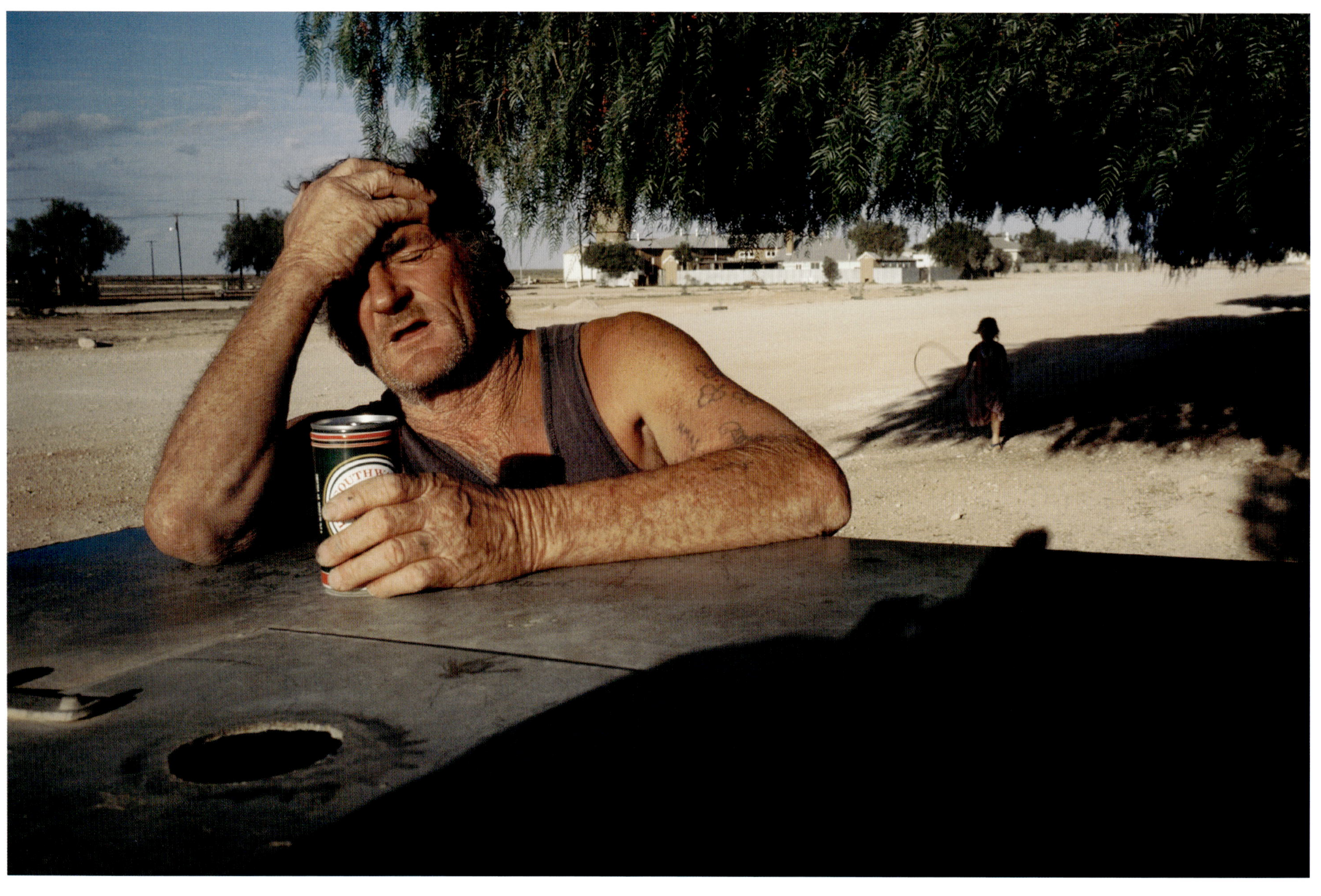

Henry Cox, Cook, Australia, 1985

Time Out

In the waning days of December 1981, my life, professionally and personally, was starting to unravel. I couldn't at first see how loose the threads really were. When I finally did, it was too late.

I'd returned from photographing Peru in November, ending the second part of a five-month freelance assignment. I had found the diversity of Peru and its people stunning. At times majestically beautiful, often raw, occasionally threatening, Peru was a high-intensity, high-adrenaline country: Its ocean coast fronted some of the driest deserts in the world. The formidable and often foreboding Andes towered over extraordinary landscapes one traversed on rock-littered mountain roads, at times barely wide enough for two vehicles abreast. And beyond the road's edge, just a few steps away, there might be a thousand-foot drop. The sky above Puno and Lake Titicaca appeared so clear it seemed possible to see beyond one's imagination. The Amazon snaked through seemingly impenetrable jungles. The Nasca lines were mysterious and of uncertain origin. The Inca realm of Cusco, Machu Picchu, and the Urubamba Valley was mystical even when assaulted by tourists. The cities were all extraordinary in their own ways: Lima, Trujillo, Arequipa, Ayacucho, Cajamarca, Chiclayo, Piura, Iquitos. And on and on. I will employ here a word that in my time has become a clichéd exclamatory description, commonly undeserving, but in this case, in my eyes and mind, the absolute truth: Peru was *awesome.*

My life was not.

I WAS SEPARATED from my wife, and upon my return from Peru, I left the home in Barboursville, Virginia, where she and I and our four children had lived for the past decade, and moved alone into a rented farmhouse in nearby Somerset. Ani Baraybar, a young woman from Lima whom I'd met and fallen in love with soon after beginning the Peru assignment, remained in Peru. Perhaps once a week we would try to speak by telephone, but both of us lacked enough of each other's language to truly communicate. We had the same problem with letters, although dictionaries helped some.

I soon had to go up to National Geographic headquarters in Washington, D.C., to work on putting together a 38-page (a common story length then, but a huge amount of space for a typical story in today's *National Geographic*) Peru story for the magazine. In Peru I had, for the first time, exposed more than a thousand rolls of film on a single assignment—somewhere around 1,300, or, over the five months on assignment, an average of 8 rolls a day. Then as now I worked day and night, seven days a week, when on an assignment. In Peru, if I was awake, I was making pictures. That assignment remains one of the most—if not *the* most—dramatic visual stimuli I've experienced as a photographer. Pictures were everywhere. I made a lot of good ones. I also made a lot of failures, but in many cases they were interesting—the kind of picture that, when you first see it, makes you say, "Oh . . . damn! Look at that. Almost!" I've always put great importance on finding interesting failures in my work, a far more satisfying harvest than simply finding some good pictures amid a lot of goddamn boring ones. I certainly make those, too, but to me an interesting failure is an indication that something good was going on within me emotionally, intellectually, or both. I may have missed the picture for some reason, often technical, but an "almost" effort is far better than not having seen the picture at all.

My picture editor, David Arnold, had most of my film edited by the time I returned; he and I got his edit narrowed down, and then, with a layout designer, we proceeded to put together the story. To say that it didn't go terribly well for me would be a major understatement. In the layout room we put pictures on the wall in the usual manner, seeking first a lead, then a sequence of pictures, and an ending. But I had serious problems with the layout designer. He wouldn't speak to me. He certainly wasn't mute, but he really wouldn't discuss the layout. That was his nature. English wasn't his native tongue, and I think he sometimes used that as an excuse, allowing him to stay remote, avoiding any discussion of my point of view regarding the layout. Communication was almost nonexistent between us, and he was basically in charge: He had power; I didn't. He also thought the pictures, in some cases, would benefit by cropping, an indelicate cutting off of a part of some pictures simply to make them fit a repetitious page design he thought good, something I considered ruinous to the integrity of the images. But I had no deciding vote. Very few pictures I've made over all the years have, I thought, needed severe, if any, cropping. I'm not a purist about that, but I crop with my eye, in the camera, when I originally make the picture. That's called composing.

The story was laid out and approved by Editor Bill Garrett, and that was the end of that. Except, of course, for me it really wasn't. I couldn't bring myself to let it be.

Although at first I'd heard many admiring comments from other photographers about my Peru pictures, as time passed I began to hear murmurings of criticism—not from other photographers, and not to me personally, but kind of like background noise that I picked up on around the various editors' offices. I was smoldering because I thought the Peru layout wasn't as good as it should be. Now I was hearing comments about how much film I'd shot and how long I'd stayed out on the assignment and how much expense money was spent, although the magazine wasn't nearly as budget conscious in those years as it has been forced to be today. I started obsessing on the criticism. And my personal life was a mess.

I was living alone. I was drinking too much. The early 1980s were years I and some of my friends indulged in the so-called recreational use of cocaine. Pot had always been popular among us, but for a period, cocaine would eat up a lot of our money and attention. Out in Minnesota my older brother, a career radio and television personality, had lost his job as a radio talk show host, and his job was his *life*. His first failed suicide was merely a short delay of his successful attempt to come.

Closely following my disappointment with how the Peru story was handled, despite its successful reception by my fellow photographers, came another event that would complete that list of what one often hears as life's most stressful experiences: the end of a marriage, a death in the family, the loss of one's home, and the loss of one's job. There may be others, to be sure, but those four are more than enough for anyone to handle at the same time; enough to drive one to drink, if one wasn't already, and I was.

The annual photographers' seminar at National Geographic headquarters—a two- or three-day traditional gathering of photographers from the staff and freelancers from around the world who contributed to the magazine—was to take place in early January. In my book *The Photographic Essay*, published in 1989, writer Erla Zwingle summed up the disaster those days would become for me:

The story, called "The Two Souls of Peru," was undoubtedly the high point of Allard's life and career. An equally profound low followed . . . At the annual National Geographic seminar in January 1982, Allard pulled the linchpin out of his career and watched the pieces fly apart . . .

He had returned from Peru in something of a trance state, enthralled by his subject and the intensity of the experience. He was frustrated by what he felt was a lack of receptiveness to his ideas about the structure of the story's layout, and also smarting from what he felt were unjust criticisms of overspending and overshooting in the field. He complained to Gilka. He complained to Garrett. To no avail.

ON THE LAST DAY of the seminar I attended an afternoon meeting held to allow magazine staff members to voice grievances behind closed doors. For some reason I didn't seem to realize it was for staff members only, not for a freelancer like me. But I was loaded for bear—a single subject, Peru, festering in my brain—thinking in some twisted way, I guess, if they want to hang me, here I am with the rope. The scene was in one of those cavernous ballrooms at the Mayflower Hotel, hard across the street from the National Geographic building on 17th Street. Gil Grosvenor, President of the Society, was taking questions from the staff. Director of Photography Bob Gilka was there, of course, as was Editor Bill Garrett.

I was sitting fairly far back. Sitting in the row behind me and just a few seats to my left was the white haired old lion of National Geographic, Melville Bell Grosvenor, Editor emeritus. He had been the magazine's Editor when I had arrived as an intern almost 20 years earlier, and had championed some of my early work. In 1966 he saw some pictures I'd made in the winter of buffalo in Yellowstone Park for inclusion in some other *Geographic* story, and ordered the editors to send me back to do my own story about wildlife in Yellowstone in winter. That story assignment was my first real look at Montana and the West, and it started my long and still enduring love affair with that part of America. Melville also assigned me to write the story, even though I don't think he had any idea whether I could actually write. I think Melville figured if a person had a camera he could be a photographer, and access to a typewriter would make him a writer. It was fine with me because I'd wanted to be a writer before wanting to be a photographer, and in retrospect he probably did me a favor by bringing my two loves together.

As Editor, Melville once sent around a memo saying that what he wanted to see in the magazine was "gold-plated postcards." That memo had made me cringe, but I knew he loved looking at pictures. One could see that in the sessions held in the projection room just outside his office when a finished story was reviewed. He might not have understood the kinds of pictures I thought were good, and his visual intellect might not have impressed the curator of photography at the Museum of Modern Art in New York City, but he genuinely loved looking at pictures.

I remember seeing Melville sitting behind me at the meeting that afternoon, and I remember wishing he wasn't there; I think I sensed this wasn't going to end well. And I seem to recall that I could hear his heavy breathing. Three months later he was dead at age 80.

During the staff meeting, as society president Gilbert Grosvenor was responding to staff members' criticisms of new restrictions on first-class plane tickets, Allard exploded. "I don't want to talk about first-class airfare," he said. "What I want to talk about is first-class picture editing." He went on to unburden himself of a number of critical opinions concerning the operation of the magazine.

Bob Gilka was livid. "Bill was pretty obstreperous," he remembers. "Some of the people around him finally quieted him down. But there was a long period after that when we didn't use Allard." Photographer Jim Blair's version of things is somewhat different: "Our general impression was that Gilka said, 'That man will never work for me again.'"

And I didn't.

WHAT I HAD DONE was clearly stupid, almost perversely self-destructive, I suppose. Although in those years I was probably sometimes considered to be difficult to have around in the layout room, my reputation as a consistent producer of good work was rock solid. Still, my role as a freelance contributor to the magazine was certainly more probationary than had I been a staff member; no freelancer is indispensable. And even before going to Peru I had told myself: It's their magazine. Just let them do whatever they want to do; you don't have any control. But I didn't do that. I let myself blow. I was carrying around all the stress of my personal life, and it became more than I could handle. And neither whiskey nor anything else was helping, to say the least. I went out that night to the seminar dinner, but for me the evening was enveloped with a great sense of loss. The dinner was held at a Geographic facility far into the D.C. suburbs, and I rode out there in a rented limousine with some of my friends. One was a freelance photographer who occasionally carried a revolver in a small black doctor's bag, for what reason I have no idea. At one point he fired it out the open window of the limo up into the wintry night sky. Crazy. A disturbing day followed by an equally bizarre night. At the dinner it was as if I had some kind of communicable disease, and people tended to shy away from me, as though they were thinking, Don't want to get too close to that guy. Thankfully, much of that night I've managed to suppress. Or maybe that's not such a good thing. I guess one learns best from one's mistakes if one can remember them clearly, painful as that might be.

The next day I wept, driving back to the farmhouse in Virginia. I felt as though I'd said goodbye to a lot of old friends.

In retrospect, my comment about "first-class picture editing" on the Peru story was unfair to the picture editor; he had done his work well enough. He picked the right pictures, for the most part. But once we got into the layout room, what had seemed so promising, so sweet and fruitful about my efforts in Peru, all now seemed bitter. We were supposed to be professional communicators, and I was suddenly dealing with someone who wouldn't communicate. What I had really meant about picture editing had to do with how the pictures were used in layout. Looking at the published story today I guess I could say, "Well, it probably looked pretty good for its time." But I always wanted my stories to look better than pretty good; I wanted them to be as good as I knew they could be. I let myself care too much, and I picked the wrong time, the wrong place, and the wrong person to unload on; the price was heavy, indeed.

Bob Gilka, the man who took me in off the street in the summer of 1964, put me back out there in the winter of 1982. As time passed, I mailed in a number of story proposals, but none were accepted. For the next three and a half years I was basically unemployable at *National Geographic* magazine. During that time I never entered the building.

Before 1982 was over I'd cashed in an insurance policy to help pay some bills, come to an agreement with my wife over a divorce settlement, and borrowed some money from my parents to make it through the year. I was a middle-aged man very much at odds with what had been my former life, but positive new things were on my horizon. Ani came to visit me and stay awhile, then returned to Peru. While she was with me my first book, *Vanishing Breed*—a collection of my photographs and writing about the American cowboy, with a foreword by novelist Thomas McGuane—was published to considerable acclaim and great sales, at least for a photographic book that's not a how-to kind of book. At first, though, all I could see were the book's flaws, the uneven quality of the printing (which caused me to ask the publisher to abandon plans for a special deluxe edition I didn't think would be worth the high retail price because of the less than excellent printing). I believe there were maybe a dozen or so copies of that slip-covered, quarter-bound-in-leather deluxe edition in existence, ones that somehow got out before the edition was aborted, and those books are collectors' items. I have some of them.

I like to think I'm an optimist at heart, but all that year I'd been hanging on to the publication of *Vanishing Breed* as a means of emotional survival, and I needed it in a way difficult to describe. I needed the book to sing; I needed and had hoped for something perfect, unblemished, pure. It wasn't that, but I came to realize and appreciate that it was a success by almost any other measurement.

In 1983 I started getting a few assignments from John Loengard, director of photography at *Life,* and I was getting asked by some ad agencies to do some commercial assignments that paid well. None were interesting enough to make up for losing the long, wandering, and serendipitous assignments I'd been used to doing for the *Geographic,* essays that I could build a body of work on, work in which I could invest my emotions, stories I could live in, which is what I think I do with a subject I really care about. I become immersed in it. In workshops today I stress to students the need to truly care about what you do. It sounds simple, but it isn't. You may not love the subject; you might hate it and want to show it strongly for that very reason. War and poverty would certainly be examples. But one cannot do superior work if one is indifferent. *You have to care.* My problem with the Peru story, besides the other stuff that was falling apart in my life at that time, was that I cared *too much.* That can become destructive.

During my *National Geographic* career I've not always had assignments I was thrilled to get; some were stories nobody else really wanted. But once I had a story I gave it everything I could. I sometimes questioned in my mind why an assignment I felt truly right for and asked for was given to a photographer I felt was not even close to being the right person. But that kind of decision is in the hands of the director of photography at any magazine. Former director of photography at *National Geographic* Kent Kobersteen used to say to me, "You can't do them all." And I'd tell him I didn't want to do them all, just the ones I really wanted. When I didn't have a good assignment on my horizon, I'd get nervous, and Kent would say, "Oh, you know you'll get something great." I'd respond that maybe the day would come when I wouldn't. In the last couple decades at *National Geographic* I've managed to get assignments I've really wanted, and that, I believe, is how I've managed to keep the juices and the passion going over the long haul: by doing stories I've truly cared about, not just another assignment. That would make it like a job. The best feeling for me is to be working on something I really love, knowing that when I finish it, I have another great one to follow. I've had workshop students tell me I'm spoiled, always working on essays they think are wonderful opportunities, and in their minds, perhaps I am. But I like to think I've earned those opportunities; I've certainly tried to.

On a lovely mid-April day in 1983, six months after my divorce, I married Ana Maria Baraybar, at that rented farmhouse in Somerset, Virginia. My best man was Jon Schneeberger, now deceased, who was my best friend and also the best picture editor I ever worked with at *National Geographic.* I loved him like a brother and miss him all the time. My children and many friends were in attendance at the wedding; there was music and dancing, at one point causing a tall bookcase to come crashing down with all its volumes, brought low by the enthusiastic dancers on the dipping and quivering heart pine floor of the pre-Civil War house.

It was truly spring in more ways than one; it was the time of a new beginning to my life and career.

Of the assignments I did for John Loengard at *Life* during the early 1980s, I most remember the story *Life* reporter Rinker Buck and I did about a Wyoming range detective, a story I'd proposed to Loengard. I'd read somewhere—I think in an in-flight magazine—about Ed Cantrell, formerly the top law enforcement officer in Rock Springs, who had been indicted for murder after shooting one of his own undercover agents. He shot the agent, named Rosa, between the eyes, just a little off-center, while the man sat in the back of a police car parked outside a Rock Springs bar. Cantrell had been in the front passenger seat. There had been an argument, and Cantrell claimed he killed Rosa in self-defense, thinking he was going to draw on him.

Some area ranchers hired the superb, if flamboyant, criminal attorney Gerry Spence, out of Jackson Hole, and although a lot of local people thought Cantrell was guilty, Spence got him acquitted. His career as a town or county law officer was over, though, and he was working as a range detective, combating cattle rustling in Sweetwater County, when Rinker Buck and I spent a couple of weeks with him.

Cantrell had been a teetotaler early in life, but after losing his son to a head-on highway wreck some years earlier, he had taken to drinking. He was a slender man of medium height, with hair cropped short and pale blue eyes that were occasionally bloodshot and sometimes appeared icy. Cantrell always carried a six-inch barreled .357 Smith & Wesson revolver in a hip holster.

One afternoon Rinker and I were on horseback along with Cantrell, who was helping a rancher friend move some cattle down along the Little Snake River close to the Colorado border. As the afternoon faded we noticed Cantrell was no longer around. Rinker and I unsaddled our horses, turned them out, and went searching for Cantrell. We eventually decided to drive down by the river. It was getting late in the day; not really daylight, not yet dark, it was becoming that time the Basque call "the time between dogs and wolves," when one's eyes and mind question the reality of the most common of objects: Is that really a rock? The river below us was almost metallic, reflecting the softly glancing silver light of dusk.

We saw his truck along the edge of the river. We drove down toward him as he came slowly up the dirt track. Buck was driving, and I told him to stop—I'd go talk to Cantrell. I got out and walked around the front of our vehicle to approach Cantrell in his pickup as he drew closer.

I didn't see it at first. It wasn't until I was within about five feet of him sitting there behind the wheel, his gray Stetson and his white shirt outlined within the cab of his truck. His left elbow was resting on the door frame of the open window, his left hand on the steering wheel. Then I saw the gun. The barrel was nestled in the crook of his left arm, and the muzzle, a hard, black hole, was pointed at my chest. His face was expressionless. His eyes were blue, cold, and distant.

My response was involuntary: "Jesus Christ! Ed! What the hell are you doing?" I raised my arms as if in surrender.

I started to move slowly backward and to my left, thinking to get back to our car. As I did, he tracked me by easing his truck forward, the gun still steadied in the crook of his arm as he steered with one hand. I realized any kind of retreat was senseless. I probably wouldn't get but a few feet before feeling the bullet, if for some insane reason, he really wanted to take me out. So I stopped, and then walked directly over to his truck and stood almost speechless in front of him. I didn't know what to say.

"Chilled your shit, didn't I?" he said flatly, at last.

"Oh . . . yes," I said, with some difficulty. "Yes, you did."

I guess Cantrell was drunk that evening along the Little Snake River. I don't know for sure and never will. But I've been around guns all my life, and the one thing you don't do is point one at anything you don't intend to shoot. And it wasn't a matter of whether the gun was loaded. You assume they always are; that's the only safe way to be with guns. And I know damn well Cantrell's gun was loaded. He had too many enemies for it not to be. I guess I still haven't forgiven him for that. Or maybe I have but I just can't forget it.

I never saw him again. He's dead now, died a few years back.

THAT STORY ABOUT ED CANTRELL ran for just a few pages in *Life*; I can't now remember just how many, maybe six or eight. Still, it was one of the few stories of substance, stories I felt good about, that I was able to do during those years I wasn't being hired by *National Geographic*.

It wasn't until Bob Gilka retired in 1985 and Rich Clarkson became director of photography that I was once again able to photograph for the *Geographic*. Rich Clarkson brought me back in. Was the exile period a bit harsh? I think so. I broke a code, I suppose, by my conduct that afternoon at the seminar. I made some professional criticisms, but not very professionally and far too openly, and they were taken personally. Either Gilka or Editor Bill Garrett could have brought me back, had they wanted to, but they didn't. I certainly learned how much I truly loved what I had been doing once I found I couldn't do it anymore, at least for the magazine that had for so long been my resource, my workplace, and my second home.

When Rich Clarkson succeeded Bob Gilka as director of photography I first got some work from the Society's Book Division and then was offered my first assignment for the magazine since 1981. There was a story about something called the Tea and Sugar Train, a weekly supply train that traveled across southern and Western Australia, stopping at desolate little railroad worker communities. Freelance writer Erla Zwingle had turned in a manuscript everybody lauded, but there were no pictures to go with it. A freelance photographer had been assigned, but the magazine wasn't happy with the pictures, and Clarkson asked me to take it on, to reshoot it. That's something I believe no photographer really likes to do, especially if the story's focus is narrow, because your subjects have already been approached by someone, and they're going to be curious about why that earlier photographer hadn't been successful. I've done it a couple of times, and I always avoid looking at the first photographer's pictures. I want it to be fresh for me.

I left for Australia, and for the next month or so, I spent a lot of time on a train, going back and forth over more than a thousand miles of mostly arrow-straight track, crossing wide-open land with not much on it. There was little to photograph on the train itself. I read a lot of books, which is a love of mine second only to music.

A train inspector named Henry Cox lived in Cook, the main railroad depot by the border between Western and South Australia. When I'd stop at Cook, "Coxie" and I would drink some beers and talk when he was home, off the job. Coxie was a rough-hewn-looking man, tattoos on his arms, with thick workingman's fingers that gripped his Aussie beer can and sometimes clawed at his forehead as he talked.

In Cook there was a public swimming pool, and while hanging around the pool at midday, when the light is not usually terribly interesting, I saw a boy wrapped in a towel, standing on the other side of a screen, or scrim, that I suppose was there to keep the outback dust from blowing in on the pool and the swimmers. It softened the light, and the picture became one of those that end up kind of asking a question. I believe the best pictures often ask questions: Just what is going on here? What is this? Who is this person? Why? If a picture carries aesthetic strength along with a question mark, I think one tends to remember it.

Every Christmas season a train inspector named Alf Harris would go out on the train dressed as Santa Claus. At one stop there were three Aborigines standing trainside as Alf looked down on them from his place in the open railroad car door. The Aborigines usually don't want you to take their picture, but I tried discreetly to make just two exposures, only two. In one, the slight but significant gesture of one of the women with a lifted little finger makes the image far better than the other one. The difference between a good picture and one that might be special is often a matter of inches, or perhaps a gesture, even as small a gesture as an upraised finger. The scattered clouds give relief to the vast blue sky and play off Santa's beard. That was so long ago I can't possibly say now whether I was aware of those subtleties; I think they are often the result of subconscious thinking and seeing. Here, again, is a picture basically quite simple, with few moving parts, but it poses a question: Just what the hell is going on here?

THE TEA AND SUGAR TRAIN STORY in 1985 got me back into the rhythm of producing essays for *National Geographic* magazine. That same year I was invited to join the photographic agency Magnum, a photographer-owned, highly respected agency representing some of the finest photographers in the world, with bureaus in New York, Paris, and London. Some of the first photographers I had studied when at the University of Minnesota were Magnum photographers, among them one of the agency founders, Henri Cartier-Bresson of "the decisive moment" fame. Another Magnum member, Dennis Stock, had been helpful when I was a student. He had taken a call that I made from a phone booth in Manhattan on my first trip to New York in 1963. I had come to New York with a small portfolio of black-and-white photographs. Back in Minnesota I was a junior at the university, and I went to New York not looking for a job; I was there searching for people who would look at my work and simply talk to me about it. I had Stock's book *Jazz Street* at home. I had looked his name up in a New York City telephone directory in a phone booth on Madison Avenue (yes, they actually had intact telephone books in New York phone booths in the sixties), got lucky, and somehow picked the right Dennis Stock in the book. And I got luckier yet when he answered the phone, allowing me to tell him who I was and why he didn't know me, and ask if he'd look at my pictures. Literally on the eve of Dennis and his wife's departure for a move to Europe he invited me to come over, where we spread my pictures out on the floor of his stripped-down apartment, his wife made us a couple of screwdrivers, and he critiqued my work and gave me great encouragement. Years later we became friends. His openness that day in 1963 was of much greater importance to me then than I suspect he realized.

After joining in 1985, I stayed in Magnum only two years before opting to leave. I was about to turn 50, Ani and I had a baby on the way, and I feared I wouldn't be able to honor the financial commitment necessary to maintain my Magnum membership. There are times I regret leaving Magnum. It was a touchstone, as photographer Bruce Davidson used to tell me. It was like a family, and even now continues to feel that way after the almost quarter century since I left it. And although I don't know nearly as many of the member photographers as I once did, I go to the annual Magnum meeting party in late June if it occurs in New York or I happen to be in Paris or London.

When my *Geographic* family relationship healed, I moved on to doing magazine assignments in a variety of places in the world. In the years to come, though, I would not find a subject that would coalesce in terms of something I could pursue and build on as I had my love affair with the American West, although for a while it seemed as though Peru might have that kind of attraction. In the mid-1980s I did return to Peru on my own and for *Geographic* and *Life*. In 1995 I photographed a new Peru country story for *Geographic*. Since then, however, I haven't pursued the subject.

In 1996, at the request of then Director of Photography Tom Kennedy, I rejoined *National Geographic* as a staff photographer, almost 30 years after I'd resigned my original staff position in the 1960s. Joining the photographic staff at the same time were Michael "Nick" Nichols, who had left Magnum after a long tenure there; and Chris Johns, a freelance photographer and frequent *Geographic* contributor. Chris would go on to become Editor in Chief of the magazine.

By 1996 there really were no other magazines I could or wanted to work for frequently, certainly not in the United States, and I decided it was to my best benefit to rejoin the *National Geographic* staff. I started looking into European subjects, Italy and France, and continued to find subjects in America that intrigued and appealed to me. And in the first few years of the new century I saw India for the first time and found myself wishing I hadn't waited so long.

I still see former Director of Photography Bob Gilka occasionally. Ironically, it's usually at the annual *Geographic* seminar lunches. In recent years I've received complimentary notes from Gilka, now in his 90s, when he's seen a story of mine in the magazine. He has encouraged me to never quit making pictures, and sometimes writes how fortunate it was for the magazine when I first came through the door those many years ago. Well, of course, it was truly fortunate for me, too. In all fairness to Gilka, he originally brought me in. And, all on my own, I took myself out, for a while. ■

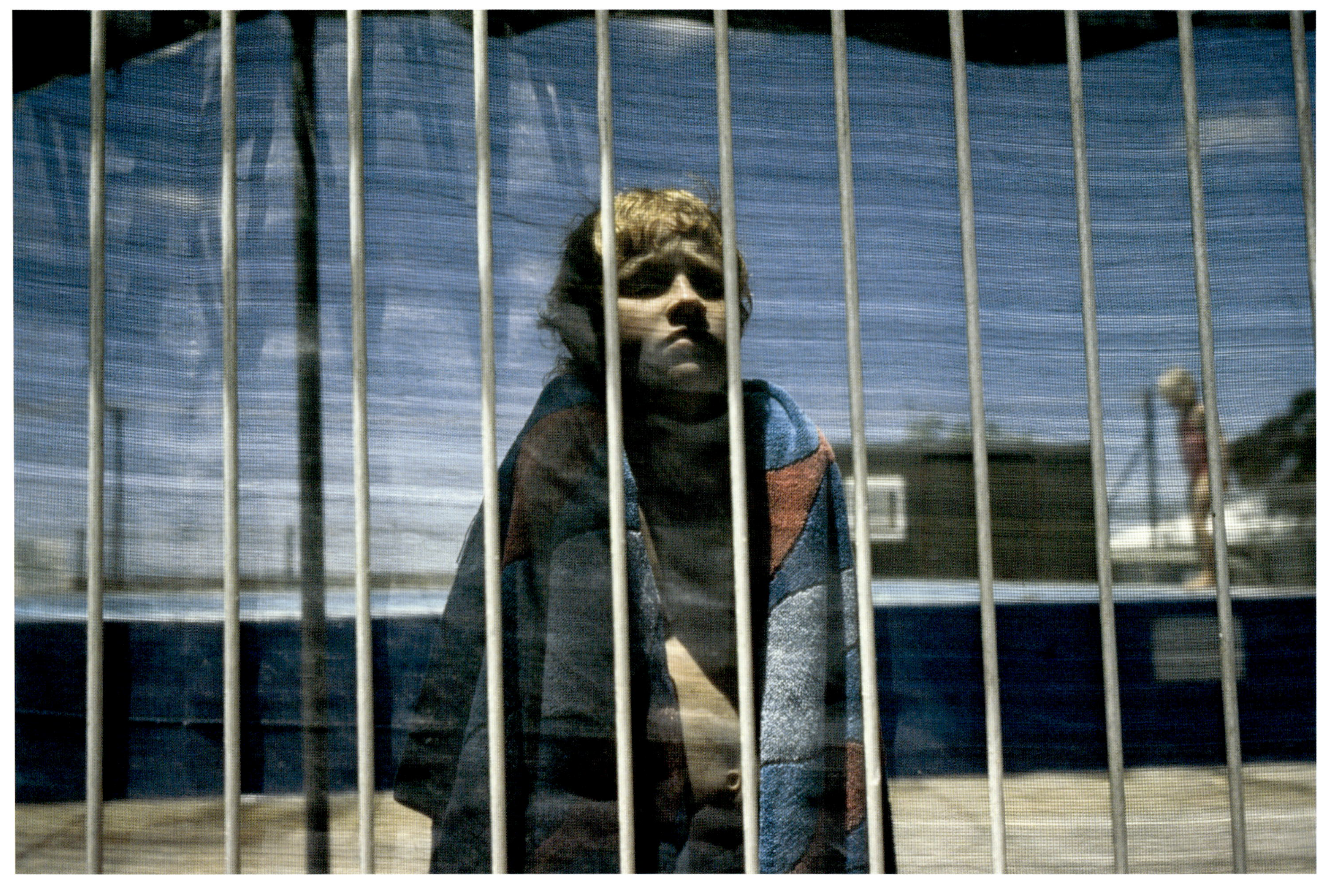

Boy at the swimming pool, Cook, Australia, 1985

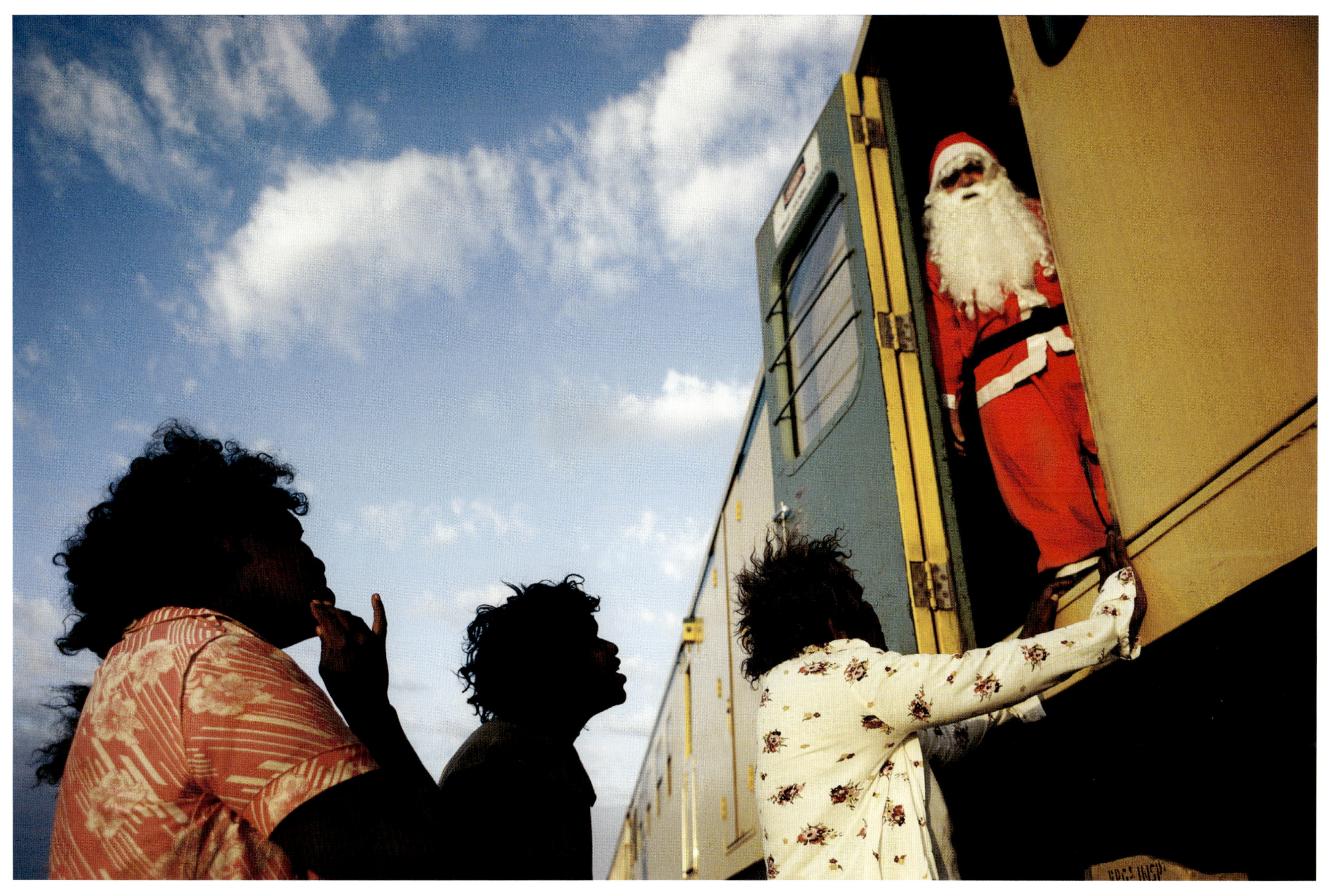

Alf Harris and Aborigines, southern Australia, 1985

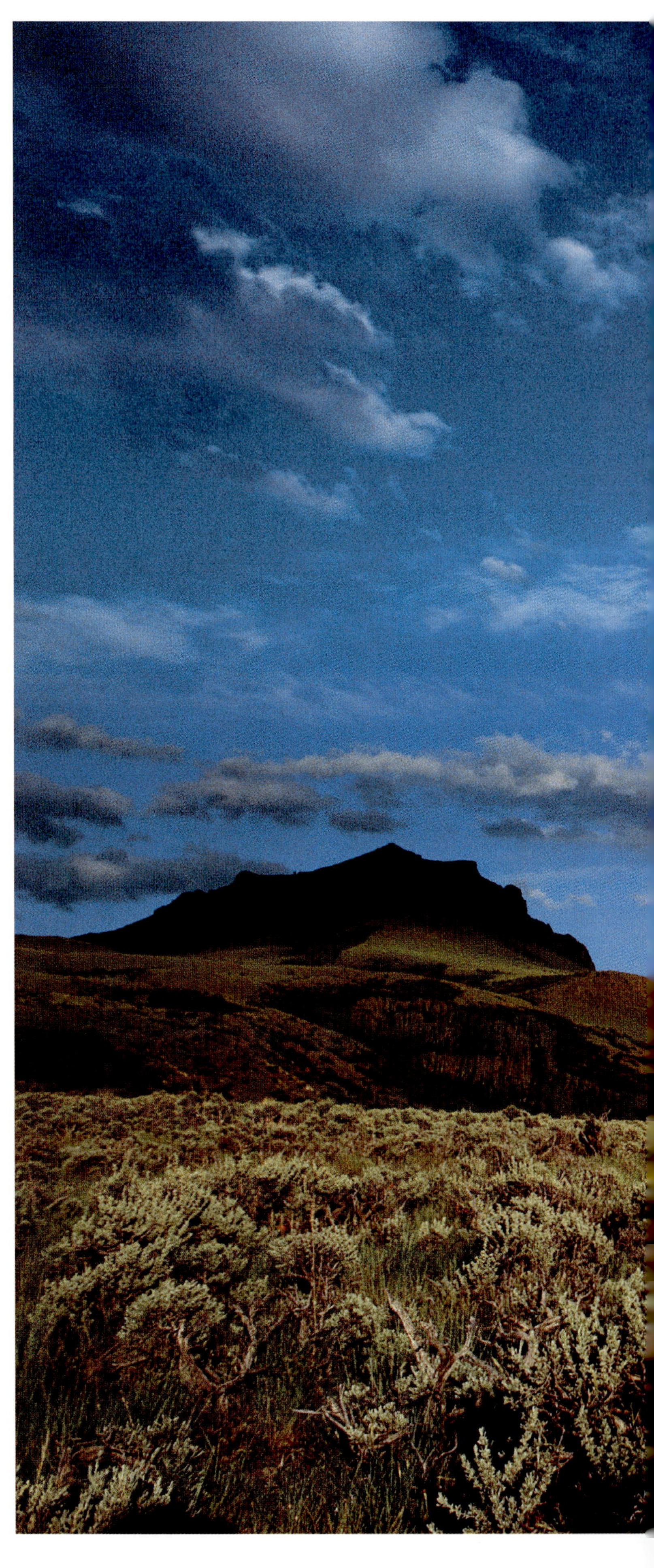

Range detective Ed Cantrell, Wyoming, 1983

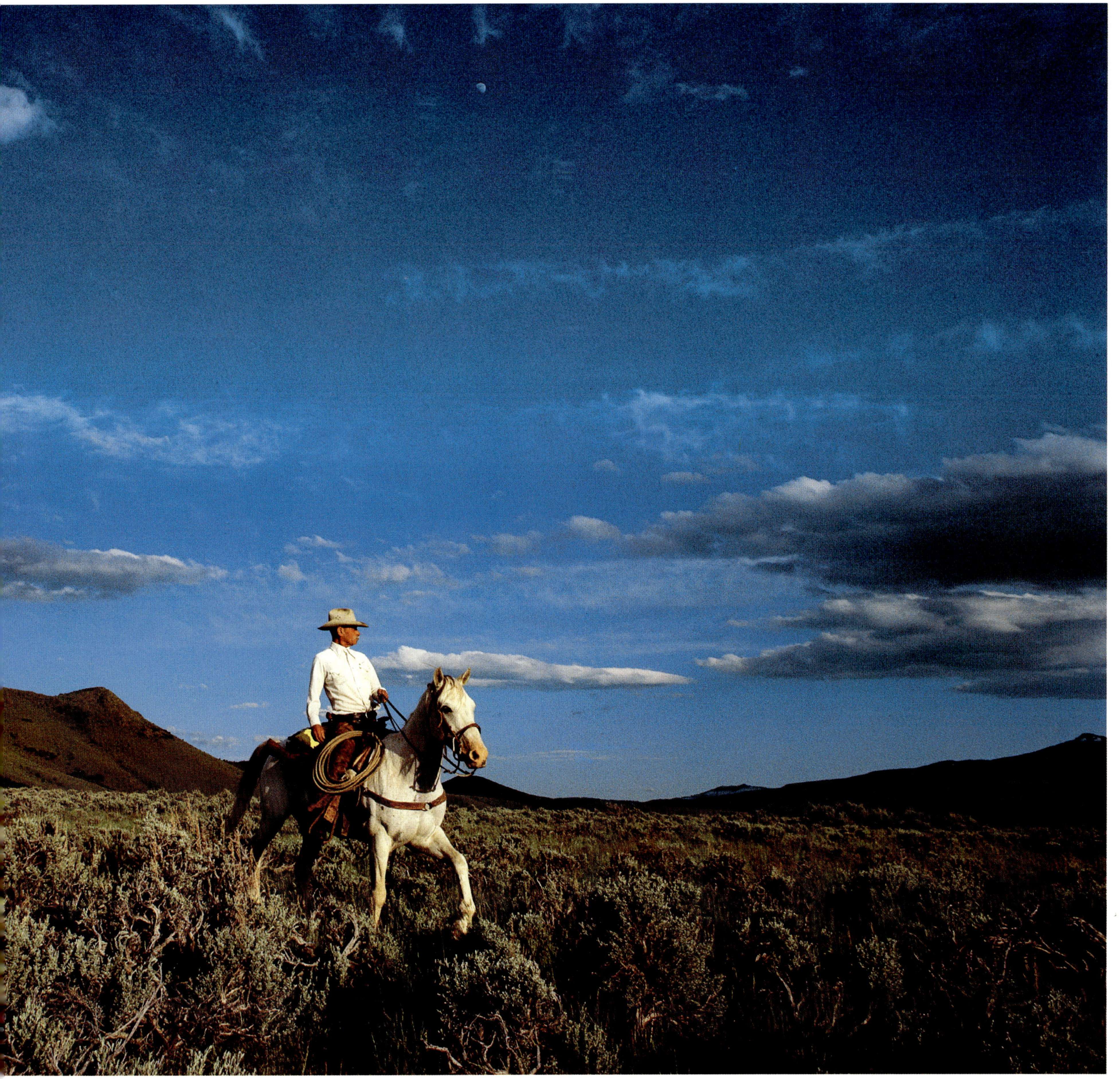

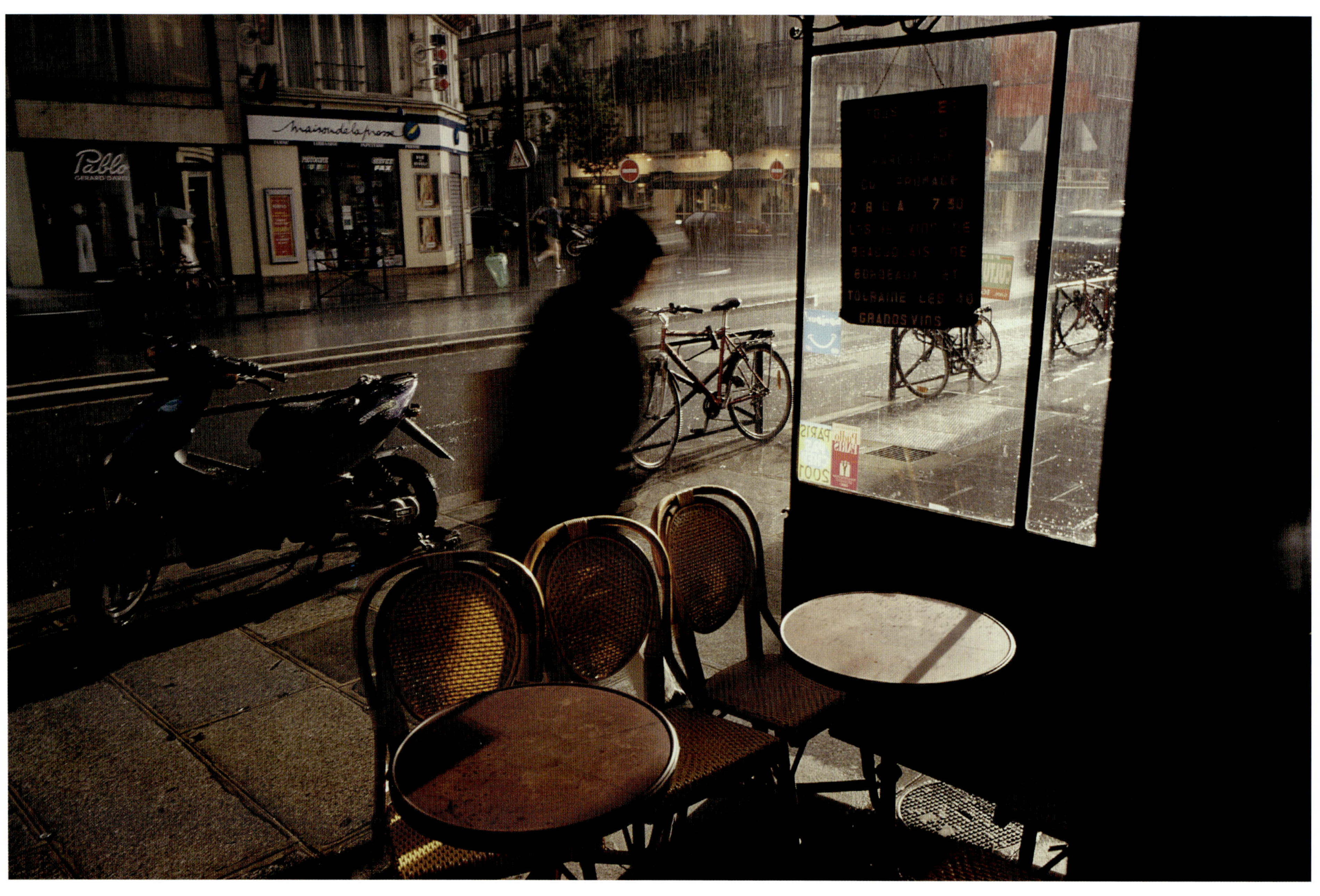

Terrace of La Tartine, Rue de Rivoli, Paris, 2002

Country of Light

We pass the bridges. Animating each bus stop, the posters and the pictures advertising perfumes, movies, and fashion magazines flicker by. The architectural charm seems to decrease as we leave the center of the city and race along, following the river. Leaving Paris, the September early morning air is bracing, full of the city's smells; the sunlight is hazy, and on the taxi's rear speakers, soft jazz accompanies me on the way to Charles De Gaulle Airport.

As I board the plane to return to the United States I see a mother and what must be her daughter, each with a cat in a crate. A plump Indian woman carries an empty birdcage in a clear plastic bag. A man I take to be in his 50s wears what seems to be a terribly obvious grayish yellow hairpiece. Next to him a young woman I guess to be French wears a tight T-shirt and no makeup, and she is beautiful in that imperfect way of so many Frenchwomen. She has full lips, like ripe fruit.

I wonder, as I have so often when I am there, are the women one sees in Paris truly more interestingly attractive than in any other city in the world? I sometimes think so. I think of Rue de Rivoli in the summer, on late afternoons when the lowering sun floods the street with a river of warm, golden light, bathing the sidewalk café tables and the faces of women on their bicycles, skirts drawn tight across their thighs, legs pedaling, faces smiling as they pass.

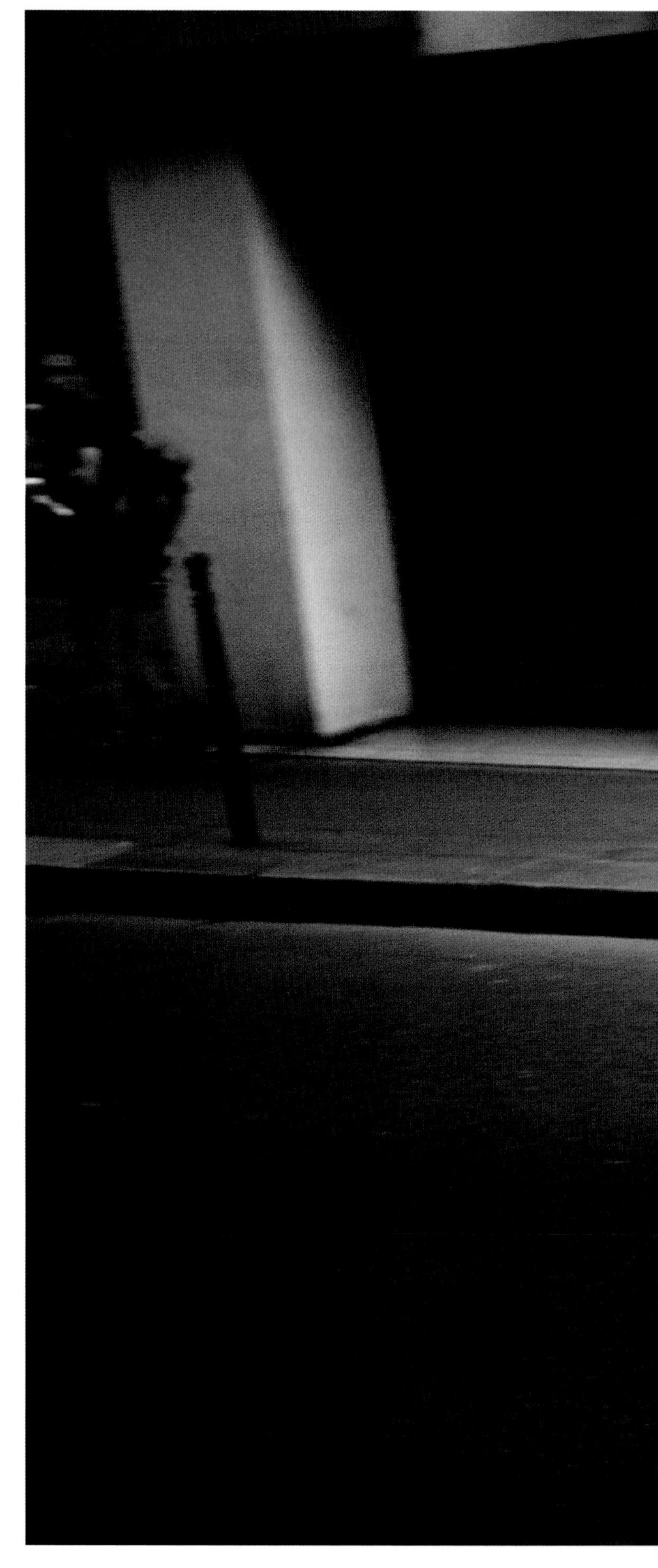

Le Marais, Paris, 2002

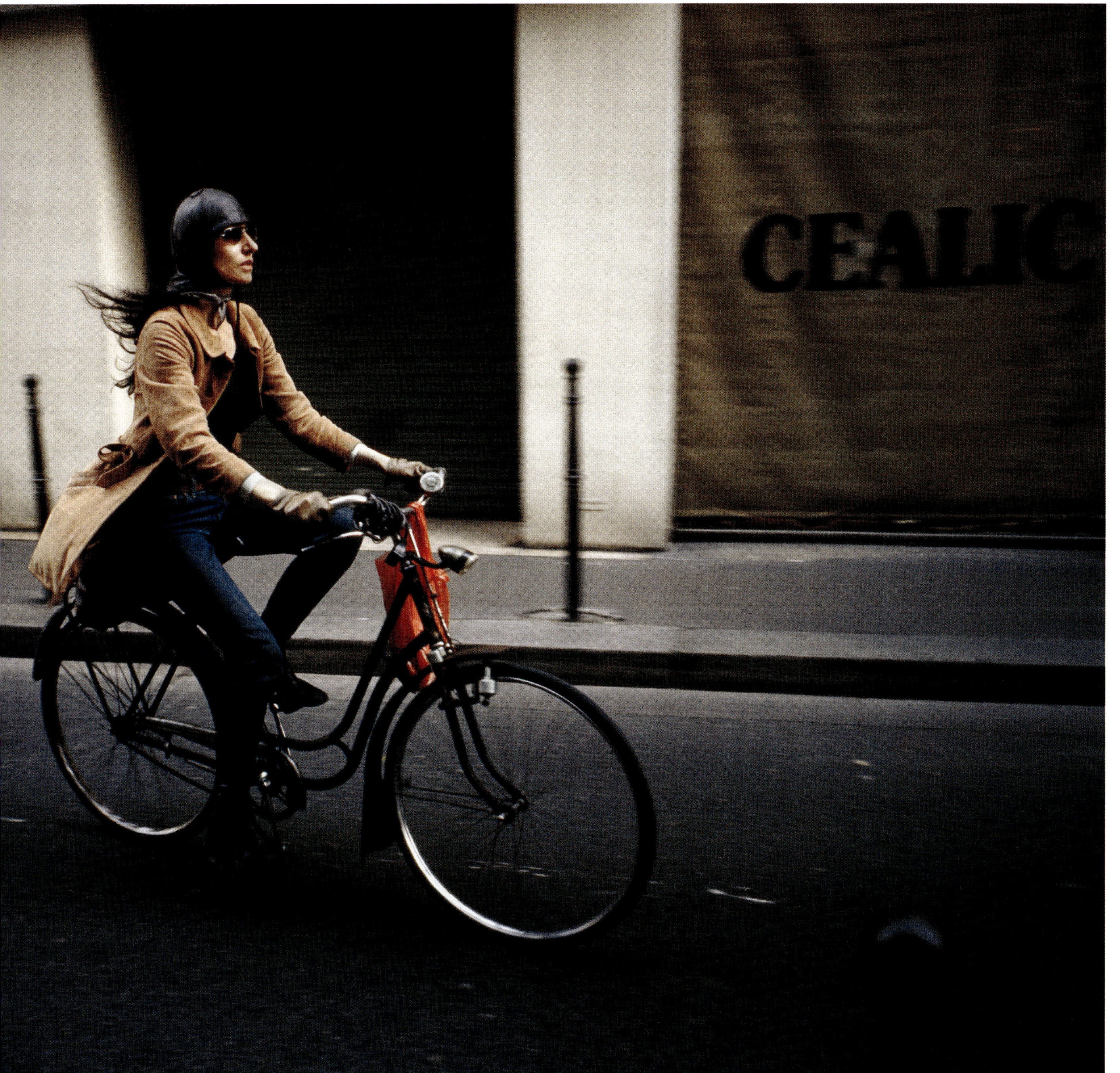
CEALIC

In Paris, you can fall in love at first sight with a woman passing by, walking her bike, a swath of soft yellow scarf embracing her throat. You don't know her, you've never seen her face before, and most likely you'll never see her again, but you simply fall in love with her Parisian beauty. Of course, we live in a world of heartbreaking illusions, and there is always present the possibility of the greatest, most devastating Parisian illusion: seeing someone on the street who appears to be unmistakably French—more than that, actually, totally Parisian, with that indefinable flair and style, that touch of something in her dress and manner, in her look—and then discovering she is from Omaha and sounds like it. Ah, the anguish of reality. It does happen.

Still, I think there is definitely a Parisian female look, especially among the young. Time and again, one sees attire with some distinctive flair, perhaps just a hair ribbon, but the right kind of hair ribbon in the right place; maybe a simple scarf, but wrapped just so; it might be clunky shoes on beautiful legs with multicolored knee-high stockings; sometimes it is something that simply shouldn't work but does.

Maybe it's attitude as much as anything. Maybe it's about not caring beyond the very present. Their tomorrows will be considered when they arrive. In the meantime it's "Look at me, but if you don't, I don't care. And you probably will look, anyway."

One evening, in 2002, while working in Paris on a *Geographic* story about the Right Bank neighborhood Le Marais, I joined my young American friend, photojournalist Chris Anderson, and his French girlfriend, Marion Durand, at La Belle Hortense, a wine bar around the corner from my hotel on Rue Ste. Croix de la Bretonnerie. Marion was dressed in an absolutely outrageous combination that seemingly could have been blown out of a cannon in an explosion of randomly chosen colors and fabrics, and yet it all worked beautifully. I can't recall it well enough now to describe it, but I might have trouble doing so even if it had been just last night; that French flair is difficult to describe. One has to see it to know it.

Marion and Chris lived in Paris then. Marion was not from Paris but from the south of France, and she had some Catalan Spanish in her blood. I remember the first time I saw her with Chris at Visa pour l'Image, the annual photographic festival held in Perpignan, France. She was petite, dark complexioned, with dark eyes and brows, and her dark hair was cut extremely short. I said to Chris, "She reminds me of Maria in Hemingway's *For Whom the Bell Tolls.*"

"That's exactly what I told her, too, when we first met!" Chris said.

Chris and Marion are now married, live in New York City, and have a baby boy named Atlas.

As I wrote this I decided to contact Marion to ask her about the French look. We exchanged emails on the subject. She didn't remember what she was wearing that night in the Paris wine bar, but she said this about the way she *might* dress:

> *You are right about the French flair. And my own explanation, or what I feel, is that it is an instinctive sense of proportion and detail: A tight shirt with sailor pants, a little dress that falls at just about the right length, fluid and suggestive, a splash of bright color, maybe violent red lipstick contrasting with a plain tee-shirt. Short hair [of course, Marion's hair is always short] to flatter a gracious neck. Perfect shoes . . . a beautiful cotton, sheer linen . . . somehow the right equation between the amount of flesh and the height of heels, a delicate mix of nonchalance and sexiness that makes the resulting silhouette look effortless. Effortless is the key.*

OK.

MY FIRST CHANCE TO PHOTOGRAPH Paris came in 1986. I had begun to work again in 1985 for *National Geographic* after about three and a half years of being unable to get an assignment.

I suggested to David Bridge, then a picture editor for National Geographic's *Traveler* magazine, that I'd like to photograph an essay based on wandering about the sidewalks of Paris. Not exactly an original idea, but *Traveler* bought it, and I was given a relatively short assignment, maybe a couple of weeks, that I stretched into four by living in a cheap hotel.

I thought then, and still do, that walking around Paris is like walking through a series of one-act plays. One passes by a couple in deep argument or passionate embrace; a poodle sprawls at the feet of its master, who is engrossed with his newspaper and coffee; a blue-clad city worker takes his break and smokes a Gauloises, and the acrid smell catches you like a fist. On Boulevard St.-Germain brilliant sunshine appears on the heels of a heavy downpour, and a striding man lifts dark glasses to his face to confront blinding sunlight that hadn't existed moments before.

I think Paris may be the finest walking-around city in all of Europe. So much of it is beautiful, and much of the city then was safe. I covered a lot of ground that summer. I spent time with the usual suspects: the Eiffel Tower, the street artists in the Latin Quarter, Boulevard St.-Germain, the cafés Les Deux Magots and Café de Flore, and on and on. Places that have been done again and again by so many photographers, but not by me, and I relished the opportunity.

IN 1988 I WOULD RETURN AGAIN to Paris, this time to photograph the world of fashion for an all-France issue that the *Geographic* was planning to run in July 1989 to commemorate the 200th anniversary of the French Revolution. As soon as they announced their intention to publish that special issue, I asked to photograph the Paris fashion world, knowing they had to include something about fashion. I made two trips that year, in spring and in fall, covering fashion shows by many of the major designers of that time. I often worked backstage. At the request of one of the *Geographic*'s editors, I hung out with two American models living in Paris—in my mind, a clichéd idea, but I did it and made some good pictures.

Tanya Pohlkotte, an American model from St. Louis and Dallas, shared a platonic relationship and an apartment on one of the large boulevards near the fashion district with a young Frenchman named Edouard, whose passion was making collages from pictures of Brigitte Bardot he'd cut from old magazines.

I'd go with Tanya on her trips to designers' studios to show her portfolio. I once went with her when she got a facial and lay, prayer-like, waiting for the treatment to be peeled off.

I'd seen Edouard's collages in the apartment, and I'd seen Tanya in a certain multicolored minidress (I think it was a Betsey Johnson dress, but I'm not sure) earlier, and thought it would be nice to put them together in one picture.

In this picture you don't see Tanya's face, only the many faces of Brigitte Bardot in the collages. You see Tanya's legs, her bottom, and her hands. Did I ask her to put her hands where they are? Yes. Did I ask her to move them? Yes. I asked Edouard to simply sit in the chair and look at her. At one point I asked Tanya to remove her dress and stand just in her panty hose, but I preferred her with the dress on.

This is a produced picture, not something I do a lot of. I arranged the collages and I set up a strobe light to augment the window light. I title pictures only when necessary for identification of my limited-edition prints so that one picture is not confused with another. I call this one "Tanya Towering Over Bardot." That seems French enough.

I loved the Paris fashion world assignment. Working around the production of a fashion show was like being in the center of a storm of beauty. Models of many different nationalities would wander into the dressing rooms, sometimes arriving not looking terribly special or pretty, but after hair and makeup, quite often they would appear stunningly beautiful.

There is great intensity backstage at a Paris fashion show, whether it is about haute couture or ready-to-wear fashions. I watched last-minute approval by an explosively intense Yves Saint Laurent of a veiled model about to take to the runway. A more relaxed Emanuel Ungaro sent out a flock of models, their slender legs clad in metallic stockings, and by mixing with the ambient light a little strobe light on my camera, I made those legs shimmer. Faces of famous models from the covers of *Vogue* and *Harper's Bazaar* hovered seemingly everywhere. After one show, black-clad designer Karl Lagerfeld stood backstage without a fan wavering in his hand—a rare public omission of that affectation—sipping champagne, while a companion raised his dark glasses either to see someone else better or, perhaps, to make himself appear more recognizable in the picture he thought I was making.

The world of fashion is a crazy one; I'm not sure I'd ever want to be fully a part of it. But in 1988 I immensely enjoyed photographing that world. It's only fair to note that my published story—written by the late *Washington Post* fashion writer Nina Hyde and poorly titled, I thought, by the editors "The Business of Chic"—in a later survey rated the *lowest* of any story published in *National Geographic* magazine since the early 1970s. I liked it, and my friends did too, but not, evidently, the readers of *National Geographic.* But I'm so damn glad I got the chance to do it.

I HAVEN'T WORKED IN FRANCE very much other than in Paris. In 1993 I worked on an essay about Provence. An inspirationally beautiful country for so many artists, Provence offered me the opportunity to play a little in my approach to landscapes, such as the poppies weaving in the wind before a background of olive—or are they cherry?—trees. In early spring, a blossoming almond tree cast spiderweb-like shadows on gray, dappled soil; and later in the season, not far from Aix-en-Provence, a slender, tortuously twisted and charred tree trunk stood, almost defiant, from a forest fire that had recently ravaged the land frequented by Cézanne when he came to paint the distant Montage Ste.-Victoire.

IN THE OFFICE OF THE MAYOR of Arles, I watched young women of the Camargue vie for the title of Queen of Arles. Dressed in the tradition of their region, they had to be able to speak Provençal. Outside, in Arles's ancient arena, horsemen of the Camargue competed.

In the arena at St.-Rémy-de-Provence, daring *razeteurs* raced across the sand to snatch a thread of yarn from the forehead of a Camargue fighting bull, its horns almost vertical in comparison with the widespread horns of a Spanish fighting bull.

In Arles, when the Place du Forum was cloaked with dusk light,

I could look down from my hotel window to the color-striped umbrellas sheltering restaurant tables below; glowing strings of yellow and red lights were threaded through the limbs of a plane tree. Later, in the Café Van Gogh, a Gypsy woman leaned against the bar and smoked a cigarette, while next to her a young couple from Paris pressed their lips together in a kiss that seemed to last forever.

MY WORK IN 2002 in the Marais neighborhood, on the Right Bank of Paris, brought me into the core of a complex array of cultures. It was then the heart of the gay community, and it had been the Jewish quarter for centuries; it was a neighborhood filled with creative people, some good restaurants, some pricey hotels, and, of course, tourists. I was doing the kind of story I most enjoy, the kind I can live inside of, every day, just by walking out of my hotel in the heart of the neighborhood and roaming the streets, looking for pictures.

Of course, there were favorite spots, places I'd haunt in hopes of finding visual treasures. For breakfast I'd walk over to Bouquet St. Paul, a café on Rue de Rivoli, to nestle behind a small table by the window and scan the *International Herald Tribune* and watch the passersby; at the bar there I'd sometimes recognize a wine bar waitress having an early drink before heading to work. For lunch I'd most likely go to Rendez-Vous Des Amis, an old bistro just a two-minute walk from my hotel. If a particular table was free I could look out the bistro's open door and use its shape to frame pictures of people coming and going on Rue Ste. Croix de la Bretonnerie. The afternoon light was often lovely around the bar just inside that doorway. Before dinner I'd have a glass of wine at La Belle Hortense or at Au Petit Fer à Cheval, wine bars across the street from one another. Then, perhaps, I'd eat a meal at Le Coude Fou or, more often, at Au Gamin de Paris, where, with luck, I'd get a table by the far wall opposite the windows and entrance; there I could read and observe other diners while I dined on *confit de canard* or rabbit, with escargots for starters.

On tango nights I'd go to the Bistro Latin, an upstairs dance hall on Rue du Temple. A kind of nondescript place with no exceptional atmosphere, Bistro Latin became more sensually alive on nights of tango dancing, when the lights would come down a little (or maybe it just seemed that way) when the floor filled with dancers. Bending and swirling, couples were joined at their torsos; a woman's calf muscle became taut but graceful as she raised a leg and pivoted her body in response to her partner's lead. The air in the hall was close and warm; perspiration glistened on a dancer's neck, where stray strands from her upswept hair lay dark and damp.

I'd hang out at gallery openings, visit the Picasso museum, wander around Place des Vosges. And some nights I'd go to one of the gay bars, such as Les Scandaleuses, a lesbian bar on Rue des Ecouffes, where men unaccompanied by a woman are not allowed. I could go there and photograph because my assistant was a woman.

On Sunday afternoons I might go by the synagogue to see if there were going to be any weddings. Jewish wedding parties always welcomed my unexpected appearances. During one ceremony I was as close to the bride as was the groom, who was either being blessed or given advice by a man I think was his grandfather. I couldn't tell, but the way the bride eyed them, she seemed leery of what the groom was being told.

And on any given day I might pass by the school on Rue des Hospitalières St. Gervais, from which, during Nazi occupation in World War II, 165 Jewish children were sent to die in concentration camps, an unspeakable, unthinkable horror that happened not all that long ago.

Most afternoons I'd make a stop at my favorite wine bar, La Tartine, on Rue de Rivoli, where in the afternoon, high school girls would sit at tables on the small terrace and play cards and smoke cigarettes. One darkish, rain-threatening day I was with my friend Beryle Mayfield, the sommelier at Duner's, one of my favorite restaurants in Charlottesville, Virginia. Beryle truly loves Paris and knows the city far better than I. He was in town for a while, and we had decided to go to the wine bar Les Fous d'en Face for what was billed as "the first annual running of the Camembert." This proved to be a contest in which rounds of Camembert were placed on a tilted sheet of aluminum; heat from a small blowtorch was applied to the underside of the sheet, and lo, the individual cheeses would begin to run, sliding slowly, very slowly, downward. Music was then played, and most of the people present seemed to enjoy it far more than Beryle and I.

We decided to leave and walk down Rue de Rivoli to La Tartine, where more than 60 wines are available by the glass. Just as we arrived, the darkened sky gave way with a tremendous downpour of rain. And then, with the rain still falling heavily, the sun came out, and the light was the color of champagne, brilliant and slightly warm. I stood in the doorway of La Tartine with my Leica, looking out over the empty terrace tables. A student passed by, a portfolio under her arm. Across the avenue a man dashed through the rain for cover. I tried to capture the wonderfully exceptional light, desperately hoping for success. I made just a few frames before the magical light expired.

I ALWAYS TRY TO STAY IN A HOTEL room that offers a view that might eventually yield a picture, perhaps the first thing I see in the morning or the last thing at night. From my room in the Hôtel de la Bretonnerie, I could watch the streets below to see what might make a picture—like the rainy afternoon I looked down on the side street intersecting with Rue Ste. Croix de la Bretonnerie and saw the hotel's sign reflected in the panes of my opened window, and on the building opposite, a solitary red window shade that echoed the color of an umbrella carried by a pedestrian passing on the street below. It was a simple moment of coincidence that fell within the graphics of the cityscape outside my hotel room window.

I RECALL A NIGHT IN PARIS in 2004. It was early October, and I'd stopped in Paris on my return home from India. I'd taken an expensive taxi ride from the Sheraton Hotel at de Gaulle Airport into the city to meet the French *National Geographic* magazine art director, Magdalena Herrera, for dinner. It was cool enough for a jacket, and after the daily steam baths of Mumbai, the Paris weather offered great relief. I had the taxi stop near the Métro St.-Paul on Rue de Rivoli, and because I was an hour and a half early, I walked up to La Tartine for a glass of wine. My favorite spot at the curve of the weathered marble bar was vacant and I could stand, watching those who passed by outside: the bobbing heads making their kiss-kiss greetings; the bicycles floating by in the curbside lane; women with scarves enclosing their necks and throats, snugged loosely just below their chins.

A woman entered the open door, and I could feel the cold air wafting off her jacket. Funny that should be so—like a breeze, actually. She stood at the bar near me. She lighted and smoked a cigarette, stroking her shoulder-length chestnut-colored hair, glancing up to view herself in the mirror behind the cappuccino machine. Most of the mirror was concealed behind wine lists and daily specials scrawled in white. The silvering of the mirror was flawed, and a single crack traversed the lower third like the horizon line of a sloping landscape. I watched her look at herself, and I wanted to make a picture of that but I couldn't. I felt I was too obvious, the moment was too fragile to stay, should I raise my camera. I had to let it go; having it in my memory would have to suffice. I could later write about it if I chose to; I could take accurate notes right then and there, and I did; and I could later revise it if I wanted to. A writer can make an observation and later shape it and reshape it to his liking in endless drafts. A street photographer, who can't control anything, might be able to take another picture—maybe another, different exposure—but he can't really change or improve what was seen in that first moment because it is gone. As a photographer friend of mine says, there is no such thing as a second first impression.

IN JULY 1986 I HAD WORKED pretty much all night on the eve of Bastille Day, and in early morning I was ending my day; I think he may have been, too. I immediately recognized him.

Crossing Boulevard Saint-Germain at Place de l'Odeon, I noticed that most of the terrace tables outside Le Relais Odéon, where I often went to stand inside at the zinc bar and sip pastis, were filled with patrons. The sunlight was fresh and bright. When I was almost across the street I saw him there, at a table near the outer edge of the terrace, his face unmistakable: skin the color of dark chocolate, eyes somewhat hooded and rather sad. A small man. Our eyes met and he smiled. I nodded in return, slowed for just a moment, then walked on.

Why didn't I stop, I thought later. Why didn't I say, "Good morning. How are you? It's a truly beautiful morning in Paris, isn't it?" But I didn't. I walked on by.

Who knows, if I'd stopped and said, "Hello, I'm a longtime admirer of your work," maybe he would have invited me to sit with him for a while, have a coffee, a croissant. Maybe we could have talked about writing—if I had dared to ask—those books of his I'd read two decades earlier while at the University of Minnesota, when I was devouring books by fine writers. Maybe we'd have talked about his many years in Paris, maybe even about the interesting attractiveness of French women, although that was early in my Paris experience, and I hadn't quite yet come to that conclusion.

But I didn't stop and we didn't talk. A year later, in the south of France, James Baldwin died at age 63.

IN 1988, WHILE WORKING on the fashion world story for the all-France issue, I was walking along Boulevard St.-Germain one afternoon, heading up to Le Relais Odéon for a pastis. I'd just passed café Les Deux Magots and saw actor Jack Nicholson, wearing his trademark dark glasses, a sport coat, and slacks, heading directly toward me, walking briskly, as if on a mission. As the distance between us closed, I nodded to him.

"Hiyah!" he said, striding by. It never occurred to me to try to stop and say anything to him. He makes great movies; I've seen most of them. And I'm sure he is another lover of Paris, but there are so many. I just kept on walking. Like I was traveling through a series of one-act plays. ■

"...walking around Paris is like walking through a series of one-act plays."

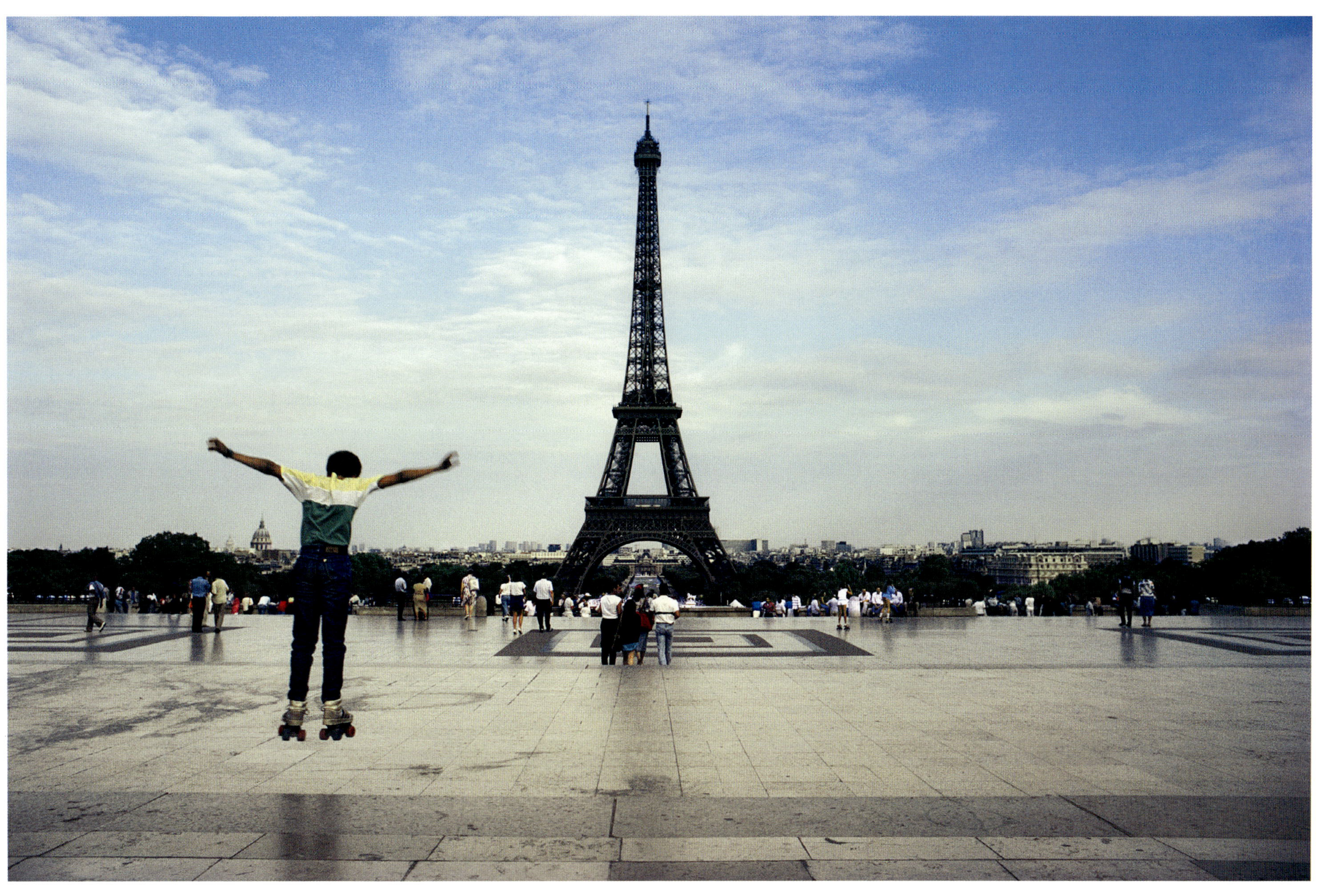

Boy on skates by the Eiffel Tower, Paris, 1986

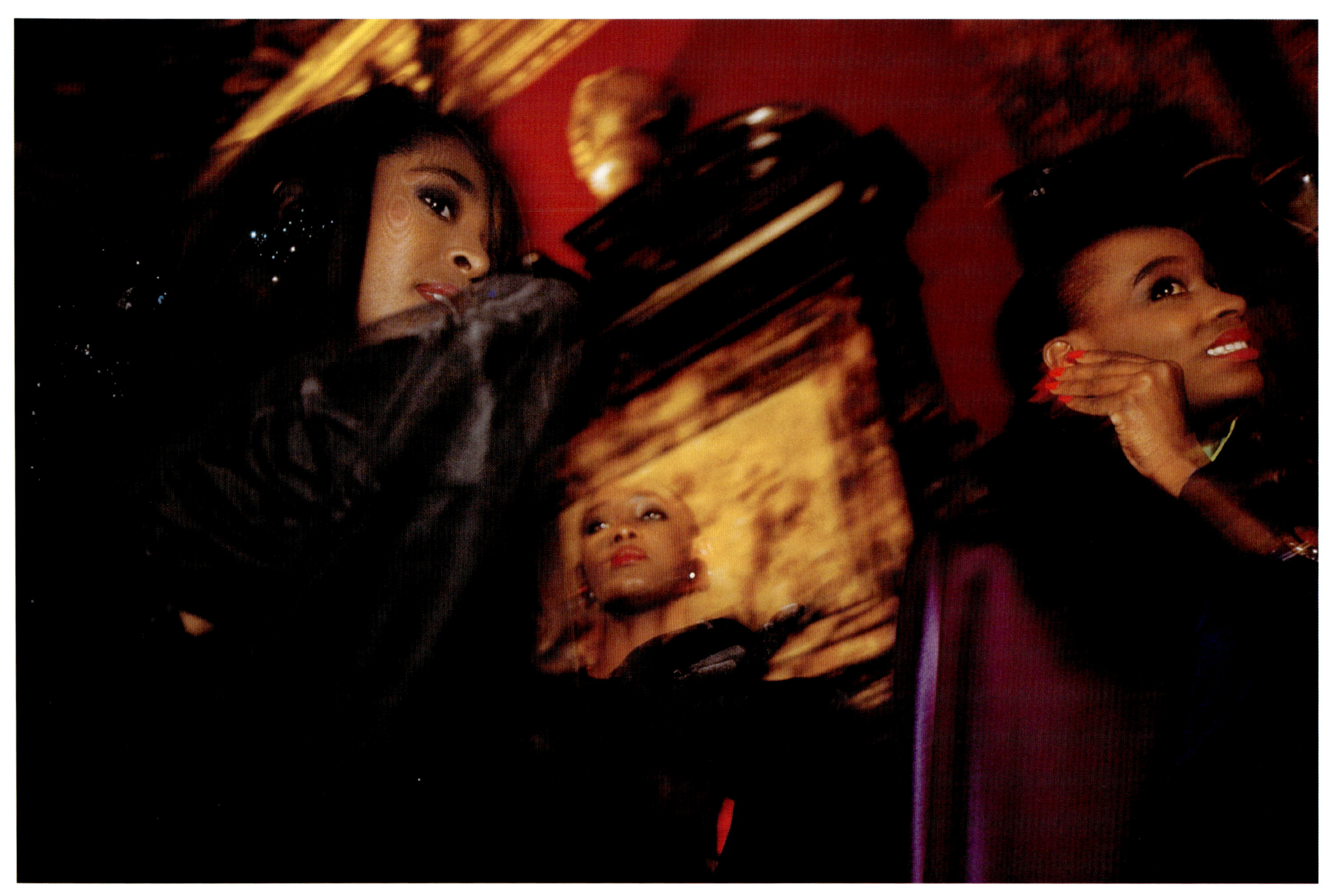

Yves Saint Laurent models at fashion show, Paris, 1988

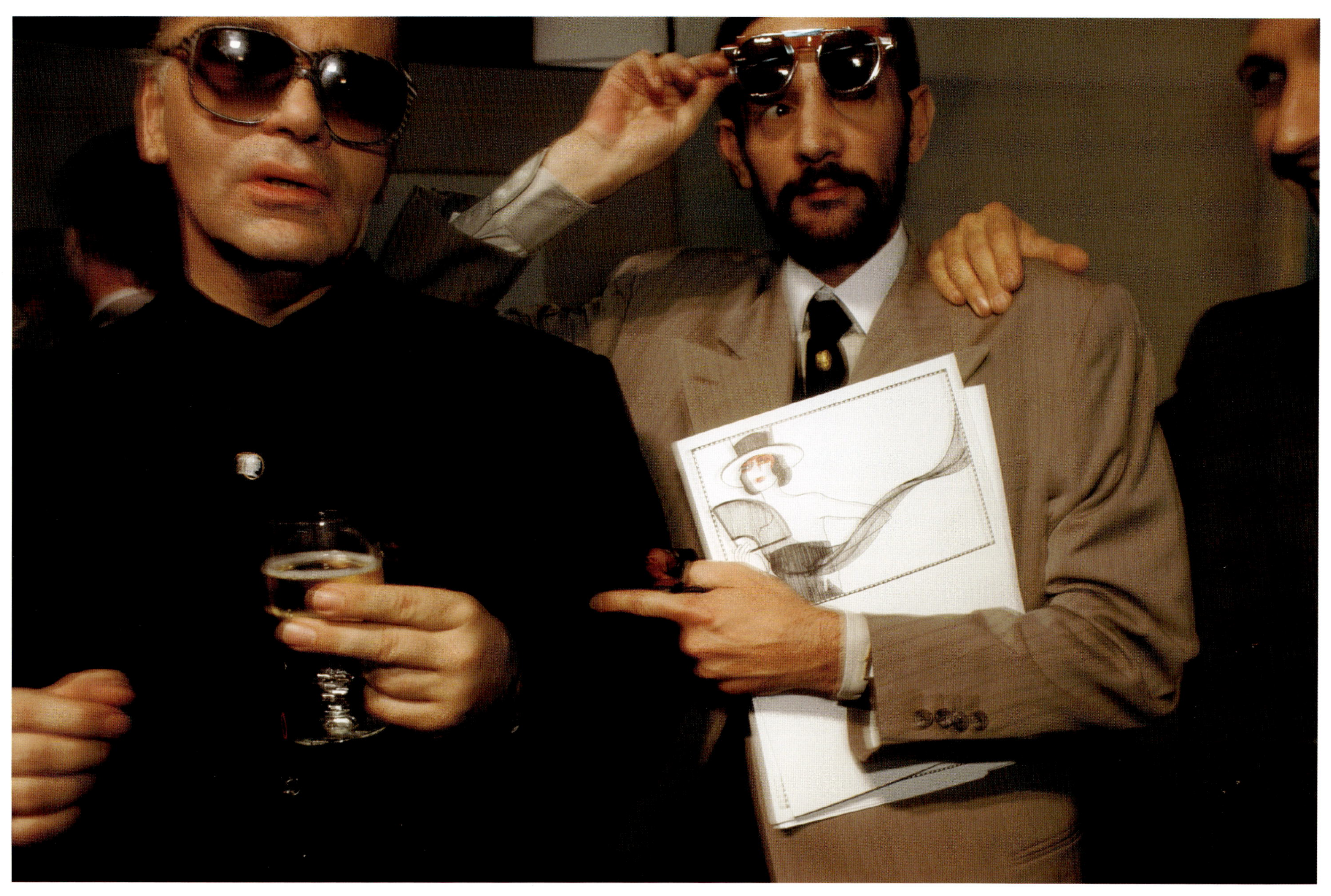

Designer Karl Lagerfeld, on left, Paris, 1988

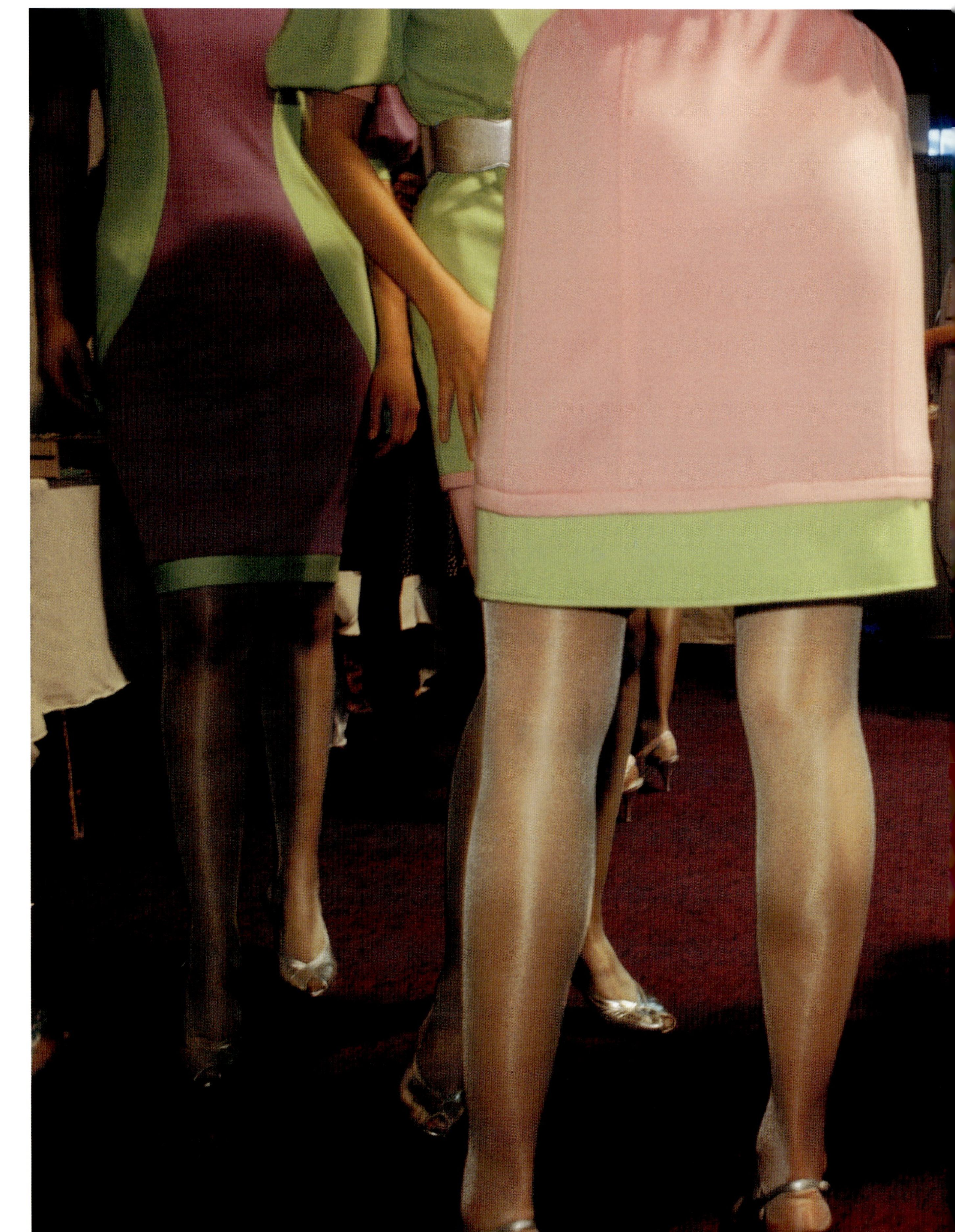

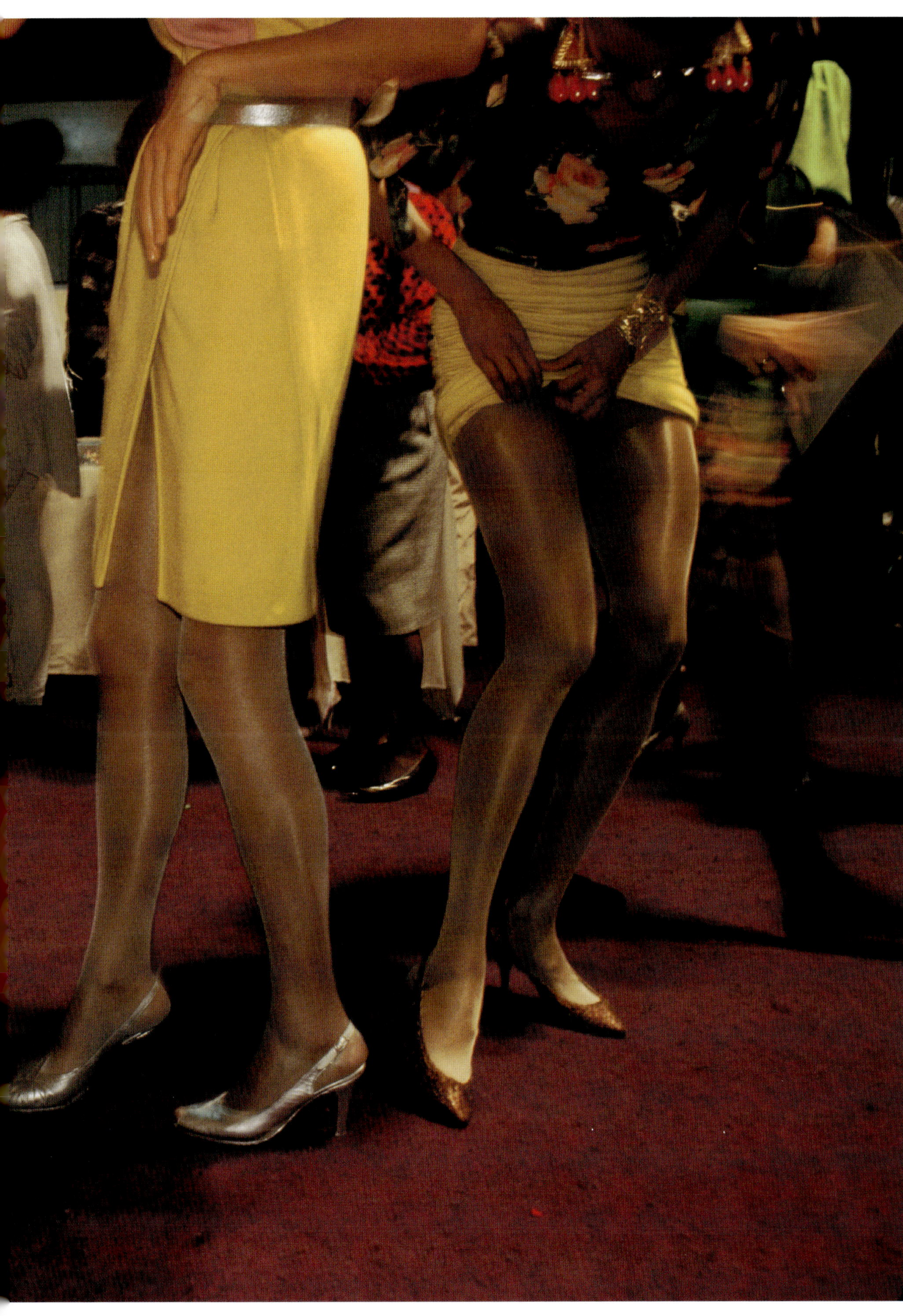

Ungaro models backstage, Paris, 1988

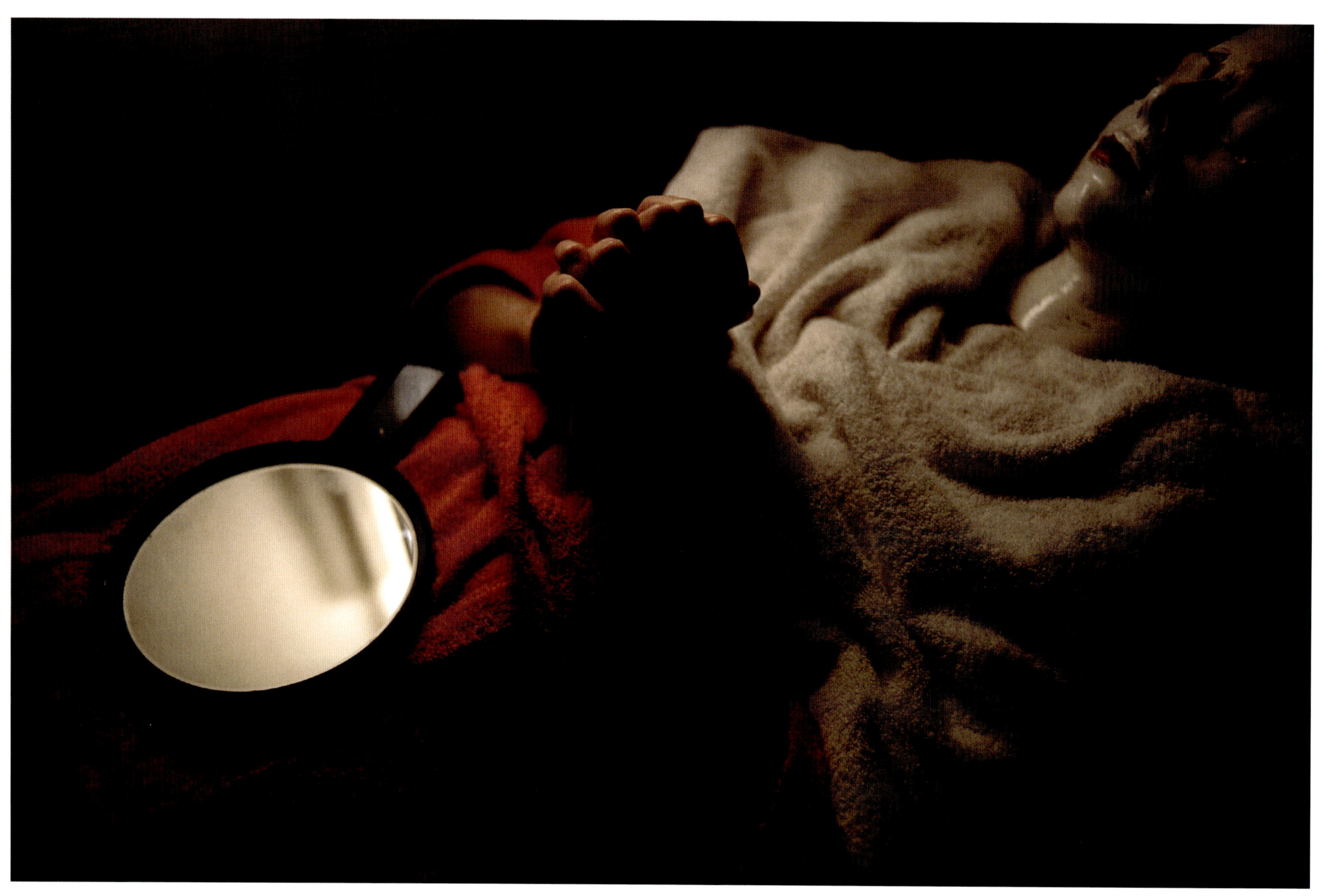

Model Tanya Pohlkotte, Paris, 1988

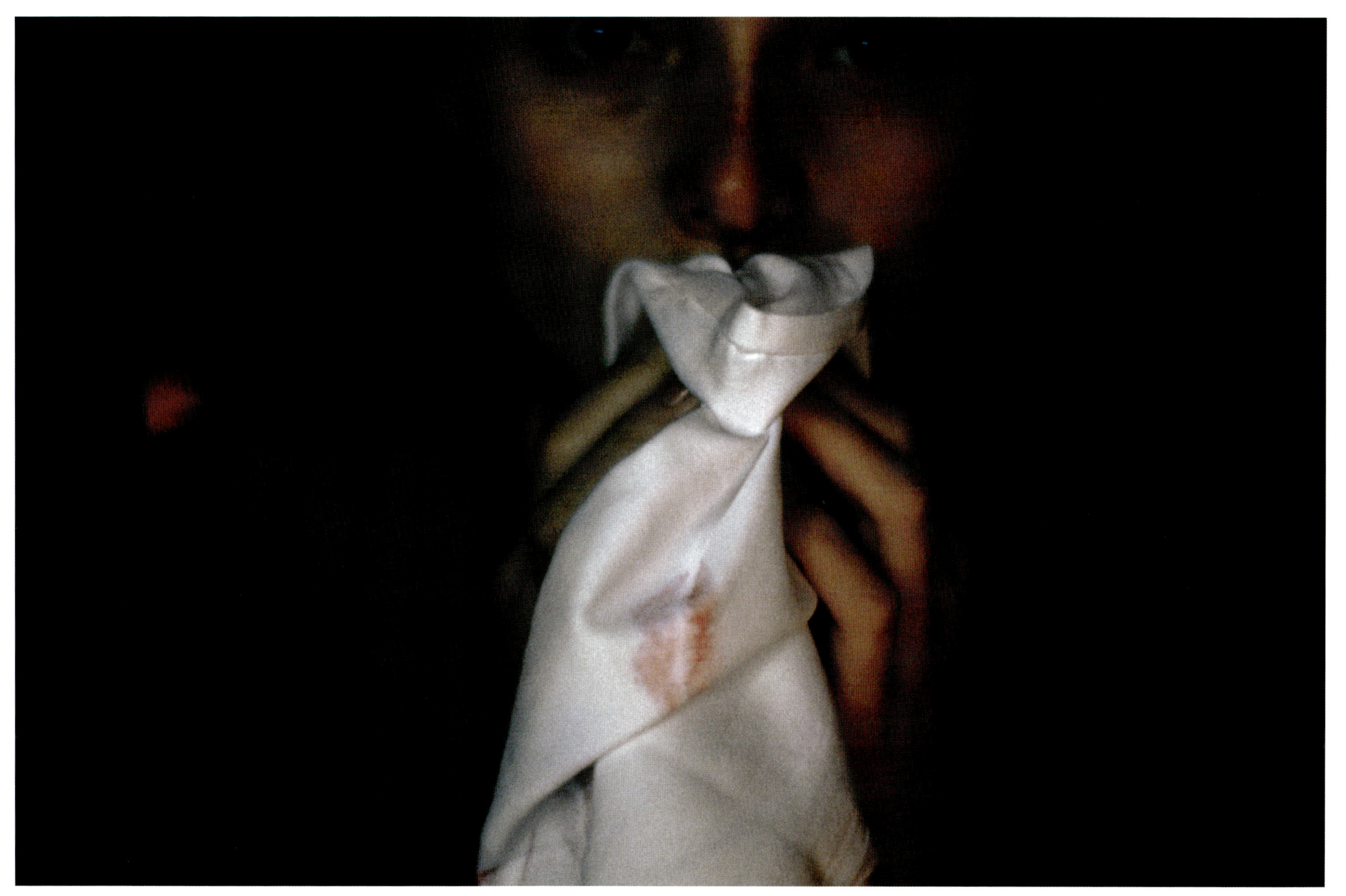

Model Tanya Pohlkotte, Paris, 1988

"...a slender, tortuously twisted and charred tree trunk stood, almost defiant..."

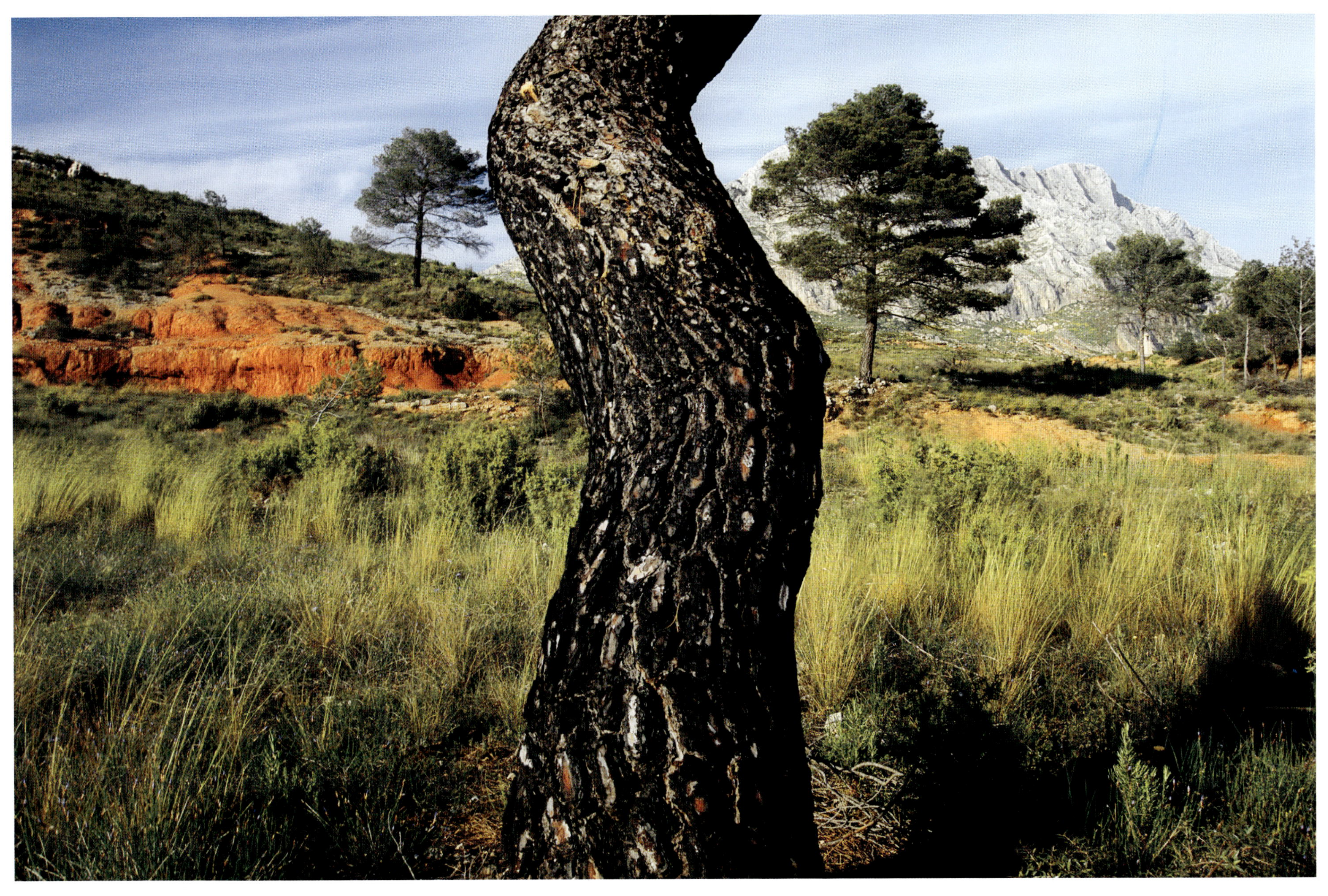

Twisted tree, Aix-en-Provence, 1993

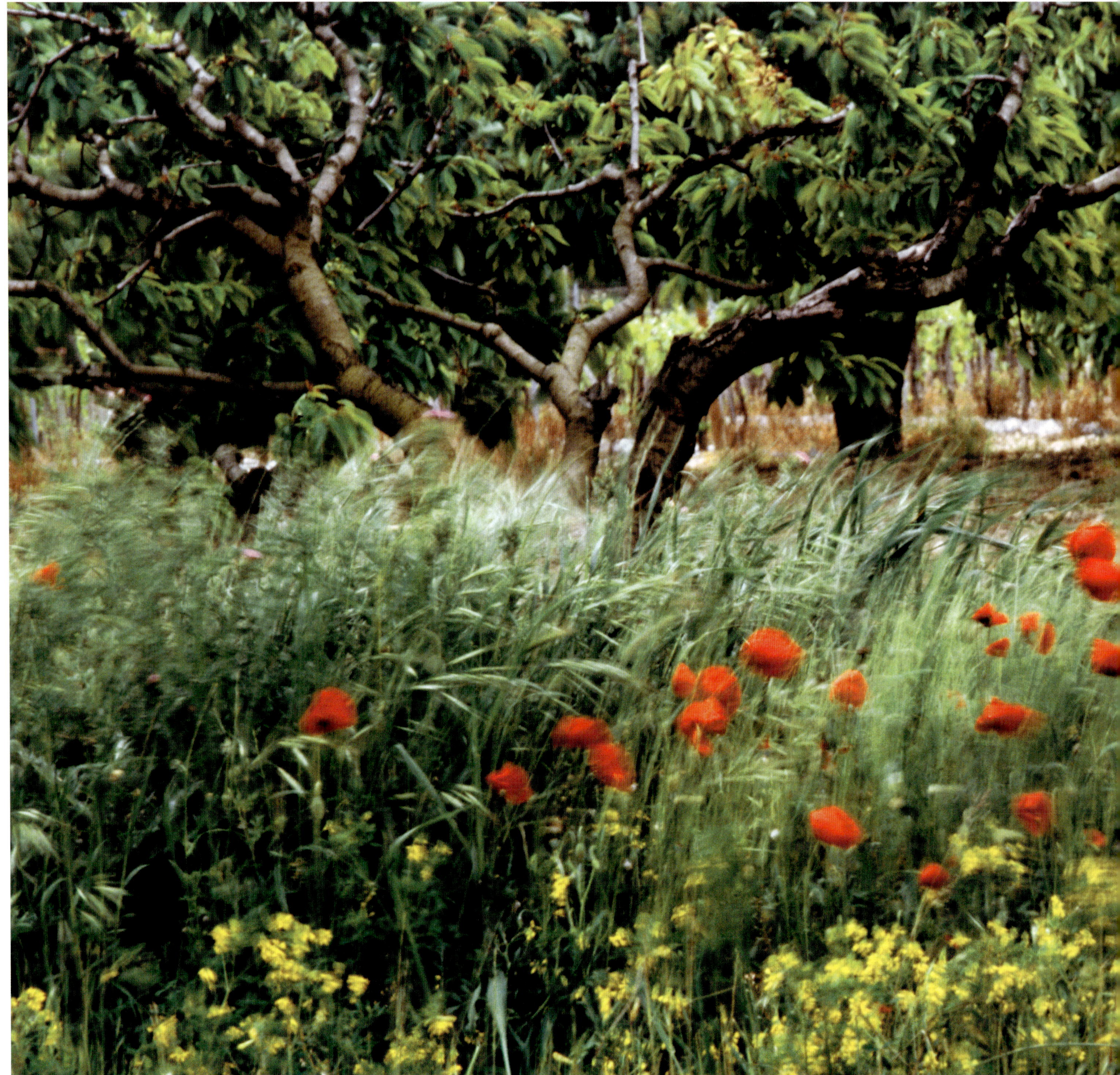

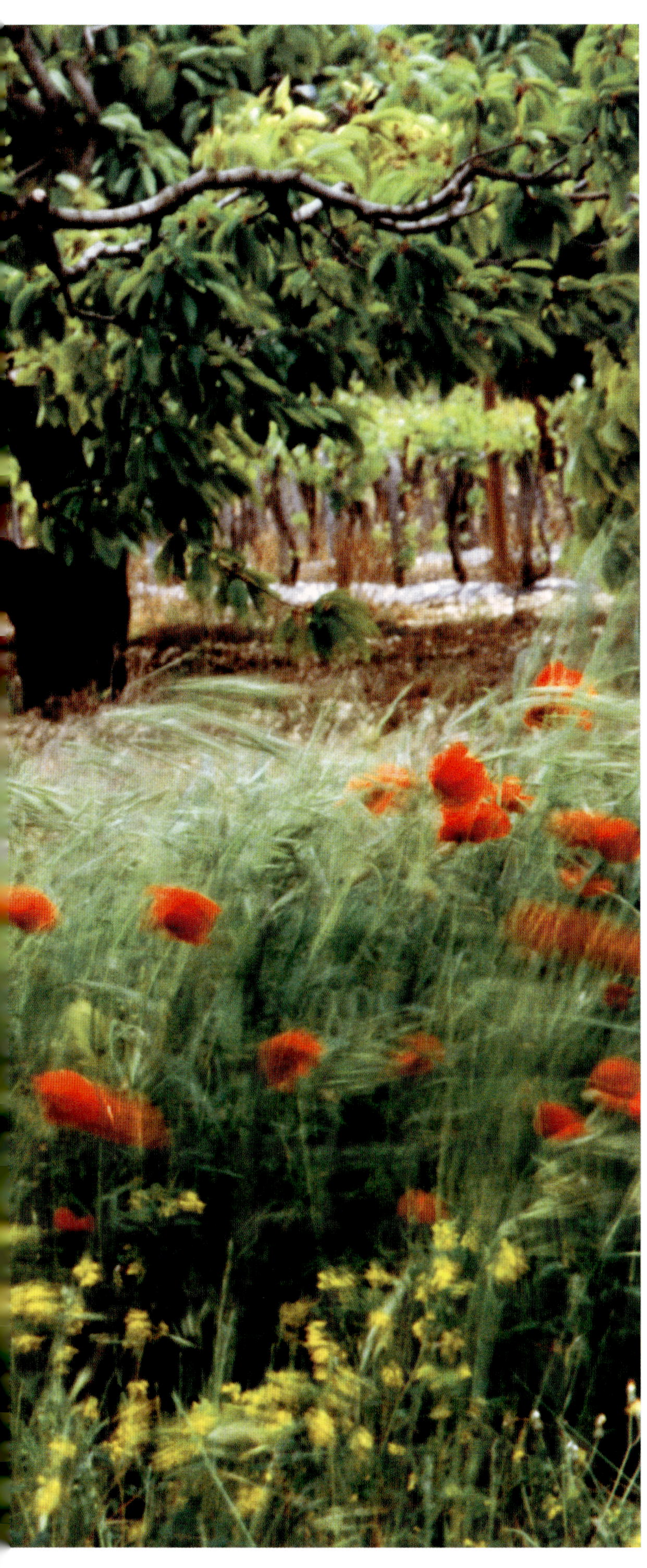

Poppies, Provence, 1993

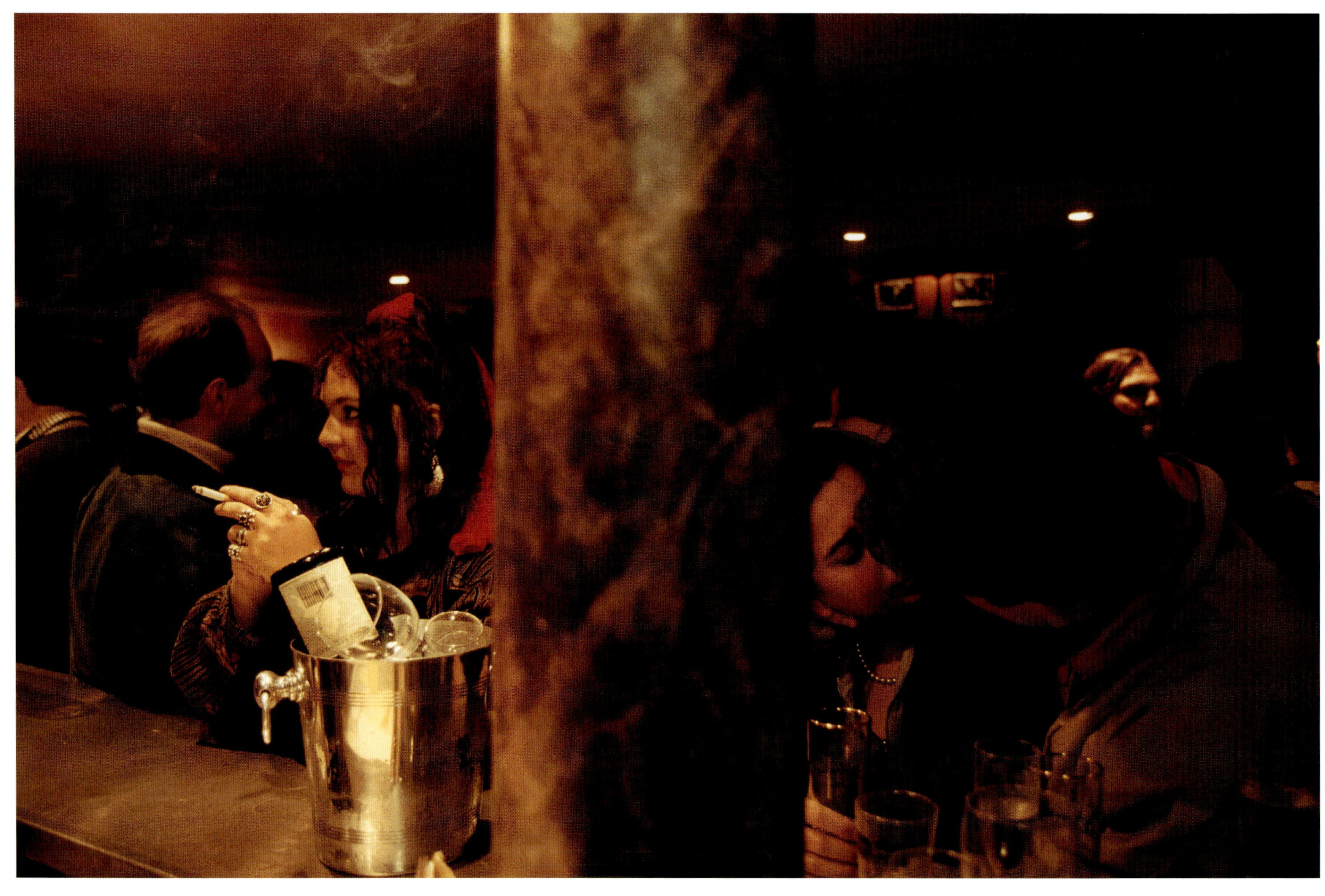

Café Van Gogh, Arles, 1993

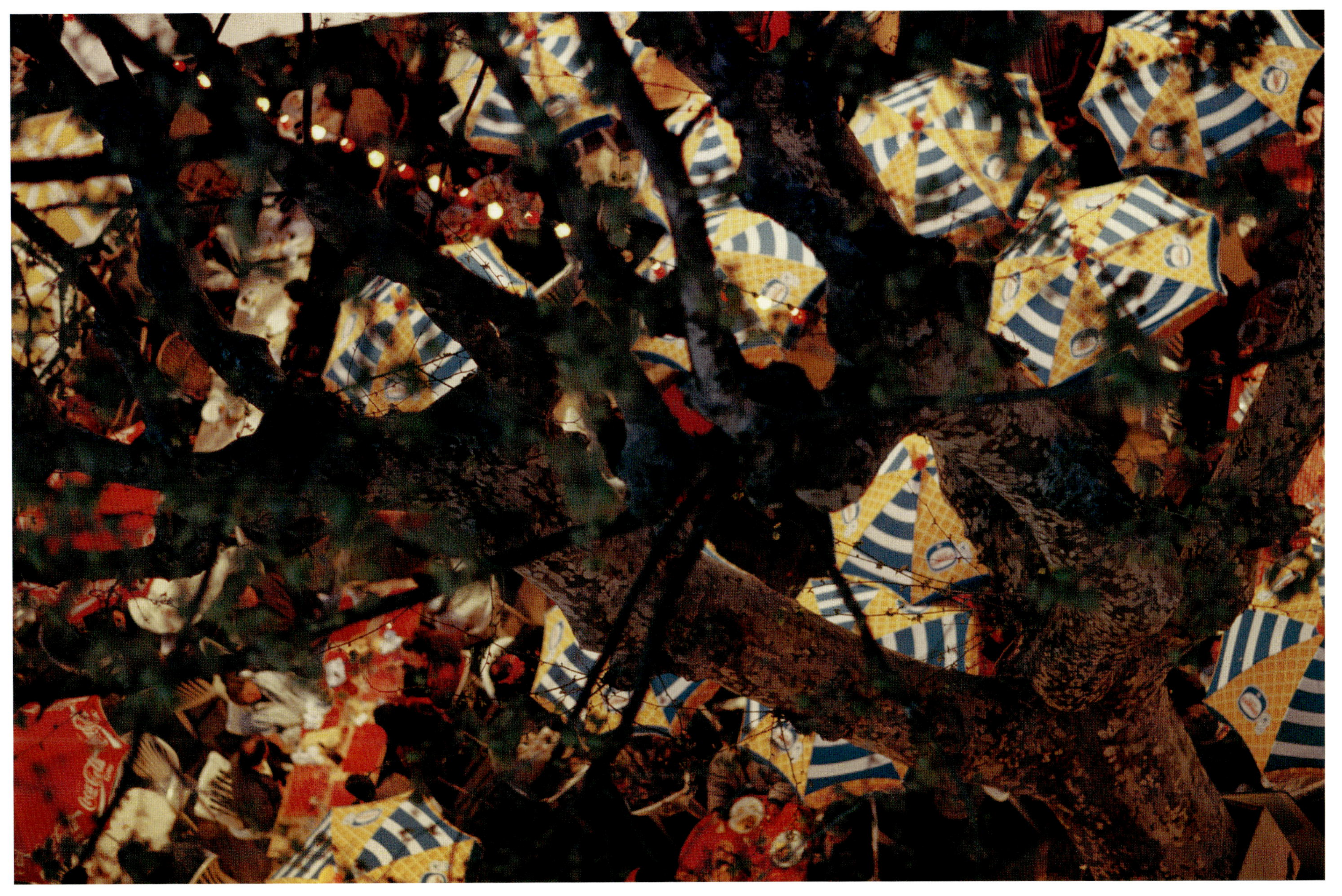

Place du Forum, Arles, 1993

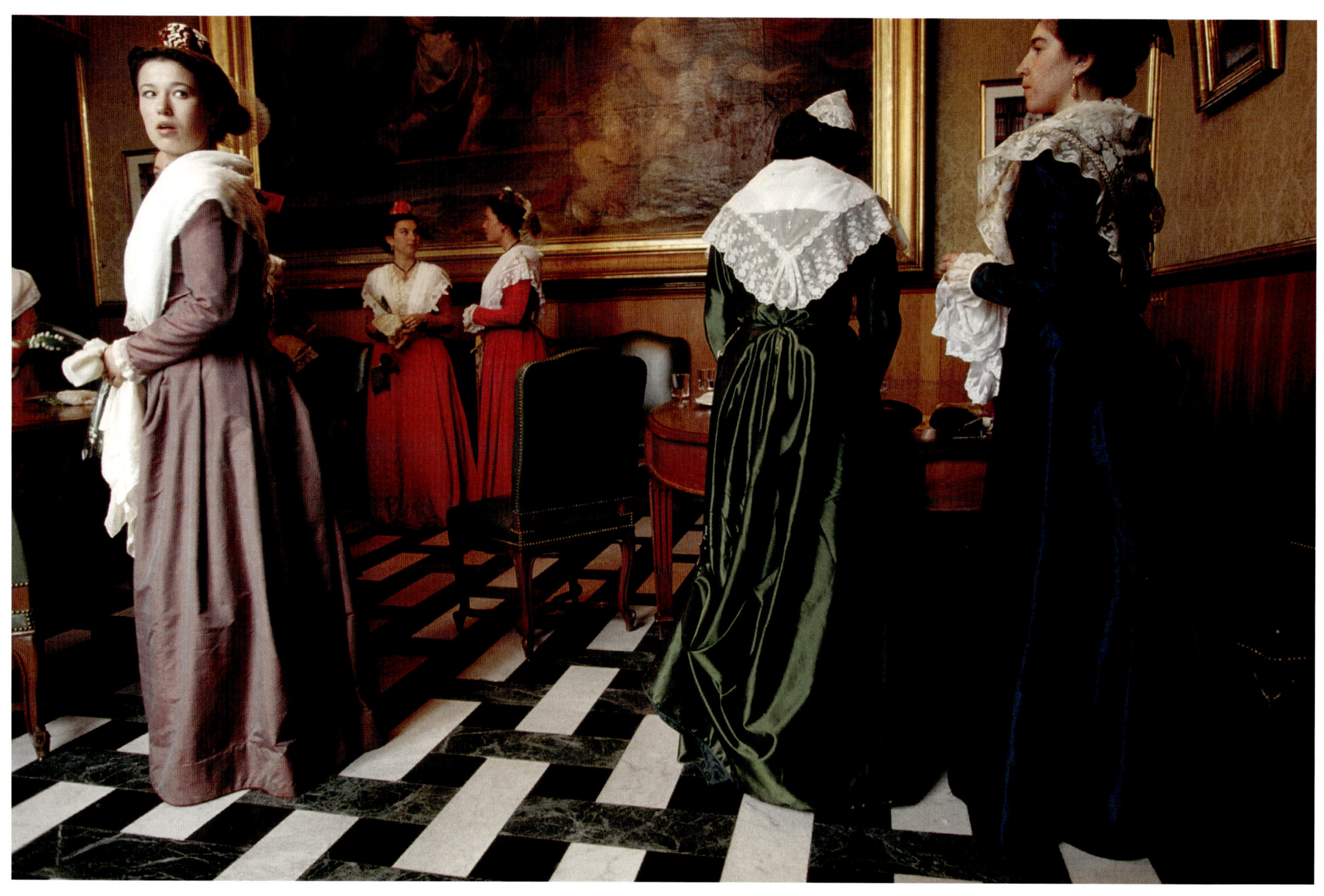

Candidates for Queen of Arles, Arles, 1993

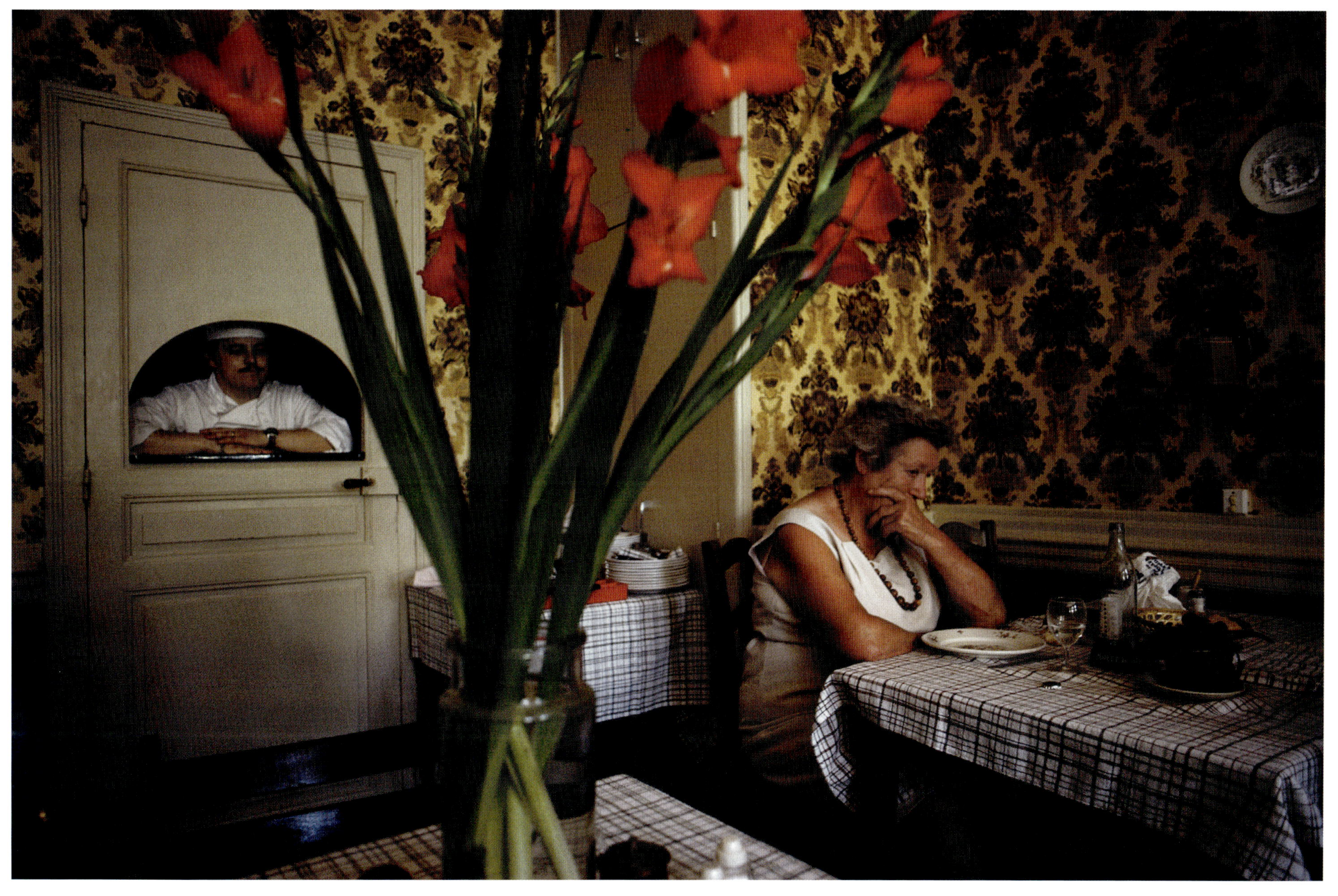

Gladiolus on café table, Provence, 1993

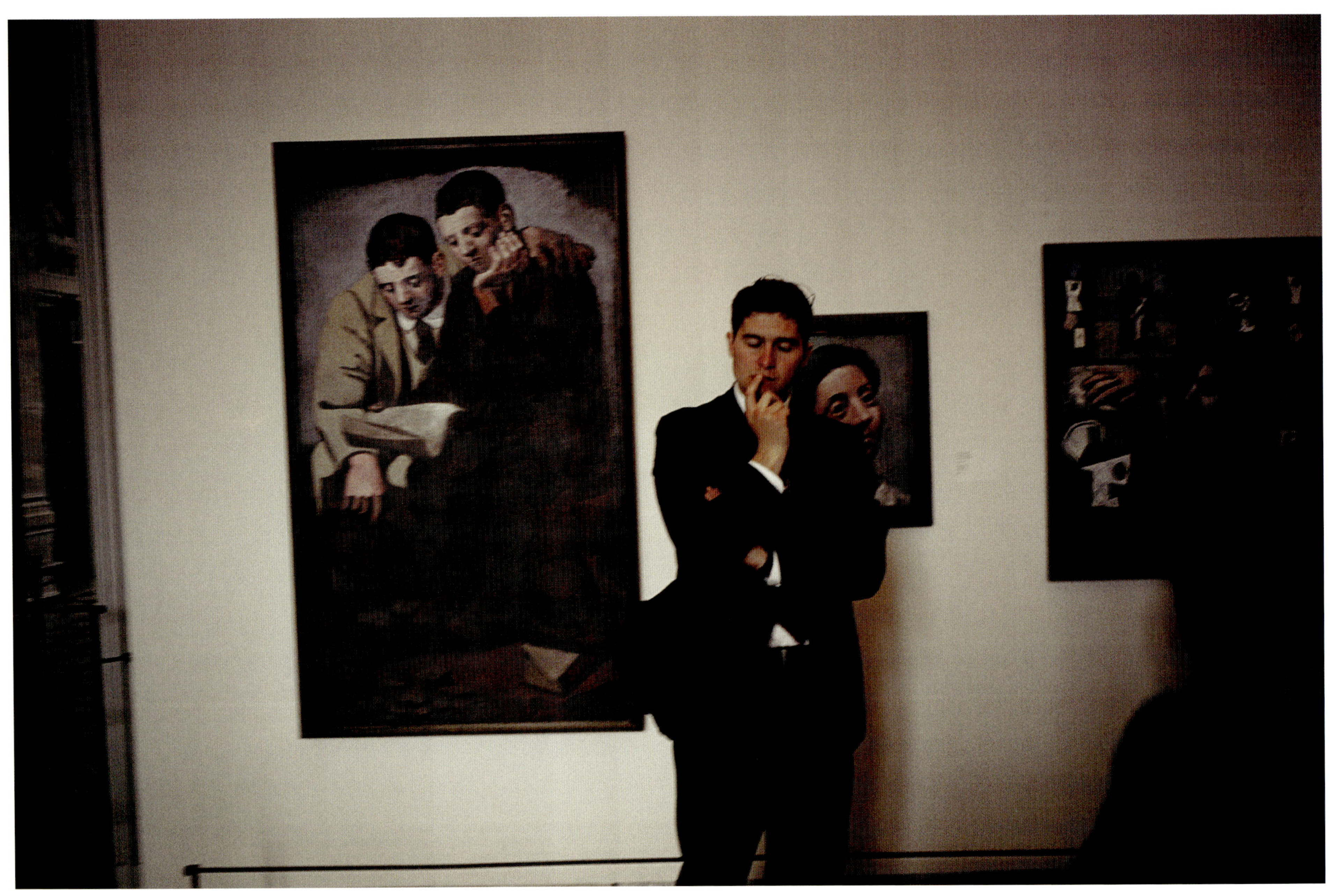

Museum Picasso, Le Marais, Paris, 2002

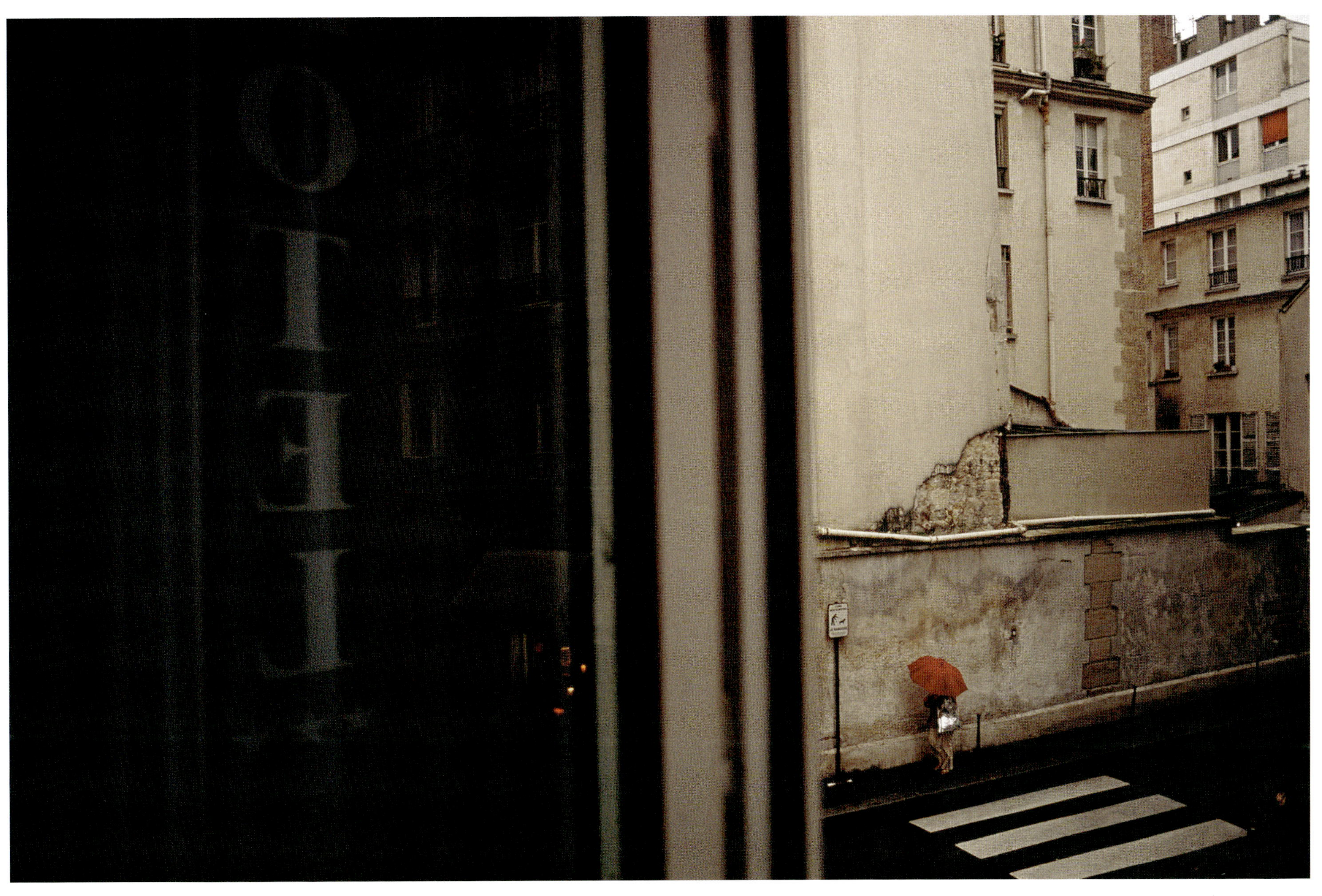

Outside my window, Le Marais, Paris, 2002

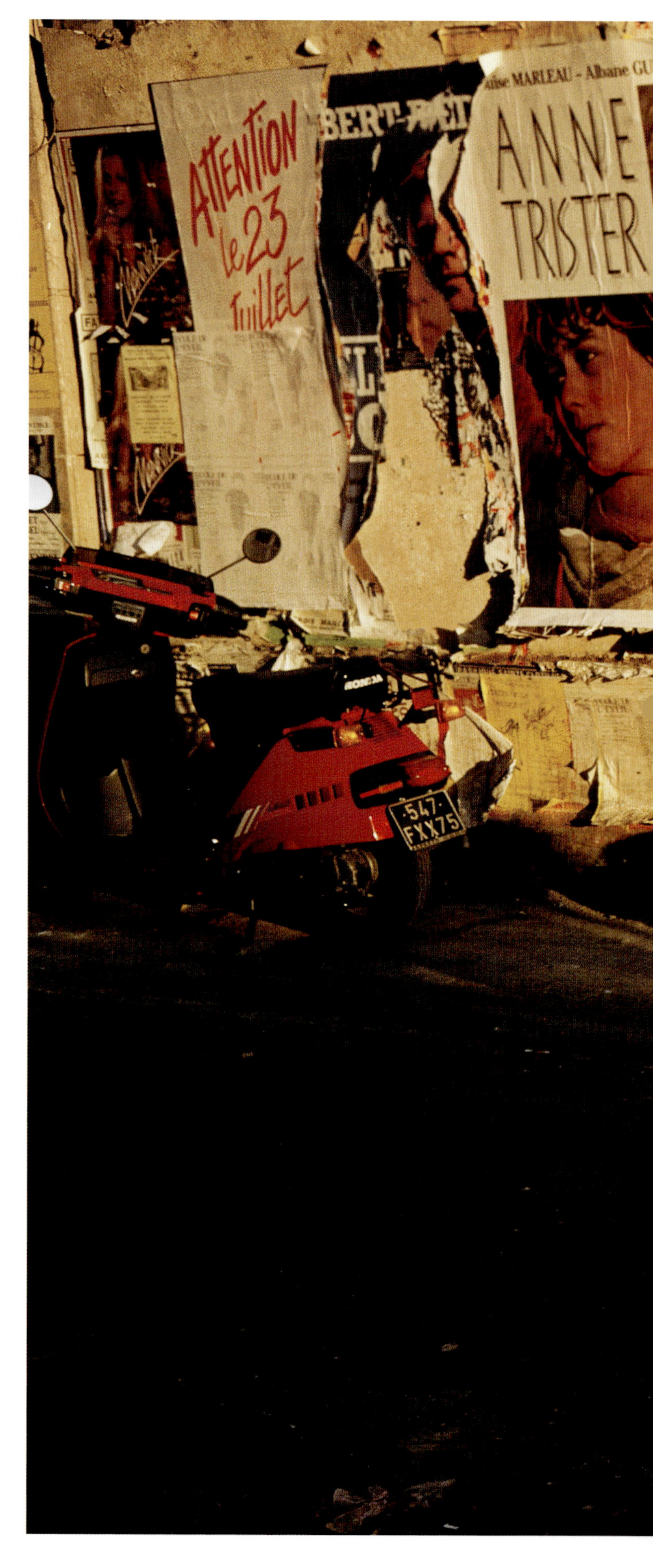

Street artists, Paris, 1986

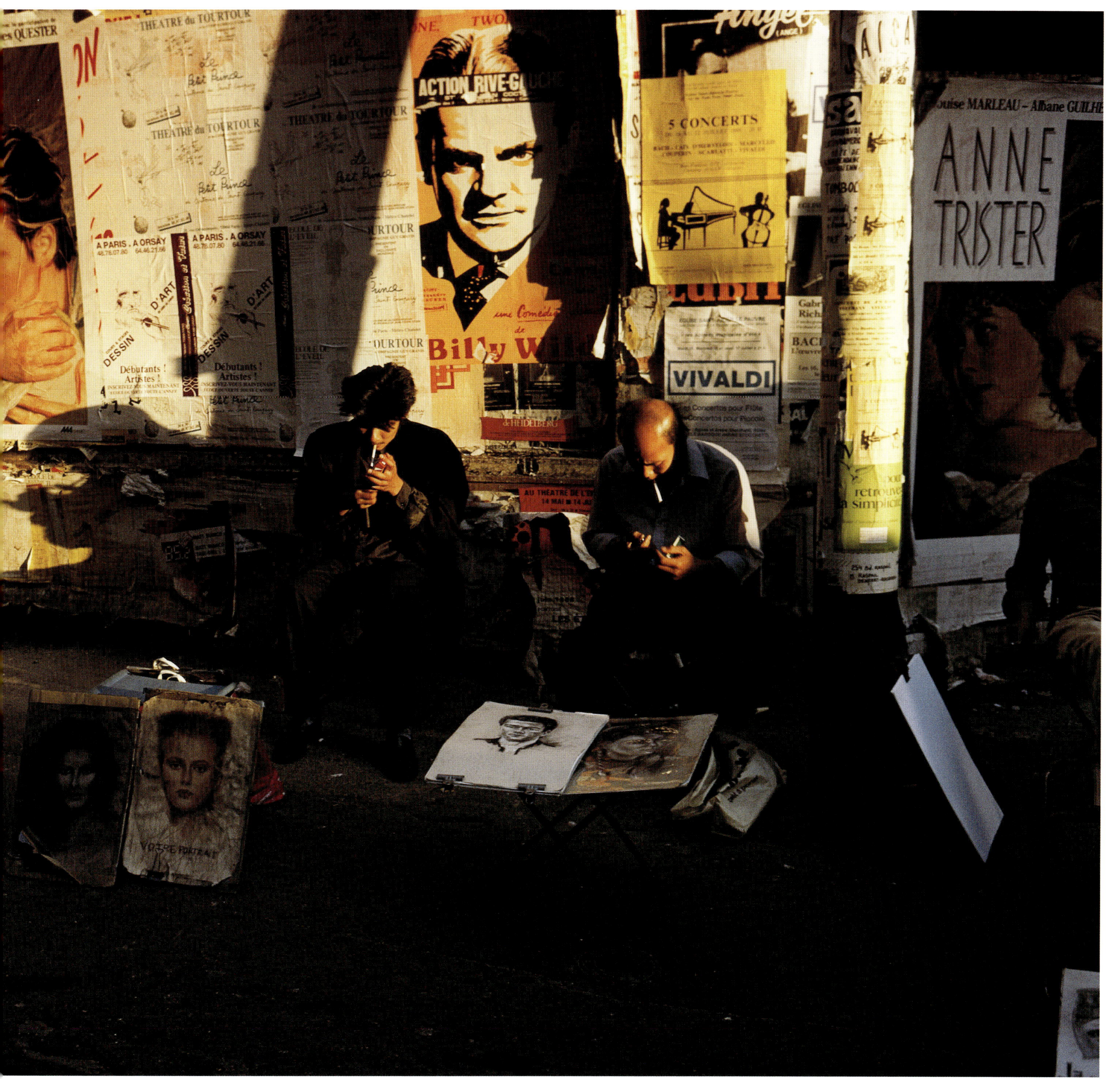

THEATRE du TOURTOUR
Le Petit Prince
A PARIS . A ORSAY
48.78.07.80 64.46.21.66
DESSIN
Débutants !
Artistes !
5 CONCERTS
VIVALDI
ANNE
TRISTER
de HEIDELBERG
VOTRE PORTRAIT

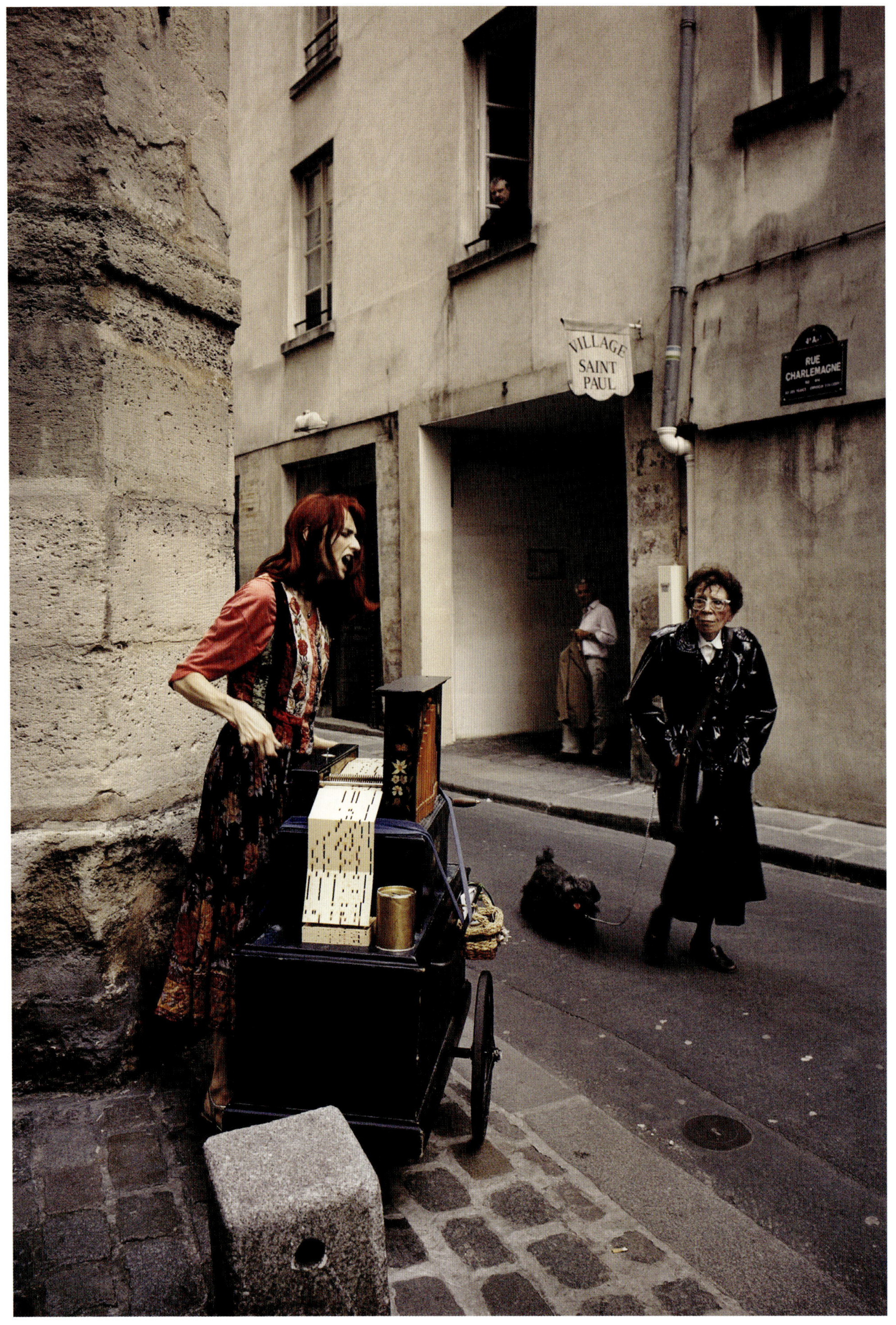
VILLAGE
SAINT
PAUL
RUE
CHARLEMAGNE

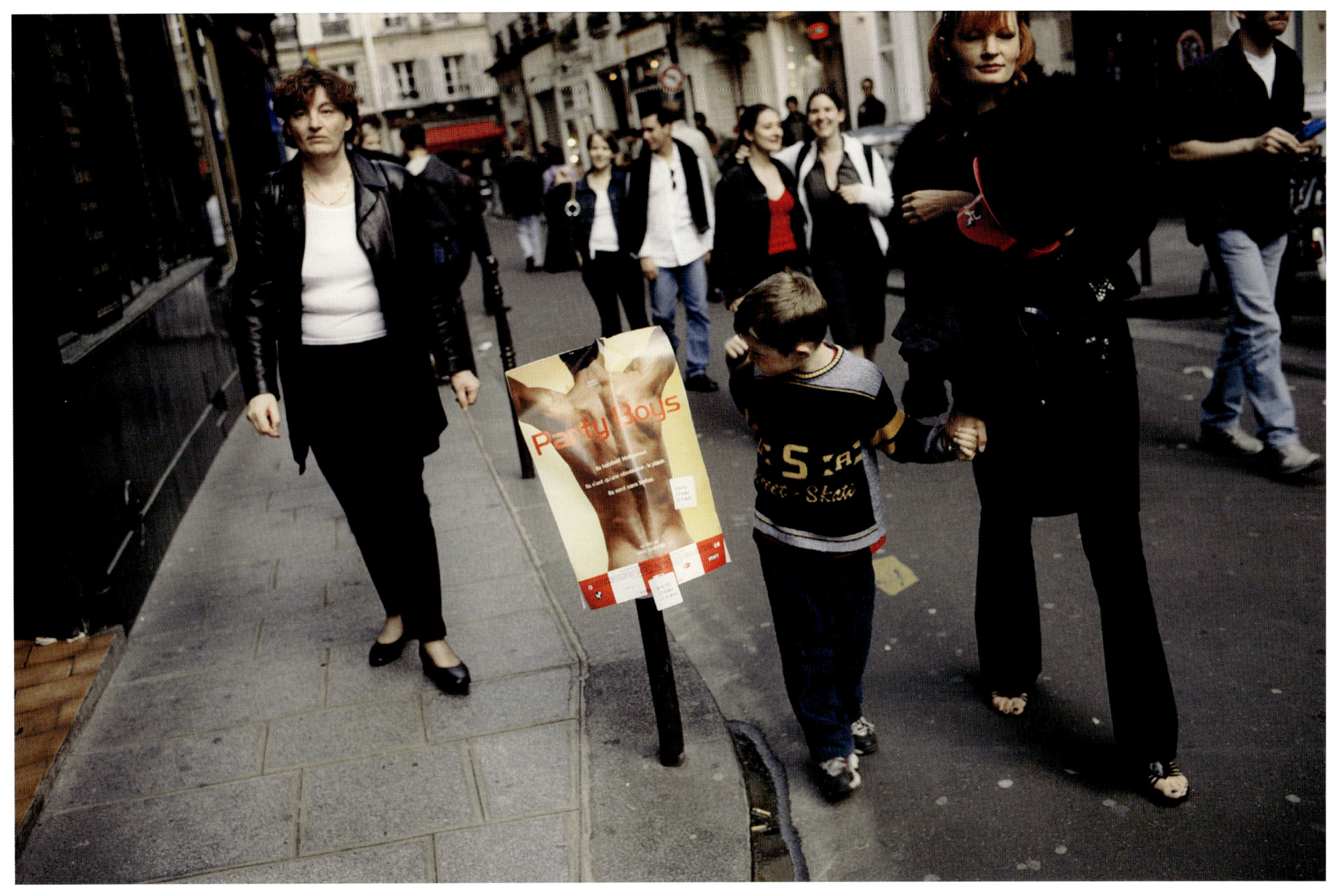

LEFT: *Street performer Dominique Alavoine, Le Marais, Paris, 2002* ABOVE: *Gay entertainment poster, Le Marais, Paris, 2002*

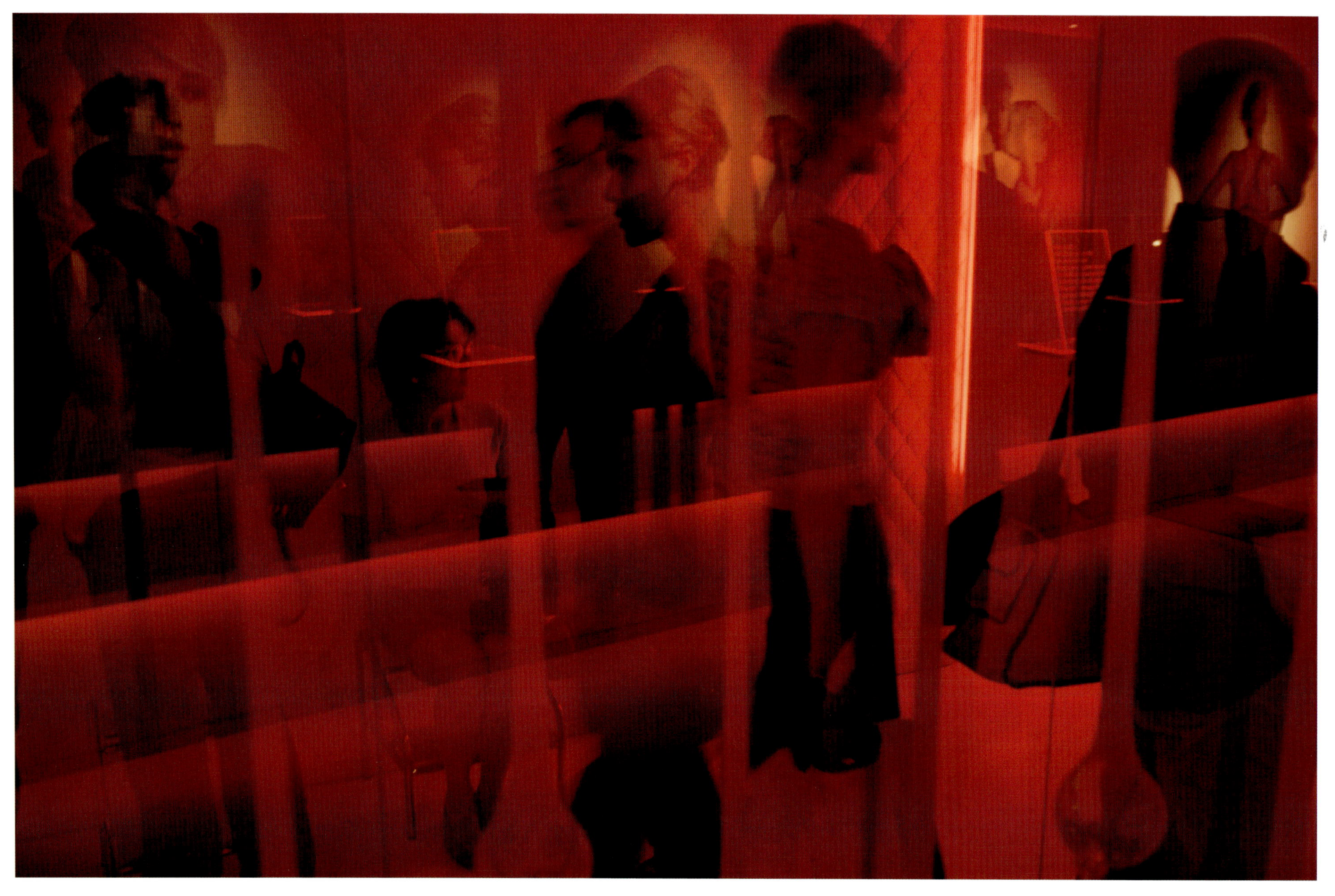

Gallery opening, Le Marais, Paris, 2002

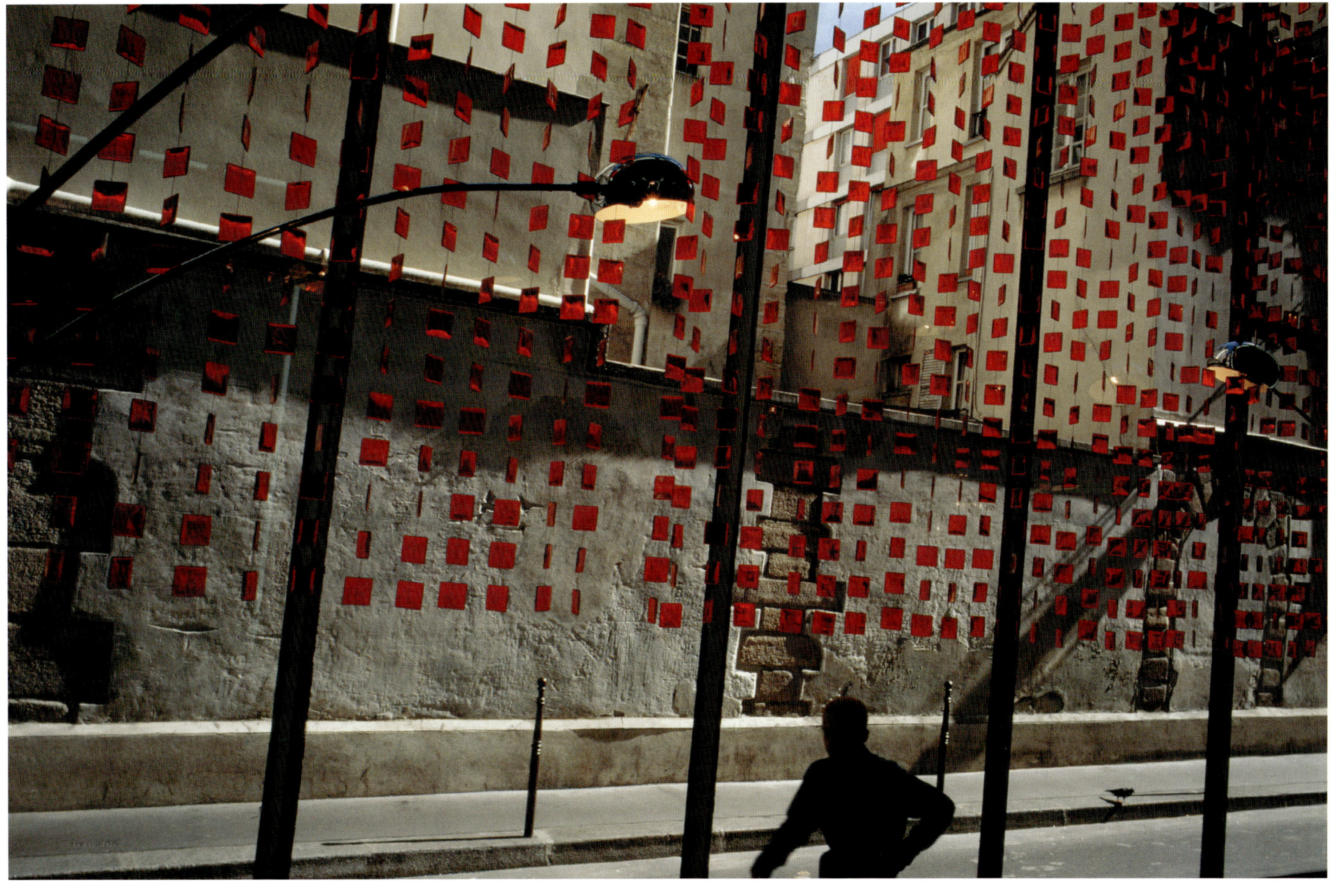

Design shop window, Le Marais, Paris, 2002

"On Sunday afternoons I might go by the synagogue to see if there were going to be any weddings. Jewish wedding parties always welcomed my unexpected appearances."

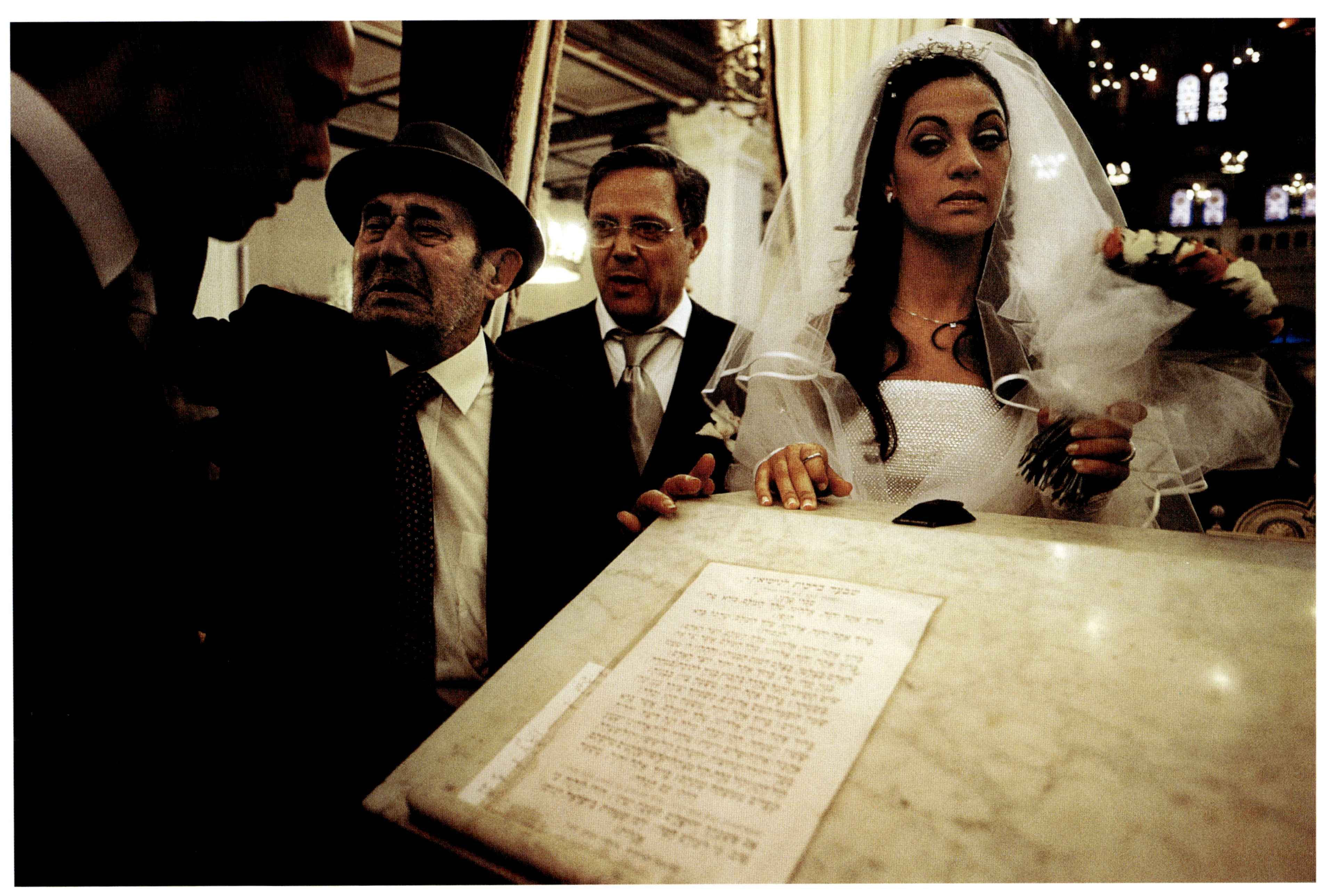

Jewish wedding, Le Marais, Paris, 2002

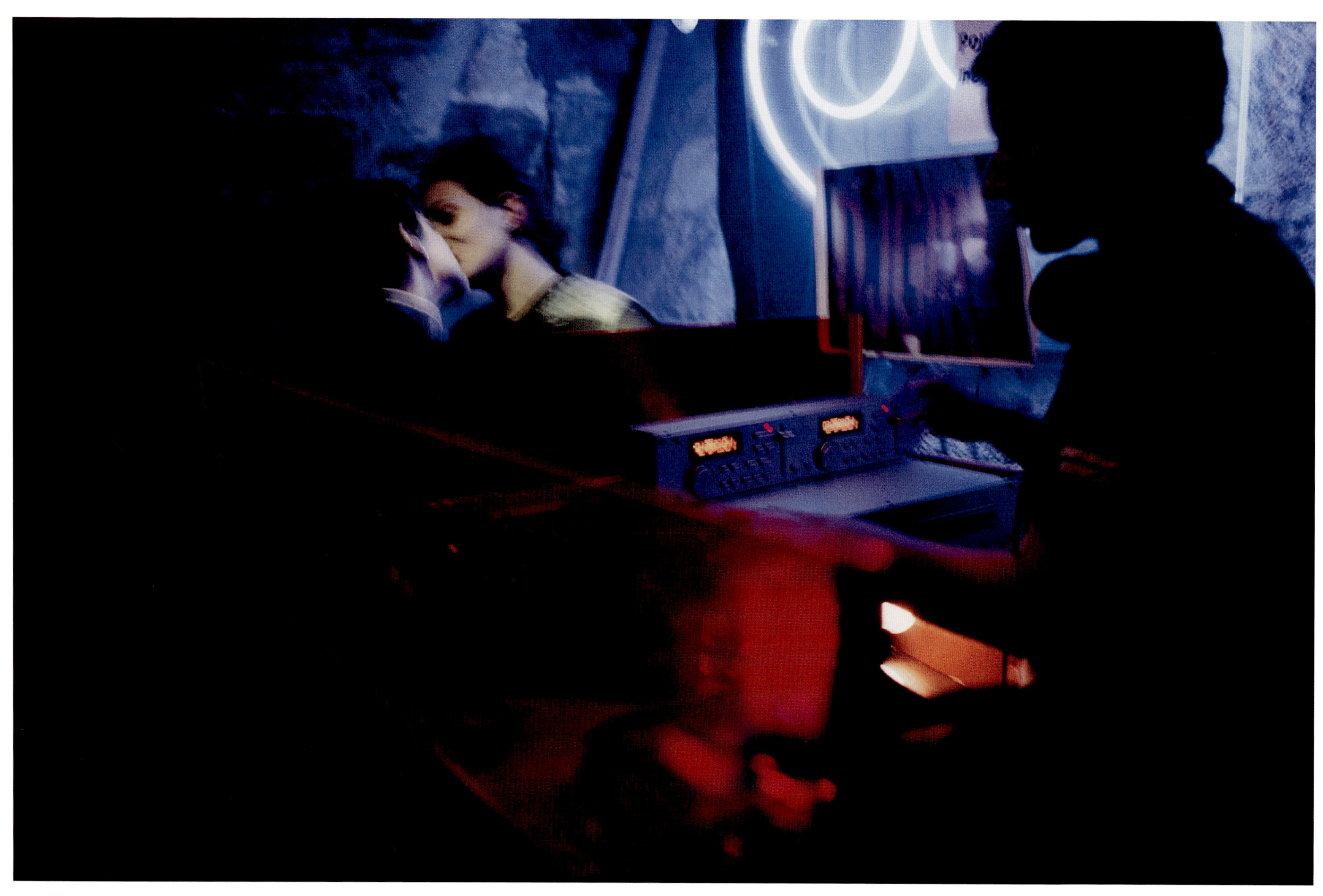

Bar Les Scandaleuses, Le Marais, Paris, 2002

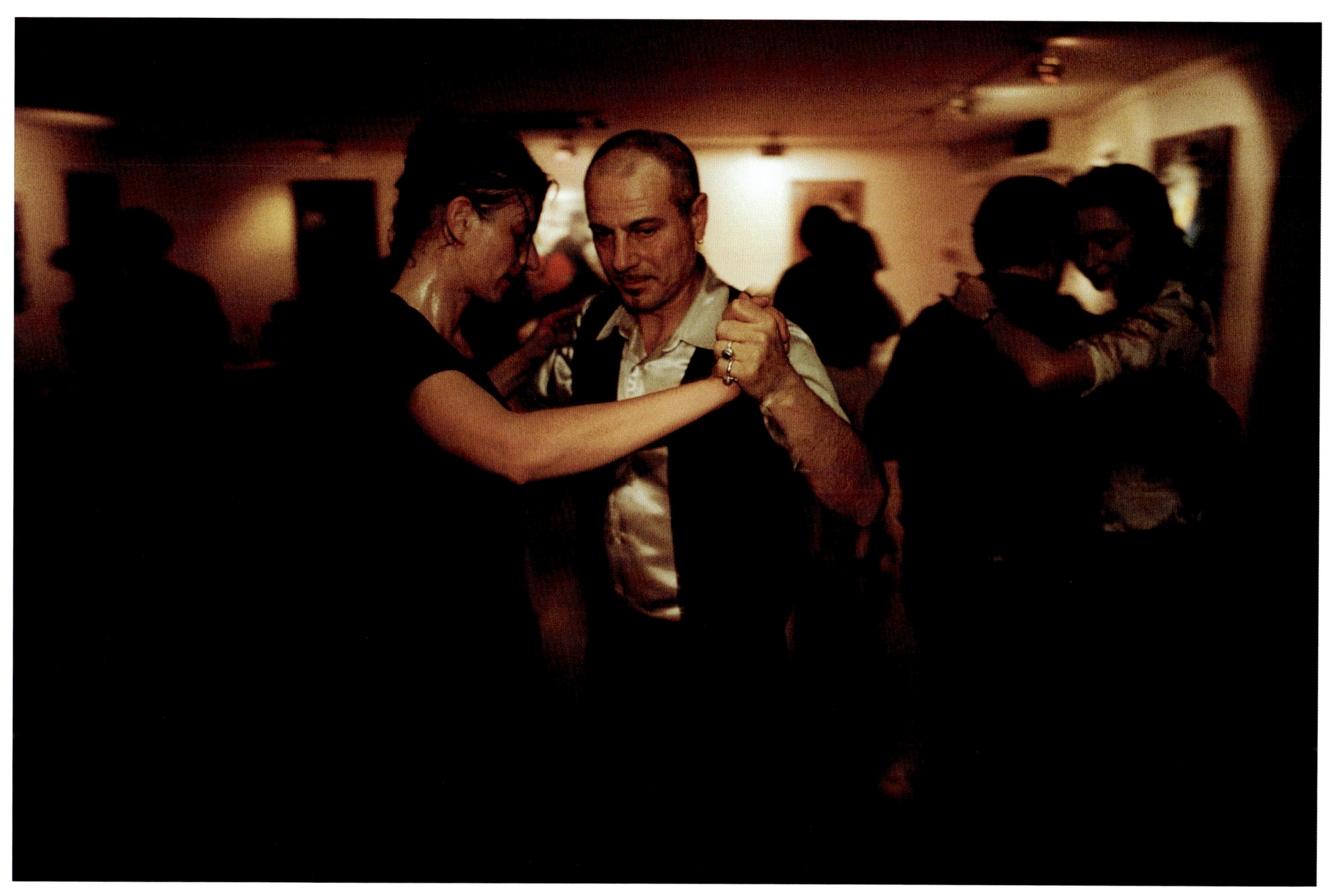

Tango dancers, Bistro Latin, Le Marais, Paris, 2002

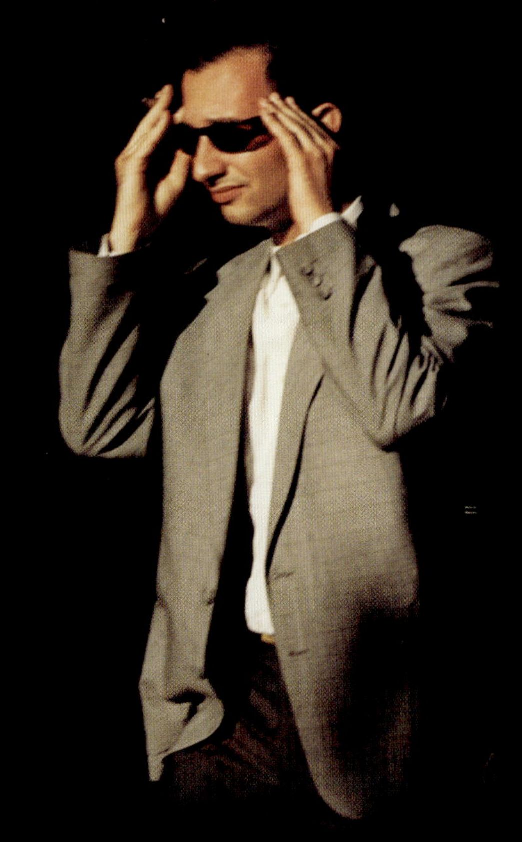

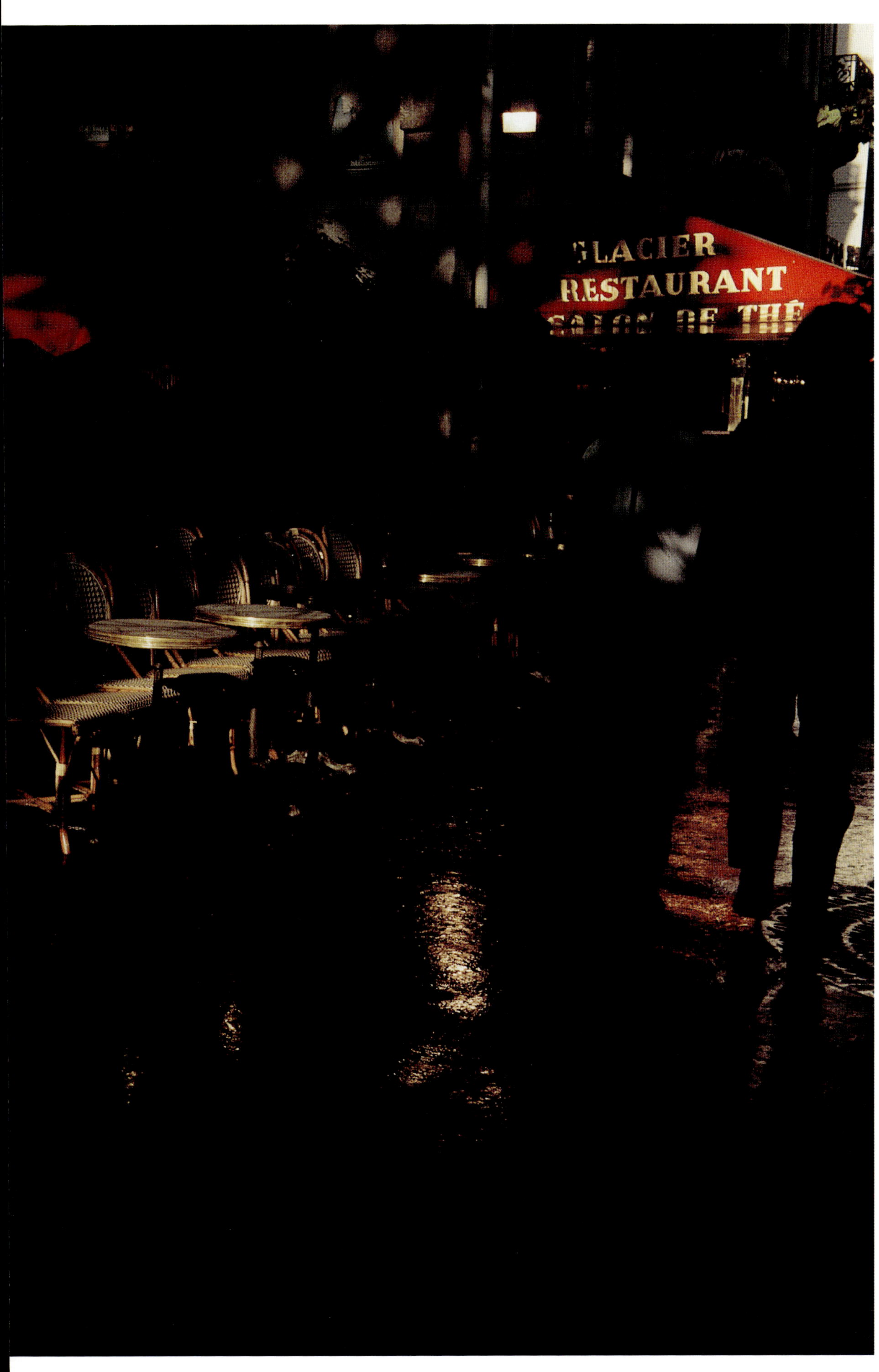

Boulevard St.-Germain, Paris, 1986

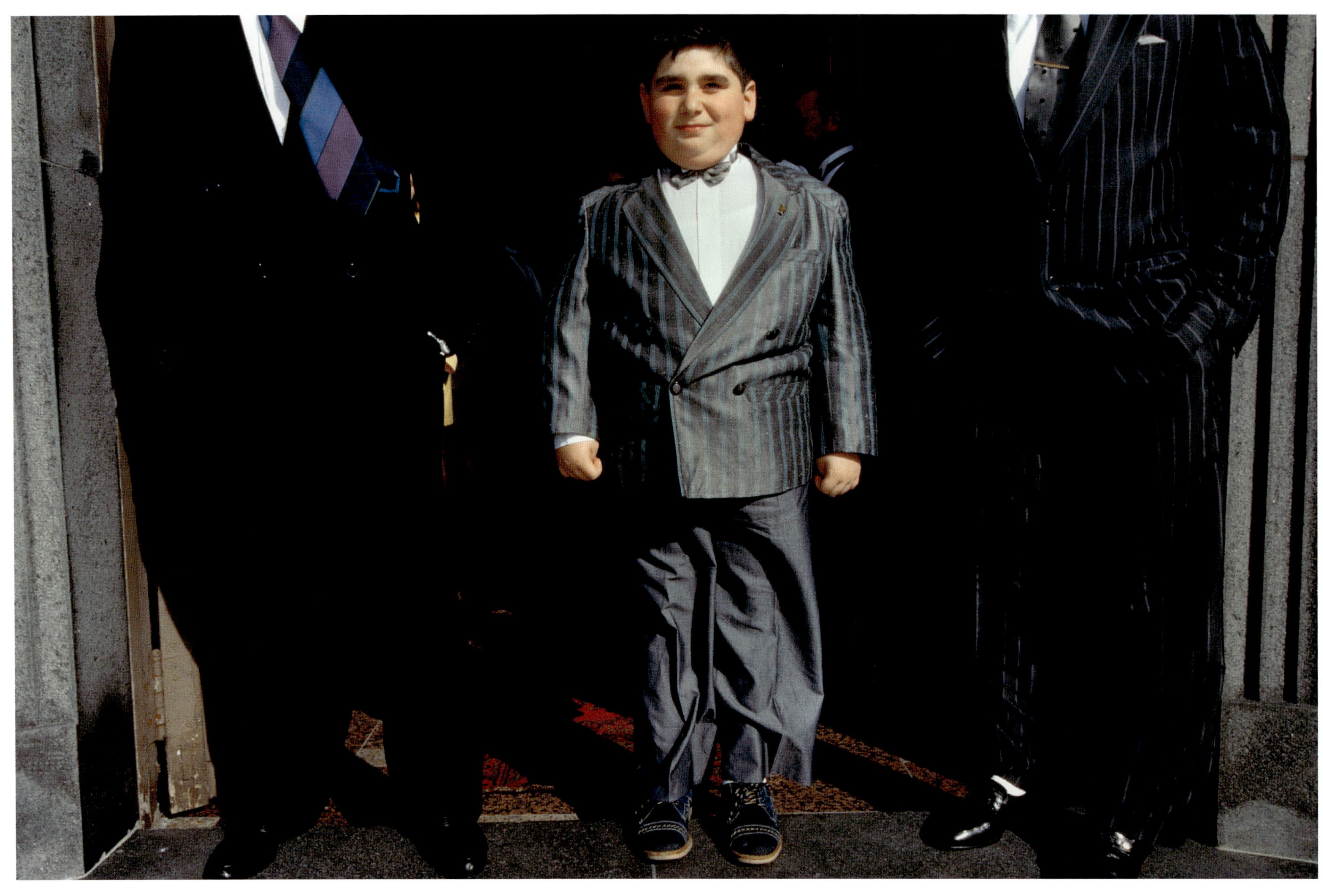

Calogero Amoroso, Sciacca, Sicily, 1994

Notes From Italy

Considering I haven't really seen that much of the country, why is it that Italy appeals to me so? I have never been to Rome, except through the airport on my way to somewhere else. Nor have I seen Naples or Milan.

I have been to Venice. I have been to Florence and Siena, to Pisa and Cortona, and many of the smaller towns that make up the alluring Tuscany. I've been to that stretch of northern Italy along the Po River. And I've been to Sicily. Still, there is much of the country I haven't experienced.

I first went to Italy in 1966 to photograph Venice for a National Geographic book about the Renaissance. I lived in a Geographic-rented ultramodern apartment with orange carpets and orange furniture, all totally out of sync with the subject at hand and yet a kind of retreat from all the splendorous antiquity and the tourists. I spent about a month in the city.

I didn't return to Italy until well into the 1980s, to teach photographic workshops in Tuscany, which I continued to do into the coming decades. In 1994 I was given a *National Geographic* magazine assignment to photograph Sicily. And in 2001 I returned to Italy once more for the *Geographic* to photograph the region of the Po River. I'd return to any of those places, especially Sicily—or for that matter, anywhere in Italy—in a heartbeat.

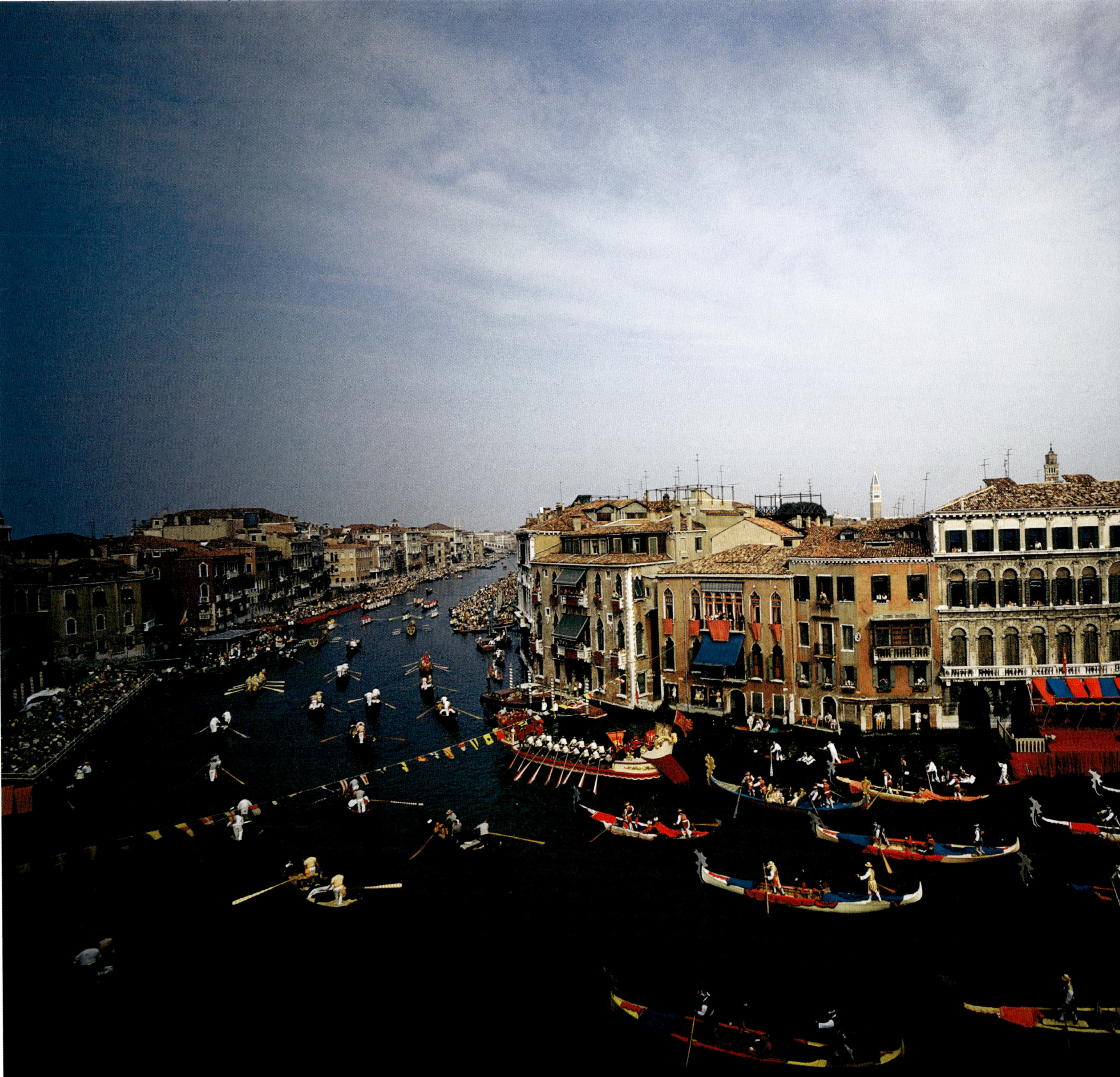

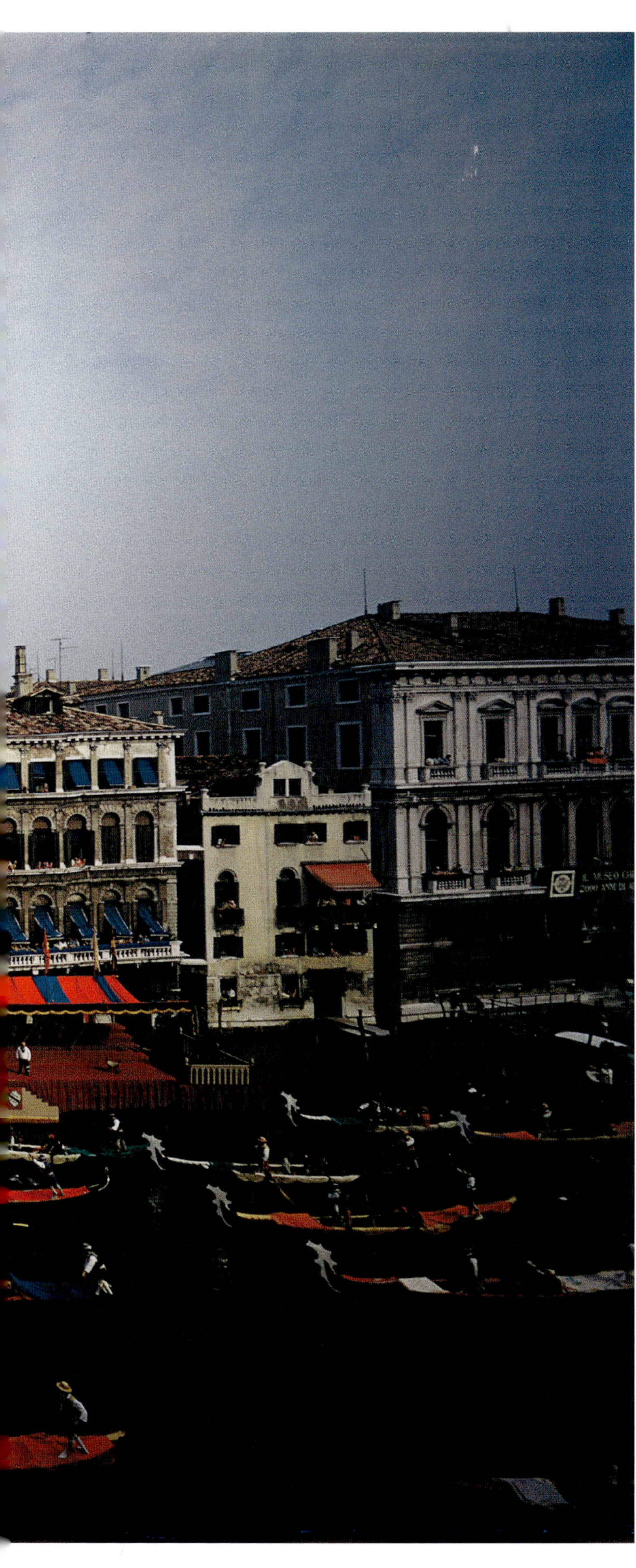

Regatta, Grand Canal, Venice, 1969

Well, as those of you who share my sentiments for the country might be thinking, Welcome to the club. Italy just seems to have that kind of appeal for a lot of people. While Paris remains my favorite city of any in the world I've seen, and I like France in general, I'll take Italy as a favorite country. There are many possible reasons: Maybe it's the food, the wine, the people and their language, the beautiful women, the magnificent duomos, the piazzas, the laughter and the street life—there is all of that and much more that in the end isn't really explicable; it's just Italy.

I LEFT THE 1994 *National Geographic* assignment to photograph a story about Sicily, thinking its offerings must be one of the best-kept secrets in world travel. True, it has a deserved reputation for being a place that can be harsh, with cities exhibiting their share of mean streets, and with a historically murderous Mafia. But fortunately, those are sides of Sicily the average traveler is not likely to confront.

Sicily abounds in antiquity, with ruins remaining from many invaders and occupiers. The streets of its cities and towns are alive, animated with humanity. Unlike parts of France, where it sometimes seems people are hidden away behind a wall somewhere, in Palermo, the people are out sitting on their front stoops or leaning from their small flowerpotted balconies that jut out over narrow streets where laundry lines dangle in competition with soccer banners, and the air is filled with an exchange of neighborly taunts and humor. At its best it is Italian theater, where everyone is in the play.

The food was often simply superb. Seafood? Well, this is the largest island in the Mediterranean. What would one think? In the spring I found marinated baby octopus almost addictive.

ON ONE OF MY TRIPS, I was in the Rome airport, transferring some equipment bags, when I was approached by two policemen.

"Where are you going to?" one of them asked.

"Palermo," I answered. "Sicily."

Their response was a pair of frowns, disapproving, evidently, of my destination.

"I love Sicily," I told them. "It's a wonderful place." Again, frowns.

"No!" one answered emphatically. "Is a bad place. No good."

It was apparent there was no way I would convince them otherwise, and I thanked them for their interest and we parted ways. To this day I believe I was right and they were wrong. True, it's their country and they know infinitely more about it than I do, but it seems in Italy that the farther north you go, the more the Italians look down on anything south of them, and Sicily, of course, is at the bottom. But it's at the top of my list of places in the world I'd like to see again.

"MASSIMO," I SAID, "LET'S GO up to that church. It might be a good place to look down on the town." Massimo Bassano, a young man from southern Italy, was assisting me as my interpreter and driver on my assignment to photograph Sicily. It was spring.

Close to our destination of Sciacca, we'd seen a church perched high upon a hill overlooking the town. When we got to the top, we discovered people in a wedding party waiting in the church doorway for the bride to arrive. Flanked by what may have been his father and maybe an uncle, a boy dressed in his double-breasted Sunday best stood staunchly and proudly as I took his picture. A ferocious wind was blowing, and the boy's trousers were pressed hard against his legs. I looked at him and thought he looked like he could someday be the mayor of this town or maybe immigrate to the United States and run some kind of business in New Jersey.

MASSIMO AND I SPENT TIME on the island of Favignana, where for centuries Sicilian men have trapped in nets and hauled from the bloodied water with gaff hooks the valuable bluefin tuna. In years past some fish caught in *la mattanza* surpassed 500 pounds, but the annual take and the size of the fish are diminishing. Today almost all the bluefin tuna harvested and transported on ice-filled barges to the main island town of Trapani are butchered by Japanese crews wielding huge axlike blades and razor-sharp knives on blood-slick floors littered with sightless severed tuna heads. The meat is then shipped to Japan.

IN OLD PALERMO, people living in the poor, rough-edged Albergheria neighborhood displayed their laundry on lines strung from the windows. Sizable white underwear flared in the breeze like strange large birds taking flight. In the city's main market of Vucciria, Massimo and I wandered the maze of isles threaded by shops and stands that offer almost anything: fish fresh from the sea that morning; half a swordfish with its rapier-like bill; slain goats, still wearing their hides, hung in rows above pyramids of various fruits. I watched and photographed a double image of a shopkeeper raising a candy-striped parasol to provide shade, using the mirror that faced his counter and showed him when someone was approaching. We stopped at a butcher shop that sold horsemeat and purchased two steaks. We took them to a market restaurant where they prepared them for our lunch. The meat was tender, lean, and sweeter than beef.

The afternoon of our first visit to the Vucciria market there was a Mafia killing only blocks away. We were jammed in traffic, and I jumped from our car to see why there were so many flashing police lights up ahead. I discovered a cluster of police at the side of a car, a plainclothes detective holding in his surgical-gloved hand a small handgun. There were two bullet holes in the window frame on the driver's side, and a long, slivery smear of blood swiped across the side of the car from when they must have removed the body.

Later during our assignment I went to a slaughterhouse that butchered horses. I'm not sure why; perhaps I wanted to compare the place with slaughterhouses I'd photographed in Peru. It was much more modern, much cleaner, and, if possible, less violent. I really didn't have the Mafia in mind; I wasn't thinking of the slaughtered horse head from *The Godfather*, although my picture of the horse being bled, with the worker in a white smock holding the knife behind his back as if hiding a weapon, seems to echo the ever present potential of violence represented by the Mafia and how embedded it is in everyday Sicilian life.

DURING EASTER WEEK Sicily's Easter processions are powerful displays of religious fervor and emotion. There were images everywhere, sometimes dramatic, often surreal. In Trapani there was a 24-hour procession with men from different social associations carrying religious icons through the streets; bands would play their brassy music, drummers rapping a staccato beat to drive them along. On Holy Thursday, before Good Friday, there was a "living procession," a tradition in Marsala since the 17th century. Three men wearing lifelike masks of papier-mâché played the role of Christ at different points on his way to the Crucifixion. A burly mustachioed man in a suit and tie, a crucifix draping his neck, led Jesus in his crown of thorns out of the church and into the streets of Marsala. The man looked off to one side as if surveying for possible trouble, gripping Jesus firmly by one arm, reminiscent to me, in some bizarre way, of the image of the lawman escorting Kennedy assassin Lee Harvey Oswald when he was shot by Jack Ruby.

RETURNING TO PALERMO from a day trip to the Greek ruins at Agrigento, I saw a landscape with layers of imagery. In the distance the low-lying hills caught some of the last sun of the afternoon; a house of some past century stood roofless near the edge of that sunlight; and in the middle distance, a passing cloud blotted out the sun, casting that area in shadow. Near us, along a fenced border, a band of sheep flowed past. I asked Massimo to stop. I dashed out into the grass in front of the fence, and then I saw the wildflowers. I grabbed a strobe light from my bag; narrowed the focus of the beam, trying to center the light on the blood-red blossoms and some of the greenery; and tried to balance all of the light variations in one proper exposure. We ended up using the picture as a three-page foldout in the published story. All of what I did regarding the composition, and the technical aspect of getting it on film, was pretty much subconscious, my reaction through practice and experience. There was no LCD monitor in the back of my Canon film camera to look at, nothing to refer to. There simply wasn't enough time to think it all out, to debate with myself about what to do. There often isn't—by the time you do, the picture is usually gone.

ON THE AFTERNOON OF A FESTIVAL in the village of Alcara li Fusi I drank beer outside a café and watched a young waitress in a polka-dot minidress tend tables where old men in coats and ties and caps sat smoking cigarettes and talking, probably about politics or maybe soccer. Their wives were most likely at home. The contrast between those old men, with their sunbaked faces, and the young waitress, her shoulders bared, her legs exposed to the edge of her thighs, was a picture of the passage of time. In the years of their youth, none of those men would ever have seen a girl dressed as this fair young one was. But in the cities of Sicily, and even in the villages, the passage of time was evident; some social mores, at least in the manner of dress, are changing. However, one is still probably wise not to look too hard or too long at any young woman passing by if she's with someone who might be her father or perhaps her boyfriend. But the young women of today's Sicily are definitely giving one increasingly more reason to look.

I AM IN SIENA IN TUSCANY on a blue-sky day sometime in the 1990s. I'm teaching a workshop in Cortona, and we always include at least one trip to Siena for the students. At the magnificent duomo, people are waiting for the door to open after lunch, most of them standing or squatting across the street from the steps. But just outside the broad wooden door on the right, a young blond woman waits as if determined to be the first to enter. Her light-colored skirt catches the sun. She's not pretty, but attractive. Her skirt is patterned with the words KISS ME, many times, in large, red letters. When a man in a shirt open at the throat unlocks and opens the door to the duomo, she walks sprightly through to a side lighted by candles and kneels quickly, then walks over to the first confessional booth, takes a seat on the bench, puts on glasses, retrieves a magazine from her purse, and reads, waiting for a priest. She wears open-toed, high-heeled sandals. Her toenails are painted steel gray, highlighted with silver glitter that catches the light. The air is filled with the smell of candle wax.

IN CORTONA, ITALIAN SCHOOLGIRLS—some of them blond, some smoking cigarettes and chattering, hands fluttering like doves in flight—stride along the narrow Via Nazionale and cross the Piazza della Repubblica. A shaft of early morning sunlight cuts a swath along the street, bathing their hair in gold. Some of the youngest in the group wear backpacks of orange and black, yellows and reds. Blue clouds of cigarette smoke rise above the bus stop, where clusters of these barely pubescent children mingle on their way to class. The sun beams like a spotlight through the darkness of a narrow side street, flashing briefly on the faces of passersby. Restaurant workers carry cartons of fresh produce; a butcher steps out of his doorway and stands like a lighthouse in his white shirt and apron.

IN SIENA, NEAR THE PIAZZA, I hear two American men, they sound like New Yorkers, at a sidewalk café table, discussing Italian women passing by, some displaying those clear plastic bra straps they wear with backless dresses.

"The one with the really nice ass . . . ," says one of the men, evidently meaning to single out a particular woman from a passing trio.

"Be more specific," his friend answers.

FORTY YOUNG ITALIAN MALES are at a Siena restaurant table that runs the length of a long outside room. They sing traditional premarital songs and raise their glasses with each vocal outburst, pounding the table, asking for the groom, then singing about the bride-to-be. Sometimes a glass can be heard shattering on the floor. None of the other diners complain but rather watch in quiet amusement. At a table near the corner, a dusky-skinned woman lowers her face to kiss the fingertips of her male companion.

THE PIAZZA IN SIENA is my favorite in all of Italy. As evening approaches, how softly the light falls on the herringbone bricks of the bowl-like square. Shop lights stand out against the blue crepuscular light. There is a different, perhaps deeper dimension to the scene in this kind of light; figures, many dressed in black, take on a depth and edge they didn't seem to have at noon under the hard-edged midday sun.

MY ASSISTANT, MARISA MONTIBELLER, and I came to refer to him as Il Posterino. He was a man we'd met on a street corner in a small village during one day's travel along Italy's Po River in the spring of 2001 as we began my *Geographic* assignment to photograph Italy's Po River country.

It was a Tuesday in April, and we thought there was supposed to be some kind of ox cart race nearby. I'd never seen an ox cart race before and thought it might be good. We assumed the races would be the next day, a holiday celebrating the liberation of Italy from the Fascists in 1943. We had stopped to ask where and at what time the races would start. So often, when we asked directions to somewhere, and how far away it was, the answer always seemed to be "One and a half hours." No matter where we were going.

The man wore a dark red sweater over a long-sleeved shirt. He looked to be in his 40s and was with an elderly woman. Across the street an old man in a yellow straw hat stood leaning against a bicycle watching us as Marisa asked the man in the sweater directions and details about the celebration. She was seated behind the wheel of our VW station wagon, which was loaded with many things, much of which we didn't have when we had started our travels two weeks earlier. The man told us the ox cart races would not be the next day but on a day in late May. He offered to show us something about the event, and left the old woman to go to his house.

Passing the curious man with the bicycle, we followed in our car as the man in the sweater walked briskly around the corner to the middle of a quiet sun-swept street of houses with closed doors and shuttered windows.

"Non cè un cane," Marisa said. "Not even a dog." In other words, nobody's here.

He told us he'd be right back, and ran to open an overhead door on what might have been a garage, had it been a little larger. He came out with a poster that he unrolled and displayed in front of Marisa at the car window. The poster had a badly reproduced picture of an ox in a yoke and a list of events and dates for the month of May 1997. The man grinned proudly and then carefully rolled up the poster and presented it to Marisa, who smiled her beautiful smile and thanked him.

He said, "Wait, I have another," ran back to the open door, went in, and reemerged with a second poster. This one had another bad photograph showing men prodding oxen forward along a street lined with people. He stood proudly again in front of Marisa, holding the poster tucked beneath his chin with one hand while his other hand surged down, pulling open the poster as far as he could reach in a dramatic effort of revelation. Then he carefully rolled it up and gave it to her. Marisa thanked him again.

But he wasn't finished. "Wait," he said excitedly, "I have another!" Marisa declined an additional poster but thanked him profusely, and we drove away.

We never did see any ox cart races, but in the days to follow, as Marisa and I pursued our story about the Po River country, we joked about the funny man who had so wished to please her. For almost any reason, or on any occasion, one of us might suddenly say to the other, "Wait, I have another!"

ON THE ROAD along the Po River in northern Italy I have nights of partial, restless sleep, tired mornings. I'm trying to read as Marisa drives, trying to let myself fall asleep, an open book between my legs. I'm unable to do better than doze briefly before jerking awake as she downshifts to zoom around a car giving up its place in the fast lane. We're going 190 kilometers an hour in a rented VW station wagon loaded down with duffel bags of clean and dirty clothes; hiking boots; extra cameras and film; and hats from the Borsalino shop in Alessandria, where the salesman's name was Dulce Angelo—Sweet Angel.

We have chocolate-covered hazelnuts from Alba, bottles of wine from Barolo and elsewhere in the Piemonte. A hundred and ninety kilometers an hour with an attractive blond Italian woman at the wheel. Marisa has her hair pulled back, held out of the way with a thick lavender rubber band, the kind you get on bunches of asparagus. Her face is triangular, and although accented with well-defined cheekbones, it is not severely angular, and is softened still more by wavy strands of yellow-streaked hair that fall along the sides of her face. Her eyebrows are plucked to a fine taper above blue eyes that tell stories without words.

Marisa sometimes put yogurt on her face at night, or for a little while between when we were finished working for the day and before we'd go to dinner. I'd see her pop out of her door to tell me something, her face all white. She had wonderful skin, yet she looked strangely exotic with her face covered in yogurt. I wanted to photograph her face then, but she wouldn't let me. It was a shame—she was beautiful that way.

We're late for a meeting with a delta rice farmer and will miss lunch if we mistakenly pass another exit. Through the poplar trees bordering the highway, shafts of hazy sunlight fall like gauze stretched taut between tree trunks. We reach Ristorante Vecchia Brenta before the kitchen closes for lunch. We are in Vercelli, the town that has the biggest rice market in all of Europe.

In the *ristorante,* peach-colored drapes are drawn back, cinched with blossomlike ties of the same color. Tables covered with green cloths creased from laundry folds create a pattern across the room; beneath tall paned windows sunlight dapples sills the color of cream. Our waiter is the kind who wrings his hands, gripping them together as he describes the offerings of the menu, smiling all the while. I have "mother-in-law's tongue," fried eel from the edge of the Adriatic Sea where the Po flows into it. A woman and a man at a table beneath a gilded mirror sit conversationless, she smoking a cigarette down to the filter, then stubbing it out and exhaling an angular funnel of gray smoke.

IN SALUZZO THERE IS A SCHOOL for music, and I concentrate on two young string players from Rome. They appear to be in their late teens; they might be 20. Each has what seems to be a perfect complexion; one is as fair as alabaster but for the slight rose blush of her cheeks. Marisa calls them strawberries.

As we traveled, Marisa invented a rating system for Italian females of different ages, based on various fruits. A "green apple" is very young, not quite ripe. A "strawberry" is young, ripe, but still showing innocence. A "peach," in Marisa's system, is anywhere from the mid-20s to the mid-30s; a "grape" will be in her mid-30s to mid-40s, and when one sees a mix of the above, that constitutes a "fruit salad." Bear in mind, now, that was Marisa's concept, not mine. She's not exactly a feminist. At that point, she was, I think, a peach.

When the conductor of the school sees me photographing the two violinists from Rome, he says, "I can see your intuition is good, and I compliment you." My intuition may have been good but my pictures of the two young women, I will later discover, are nothing special. Sometimes the pictures just don't come together, despite the appeal of the subject matter.

WE ARE ON A BEACH along the Po below Ferrara, just inside the delta. The sand is neither tan nor gray but some vague in-between color, perhaps a bit closer to that of powdered cement mortar. The people on holiday seem equally colorless in their beach attire, still showing the browns and blacks of a long, chilly spring, almost as lacking in color as they were on the streets of Turin a few weeks earlier. But here and there I see a bathing suit of fluorescent orange or lime green. At not quite five in the afternoon, the sun is softened and diffused by scudding clouds that pale the blue of the sky and cast translucent shadows across the sand. Nearby, a blonde, her hair pulled back and tied, a scruff of yellow escaping out against the light, takes a cell phone from a plastic bag resting inches from the face of a dark-haired man asleep at her side. She punches in some numbers and then abandons the effort, replaces the phone in the plastic bag, and rolls over on her back, her breasts moving like sea swells as her body shifts position. She is full-breasted in a two-piece bathing suit that matches the color of the sky.

IN CREMONA THERE IS A SCHOOL for violin making. Cremona is the birthplace of the violin and where the greatest violin makers—Andrea Amati, Antonio Stradivari, and Andrea Guarneri, in the 15th, 16th, and 17th centuries—created violins now treasured beyond price. Today many fine stringed instruments can be seen hanging in shop windows, hand-crafted of fine-grained woods, amber and honey colored; their elegantly beautiful shapes seem as graceful and as delicate as falling tears. They are beautiful just to look at; what a joy it must be to be able to play them. When I look at my picture of violins in a Cremona shop window, I think of my late brother, Bruce, a wonderful violinist who could make his sing, and how much I miss hearing the beauty of his music.

FERRARA IS A CITY OF BICYCLISTS. It seems everyone traverses Ferrara on a bicycle, although I'm sure that's an exaggeration. In the morning I watch bicycles and their riders pass under a stone archway, the tires softly whispering. Sometimes a faint bell sounds as the circular shadows glide gracefully along; there's a floppy-eared dog in a handlebar-mounted wicker basket, a bag of fruit from the nearby market nestles in another, and a woman's shapely legs stand out among her fellow commuters. Seeing how smoothly and efficiently the people of Ferrara commute by bicycle makes me feel that getting into a car here represents a certain kind of crudity, something not truly necessary. Then, again, should it start to rain . . .

WHENEVER WE WERE IN TURIN my assistant and I would daily check out the coffee shops and parks, crossing the piazzas, in and out of the cafés, looking for pictures. I'd drink cold beer and eat salted almonds and warm hazelnuts at the bar in the Hotel Turin across from the railway station, while listening to the CDs they'd play. With luck I'd hear some Paolo Conte songs; without it, perhaps a plain, emotionless version of "Somewhere Over the Rainbow" played by a Bobby Hackett–like cornet player, backed with a thick layer of strings that poured out like syrup. One afternoon Marisa was chewing on the cuticles of her fingers and listening to the English lyrics of a pop song, but she couldn't catch them well. I can't now remember who the singer was, but Marisa didn't understand all the lyrics.

"What did she say?" she asked me, as the song played. "What did she just say?"

"I think she said, 'I hate you,' " I answered.

"Oh," Marisa said, "It's a love song."

WHEN IN TURIN we'd go to check the blossoming apricot trees in Valentino Park, always hoping to be there when the soft, pink blossoms were ready to fall, but it never seemed to happen. Then, one day when we were there, a breeze swelled, and it was as though pink snow was falling all around us. Marisa was like an excited child, jumping up and down in delight with the beauty of what we saw. It lasted only a few minutes and then was still again.

IN EARLY SEPTEMBER 2001, during my fall trip for the Po River assignment, Marisa and I were staying at a bed-and-breakfast on the far eastern edge of the delta. We had nice rooms, clean and quiet, with no television; none was needed in such a beautiful place, although it's nice to be able to catch some news if they have CNN.

On a lovely afternoon, around three o'clock, I was reading a book in the open courtyard of the inn. Marisa was somewhere, I didn't know where. We were waiting for the light to get good, and then we'd go out for a drive, looking for pictures.

"Bill, you'd better come in here."

Marisa, her face somehow different from the one I thought I knew, had emerged from the patio doors leading to the owners' living room, where she and they had been watching television. I went in and took a seat. CNN, with only Italian commentators, was showing the twin towers of New York's World Trade Center aflame, huge billows of smoke rising into a clear, blue sky. They showed how an airliner had plunged into one of them. They showed it again and again. And then, oh my God, one after the other, the towers fell, collapsing upon themselves. All the commentary was in Italian, so I couldn't follow the explanations. Marisa filled me in, but I could only sit mute and watch the surreal horror of it all. And then I couldn't watch any longer. I got up from my chair and walked out to the iron gate separating the inn from the parking area. I leaned upon that gate and I came apart. I sobbed. What was happening? A nightmare was taking place within my country, and I was on the outside, looking in. Later I learned about the other planes, about the crash in Pennsylvania, about the Pentagon. In retrospect I don't recall feeling that I should have been there, in New York or Washington, to document what was happening. Had I been, of course I would have. But that afternoon, leaning against that gate, I didn't feel like a photojournalist; I felt like a man whose country would never be the same; I felt engulfed with the fear of what in the world will it be like now for my children?

I asked Marisa to drive me to the nearest town. I needed to buy a shortwave radio, something I always traveled with in the early years of my career. But now, with CNN in English being available almost everywhere I went, I'd not been carrying a radio in recent years. I found one in town. I listened to the reports, so unreal, so devastating. I smoked some cigarettes and drank some whiskey and felt hollow inside and terribly far away from my country, from my wife, my children—my four oldest approaching their 40s, the prime of their lives; my youngest, only 14 years old, just beginning. What was happening to their world, their future?

Late that evening I learned through a telephone call from Mike Yamashita, a photographer friend in America, that my friend Ann Judge, who had headed the Travel Department at National Geographic, and another National Geographic employee whom I didn't know had been taking some Washington, D.C., schoolchildren on a field trip to Los Angeles, but the terrorists aboard their plane had turned it back and plunged it into the Pentagon. Ann used to walk around the Travel Department office with her shoes off, always in stocking feet, pretty and pert, capable of handling any kind of travel problem I might have; Ann could always fix it. When I was up in Washington to edit or do a layout, we'd have a drink out on the patio of a place called Herb's on 17th Street and Rhode Island Avenue, a block away from the Geographic. Now she was gone.

In my career I've often been alone but seldom lonely. That's not necessarily a good thing, I suppose. Maybe if I were not so capable of immersing myself in my work I would feel more pangs of lonesomeness for those I love, for those who need me. I loved being in Italy in 2001. But on that September day, and on many following days, I felt very much alone and lonely. I am still too capable of being by myself, but as I age I realize how much I have missed in being so. In a way of life that has offered me so much, I have not always taken the best. ■

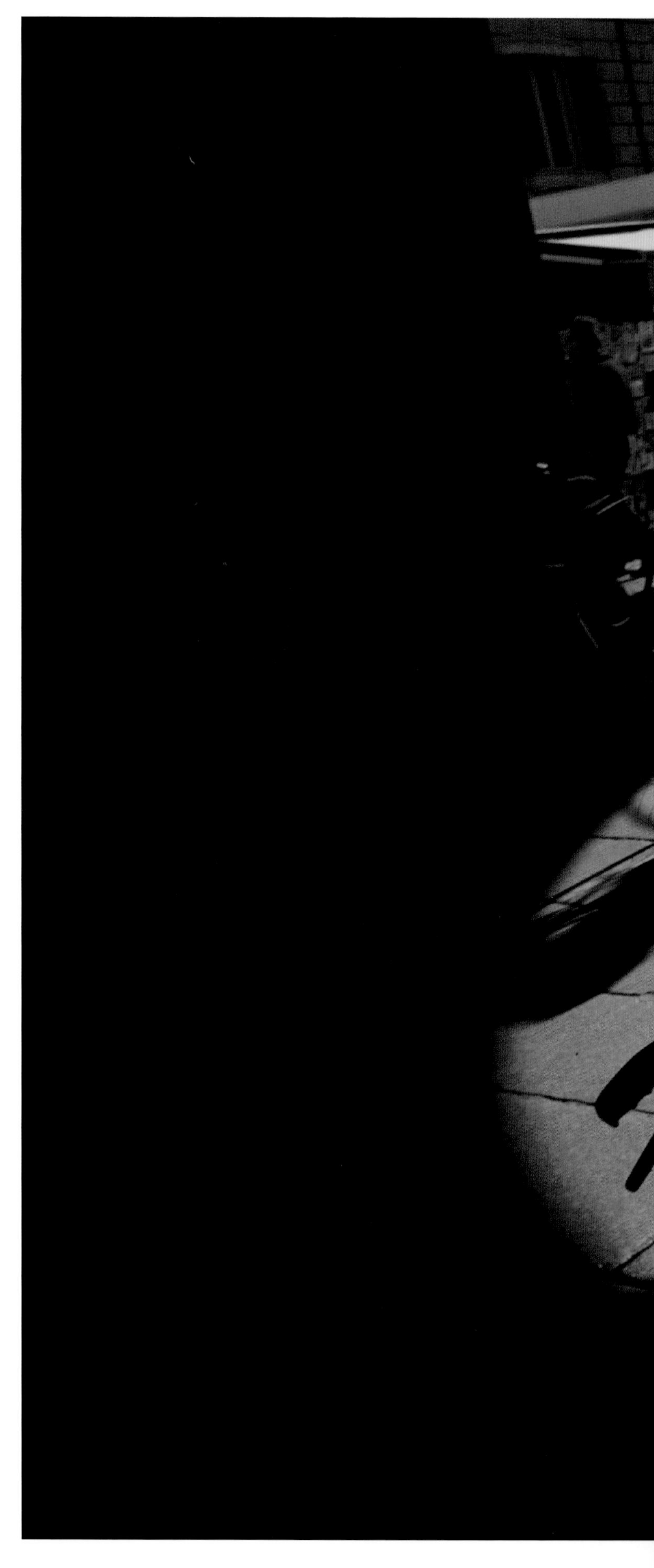

Bicyclists, Ferrara, 2001

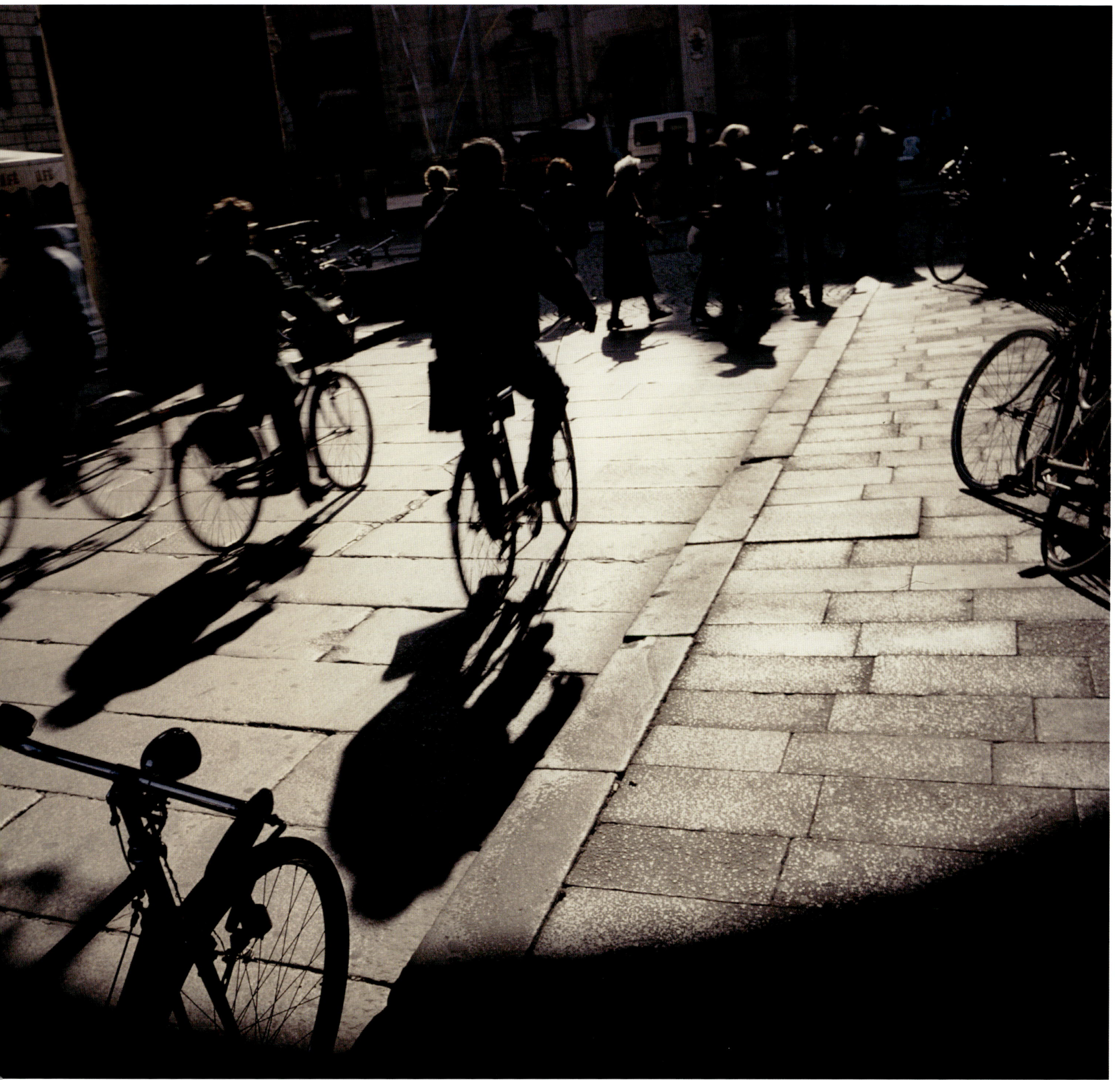

"In my career I've often been alone but seldom lonely. That's not necessarily a good thing, I suppose."

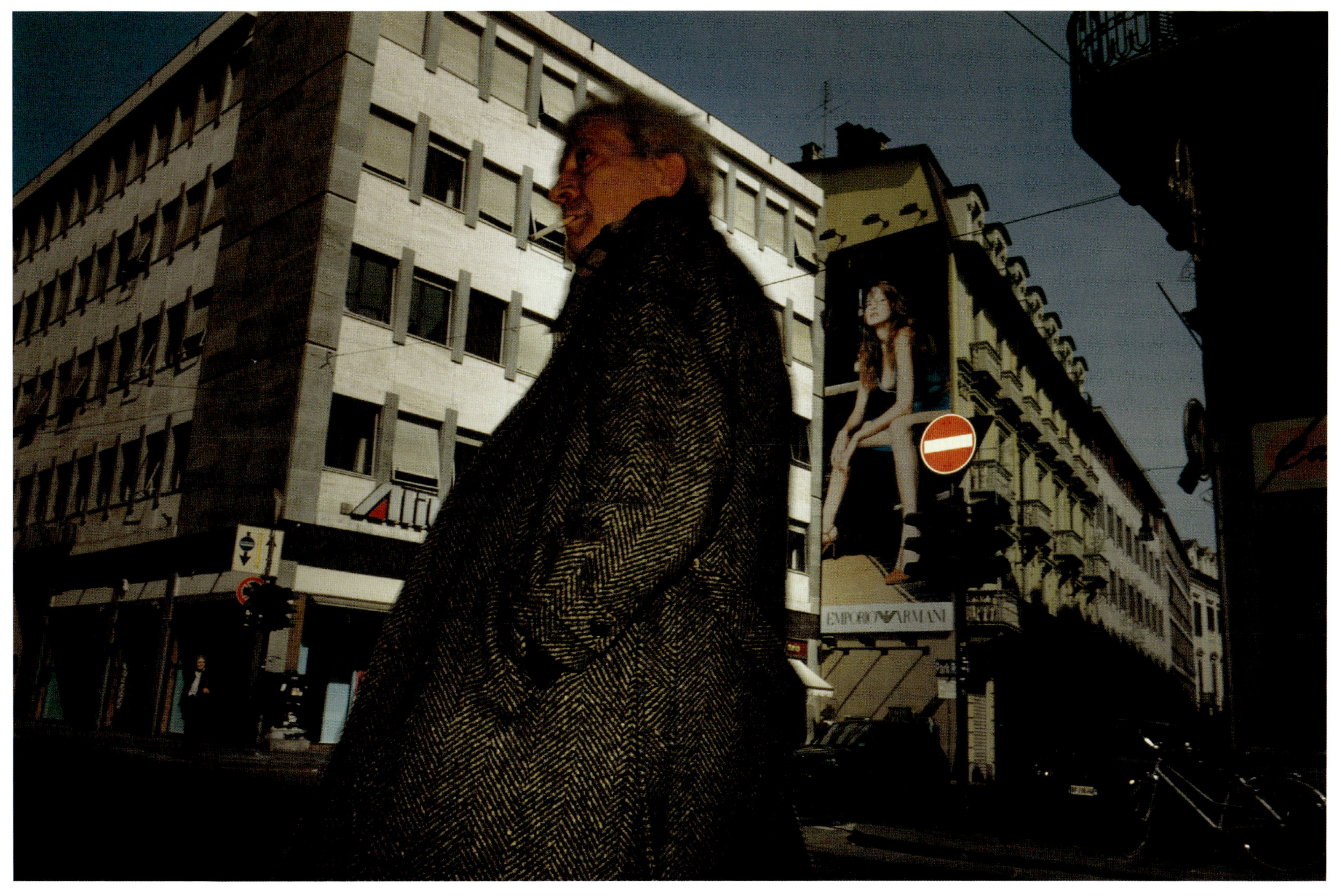

Man in an overcoat, Turin, 2001

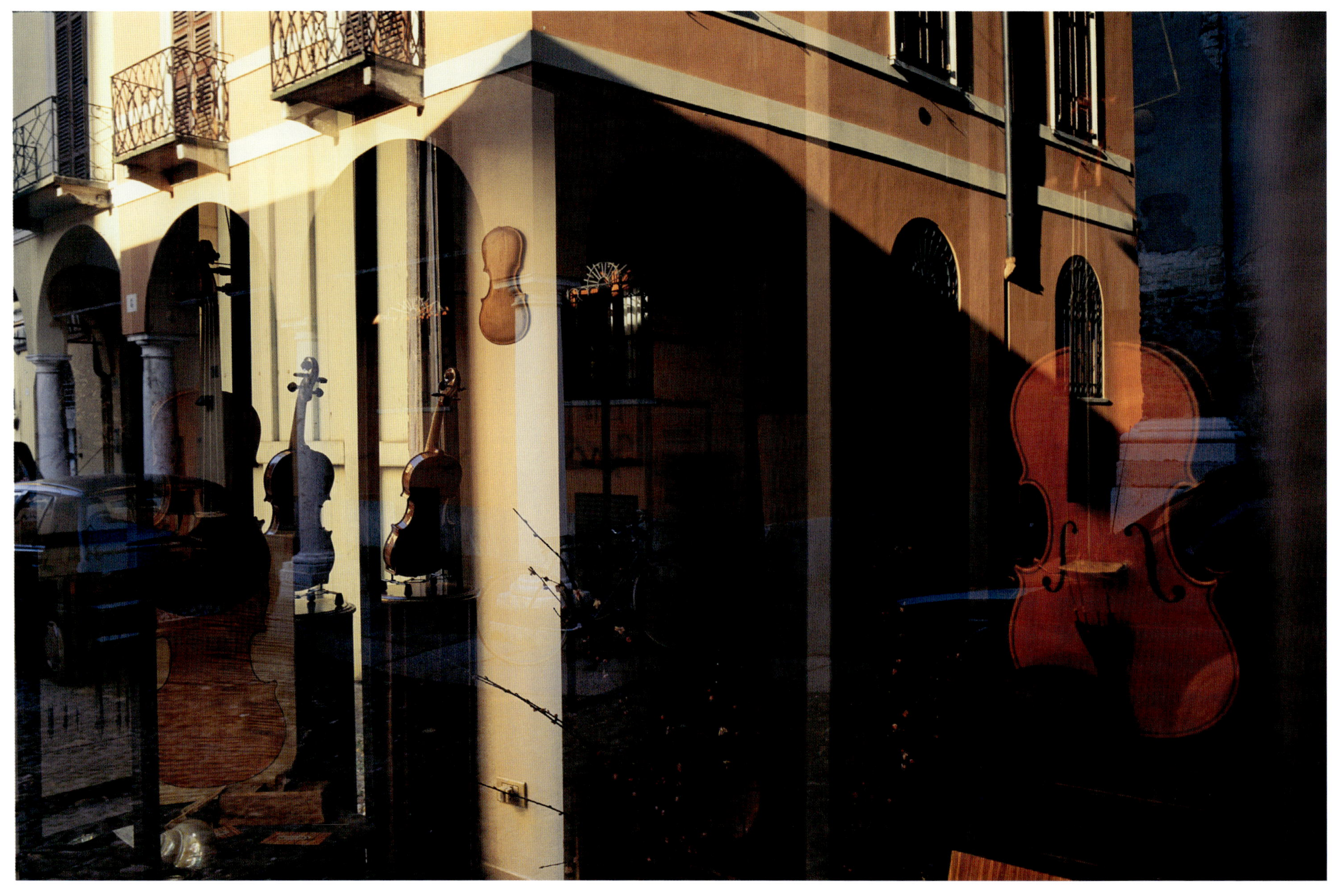

Violin shop, Cremona, 2001

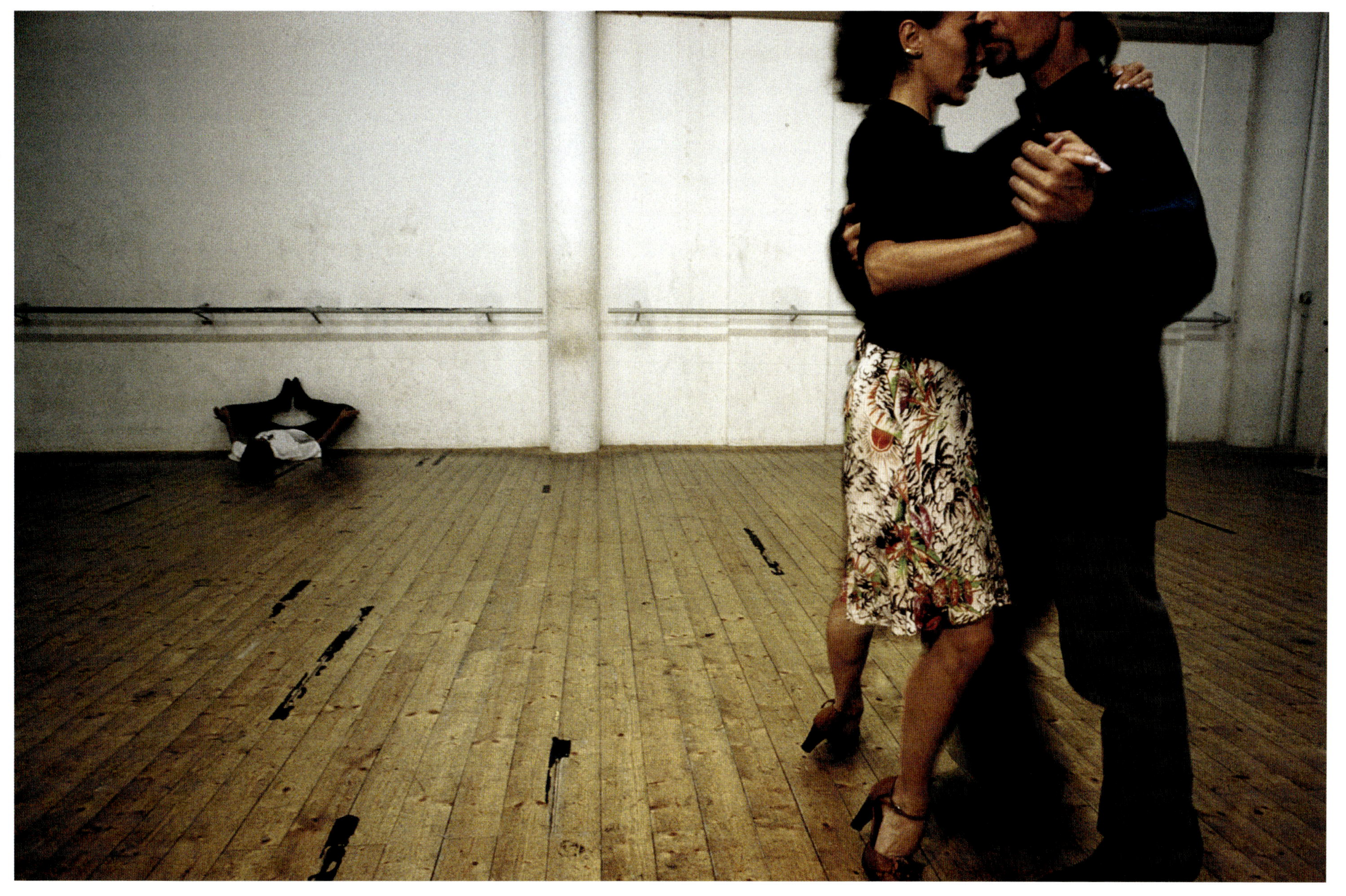

Tango class, Turin, 2001

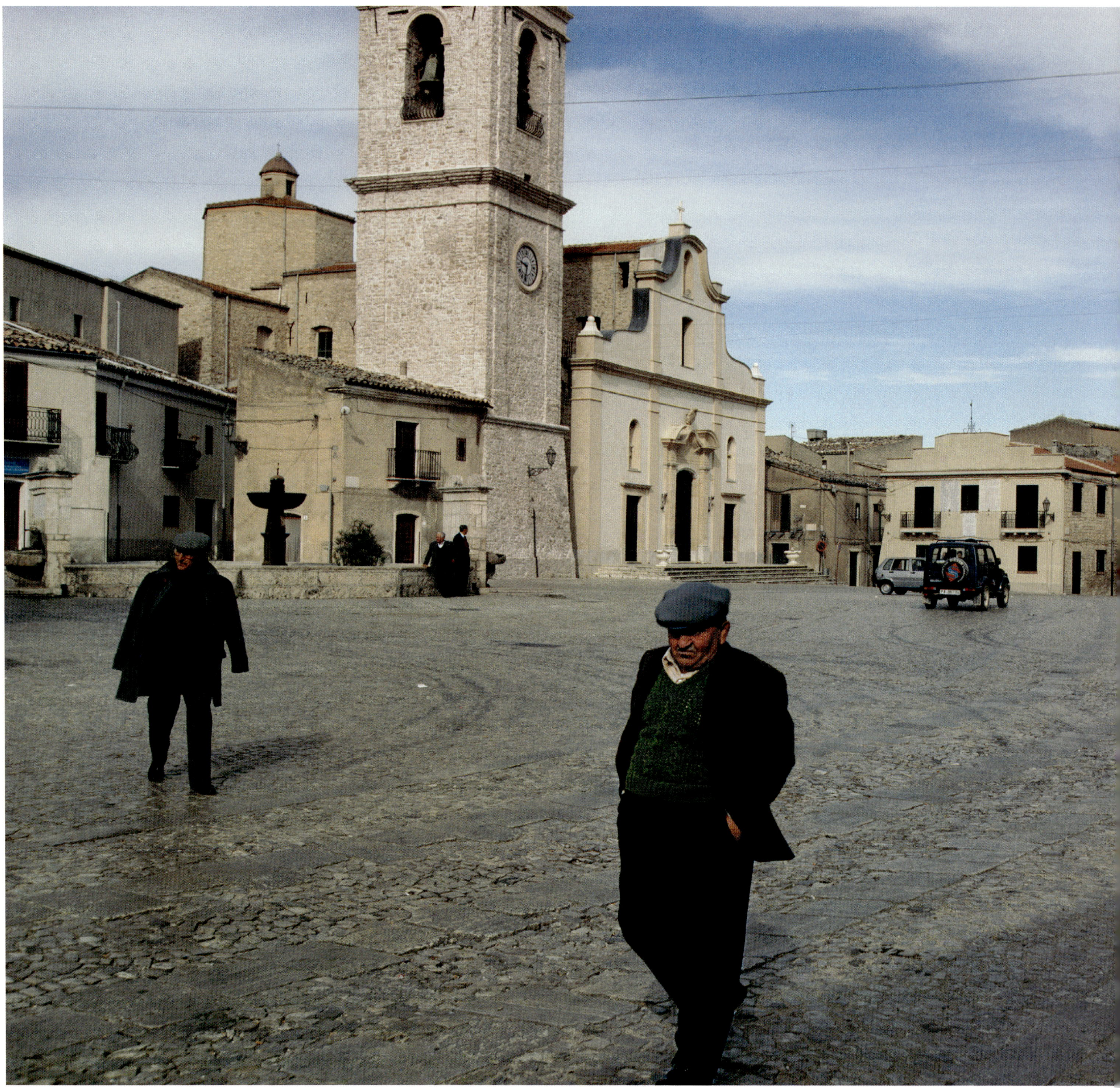

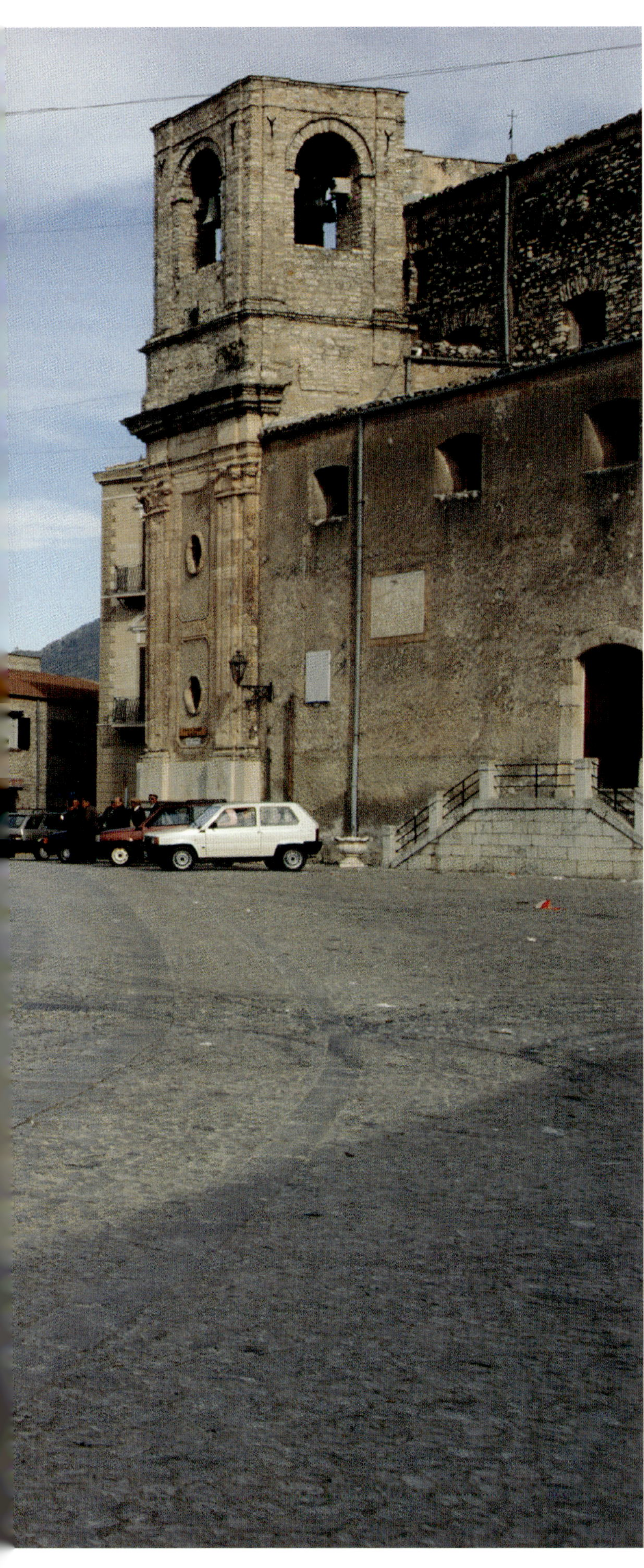

Palazzo Adriano, Sicily, 1994

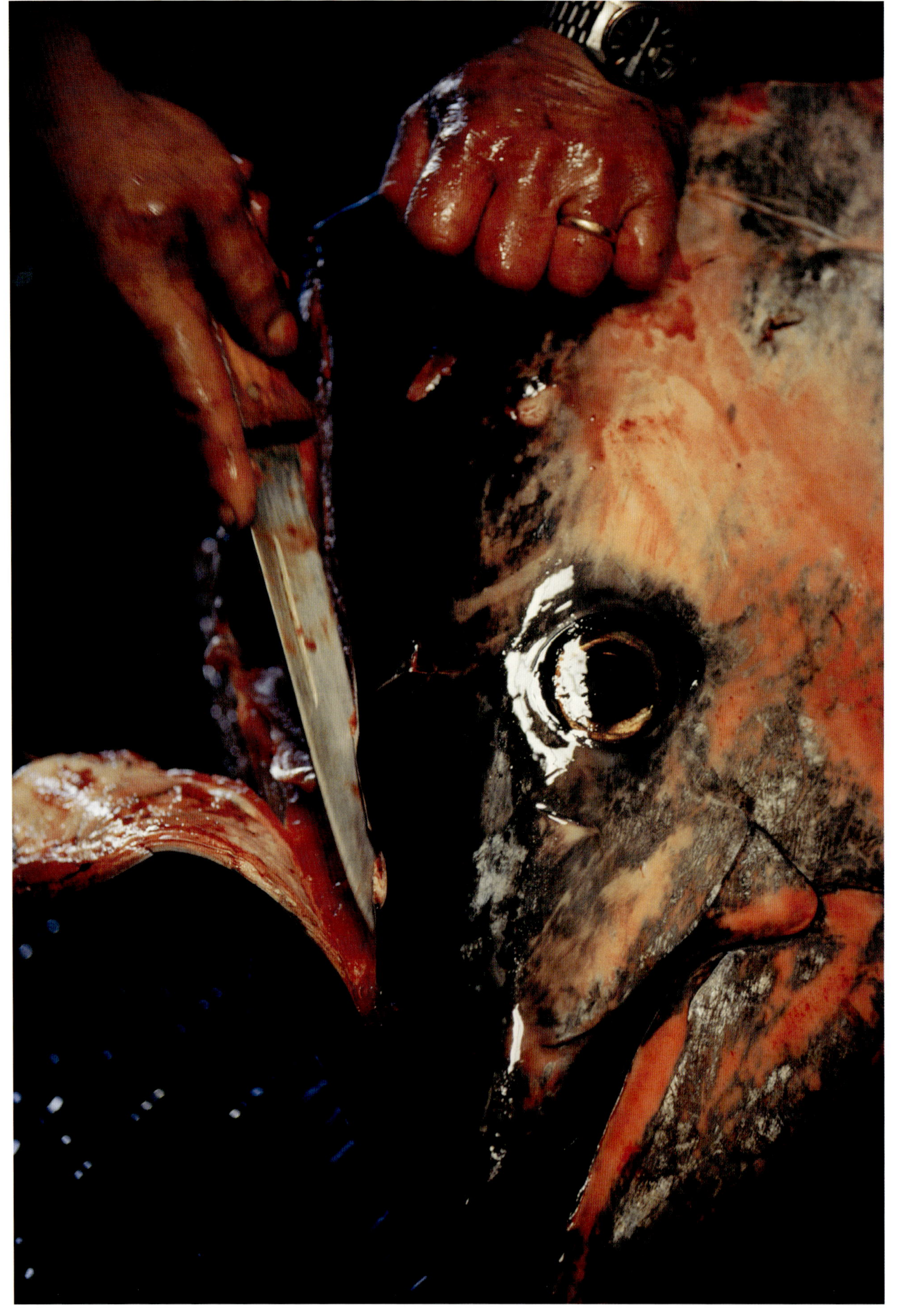

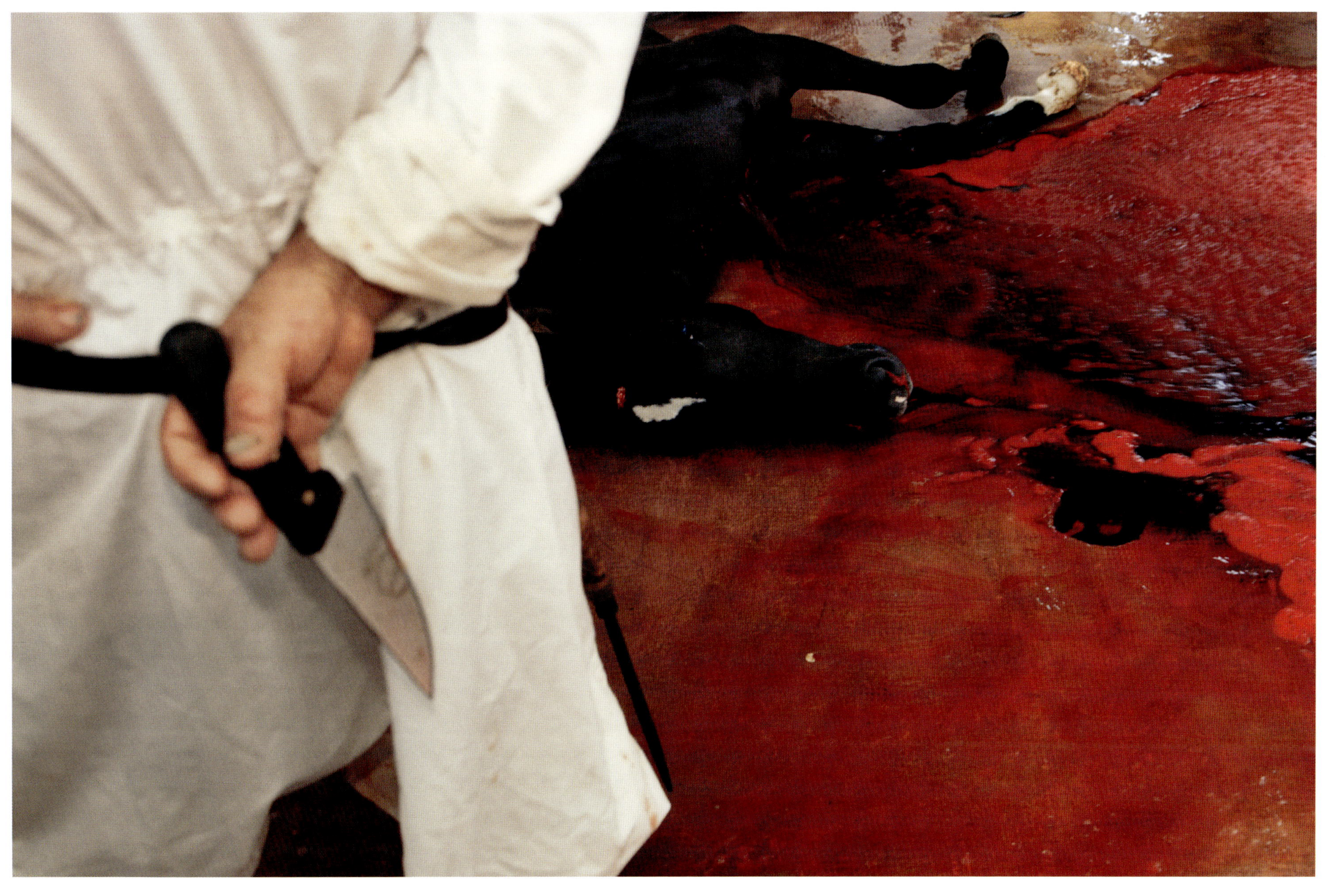

LEFT: *Butchering bluefin tuna, Trapani, Sicily, 1994* ABOVE: *Slaughtering horses, Palermo, Sicily, 1994*

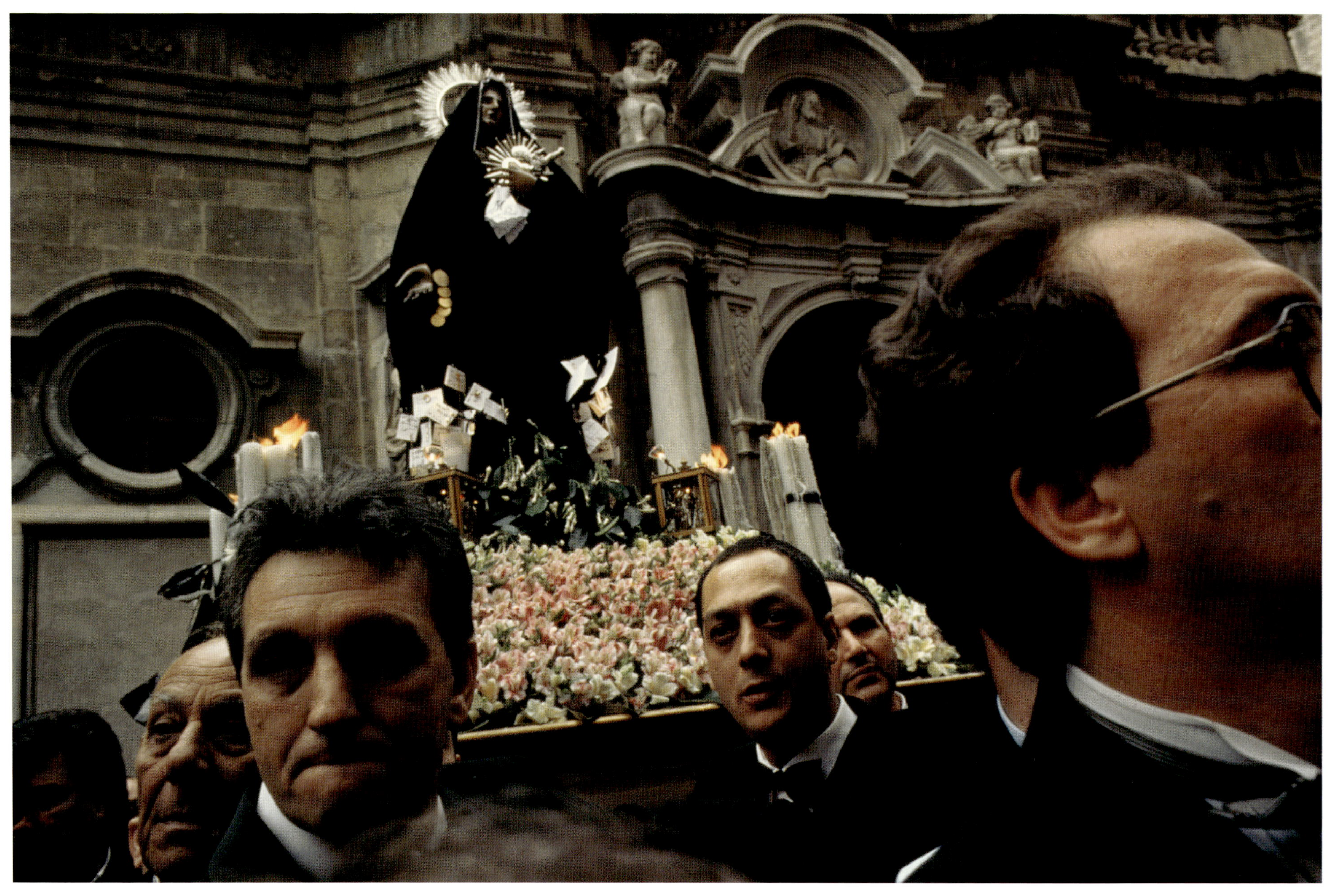

Easter procession, Trapani, Sicily, 1994

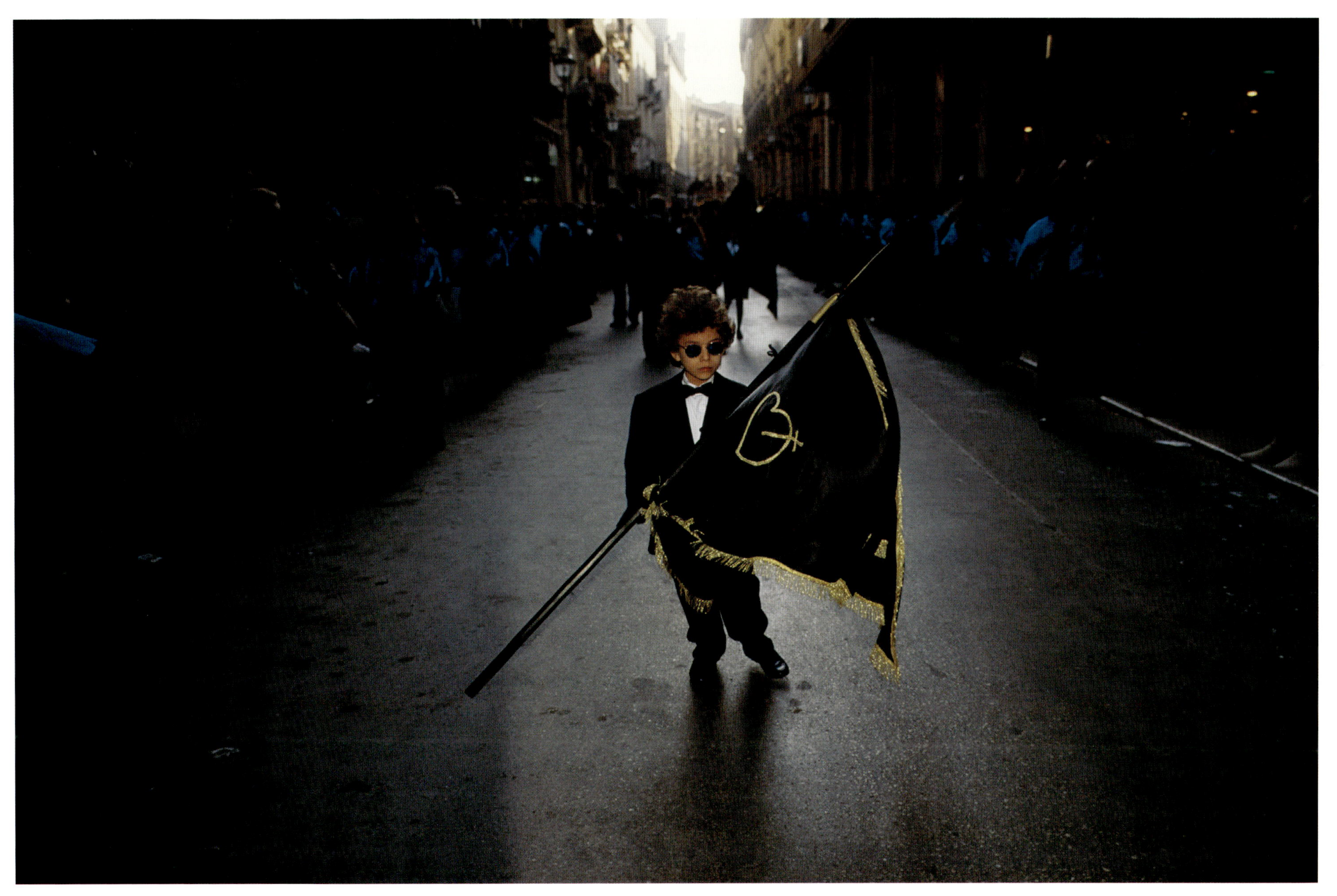

Boy with a flag, Easter procession, Trapani, Sicily, 1994

"Sicily's Easter processions are powerful displays of religious fervor and emotion. There were images everywhere, sometimes dramatic, often surreal."

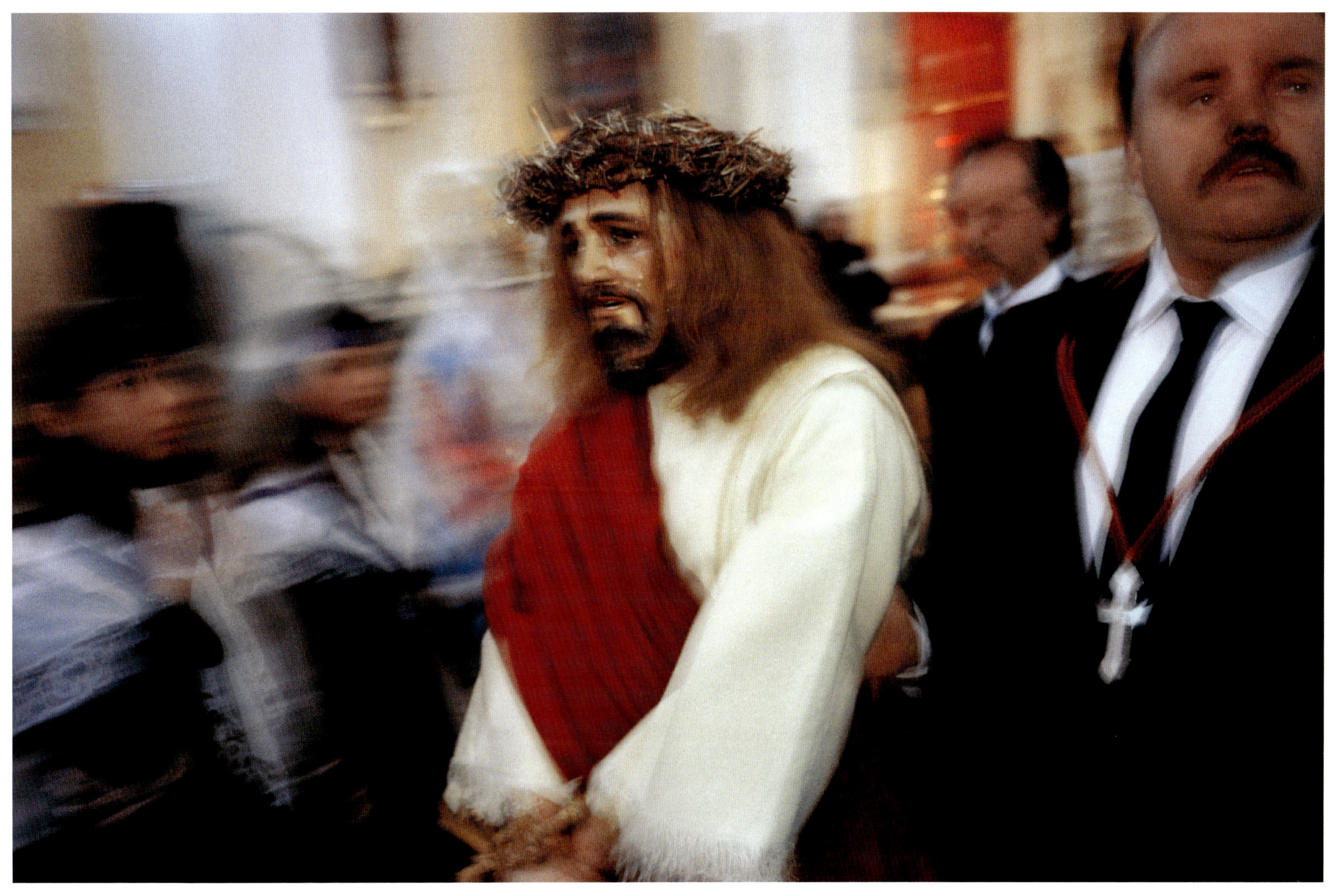

Taking Christ by the arm, Easter procession, Marsala, Sicily, 1994

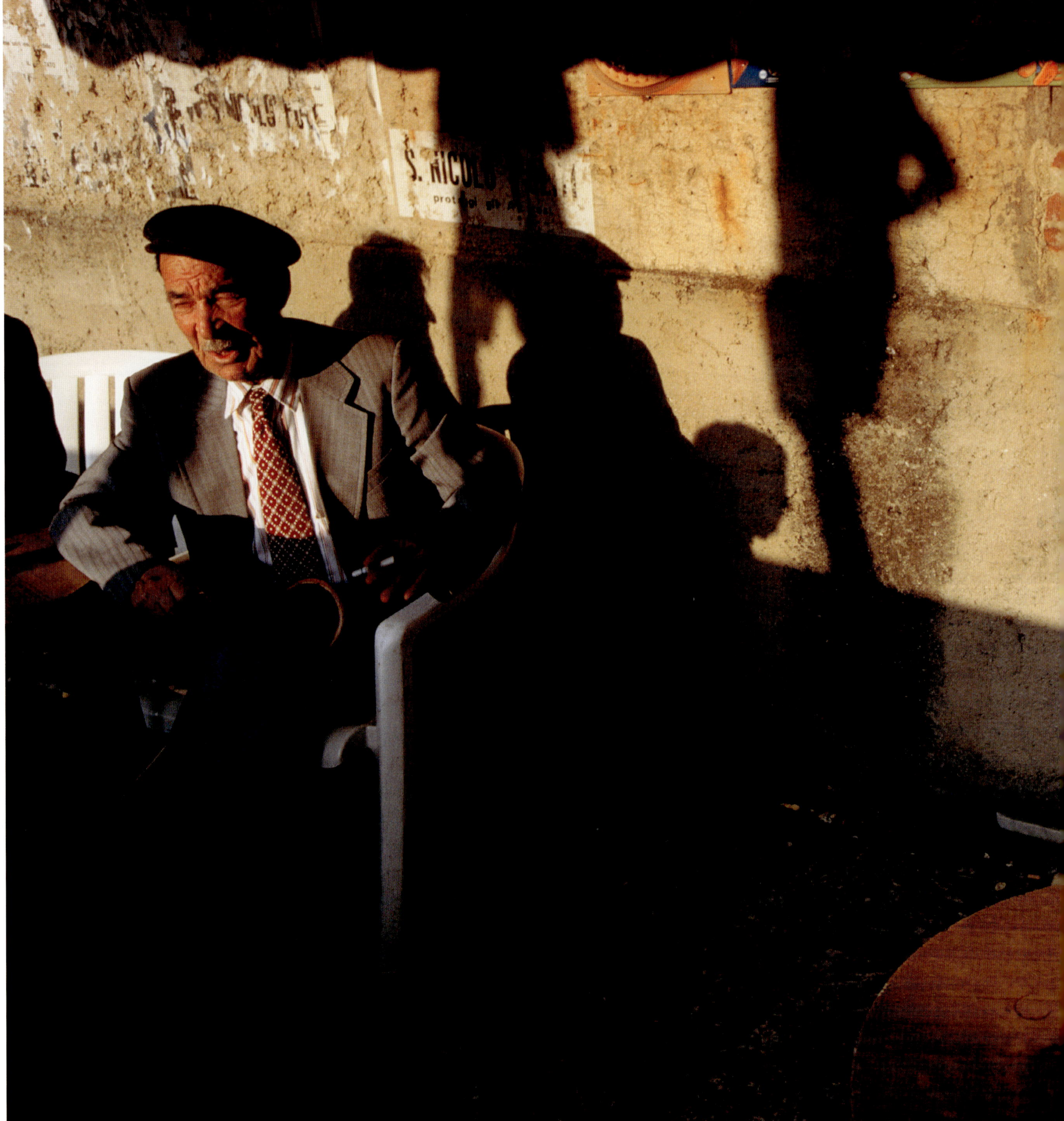
S. NICOLO

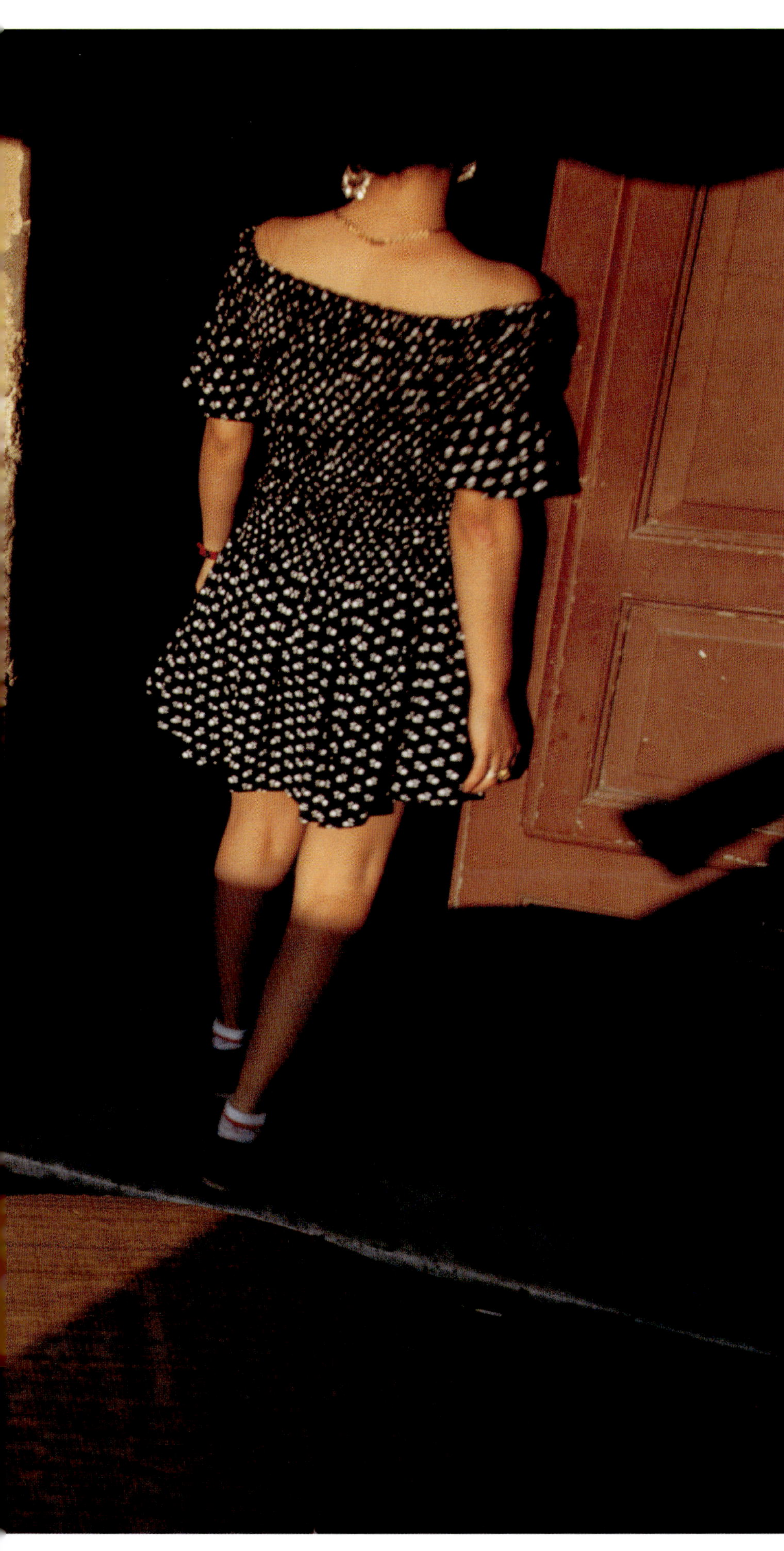

Café waitress, Alcara li Fusi, Sicily, 1994

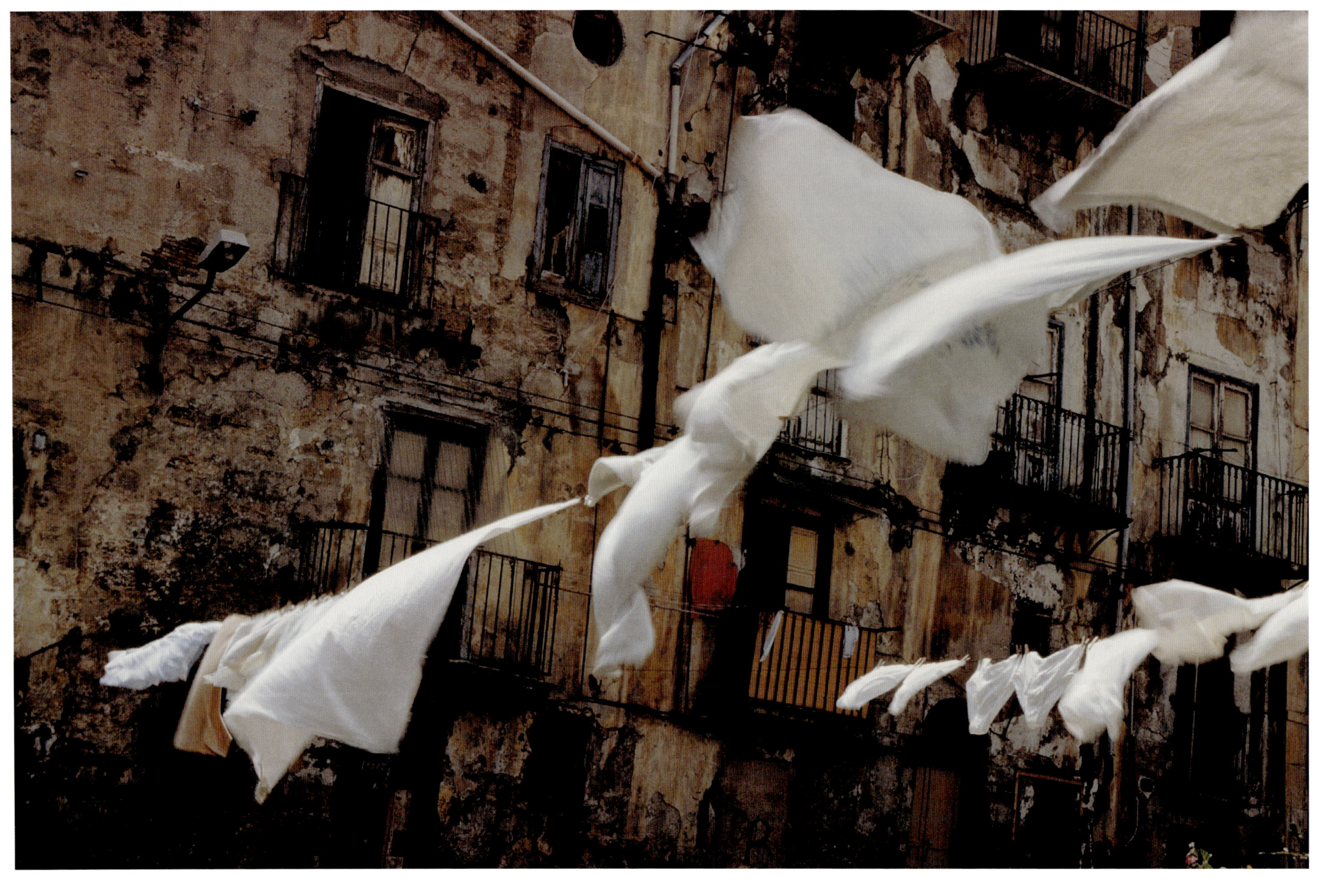

Wash lines in Albergheria neighborhood, Palermo, Sicily, 1994

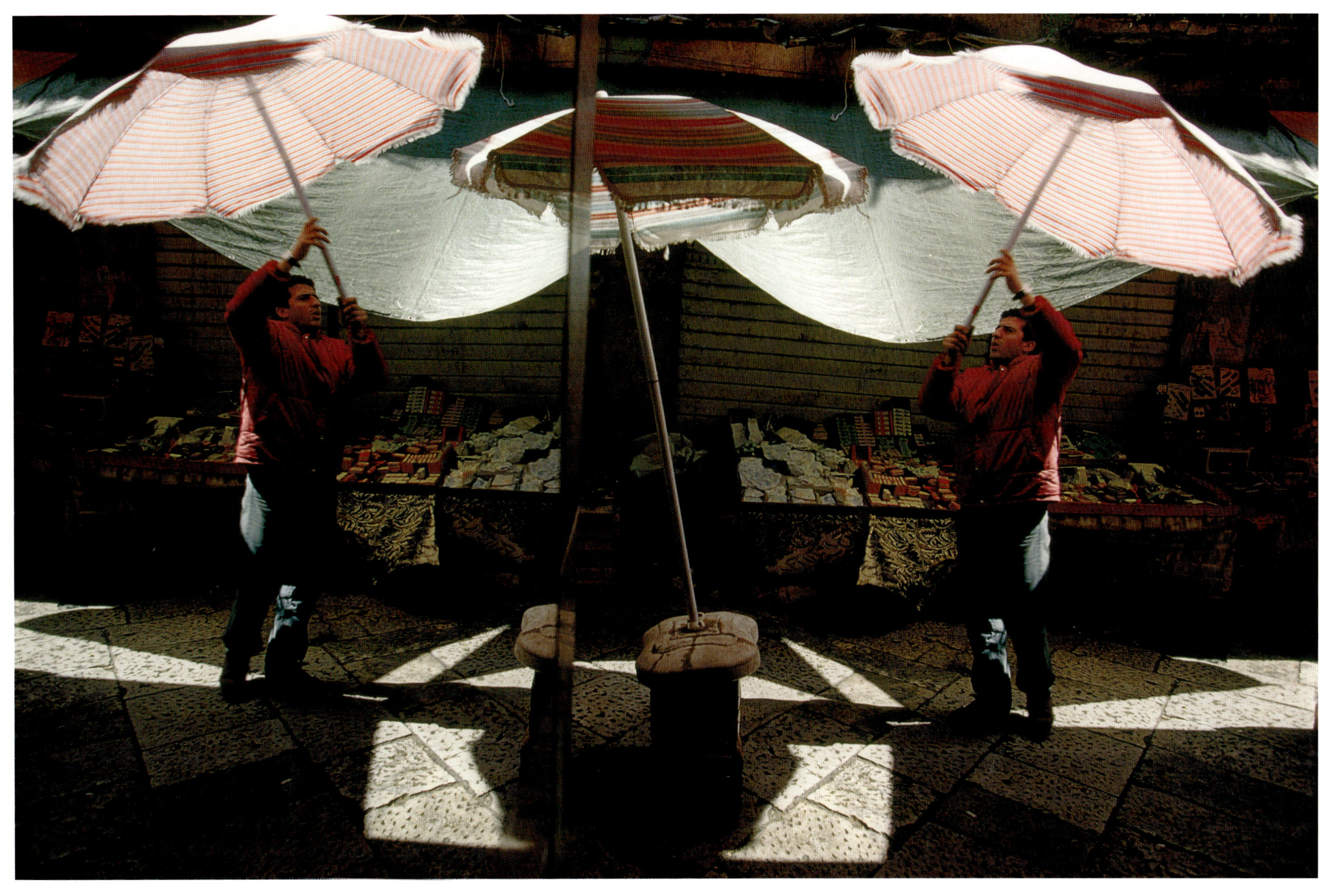

Vucciria market, Palermo, Sicily 1994

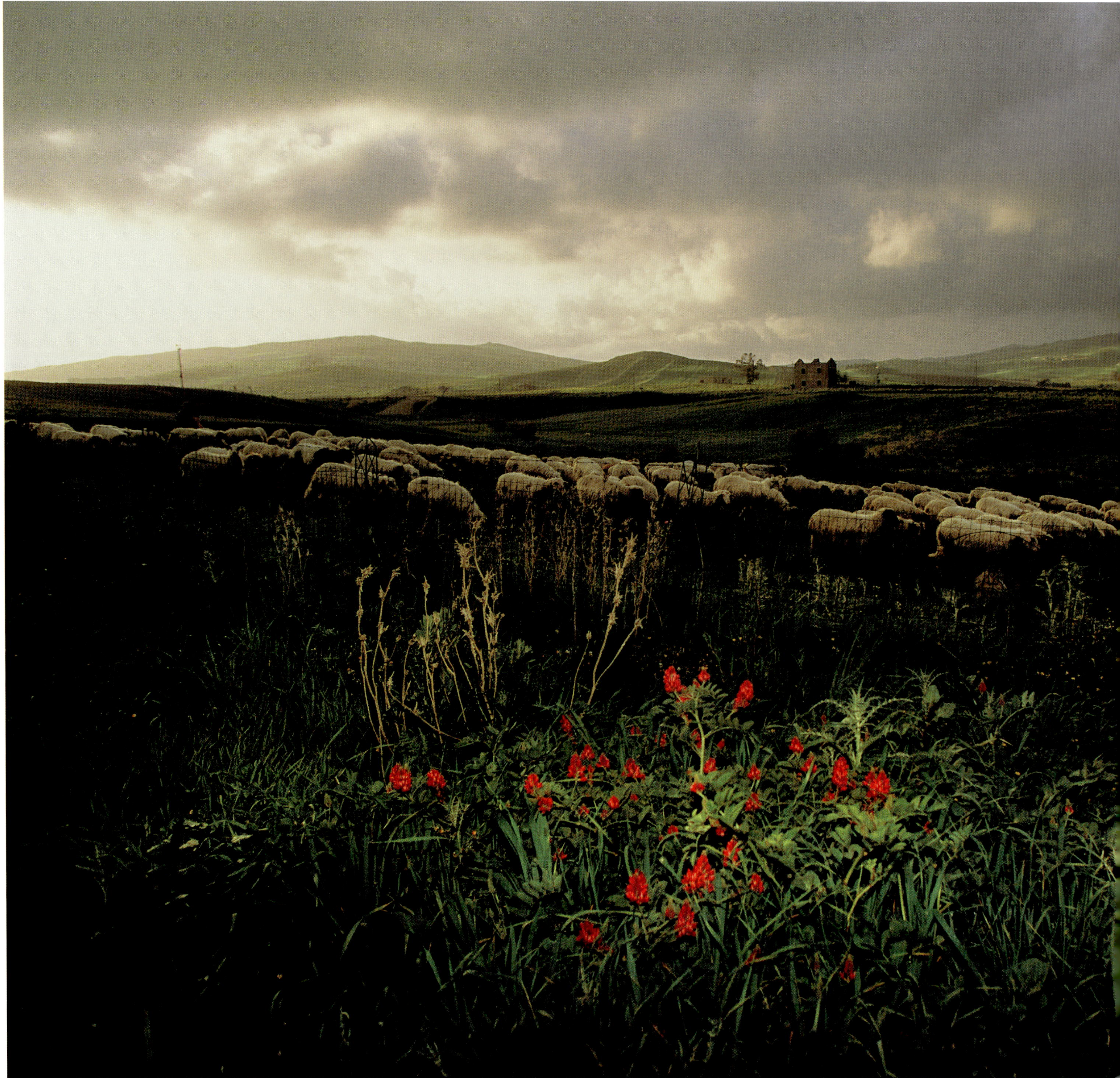

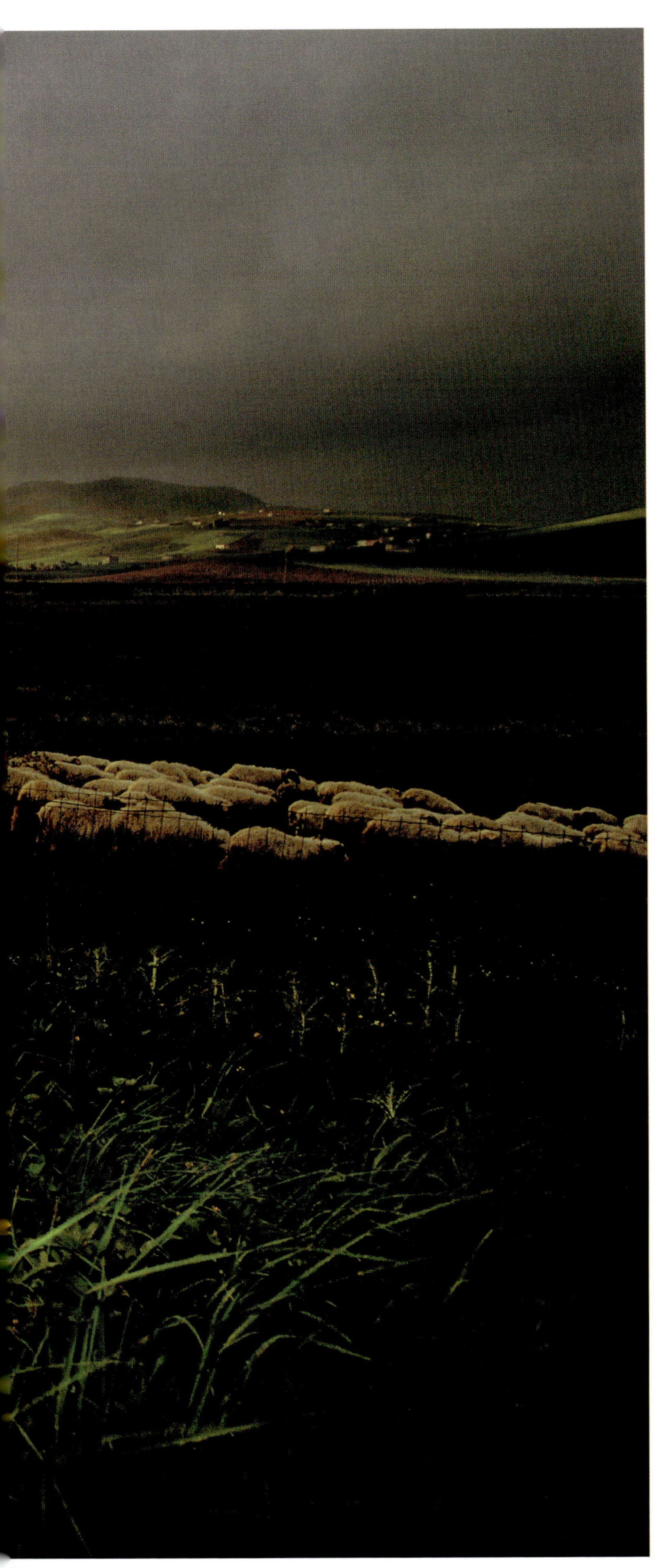

Wildflowers and sheep, Agrigento, Sicily, 1994

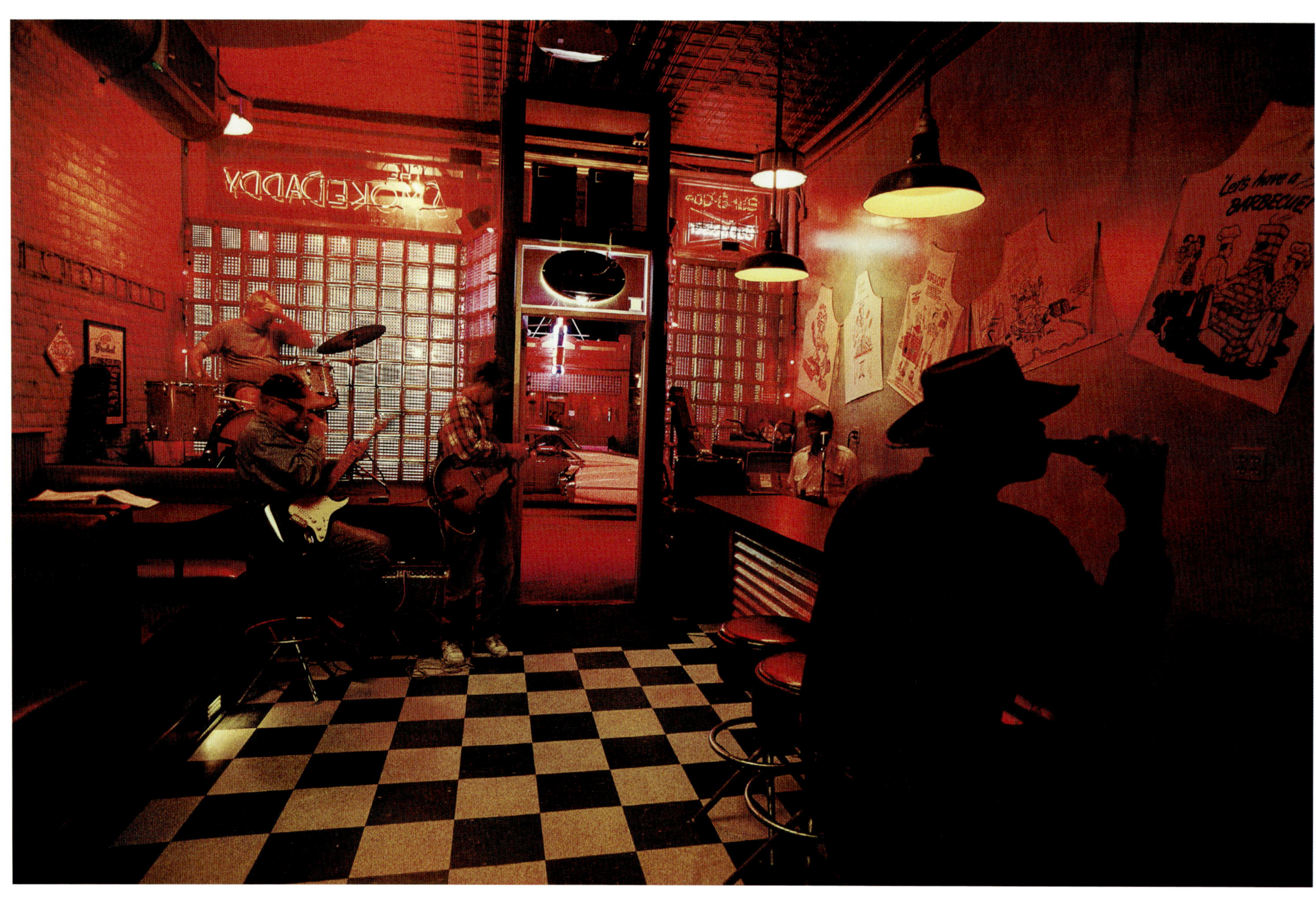

Smoke Daddy blues bar, Jimmy Lee Robinson foreground, Chicago, 1997

Music, Frank Sinatra, and Me

Come fly with me, let's fly, let's fly away
If you can use some exotic booze there's a bar in far Bombay
Come fly with me, let's fly, let's fly away

—Sammy Cahn and Jimmy Van Heusen

On a wall in the music room of our house in Virginia, centered above the 48-inch upright Yamaha piano I hope someday to learn to play, hangs a framed black-and-white photograph made by Los Angeles photographer Bernie Abramson. In the picture a man is playing a piano. Another man is sitting alongside the piano, singing, his head tilted back a little, eyes closed. He holds a drink in one hand. He's impeccably dressed. One of those shirt collar pins popular in the 1950s shows beneath the knot in his tie, and a narrow wedge of white handkerchief protrudes from the breast pocket of his suit coat. He wears a ring on the little finger of his right hand, and a thin watch on his left wrist is faintly visible beneath the French cuff. It appears to be about 1:15. I assume it's at night. The man playing the piano is Nat "King" Cole. He's smiling warmly, and I think he's singing along, but it's hard to tell for sure. Behind them rows of wine bottles stand on a tier of shelves; others in straw baskets hang in clusters from the wall. They're in a restaurant called the Villa Capri in Hollywood, California. It's December 12, 1957, and Frank Sinatra is celebrating his 42nd birthday.

During the decade of the fifties—while American audiences slowly abandoned the big band music that spilled from radios and filled dance halls and ballrooms from the 1930s through the war years of the '40s, and while popular music on radio became increasingly bland and cute, with stations giving great play to novelty songs such as Patti Page's "How Much Is That Doggy in the Window?"—Frank Sinatra produced one incredible record after another of songs written by the composers and lyricists of what is now known as the Great American Song Book: Irving Berlin, George and Ira Gershwin, Cole Porter, Rodgers and Hart, Hoagy Carmichael, Duke Ellington, Harold Arlen and Johnny Mercer, Matt Dennis, Sammy Cahn and Jimmy Van Heusen, and so many others. Starting in 1953, when he moved from Columbia to Capitol Records, Sinatra recorded these "standards," some old, some new, with many of the finest arrangers, conductors, and studio musicians in the business. He was no longer the 1940s bobby-sox heartthrob crooner with an appealing, if kind of thin, voice. Maybe because of the cigarettes, the whiskey, and the maturing years, his voice darkened and deepened. He was approaching the period in his extraordinary career when he would be deemed the finest interpreter and performer of American popular songs—ever. Rock-and-roll had arrived, of that there was no doubt. Chuck Berry brought it in. And Elvis. Buddy Holly had come on the scene. Electric guitars would eventually rule. But rock-and-roll hadn't quite yet taken over. And Frank Sinatra was the best there was in popular music.

And me? In 1957? Well, I was 20 years old. I worked as a construction lineman for the Northwestern Bell Telephone Company, riding to the job site each day with a line crew on a truck out of a company garage in north Minneapolis. I was often late to work, not a sign of loving one's job. My sister thought I should go to college, but I had barely graduated from high school, and my grades were far too low to get into the University of Minnesota. I hadn't thought much about college. I had no direction, so I just kept climbing telephone poles, enjoying the work on days when the weather was nice, not so much when it was not. I actually wasn't too crazy about heights, although on a bet between me and some of my buddies in high school I once proved I could climb to the top of a 13-story ladder—not a fire escape, just a steel ladder that ran straight up the brick wall on the back of a downtown Minneapolis hotel we always passed by on our way to a poolroom off Hennepin Avenue. I recall that it was a late summer night and that I never did collect on the bet, which I think was $12.

I hadn't done much of anything since getting out of high school. The first summer I worked at a record store in downtown Minneapolis, a job I enjoyed because I could listen to music all day long. But it didn't pay enough, so I hired on with the telephone company. My parents thought that was good because they lived through the Great Depression years and thought any job with the city or a utility company represented job security, and I suppose in 1957 they were right about that.

So there I was, climbing poles, getting razzed at lunch if I chose to read a book instead of playing poker with the crew. I really liked playing poker, but I was enjoying reading a lot of books I should have read when I was in high school. I was devouring Hemingway, Fitzgerald, Steinbeck, O'Hara, some Faulkner. Part of me thought maybe I'd like to be a writer.

Oh, and I got married. Five days after my 20th birthday. My wife, Mary Catherine Burns, was 19. We'd met at a dance when we were both still in high school. She was from the south side of town, I was from the north side. We moved into an upper duplex on Emerson Avenue on the north side of town, just a few blocks from where I grew up, if, in fact, I had.

Sometimes we'd go across the river to the Prom Ballroom in St. Paul to hear one of the big bands that still came around, like Ray Anthony, Les Brown, or Stan Kenton. If the Four Freshmen came, my friends and I never missed them. Their sophisticated harmony and musicality was so much better than most popular vocal groups'. My wife and I didn't have much furniture, but we had a high-fidelity record player with a single big wall-mounted speaker. It wasn't stereo, which was going to be the next big thing, but it had good sound, and I listened to a lot of Frank Sinatra. We had a small black-and-white television set, and Sinatra had a weekly show I tried not to miss.

Now, at this point you have a right to ask—what the hell does all of this about Sinatra and music have to do with photography in general and my pictures in particular? A lot, really.

Music has been a driving force in my entire life. If I were not a photographer and writer I would most likely have a profession in music. I was raised in a family where music was vital, part of our daily lives. My parents were amateur musicians; my father, who immigrated to America from Sweden in 1905, at age six, played accordion, my mother the piano, and they made a few extra dollars playing at Scandinavian lodge meetings and dances. My sister, who plays piano, has a lovely voice and sang in high school, in church, and later in community theater productions. My younger brother was a brilliantly gifted musician, a superb violinist and trumpet player, playing professionally from age 12 until his death at age 64 in 2008. Although I never took formal music lessons, something I now regret, I played trumpet by ear. And I sang. As a kid I used to listen to my sister's radio on the dresser in her bedroom when I was home alone, and I'd pretend one of her hairbrushes was a microphone and sing along when they played songs I liked. I loved to sing and still do. I perform with my daughter Terri, a singer-songwriter living in Charlottesville, Virginia, working local gigs with her and her fine band musicians when I can.

I was in a vocal quartet in high school, and then a trio after graduation. Jerry Longie, who sang lead in the trio, worked downtown at a parking lot with a garage that had a car elevator, and we'd practice in the spacious elevator because the acoustics were good. Across the street was Freddie's Supper Club, and one winter night, when the Four Freshmen were booked there, Jerry persuaded them to come to the parking lot to listen to us sing our arrangement of "Autumn Leaves." For some reason we did it in the parking attendant's small booth, the door cracked open to accommodate our trio and three of the Four Freshmen, who walked over between sets. I remember Bob Flanagan, who played trombone and sang high lead in the Freshmen, standing in a fine black overcoat with the collar turned up against the cold, listening. He was complimentary, and that made our night. "Well," he said, "I hope to see you on the road."

We'd do a few gigs here and there in the city, but none of us were adequate instrumentalists, so we had to sing a cappella. That had its limitations, and within a year or so the other two in the trio wanted us to find a guitarist, hit the road, and try to make it big in the music business. "I want to be a star," one of them said to me. I decided to stay at home. But I wished them luck. They did go on the road, and for a few years had some modest success playing folk music clubs around the country. It was around 1960 when we split up, and by that time I had quit my job at the telephone company and enrolled at the Minneapolis School of Fine Arts, getting accepted on the basis of a few drawings.

I could always draw well as a child. Art was my easy course in high school. I could skip class to go smoke cigarettes on the school roof and still get an A. But during that year at the School of Fine Arts I took a mandatory course in English composition and became more interested in writing than the art courses. The following year I transferred to the University of Minnesota, thinking to major in journalism. I was on the edge of finding a direction that would eventually lead to a life and career of doing something I would truly love. A career, not just work or a job. It's never really work if you're doing something you love. And I've never thought of what I do as a job.

As the result of hearing a lecture about photojournalism by a young, enthusiastic associate professor named Smith "Smitty" Schuneman in my sophomore year at the U of M, I signed up for a beginning photojournalism course. Schuneman had spoken about the bringing together of words and pictures, and how the combination can have a strength beyond that of either discipline by itself. I became enraptured with photography, and my ambitions centered on wanting to be a photographer. I took everything I could in photojournalism and everything I could in photography in the university's art school. And part of me still wanted to be a writer. As the school years went by, our family eventually grew to four children, all a year apart in age. During those years I earned, at best, a modest income driving a taxicab during the school year and a beer truck in the summer. We had moved to a low-income housing project not far from campus, and by the economic standards of the time we were living below the poverty line. Still, we got by. But in none of my deepest dreams, then, did I ever visualize myself doing what Sinatra sang about in one of my favorite songs of that time:

Come fly with me, let's float down to Peru
In llama land there's a one-man band and he'll toot his flute for you
Come fly with me, let's take off in the blue

In a fairly short time, I'd be doing just that.

IN THE SPRING OF MY SENIOR YEAR, 1964, I journeyed to Chicago, New York, and Washington, D.C., showing my portfolio of black-and-white photographs, looking for a possible job upon graduation. Someone at an industrial company magazine in Chicago wanted to hire me as both a photographer and writer, but it turned out the job had already been offered to someone else. In New York, I was encouraged by various magazine picture editors I saw. When I told the picture editor of *Look* magazine that I was going to Washington, she suggested I try to see Yoichi Okamoto, then head of photography for the U.S. Information Agency and later President Lyndon Johnson's personal photographer. I didn't have an appointment with Okamoto, but he was in and agreed to look at my work.

Okamoto immediately called Bob Gilka, director of photography at *National Geographic* magazine, asking him, "Do you want to see a good people photographer? Well, damn it, I wouldn't send him over if he wasn't any good. One o'clock tomorrow? OK. Let's have lunch one of these days." That brief telephone call changed my life. The next day, when I showed Gilka my portfolio, he offered me a summer photographic internship.

Gilka saw on my résumé that I was 26 and had four kids. The internship was supposed to be for a college photojournalism student with maybe a year left in school, somebody who showed promise and might benefit from the experience of spending the summer at the magazine. Still, he offered it to me—but with reservations.

"If you can get anything else," Gilka said, "take it. Because this job doesn't offer much money and it's all over in the fall." I wasn't cocky, but the time spent in Chicago and New York had given me a certain confidence. "Well," I replied, "I've been busted for five years, another three months won't kill me. And you just might want to keep me."

And that's pretty much how it worked out. A three-month internship led to a six-month contract, which led to a staff position that I held from 1965 until fall of 1967, when I felt the need to be independent, resigned my staff position, borrowed some money to buy cameras, and became a freelance photographer. My passion for making pictures and sometimes writing about them was burning deeply, and all along those fires were being fed by music. My tastes—then as now—were eclectic. Pop, some jazz, I really hadn't heard any blues yet, a little classical, although I wasn't exposed to much of that either. In 1963, my senior year at the university, I worked for a Minneapolis television station as a part-time news cameraman, carrying around one of those windup Bell + Howell 16mm cameras. On the day John F. Kennedy, a hero to my generation and the first President I ever voted for, was killed, I filmed reactions around the city. When the film was edited, I suggested accompanying it with the beginning of the second movement of Beethoven's Seventh Symphony, where the strings appear so elegant and soft at first, and then rise up the scale in ever increasing volume, until they are almost weeping. The newsroom director went along with my suggestion and aired my film with just that music, no commentary.

What was it that Duke Ellington once said? "There's only two kinds of music. Good and bad." Any music that sounded good to me was what I wanted to hear. I always had to have it, although I was slow to warm to rock-and-roll.

Of the wonderful recordings Sinatra made in his long career, for me two albums made in the 1950s, both arranged and conducted by Nelson Riddle, stand out above all others: *In the Wee Small Hours of the Morning* and *Only the Lonely.* Many appreciators of popular music consider them to be among the finest ever made. Each contain beautifully written songs that Sinatra treats with exquisite respect for the lyrics, using his unsurpassed phrasing and breathing technique to deliver the songs with heartrending intimacy. Sinatra pioneered the "concept" album, building a thematic collection of songs that carry a mood from beginning to end. The theme in *Only the Lonely* is achingly, perhaps devastatingly, melancholy. A screenwriter friend of mine in Montana says it's impossible for him to sit alone and listen to that album. It's too dark, he says.

In "It's a Lonesome Old Town," from *Only the Lonely,* the sound of a trombone figures throughout the song, especially in a solo passage, playing over a faint layer of strings, that is haunting. Arranger Riddle, a former big band trombonist, used the voice of that instrument often. Here it is not some brassy trombone marching through River City in *The Music Man.* In "It's a Lonesome Old Town" it is a solitary lament, something reminiscent of an Edward Hopper painting, where a man might be seen sitting alone in the night on the edge of his rumpled, unmade bed in a sparse walk-up apartment, in his shirtsleeves, tie undone, cast in pale blue light falling through a window looking out on a dark street and the neon sign for the bar down below. In one of his works, Dylan Thomas wrote, "For at night the heart comes out, like a cat on the tiles." It's that kind of sound, that kind of song.

I've always felt photographers can learn so much from good writers, good painters, and good music. Ultimately I think our photographs reflect much of what we expose ourselves to and absorb: what books we read, what paintings we look at, what music we listen to—all of that is somewhere inside us, influencing how we see and express ourselves in our pictures. I want an image to have the harmony and economy of a well-crafted paragraph, the grace and sense of balance found within the geometry of a fine painting. I want my pictures to have intimacy, and at their best, I really want my pictures to sing. When you can put together a group of photographs that truly have voices that evoke an emotion, a human condition, and sequence them on the pages of a magazine or, better yet, in a book, you can have, I think, the equivalent to the arrangement of songs on an album. This is where the writer, the magazine layout designer, or the book designer can bring their artistry to bear much as the lyricist, the musical arranger, and the conductor bring out the best in a singer. The best pictures last because they sing, and some people will remember them as they remember songs. Maybe that's a stretch. But I believe it; it works for me to think that way.

Ironically, over my years of doing essays for *National Geographic* about people and their cultures, I've done only one that specifically dealt with music, and that was in 1997, when I had the privilege of photographing the world of black blues music for a story called "Traveling the Blues Highway." Although I was raised in a family of musicians, I didn't grow up with the blues—unless, of course, you count the tendency toward melancholy I inherited from my Swedish-born father. I entered the world of the blues with a general love of music but not much knowledge of this particular musical form. I came away a year later intoxicated with a new love, the kind you know will last forever.

In the past, when asked what my favorite assignment was, I really couldn't single out just one. But today I would probably say, "Yeah, the year I traveled around listening to good blues music and photographing the places where I heard it." Juke joints and blues festivals in the South and up north in Chicago. Stay up late, drink some beers, listen to great music, and make pictures. Get up late the next morning and do it again. Assignments like that aren't running around in bunches.

On that assignment, as on others over my career, I had to remind myself of something: When you're surrounded by rich visual material, that's when you really have to be selective. The hunter who flushes a covey of quail and quickly shoots at the many birds flying off often misses them all because he didn't pick *a* bird. You have to pick *a* bird, pick *a* picture and think only of it, really concentrate and look at it. Of course, it may be but a moment in time; still, pick a bird. And then move on. During that "Blues Highway" assignment, when the music was great, which was often, and there were pictures everywhere, and I was having a wonderful time, I'd try to remember: Be careful, slow down. Everything's great, but are you really making great pictures? Are you *really* seeing them, are you being truly selective?

A decade before starting the "Blues Highway" essay, I was working on a story about William Faulkner's Mississippi. On Easter Sunday in 1987 I was photographing in a juke joint, a house owned and lived in by African-American blues musician Junior Kimbrough and his family. On most Sundays local bluesmen gathered to play in the living room, and people danced. Early in the afternoon I photographed one of Junior's daughters, Paula, in a back bedroom of the house. Her brother David was sitting on a cot covered with a *Star Wars* blanket, kissing his girlfriend. Someone was passed out on a wrinkled bed by the side of the room, and Paula, in a silvery outfit and wearing a scarlet hat, her Easter outfit, stood posing, one hand resting jauntily on a hip, and leaning on the other arm thrust out to the closed door behind her. I didn't want her to pose but realized that, in fact, her somewhat exaggerated pose was really completing the picture. Later, after dark, a couple danced, sweaty and close beneath the warm yellow light of a single bare bulb ceiling light. Bottles of moonshine whiskey were being passed around, and the walls of that small Mississippi house were still throbbing with music when I left deep in the night. Ten years later, while working on the *Geographic* "Blues Highway" story, I again visited Junior Kimbrough's juke joint, no longer his house but a separate place. While rivulets of sweat snaked down my back in the sweltering Mississippi night, I watched an attractive young African-American girl just a few feet from the band sensuously sway and bend to the rhythm of a slow blues while heavy-bodied women at the back of the room cooled themselves in front of an industrial-size floor fan.

On Chicago's South Side I was making pictures in a blues club called Smoke Daddy. A classic, cream-colored 1960s Cadillac was parked at the curb, its almost lethal-looking fins visible through the open door of the bar.

Three circular lights, two yellow, one white, descended from the ceiling to illuminate a checkerboard-painted floor. Seated at the bar on the right, three bar stools down from the end and silhouetted in the motion of drinking a beer, was Jimmy Lee Robinson, a bluesman who was to take his own life about a year or so later.

I came across Bobby Rush a couple of times while working on the "Blues Highway" essay, once when I photographed him from the crush of a crowded Rum Boogie Café on Beale Street in Memphis, once again on the road in Mississippi. Rush, then in his late 50s, was one of the most energetic blues performers I encountered. He worked a lot of what was considered the Chitlin Circuit, smaller festivals and clubs that draw a high percentage of African-American audiences. Other big-name blues artists, such as B. B. King and Clarence "Gatemouth" Brown, often drew a majority of white enthusiasts at blues festivals, especially up North.

Rush was the consummate showman: blousy-sleeved, colorful shirts; slick black hair and mustache; apportioning out harp licks between lyrics, his lean body in a widespread stance with thrusting hip movements, a bit risqué but never over the top. For sexual emphasis he always had a couple of young African-American women who took the stage at various times to dance. Actually, they shook more than danced; they moved their bottoms with a ferocity that seemed almost motor driven, exaggerated by skintight outfits that became explosions of color in motion. At a blues festival in Greenville, Mississippi, prime country for the Jackson-based Rush, his dancers, Dianne and "Scandalicious"—how I loved that name—were just finishing one of their between-songs costume changes inside the band's bus. Scandalicious, in a lemon-lime-colored outfit, was checking her face in the bus's rearview mirror and adjusting an earring, while Dianne, in pink pants so tight across the front they seemed cleaved, was just finishing retouching her face, and held a tiny compact and puff in her scarlet-nailed fingers. The scorching Mississippi Delta afternoon sun cut through the bus windows in a blast of white light. On her right arm Scandalicious wore a watch on her wrist and some kind of Egyptian-like silver-wired clasp encompassing her upper arm. Looking at that picture now, I wonder: Is Scandalicious left-handed, and what kind of music did the ancient Egyptians listen to?

Clarence "Gatemouth" Brown, I was told, could be very difficult; he didn't suffer outsiders very well and did *not* want to be referred to as a blues musician. In truth, he was a versatile performer. He could play jazz, he recorded some big band arrangements on some of his many albums; there didn't seem much the then 73-year-old Louisiana-born musician couldn't do or hadn't done, musically. I first met him at a blues festival in Memphis, walking up to him as he stepped out of his dressing room trailer, the distinct, sweet fragrance of pot exiting with him. I got right to the point and told him I understood he didn't want to be considered just a bluesman, but that of all the CDs in my car, the one that probably got the most play was a single cut, something by him called "Think I'd Rather Have the Blues," with a big band arrangement that had lots of brass and swung in the ways of Count Basie or Sinatra with Nelson Riddle. I didn't mention Sinatra, although I think Gatemouth would have approved. We got along fine.

That afternoon I convinced the stage crew at the tent where Gatemouth was going to perform that I needed to work the edges, be in the wings and not down in the pit in front of the band. I always want to be around the edges of any performance, because that is where the most interesting images are found: within the tension and backstage interplay surrounding the performance, not the performance itself. The stage crew believed me and trusted me, I guess, not to get out of hand. That's how I made the picture of Gatemouth ending his set that closed the Memphis festival. I was all but playing in the band at the end of his last song, and when he finished, I stepped out onto the stage behind him. When he turned and saw me, between himself and his drummer, he flashed that Gatemouth smile and his eyes glimmered. It was almost like he expected me to be there. To play my part.

The first time I saw the late Junior Wells, one of the most famous Chicago bluesmen, was at the bar in the Checkerboard Lounge on Chicago's South Side: white, five-buttoned sport coat; handkerchief in the breast pocket; black shirt with a white collar; black fedora; a large gold medallion hanging by a chain over a multicolored tie. He was something to see, and I knew right away that I had to portray him. Junior was a big clothes man, foppish in a classic sense; I would have loved to see his closet. It was said he could be set to leave his house, be almost out the door, and then suddenly change his mind and his entire outfit for reasons known only to him.

Junior Wells put the Checkerboard Lounge on the blues map with his performances there over the years, but he wasn't playing that night. This was early summer of 1997. I saw him briefly at the Chicago Blues Festival but had no time to work with him. I was due back in Chicago in the fall and decided to get with him then, but before I got back he became ill and slipped into a coma from which he never emerged. Junior died in early January 1998, and the last time I saw him he was lying in a casket in a Chicago funeral home. Upon hearing of his death I had called his family and asked if I could come to photograph his funeral.

Junior Wells was definitely a hat man. I don't think I ever saw a picture of him without one on his head. That's why, when I arrived at the funeral home in Chicago for the viewing, I wasn't surprised to see him lying there, stylish as ever, a hat on his head. I'm from Minnesota, and open-casket funerals were common in our community when I was growing up. I didn't like them then and I don't like them now. But, if I *were* an open-casket guy, I would go out like Junior, because I *am* a serious hat man. I own and wear a lot of them: stylish hats, hand-shaped crowns and brims, fine-quality felt. I'd have them put on my best, a silver belly 10X with a Montana crease and full pencil rolled brim, custom-built for me in Billings, Montana, by Rand's Custom Hats. I suppose I could leave that hat to one of my sons, but it would really dress up the casket nicely. However, I'm not going that way. Ashes it will be. Scatter some of them in central Montana, and the rest can be slipped under a patch of sod in the family plot in Union Cemetery near Cambridge, Minnesota, where my folks' ashes are absorbed. My boys can flip for the Rand hat and divide up the rest of them. Other than that, gather together and play some good music. Live music would be best, but if not, just make it good and varied. Including a little blues and some Sinatra from the fifties would be nice. ■

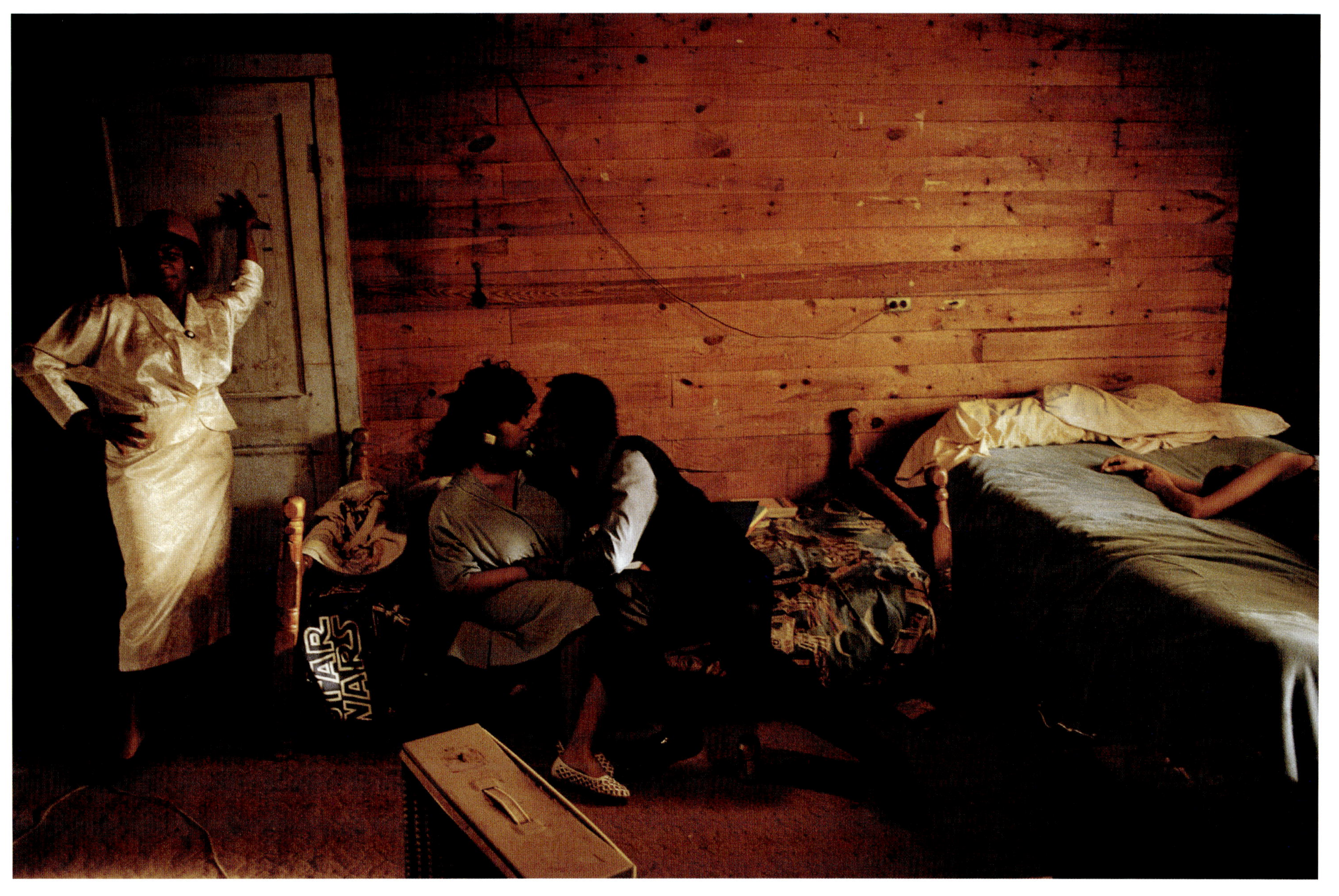

Paula Kimbrough in her Easter dress, Junior Kimbrough's juke joint, Holly Springs, Mississippi, 1986

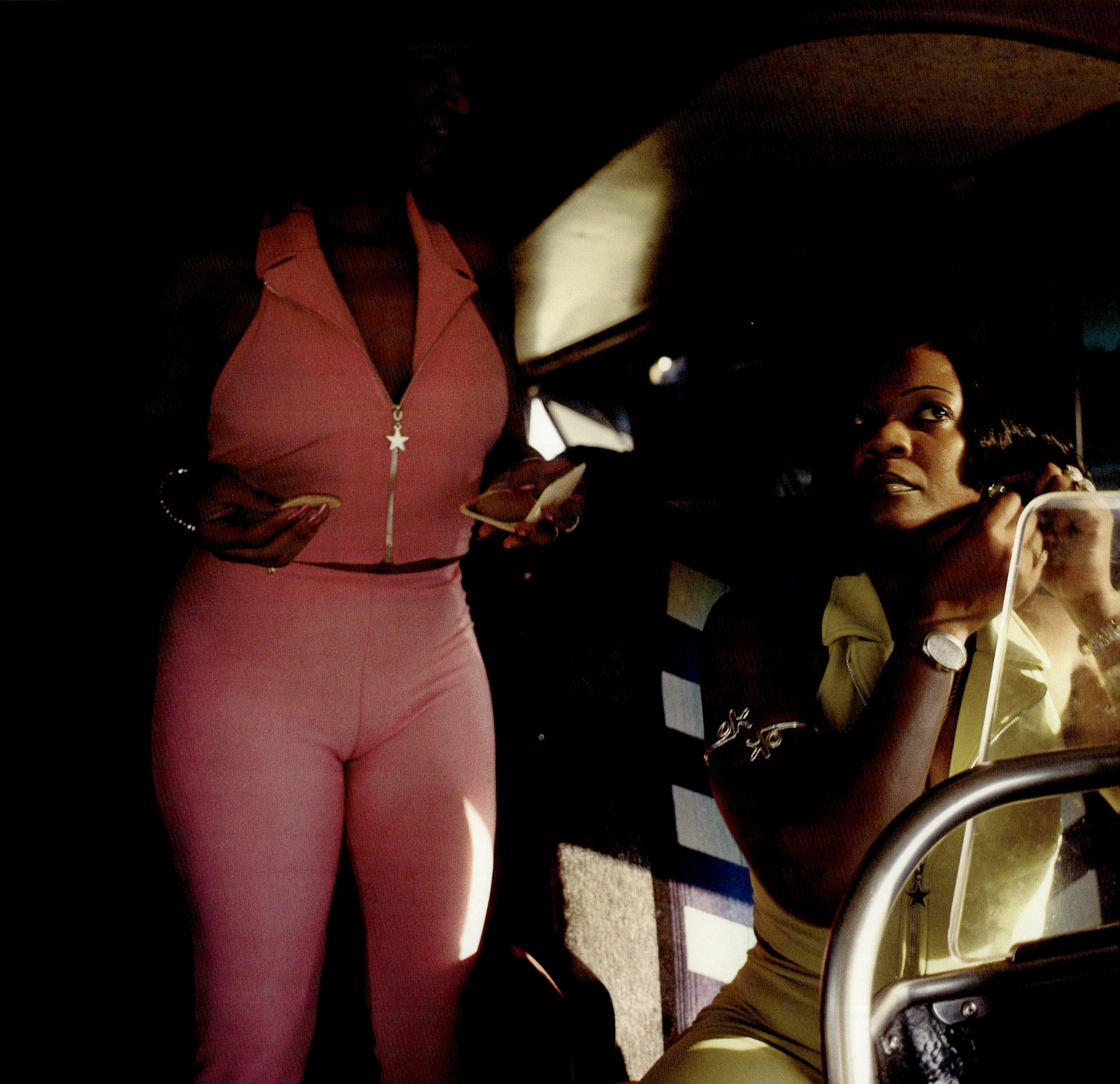

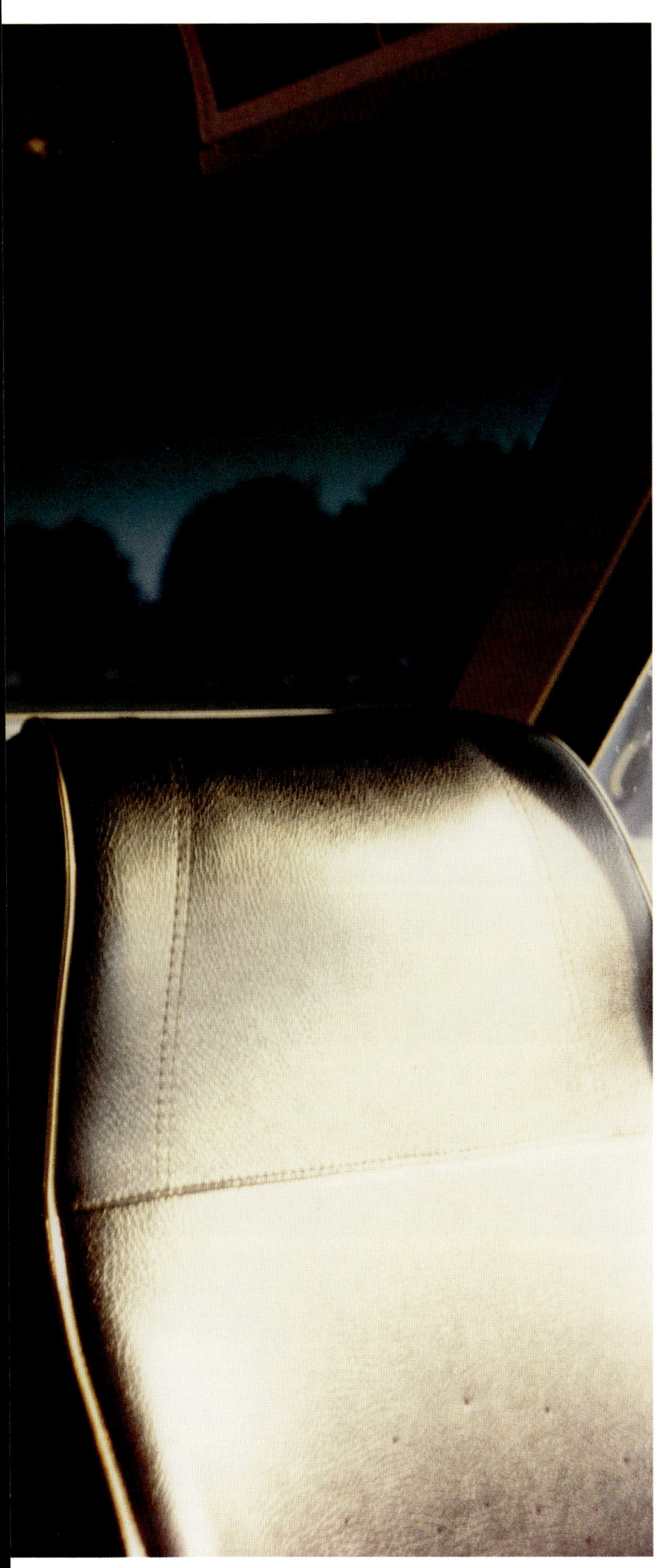

Dianne and Scandalicious on the Bobby Rush bus, Greenville, Mississippi, 1997

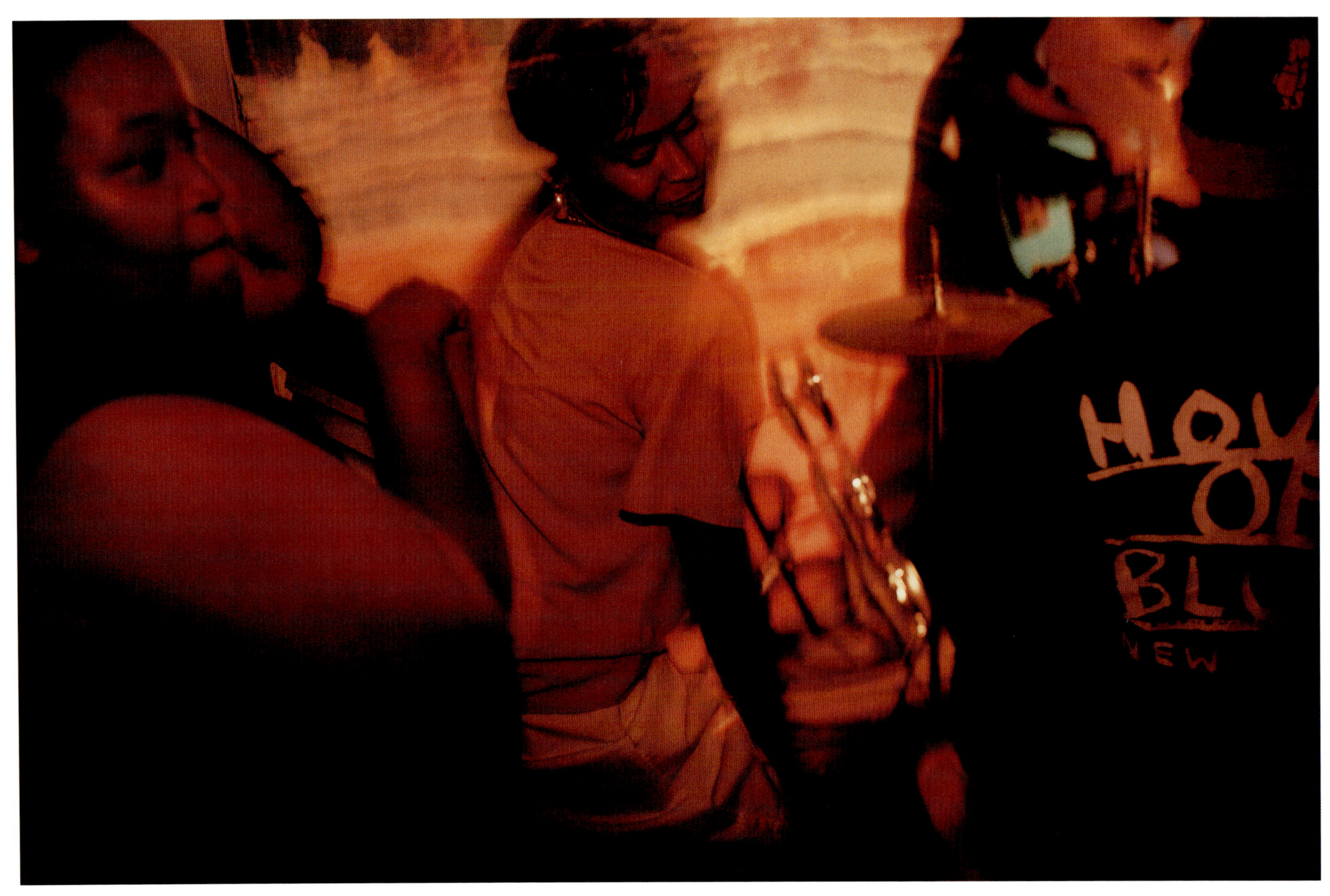

Junior Kimbrough's juke joint, Holly Springs, Mississippi 1997

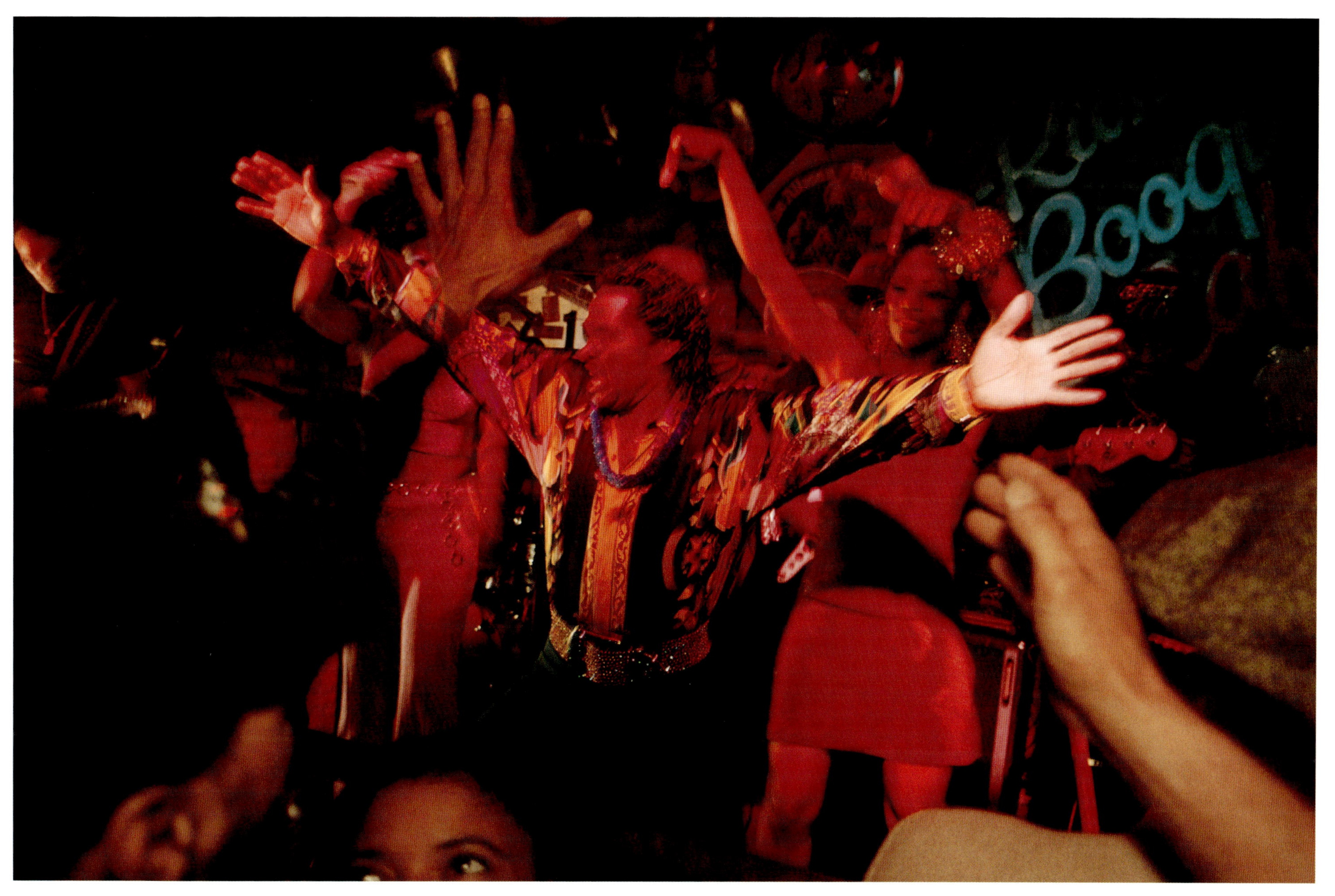

Bobby Rush, Rum Boogie Café, Memphis, Tennessee, 1997

"...music has always been a major and necessary force in my life. If I were not a photographer and a writer, if I were lucky enough, I'd make music my work."

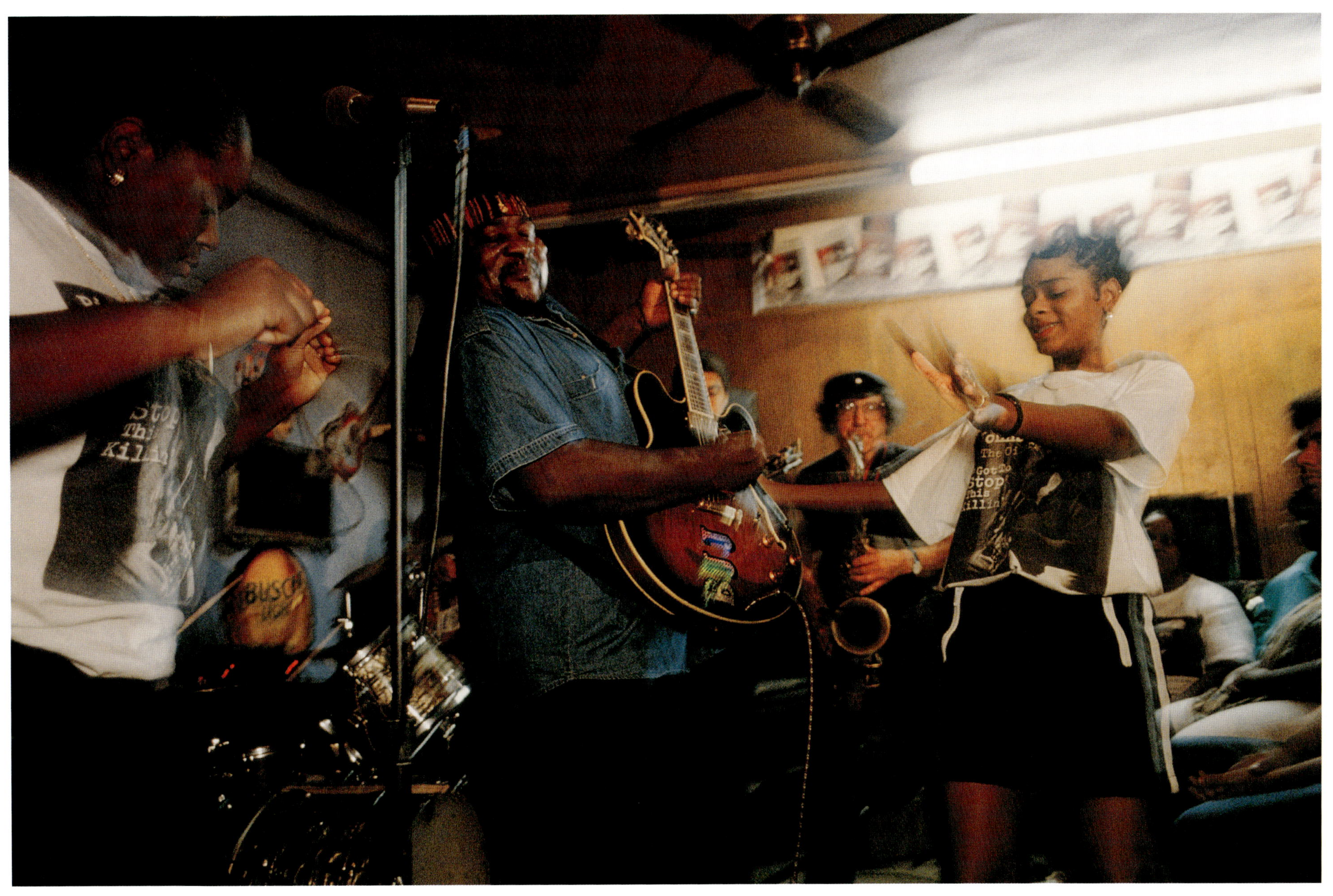

Big Jack Johnson and his granddaughters at Red's, Clarksdale, Mississippi, 1997

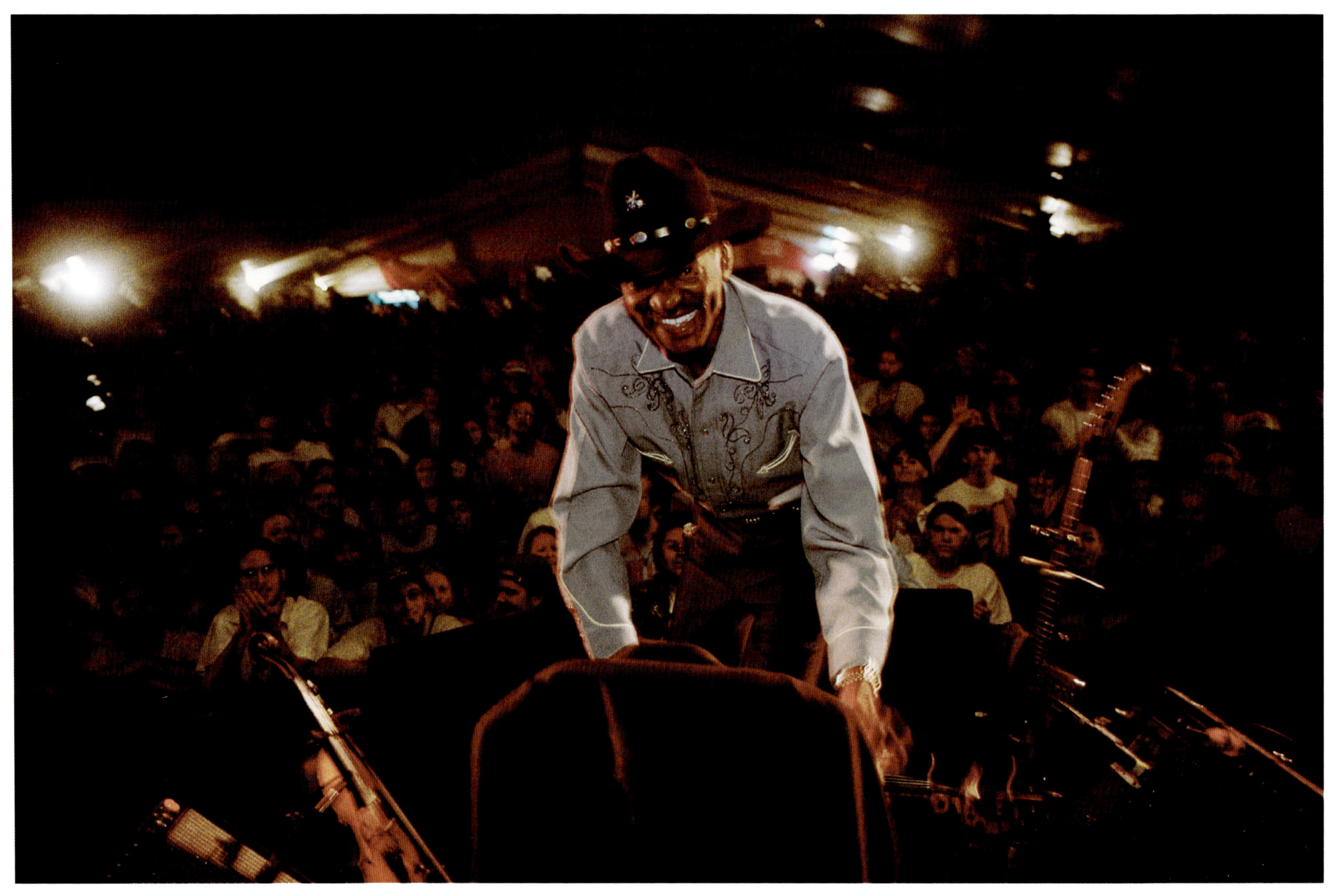

Clarence "Gatemouth" Brown, Memphis, Tennessee, 1997

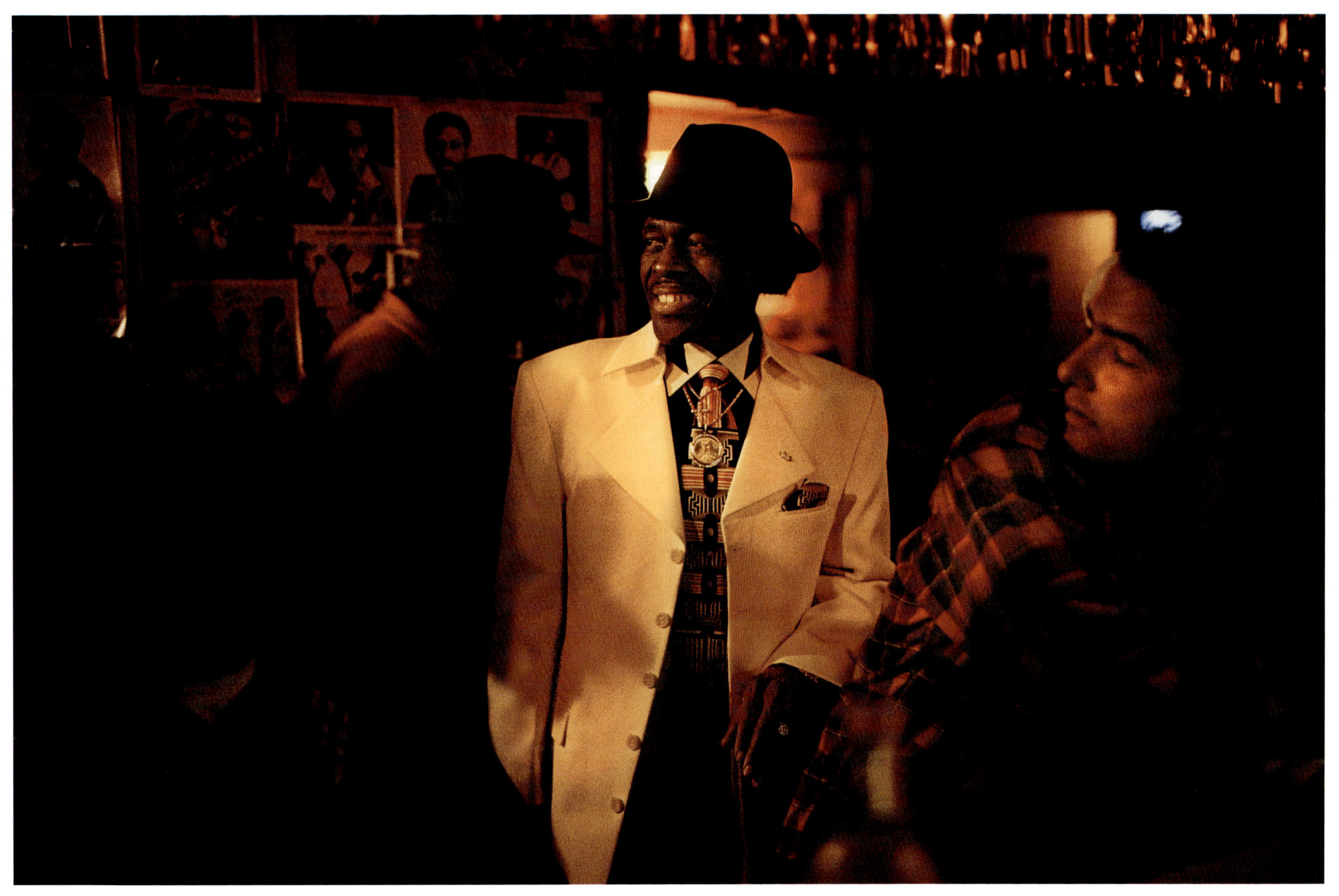

Junior Wells, Checkerboard Lounge, Chicago, 1997

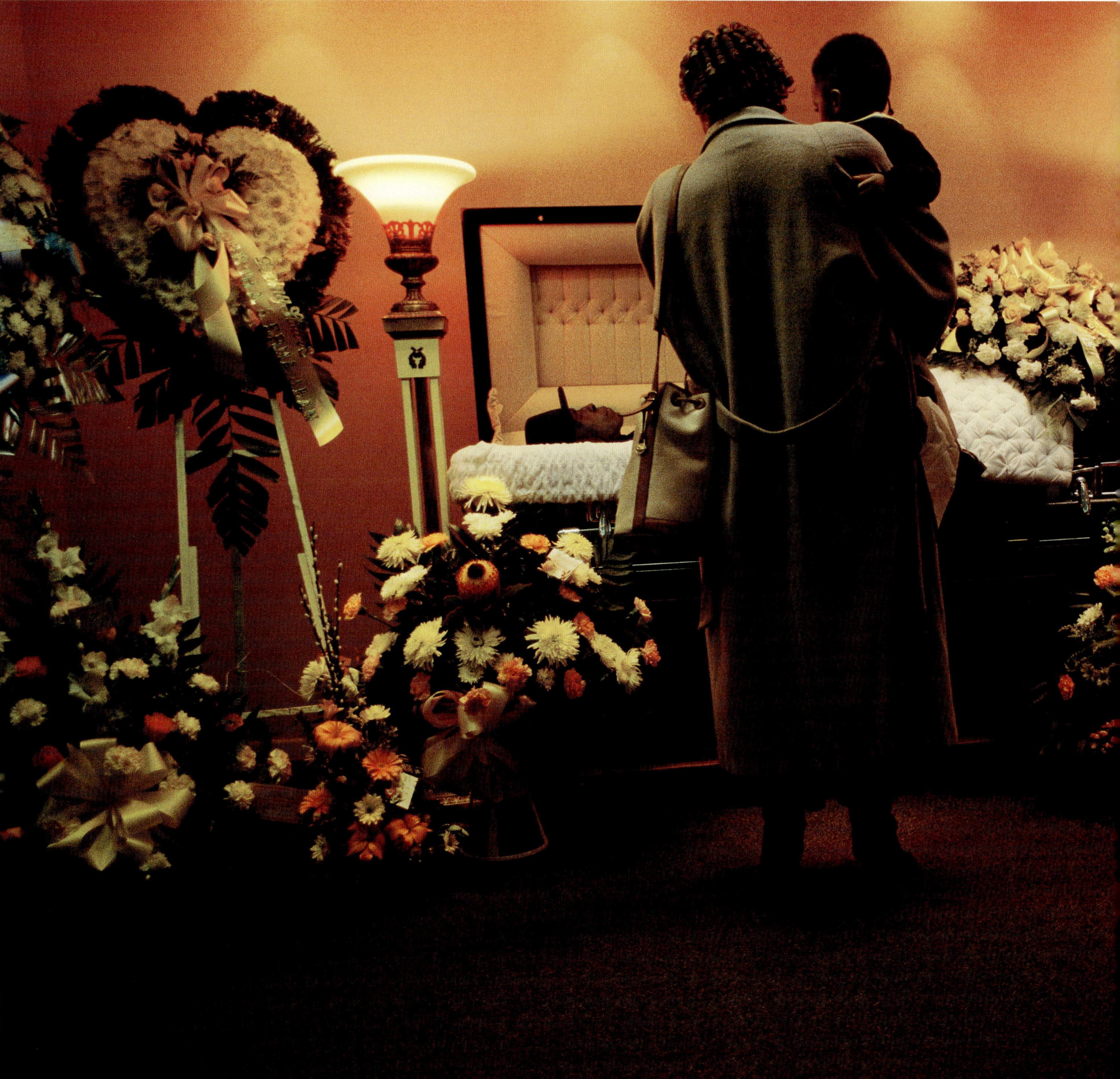

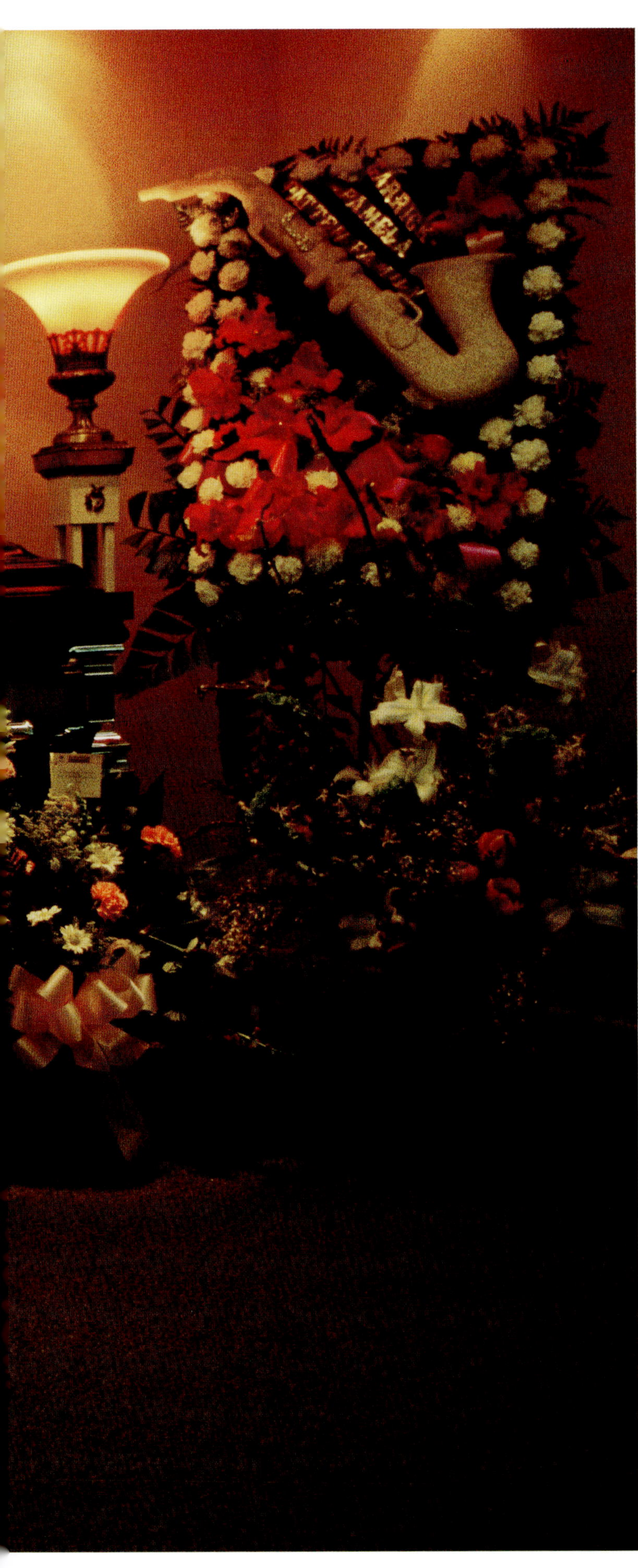

Funeral of Junior Wells, Chicago, 1998

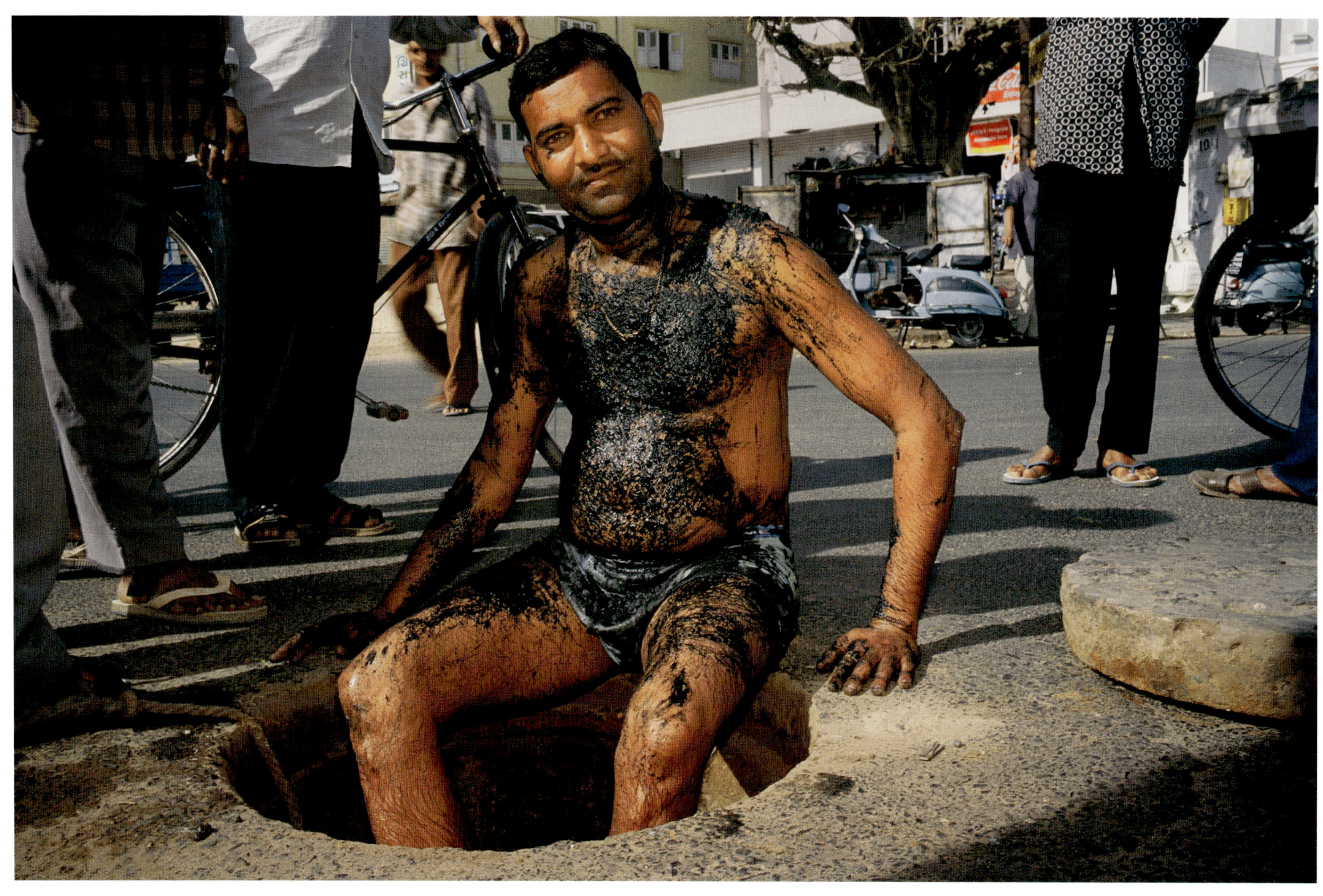

Amrutbhai Savasya, scavenger caste, Gujarat, 2002

Observations on India's Untouchables

"The Economic Survey 2001 claims that poverty reached an all-time low of 26 per cent in 1999-2000. According to the latest estimates, the number of poor people in the country stands at 260 million."

—*Times of India*, February 27, 2002

In 2002 I worked on an essay about Le Marais, a relatively small but chic Right Bank neighborhood in Paris. That same year I also had the privilege of photographing an essay about India's Dalits, more commonly known as the Untouchables, those 160 million souls born into the dark bottom of India's massive social structure, the Hindu caste system. Going back and forth between the two subjects was like working on two separate planets.

Le Marais—abounding in beautiful historical architecture, sophistication, and wealth, with pricey hotels, antique shops, and restaurants—has the immaculately manicured Place des Vosges, with its fountains and grassy geometric carpet with benches beneath the trees, the arches of the covered walkways open to sidewalk cafés and shops. A few minutes away, on Rue de Rivoli, one can linger endlessly over coffee and observe the beautiful Parisian girls in summer dresses pedaling their bicycles into the late afternoon sunlight. Here, within this 360-acre pocket called Le Marais, in one of the world's greatest cities—and my favorite—is the continuation of centuries of Jewish history and the heartbeat of Paris's gay community. Here live and work those of many racial and religious varieties, their social interaction seemingly without borders, if not totally lacking prejudice.

Leaving Paris, I would fly off to the vastness and intensity of India, with its extraordinary variety of landscapes, often beautiful, at times harsh, sometimes both—a country embroidered with many languages and religions, at whose center exists an ancient and often fanatically rigid sense of identity and dictation of one's place in the social order. At first, for some reason, I thought with a bit of time I could understand it all. I soon came to wonder, how wrong could I be? How much time is enough? I'm not sure I understood anything about India except that the country was almost beyond comprehension for me, a first-time visitor from the Western world. India was immediately intoxicating, incredibly confusing, jaw-dropping, and almost insane in its visual stimulation. "My God," I would often exclaim, when with someone else, "did you see *that?*"

As writer Tom O'Neill and I began to search out examples of India's caste system, still brutally intact after 1,500 years, we met many wonderfully gentle and gracious people who welcomed us into their lives and often very modest homes. We visited Untouchables who have been forced into some of the most menial and often repulsive endeavors simply to survive: jobs that higher caste members will not do but Untouchables must, for the simple reason that they were born into it. If a man is a Bhangi, a member of a scavenger caste, he will spend his life cleaning up human waste, because *his* father spent his life cleaning up human waste, and *his* father before him, an uninterrupted lineage coursing back through their ancestry and the history of human waste in India.

It is an Untouchable who will remove the dead and rotting animals from the streets; tan the hides of cattle; scavenge the garbage for any item conceivably useful or edible; wash used clothing for a higher caste man to sell at profit in the markets; clean the sewers of a city and the open latrines of village homes. An Untouchable will see to the cremating of the dead and disposing of the afterbirth of the newly born.

As I pursued my first assignment in India, I wrote observations in my notebooks, vignettes of what I saw and felt while entering an incredible world where pictures were everywhere, yet because I was concentrating on the lives of the Untouchables, the things and people I saw in my daily travels might not always be part of my story. Even though one of every six Indians is a Dalit, they exist in a country of one *billion* people. From my very first cab ride in New Delhi, looking out my door window, I would see incredibly visually exciting images of places and people. But I would wonder: What am I seeing? Who are those people over there? Is that an Untouchable? So, to pursue my subject, I would go, with the help of some nongovernmental organization, to a village or a place in a city where they would introduce me to Untouchables whom I could meet and photograph.

Untouchables really don't look any different from anyone else in India; a man may appear healthy and handsome, a woman pretty, a child well scrubbed and cute as a puppy. They may well have the same skin color as an upper caste member. It is by their names, backgrounds, where they live, and occupations that they will eventually be identified by those of higher castes. Their inescapable fate seems indelibly stamped upon them at birth.

IN NEW DELHI, the hired driver is hacking and sneezing the first two days we are out; the car's horn is wheezing, too, but on the third day the driver's health seems greatly improved, and the horn also sounds stronger, as if the two of them are related. Along the streets are groups of giggling schoolgirls in uniformed saris or snow-white blouses above solid-colored skirts and knee-high stockings. There are vendors of everything imaginable under the Indian sun. Rumbling out of all the multi-starred hotel driveways are white Ambassador Classics, unchanged for 50 years; the four-door tubs putter along, their drivers choosing to remain in high gear instead of shifting down for what would offer extra acceleration when needed. They seem to expect relinquishment of the road to them by other drivers and riders in their path.

"GIVE ME SOME MONEY and I'll eat a banana," says the dirty-faced little boy begging along the road to Sikar, Rajasthan.

A CAT LIES CRUSHED at the edge of a road going north out of Jaipur. Camels are driven by men whose heads are wrapped in scarves and shawls against the early morning cold. We pass a community of Untouchable brick kiln workers with their camels and goats and kids. We are told a ten-year-old girl (it's said nobody truly knew her age) was killed from a fall in a brick kiln nearby. A broken neck? Who knows. They took her to the nearest town for an immediate funeral and cremation.

IN AN UNTOUCHABLE VILLAGE of hide tanners, blackbirds whirl and dive in tight formations, sweeping back skyward behind the woman cooking an adhesive made from animal parts; how strong it smells, the stench of animal hides, the smoke and steam, how it burns and bites the eyes and throat. She does this all day long.

THERE ARE FIVE DEAD DOGS on the morning drive to Sikar. And a cat. A man rinsing the dust from his throat holds a metal pitcher up over his face and pours water down into his mouth, then spits a long stream out onto the ground, where on impact it blossoms into the irregular shape of a faint damp cloud on the dusty street fronting his tea shop. A burro forages through scraps of paper and plastic and finds a banana peel. A cart donkey leans into its traces, a young man urging it on with a stick, hammering its rump. Attempting to get traction, the dirty-white animal leans forward at an extraordinary angle, hooves scraping and slipping, struggling for purchase, managing to stay on its feet in the midst of all the hectic movement of vehicles, people, and beasts of burden that flow steadily by its flanks, coming and going.

MEN RIDING DOUBLE on a trio of motorcycles with *vhols*—bright steel containers hanging off both sides of the rear wheels—are bringing milk to Jodhpur. Swaddled in their shawls, some squint into the early morning sun; others hide behind round, dark glasses that look like something German tank commanders might have used in World War II. The road surface is ragged, and camel carts jounce roughly in the wake of lumbering trucks and seriously overcrowded buses.

OUR DRIVER IS A SMALL, SLENDER MAN, light mahogany in color. He has a mustache, and, with one wandering eye, his creased face reminds me a bit of the fine American novelist and poet Jim Harrison, although I've never met Harrison—I'm only going by the pictures on the dust jackets of his books.

NEAR THE PAKISTAN BORDER there is a dead cow on a road fenced on one side by a few strands of barbed wire that hang like remnant threads of an abandoned spiderweb. Here and there on the other side of the wire are land mine warnings, red triangular signs on steel stakes driven into the desert sand like roadside memorials marking past tragedies.

AN ABANDONED NEWBORN baby girl in Bihar, left under a bridge, where she might first have been discovered by a dog or maybe a pig, luckily was found and is brought to a shelter that serves as a kind of rehabilitation center for Dalit midwives. Because Hindus consider contact with blood defiling, most Indian midwives are Untouchables and have traditionally been paid more for disposing of a female baby than for delivering one. At the shelter where they brought the thrown-away baby, women are being taught that killing girls is wrong. The silver-haired midwife I photograph with the baby has large, strong-looking hands that dwarf the tiny swaddled infant, who resembles a miniature elderly person with worried eyes. Someone tells me that a common way for a midwife to dispose of an unwanted girl baby is to sever its spinal cord with a twist of her hands, like wringing a wet towel. I try to forget that right away, but can't possibly. Not for a long time, maybe never.

IN THE UNTOUCHABLE VILLAGES we visit some residents and drink tea with milk and lots of sugar from cups of stainless steel. In even the poorest homes we are offered the hospitality of tea, crackers, and smiles. But away from the solitude of a village, in the crush and rush of heavy city traffic or on a highway thick with travelers, hostility can rise up from some seemingly innocuous event. A motorbike rider rams into our car from behind on a small town street, sending him sprawling and bending a wheel on his bike. In moments, a small crowd has gathered, encompassing our vehicle, and half a hundred eyes are examining the evidence and possibly forming a jury; if just one voice starts a harangue against the foreigners it could soon be joined by an intensely harsh chorus of negativity. In such an instance I am reminded of a quote from Anglo-Indian writer Ruskin Bond: "India is more than a land. India is an atmosphere. Over thousands of years, the races and religions of the world have mingled here and produced that unique, indefinable phenomenon, the Indian: so terrifying in a crowd, so beautiful in himself."

THERE IS INDIAN POP MUSIC on the car radio. Our driver has just speedily circumnavigated a sleeping goat. A road-killed dog stretched out dead in the morning was noticeably flatter when we passed it again driving back at midday. Patches of light dapple the ground beneath the trees on both sides, each burst of brilliance revealing another scene of India. The tamarinds edging the road are girdled by red and white paint, like barber poles, or the wing markings of a World War II British Spitfire fighter plane. There seem to be endless kilometers of road construction but only an occasional earth roller as evidence of work in progress. There are numerous bright, red-lettered signs announcing DIVERSION or BUMP. In the *Times of India* there is a story about an accident in Uttar Pradesh, where 16 people were crammed into a jeep that was hit head-on by a speeding bus, killing 11 people in the jeep. The bus driver "absconded" and was currently being sought.

A YOUNG BOY STRIDES so casually, with brown, storklike legs, across the road, clearing the oncoming vehicles by the slimmest of margins, paying no mind to the horns that sound again and again. In the cities and towns of India, it seems one could succumb to madness from the endless horns: a honk, a yap, or a squeal, bark, bleat, or rasp. Welling up from some impossible gridlock of travelers, the sounds of those horns rise in number and volume until it becomes the unrelenting cacophony of 5,000 goats crazed by starvation, all demanding their mother's teat.

THE NASHVILLE SOUND—top-40 country music—is playing in the lobby of the Park Inn in Uttar Pradesh. At the desk a lovely, almond-eyed woman cashes my traveler's checks. Her teeth are milk white, her skin the color of coffee and cream. I find her beautiful and think of a line from novelist David Davidar's *House of Blue Mangoes:* "Fair in a land where the paleness of a woman's complexion outweighs every other attribute." Beauty, I guess, is so often dependent upon the eye of the beholder, judged and valued by the culture that spawned and formed one's visual preference or prejudice.

IN A TEMPLE THERE IS A WOMAN who washed her feet in the temple elephant's urine. I don't know what that was supposed to be about. Good luck, perhaps?

IN BIHAR, ONE OF INDIA'S POOREST states, I photograph in a rock quarry where slender women in saris, with heavy, rock-filled metal pans balanced on their heads, walk single file to a loud, growling, machine, where they dump their loads onto a conveyor belt that will carry the rocks into a crusher, grinding them into gravel. The women return for more, walking gracefully in a fog of choking gray dust that covers them and a small boy who plays nearby, the little one pale as a ghost.

IN THE BRICK KILNS of Rajasthan, women with faces coated and textured as if with some kind of makeup, their wrists ringed with many bangles whose sparkle is muted beneath layers of clay dust, unload wooden wheelbarrows filled with rough, red bricks and pile thousands of them, stack after stack, until at day's end they have earned perhaps two dollars. They, too, have children I sometimes see walking or playing along the wheel-furrowed dirt road running between the kiln's black-spewing smokestack and the small huts where the families eat and sleep. The road is littered with the rubble of broken bricks.

IN DELHI, A SMALL BAREFOOT GIRL with dirty, sleep-tousled hair hugs herself against dawn's chill. A man behind her carries on his back a burden of clothes, fresh from being beaten clean at the water's edge of the Yamuna River, to a pile of fire-heated rocks where he will steam them. He and others of the Dhobi caste will wash dirty clothes all their lives. They live along the river in crude, tin-roofed huts with their families. I step very carefully, because excrement, human and animal, is everywhere. It's not yet full light, and I walk as though on eggs, praying not to misstep or slip on the dew-slick earth. A one-eyed dog sits on its haunches, watching me.

THERE SEEMS NO LIMIT to the suffering inflicted on Untouchables. Sometimes it is death, sometimes, something seemingly almost worse. In Uttar Pradesh, I met a young, terribly scarred Untouchable man named Ramprasad whose story is like some scene out of a horror movie. One day he and three of his friends were checking fish traps they'd placed in a pond supposedly for the use of anyone. But upper caste villagers came upon them and decided the Untouchables had no rights there. The penalty they inflicted was inhumanely severe. The mob doused Ramprasad and one of his friends, Ramlakan, with acid. The friend thought to dive into the pond, washing away much of the acid but still leaving ugly blistering scars on his back and arms. Ramprasad, in panic, ran, and as he did, the flesh and the eye on one side of his face literally melted, changing the handsome young man and his life into a waking nightmare. I don't think his attackers were given any significant punishment; maybe a few months in prison. The positive side of this story, if there is one, is that in the United States a reader of *National Geographic* magazine saw the story about the Untouchables and Ramprasad's picture and arranged through a church organization to raise funds and get Ramprasad reconstructive plastic surgery by Indian doctors who donated their time and skills. They attempted to reconstruct his face, smooth some of the scars, and built him an artificial ear and eye.

IN RAJASTHAN, LAXMAN SINGH, a laborer who protested not being paid for his construction work on a home for a village council president, was beaten with stones and iron rods by friends and relatives of the village official. He lay untreated on a local hospital floor for three days, losing both legs to gangrene. When I photographed him he had been taken in by a sympathetic higher caste member and allowed to hide in a farm shed, afraid of being discovered by his attackers, who might well kill him to keep him from testifying in court. He sat, both legs gone below the knees, beneath a concrete counter laden with stainless steel kitchen utensils and dinner plates, tucked away, as one might place a garbage container.

IN GUJARAT I FOLLOWED Amrutbhai Sarasiya—a Bhangi, a member of the scavenger caste, the lowest of the hundreds of Untouchable castes—as he made his rounds unclogging sewers in Ahmadabad. I watched him descend into the sewer on a rope, immersing himself in excrement, to use a simple metal bucket to remove the waste, bucketful after bucketful. When finished, he sat for a moment in his filthy briefs, on the edge of the sewer opening and looked at me as I photographed him coated with sewage. Around his neck, shimmering in the morning sunlight, was a thin gold chain. I noticed how the chain glimmered, but I also noticed how his eyes did, also. This man's pride seemed undiminished by his position in the world. Later I followed him through the neighborhood as he sought a place where he could clean himself, being turned away from several wells before someone, finally, granted him his simple request. ■

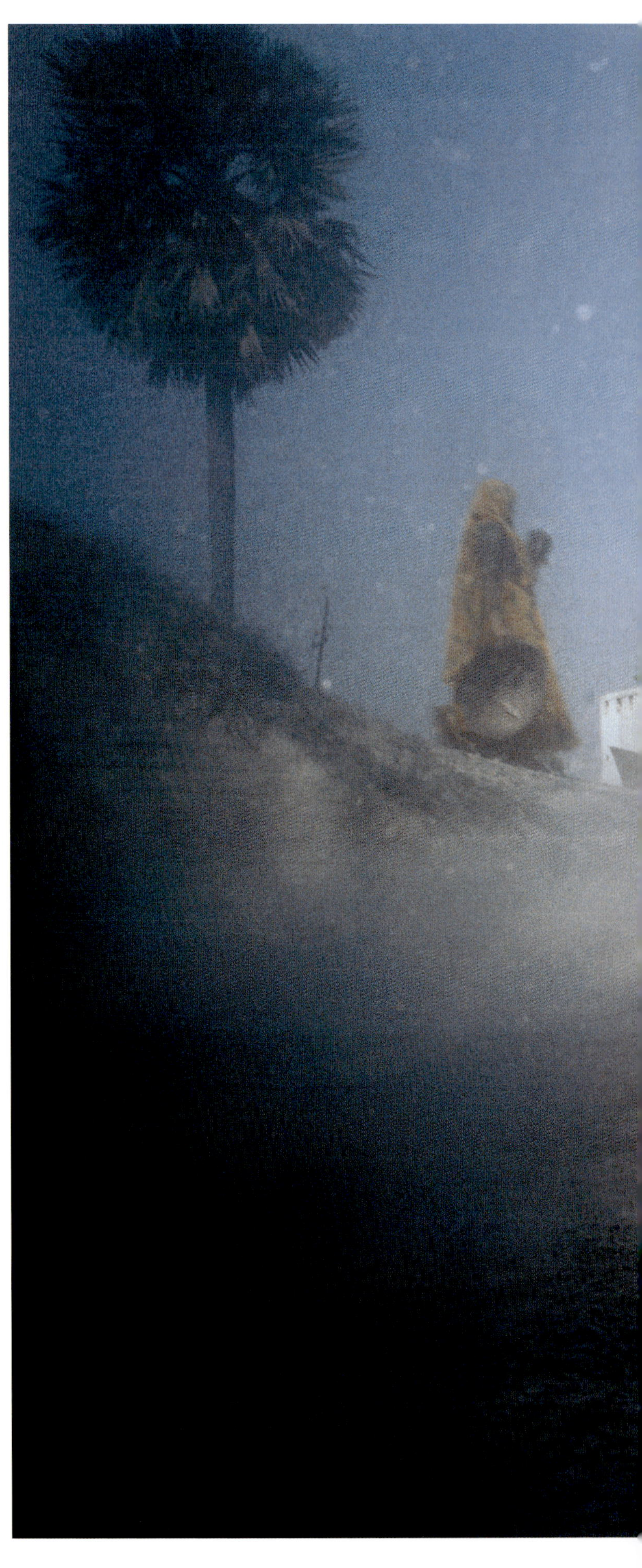

Women in a rock quarry, Bihar, 2002

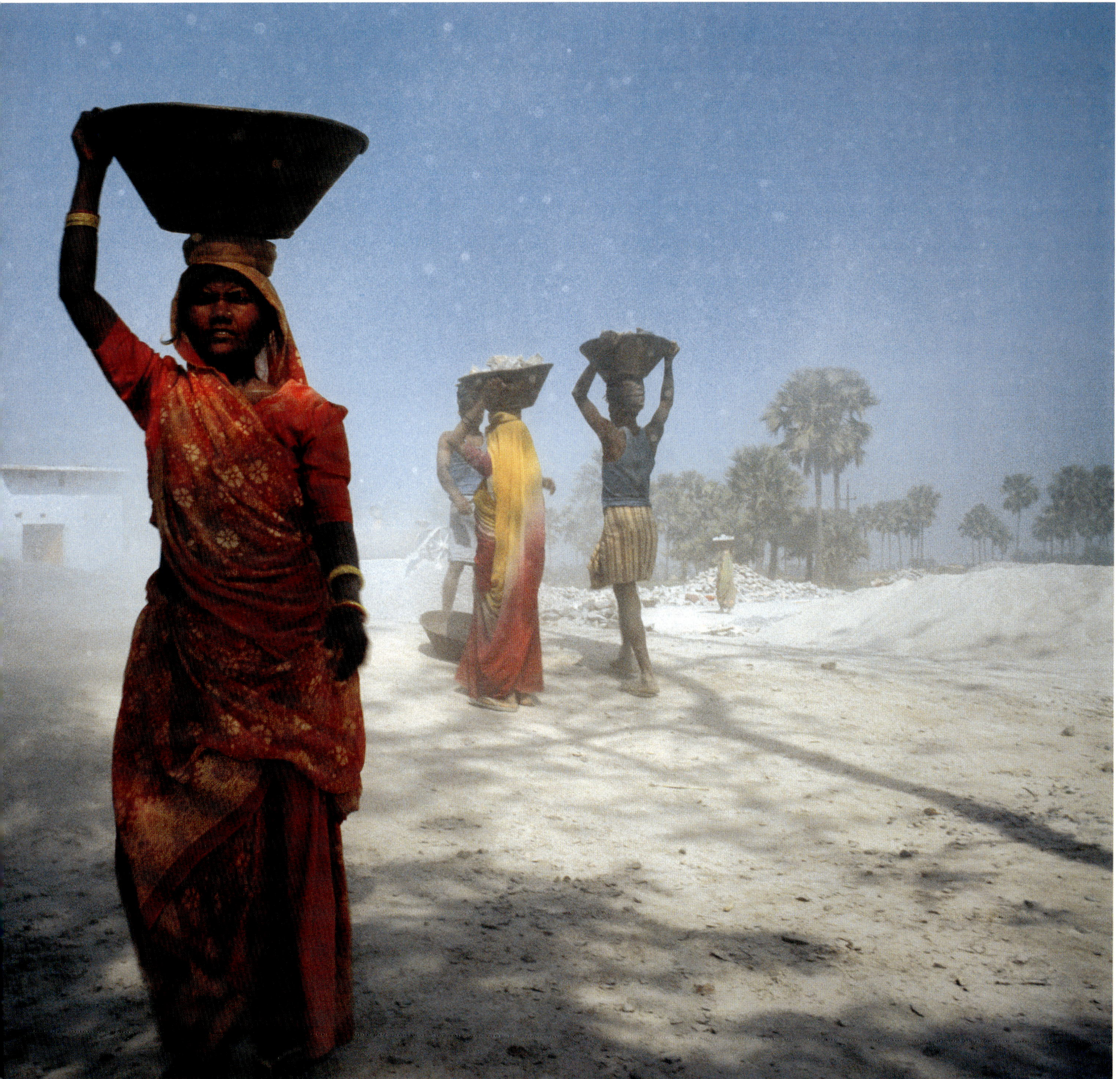

"The women return for more, walking gracefully in a fog of choking gray dust that covers them and a small boy who plays nearby, the little one pale as a ghost."

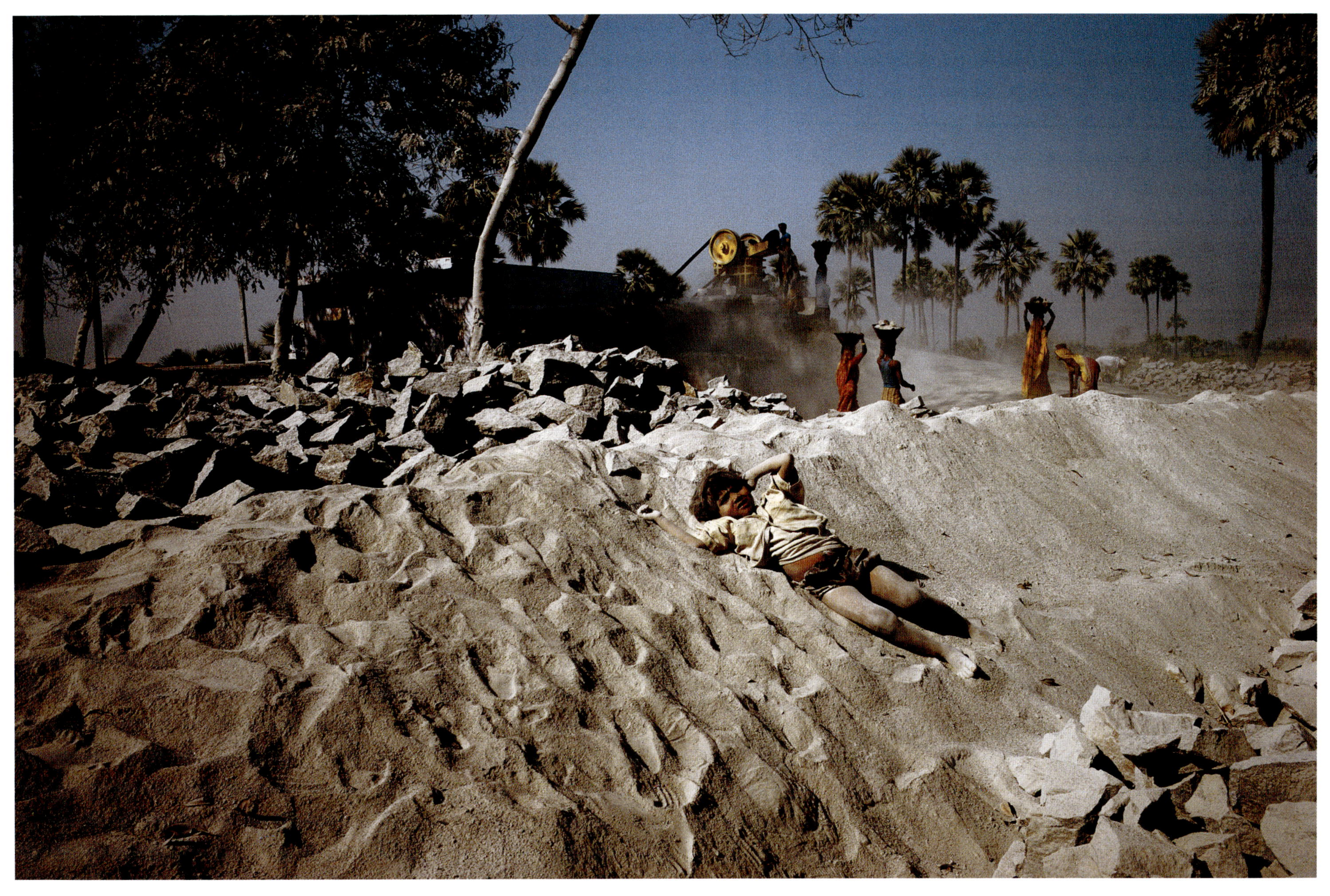

Boy playing in quarry dust, Bihar, 2002

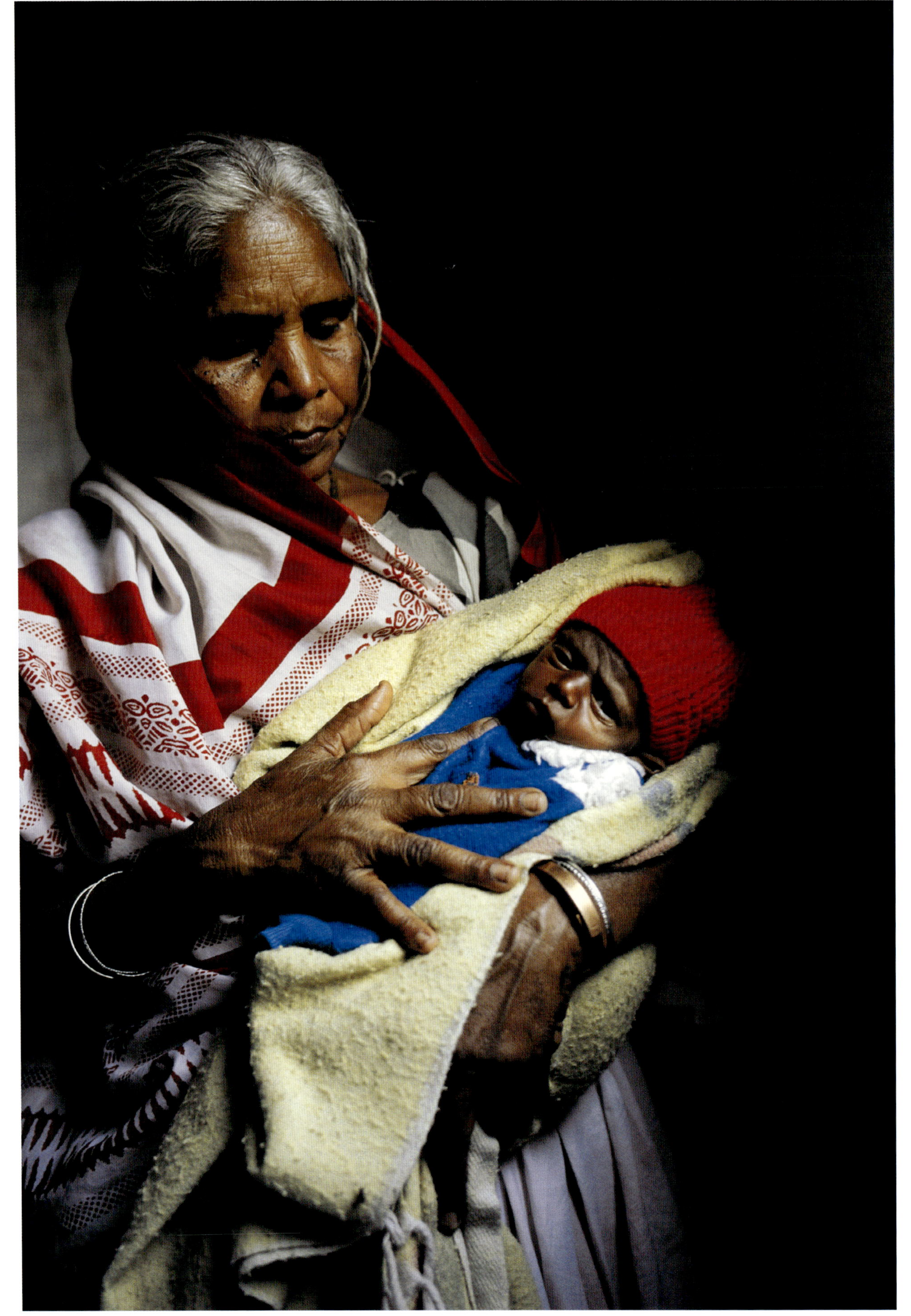

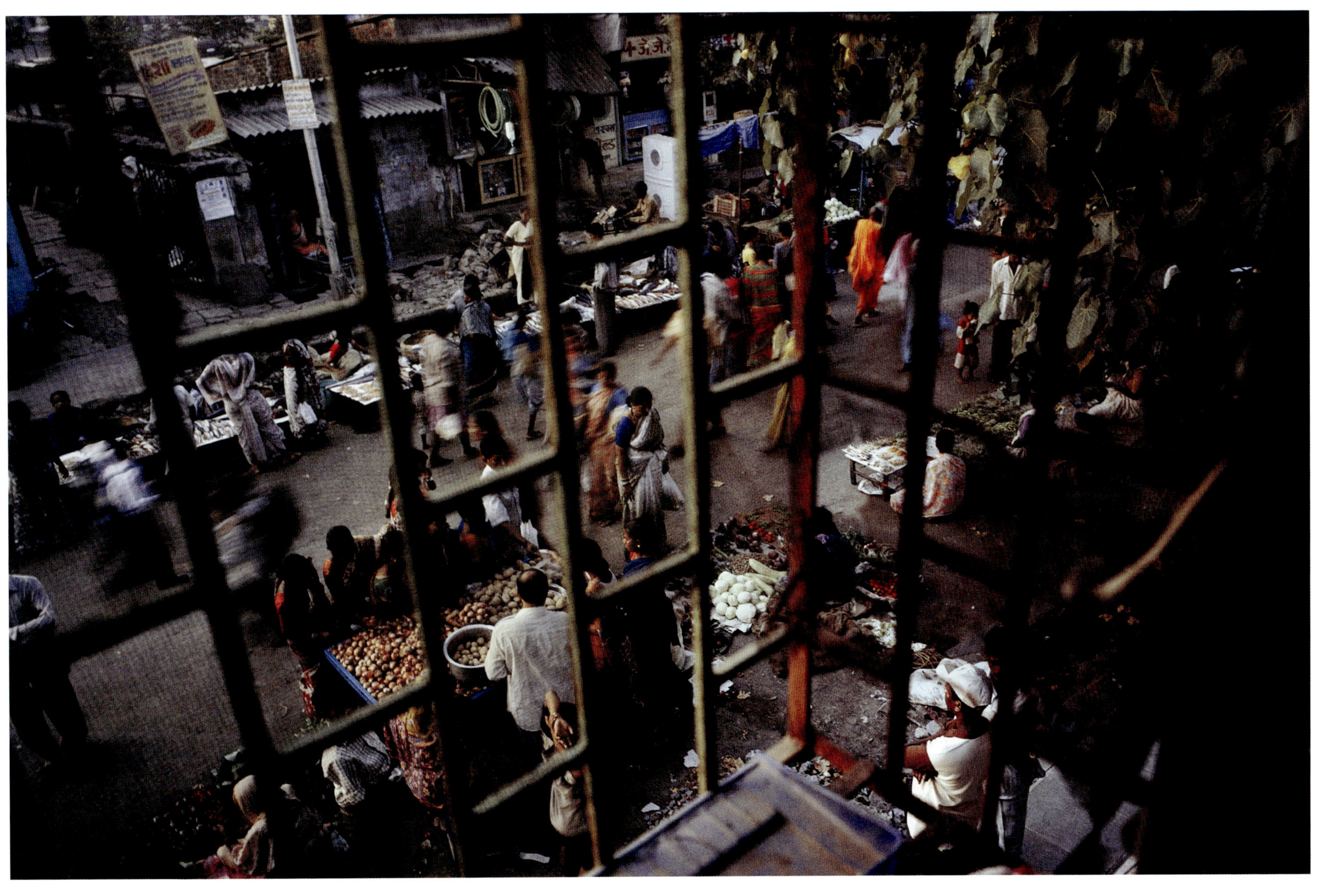

LEFT: *Untouchable midwife with discarded baby, Bihar, 2002* ABOVE: *Street market in Untouchable neighborhood, Mumbai, 2002*

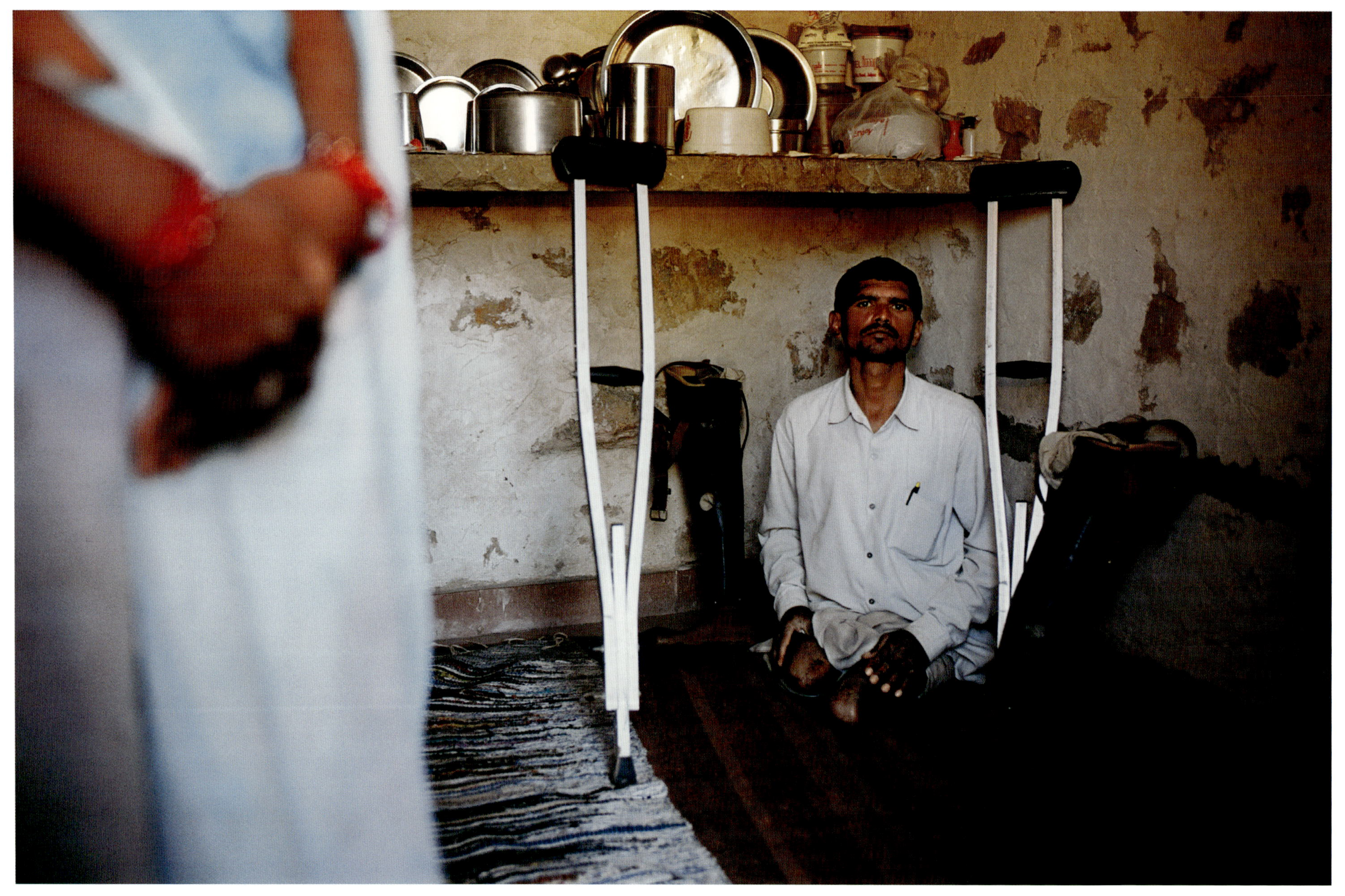

Laxman Singh, Rajasthan, 2002

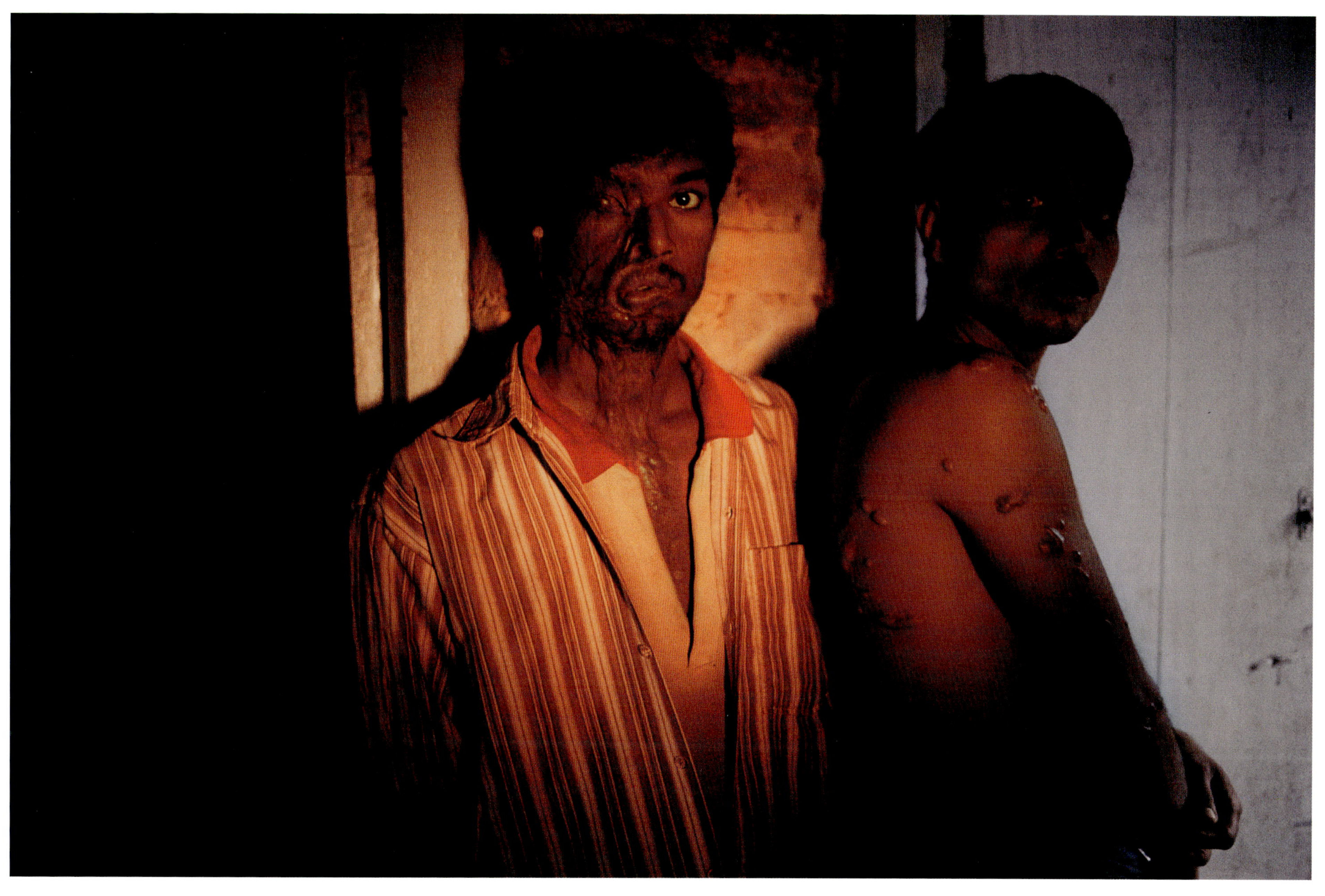

Ramprasad and Ramlakhan, Uttar Pradesh, 2002

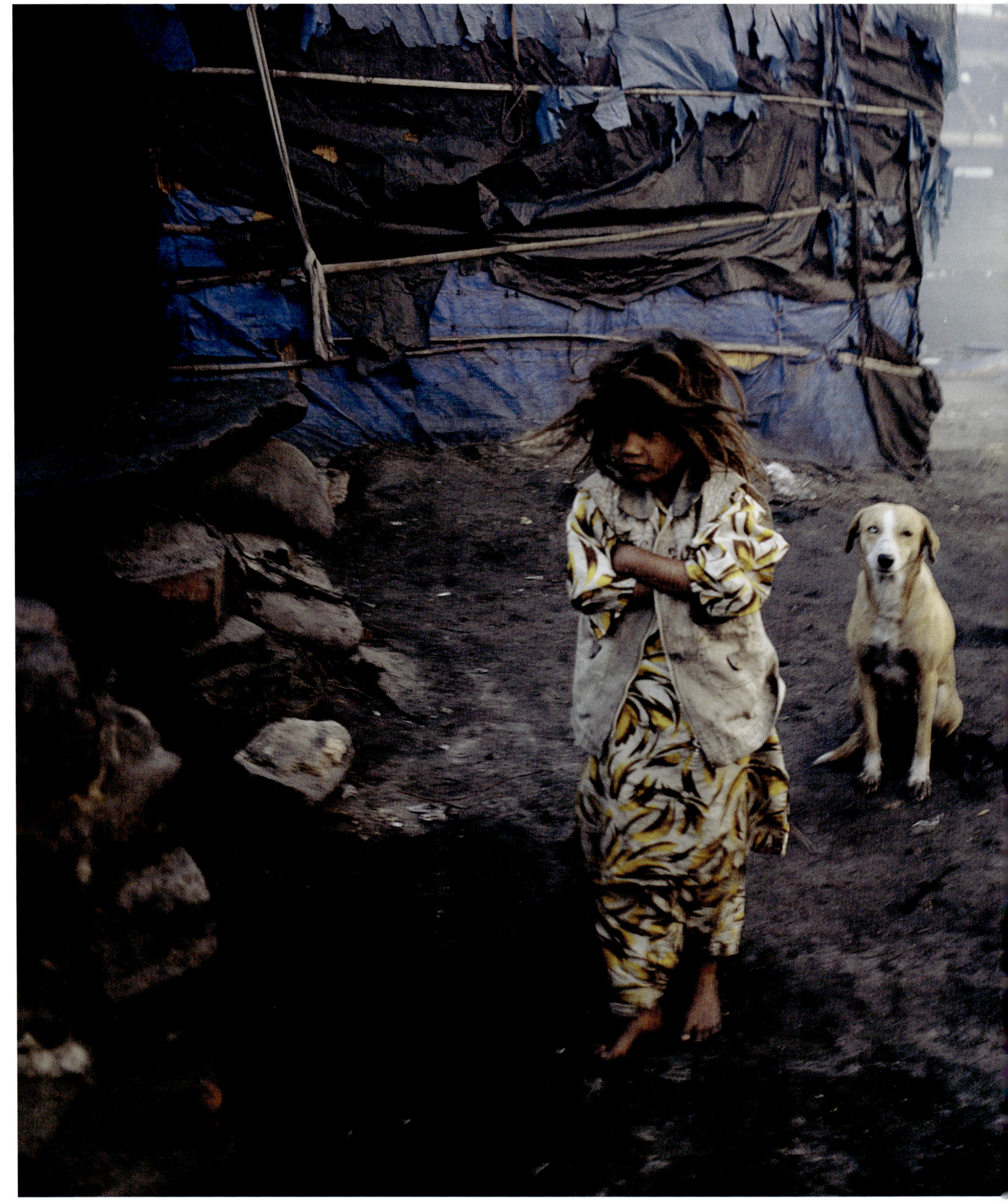

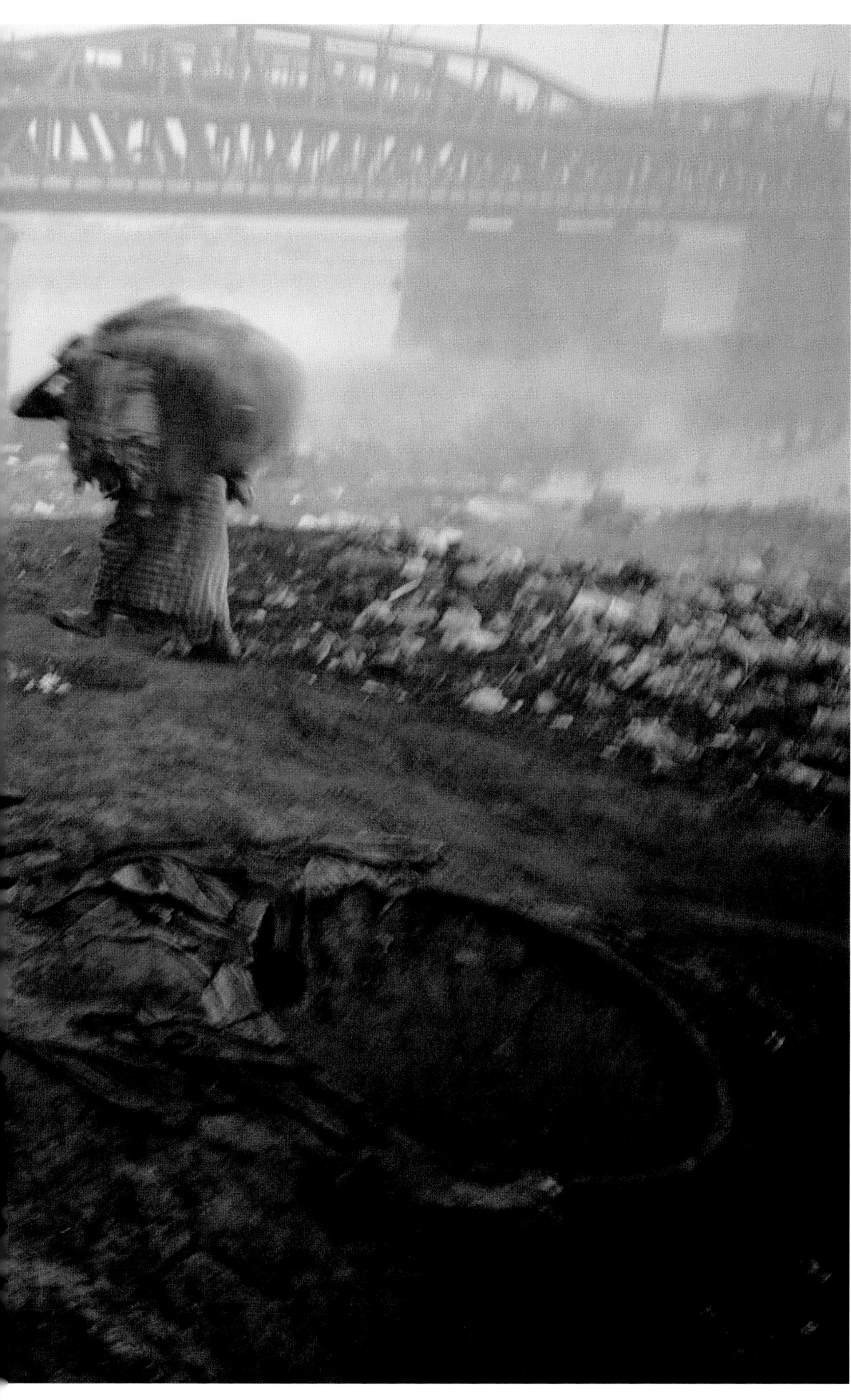

Child of the Dhobi caste, Yamuna River, Delhi, 2002

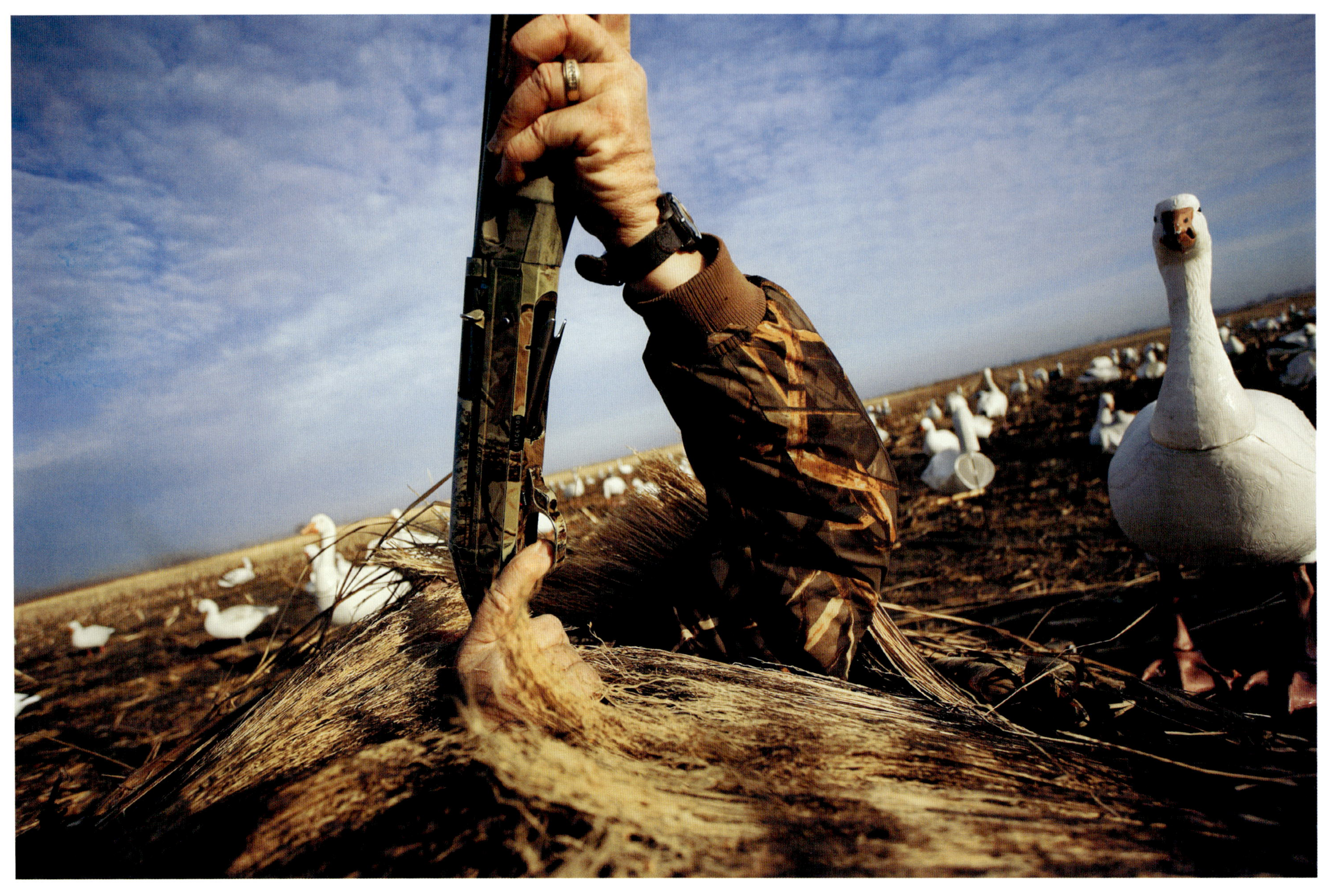

Snow goose hunter, Iowa, 2007

The Season of the Hunter

Autumn has always been my favorite time of the year, especially October, when the air sharpens and leaves begin to color. Dusk still comes gently. Darkness doesn't just suddenly descend as it seems to at the end of those short days of winter. And the light takes on a particular seasonal beauty of its own. My writer friend Bill Kittredge has referred to the October light in Montana as being holy, and imagines himself "healed to the glory of things in this light." To that I say, amen.

Autumn is also the season of the hunter. Growing up in Minnesota I was introduced to hunting by my father. Although he subscribed to one of those outdoor magazines that extolled the adventuresome rewards of hunting big game and fishing for trophy bass, my dad sought only panfish and hunted only pheasant, and for those brilliantly colored ring-necked birds, just a few days each year: opening weekend and maybe another couple of days during the season. He usually hunted with Andy, our family dentist. I don't think either Andy or my father ever went out in the field because they had to put meat on the table, but probably for the camaraderie, the opportunity to tuck some Copenhagen between cheek and gum while walking the edges of sloughs and across the jagged yellow corn stubble fields. To sit with their leather, high-topped boots removed and drink some beers and a few shots of whiskey in a small country motel at the end of the day's hunt.

WHEN I WAS 12 my father took me to the woods on his brother's farm to hunt squirrels. I had my Christmas gift of the year before, a single-shot .22 rifle from Sears. He carried his Winchester Model 12, a 30-inch barrel, full choke, 12-gauge pump with most of the bluing gone and the wrist of the scarred walnut stock darkened by the grip of his right hand. That shotgun now rests in my bedroom closet, almost never used but cherished.

Uncle Hank's 160 acres of sandy soil was near a farming hamlet called Isanti, about an hour's drive north of our home in Minneapolis. On his farm were some woods, larger than a grove but not a deep woods, maybe five or ten acres. Those woods were full of gray squirrels and their larger cousins, the fox squirrels, with their reddish fur, bushier tails, and seemingly noisier voices when chattering in alarm. The trees were mostly oaks, some maples, a few scrub pines and cedars, but mostly oaks, and they bordered a large field my uncle always seemed to have planted in corn. In autumn the squirrels fed on acorns from those oak trees and corn from that field. What squirrels we brought home that day and on other forays we cleaned either out behind the garage, where we could wrap the hides, tails, heads, and guts in newspaper and dispense of them in the garbage can, or, if it was dark, we cleaned them over newspapers on the concrete floor of our unfinished basement, which always smelled of laundry. I learned to skin and clean the squirrels, becoming accustomed to the pungent stink of the entrails, and when I soaked the liver-colored carcasses in salt water overnight, how their limbs were fine boned and delicately tapered.

WHEN MY MOTHER COOKED THEM and served them with some kind of white sauce, or gravy—it seemed then that most of the women in our heavily Scandinavian neighborhood served a lot of meals that included a white sauce—the squirrels were delicious. After moving to Virginia as an adult, I learned how equally good they could be in a classic southern Brunswick stew. Carrots, celery and onions, some tomatoes, a few small potatoes, and squirrel, mixed with pieces of chicken, slices of apples and bacon, simmered until the meat fell off the bones, tender and tasty.

I still hunt in the fall if not away on assignment. In the mid-1990s I began to hunt in Montana and continue to do so today. In truth I'm not a really skilled hunter. I'm not a finely tuned woodsman who spends countless hours studying the prey and its habitat. I can detect a deer scrape or rub, but I can't read the woods like those who make it their life. And most of my big game hunting in Montana is in open country, as opposed to the woodlands of the Midwest and the South. I'm not terribly proficient with a shotgun, so I don't do much damage to Montana's game bird population. I can usually—but not always—shoot a rifle pretty well. Like any decent hunter, I try to kill as cleanly and as humanely as possible.

SO, WHEN ASKED, "DO YOU HUNT?" of course I answer yes. I won't try to explain or defend why (not that I believe it needs defending), because others have written intelligently about what hunting represents, and why they do it. I don't know that I can improve on anything that has already been said clearly and well on the subject, and I certainly don't want to add to the abundance of badly written attempts to justify hunting. I will say this: I am a carnivore, and if I didn't eat what I killed I wouldn't hunt. I enjoy the taste of wild game, lean, fed on nature's offerings, and, in Montana, flavored by the wheat and barley crops that are often part of both the landscape and, thus, the habitat. If I go into a restaurant today and see venison or pheasant on the menu, I won't consider ordering it, because I know it's farm raised, not wild. It's illegal to sell wild game in restaurants in the United States, and to my taste, farm-raised venison or pheasant is bland.

Hunting—with the arguable exception of some rural residents struggling through truly difficult economic times—is not needed for the survival of our populace, but for some it offers a kind of fulfillment difficult to explain. I suppose by now, in my early 70s, I should have tired of hunting, but I haven't. I could say it's because I need the game meat to fill my freezer, but that freezer in my garage in Missoula would probably be kept filled through the graces of my Montana Hutterite friends who hunt. I guess I'm drawn to hunting, to the woods and plains and fields as if by nature. I simply enjoy being out there. So I go for the pleasure of the outing and taking part in a process as old as the earth itself.

A large part of the appeal I find in hunting is in the enjoyment of the landscape within which I hunt. At times it is also in the companionship of dogs. To see Buster, my English springer, burrowing through the brushy tangle of a Montana coulee, trailing a pheasant rooster on the run, or quartering back and forth at a sprint across the tall grasses—

bounding up at times to look about, back down again, nose to the ground, snorting and snuffling as if vacuuming for the scent of the prey, doing what his species was bred for centuries ago and enjoying it with the enthusiasm with which dogs always seem to put human effort to shame—is to see something beautiful and as much a part of the natural world as anything might possibly be.

In 2006–07 I photographed for a *National Geographic* story about hunters and the need for hunting to maintain a balance in game populations, and about the value hunting represents in supporting conservation. My travels sometimes took me into country that was once inhabited by a game species driven out by population pressure, such as the elk that once were found in the East but long ago vanished in a westward migration. In reclaimed coal-mining country of western Kentucky I photographed an elk hunt made possible by a highly successful elk-reestablishing effort started in 1997 by the state of Kentucky and the Rocky Mountain Elk Foundation, based in Montana. Today there are more than 11,000 elk roaming approximately two and a half million acres over 13 counties.

Working on that essay I was sometimes in country that once was the hunting grounds of the High Plains Indians, many of whom lived seminomadic lives, going where the game was. One such area was the Judith Basin country of central Montana, where the organization Pheasants Forever rejuvenated an area of about 800 acres of habitat for pheasant and grouse, making it available for public use. Later, for a National Geographic book about places one might consider "paradise," I wrote about a picture showing hunters and their dogs walking through the tawny fields of that conservation project near a place called Coffee Creek:

Once upon a time—a good century-and-a-half before the fence in this picture was built—immense herds of buffalo still swept across central Montana in endless humpbacked waves of brown. Crow and Cheyenne and Blackfeet, their bodies and horses gaudily painted for hunting or fighting, rode through grasses sometimes belly-deep to their mounts. How spectacular that must have been to see—a vision of a Western paradise inhabited by very few. From what we know in retrospect, those first Americans didn't think of this land in the way we've traditionally been taught to think of ownership. It was both simply and profoundly country they lived in or went to for different reasons at different times; perhaps to ride against their enemies and earn honors by stealing their horses, or to hunt buffalo. As the curtain descended on the 19th century, with the coming of the first settlers and cattle, the telegraph and the railroads, and a conscious effort by the government to rid the land of the Indians' commissary, the buffalo were eliminated. The land probably seemed a lot less like paradise then to those who had known it at its best. That was very long ago. To me there are parts of Montana such as this landscape with Square Butte anchoring the horizon that are still capable of instilling a feeling of wonder at the beauty of the land, the sharp edge of pristine air and—when one's vision isn't grayed by the ashes of a forest burning because of human carelessness or an act of nature—the possibility of seeing seemingly forever. It isn't the same as it once was, of course, but it's good enough still to make one almost tremble at the thought of just how wonderful it must have been.

THOSE WOODS IN MINNESOTA where I hunted squirrels as a boy didn't last long after I grew up. The small family farms that made up that community are mostly gone now, replaced by housing developments within commuting reach of the Twin Cities. Today, finding access to a place to hunt wild game has become a major issue among hunters across the land. Many farmers and ranchers in the Midwest and West who have wild game on their land now help meet the constant struggle for economic survival in agriculture by asking pay for permission to hunt. This, of course, could eventually lead to a time when only those who can afford to pay to hunt will be able to do so. Hunting for the average working man will never again be what it once was for my father's generation and mine.

As a boy I learned some things from my father about hunting that didn't necessarily have to do with coming home with food for the table. My father used to stop at farms and ask permission to hunt, and was just about always granted it. George Allard was a modest man who liked people. He always brought candy for the farmers' children, and he always closed any farm gate he opened. I'm sure anyplace he went he conducted himself with grace and gratitude. He was an intelligent although not a greatly sophisticated man. A blue-collar worker, he had only an eighth-grade education. But he taught me something vital to understanding hunting: It really isn't about killing. ■

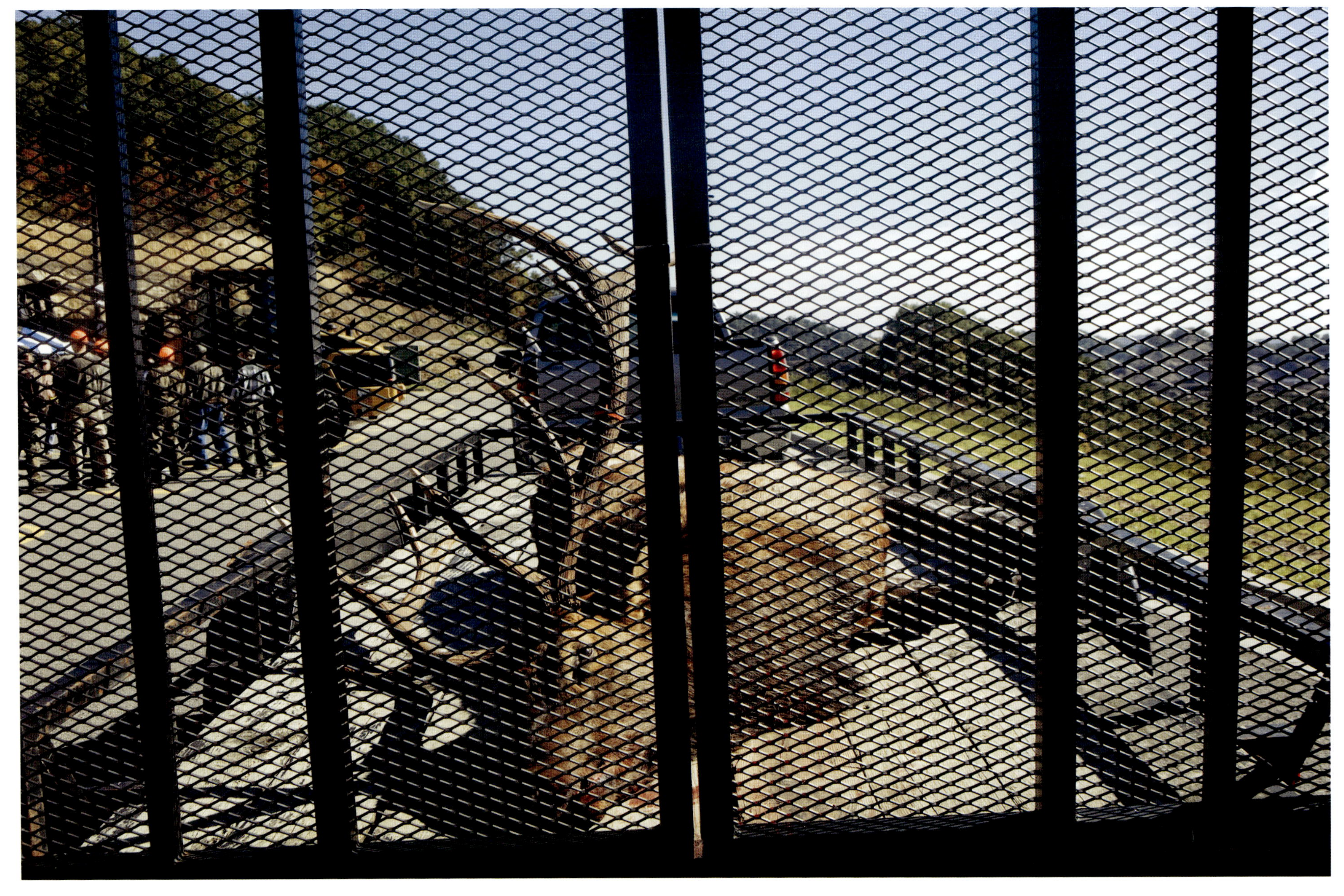

Bull elk in a parking lot, Kentucky, 2006

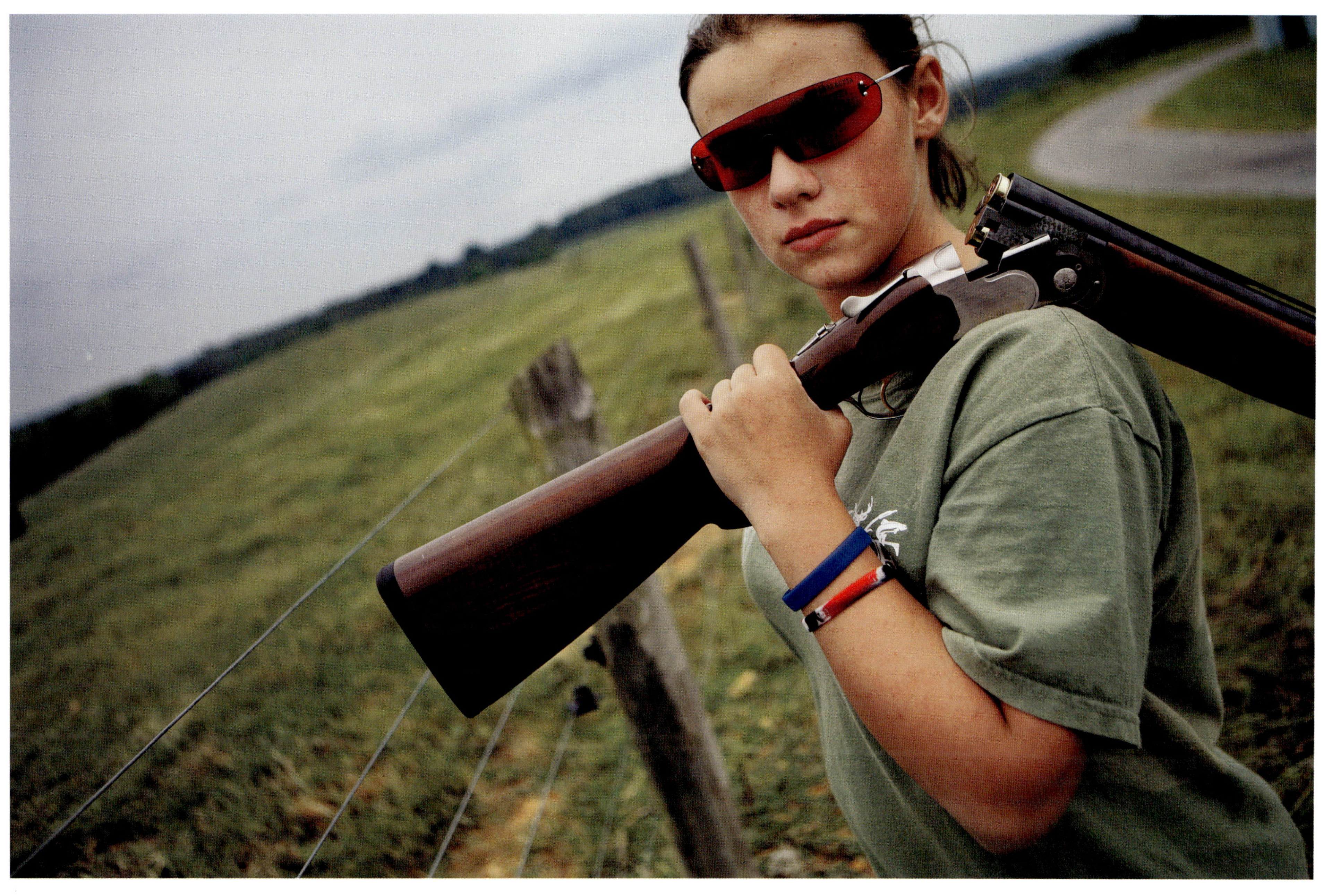

Mallory Martin, dove hunter, Tennessee, 2006

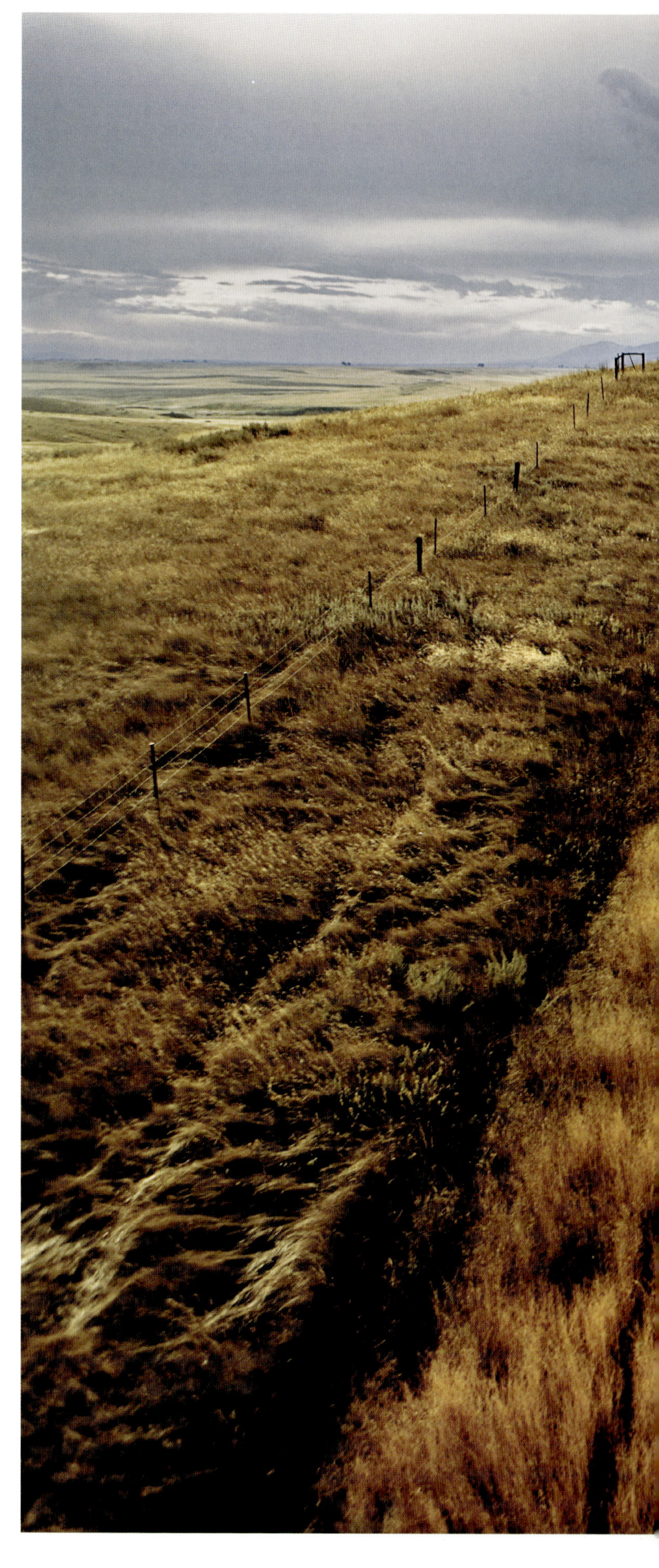

Bird hunters, Coffee Creek, Montana, 2006

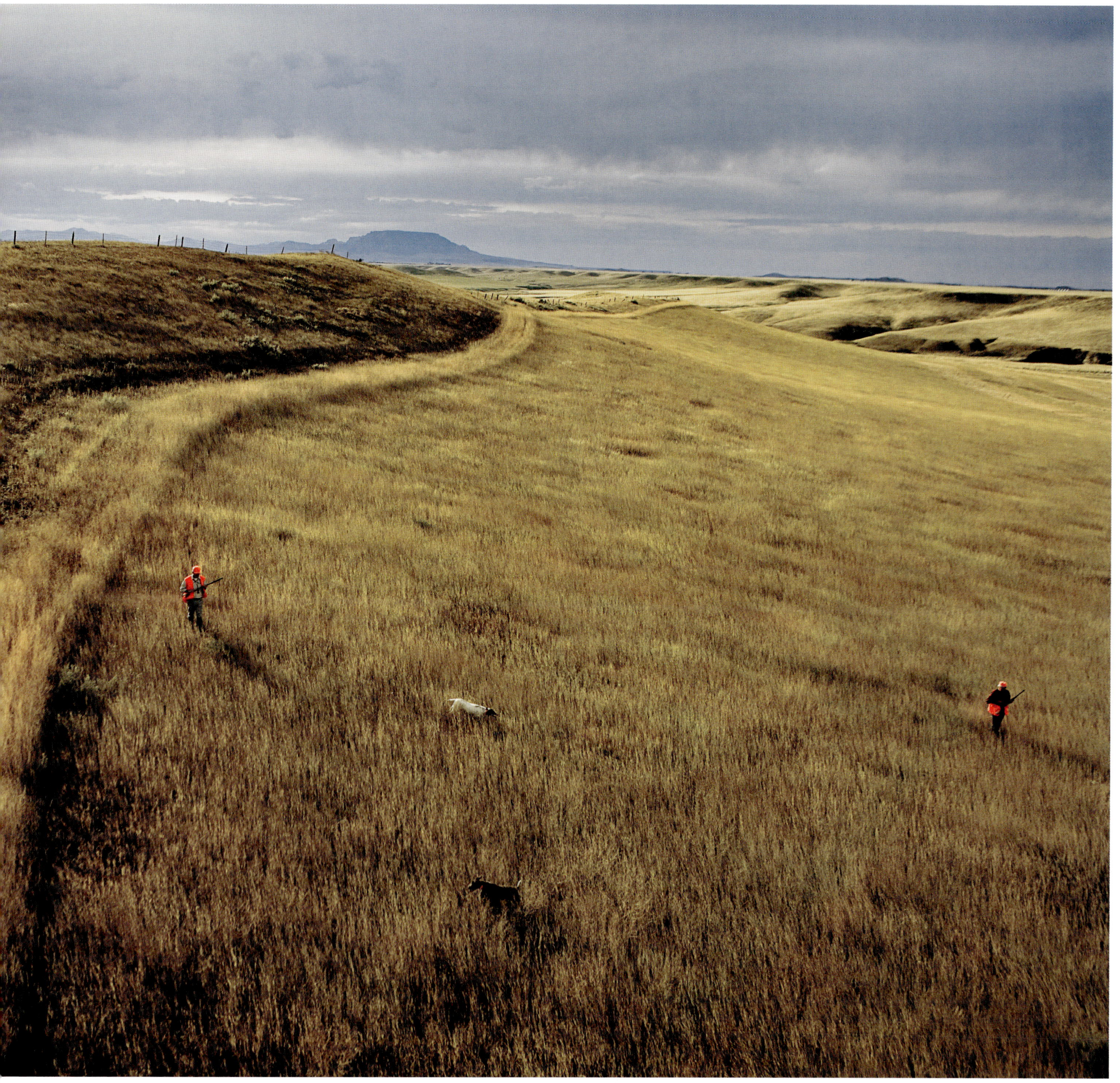

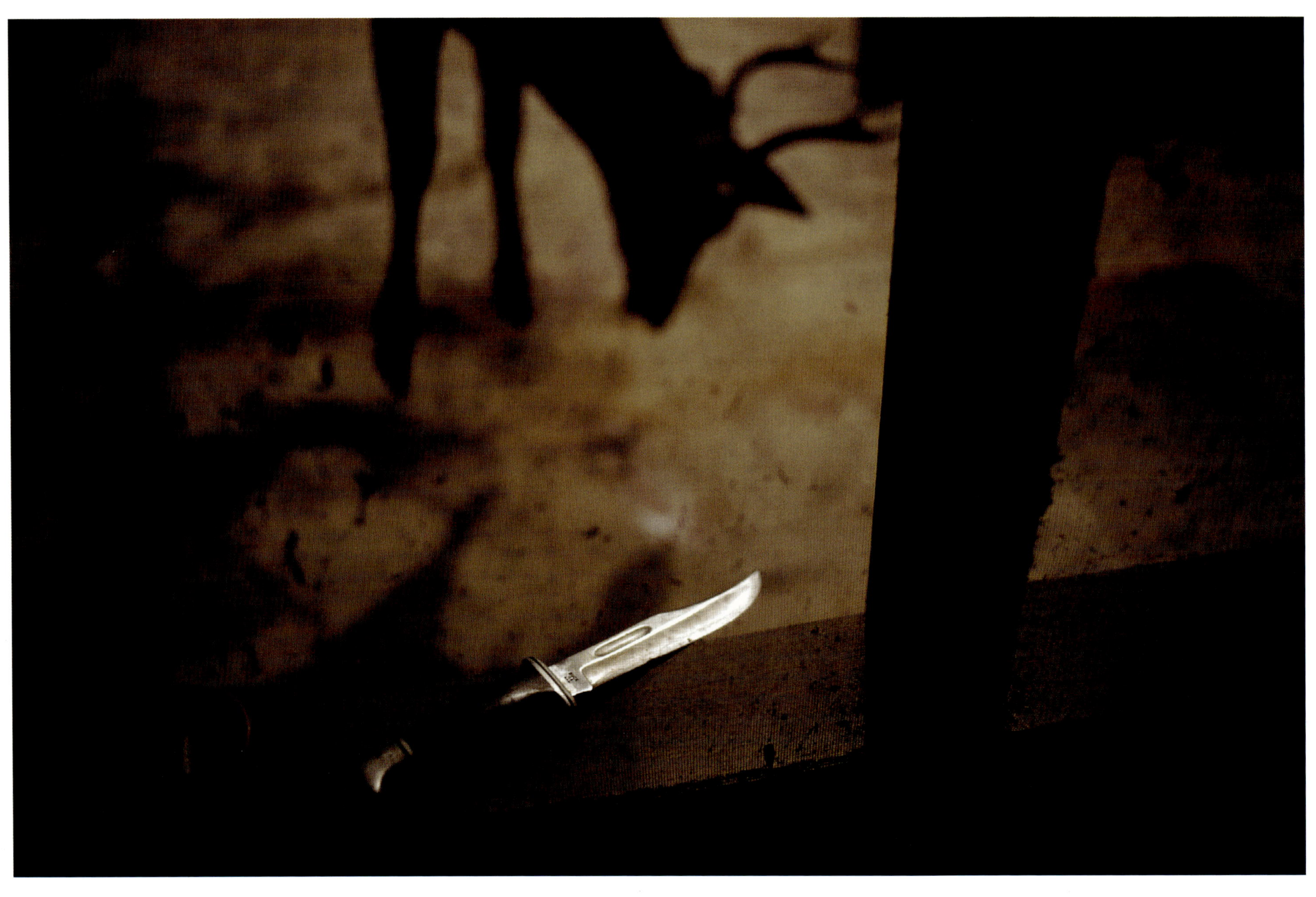

Deer-hunting camp, Mississippi Delta, 1987

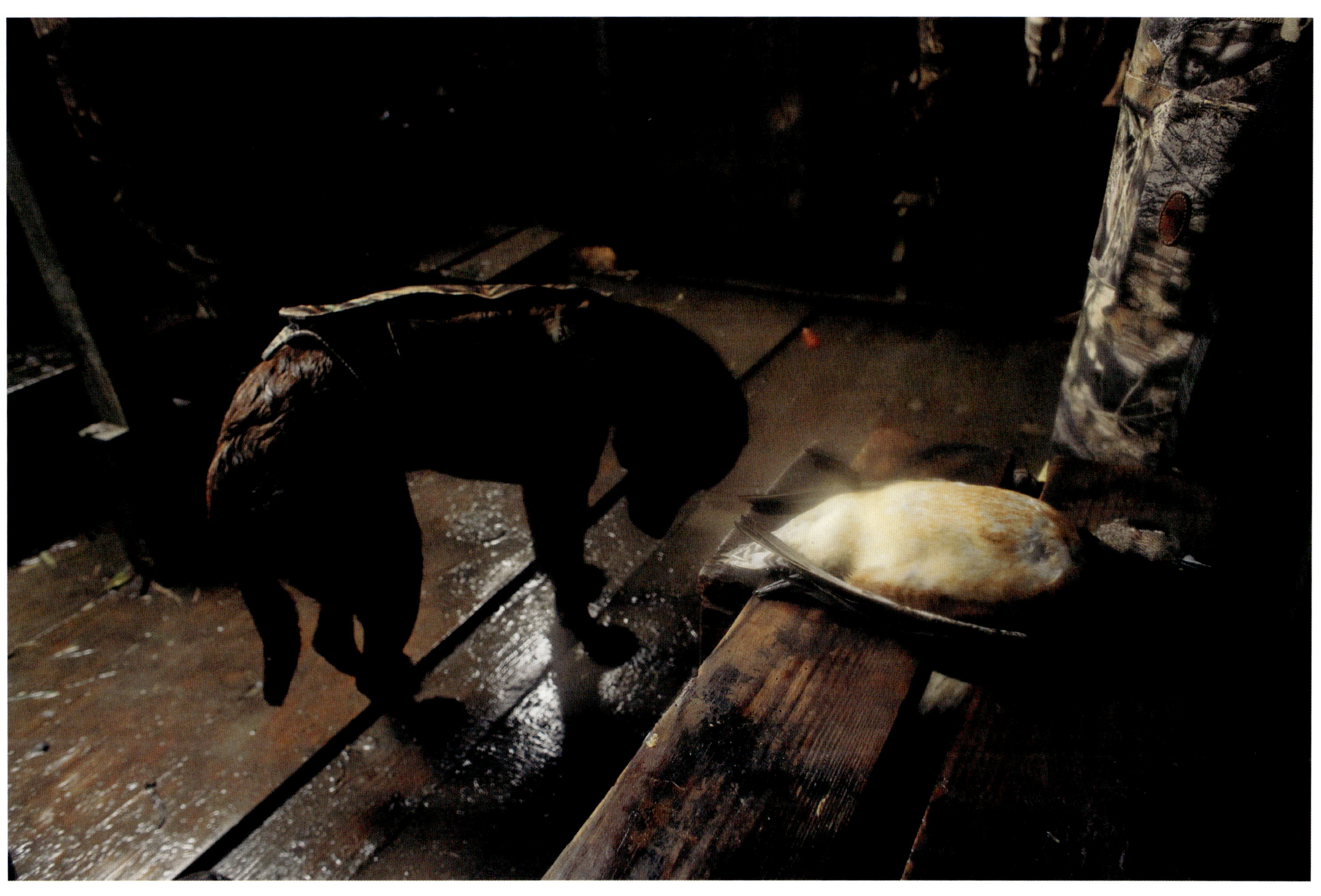

Duck-hunting blind, Arkansas, 2007

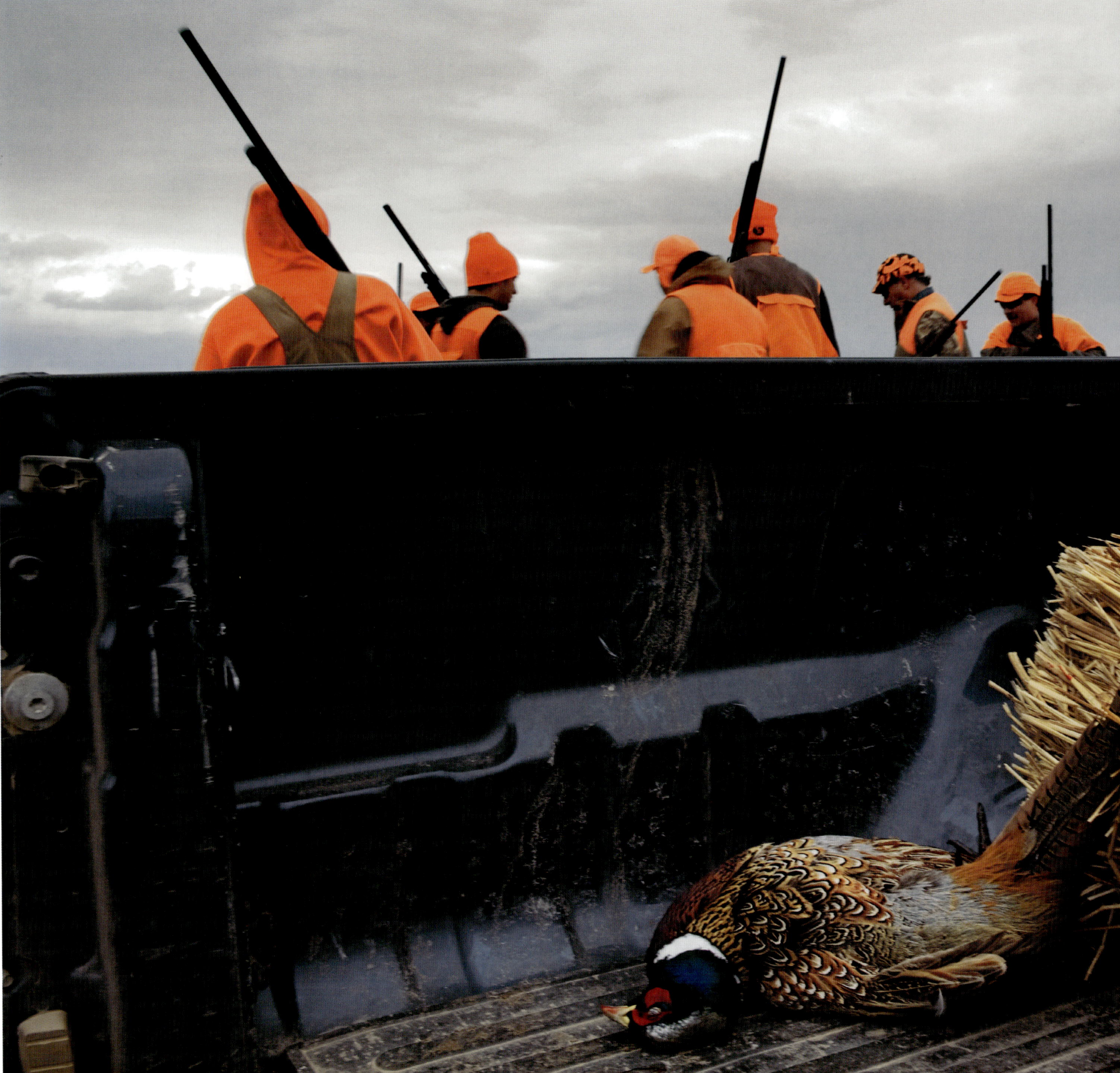

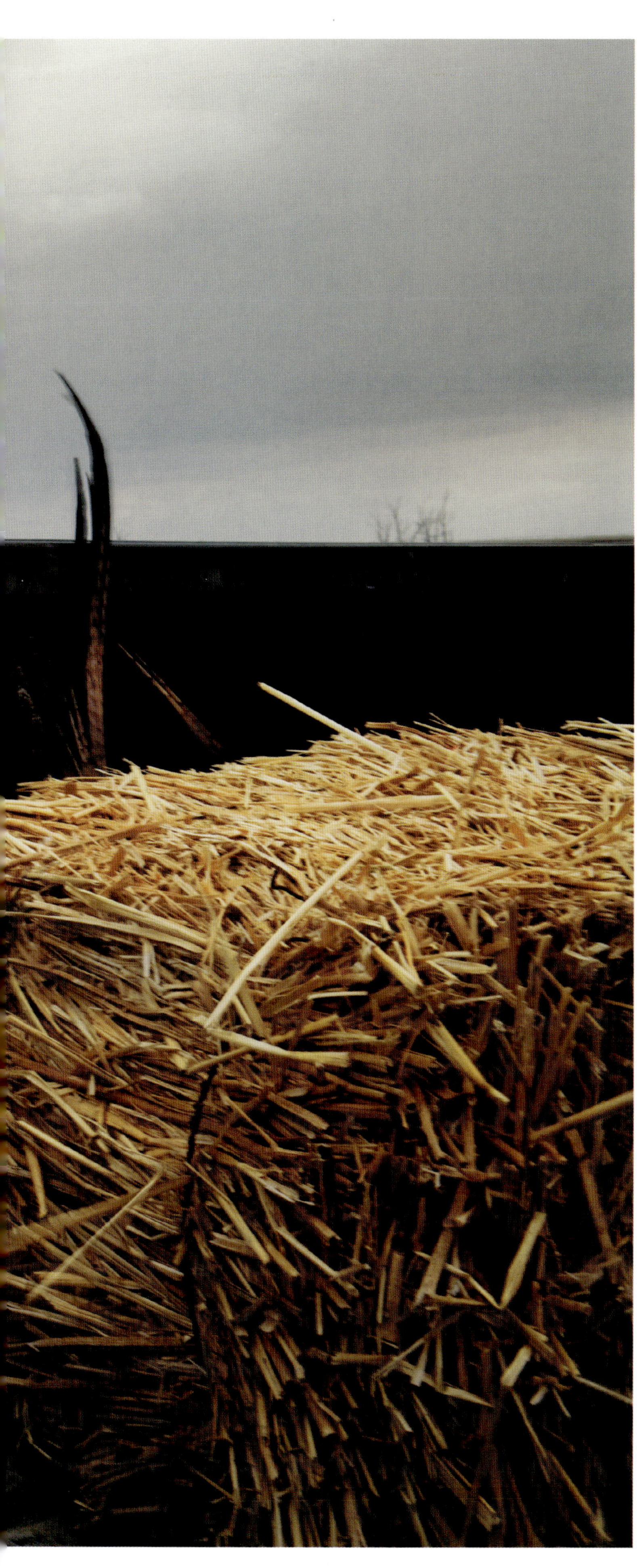

Pheasant hunters, South Dakota, 2006

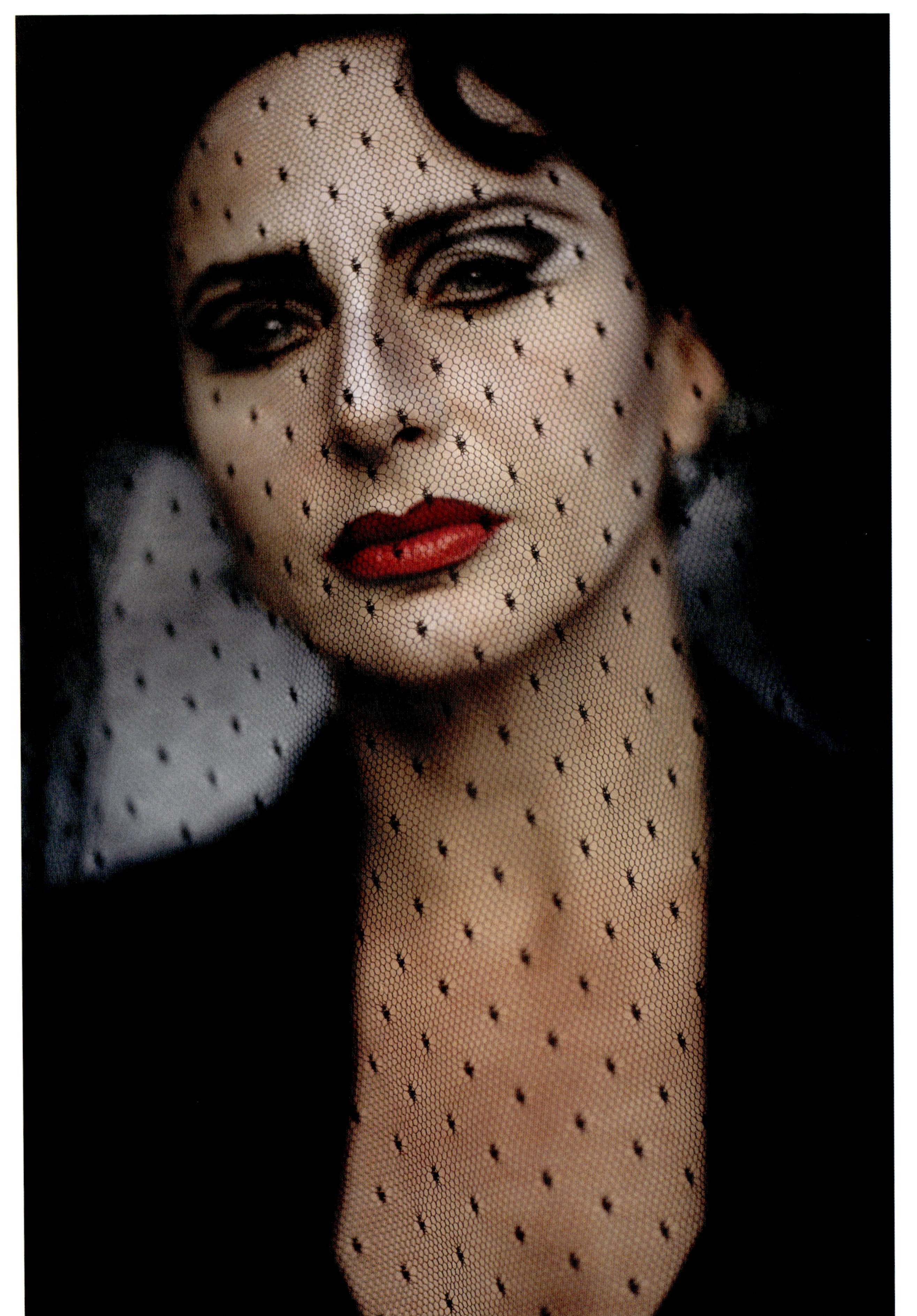

Her Picture in a Frame

The sun come up, it was blue and gold,
The sun come up, it was blue and gold,
The sun come up, it was blue and gold,
Ever since I put your picture in a frame

—Tom Waits and Kathleen Brennan

It's fair to say that over my 46-year career I have been known primarily for pictures of the masculine world: cowboys and buckaroos in bars and cow camps out West; rodeo riders; baseball players; blues musicians—that kind of thing. But actually, I have probably most enjoyed photographing females. The feminine face, seen either as a portrait or as one of the primary elements within a broader composition, has given me great personal and artistic satisfaction. Watching for interestingly attractive female faces, ones that create within me the desire to look more closely and possibly portray them with my camera, is almost an addiction in my daily life.

Although sometimes unquestionably beautiful, a face may often be attractive because of its imperfections. I will know it when I see it, and I might see it anywhere. In a supermarket I may leave an aisle down which I've been pushing my cart searching for cinnamon sticks and slivered almonds—which I need—to look again at a face that just passed by, rounding the corner where towers of buy-one-get-one-free potato chips are stacked, heading up the aisle for condiments and canned vegetables, none of which I need. But I do need to see that face again. So I follow. Actually, as the primary cook and grocery shopper in our family, I pick supermarkets in both Charlottesville, Virginia, and Missoula, Montana, where we divide our living time, partially based on the

Benedetta Buccellato, Sicily, 1994

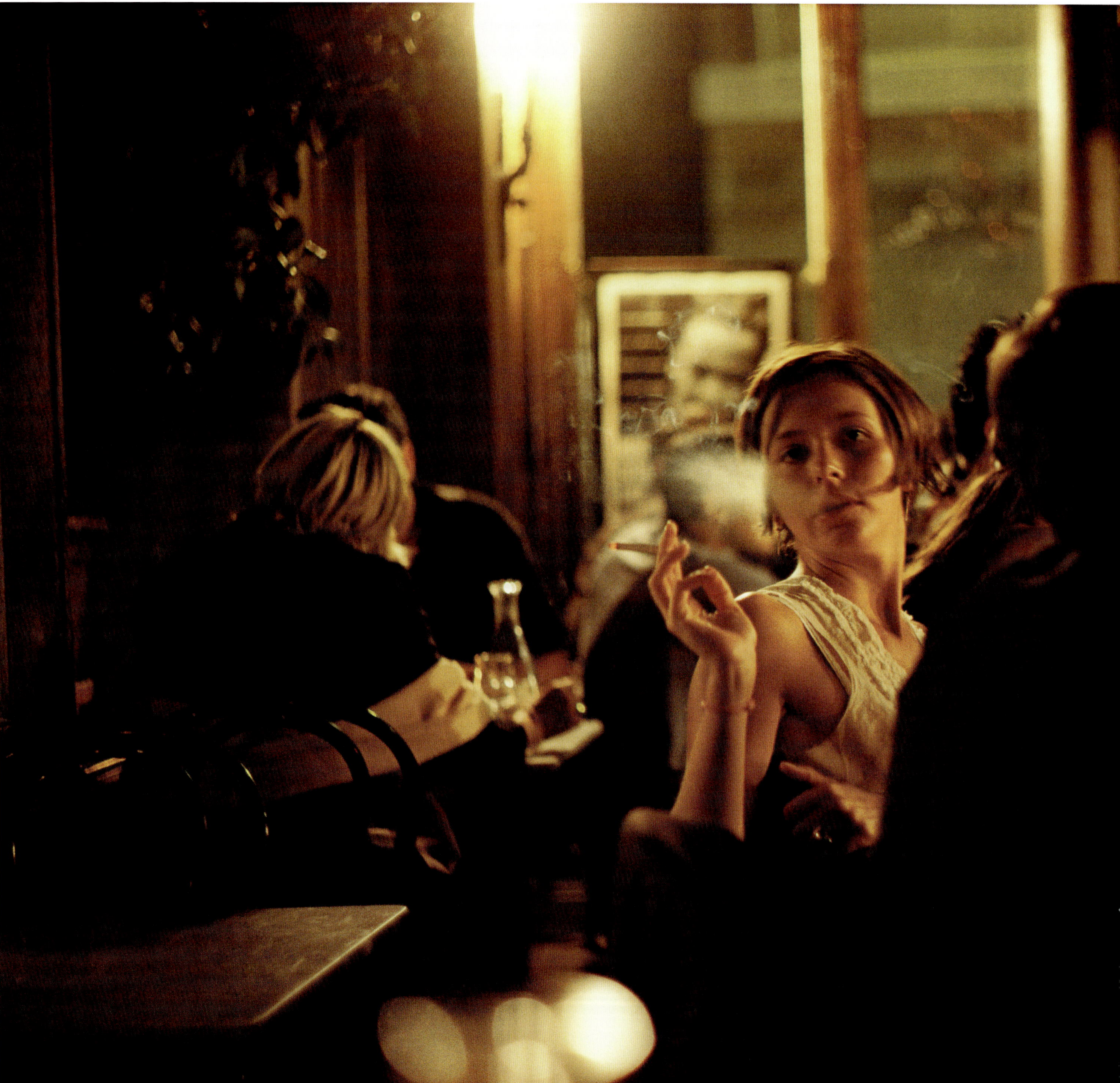

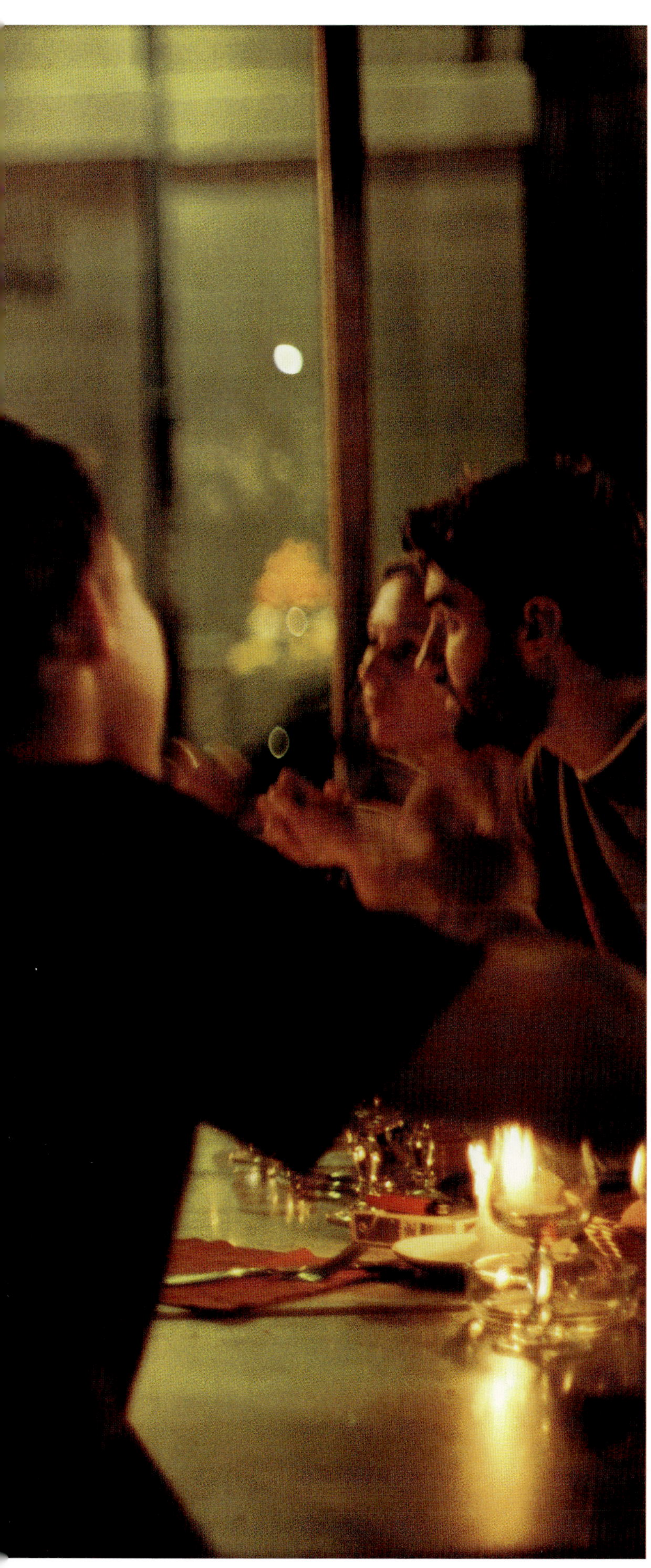

Girl smoking, Au Gamin de Paris restaurant, Le Marias, Paris, 2002

possibility of seeing someone like that. It's certainly not a hobby. And you can judge for yourself, but I wouldn't call it stalking. It's merely looking. That's what "street shooters," which is what I am thought of in the profession, do. We watch people and what they do, how they look and where they go, and how they may form a picture worth making. It's what I do for a living. Sometimes it leads to life-changing occurrences. I met my second wife this way, although not in a supermarket, and I definitely wasn't looking for another wife. But more about that later.

Many of the images in this chapter of the book are what I consider "found" pictures, made serendipitously, as they occurred, without any request on my part, somewhere along the road, somewhere in the world. It could be in Paris, in a restaurant, or backstage at a fashion show. Perhaps along a country road in Mississippi, or maybe at a lake in northern Minnesota. It could be anywhere. It might be a picture made in a glance.

These pictures certainly aren't all what is commonly thought of as a portrait in the formal sense of the word. There are other pictures here, however, that I made of someone I'd seen somewhere and photographed specifically by request.

Sandrine Gataleta, the young woman standing in a hotel room in Arles, France, for instance. A tall, striking woman, with a mass of jet-black hair, she tended bar at the Café Van Gogh, just across from the Hotel du Forum in the Place du Forum. It was 1993 and I was working on a photographic essay about Provence. I was intrigued by a vacant room in my hotel that I'd seen through the open door when it was being tended to by the housekeeper. The wallpaper was of pinks and greens—Matisse colors.

I asked Sandrine to pose; she hadn't seen the room. She arrived clad in black. A multicolored scarf snugly encompassed her slender neck. Her lips were bright red. She stood bathed in the light from a window next to a dresser. The room and the light embraced her. Looking at her now, head-on, a direct confrontation between photographer and subject, I see that a very narrow slice of negative space separates the slight swell of her belly from the dark frame of the dresser mirror that reflects the patterns of the drapes and walls in a series of repeated curves and verticals. The tiniest bit of space can be seen between the bend of her left arm and her back. All compositions are like puzzles with many pieces, and it falls to the artist to put them together as he or she thinks best.

THIELE ROBINSON WORKED AT ONE TIME as an assistant for my friend, wildlife photographer Tom Mangelsen, in Jackson Hole, Wyoming. Thiele traveled the country and the world with Tom for several years before leaving Wyoming for California. In the fall of 2004 I was teaching at a Rich Clarkson workshop in Jackson Hole, and Tom hosted a wine and cheese party for the faculty at his wonderful cabin beneath the Tetons. I met Thiele there and was struck by her unusual beauty. After the party she chauffeured me to where we were to have an evening workshop presentation.

I was scheduled to do two workshops for Clarkson that year. "When I come back for the next workshop," I told her, during the brief drive, "I'd really like to do some portraits of you."

"I don't know," Thiele said. "I'll have to think about that." She said she'd never been photographed before.

Later, I guess I mentioned it to Tom, or maybe Thiele did, but Tom eventually told me that he told Thiele: "If Bill Allard wants to photograph you, I really think you ought to do it." So when I next came back, she did.

We spent part of a day in her mother's house, up above Jackson Hole, moving around from a window by the front door, to the kitchen, and finally to a window seat by a large, dark divider screen with animals painted on it. Thiele had changed from jeans into a simple black dress, and she wore a gold cross on a slender gold chain. It was during the last few minutes that I seemed to find my way with her face and the space I'd chosen.

The session was a little awkward for me because I was using a digital camera loaned to me by one of the workshop's sponsors; the feel of the camera was unfamiliar, and because I'd never used a digital camera before, I kept forgetting I could look at the image in the LCD monitor. The portrait I selected as the best from my work with Thiele was eventually published by *American Photo* magazine.

In 2005, a year after my portrait session with Thiele, I began using digital cameras exclusively as I started my Hutterite assignment for *National Geographic.* I have not used film since then, and probably won't ever again. One reason I abandoned photographing with film was that Kodak was discontinuing the wonderful Kodachrome emulsions I'd loved and used for so many years. With those tools gone, it seemed time to move on.

THE YOUNG COUPLE ON A COUCH, gazing into each other's face, was the first thing I saw when I walked into a back room at an Ole Miss fraternity house. I'd gone there to photograph a Christmas party while working in Oxford, Mississippi, on an essay about William Faulkner in 1986-87. As a student at the University of Minnesota in the 1960s, I didn't belong to a fraternity. In fact, upon graduation, I was 26, married, and had four children, ages one through four; I was not exactly fraternity material. Before making this picture I had never been in a fraternity house anywhere, and I haven't been in one since. But I do like this picture. And with all respect to the young woman, I sometimes think that maybe that was what Faulkner's tragic character Temple Drake might have looked like as she boarded that train in Taylor, Mississippi, bound, ultimately, for a brothel in New Orleans.

THE PICTURE OF A YOUNG WOMAN blowing smoke over her shoulder in a Paris restaurant is a visual gift I received one evening in 2002. Au Gamin de Paris, a favorite restaurant of mine in the Marais neighborhood, was just around the corner and down the street from my hotel on Rue Ste. Croix de la Bretonnerie. I was dining alone, as I often do, reading a book, with a Leica sitting on the table in front of me. I never dine alone without a book and a camera. If I'm not alone I probably won't have a book on the table (although there will likely be one in my bag), but I always have a camera within reach. For some reason I was evidently watching her and her young friends. It's been a few years now, and I don't remember it well; maybe she had made that motion of turning to exhale her cigarette smoke a time or two before, and I was watching and waiting. Could be. Looking for pictures is always a little bit like hunting: watching and waiting. When she turned this time, her eyes and mine met just as I raised the camera. Usually in a candid photograph you hope not to have anyone looking at the camera. But in this case the momentary contact her eyes had with mine is the essence of the image. It gives the viewer personal contact with the girl in the picture and makes it somehow intimate and complete.

IN 1994 I WORKED IN SICILY. I loved being there, and one day I went to see the ancient outdoor Greek theater in Syracuse. An actress, Benedetta Buccellato, was slowly walking back and forth behind the set in soft dusk light. She wore a black veil in contrast with her deep red lips. I stepped quietly into her path and walked backward for a few minutes, not close, trying to gracefully give her enough space, photographing her face as we moved slowly together. We exchanged not a single word until I stepped aside, saying, *"Grazi."* She nodded to me and continued into her space and character. There is little to say about the making of that picture, especially considering its ultimate success as a cover of *National Geographic* magazine and its subsequent popularity and acclaim. A friend of mine, not a photographer or writer but a longtime observer of *Geographic* commented: "A beautiful woman on one cover is worth ten months of monkeys."

Some pictures have long stories behind them, others are the result of moments simply measured in fractions of time. In this case I was there, I was accepted and allowed to look, and ultimately the subject gave herself to me. It's as simple as that. I believe many of the best pictures are given, not taken.

THREE GIRLS ARE IN THE WATER of Little Floyd Lake near Detroit Lakes, Minnesota. It is 1995 and I am traveling around up North, trailering a 17-foot boat, staying at different mom-and-pop resorts, working on a book about the Minnesota lake country to be called *Time at the Lake: A Minnesota Album.* Two of the girls are occupied with a couple of floatable tubes, one of them suspended in the air above the child's outspread arms. They have their backs to me and wear water-soaked T-shirts that cling to their torsos and perhaps warm them just a bit. No one else is visible on the calm lake water that ripples gently around the children. The older girl stands alone, knee-deep in the water, hands clutched together. It's getting to be dusk. She looks cold, and by the set of her jaw, her teeth may be chattering. It's early July up North.

IN 1987, WHILE WORKING on my Faulkner's Mississippi essay, I was driving near Oxford and saw a young couple on a four-wheel ATV racing alongside the highway. She was blond, with long hair flowing back behind her as she clung to the bandanna-wearing young man driving. They turned off on a gravel country road and I followed in their dust, pulling alongside when they stopped on the shoulder.

I explained to them what I was doing: making pictures about life in William Faulkner's Lafayette County. I got the feeling they were not familiar with his work, but I thought she was kind of special. I asked if I could make a few pictures. At one point as I photographed her, she ran her hands up through all that blond hair while looking at me. He looked at me too, but I think he was wondering just what the hell this was all about. I think she knew.

In Faulkner's *The Hamlet*, there is a young woman named Eula Varner. Faulkner scholar Cleanth Brooks describes Eula, a creature of northern Mississippi, as "a woman of fabulous beauty and seductive power, though unself-conscious and almost unaware of that power," and "a kind of rustic Aphrodite."

Faulkner describes Eula as "honey in sunlight and bursting grapes," and says that she listens "in sullen bemusement, with a weary wisdom . . . to the enlarging of her own organs." She is, he says, "a soft ample girl with definite breasts even at thirteen and eyes like cloudy hothouse grapes and a full damp mouth always slightly open."

All of that may be way too much to attach to this young woman I photographed for only a few fleeting moments, but I found her visually stimulating, and I'm glad I followed her down that Mississippi highway.

THE 12-YEAR-OLD DAUGHTER of a Brazilian rain forest settler leans wearily on the rough, unfinished wooden window frame of her house. It was 1988 and I was photographing life in the rain forest of Rondônia, Brazil, which was being threatened by increasing pressure from people leaving the cities and coming to the frontier with hopes of farming. After clear-cutting the trees from the land, most homesteaders would experience a good crop or two, and then the land, not meant for farming, would exhaust itself, the farms would fail, and the people would have to leave.

The girl's name is Bernice, and she had malaria and had had it before, 15 times in the year and a half her family of five had lived in the Rondônia frontier; it kind of comes with life there. Her father has German blood, which apparently accounts for the blond hair of his three children. I was outside the house, photographing the mother and one of her daughters, a three-year-old. As I spoke to the mother, the face of a beautiful blond child appeared in the open window. It was Bernice. She had hair the color of farm butter, and eyes that were not green, not hazel, but seemingly a mix of both. She had sensual lips for a child. She will be a beautiful woman, I thought then. But she was sick, and you could see the sickness in her eyes. I made many portraits of her. She didn't seem to mind, and she didn't attempt to pose. Just before I stopped, I noticed marks on the palm of her left hand, words written in blue. "She was supposed to take a test in school today," her mother said. "But she couldn't go to school because of the malaria attack." The notes were to help her memorize what she needed to know for the test, maybe help her a little if she forgot.

I sometimes wonder how this girl fared. How long did her family make it? Are they somehow still there? Is she still beautiful?

I PHOTOGRAPHED PROSTITUTES in a Brazilian rain forest brothel called Caramine's in 1988. I went there one night and asked to take pictures. I think I had to pay a little money, but not much. The brothel was a couple hundred yards down a dirt street from the hotel I was staying at. I remember the small frontier town was full of some of the worst-looking stray dogs imaginable—mangy, one-eyed, potbellied, and wormy dogs and their pups. They'd sprawl out in the middle of the dirt roads and move only under threat of imminent death by passing vehicles.

The prostitutes' rooms were very dark, the prostitutes, some of them, very young. I photographed them on the beds in their rooms with virtually no direction from me, and with a flashlight my only light source. I was photographing a nude in one of the back rooms when the sound of breaking glass came through our locked door. The room was next to a large bar and dancing area. Then came the sound of a shot. I had to stop working so the girl could get dressed and we could get out a back door. I had hoped to work longer, but not that night. I got out of the place and never did determine just what happened.

Years earlier, in 1970, while traveling by motorcycle along the U.S.–Mexico border for a *National Geographic* story, I photographed in a brothel in Nuevo Laredo, just across the Rio Grande from Laredo, Texas. A naked young woman in silver slippers lying atop a rose-colored bedspread assumed a quite elegant pose all on her own without my asking.

IN 2004, WHILE PHOTOGRAPHING in Bollywood, I met Kareena Kapoor. She was one of India's biggest Bollywood movie stars. She was only 23 when I photographed her in a Mumbai apartment she shared with her mother. Already an accomplished actress, Kareena comes from a family that truly ranks as a Bollywood dynasty, with her grandfather, father, and sister having enjoyed great success and acclaim in the industry. I found Kareena totally unassuming, not at all caught up in her fame. I had asked to be able to photograph her at home, and for her to wear no makeup, and she complied (just a little black around the eyes). A female Indian journalist friend had told me long ago, when I described how I wanted to photograph some of the actresses without makeup: "They'll never do it!"

Kareena kept our appointment made weeks earlier. We spent the better part of two hours talking as I made photographs of her face, giving her almost no direction. The light was not what I'd hoped for that day. I used no lights, just tried to work with the available window light, and it turned out to be a gray Mumbai afternoon. I was kind of exploring her face, thinking perhaps to have another session on another day; but that was not to be. Kareena had a natural beauty I found arresting. Her lips were extraordinary—full and lush. Ironic, considering there is almost no kissing in a typical Bollywood film. But they say that's changing.

DURING THE SAME ASSIGNMENT I saw a picture of Bengali actress and former model Bipasha Basu in the *Times of India* entertainment section one day at breakfast in Mumbai. It called Basu one of the "hot" current Bollywood stars. She certainly looked good in the newspaper, an interestingly beautiful face, sexy. I decided to see if I could arrange a portrait session, and I had my assistant make contact. As I did with Kareena Kapoor, I requested to do some portraits of Bipasha where she lived, and with no makeup. We made an appointment, which a short time later was canceled. We made another, and it was postponed. Finally, she agreed to meet us, not at her home but at a sound studio where she was scheduled to do some voice dubbing for a film she was working on. It was not what I'd hoped for, but I said OK.

My assistant and I arrived at the sound studio much earlier the day of the appointment to see what we had to work with. Not much. The studio's lobby was drab—no color, no graphically interesting architecture, nothing that promised a good portrait session atmosphere. Just outside the studio, however, was a kind of gardenlike area with greenery. But there were mosquitoes—lots of mosquitoes. Too bad, I thought. And then we waited for the actress to arrive. And waited.

I was about to give up and leave, when Bipasha finally appeared, a good couple of hours late. She wore jeans and a white tank top, and she had a small pink purse strung on a silver chain over her shoulder. She had on a little eye makeup and some lip gloss. Her long hair hung down, falling along the curves of her breasts. She seemed nice, just really late. I tried to make some decent portraits in the lobby, but nothing seemed to work. Just because somebody looks good doesn't mean the portrait will be. Finally, knowing what was in store, I said, "Let's go out into the garden."

Outside, I started to make some portraits I was feeling fairly good about. But the mosquitoes were fierce. She was starting to clutch at her arms, fending off the bites but not complaining. After a few minutes, I thought, enough. I can't put her through any more of this; she was just really late, she didn't kill anybody.

"It's too bad," I said, continuing to make one more portrait or two, "that we couldn't have done this in your apartment."

She looked at me and didn't say anything.

"I'll bet you don't have any mosquitoes in your apartment, do you?"

I saw just the faint hint of a smile. It's in the portrait.

ALTHOUGH I PREFER not to have eye contact with a subject when making a candid portrait, there are many times when I want to produce a portrait with the full knowledge of the subject beforehand. When posing someone, I don't always ask her to look at the camera; I ask her to look at me. I'm making the picture, not the camera. With that kind of portrait, like Sandrine Gataleta, Thiele Robinson, or the prostitutes in Brazil and Mexico, I want to feel some kind of connection between myself and the subject. My hope is to take that connection and make a picture that introduces the person in the photograph to the viewer—even if the viewer is another country or language removed. So, it's through me that you see and meet her.

I'm always looking. As I write this chapter I think of someone I saw just this morning when I had breakfast at The Shack in Missoula. Short, tousled blond hair, she had an intricate pattern of colorful tattoos running up her right arm and on to her shoulder. Pale skinned and interestingly pretty. I introduced myself, gave her my card and requested she look me up on Google, hoping she'd respond positively. She did and I hope to photograph her sometime this summer. Maybe in time for this book: We'll see.

IN MARCH 1981, just a few days after the assassination attempt on President Ronald Reagan outside the Hilton Hotel in Washington, D.C., I left my home in Virginia to start a *National Geographic* assignment to photograph a country story on Peru. I had been kind of gravitating south after deciding to seek subjects away from the American

West, where I'd concentrated so much of my work during the 1970s. I'd felt my photography wasn't growing and I needed a new inspiration. I did work in Costa Rica and Mexico, each of them offering me a different, stronger color palette than I'd become accustomed to in places like Montana and Nevada. I had lobbied for the Peru assignment as soon as I was aware of its existence, although I really didn't know much about the country. But something inside me said, You must get the Peru assignment. I did, and it would ultimately change my life in several ways. At home my marriage to the woman I'd met in high school and who had been my wife for more than 20 years was unraveling.

I arrived in Peru in time for the famous Easter celebrations in the Andean town of Ayacucho. Easter week traditionally attracts thousands of tourists who come to see the processions and the street paintings of Jesus so painstakingly created out of flower petals, coffee, and chalk of different colors, which cover and beautify the surfaces of the streets around the Plaza des Armas. On the evenings of Good Friday and Easter Sunday, candlelight processions of men struggling beneath the weight of the religious icons they carry will sway and wind through the crowded narrow lanes, and more than once will walk across the faces of Christ and his angels.

One afternoon I was standing on the steps of the cathedral that dominates the Plaza des Armas. I was people-watching. I saw a slender young woman by herself, slowly strolling around the plaza. She wore a khaki, army-type shirt with the collar open and the tail outside her jeans. She had raven black hair and a lovely face highlighted by sculpted cheekbones. My impulse was to follow this attractive, dark-eyed woman, and I did, at some distance. In and out of shops, around the plaza a full turn, I lost count of how many places we'd entered and left, and after what seemed forever, I finally asked as she exited a shop: "Do you speak English?" "No," she replied, curtly, and walked on by, increasing her pace somewhat. I stayed back. I let her go. But that was a face that had captured me somehow. Just how much I had no clue at the time.

Several days passed before I saw her again. I was with a bodyguard assigned to me by a local politician. Spring of 1981 was a time of the early stages of Sendero Luminoso: the Shining Path guerrilla movement, inspired by a professor at one of the universities in Ayacucho. At the beginning it was ominously ugly—at dawn on some days, dead dogs were found hanging from lampposts—but it was not yet the truly brutal assault on humanity that it became for a number of years, when entire families were slaughtered in the name of a kind of revolution nobody seemed to really understand. The bodyguard—certainly not requested by me—carried a nickel-plated, snub-nosed .38 special in the back of the waistband of his trousers. He spoke some English and for a few days stayed rather close to me. I was later able to have him removed from his assignment.

He was with me, however, when I next saw the woman I had followed earlier. She was in the plaza again, carrying a paper bag of popcorn. I said hello. She replied by offering me some popcorn. Progress in the form of popcorn, I thought. Her name was Ana Maria Baraybar. She was Peruvian, with a Spanish Basque name. She was an industrial psychologist, lived in Lima, and was in Ayacucho for the Easter holidays. Her friends called her Ani. Through my bodyguard we talked a little, and I invited her to a folklore festival to be held at my hotel that evening. Ani and a female friend she was traveling with accepted. And that was the beginning.

When I came to Peru, the last thing I needed was a serious relationship, and it's the first thing that happened to me in a country where I didn't speak the native language and the woman I was about to fall in love with didn't speak mine. I had once thought that if for some reason I found myself unmarried I would never marry again unless that person was in the same profession as mine, because mine is a demanding and difficult one to follow, and certainly to share. Well, life isn't like that, is it? What we think we're going to do is not always what we end up doing. That was in 1981. I spoke only a little bit of Spanish and Ani spoke no English. We married in 1983. She now has a master's degree from the University of Virginia and speaks perfect English. Ashamedly, I still speak only a little bit of Spanish. We have been married for more than 25 years and have a son who exhibits the same large eyes, olive skin, and general goodness as his mother. It certainly hasn't all been smooth; Ani and I are different in many ways, both culturally and in our personalities. But her face still captures me as much as the time I first saw it. Her smile can still brighten any room she enters, and she remains the light of my life. ■

I love you baby, and I always will,
I love you baby, and I always will,
I love you baby, and I always will,
Ever since I put your picture in a frame
—Tom Waits and Kathleen Brennan

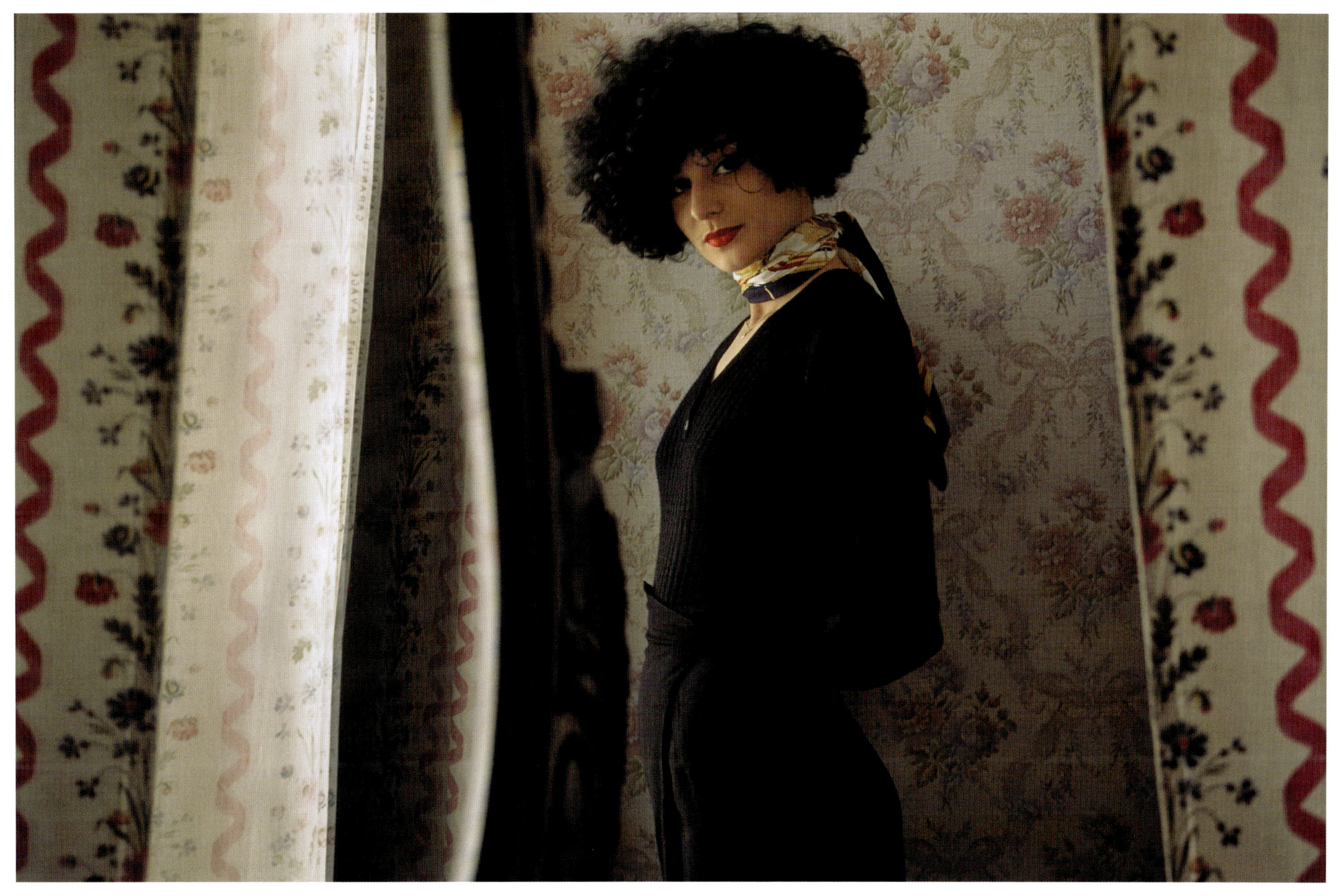

Sandrine Gataleta, Arles, 1993

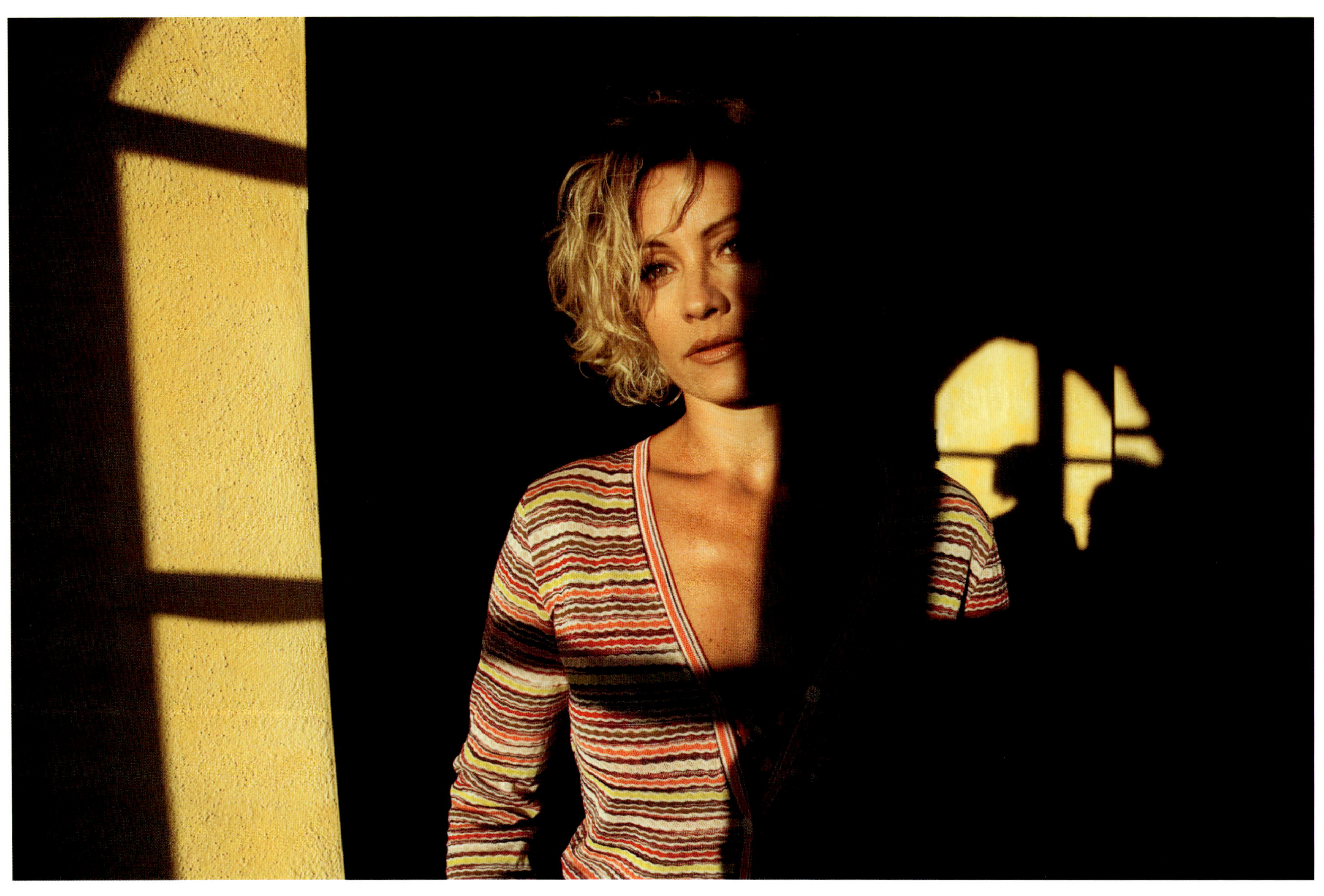

Francesca Calligaro, Tuscany, Italy, 2005

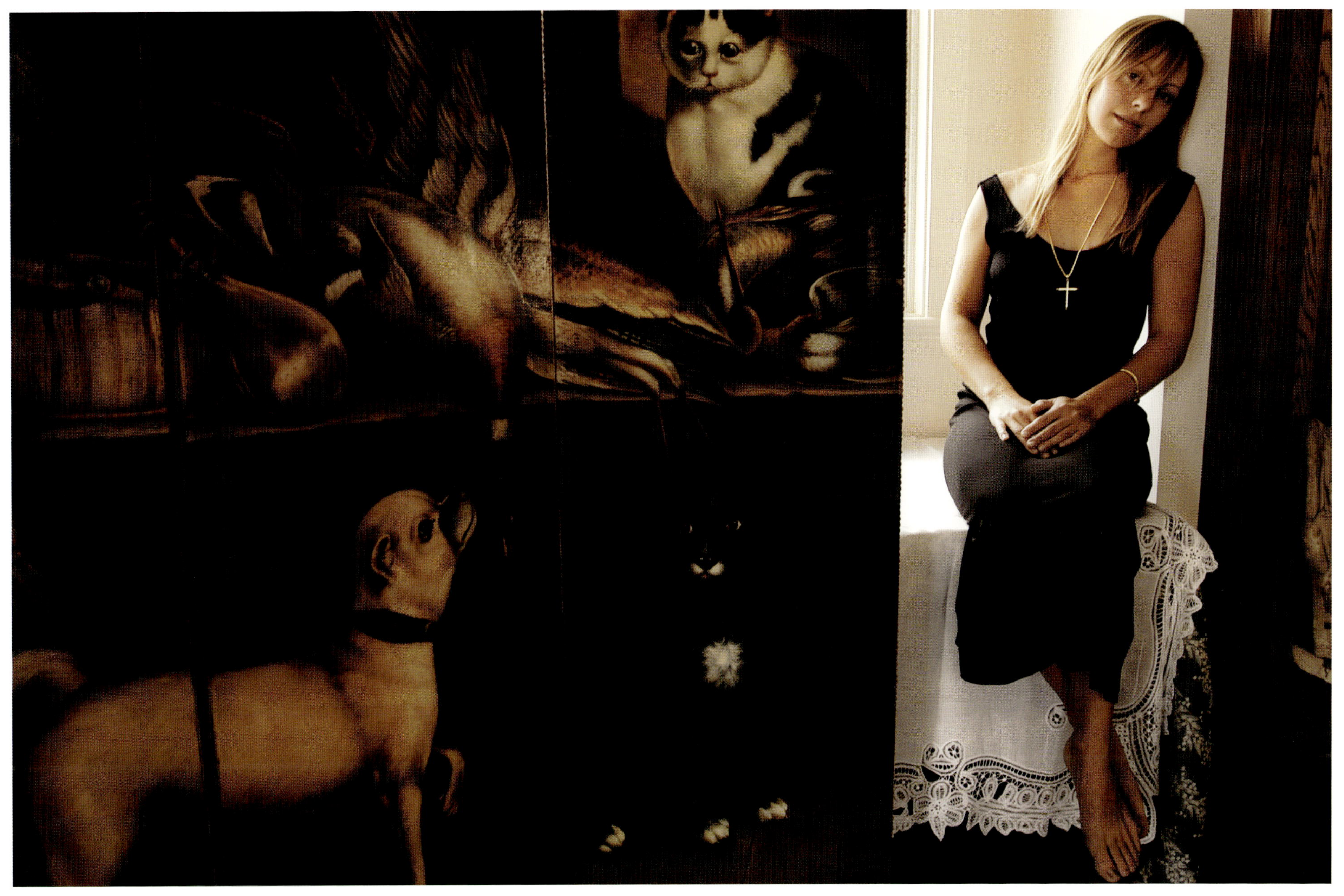

Thiele Robinson, Jackson Hole, Wyoming, 2004

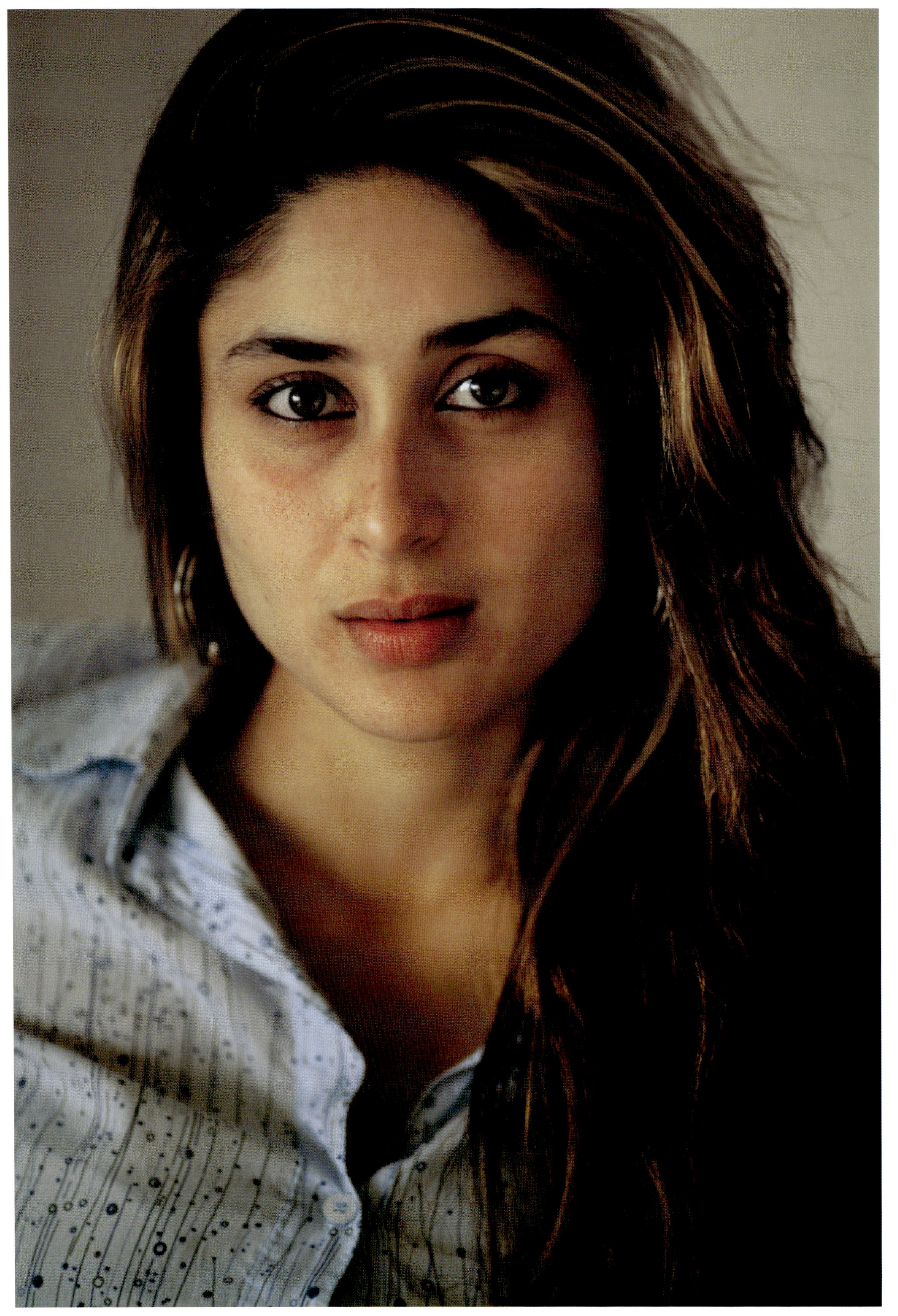

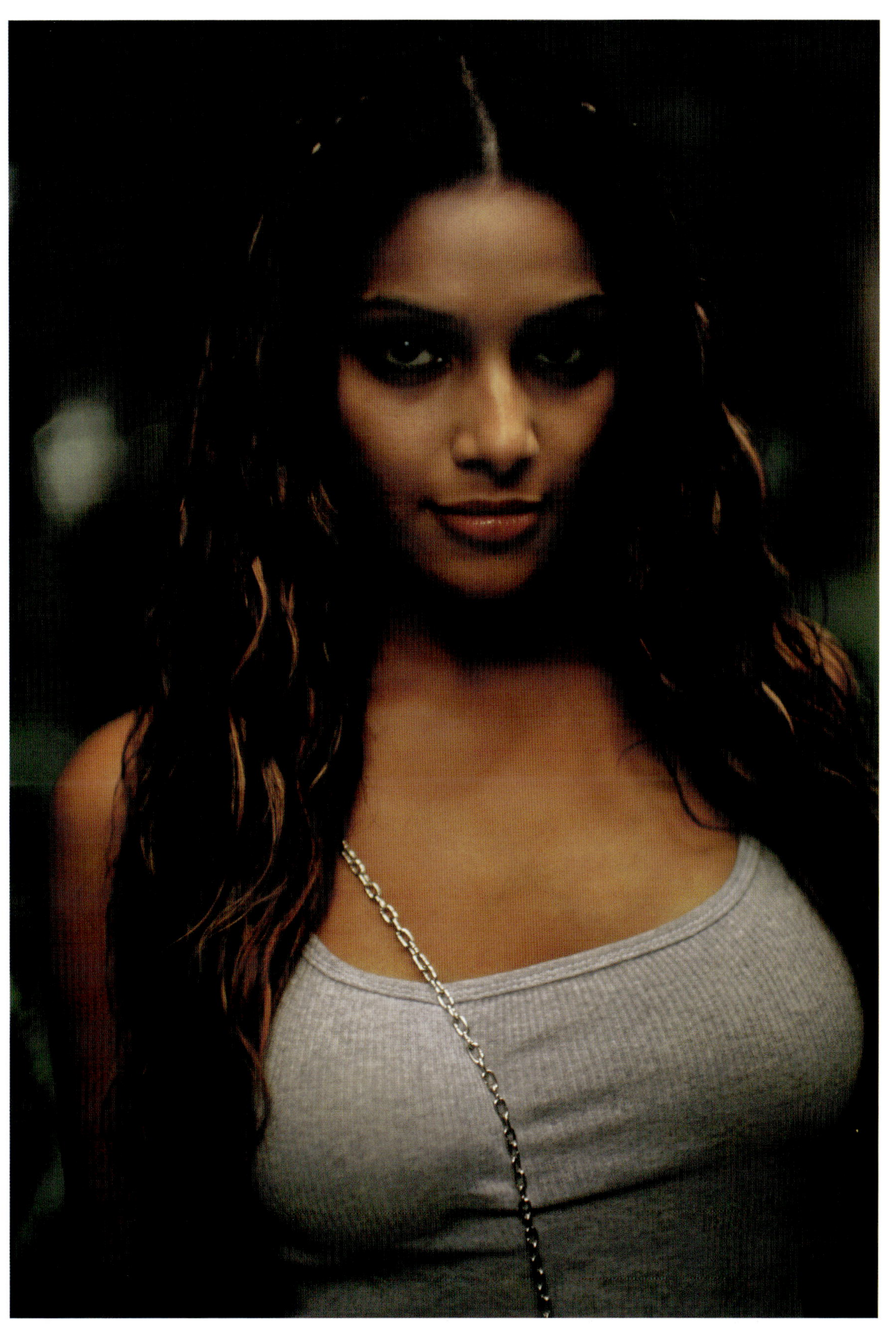

LEFT: *Kareena Kapoor, Mumbai, 2004* ABOVE: *Bipasha Basu, Mumbai, 2004*

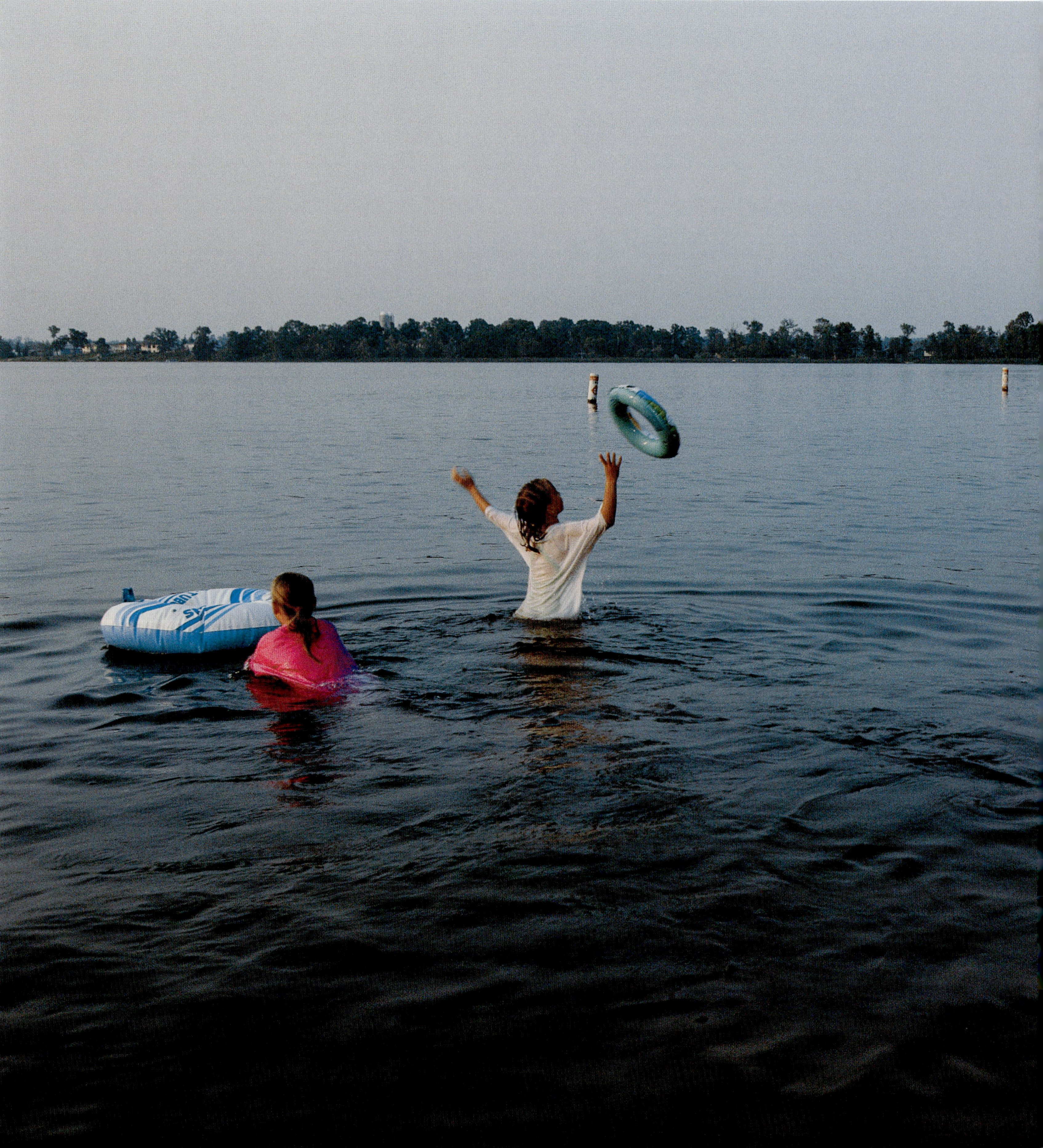

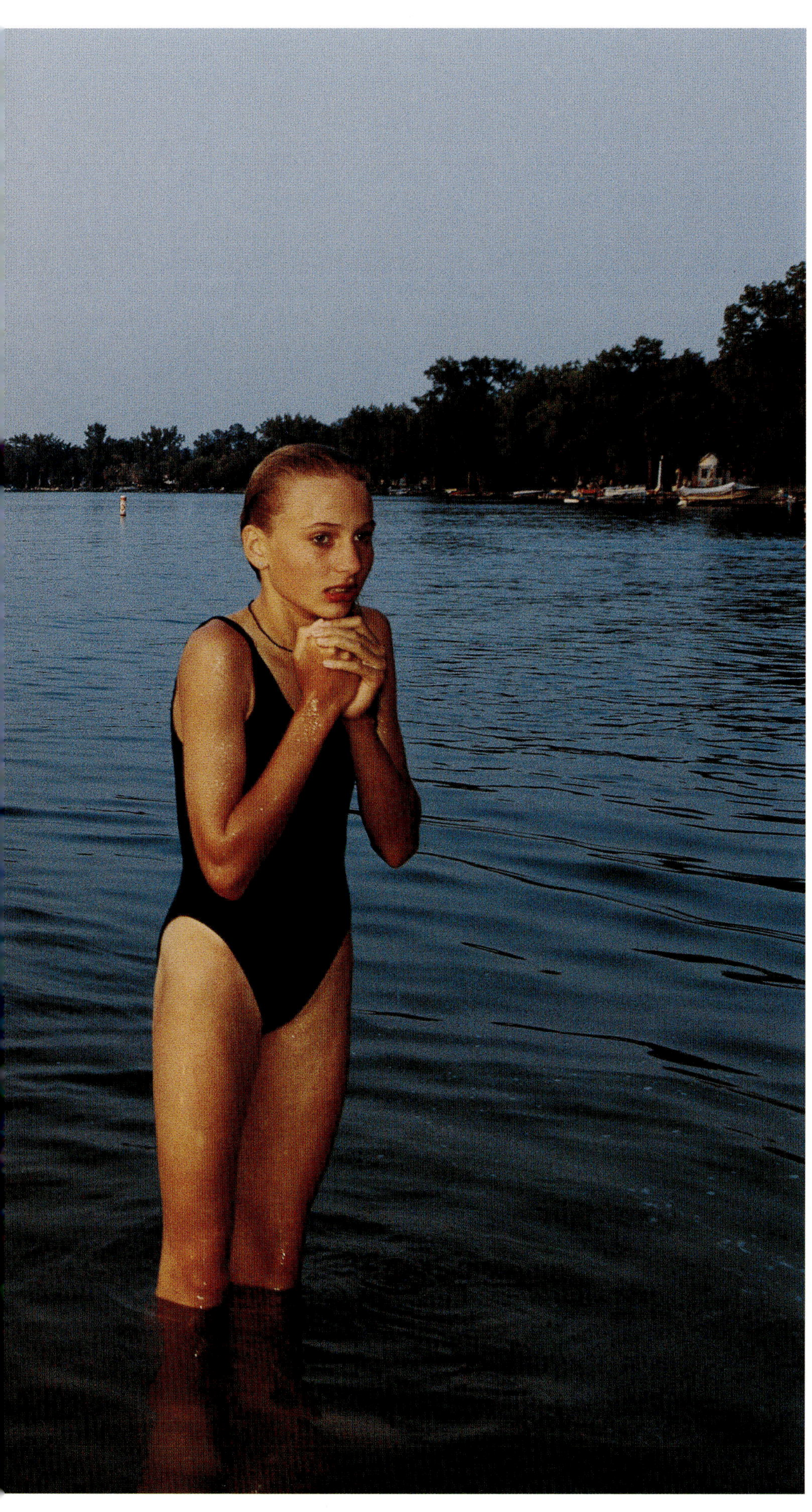

Three girls in Little Floyd Lake, northern Minnesota, 1995

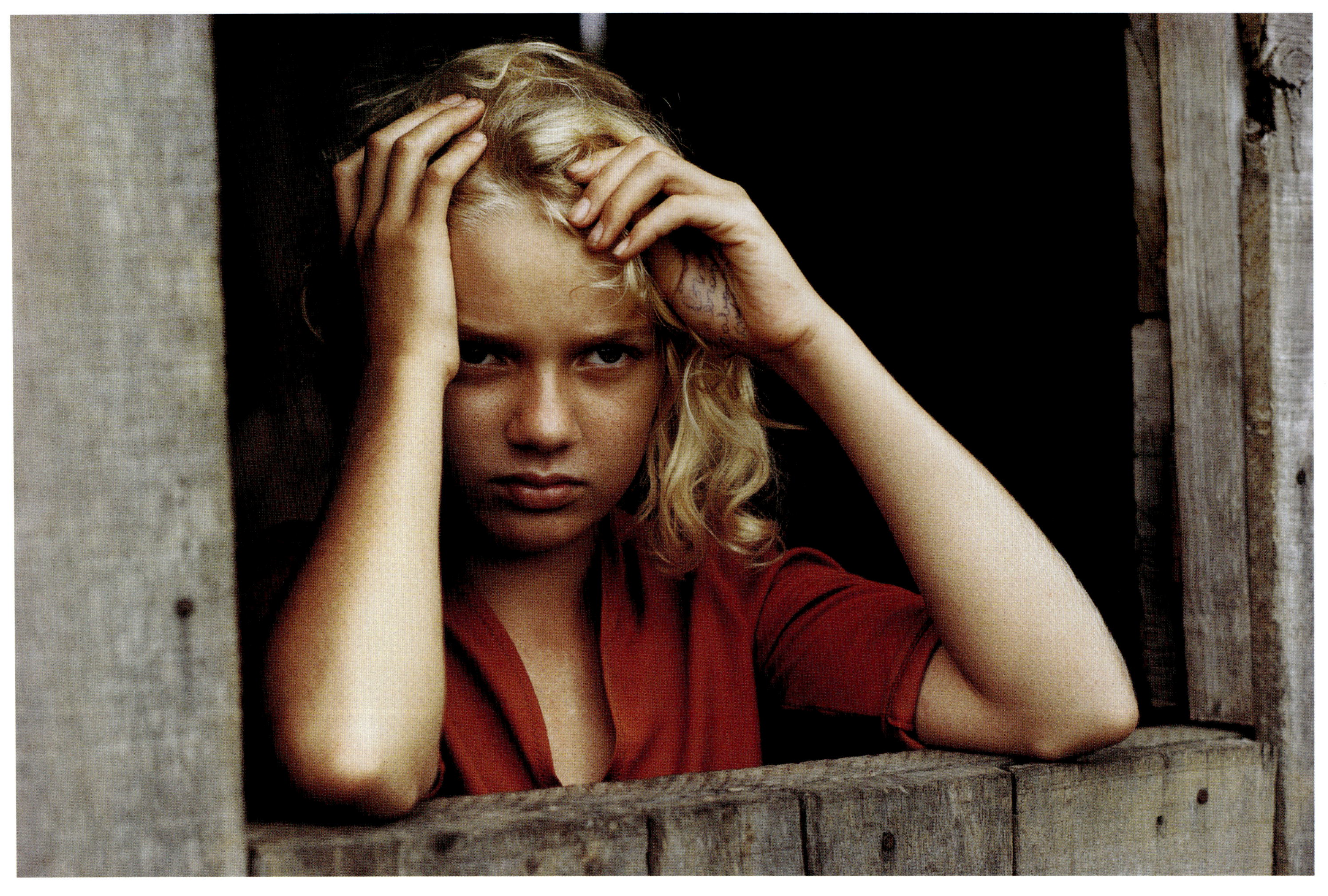

Bernice has malaria, Rondônia, Brazil, 1988

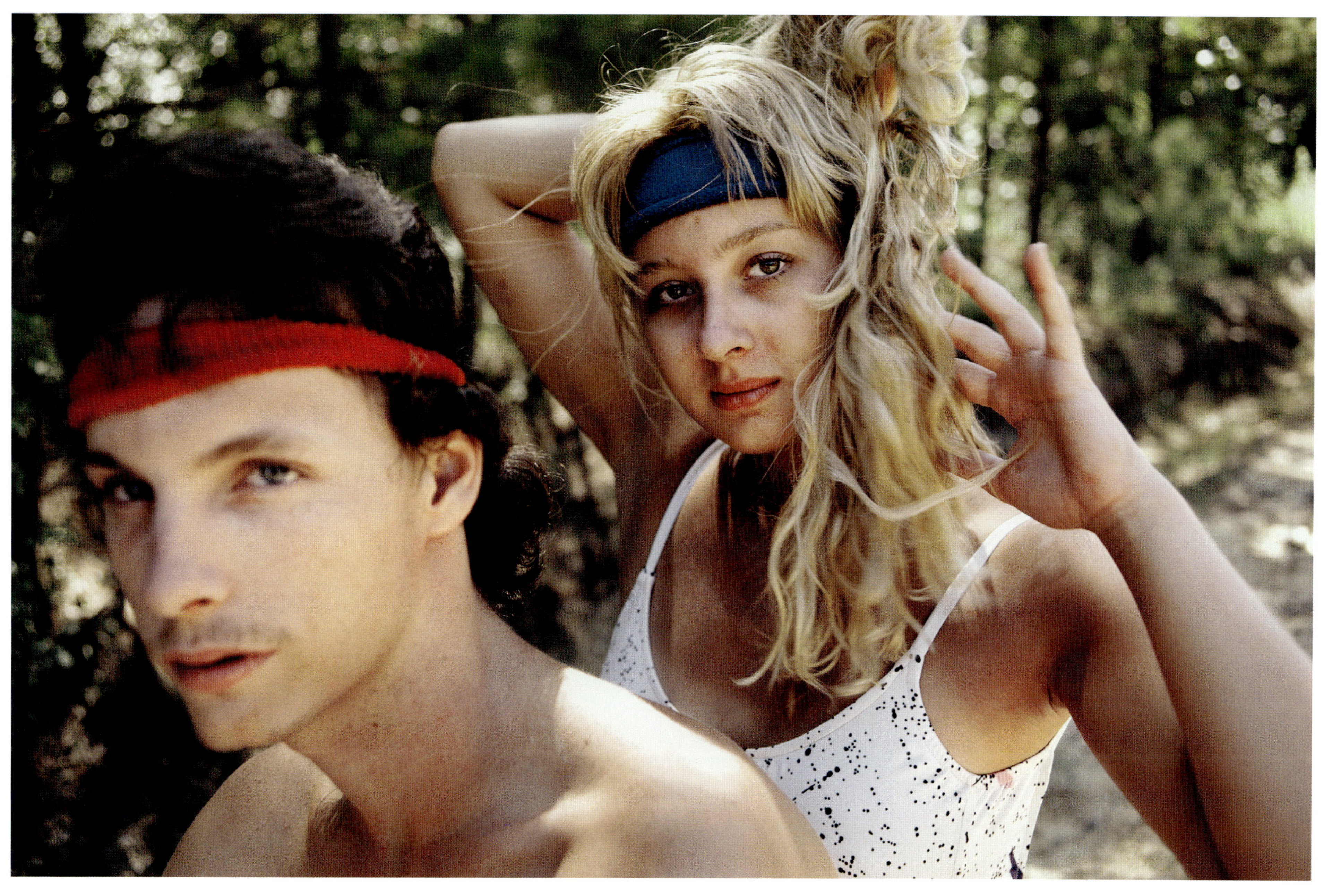

Blond girl with boyfriend, Oxford, Mississippi, 1986

"Some pictures have long stories behind them, others are the result of moments simply measured in fractions of time."

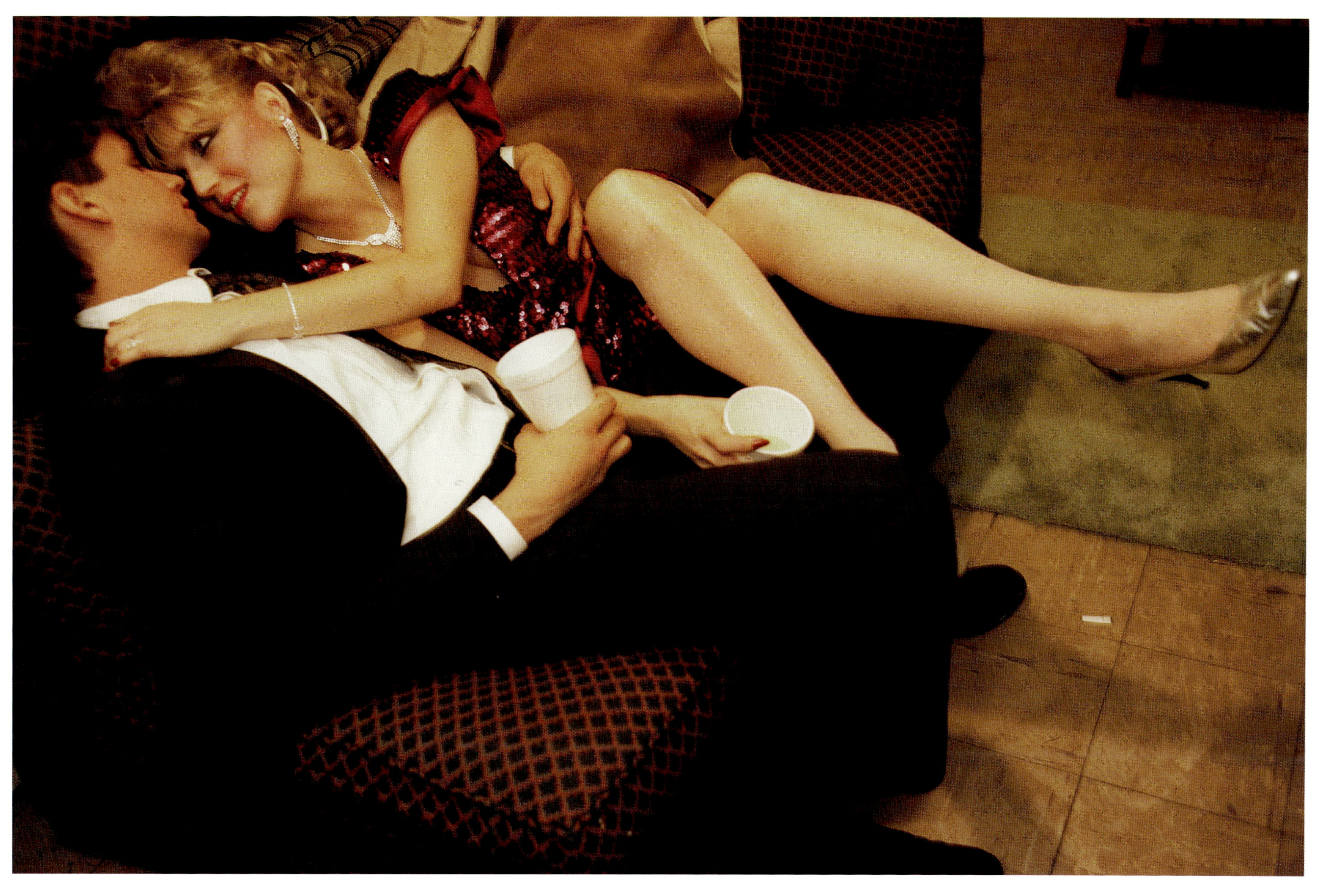

Ole Miss fraternity party, Oxford, Mississippi, 1986

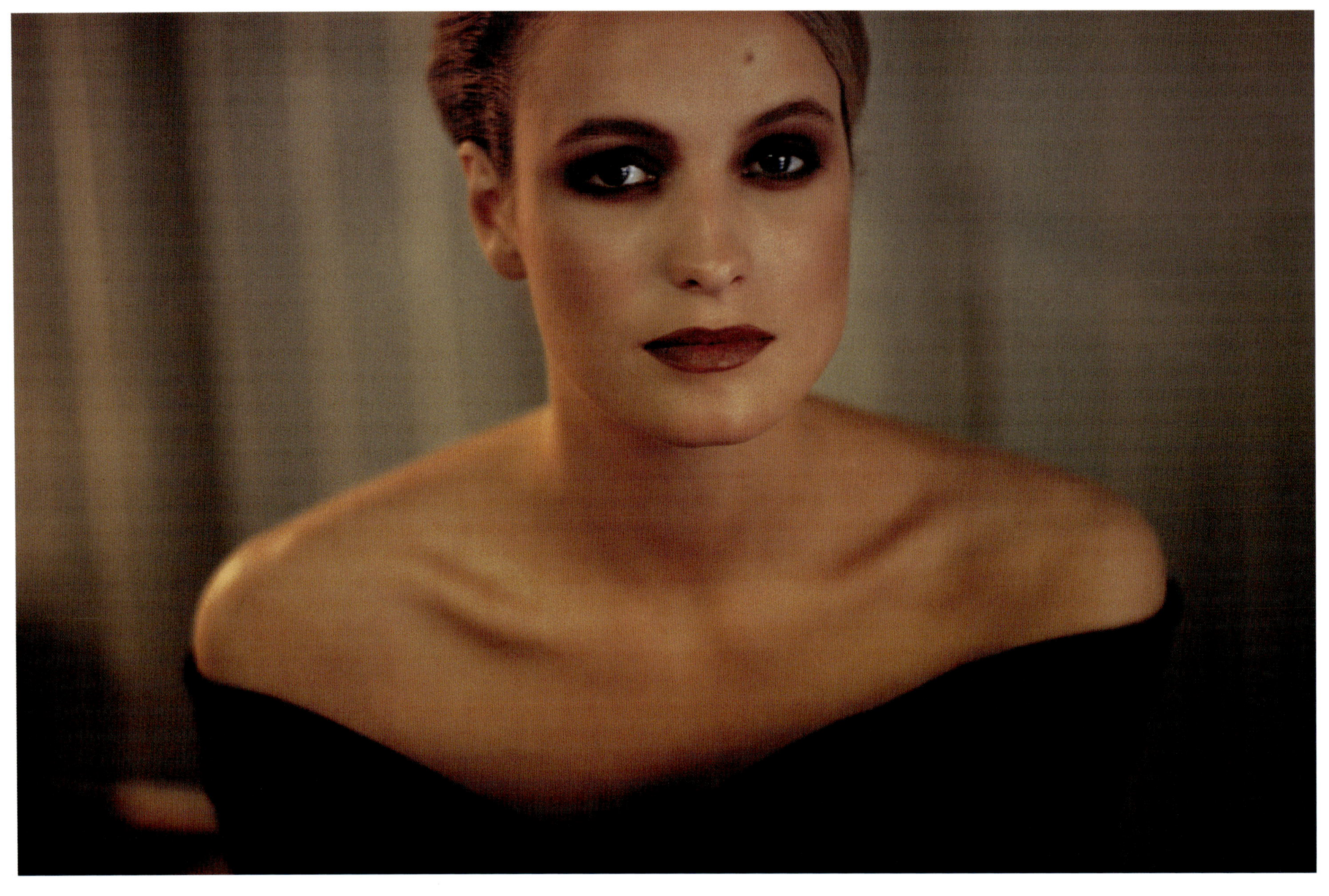

Model backstage, Paris, 1988

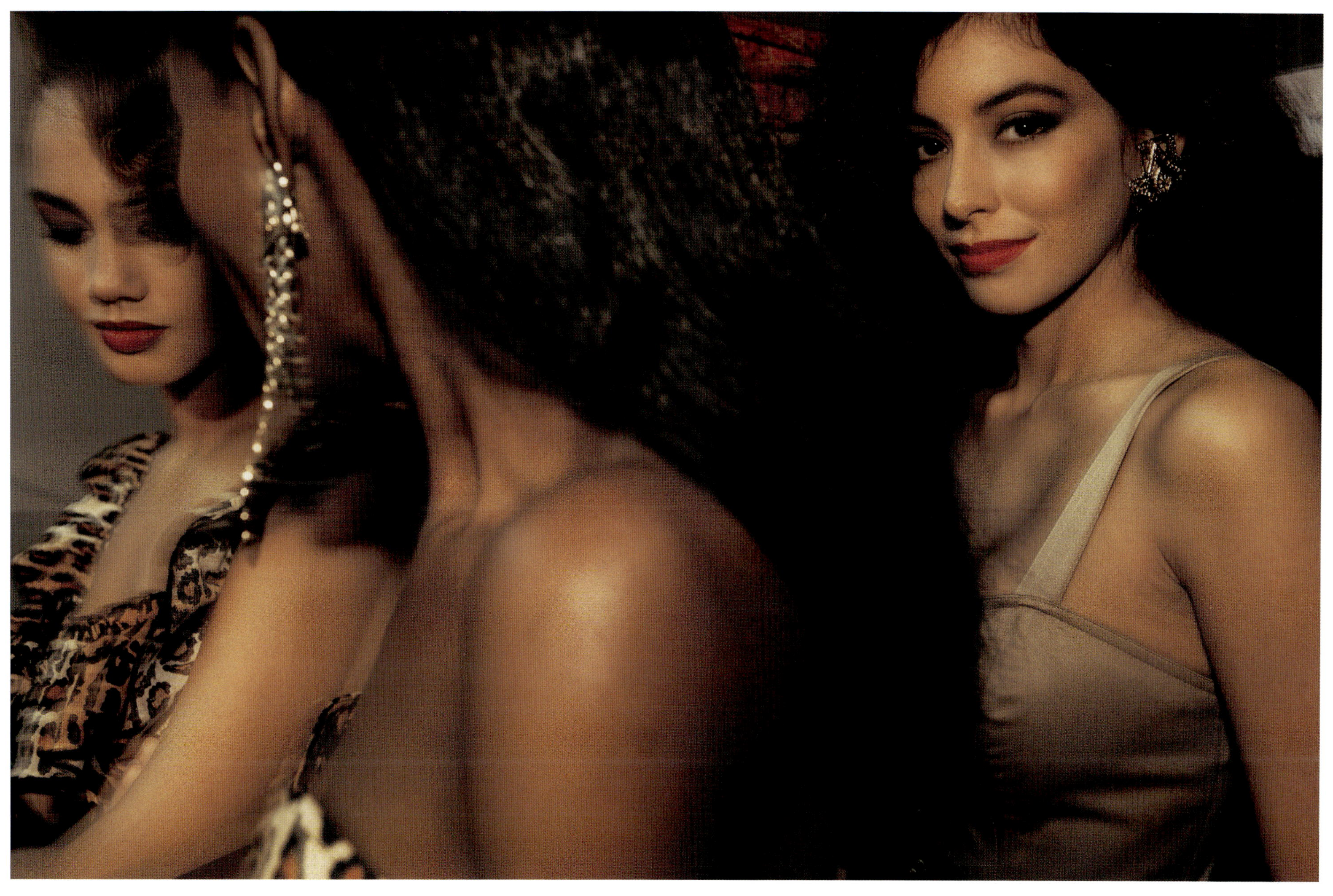

Patrick Kelly models backstage, Paris, 1988

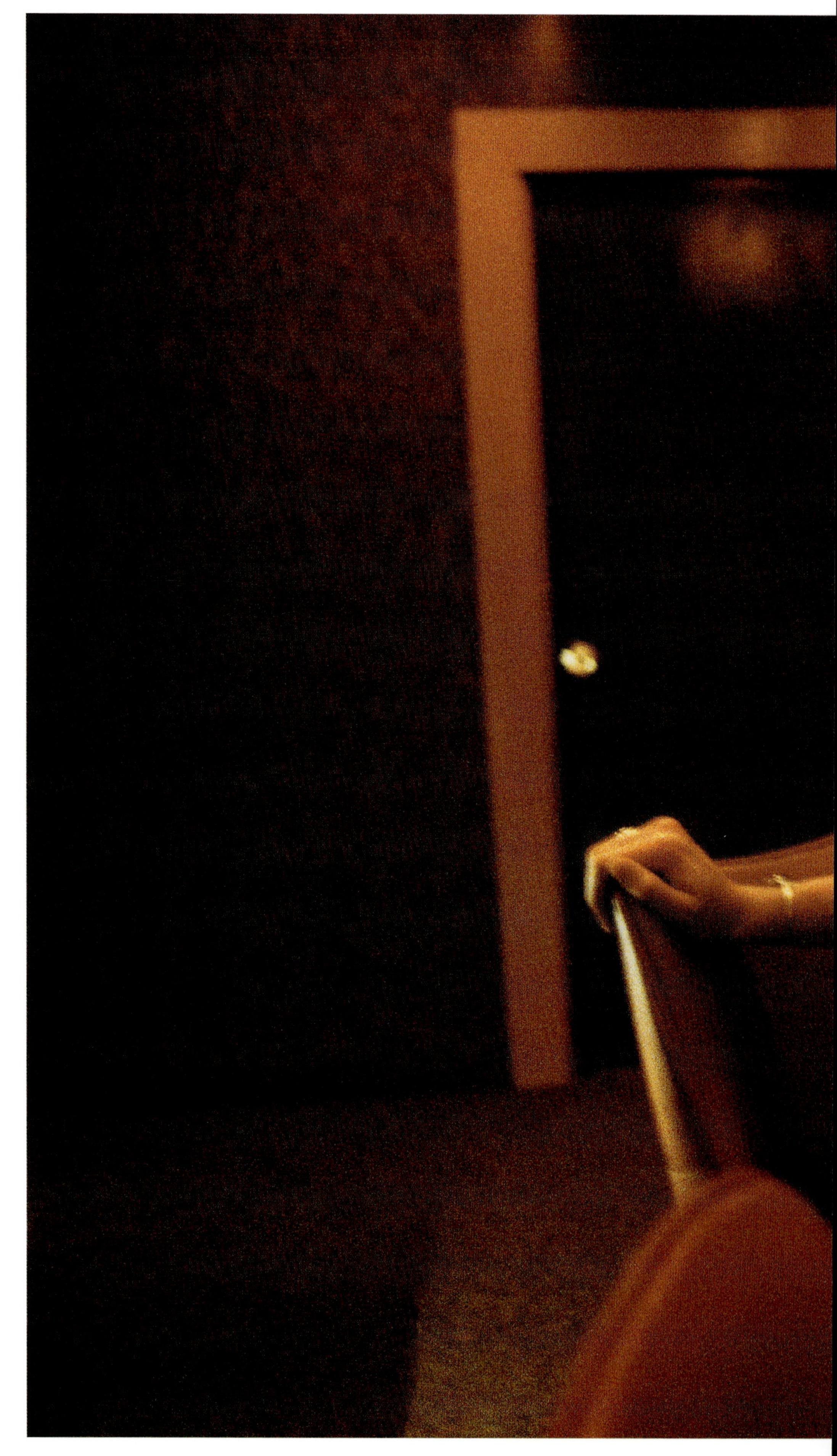

Elko, Nevada, 1979

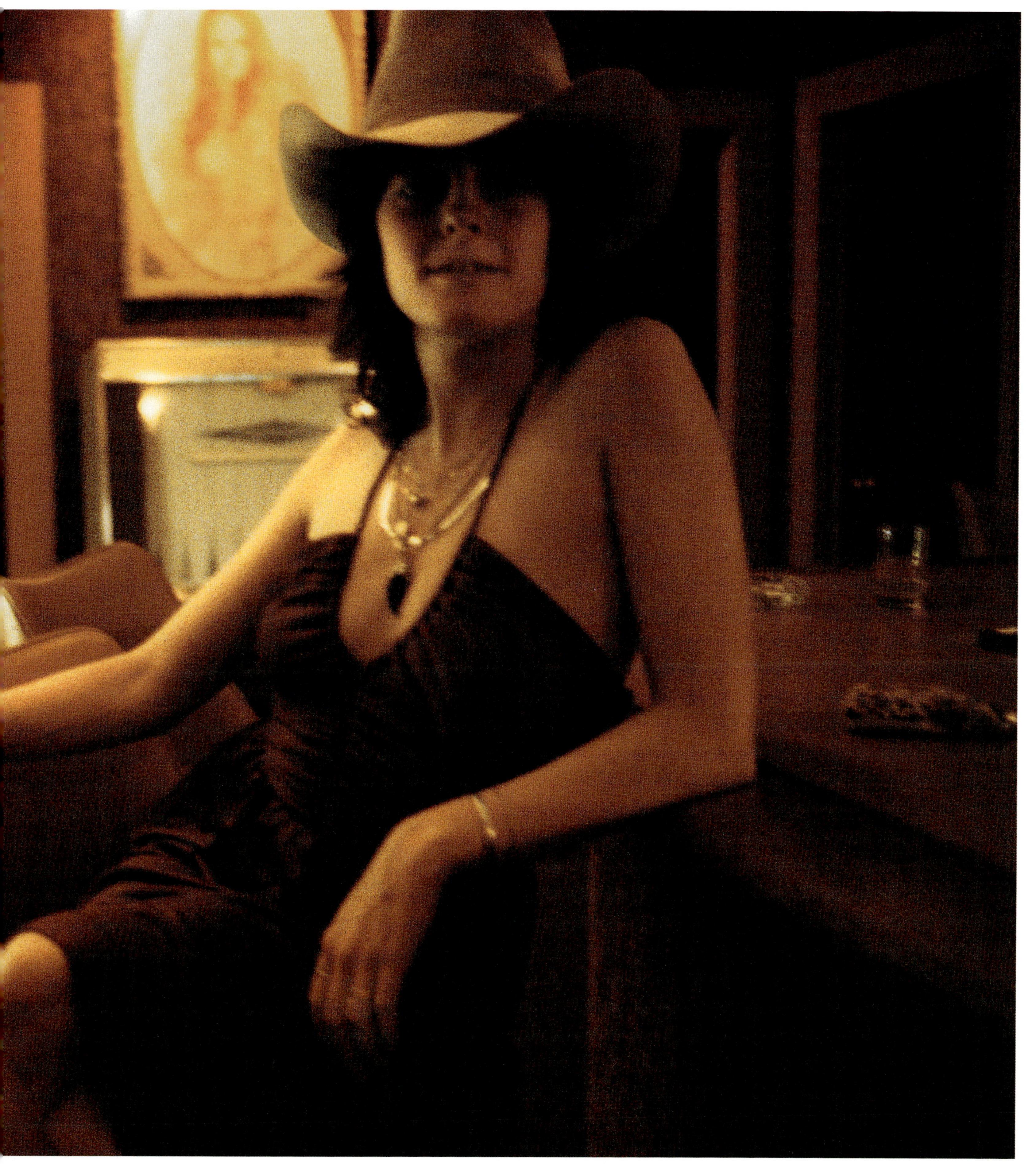

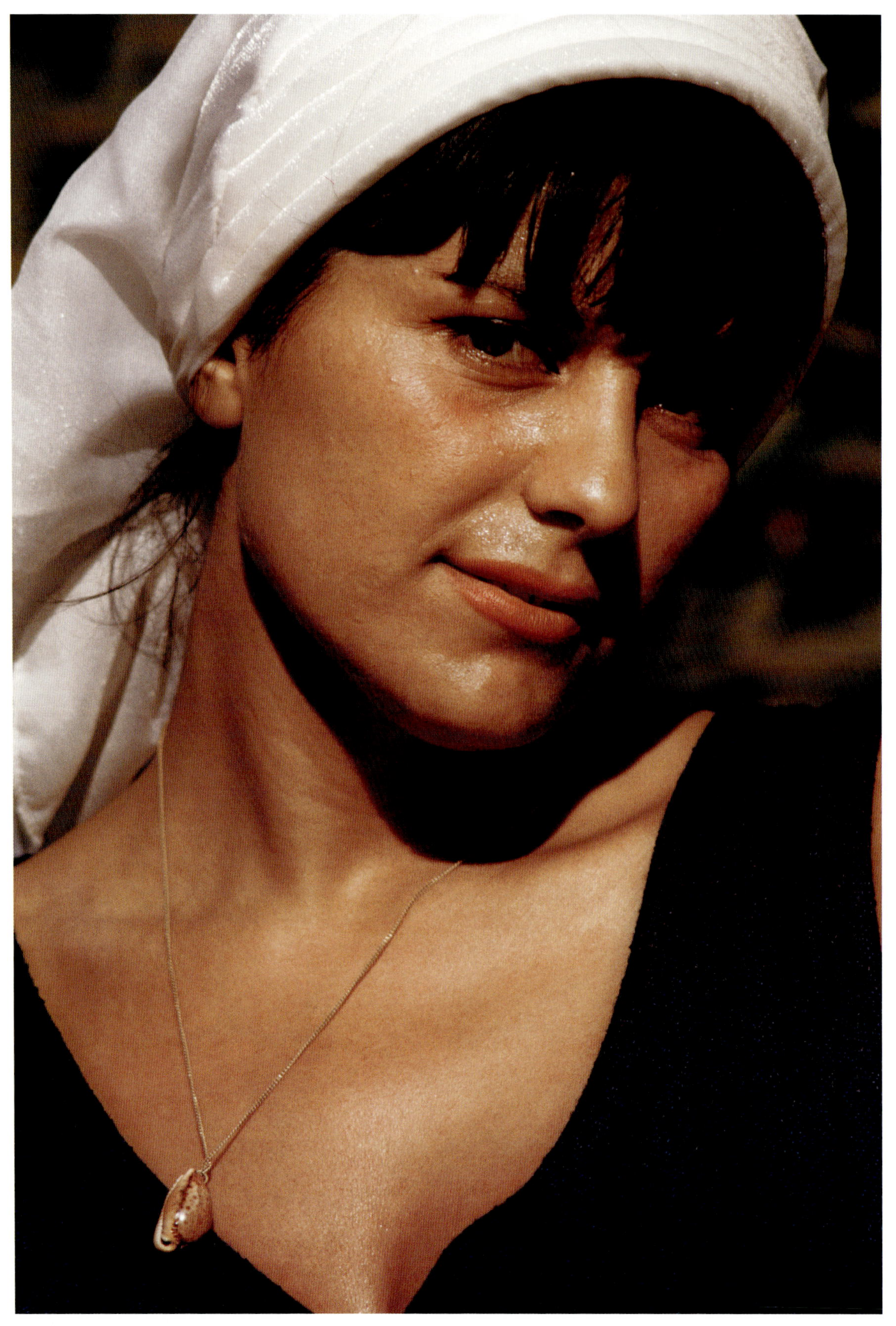

ABOVE: *Woman from Istanbul, Turkey, 1966* RIGHT: *Beauty contestant, Limassol, Cyprus, 1992*

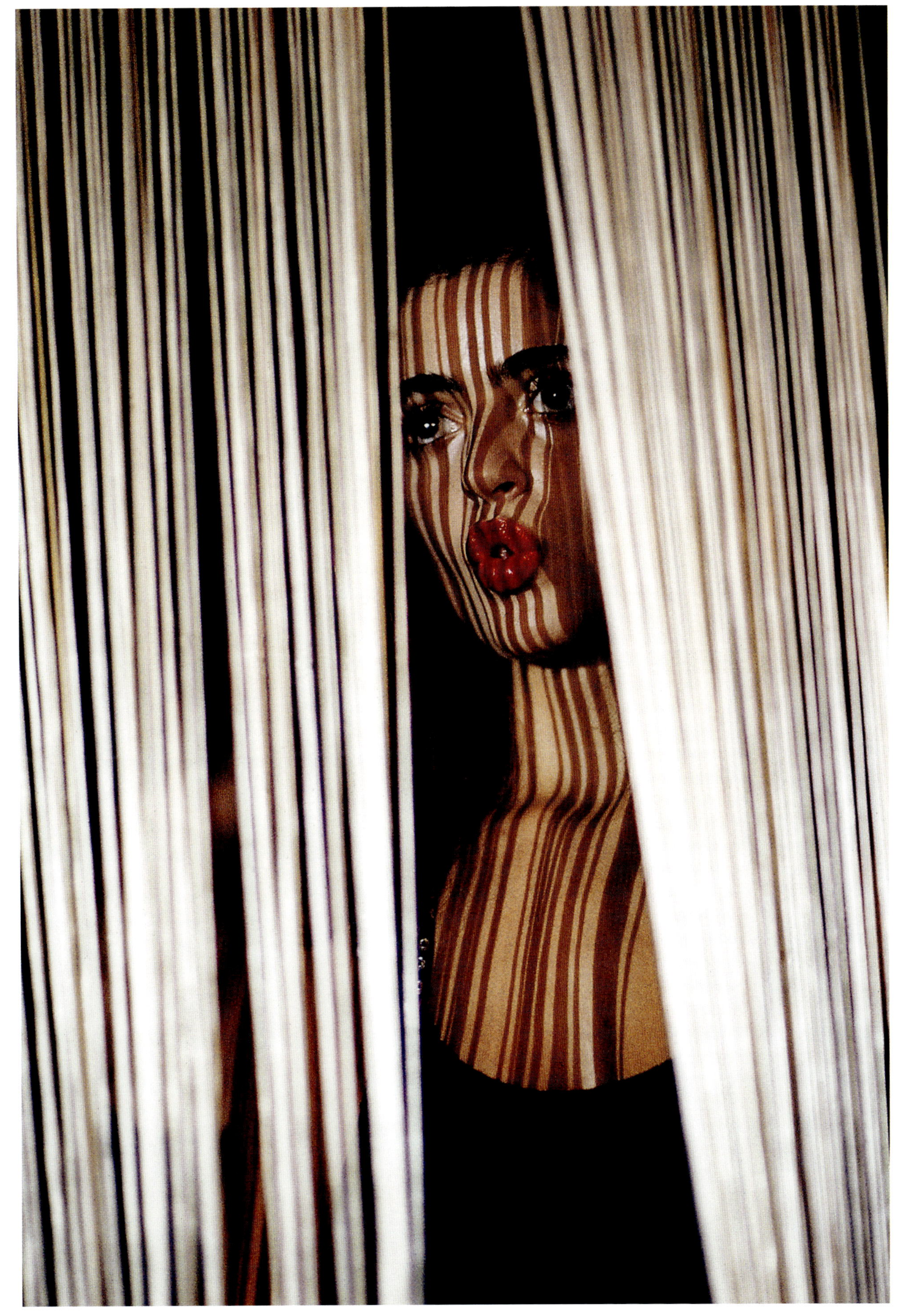

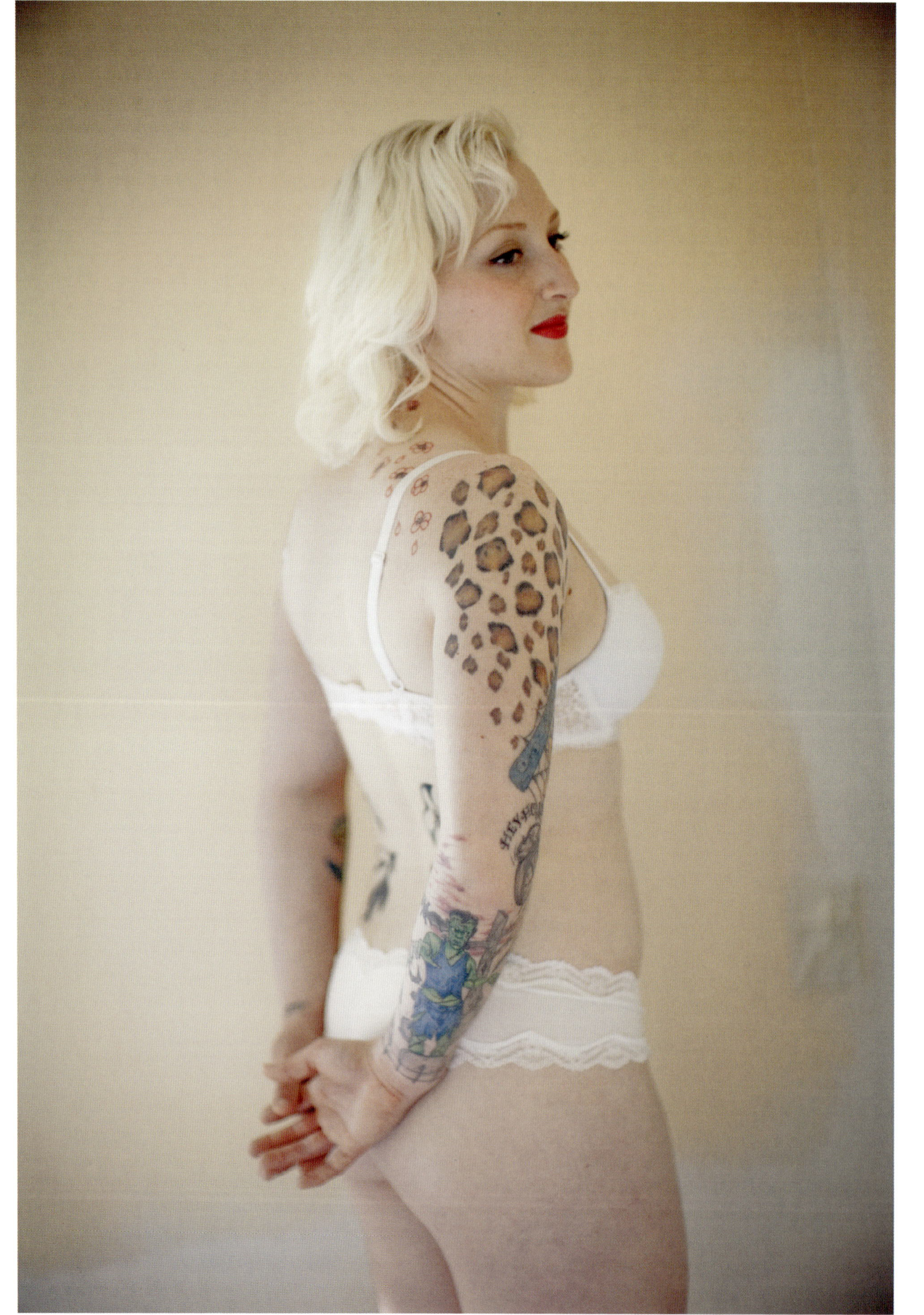

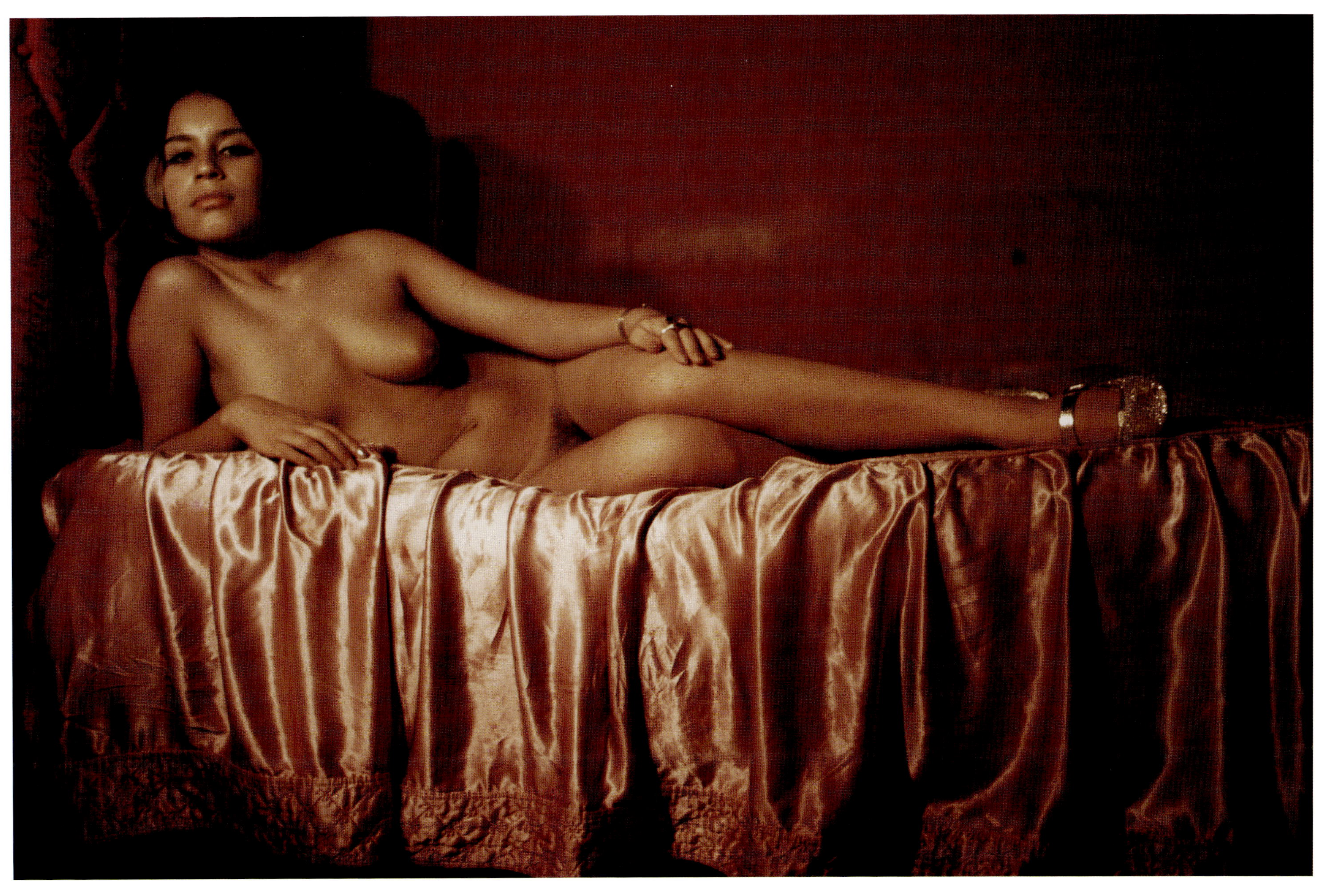

LEFT: *Indigo Maynard, Missoula, Montana, 2009* ABOVE: *Brothel, Nuevo Laredo, Mexico, 1970*

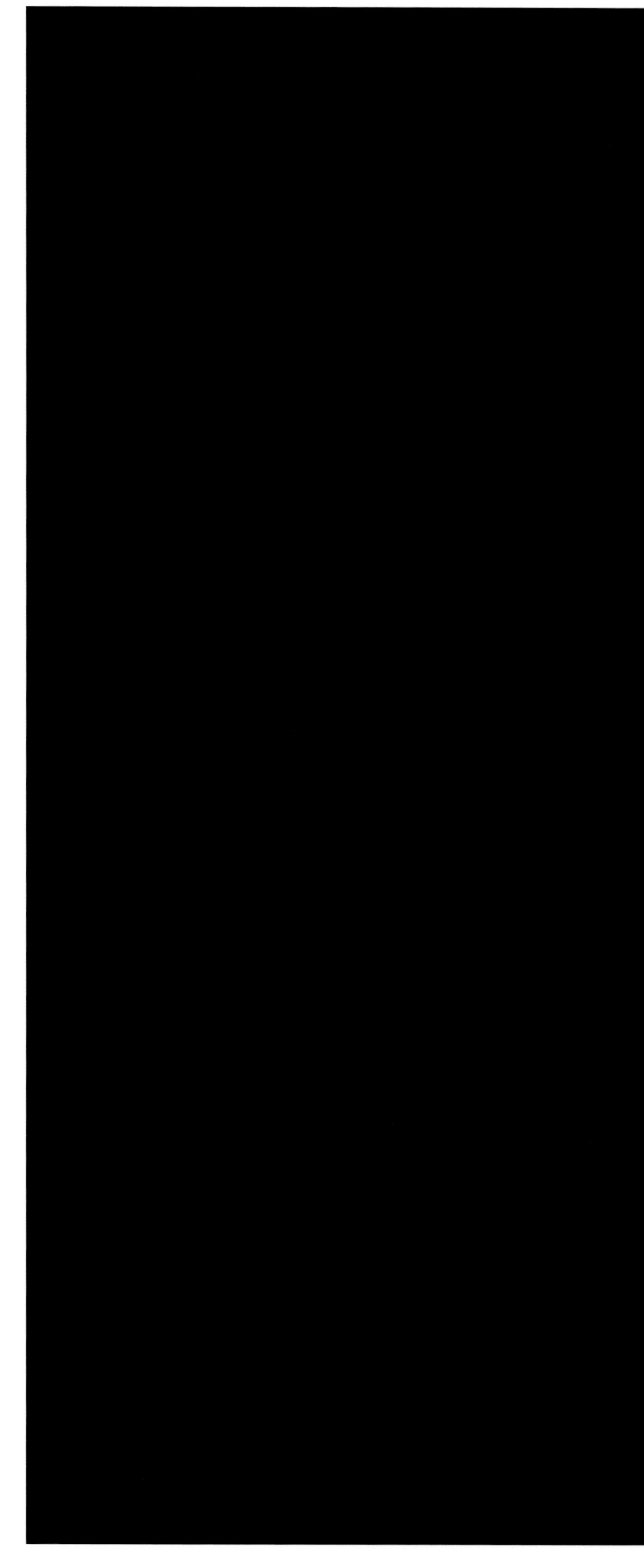

Brothel, Rondônia, Brazil, 1988

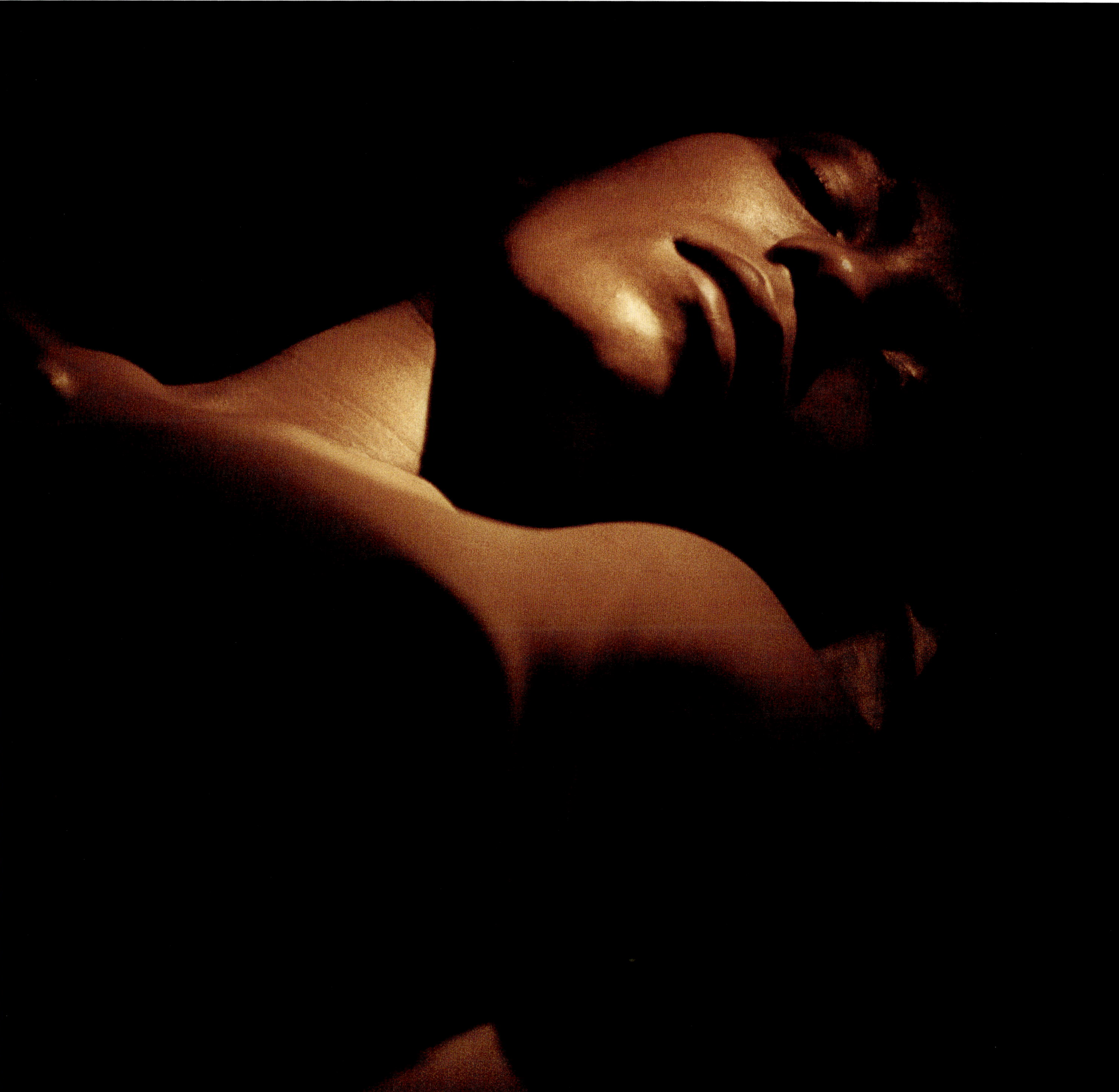

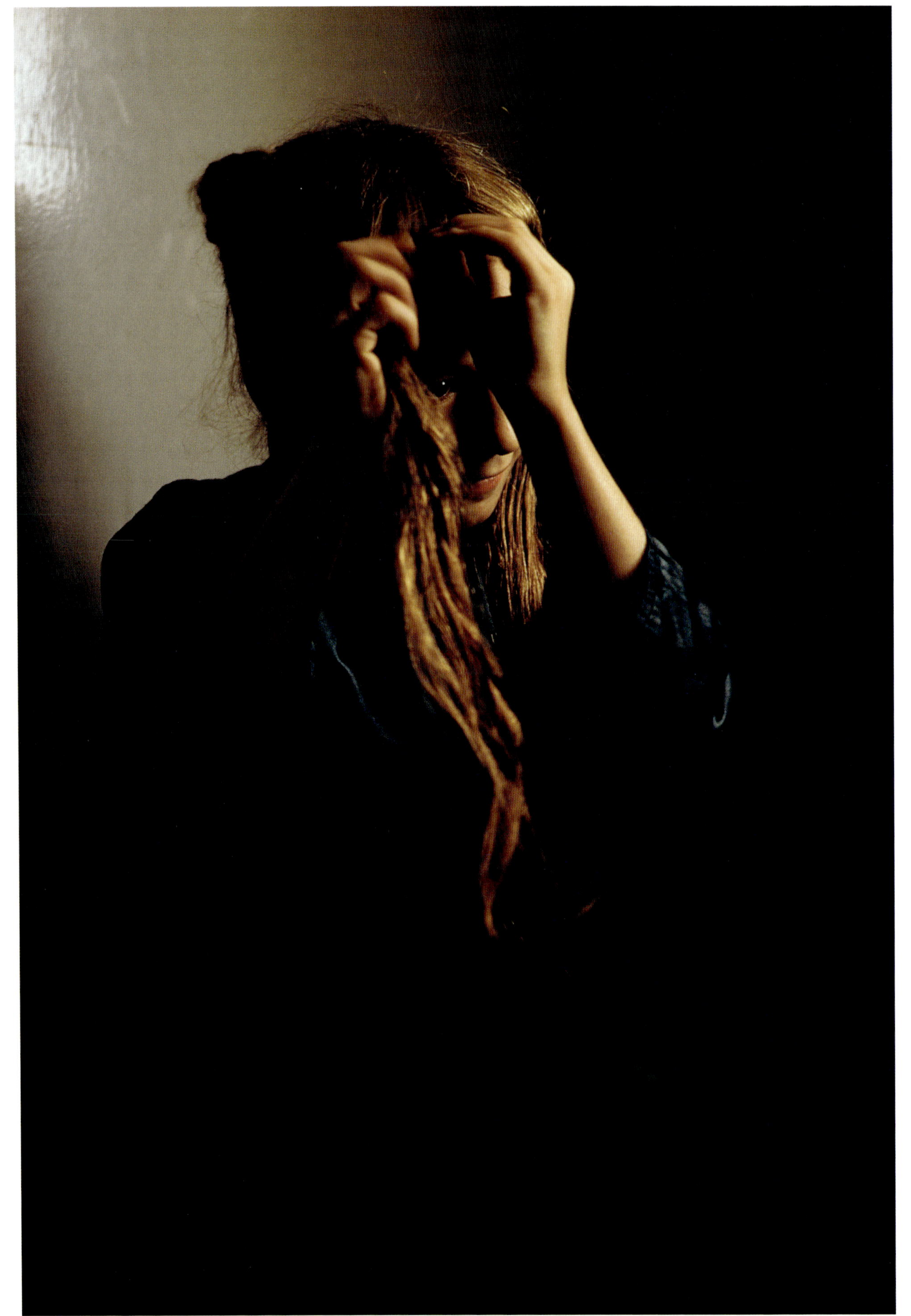

Hutterites

There is sadness in this chapter. But there is laughter, too.

Of all the stories from all the assignments I've had over my career, one became a part of my life that carried beyond either journalism or art. My relationship with the Hutterites of Montana began in 1969 with a story I photographed and wrote for *National Geographic.* That relationship continues today—and it is an extremely close one. In some ways being accepted into the Hutterite community is akin to having another family—a large, extended one—although our lifestyles are greatly dissimilar.

Along with other pacifists, the Amish and Mennonites, Hutterites emerged from the Anabaptist movement of 16th-century Europe. The first Hutterites to arrive in North America came in the 1870s, fleeing religious persecution in Europe. Unlike the other Anabaptist groups, the Hutterites live communal lives. Noted for their plain, Old World clothing—long dresses for the women, hair concealed beneath head scarves; the men in homemade black coats and pants—there are now more than 400 Hutterite colonies, representing three separate sects, in the western United States and Canada. Although the first colonies were founded in Montana, there are more in Canada, and probably because of this the Hutterite elders—the men elected by other male members to keep watch over the conduct of the colonies—reside mostly in Canada.

Kathy Walter, Spring Creek colony, Lewistown, Montana, 1969

The Hutterites' acceptance of me and my cameras came easily in some ways, more slowly and with more difficulty in other ways. The kids always liked to be around me; most of the young women didn't mind me photographing when they were cooking or making soap, or butchering geese or ducks. Eli Walter, preacher at Surprise Creek Colony in 1969, used to warn me sternly, "No pictures of the women!" But when I looked at him I would always see a twinkle in his eyes. Sometimes this was followed by the demanding and ridiculous question "How many horses did you steal today?"

The first time I came to photograph a Hutterite prayer meeting at a colony called Spring Creek, near Lewistown, Montana, nobody showed up. The second time I attended, it was mostly children and the preacher, not many adults. Even though I was using a Leica 35mm rangefinder camera, with possibly the quietest shutter made, each time I squeezed off an exposure within the silent intimacy of that one-room schoolhouse that also served as the church, it sounded like a cannon shot to my ears.

That first *Geographic* story about these people, "The Hutterites: Plain People of the West," was published in 1970. My interest in the American West continued to flourish throughout that decade and beyond, and I'd occasionally stop to see my Hutterite friends if I was in their part of Montana. As the years passed and it became apparent that Surprise Creek Colony had grown so large the members would have to divide and begin a new colony elsewhere in the state, I decided it would be good to do a new story about them—a story that I would write as well as photograph.

In June 2006, *National Geographic* published "Solace at Surprise Creek," my second story about the Hutterites of Montana, and perhaps the most personal story I'd ever written for publication at that point.

In this chapter I will draw upon excerpts from that 2006 story (in italics) and interweave observations and remembrances from my first visit and from other times with my Hutterite friends over the many years.

SUMMER 2006

Thirty-seven years ago I went to the grasslands of Montana to photograph the Hutterites of Surprise Creek Colony. I found a place where people practice what their elders have preached for centuries: Live simply, share everything, and trust in God. Now I find myself returning to the comfort of my lifelong friends.

SUMMER 1969

There is a man on the moon, thousands of young people are swarming to Woodstock, and thousands more are protesting the war in Vietnam. I'm in central Montana, documenting the lives of a pacifist religious group, the Hutterites, who live in a colony called Surprise Creek. Their lives are far different from mine, and probably yours. And yet this Hutterite assignment will result in a friendship that lasts my lifetime. I'm a young man, married, and the father of four children—two sons, two daughters, all about a year apart in age. Scott, our firstborn, is nine.

FALL 2004

We're not going to the moon now, there's a new war on, and the joke about Woodstock is that if you remember being there, you probably weren't. I'm no longer young, and I have another marriage and another son. Scott is 44 now and beginning to die, but we don't know that yet. At least we try not to think about it.

Today I'm in my pickup truck, my English springer pup [Buster] beside me, headed for Montana to do a new story about the Hutterites of Surprise Creek. On the way, I stop outside Minneapolis, where Scott lives with his wife and two kids, to spend time with him.

I'm having second thoughts about the Hutterite story, and driving back to Scott's house after a Twins game, I talk to him about it. "Am I going back to the same well by doing a Hutterite story again?" Scott has melanoma; the worst kind [of skin cancer]. He turned bald early in life, but beneath his Twins cap tonight he has plenty of hair on the sides and back of his head. He still has eyebrows and looks healthy and handsome. "Dad," Scott answers, knowing how close I am to the Hutterites, "when will you ever again get a chance to do something so personal?" "Yeah," I say. "That's true." Just how true neither of us can possibly know, and I leave in the morning for Montana.

Days later in Darius and Annie Walter's tidy frame house at the colony, I feel at home. I've returned to the colony many times over the years, sometimes flying out with my dog Sarah, to bird hunt and visit. I've always stayed at the Walters.' My daughter Terri calls the Hutterites and the Walters "your other family."

Darius, 65, is sitting in his place at the kitchen table. A couple of years my junior, he's one of my best friends. Bearded, as married Hutterite men must be, Darius wears the suspenders Hutterite males of all ages wear. He's heavier than he once was, and more flushed in the face, but he has the full head of silvery hair and the twinkling eyes, warm smile, and keen sense of humor of his late father, Eli, the colony preacher when I first arrived . . .

Darius is gripping a wireless phone, one of two phones in colony homes; the other is in the home of preacher Sam Hofer. On the other end of the line is a man from Texas who has called several times, persistently seeking to join the colony. It's rare for an outsider to become a member; Hutterites don't encourage converts. "You're wastin' your time," Darius says gruffly into the phone. "It's hard enough if you're born a Hutterite. I got guys breakin' the rules all the time. We don't do it and that's that. There don't need to be any 'How come?' "

"How come?" does not apply to the Hutterite world. There's little place here for individualism in dress, thought, or other personal rights most Americans treasure. The colony owns all assets, so there's no private property, no personal bank accounts, few personal belongings—and little privacy. On the other hand, everyone is clothed, fed, and given a sense of belonging.

The Hutterites are one of the oldest communal groups in North America today. Rather than losing young people, their population is growing. Since I first came to Surprise Creek, it has grown from about 50 to 125 members. Now it's branching out. A new colony, Prairie Elk, is being established about 300 miles away in northeastern Montana . . .

Darius . . . seems more relaxed when I see him at Prairie Elk. When I first met him he was a farmer. Then, when the old boss at Surprise Creek died in 1994, Darius was voted in to replace him. It's not an easy job. He's the enforcer of many rules and the overseer of colony debts. Every morning he sits in his office just off the kitchen, paying bills, assigning jobs to the men, and managing colony affairs. Sometimes the pressure shows, and I wonder if he'd have been happier staying a colony farmer.

SUMMER 2008

Darius Walter no longer sits in the kitchen of that house at the Surprise Creek Colony near Stanford, in central Montana. By 2006 Darius and his wife, Annie, and all his sisters and brothers and their children had moved to the 7,000-acre Prairie Elk Colony established near Wolf Point, on the south side of the Missouri River. Two-lane Highway 528 runs past the Prairie Elk sign at the end of the driveway into the colony. The colony gets mail delivery on Monday, Wednesday, and Friday. Annie and Darius Walter live in the main house; all the other colony members live in nicely furnished trailer houses. A church has been built.

After 2005, when I had lived for several months at Surprise Creek with Darius and Annie and their then unmarried daughters, Annie Marie, Debbie, and Linda, and sons Ben and Bill (who married while I was there), I continued to come back to both colonies to hunt and visit or to attend a wedding or a funeral.

When a Hutterite girl marries, she always goes to live at her husband's colony, sometimes many miles away from her family and home colony. One daughter of colony preacher Sam Hofer moved to her husband's colony in Canada's Northwest Territories, a 14-hour drive from Surprise Creek.

In 2007, my wife and I bought a little second home in Missoula, answering a longtime desire of mine to live at least part-time in Montana.

It's a 1,000-mile round-trip between Missoula and Prairie Elk Colony at Wolf Point, so we don't visit as much as we'd like.

FALL 2004

It's late afternoon [at Surprise Creek], and I've fed, watered, and crated my pup in the grass behind the Walter house. I'm surrounded by some of the smallest kids in the colony, boys in homemade caps and jackets, girls in long dresses and the head scarves that cover their braided hair. The little kids address me by my full name when they have a question, and they usually have many.

"Bill Allard, is that Sarah?" It's seven-year-old Rene asking about my dog. "No," I say. "Sarah died. This is Buster." Respectful silence follows, but I know it will end. "Bill Allard," says Gregory, six, "can Buster hunt pheasants?" "Well, he's just a pup. But I'm going to find out." "Bill Allard," it's nine-year-old Ryan this time. "When you go hunting, can I go with you?" "No, not today." They know what I'm always going to say to that question, but they have to ask anyway. I guess I'd miss it if they didn't.

They're going to butcher 300 turkeys this cold morning. There's a lot of killing at a sustenance colony like Surprise Creek, most of it done for colony consumption. Almost everybody helps with butchering. Inside the slaughterhouse, the floor is shiny and slippery, splotched with red. The sweet smell of blood mingles with the smoky odor of wet feathers. Outside the slaughterhouse, young women with long wooden poles stir headless turkey carcasses in a large steel trough of steaming water. Rita, the handsome young mother stirring the trough, has a thin streak of blood crossing her cheekbone, almost like a scratch. It's turkey blood. A splatter. I think of taking my handkerchief and wiping it from her face, but of course I don't.

SPRING 2005

In Minnesota, Scott is undergoing treatment. His hair and energy are gone. He can't eat much or keep down what he does eat. He's in pain and can't sleep. The pain lessens and sleep comes when doctors start the morphine. I'm with him for a week in early May on my way to Montana again. We go back and forth to the Mayo Clinic in Rochester a couple of times. In his living room I massage his swollen legs and feet as we watch a ball game on television. When I hug and kiss him goodbye, I say I'll see him on my drive home in June.

In Montana, the spring rains have been generous to the Judith Basin, and it rolls out fresh and green. Square Butte and the Highwood Mountains rise off to the north of Surprise Creek. In the Walter house [daughter] Debbie is going out to shake the small rug that lies in front of the kitchen sink. I hear the soft padding of her stocking feet as she crosses the floor that always looks spotless . . .

Although women don't have a vote in colony affairs—only the baptized men, the "brothers," do—they share a community among themselves. Their camaraderie may be even stronger than the men's. When the women are gardening or cooking together (they do it all), they often sing. You aren't likely to hear songs from the men in the fields or the cow barns. I sense no female opposition to male domination at Surprise Creek, but maybe I just don't know enough of the women well enough. I ask Annie Marie, Darius's unmarried, 35-year-old daughter, if she resents the fact that women have no say in colony affairs. "No," she says, "I wouldn't want to take the blame if something goes wrong." . . .

Late this afternoon there's a baseball game going on in a makeshift field behind the colony school. The field is mostly in shadow, but behind the backstop the conical metal grain bins catch the lowering sun and stand like giant chess pieces touched with gold. Boys and girls of mixed ages play. As usual, no score is kept, and the game goes on until other demands halt it. Today a couple of outfielders have to leave to memorize verses for German school. The catcher has to go help unload potatoes.

Colony members sometimes watch ball games on TV in one of the bars in nearby Stanford, and once in a while the two non-Hutterite teachers from the county school system who teach the younger kids bring a television to the school. No radios are allowed in trucks or vans, although radios are found in most homes to listen to news, weather, and the occasional ball game. Some men have cell phones but these might not meet the approval of the Hutterite elders in Canada . . .

Colony life works for most because children are indoctrinated at a young age to believe that every member must submit to the rules of the church. Sometimes a member can't take this life of submission and leaves, but most "runaways" eventually return. I ask one Hutterite woman, not from Surprise Creek, if she's ever considered leaving. "Many times," she admits. "There must be more in life than this." Then she tells me something quite surprising—she has always wanted to be an FBI agent.

On the last Sunday in May, there is to be a wedding at the colony. Billy Walter, 27, Darius and Annie's youngest son, is marrying Karen Hofer, 28, from a nearby colony. As the wedding draws near, I take a room at the Sundown, a mom-and-pop motel five miles out on Highway 87. The Walters need space for guests from other colonies. I hear that Billy's sister Linda is not happy with the wedding cake. She says thinking about it kept her from falling asleep last night. I've been having trouble sleeping, too.

Scott died this afternoon, the day before the wedding. I know in the morning he is going to leave us because of a phone call from my daughter Terri, who is with him. His condition worsened so suddenly that it is impossible for me to get to Minnesota in time. I speak to Scott by phone several hours before he passes away, surrounded and comforted by his wife and children, his mother, sisters, and other loving relatives. There will be no funeral; a memorial will be held in two weeks. Now I face the choice of going back to the colony and the pre-wedding activity, or grieving in whiskey and solitude at the Sundown. I call Annie Walter and tell her about Scott. I say I'll be at the colony soon.

When I get there, the house is full of visitors. Annie, always calm and soft-spoken, tells me to go into Darius's office to see the wedding gifts that have filled the room. No one else is in there, and I've seen some of these gifts earlier—linens, various appliances, dishes, cleaning buckets and bottles of detergents, a garden hose—practical items for a practical life. I turn to leave and Darius is behind me like a wall. His eyes are brimming. "I'm so sorry, Bill," he says softly, embracing me. I can barely get my arms around him. I feel his beard against my cheek. For a moment, my heart lurches and my legs want to quit me. I lean into his embrace. Then I have to leave the house and go outside.

In the yard, I see the bird feeder where this morning there were yellow finches. Balloons are tied to the wooden posts alongside the house, and little Carolyn Walter in her new shoes and cool sunglasses is parading among the guests. Her face glows. The broad sky is a brilliant blue with clouds scattered above the horizon like white pillows strewn at random. It's such a beautiful day.

This evening there will be a shivaree—a big meal, singing, beer drinking—but I can't go. Not tonight. I stay for supper and, finally, I go to the Sundown to do what I didn't want to do before.

FALL 2005

Harry's Nightclub sits at the junction of Highways 528 and 13, close to the southern banks of the Missouri. A Miller Lite banner hanging out front proclaims, "Welcome Hunters" in bold black letters on a background of blaze orange. Off to the northwest sits the historic steel-spanned Wolf Point Bridge, built in 1929–1930 but replaced in 1999 with a modern structure. It is the largest and most massive steel through truss bridge in Montana, and the 400-foot span of the old bridge is the longest in the state. It is, indeed, a monument to the past. Herds of buffalo once crossed the river here. Crow Indian war parties on their painted ponies forded here on their raids. For travelers in this area the winters of years ago were treacherous because over the ice was the only way to cross the river until the bridge was built. There were ferries in the summer.

At Harry's I stop to drink a red beer—beer and tomato juice. It's refreshing but not as good as it would be with some of the Hutterites' homemade tomato juice. I can never get the kind of Tennessee sour mash whiskey I like at Harry's. The owner won't stock it. "It makes 'em crazy," she once told me.

On my drive out 528 I see five gaudy pheasant roosters strutting along, pecking gravel from the shoulder on my side. Just beyond them a wide swath of crimson is smeared across the yellow stripe in the middle of the road, evidence of where an unfortunate driver and an even less fortunate deer met their darkened fate on this narrow stretch of highway, where night driving is challenging and sometimes nerve-racking; so many deer come out to graze, crowding the shoulders, and they cross with a nonchalance that often proves deadly to them.

I'm about a dozen miles from Prairie Elk Colony, and in a few days some of the Walter boys and I will go out for deer on opening day of big game season. I think back to about a year ago when I was bird hunting at Surprise Creek Colony and Curtis Walter was with me. He must have been about 12 then. Curtis is the son of Terry, Darius and Annie's second oldest son. Hard of hearing, Terry talks pretty loud and is strong as an ox, with large, muscular forearms.

On that autumn afternoon I was hunting pheasant along the edge of Surprise Creek, just above the sheep barn. I told Curtis and his younger brother, Ryan, they could go along with me if they'd walk along with my dog, trying to flush pheasant from the thick willows, while I walked an easier route along the edge of a field just above the creek.

I noticed Curtis was developing a tendency toward swearing, nothing truly obscene, just a starting-out level of profanity.

"Wanna shoot that magpie?" he asked, as a black-and-white bird winged up out of the willows. "Shoot it and take it home for a rooster. That's what a city slicker would shoot at. Guys from the cities." I don't know how many "guys from the cities" Curtis knew at that point in his young life, but he seemed convinced that's what they would do.

"Oh, piss!" he exclaimed suddenly. "Oh, shit! There they go!" Four long-tailed, brilliantly colored pheasant that had been out feeding were quickstepping their way back into hiding in the thick maze of willows bordering the furrowed field just sprouting a green tinge of winter wheat.

"Watch your tongue, Curtis," I said. A black-and-white blur exploded off a willow branch and flew low above the creek.

When he was around seven or eight, Curtis used to follow me all over Surprise Creek Colony when I came to visit. In the evenings, after dinner, Darius would get about midway through reading the *Great Falls Tribune*, then end up stretched out on the living room couch, newspaper still clutched in his hand, asleep but not snoring, and I'd take Sarah out in the night for a run. We'd walk past the milk barn, where the old log horse barn used to stand when I first came in 1969; I wasn't there when they tore it down in 1971. They say after all the timbers had been removed and only the flooring remained, hundreds of rats fled when they ripped it up. Colony members stood around the edges with sticks to beat the fleeing rodents to death.

On beautifully clear nights, under a full moon, after I crossed the timbers bridging Surprise Creek, just above the laundry house, I'd let Sarah run, keeping an eye on her so she wouldn't bolt off after a rabbit and run into a coyote, although they're kind of rare around the colony. Surprise Creek Colony raises a lot of sheep, and the boys keep the coyote population down with their rifles. Sometimes when I was out with Sarah, I'd hear Curtis calling: "Bill Allard, where are you?"

Some nights, if I really needed to be alone for a while, I wouldn't answer.

FALL 2005

It's opening day of deer season, and I'm hunched down beneath a small cottonwood tree close to the edge of a clear stream feeding into Prairie Elk Creek. To my right are some small bluffs overlooking the creek, and off in the distance is a big stretch of timber on rancher Tom White's place, which borders the Missouri. Tom's a good friend of Prairie Elk Colony. I'm hunting with Bill and Dan Walter and a non-Hutterite friend of theirs. We're hoping the hunters Tom has on his place will push deer out of his timber and across a wide, open area between them and us.

The morning air is cold and sharp and there's a slight breeze in my face, which means any deer coming my way from Tom's place will have the wind at their backs, which is good for me. Within moments of there being enough light to shoot legally, I hear a distant shot from the woods. Then—two more. Then—nothing.

As deer tend to do, two suddenly appear seemingly out of nowhere; they must have burst from their sanctuary in the woods somewhere below my sight line and then come up through the dried grass, and now are crossing that open and dangerously vulnerable ground—a doe and her yearling, bounding with that beautiful grace that white-tailed deer possess. They come straight to me. The yearling falters at the edge of the feeder creek, not sure which way to go; the doe moves on but slows to a canter, and with the wind behind her, she doesn't sense me even though I could almost lean out and touch her as she passes. No bucks, however, and I am hoping for a buck.

An hour or so passes with no more deer in sight. Then I hear Dan's voice in the distance, and I spot him walking hurriedly along the bluff above the creek. I hear something about "fire." Then something about "a family on fire." Billy appears, coming toward me quickly. He tells me smoke has been seen rising from the direction of the colony. We have to get out of here and get back to the colony. Dan has already hiked back and taken the pickup truck we came in. We are afoot and are walking quickly in the direction of the road. A family's house on fire? I think. What does that mean? Please, no, no, please, no, I think, and my heart is pounding as we march out to the road heading back to the colony. I have photographed many different episodes of life on a Hutterite colony; intimate moments, times of joy and times of sadness, but I don't want to have to record the calamity of a house fire. I can only imagine what is coursing through Billy's mind and how his heart must pound, and yet his eyes appear calm. Like his brother Ben, a man of very few words, Billy sometimes seems unflappable.

When we get down the road a ways we are immensely relieved to discover the smoke is not from the colony but from a semitrailer truck that had been carrying some of those huge, round hay bales; some of them had rubbed up against the truck's exhaust stacks and caught fire. Someone has come with a front-end loader to push off the burning bales that now lie smoldering on the ground. Young Jake Walter has arrived from the colony with the orange 1960s International fire truck provided by the county and kept at the colony. Jake stands grinning in his yellow firefighter's slicker and helmet. I take his picture as he poses proudly by the old truck.

Later that day we go out again looking for deer and I get myself a nice six-point buck the colony will hang for a while to age and then butcher for me. I'll feed well off that venison, which tastes so good because that deer spent its life feeding on the wheat and barley of McCone County, some of it from the fields of Prairie Elk Colony.

FALL 2005

One day, close to noon, I'm cruising along Highway 87 when I get a call on my cell phone. It's Darius.

"Bill, where are you?" he asks.

"I'm on my way to Lewistown to get a couple of things," I say. I'd forgotten to tell him or Annie I was going and wouldn't be at the colony for lunch.

"Don'tcha know we're havin' fried chicken for lunch?" he exclaims, as if I'd forgotten some important anniversary.

"I can't make it," I say. "I'm too far down the road. But thanks for calling."

And in fact, I had forgotten it was Saturday, and at Surprise Creek lunch is often fried chicken on Saturday, and it is always sinfully good, no matter who is cooking. Not that either Darius or I really need any fried chicken, portly as we both are (Darius a good deal more than I, but I'm certainly not slender). On another day I hear lunch will be "the walkers and the talkers"—goose beaks and feet in a broth. My tastes in cuisine can be quite eclectic, but I've never really taken to that dish. On Tuesdays at Surprise Creek, breakfast is almost always bacon and eggs, and just about every man shows up for the second of two bells that announce breakfast is being served, almost as if they can smell the fare from the confines of their homes.

FALL 2005

Before I leave Surprise Creek [to go to Prairie Elk on my way back to Virginia], I have dinner with Sam Stahl and his wife, Bertha. Several years back, their 23-year-old daughter, Kimberly, left in the middle of the night to marry a Hutterite runaway from Canada. As we finish dinner, Sam says, "I told her, 'Sweetheart, he left the colony. What has he to offer you? What's the future?' " Sam's voice lowers to a whisper. "Why couldn't it have been some other way instead of heartbreak and tears and everything else?"

"You know, Bill," Bertha tells me the next morning, "Sam and I were thinking last night that we talked all about our daughter, but we never said anything to you about losing your son. I'm so sorry we didn't." I assured her that was fine. We both know about heartbreak and tears. And everything else. There really isn't much you can say.

MARCH 2006

Leonard Walter, only 54, and the second youngest of Darius's six brothers, died of pancreatic cancer. Leonard loved to talk and, like some of the other Hutterites, he loved to drink. Most Hutterite families make their own wine. Annie Marie Walter makes really good wine from rhubarb and bing cherries, strawberries and wild plums, chokecherries, and peaches and apricots. A lot of the Hutterite guys have a private stash of liquor somewhere. One man might keep a bottle of grocery store ruby port wine out in the high weeds behind an abandoned refrigerator or stove, and if it's in the winter months, drinking from that bottle is like pouring syrup down your throat, and you really feel its warmth when it hits your stomach. Certainly not everyone in a colony has a drinking problem, but it's fair to say Leonard probably did as he got older.

Leonard was good natured and always a talker, ever since I knew him when he was just a kid back in 1969. He left a lot of friends, many of them non-Hutterites. It was said he had a good heart; it seemed that everybody knew Leonard and everybody liked him. He usually knew where the game was when it was time to hunt. He had gone with me when I hunted antelope on Shorty Harlow's place that previous fall. Shorty, a gregarious and feisty rancher in the Geyser area and a good friend of the members of Surprise Creek, always welcomed me to hunt on his place. I'd see him sometimes at the Cabin Creek bar in Geyser. At Shorty's place after an antelope hunt we'd drink a little Canadian whiskey and tell a few stories to each other.

I came out from Virginia for Leonard's funeral. I photographed Leonard as he lay in view in Darius and Annie's living room the day before the funeral. I tried to be as unobtrusive as I possible could, but it was a difficult task. Hutterites from Surprise Creek and other colonies filed into the room to pay their respects; some wept, some gathered later in the kitchen to reminisce about Leonard. When Leonard lay in view in the colony church that night, many of the young Walter girls—Abby, Julie, and others—sadly wept during the religious service, unable to keep the somewhat stoic faces managed by the men. In this church where I'd witnessed Billy and Karen's wedding, which I couldn't photograph because preacher Sam Hofer wouldn't allow it, I lifted my camera once or twice during the service to make a farewell picture. I didn't ask; I just did it.

They buried Leonard up in the colony cemetery in a plain pine casket made by his carpenter brother, Paul, who makes clocks, beautiful furniture, and all the caskets. I photographed as Levi, Jake, and Matthew Walter shoveled earth from a truck looming over the grave. By its edge stood Mary Walter, who with her sister Rachel spent so many years living in the same house with their brother Leonard. Her face was twisted in sadness as the dirt tumbled down.

SUMMER 2007

I'm staying at the Sundown motel again; I'm here for the wedding of Linda Walter, youngest of Darius and Annie's five daughters. Debby Walter got married the year before and is living on a colony near Harlem, up on Montana's Hi-Line. Linda is marrying Marvin Hofer, son of the new Surprise Creek Colony boss, Jake Hofer. Linda and Marvin grew up together, and Linda will stay on the colony she was born into. I was really hoping Preacher Sam would let me photograph the wedding ceremony; it certainly would be OK with the bride and groom and, I believe, the parents of both, but Sam said no.

At the Sundown out on 87, on one side of the neon sign mounted on the motel's roof, only the letters *MO* are lighted in bright orange. On the other side of the sign, just the letters *TEL* glow, outlined in the dusk against the Highwood mountains miles away. I've just come back from the wedding shivaree held in the colony kitchen, where all the tables were crowded with Hutterites from Surprise Creek and other colonies, as well as with friends and neighbors from around the Judith Basin country. A lot of songs were sung, a lot of beer downed, and lots of food consumed. At the head table sat Linda and Marvin, their parents, preacher Sam Hofer, and sisters and brothers of the bride and groom. I watched my friend Darius as the celebration continued late into the night. It had been an extremely difficult day for him.

Earlier that afternoon I was in the crowded house I knew so well. It was Martin and Becky Hofer's house now, of course. As toasts were made around the kitchen table and Hutterite women from various colonies chatted in the living room, the darkening sky outside became an issue. It started to rain and the rain then turned to hail. I stood by the kitchen window where for years Darius had sat, observing who came and went on the colony. I watched and heard the hail pinging off the roof and the side of the house; I saw white slush pouring off the roof outside the window, and the ground becoming increasingly white. This went on for maybe half an hour, and everybody knew what this could mean for the ranchers and farmers in the area. Their wheat and barley had been looking really good, and the promise of bumper crops had been talked about, especially at the new Prairie Elk Colony in Wolf Point. But what was happening way over there, 300 miles away? The same kind of storm? It didn't take long to find out.

The storm ceased. After a while, Darius was in the back bedroom he had shared with Annie for so many years. He called me in. His eyes were moist. "Joe called," he said softly, referring to his brother who had stayed at Prairie Elk while many of the other Walters at the new colony had traveled to Linda and Marvin's wedding. "He said there isn't a trailer on the colony that doesn't have broken windows. It's really bad." He looked like a man who had kind of lost his breath. This man of gruffness and sometimes bluster was on the verge of tears.

The vast fields of wheat and barley, durum, and field peas on the Prairie Elk Colony had been lush, potentially a bumper harvest. In the space of less than an hour the colony lost 95 percent of its crops. None of it was insured. Plans for a new hog barn at the colony now seemed distant, and financial survival threatened. Surprise Creek lost some crops too, but not as severely as Prairie Elk did.

Back in my room at the Sundown, I couldn't help but think that Darius—who was about to lose a daughter, who would no longer be around each day to help tend to him and comfort him as his daughters all had before leaving to start families of their own—now had suffered the loss of almost all of the bounty he and the new colony members had worked so hard for. Just like that.

MARCH 2008

Both colonies lost one of their oldest and most beloved members when Aunt Mary Stahl, the never married sister of the former colony boss Joe Stahl, was killed in a car wreck in the winter of 2008. Sally Hofer, Rachel and Mary Walter, and Aunt Mary were returning to Wolf Point from Great Falls when the Chevy Suburban Terry Walter was driving near a place called Bohemian Corners hit ice and strong winds at the same time, flipped, and rolled. Mary Walter suffered broken bones and bruises, Rachel and Sally Walter were badly bruised, and Aunt Mary, 92 years old, was thrown out and killed. I don't know for sure, but it's doubtful anyone was wearing a seat belt.

In 1969, when we all were much younger, Aunt Mary and a bunch of us would gather in cowboy Jake Hofer's colony room, illuminated by a single bare bulb dangling from the ceiling, to sing and drink a few beers.

I'd try to make a few pictures in the dim light of that bare bulb. Preacher Sam Hofer was the assistant preacher then, and he'd come. Somewhere I have a cassette tape of Sam singing Willie Nelson's "Blue Eyes Crying in the Rain." Sam didn't sing it as well as Willie, but he did know all the words. One of the Stahl girls would play guitar, and Aunt Mary would play her harmonica. "Red River Valley" was a favorite of hers. I gave her a harmonica for Christmas one year. In the key of C.

I think Aunt Mary had a crush on me over the last ten or fifteen years. Whenever I'd come over to the house at Surprise Creek she shared with Rachael and Mary Walter—the never married sisters who took care of Aunt Mary and later shared a trailer with her when they moved to Prairie Elk—she'd want to kiss me on the mouth, which I politely resisted. Aunt Mary, like a bunch of the Walters, especially Rachel and Mary, was always a New York Yankees fan. I've always wondered why some of the most rural people I've known in my life devoted themselves to the most urban major league team of them all. Doesn't seem logical.

FALL 2008

I've known David Hofer, the chicken man at the Surprise Creek Hutterite colony near Stanford, Montana, since 1969, when he was just big enough to help hold down a calf at branding time. I was having an elk roast dinner one night with David in the colony home of his cousin, Marvin Hofer, son of colony boss, Jake Hofer. We were about done and ready for dessert when Dave got to talking about a barbecue he'd been to years ago, put on up in the Little Belt mountains by an attorney from Stanford.

"It was up on the top of the mountain, and I think half of Stanford was there. They were roasting a pig and had it on one of those barbecue deals you have to turn by hand. I guess they'd thrown in some chicken, too, and some other stuff. I stood in line to get some barbecue when they were ready to open up the pig. But when I looked in, I thought it didn't look right. I didn't want to eat what they gave me. I was thinking maybe they didn't throw the pig in the cooler before they cooked it and it had gone bad and maggots had got to it. I walked over to where nobody could see me," he said, "and I scraped off part of what was on my plate into the grass. Damn! I thought, maggots! Ya know," he said with a recollecting grin, "I found out later it was really just white rice."

FALL 2005

"People either like 'em or dislike 'em," says Bill Rathert, the co-owner of a car dealership in nearby Wolf Point. "The rumor is that some of the young guys drink, but that's the same as the rest of the country. I feel sorry for the women, though, 'cause they're kind of confined. But the Hutterites will do anything for you. They're not afraid of working. They're good people."

They are good people, I think, alone in the main house on my last day at Prairie Elk. I see the Corn and Soybean Digest *perched on the armrest of the living room couch, and on a small table in the corner are eight well-worn German prayer books, the bindings of several strengthened with tape. Most have the names of the owners: Paul and Rachel Walter, Darius and Annie Walter. . . .*

I pull away from Prairie Elk with Buster stretched out on the seat beside me. Geese are coming up off the river, black against gray in the surly sky. The last day at Surprise Creek, when I was saying my goodbyes, I came across five-year-old Jaden Walter playing outside the kitchen. "Bill Allard, where are you going?" he asked. "I'm going home," I told him. As the truck warms up and my road music plays, I think, yeah, that's right. I'm going home—leaving one for another. I'm pretty lucky. And I know I'll be back. ■

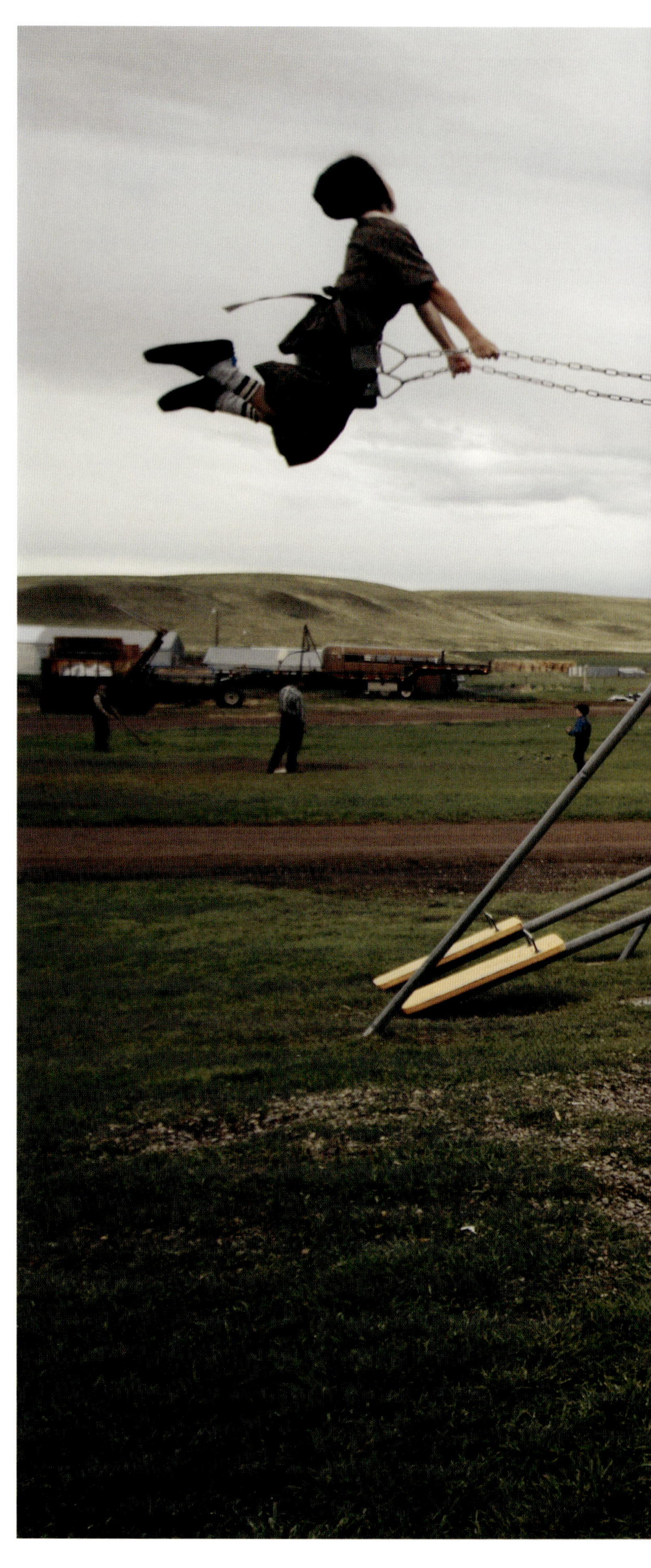

Girls on the swings, Surprise Creek Colony, Stanford, Montana, 2005

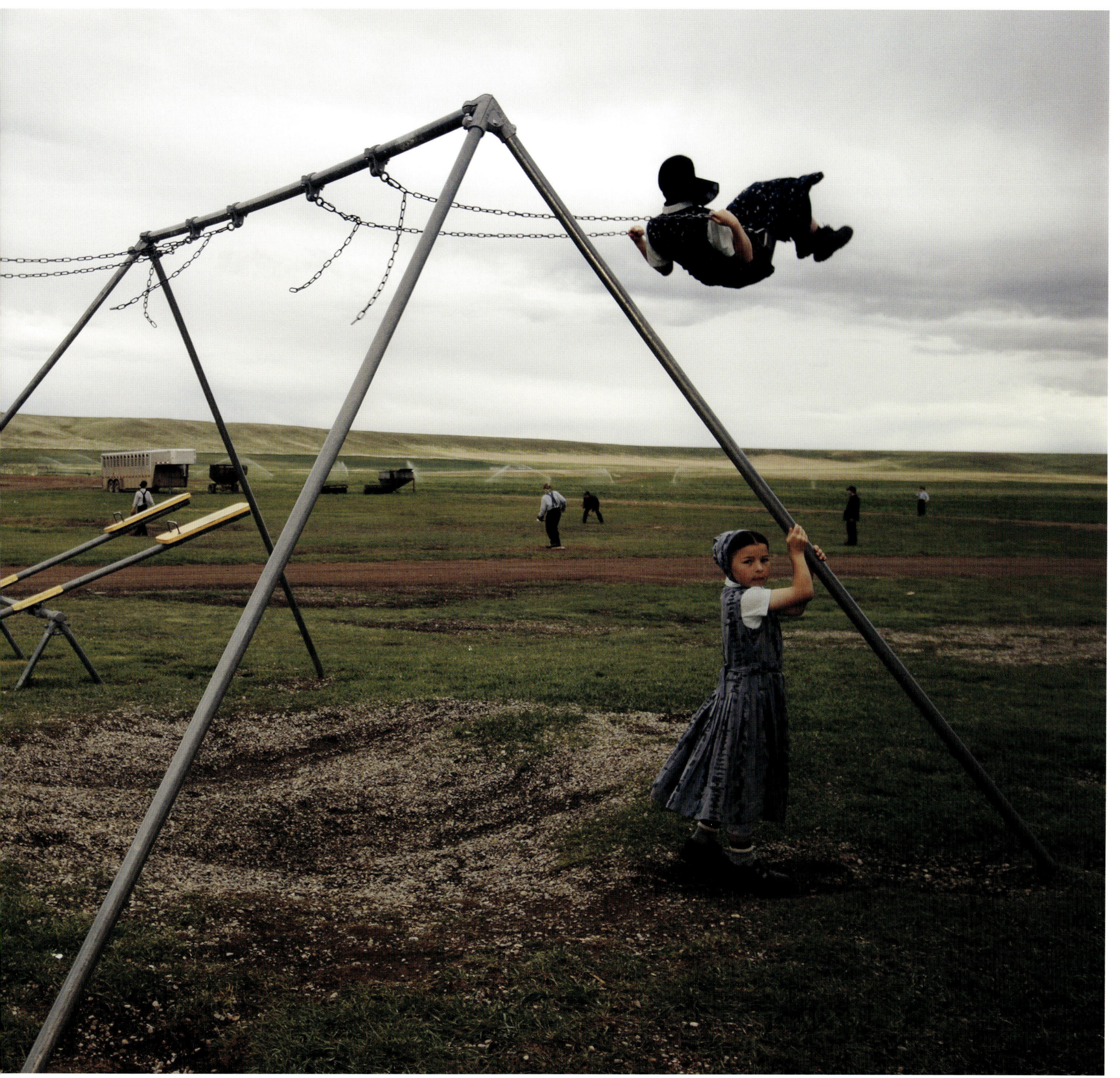

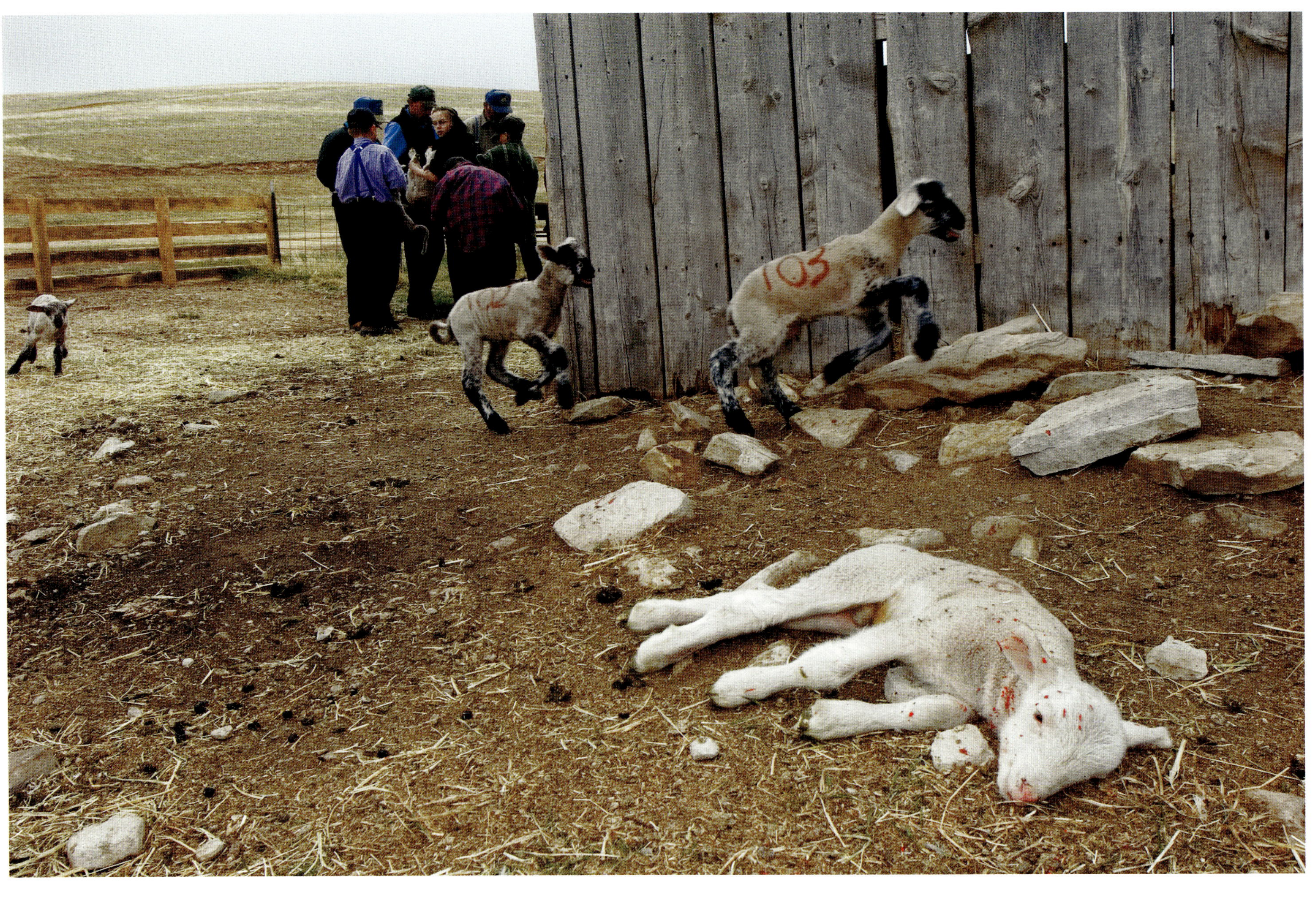

Docking the lambs' tails, Surprise Creek Colony, Stanford, Montana, 2005

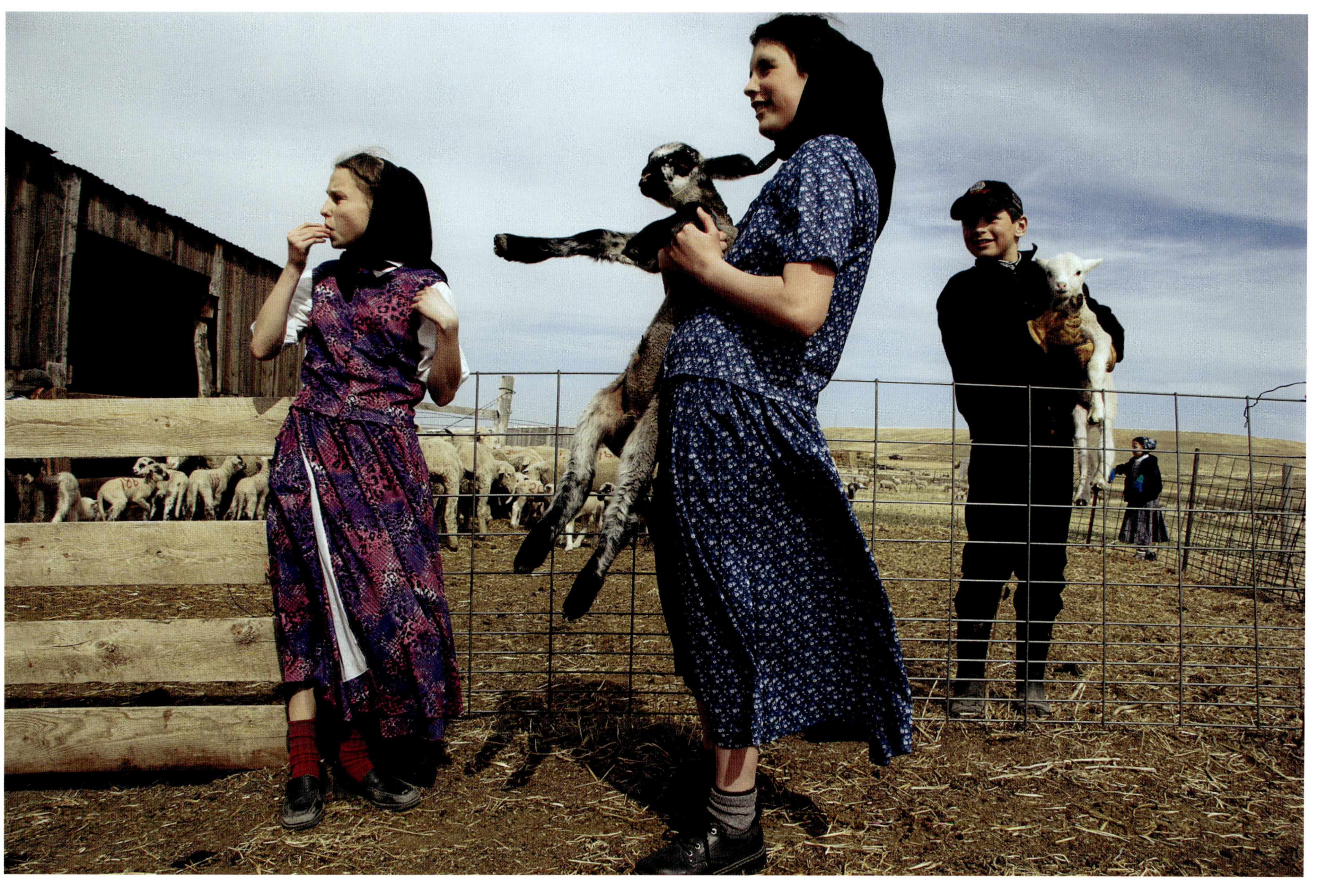

Rachel, Stephanie, and Curtis, Surprise Creek Colony, Stanford, Montana, 2005

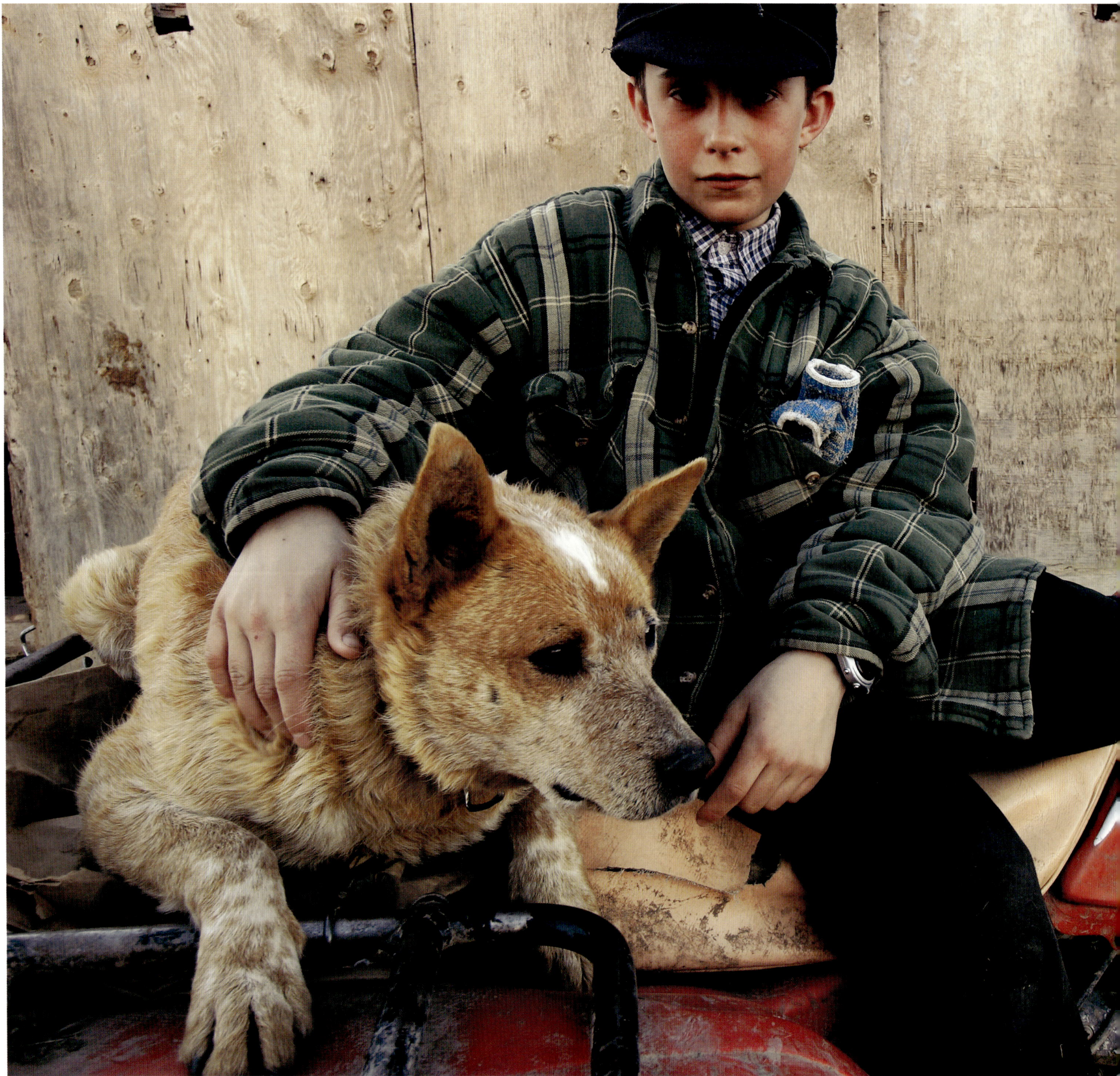

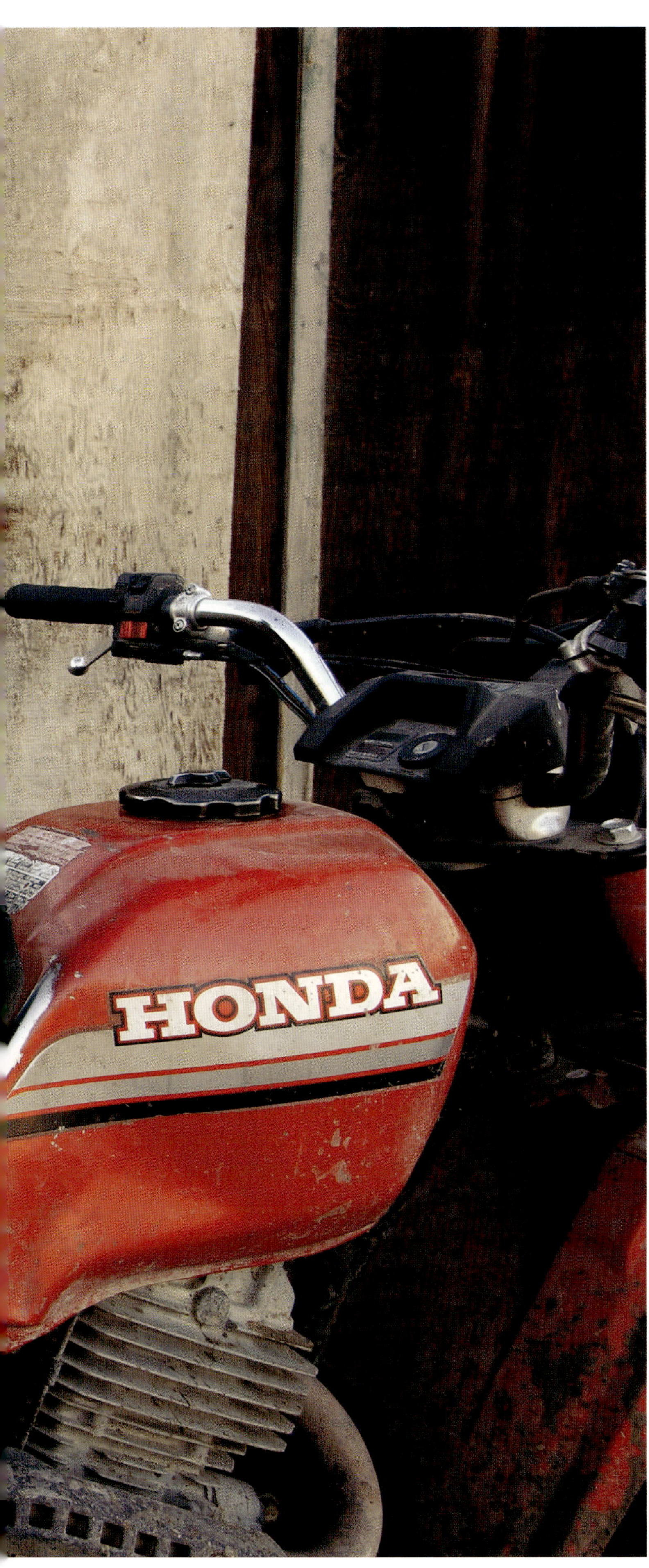

Kelley Hofer and Cactus, Surprise Creek Colony, Stanford, Montana, 2005

"I ask Annie Marie, Darius's unmarried, 35-year-old daughter, if she resents the fact that women have no say in colony affairs. 'No,' she says, 'I wouldn't want to take the blame if something goes wrong.'"

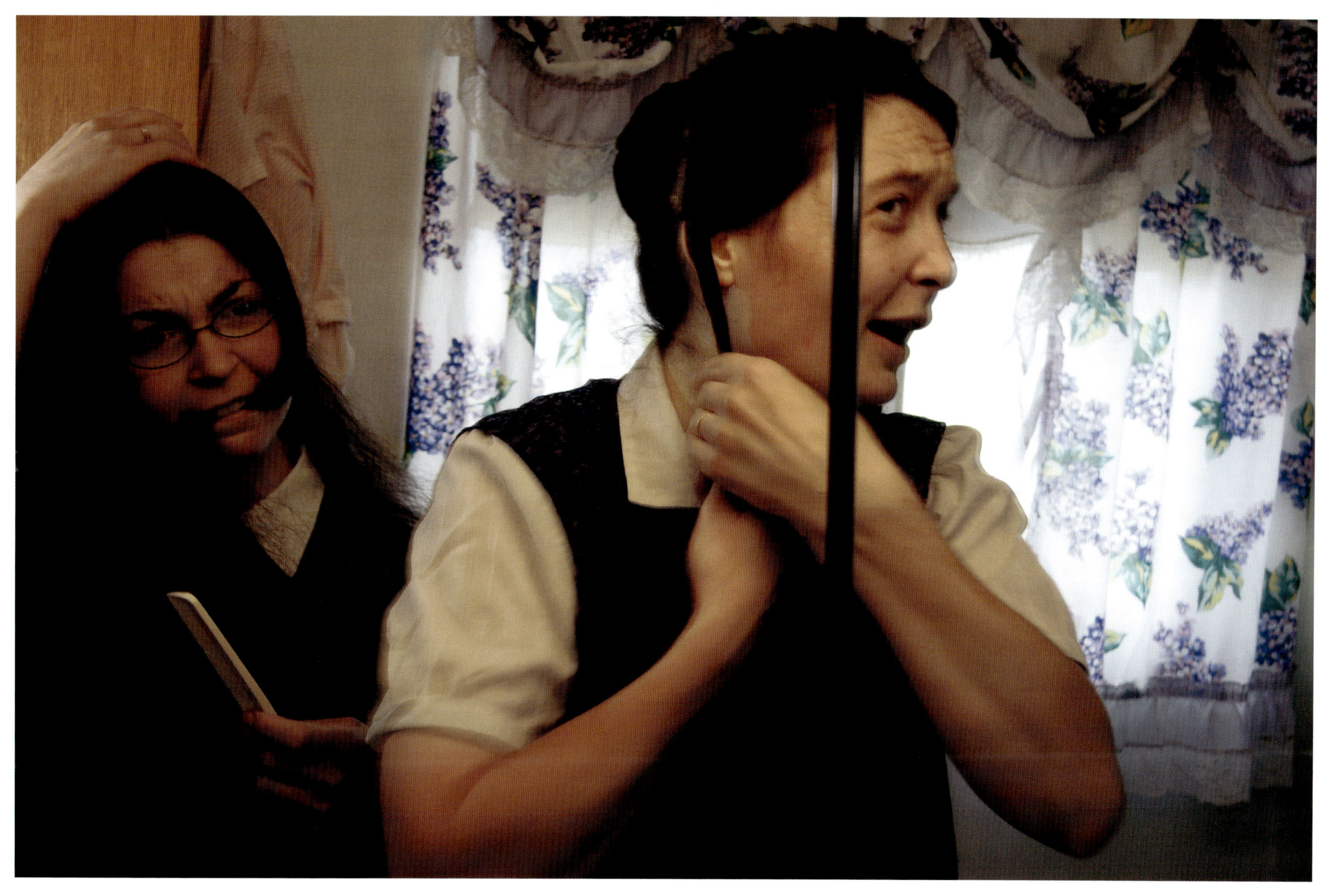

Linda and Annie Marie Walter, Prairie Elk Colony, Wolf Point, Montana, 2005

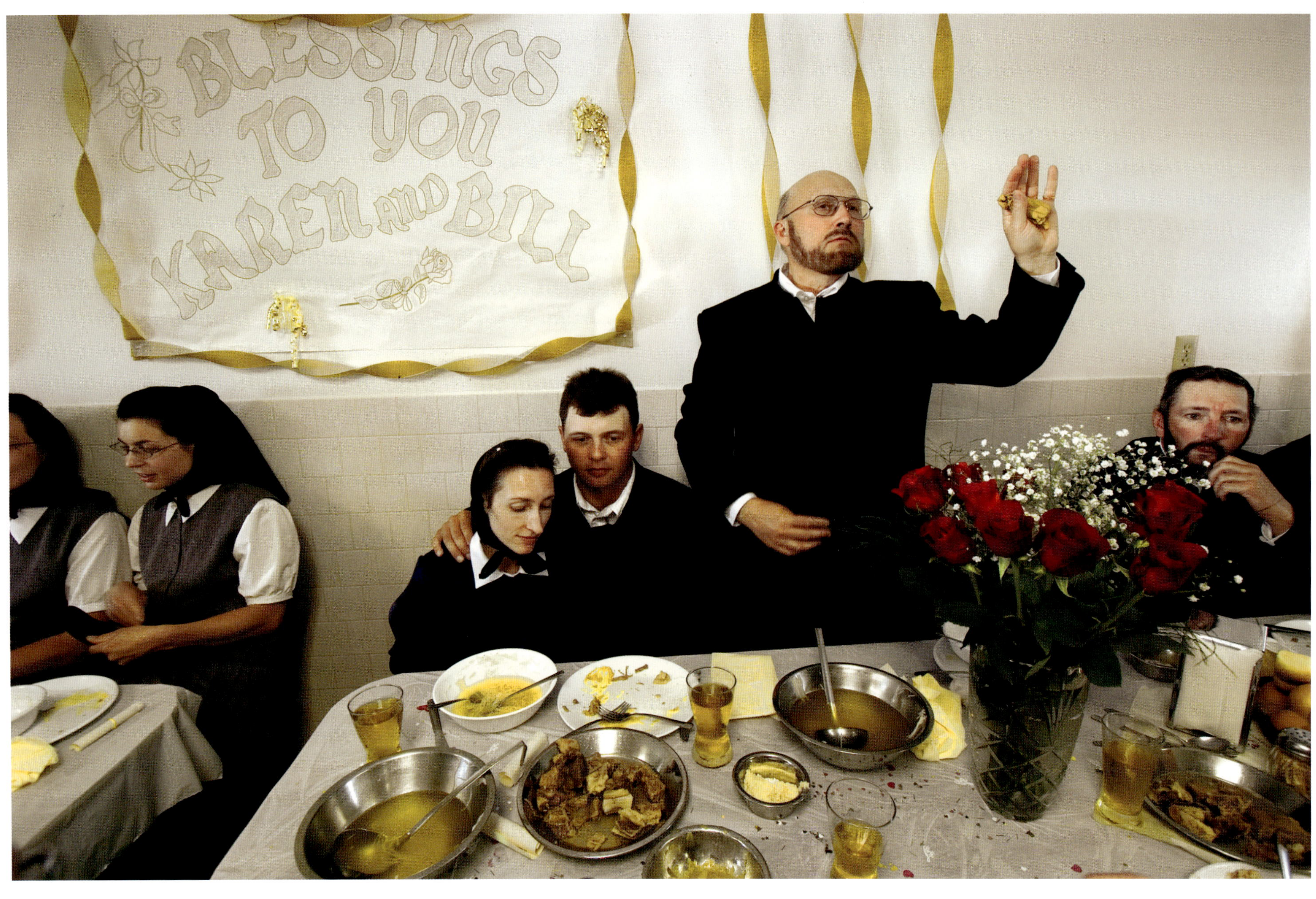

Wedding of Bill Walter and Karen Hofer, Surprise Creek Colony, Stanford, Montana, 2005

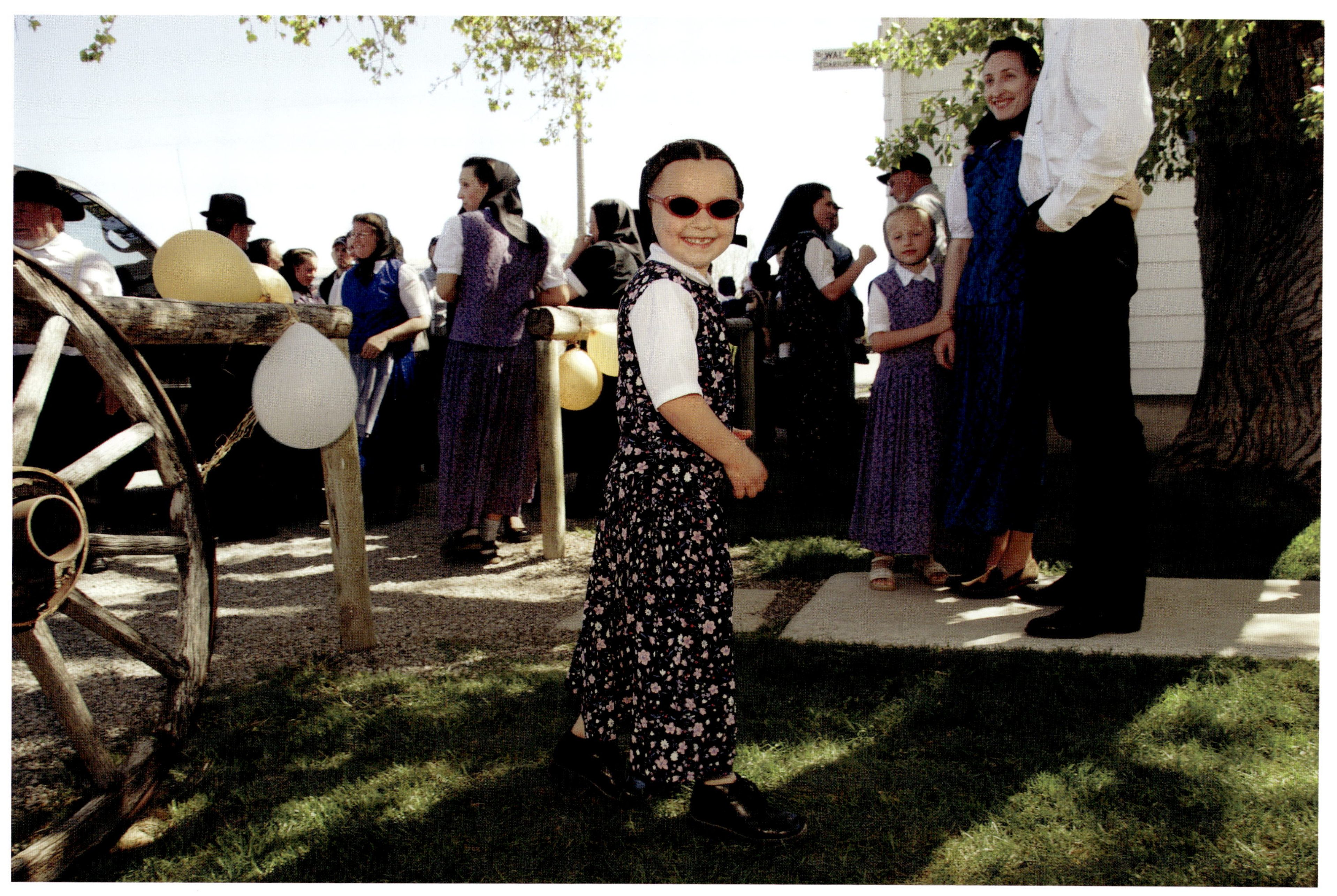

Carolyn Walter, Surprise Creek Colony, Stanford, Montana, 2005

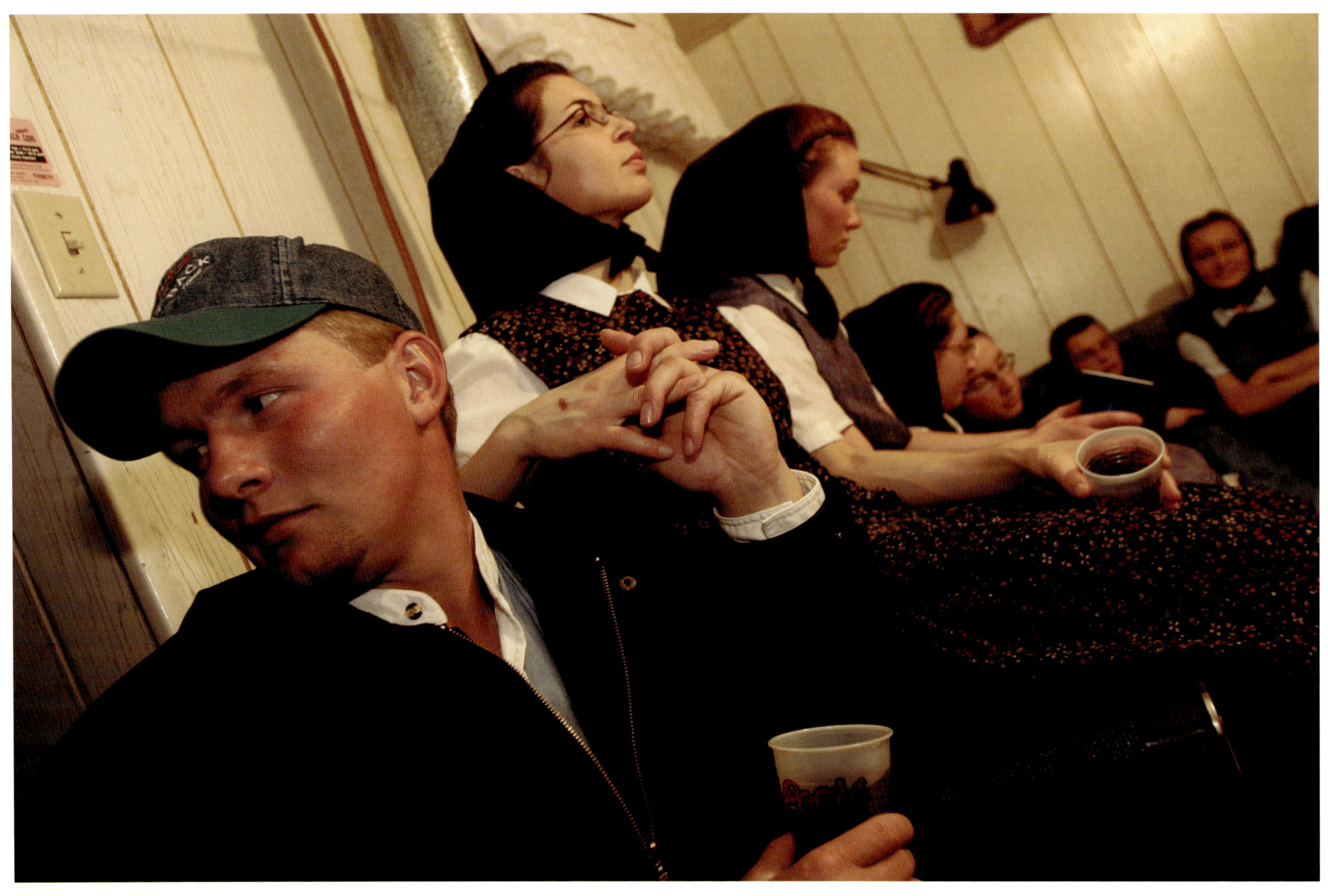

Marvin Hofer and Linda Walter, Surprise Creek Colony, Stanford, Montana, 2005

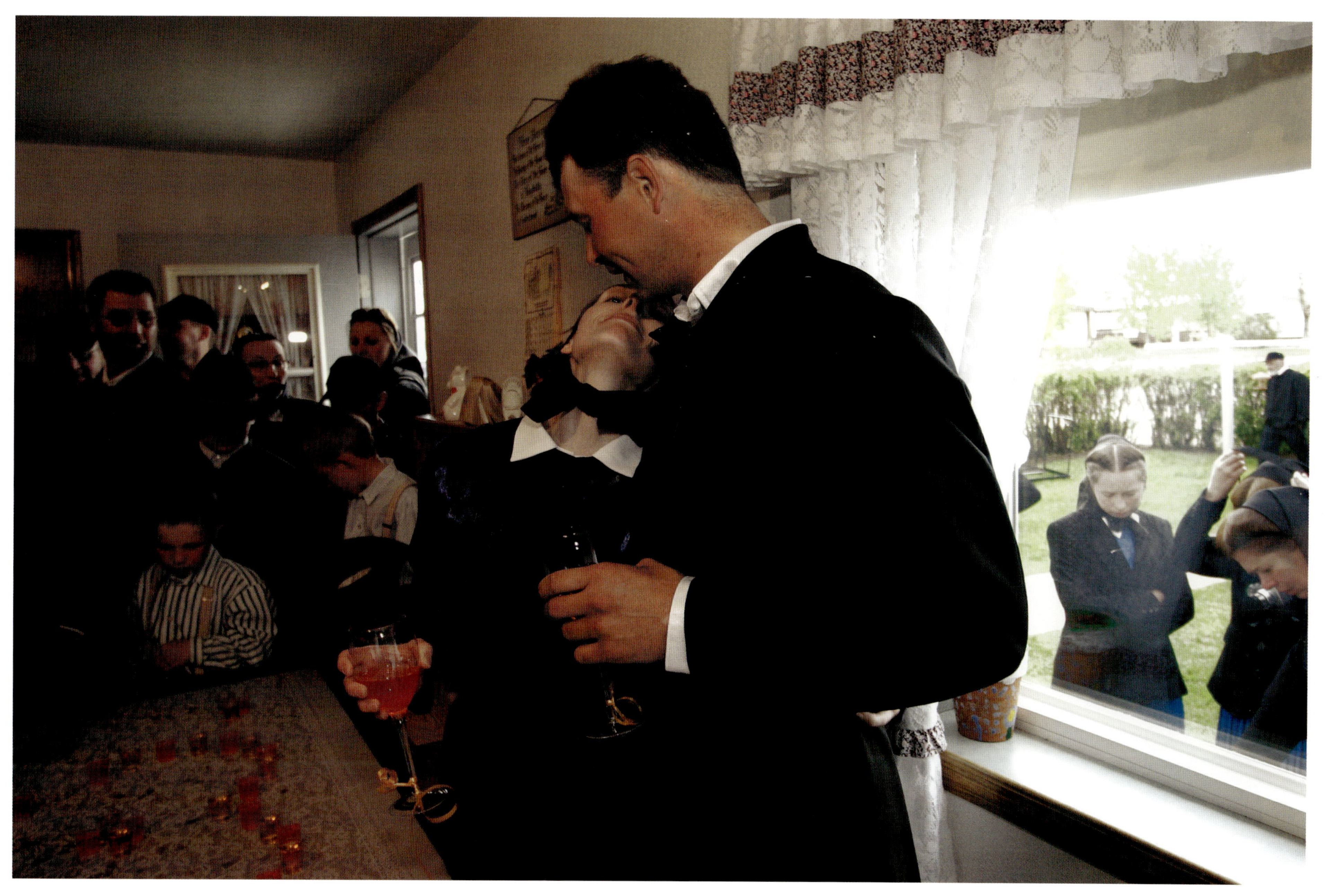

Bill and Karen Walter, Surprise Creek Colony, Stanford, Montana, 2005

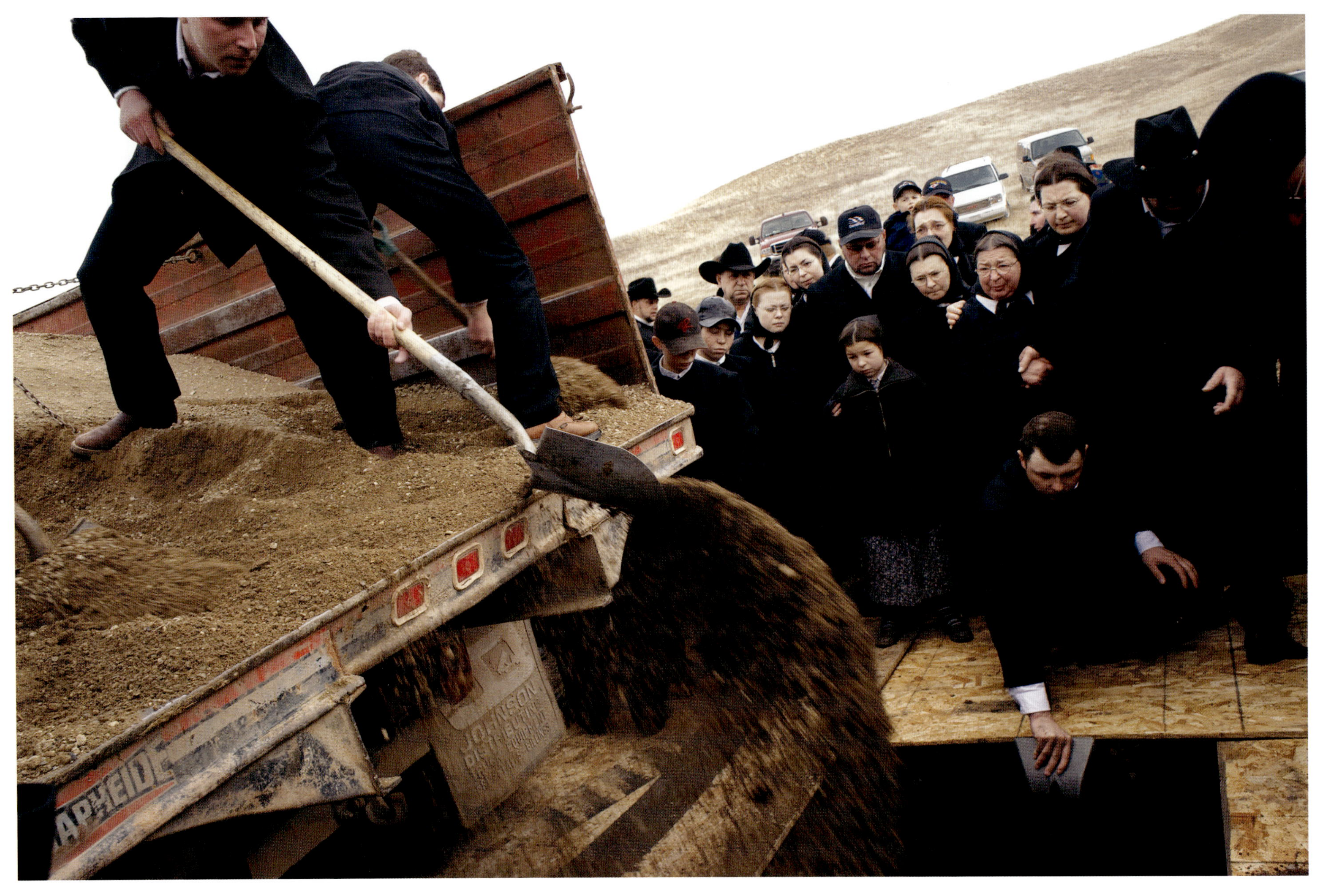

The burial of Leonard Walter, Surprise Creek Colony, Stanford, Montana, 2006

ACKNOWLEDGMENTS

MY LIST OF ACKNOWLEDGMENTS must begin with gratitude to all the people who are found in the words and pictures within this book. As I say elsewhere early on, I've heard a lot of good stories over the years, and many of my best pictures were given, not taken. For all those stories and visual gifts, I feel tremendous gratitude. Some specific individuals must be thanked, of course, but the list is one doomed to omit some who should be included but are not. I'll try my best. Let's start with those who were or are in my workplace, so to speak:

All of the seven editors in chief I've worked for at the *National Geographic* magazine since 1964, starting with Melville Bell Grosvenor, up to today's Chris Johns. To say that the magazine has evolved tremendously in relevance and visual intellect over all those years would be quite an understatement, in my opinion.

John Q. Griffin, president of publishing, has set a goal of producing fine books under the National Geographic imprint; Nina Hoffman, president, Book Publishing Group, leads the Book Division in seeking that goal. David Griffin, this book's designer, is a true lover of books; he is also director of photography for *National Geographic* magazine, the fifth director of photography I've worked for over the decades. Barbara Brownell Grogan, vice president and editor in chief of Books, has been my text editor for this book as she was for my previous one, *Portraits of America*. She has guarded my voice well, taking my many last-minute changes, sometimes assisted by her devoted assistant, Bridget English. Trish Dorsey, illustrations specialist, and especially Judith Klein, editor, also were indispensable. Marianne Koszorus, the Book Division's director of design, fully supported my hopes for the best possible cover for the book. Gary Colbert has sought to get the best paper and printing he could under the ever present stress of production cost increases; Chris Brown has given me his all in pursuit of the reproduction needed to get my pictures translated to the printed page. In photography, especially color photography, reproduction is not just something, it's everything.

Former director of photography at *National Geographic* magazine Robert E. Gilka gave me my first job as an intern at the Geographic and the first assignment that led to a long career of doing something I truly love. I always tried to repay him with the best work I could do.

I have too many good colleagues among my fellow photographers, writers, and editors to try to list. They all know who they are, and I hope they realize how much I treasure their talents, friendship, and inspiration. One photographer, the late Dennis Stock, of Magnum, welcomed me and my photographs into his New York City home almost 50 years ago when I was a junior in college and a beginning photographer looking for a response to my work; my time with Dennis was priceless. I regret he didn't get a chance to see this book, and I can only hope I may have been of similar help and inspiration to another young beginner sometime during my career.

One man must stand out not just for his friendship but for his role in bringing me back into a career pursuit I'd temporarily lost for a while. Rich Clarkson, who served for too short a period as director of photography at *National Geographic* magazine, made bringing me back to work there a priority when he arrived. Thanking him for that is something I can never adequately do.

Going back to the very beginning, my parents, George and, especially, my mother, Willie Allard, although not professionals themselves, always stressed to their children the need to do the best they could and to not settle for less. My sister, Ann DeGray, was persuasive in moving me forward as a young man toward a more productive life than I might have found on my own initiative. Two teachers at the University of Minnesota were instrumental in my development as a photographer: Jerome Liebling and R. Smith "Smitty" Schuneman, although greatly different in their teaching ways, sought the same goal of excellence. Smitty also became a mentor and remains to this day a great friend. There was an English composition teacher at the Minneapolis School of Fine Arts whose encouragement fanned the flames of my initial aspirations of being a writer. I had her for only one brief class, and I'm ashamed to say I can't now recall her name, but she mattered.

Out in Montana I have much to be thankful for among my Hutterite friends at Surprise Creek and Prairie Elk Creek Colonies. I've spent so many treasured days with the Darius and Annie Walter family. Over the years they have opened their home to me as though I were family. In Missoula, Montana, Swede Anderson is the kind of friend who is always there to help when needed. And Al, Angie, Cheyenne, and Ryan at the Kettle House brewery on the Hip Strip in Missoula, where they pour that unsurpassed Cold Smoke Scotch Ale in a wonderfully unpretentious atmosphere, where the late afternoon sun comes in through the windows facing Myrtle Street and falls upon the bar like some kind of holy light, turning a glass of beer into an almost electric amber vision.

Finally, my wife, Ani, and my children, Chris, Terri, David, and Anthony, all have given me unequivocal love and acceptance of my many long absences. Time can't be replaced, and it's impossible to thank them with more than my love in return.

And our Scott. We miss him. We loved him so and always will. ■

PREVIOUS WORKS

Portraits of America
Time at the Lake: A Minnesota Album
A Time We Knew: Images of Yesterday in the Basque Homeland
The Photographic Essay
Vanishing Breed: Photographs of the Cowboy and the West (Nominee, American Book Award 1982; Winner, Wrangler Western Heritage Award for Outstanding Western Art Book, 1983; Leica Medal of Excellence, 1983)

AWARDS

University of Minnesota Outstanding Achievement Award, 1994
Joseph A. Sprague Memorial Award, 2002
University of Minnesota School of Journalism and Mass Communications Award for Excellence, 2004

WILLIAM ALBERT ALLARD: FIVE DECADES

By William Albert Allard
Foreword by William Kittredge

Published by the National Geographic Society
John M. Fahey, Jr., President and Chief Executive Officer
Gilbert M. Grosvenor, Chairman of the Board
Tim T. Kelly, President, Global Media Group
John Q. Griffin, Executive Vice President; President, Publishing
Nina D. Hoffman, Executive Vice President; President, Book Publishing Group

Prepared by the Book Division
Barbara Brownell Grogan, Vice President and Editor in Chief
Marianne R. Koszorus, Director of Design
Carl Mehler, Director of Maps
R. Gary Colbert, Production Director
Jennifer A. Thornton, Managing Editor
Meredith C. Wilcox, Administrative Director, Illustrations

Staff for This Book
David Griffin, Art Director
Judith Klein, Editor
Bridget A. English, Assistant Project Editor
Trish Dorsey, Illustrations Specialist
Robert Waymouth, Illustrations Specialist

Manufacturing and Quality Management
Christopher A. Liedel, Chief Financial Officer
Phillip L. Schlosser, Vice President
Chris Brown, Technical Director
Nicole Elliott, Manager
Rachel Faulise, Manager

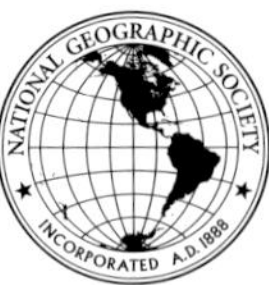

The National Geographic Society is one of the world's largest nonprofit scientific and educational organizations. Founded in 1888 to "increase and diffuse geographic knowledge," the Society works to inspire people to care about the planet. It reaches more than 325 million people worldwide each month through its official journal, *National Geographic*, and other magazines; National Geographic Channel; television documentaries; music; radio; films; books; DVDs; maps; exhibitions; school publishing programs; interactive media; and merchandise. National Geographic has funded more than 9,000 scientific research, conservation and exploration projects and supports an education program combating geographic illiteracy. For more information, visit *nationalgeographic.com*.

For more information, please call 1-800-NGS LINE (647-5463) or write to the following address:

National Geographic Society
1145 17th Street N.W.
Washington, D.C. 20036-4688 U.S.A.

Visit us online at *www.nationalgeographic.com*

For information about special discounts for bulk purchases, please contact National Geographic Books Special Sales: *ngspecsales@ngs.org*

For rights or permissions inquiries, please contact National Geographic Books Subsidiary Rights: *ngbookrights@ngs.org*

Library of Congress Cataloging-in-Publication Data

Allard, William Albert.
William Albert Allard, five decades : a retrospective.
p. cm.
ISBN 978-1-4262-0637-5
1. Documentary photography. 2. Portrait photography. 3. Landscape photography. 4. Allard, William Albert. I. National Geographic Society (U.S.) II. Title. III. Title: Five decades. IV. Title: 5 decades.
TR820.5.A45 2010
779.092--dc22
2010011630

Printed in China

10/TS/1